Praise for *Age of Inference: Cultivating a Scientific Mindset*

This volume takes on one of the thorniest existential problems of our time, the contradiction between the exponentially growing amount of information that individuals have access to, and the diminished capacity of those individuals to understand it. Its chapters provide the reader with an introduction to the relationship between knowledge, science, and inference; needed new approaches to learning science in our new data rich world; and a discussion of what we can and must do to reduce or eliminate the growing gap between the inference have's and have nots. It is not too much to say that how we resolve the issues outlined in this volume will determine the future of our species on this planet.

—Joseph L. Graves Jr.
Professor of Biological Sciences
North Carolina A&T State University
Fellow, American Association for the Advancement of Science: Biological Sciences
Author of *The Emperor's New Clothes: Biological Theories of Race at the Millennium*

In *Age of Inference: Cultivating a Scientific Mindset*, the reader is immediately drawn into the need to prepare students and educators for utilizing massive and growing amounts of data to solve human problems. The editors explore the human interface with robotic technologies embedded in our daily routines and ask us to consider where humankind will end up in the future, if we, as educators, are not prepared to cultivate the skills of scientific and logical reasoning in conjunction with society's increasing reliance on artificial intelligence. The text is packed with reasoning-based applications and strategies for use with preservice teachers, in STEM teacher development, and would also offer a timely book study with superintendents and campus-based leaders for addressing the complexities of human change that we face today.

—Karen Embry Jenlink
Emeritus Professor of Doctoral Studies
Stephen F. Austin State University
President, Association of Teacher Educators (2017–2018)
World Federation Association of Teacher Educators,
Board of Directors (2020–2023)

Age of Inference is useful for science teachers and pre-service teachers who want to examine issues with scientific literacy in the public and develop strategies for utilizing the vast quantities of data available to all citizens. Through the stories, experiences, and research-based methods shared by the authors, the reader recognizes the cruciality of cultivating a scientific mindset where not only knowing, but doing quality science in the classroom can produce citizens capable of scrutinizing and employing scientific information for personal and societal decision-making.

—Jean Becherer
Veteran Biology, Ecology, and Forensic Science Teacher
Belleville East High School

How do we know what we know and how can we use that knowledge to make well-informed decisions? How do we prepare students to tackle illustructured societal issues that simultaneously present too much information, yet almost always leave us with unanswered questions? *Age of Inference* interrogates these questions through historical, philosophical, and pedagogical lenses. Making meaning is infused throughout. Through reflective questions, readers delve more deeply into the material, consider its implications, and think about their own learning.

—Bora Simmons
Professor Emerita, Environmental Education
& Teacher Education Northern Illinois
University Director, National Project for Excellence
in Environmental Education

In our world and society of exponentially growing problems, we need a scientific mindset more than ever before. Big data is not enough for addressing dangers to the environment or tackling threats to democracy; we need the ability to draw sound inferences from the data. Knowledge alone is not enough; we also need critical reasoning. Cultivating a scientific mindset requires fundamental changes to the way we teach and learn. This important and well-written volume shows how.

—Ashok Goel
Professor of Computer Science & Human-Centered Computing
Georgia Institute of Technology Editor of AI Magazine Founding Editor
of AAAI's *Interactive AI Magazine*

If you are a science teacher concerned about the implications of information overload, analysis paralysis, and intellectual complacency on our health, economic future, and democracy, then I recommend this book. In a time of abundant information, fake news, and conspiracy theories, science as a way of thinking and knowing is critical for the new Inference Age. This book's exploration of how we know including standards of evidence, practical application in the classroom, and speculation about the future is an important read for science educators.

—Michael Svec
Professor for Physics and Astronomy Education Furman University
Fulbright Scholar to Czech Republic

If you care deeply about science education and the public understanding of science, this book is for you! Important and timely, the editors have assembled an engaging set of essays that illuminate the role and significance of inference in science. Each chapter moves the reader forward to a deeper understanding of inference in accessing, conceptualizing, and applying scientific knowledge. As a collection, the book provides a compelling case for the Age of Inference as the next evolutionary step in public access to knowledge and challenges the reader to be a participant in promoting scientific knowledge ethically and responsibly in a climate of information overload.

—Randy L. Bell
Professor of Science Education & Associate Dean of Academic Affairs
Oregon State University

As opposed to those only purporting to focus on scientific thinking, this book truly does just that. The authors in three sections take up the notion of what it means to think in science versus thinking like a scientist and highlight the value in becoming a practitioner of science regardless of one's ultimate profession. During present times, novices are making decisions in the vein of experts but are often not trained to do so. As the next generation of educators and science communicators contemplate their futures, *Age of Inference: Cultivating a Scientific Mindset*, provides a compelling case for the reconceptualization of individualized education through broad commentary and specific cases. With this, major challenges not only for students but also the public at large are discussed. Those trained in the sciences will recognize essential aspects of their training; aspects that are rarely featured in standard content-focused textbooks. Further, major issues such as confronting uncertainty and increasing diversity are broached. With helpful discussion questions at the end of each chapter, this book can be used in a diversity of settings. In summary, *Age of Inference: Cultivating a Scientific Mindset*, moves beyond a consideration of developmental age, and treats the current period of human innovation as an age where information overload poses a fundamental problem that will take members of the education community and public to enact a sea change of how humans reason with information.

—Rebecca Jordan
Professor, Community Sustainability
Michigan State University

Published in 1667, the *Saggi di naturali esperienze* (Essays on Natural Experiments), was the one and only publication from one of the world's earliest scientific academies, Florence's Accademia del Cimento (Academy of Experiment). This book reflected the Accademia's crucial work in promoting rigorous experimentation and argumentation as the foundation of modern Galilean science. Today, given the rapid changes we see during the transition from the Information Age to the Inference Age, there is a need to reinvigorate our conversations around the place and practices of science and science education in contemporary societies. And in these turbulent times, the need for these conversations will only increase. This book is an important and timely addition to this work. My congratulations and thanks to the authors for their work and vision.

—Wayne Melville
Dean of the College of Education
Lakehead University–Ontario
Co-editor of the *Journal of Science Teacher Education*

Inference is perhaps one of the most important concepts essential to teaching and learning in the discipline of science. *Age of Inference: Cultivating a Scientific Mindset*, edited by Philip Short, Harvey Henson, and John McConnell, brings together a collection of scholarly works on the importance of inference in science. Understanding how scientists make inferences, and in turn bringing inference to the foreground in science classrooms is extremely important to how students learn science. The contributing authors for this book are exceptional experts in their field and offer the reader a critically important insight into the essential nature and importance of inference. A higher-order skill, inference is a prerequisite for preparing students of science and the 21st century skills necessary to scientific understanding, research, and discovery. The contributing authors for the book have presented an important collective insight concerning inference and the use of evidence to answer important questions in the quest for scientific knowledge.

—Patrick M. Jenlink
Regents Professor
Stephen F. Austin State University

Age of Inference offers multiple disciplinary perspectives that are showcased in a space for reader exploration. Connections engage the reader with content, concepts, and educationally "what could be on the horizon." It sparked new questions and prompted me to contemplate possibilities for moving forward with integrated and interdisciplinary functionality.

—Andrea Burrows
Professor Secondary Science Teacher Education
Associate Dean for the College of Education University of Wyoming

Age of Inference

Age of Inference

Cultivating a Scientific Mindset

edited by

Philip C. Short
Austin Peay State University

Harvey Henson
Southern Illinois University Carbondale

John R. McConnell
Austin Peay State University

INFORMATION AGE PUBLISHING, INC.
Charlotte, NC • www.infoagepub.com

Library of Congress Cataloging-in-Publication Data

A CIP record for this book is available from the Library of Congress
http://www.loc.gov

ISBN: 978-1-64802-797-0 (Paperback)
978-1-64802-798-7 (Hardcover)
978-1-64802-799-4 (E-Book)

Printed in the United States of America

CONTENTS

Foreword ix
Miranda Feliciano Tyson

Acknowledgments and Dedication xi

SECTION I

INTRODUCTION: THE NATURE OF KNOWLEDGE, SCIENCE, AND INFERENCE

1 The Age of Inference 3
John R. McConnell, Sarah B. Dugger, and Philip C. Short

2 Nature of the Scientific Enterprise 17
Harvey Henson

3 The Nature of Science Education: Relativity of Theory 39
Philip C. Short

4 Mathematics: Language, Modeling, and Comparison Assisting Inference 59
Mary Barone Martin, Tammy Jones, Dovie Kimmins, and Teresa Schmidt

5 Statistics: Developing Impactful Teaching and Learning 75
Mary Barone Martin, Tammy Jones, and Teresa Schmidt

6 Statistics: Assessing Success in the Inference Process 91
Mary Barone Martin, Tammy Jones, and Teresa Schmidt

SECTION II

APPLICATION: FRAMEWORK FOR SCIENCE IN A DATA-RICH WORLD

7 Children's Literature Resources to Support Authentic Science Practices and Environmental Decision-Making: The *Conservation Tales* Series 109
Tom J. McConnell and Barbara Giorgio-Booher

8 Supporting Statistical Literacies in the Context of a Data Visualization Project With Elementary Students 131
Lynn Hodge, Joy Bertling, and Shande King

9 Green Literacy K–5: Nurturing a Scientific Mindset...................... 141
Jennifer Cullerton Johnson and Mary K. Gove

10 Complex Multimodal Text Sets to Support Science Literacy 157
William Romine, Amy Lannin, Torrey Palmer, Delinda van Garderen, Rachel Juergensen, Cassandra M. Smith, and William Folk

11 Power Up or Put Away? Using Mobile Phones for Authentic Student Investigations 183
Kristin T. Rearden and Blanche O'Bannon

12 Self-Regulated Learning Theory to Build Scientific Mindsets for Diversity in STEM 195
Giuseppina Mattietti and Erin E. Peters-Burton

13 A Case for the Model-Based Reasoning Classroom........................ 213
Arthur Beauchamp and Cynthia Passmore

14 Cultivating a Scientific Mindset Through Inquiry-Based Science Learning Utilizing Nasa Resources for Educators 223
Leslie Huling and Virginia Resta

15 Bridging the Disconnect Between How We Do and Teach Science: Cultivating a Scientific Mindset in an Era of Data-Driven Education 239
Jana Bouwma-Gearhart

16 The Scientific Method Card Game: Applications for Any Educational Context 265
Kallina M. Dunkle

17 Toward a Design-Centered Scientific Mindset: Closing the Opportunity Gaps via 3D Design and Printing in STEM Teacher Education 279
Lingguo Bu, Harvey Henson, and Euginia Nyirenda

SECTION III

CONCLUSION: THE FUTURE FOR INFERENCES AND ACTIONS

18 Developing Critical Literacy Skills Among Diverse Learners During the Age of Inference 299
Laveria F. Hutchison

19 Content and Pedagogical Knowledge for Teaching Confidence Intervals in a Post $p < 0.05$ World 317
Jennifer J. Kaplan and Kristen E. Roland

20 The Multidimensional Learning Goals for Making Inferences With Data 347
Ryan Seth Jones, Anna Strimaitis Grinath, and Fonya Scott

21 Expectations and Disciplinary Blends 355
L. Jeneva Clark, R. Alexander Bentley, Nicholas N. Nagle, and Vasileios Maroulas

22 Machine Learning: A New Lens for Integrating Computational Thinking and Science in the High School Classroom 369
Michael Daley, Zhen Bai, Raffaella Borasi, and Dave Miller

23 Becoming a Postmodern STEM Teacher Leader in the Age of Inference 385
Rebekah Hammack

24 Seeking Homeostasis in a Heteroscedastic World: A Sense of the Stakes in the Age of Inference 393
Philip C. Short, Donna F. Short, and John R. McConnell

References 411

About the Editors 461

About the Contributors 463

FOREWORD

"I'm not a science person."

A common first-day conversation with my 9th graders.

"What do you mean you aren't a 'science person?'"

"I dunno, I'm just, not good at that stuff, you know?"

We've all heard it before: a "science person." But what does that term even mean? Does it mean you "like" science? "Love" science? Are "good at" science? A combination of the above? Is it like being a cat person or a dog person, branded by society as an unchangeable personality trait?

That then begs the question: What is science?

Sometimes, we ask our students that too, and their responses tend to vary.

"What do you mean . . . it's science."

"Don't you do . . . experiments and graphs and things like that?"

"Like . . . a subject in school."

None of their responses are incorrect or inaccurate—science is, indeed, science. It does, in fact, involve a lot of experiments and graphs and "things like that." And it is, last I checked, a subject that is taught in schools. But students often miss what, fundamentally, we work for 10 months to instill in their still-developing brains:

"Science is a way of thinking."

As a teacher, I recently participated in a professional development session on what's called project-based learning (or PBL for short). PBL is a pedagogical method in which "students gain knowledge and skills by working for an extended period of time to investigate and respond to

Age of Inference, pages ix–x

an authentic, engaging, and complex question, problem, or challenge" (PBLWorks, 2022, para. 3). The workshop involved dozens of educators from across the United States who taught everything from early childhood English language arts to high school engineering. Together, we spent three consecutive Saturdays on Zoom integrating PBL into existing units of our respective content areas.

When walked through PBL, however, I was struck by the nagging feeling that this was all very familiar. On the first day, our facilitator reviewed the Seven Essential Project Design Elements. Students (a) pose a meaningful problem or question; (b) find resources and conduct research; (c) investigate an issue with real-world authenticity; (d) express their own ideas in their own voices; (e) reflect on their process and progress; (f) give, receive, and apply feedback; and (g) present their work to people beyond the classroom (PBLWorks, 2022).

If this also seems familiar to you, that is probably because my facilitator, along with many other experienced educators, spent hours workshopping the steps of the scientific method—a concept that, according to the Next Generation Science Standards (NGSS), is ostensibly covered in elementary school.

But my fellow educators, clearly, had never really thought of learning that way before. This isn't inherently their fault—after all, as will be addressed later in this book, science curricula in and of themselves are not equitably taught across the United States. But in order to be better educators, we all, regardless of content area or grade level, need to internalize a different way of thinking.

A scientific way of thinking.

"What?"

My students are, understandably, confused.

"What are you talking about?"

It takes time to instill a new way of thinking—as it does with any change in cognition. But if you have asked enough questions to lead you to this book, you are well on the right track to changing yours.

—Mx. Miranda Feliciano Tyson
Special Education Science Teacher
New York City

REFERENCE

PBLWorks. (2022). *What is project-based learning?* https://www.pblworks.org/what-is-pbl

ACKNOWLEDGMENTS AND DEDICATION

The editors of this book would first like to salute this era's young champions of free, analytical, and science-informed thought around the world. We acknowledge and admire them represented by the following individuals, for seeking equitable solutions to problems affecting all populations—the young people who are asking the global community to "follow the science."

Alexandria Villaseñor, Anuna De Wever, Autumn Peltier, Bruno Rodriguez
David Wicker, Eyal Weintraub, Greta Thunberg, Mari Copeny
Helena Gualinga, Holly Gillibrand, Isra Hirsi, Haven Coleman
Jerome Foster II, John Paul Jose, Kallan Benson, Jamie Margolin
Lilly Platt, Luisa Neubauer, Mari Copeny, Leah Namugerwa
Vic Barrett, Xiuhtezcatl Martinez, Xiye Bastida, Saoi O'Connor

This volume would not have been possible without the help of many people and supporting institutions. Certainly, we appreciate our contributing authors who poured creative energy into the chapters with a display of honest critique and collaborative spirits throughout the project. Our gratitude goes out to Mx. Miranda Feliciano Tyson for composing the book's foreword and to Kristina Johnson Parish for turning our central themes into the perfect abstract illustration for the cover. Ji "Jacinta" Ma was an efficient organizer in the early stages while Tasha A. Berry has been an invaluable reviewer of documents and manager of multiple, varied tasks at the culmination of the project. This work was encouraged by support from the

Age of Inference, pages xi–xii

Austin Peay State University Jack Hunt STEM Center, the Southern Illinois University—Carbondale STEM Education Research Center, and the ATE/NASA EPDC Commission on STEM Education in the Future. We dedicate this effort to all of our teachers—and to all of our students, to whom we hope to reflect the same kind of love and generosity that was shown to us.

SECTION I

INTRODUCTION: THE NATURE OF KNOWLEDGE, SCIENCE, AND INFERENCE

This section of the book introduces the epistemology of human existence: how we know what we know, what causes us to think what we think, and what standards of evidence we should use in seeking the truth about ourselves and the world in which we live.

CHAPTER 1

THE AGE OF INFERENCE

**John R. McConnell, Sarah B. Dugger,
and Philip C. Short**

If you can look into the seeds of time, and say which grain will grow and which will not, speak unto me.

—William Shakespeare

Information is now a commodity (Kross et al., 2020). With the click of a mouse or remote control, anyone can access a trove of information. People possess at their disposal increasingly large amounts of information, or data (Figure 1.1). This access to large amounts of data, once considered an advantage, can also present a hindrance if the data are not collected, organized, analyzed, and interpreted properly. With ubiquitous access to data, the onus now placed on students and teachers of science, as well as science institutions, is to use the "right" sorts of data to make the "right" sorts of decisions (Rivers et al., 2020). Education is becoming less like a checkers game and more like a chess match, where the best players are those who can anticipate next moves and act accordingly. To keep pace with and stay ahead using science and innovation, the ability to estimate future trends is paramount.

Age of Inference, pages 3–16

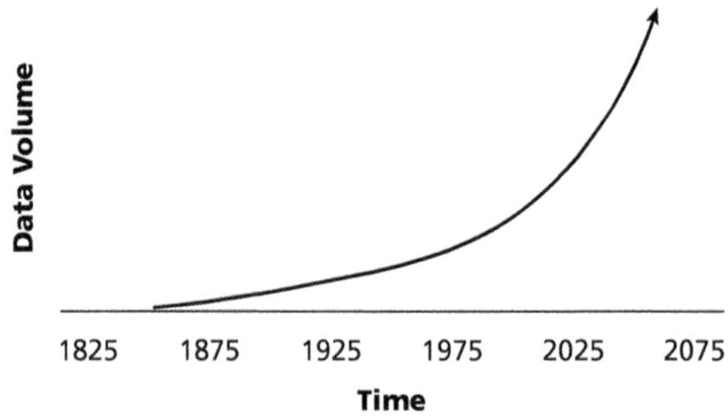

Figure 1.1 Proliferation of data.

HISTORICAL PROGRESSION

Humanity has entered and exited many eras throughout history. As with the agricultural and industrial eras, we certainly are, in some ways, still immersed in and dependent upon the developments and tools of previous ages. However, we have entered times that may be better described by the next set of tools necessary to advance further. The recent decades of technological advancement have delivered most of the world's available information to our fingertips; nevertheless, far too many remain ignorant of the approaches and abilities necessary to discern the validity of the data. Fewer, still, lack the capacity to parse that information in useful ways. Flawed conclusions are drawn daily as are the ideological lines that preclude constructive dialogue in society.

The ability or inability to "infer" from multiple data sets, bodies of information, and diverse perspectives may be a determinant to whether the Information Age propels our species forward toward sustainability, security, equity, and better decision-making—or whether the inundation of information overwhelms the global citizenry like "drinking from a firehose." It is often said that we entered the Information Age a few decades ago, but we would ask if that description still defines us today (Bi, 2019).

Some may say we have entered a new era where an inundation of information has compelled us to develop new tools to help us make sense of this information and to be able to solve new problems and make better decisions (Bi, 2019; Starčič, 2019). Science, which has always espoused a systematic approach to drawing conclusions, is as important as ever and requires a certain mindset that allows for a degree of comfort with the limitations within which it must operate (Doerr et al., 2017; Kalman, 2010). The latest tools we have developed to help society, while still steeped in scientific principles, have evolved to the point they mimic human logic and learning. The development of these tools marks the birth of a new era, the

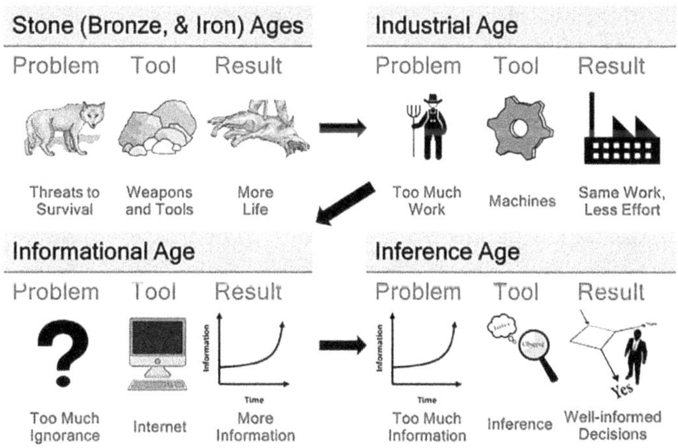

Figure 1.2 Progression of human challenges, tools, and results.

Age of Inference. The swift progression from the Information Age to the Inference Age, near the turn of the 21st century, advanced the requirement of tools with more sophisticated reasoning capabilities to make sense of all the data at our disposal (Figure 1.2). Whereas the invention of the steam engine by James Watts in 1769 helped to usher in the Industrial Revolution and the advent of the telephone by Alexander Graham Bell in 1875 helped to expedite the exchange of information, a single development to signify the start of the Age of Inference is harder to pinpoint. In fact, its development is still taking place at a spectacular, breakneck pace (Starčič, 2019). It is from the technologies of these previously established eras that we are now steaming ahead with the development of a new type of engine, one with information as its power: the inference engine.

CURRENT PROBLEMS

The consequences of the Information Age are unprecedented and profound. The advent of the internet has brought on an overload of information, analysis paralysis, and intellectual complacency. This is certainly pronounced in the younger generations, where students are quick to google an answer. Patients are prone to diagnose themselves via what they can gather online. Educators are tempted to adopt lesson plans at the click of the mouse. People may be quick to access information that helps them, but they may then forfeit the ability to make sense of it, consider it critically, or use it appropriately. The democratization of information has created an imbalance between expert and novice, with the accessibility of information equal to both but without the experience and expertise needed by the latter (Kross et al., 2020; Patterson & Gray, 2019).

Information Overload

With the immediacy at which information can be obtained and work can be conducted, current generations are losing their abilities to focus and concentrate on prolonged tasks. Surfing the internet, binge-watching television shows, and endless streaming and consumption of online content has created a shortened attention span and a desire for instant gratification. This abundance of information has paradoxically caused a reduced capacity to process information. "Information overload occurs when the amount of input to a system exceeds its processing capacity. Decision makers have fairly limited cognitive processing capacity. Consequently, when information overload occurs, it is likely that a reduction in decision quality will occur" (Speier et al., 1999, p. 338).

In addition to the rapidly growing abundance of information, other issues are contributing to information overload in this hyper-digital age. The ease of disseminating information over the internet, new online channels for distributing this information, and the large amounts of historical data are but a few reasons (Swenson, 2004). Information overload affects both individuals, distracting them in their work (Speier et al., 1999) and confusing them in their personal lives (Paul & Herbig, 1994), as well as institutions, where poor information management can lead to bad decisions (Mulder et al., 2006).

Analysis Paralysis

In a world where information is ubiquitous, there is always more information to consider. With an exponential number of choices before us, and with an exponential number of options per choice, the process by which we make decisions becomes more complex (Kross et al., 2020). Whether due to the complexity of the decision before us, or because of the fear of making the wrong decision, it is easy for us to simply request more information and defer decision-making. Simpler yet, it may be easiest to have *something else* make our decision. With information so easily called up by our devices, our desire for immediate reward has increased, and this demand for instant search results and social media likes may preclude our willingness to carefully scrutinize information for accuracy and interpret social interaction for meaning.

Defaulting to a search engine and allowing others on social media to preordain decisions have allowed people to distance themselves from the decision-making process. It also gives them a scapegoat to blame when a decision goes awry. To this end, it seems as if both the desire and ability to analyze information wane in light of the glut of information available at the tap of a button. Furthermore, as the time needed to digest information increases with the vast amount of data available, the time available to evaluate information decreases, and the dilemma of accepting what one reads at face value without properly vetting the information manifests.

Intellectual Complacency

Just like individual people, many institutions, including educational ones, are data-rich but analysis-poor. On the heels of amassing vast amounts of data, individuals and institutions can become complacent with the due diligence that is often necessary for understanding their environments. The drive to make data-driven decisions does come with its drawbacks. First, the bigger the dataset, the easier it is to find support for a particular hypothesis one chooses to test. Second, number crunching may be allowed to substitute for thinking and judgment. Data-driven decision-making must still be a rational approach based on experience, context, and a deep understanding of the underlying factors and assumptions of the problem (Rivers et al., 2020). With the deluge of information on television, the internet, social media, and so forth, one can actually end up knowing more and more about less and less, and the schools in which we teach our students are not impervious to this.

If I have seen further, it is by standing on the shoulders of giants.

—Isaac Newton

SOLVING PROBLEMS IN THE AGE OF INFERENCE

To solve meaningfully original problems, scientists must know what has been studied, how they were studied, and what directions those studies provide. Based on the findings of past research, scientists can determine where and how to make contributions to their respective fields of study. Yet, they face a paradox when addressing problems: An answer to one question leads to other questions. A solution to one problem exposes other problems. An outcome of one study unveils the potential for many others. This paradox only intensifies when the proliferation of information, questions, and answers occur, and this has brought on the necessity for more sophisticated, computationally demanding techniques and methods of analysis (Starčič, 2019).

Inference Engines

The Age of Inference has introduced new problem-solving tools that harness the power of technology, and the most fundamental of these are called inference engines. Inference engines, at their most basic level, are simply computer programs that use logic to infer answers to questions from data. The database that is queried by an inference engine is composed of metadata that are labeled or tagged so that they are searchable (Barr & Feigenbaum, 1981). In effect, an inference engine can search for existing connections between packets of data in a fraction of the time that a human could find those connections (Barr & Feigenbaum, 1981). The caveat, however, is that humans need to be equipped and well-versed in interpreting the connections and applying them to pertinent life situations. Data are only as good as the interpretations derived from them; therefore, inference engines are only as effective as they are able to help identify and analyze, within the inference engine's capabilities, chunks of information that allow people to derive meaning from that information.

Machine Learning

Machine learning takes the connections identified by inference engines a step further. Unlike logic-based methods, machine learning is probabilistic and uses statistical models rather than deterministic rules. The goal of machine learning is to make sense of the structure of datasets where structure does not yet exist. Computers are able to analyze copious amounts of data in a fraction of the time required by human brains. This capability allows machines to analyze data sets so that extrapolations can be made and predictive models can be created, tested, and improved. Machine learning can identify error in modeling with the incorporation of new data sets. Applications are valuable in industries such as engineering, healthcare, transportation, government, finance, and retail, while the implications of using machine learning in the field of education and other social sciences are just beginning to be realized, especially regarding differentiated instruction and assessment.

Artificial Intelligence

Artificial intelligence (AI) is the cutting edge of technological development with regards to inferential tools of reasoning. Simply speaking, AI employs the use of an artificial neural network (ANN), which is like a sophisticated regression model where the regression coefficients are weights

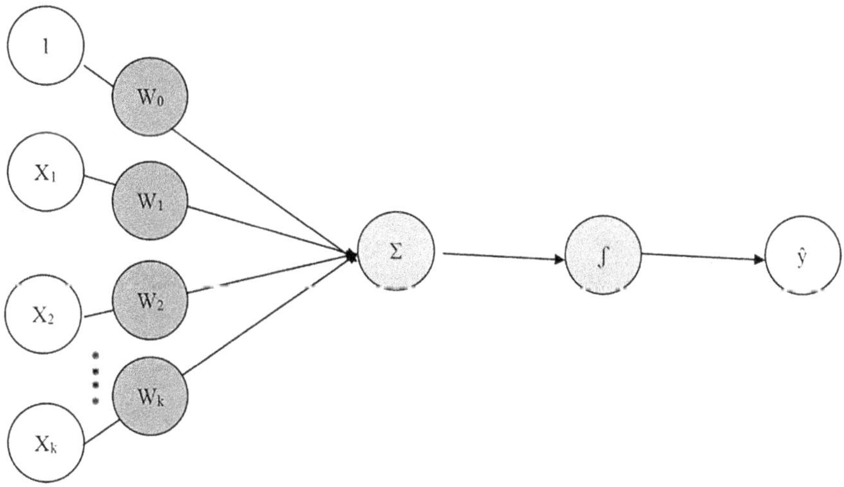

Figure 1.3 An artificial neural network.

($W_0 \ldots W_k$, see Figure 1.3) and can change. These weights change depending on the data coming into the model, and this signifies "learning."

As you can see, an ANN is a multilayered mathematical model inspired by the human brain. Like the neurons in our brain, they receive information (data). Input nodes are analogous to dendrites in neurons and are represented by the leftmost circles in Figure 1.3. While the leftmost circles are inputs, the rightmost circle is the output, analogous to the axon. Each circle in the hidden layers (Σ and ∫) represents a function that the inputs go through, ultimately leading to the output. Of course, the output can then serve as an input to another neuron, or ANN. To optimize the model, training must occur where various techniques are used to adjust the weights. Once optimized, ANNs are very good at finding patterns in huge amounts of data, usually supplied in real time and from various sources. This is what powers software used for facial recognition, autonomous driving, search algorithms, and so forth. Of course, there is a certain amount of error inherent in an ANN, just like with our own thinking (Carlini & Wagner, 2017; Nguyen et al., 2015; Szegedy et al., 2014). Since an institution with huge amounts of data might rely heavily on understanding the meaning behind those data, it is important to build, test, and verify the model makes sense, and this requires a vast number of considerations that even good human reasoning involves.

A good forecaster is not smarter than everyone else;
he merely has his ignorance better organized.

—Anonymous

IMPLICATIONS FOR EDUCATION

In education, there are several promising uses for AI, namely hyper-individualized learning, adaptive assessment, and teacher- or school-level value-added assessment systems. All of these focus on using data to identify patterns in student learning and other education data. These patterns are used to identify current strengths and weaknesses of students, teachers, and schools, and to provide feedback to these constituents (Louhab et al., 2018; Luckin & Cukurova, 2019). One of the most exciting and promising uses of AI involves not just the ability to personalize education for learners but also the ability for AI to improve equity of education for all learners.

Hyper-Individualized Learning

Personalized learning, differentiated instruction, hyper-individualized learning: Many times, these terms are used interchangeably when it comes to describing the push to address the needs of individual learners. These terms, however similar, are not synonymous. Personalized learning, conceptually, refers to a dated, albeit well-intended, process developed as a response to the standards-based pedagogy that gained a foothold in education during the last century. Originally designed to address and adapt to the specific needs of learners, personalized learning fell short as students were progressively more isolated and separated from the cooperative exchange of ideas so fundamental to deep, critical thinking processes. Differentiated instruction gained ground as an effective teaching practice with the move to inclusion classrooms. It refers to the practice of adapting instruction to meet the needs of each group of diverse learners in the classroom. Differentiation tends to work in conjunction with personalized learning, but the emphasis is more focused on specifically tailoring lessons to reach the same standards but in ways specific to the different types of learners in the classroom.

The drive to adapt learning environments into more individualized scenarios has grown as standards-based curricula have taken a foothold in education. The use of technology-driven individual programs, adaptive assessments, and self-paced curricula to differentiate learning has effectively turned many teachers into facilitators instead of content teachers. This occurs when schools allow teachers to solely provide online or other technology-driven programs for their students instead of integrating technology with standard lessons. Hyper-individualized learning is a term that has recently come to the forefront of education as more and more schools are adopting one-to-one technology for students. This practice, designed to facilitate mastery of learning standards, melds personalization and differentiation by focusing on individual learning plans for each student. Many schools are practicing this by using only technology-based learning with the teacher assuming the role of facilitator. Other schools are implementing this by trying out flipped classrooms. Publishers are launching digital resources for students that present study materials in different ways based on previous student responses, and the more the students use the study materials, the more the program identifies their strengths, weaknesses, and learning styles. No matter which form hyper-individualized learning takes, there are both benefits and pitfalls. Some of the pitfalls are isolation, academic dishonesty, lack of critical thinking, and reliance on search engines for information. However, if hyper-individualized learning is implemented as a fusion of traditional lessons, technology-based learning, and collaborative learning that involves deep, critical analysis of information, it can be a powerful tool to increase student achievement and advance critical thinking skills.

What does impactful hyper-individualization look like? It involves scrutinizing mastery of standards through frequent formative assessment and adjusting programs as needed to address any areas that need enrichment or remediation. Similar to establishing an individualized education plan for students with disabilities, forming an individualized learning plan for each student (one that is tweaked regularly) will lay the foundation for auspicious academic achievement. Additionally, allowing students to track their own progress, that is, self-assess, through their hyper-individualized learning plan can yield transformative increases in their academic achievement (Hattie, 2012). Furthermore, implementing classroom discussion and feedback to enhance hyper-individualization yields an even greater impact (Hattie, 2012). Imagine how powerful learning can be when students not only progress through their learning plan and track their progress but also are able to carry out classroom discussions about their learning in a demonstration of their critical thinking and metacognition.

Adaptive Assessment

Adaptive assessment is designed to grant students an assessment experience that is tailored to their individual learning accomplishments and to provide teachers with assessment data specific to their students' learning and capabilities. By design, adaptive assessment means using a branching assessment whereby the answer to each assessment question determines which question a respondent answers next (Doble et al., 2019). Subsequent question items may be more or less difficult, depending on the previous answer, to zero in on the true ability of the student for the standard the line of questioning is measuring (Doble et al., 2019). Adaptive assessments can be used to drill down into the strengths and weaknesses students have in order to identify areas where remediation is needed, areas where mastery has been met, and areas where enrichment would be appropriate (Hubalovsky et al., 2019; Louhab et al., 2018; VanMeveren et al., 2018). Using adaptive assessments in the classroom gives teachers access to actionable data that they may implement to customize learning experiences and maximize the impact of those learning experiences by meeting students at their level of need (Hubalovsky et al., 2019; Khosravi et al., 2020).

Adaptive assessment in education has many implications in the classroom. This type of assessment generates data that may be categorized according to various factors such as learning standards, base skills, and interpretive skills. As teachers are freed from the drudgery of grading, analyzing, and interpreting assessments when using adaptive assessments that are computer-based, they are able to incorporate practices such as individual conferencing and small group work to further explore areas of need and mastery as identified by the adaptive assessment (Matthews et al., 2012). It is important to note that computer-based adaptive assessment does not replace human interaction in student evaluation; instead, it should enhance it (Descritan et al., 2015). Educators have the responsibility of establishing strong relationships with students so that conversations about growth areas and mastery areas will result in more student learning.

Education Value-Added Assessment Systems

Value-added assessment systems have risen to the forefront of education as federal policies such as the No Child Left Behind Act (2001) and the Race to the Top Act (2011) have encouraged implementation of accountability systems tied to funding from various federal, state, and local agencies (Paige et al., 2019). In this test-heavy environment, different models for assessing the annual yearly progress (AYP) of students and overall effectiveness of schools are used by different states. Some of these models are hierarchical regression models and some are mixed models (Sen et al., 2017).

One of the most widely referenced models is the complex regression model from Tennessee, the Tennessee Value-Added Assessment System (TVAAS; Paige et al., 2019). The accuracy of these models has come into question of late as mass standardized testing issues have devalued and discredited resultant data in some states (McConnell et al., 2019). Regardless of which model an educational agency uses, value-added assessment systems utilize standardized testing data to calculate an effectiveness level for a school or district. Some of the models attempt to account for confounding variables such as socioeconomic status in order to level the playing field for test scores. Most models used are mathematically complex and rely on linear comparisons between annual test scores.

State and local education agencies have different policies in place for how resulting scores are used. Some scores are used as part of a larger metric that represents teachers' level of effectiveness. This level of effectiveness score, in turn, may be used by some districts for hiring and firing purposes as well as pay incentives. Because of the high-stakes nature of standardized testing and its tie to value-added models, many teachers have resorted to *teaching to the test* in order to artificially inflate their students' test scores and their resultant effectiveness scores.

Campbell (1976) cautioned, "The more any quantitative social indicator is used for social decision-making, the more subject it will be to corruption pressures and the more apt it will be to distort and corrupt the social processes it is intended to monitor" (p. 50). Thus, it behooves education agencies to discover ways to evaluate student achievement and teacher/school effectiveness that is without bias.

Cross-Curricular Connections

Information acquisition, assimilation, interpretation, and application are fundamental skills not only in the science classroom but also in other core content areas. They are likewise essential parts of executive functioning skills used throughout life. Sound problem-solving skills can be established in mathematics and science classrooms in the early years and applied in liberal arts classrooms as students mature in their critical thinking abilities. These crucial skills can be fostered by providing opportunities for students to ask questions, propose answers, discuss and defend positions, and make inferences from research to support positions and reframe answers. Students can no longer be expected to be rote memorization machines who spout canonical responses to basic questions. In core subject areas, teachers have the critical responsibility to help students learn to explore the cavernous sectors of their brains and weave together the information stored in those recesses into complex, synthesized solutions to problems (Kloos et al., 2019). In literature, this could be addressed by comparing themes across multiple literary works. In history or social studies, this could be addressed by proposing a solution to a problem faced by different groups of people in different eras. In math, students could propose multiple different approaches to solving a problem and defend which approach is the most useful. In science, students could propose a model for a scientific process and then design and conduct experiments to support or provide adjustment for their model (Krajcik & Czerniak, 2018). But, no matter the subject area, students need diverse opportunities and time to practice these skills so they will have the confidence to use them when needed.

Teachers are learners just as students are learners. It is crucial to ensure they are well equipped in their use of inferential reasoning abilities. Educators who routinely take in information and teach that same information, without taking the time to process it, do students a great disservice by not challenging them to utilize critical thinking and inferential skills, with or without technology (Mansour, 2020). Modeling creative thinking and processing of information and allowing plenty of time for students to practice these skills both individually and collaboratively will go a long way in helping students become absorbers of information rather than reflectors of information.

It is better to foresee even without certainty than not to foresee at all.
—Henri Poincaré

COMFORTABILITY WITH UNCERTAINTY

A major obstacle to applying machine learning algorithms and AI to real-world problems, which can be viewed as representing the forefront of current progress in inferential problem-solving, is the ability to do so with due consideration of the contextual, sociological, psychological, and less observable, tangible, and measurable factors that we as human beings often ponder (Hicks & Irizarry, 2018).

Consider, for example, our current navigation systems that rely on constantly changing inputs to produce optimized outputs. At first, these systems only offered one "best" route for navigation. As development progressed and more information was integrated with these systems, these navigational tools then began offering alternate routes from which the user could choose. Now, with even more additional layers of information within these systems, the types of maps and methods of travel (car, public transit, walking, biking, etc.) that these navigational tools use can even change, thus illustrating that the correct user-specific path and means by which this path is taken are dependent on context. The possibility of how this evolution of *decision-making* by technology—this advanced inferencing accomplished by machines but programmed by human beings—can more closely mimic, say, what a curious child independent of a well-defined desired outcome might consider and still be rendered "correct" remains to be seen.

Instead of providing solutions, the urge for certainty often creates new problems for completing highly complex tasks or resolving individual, nuanced decisions. How we are able to create and program machine learning algorithms to test knowledge in and apply results to different contexts and "alter their learning" as necessity and objective reason demand also remains to be seen. Transferring the higher stages of knowing, where one can tolerate ambiguity and uncertainty in one's thinking and doing, view one's own thoughts and actions critically, and still make well-informed and rational decisions, to the development of machine learning and AI will certainly take a phased and measured approach. Instilling higher-order epistemological adherences of knowing to those creators of such models—our future scientists and computer programmers—will be just as critical.

> *When a flower doesn't bloom, you fix the environment in which it grows, not the flower.*
>
> —Alexander Den Heijer

EQUITY IN EDUCATION

Furthermore, how do we do this for our students so that it is equitable and accessible for all? Relatedness of topics, motivating all students to engage holistically and metacognitively with their learning, and the teacher's approach to creating a certain type of learning environment all come to mind. However, inasmuch as knowledge and skill attainment requires a certain type of mindset, it seems to bear that *one's approach to solving problems* can be applied to new situations. How this might manifest in machines seems less certain, as they are constrained to the software coding on which they depend (as if this is so different with humans).

With regards to the factor that is probably most in control of the teacher (i.e., the type of learning environment he or she can create for the students), certain considerations come to mind. What type of teaching strategies can propel all students to adopt a more multiplicitous, relational, or reflective way of thinking? What sort of prompts, activities, or even assessments might move the neediest of students to think beyond their current confines of knowledge acquisition? Surely, some types of learning must involve rote memorization, regurgitation of facts, and singularly correct answers (as in learning the alphabet or multiplication tables), but other types of learning involve alternative solutions, argumentation, weighing evidence, and factoring in the empathic and contextual aspects of a complex problem.

Perhaps what is most important in the end, as students progress through their understanding of a subject area, is that they are all challenged appropriately, supported proportionately to their abilities, and encouraged to fail (Leung, 2019). As scientists, we know that every inquiry starts with a problem and that the method by which any problem is solved, on a fundamental level, is fairly standard. However, behind every theoretical perspective, statistical analysis, and clinical intervention is an anecdote that can make the topic come to life for the student. Because of this, it is usually through a constructive and shared struggle, even a collection of failures, that the best learning takes place.

Every student has unique perspectives and abilities that can be shared with others, and teachers should facilitate a collegial environment in which these varying viewpoints and talents can be exposed and developed (Patterson & Gray, 2019). Students ought to challenge the teacher as much as the teacher challenges the students. If students know that their contributions will be respected, their untethered curiosities are important, and are removed of the insecurities that sometimes surround uncertainty, then this may best allow them to grow in their learning, specifically, *their learning how to learn, how to solve ambiguous problems,* and *how to develop the inferential tools* that are becoming ever more ubiquitous. The capacity of the next generation to use these tools will be an important indicator of success in this fast-evolving Age of Inference.

REFLECTIVE QUESTIONS

1. What intended benefits and unintended consequences did the Information Age have on society? How have these shifted the knowledge, skills, and dispositions of its people?
2. What are the different good and bad ways inferential technologies (like automation, machine learning, and artificial intelligence) have influenced your life? How might this change further in the future?
3. The next chapter talks about the nature of a scientist's work. In your opinion, what ways will it remain the same and what ways will it change? What working principles do you think will be needed to thrive in this type of work?

CHAPTER 2

NATURE OF THE SCIENTIFIC ENTERPRISE

Harvey Henson

This is the greatest discovery of the scientific enterprise: You take hydrogen gas, and you leave it alone, and it turns into rosebushes, giraffes, and humans.

—Brian Swimme

Observing the physical world, systematically investigating natural phenomena through scientific inquiry, and developing a rational worldview that is informed by shared and reasonable explanations is the goal of science. Science is complex and diverse, patient until the fruit of evidence is obvious, delivered, and accepted. The scientific enterprise is a human enterprise of making sense of the physical world through inquiry and intellectual expansion. The goal of the scientific enterprise is to construct new knowledge, solve problems, advance human understanding, and cultivate the scientific mindset wherever possible but especially among our students and educators.

Age of Inference, pages 17–38

SCIENTISTS AS EDUCATORS; EDUCATORS AS SCIENTISTS

Nothing has such power to broaden the mind as the ability to investigate systematically and truly all that comes under thy observation in life.

—Marcus Aurelius

I'm a scientist, specifically a geophysicist; and I'm an educator. Each semester on the first day of science methods class, after introductions and icebreakers, I ask the preservice teachers to imagine and describe what they think a scientist looks like. Their responses and colorful drawings are most typically caricatures of nerdy, goggle-wearing, men in lab coats playing with test tubes. After exploring the topic further and guiding the students toward a more appropriate and diverse description of a scientist, I then ask, "Are you a scientist?" During the early years of teaching, I was surprised that my students did not self-identify as scientists and did not understand that educators and scientists might complement a single person, or profession. Occasionally, an emphatic, "Yes, I'm a scientist. I think we all do science," or some similar response, bursts out of these classroom discussions to stimulate enlightening deliberation and argumentation. Such responses are hopeful confirmation of the crucial work required if we are to advance toward the critical goal of a more scientifically literate nation and world (Hackling et al., 2001; Hurd, 1998; National Research Council, 2012; UNESCO, 1993).

Indeed, experience and research suggest our preservice students have a poor understanding of the nature of science (NOS; Al Sultan et al., 2018; Lederman, 2014; Lederman & Abd-El-Khalick, 1998; Schwartz et al., 2004). They suffer from misconceptions, possess limited science content, endorse negative attitudes, and struggle with who and what scientists are (Abd-El-Khalick & Lederman, 2000; Al Sultan et al., 2021; Amirshokoohi, 2016; Kazempour & Sadler, 2015). Findings of many science teacher educators and researchers echo these perplexing outcomes as described thoroughly by colleagues in subsequent chapters.

As McConnell argued in the previous chapter, the present Age of Inference requires a new mode of making sense of the world around us, and our teachers must be able to exercise a scientific mindset while developing the same outlook within their students. So how do we help our preservice students and teacher colleagues improve efficacy, attitude, and content knowledge with respect to the nature of scientists (NOS)? The field generally agrees that STEM educators need to acknowledge this dilemma plaguing science education and must act to implement inquiry-based science instruction aligned to the Next Generation Science Standards (NGSS; NRC, 2013a). For example, Short (Chapter 3, this volume), "The Nature of Science Education: Relativity of Theory," presents a thoughtful discussion contrasting the inadequacies of traditional science instruction with teaching methods aligned to the NGSS science and engineering practices to more effectively teach students.

The NGSS (2013), a framework to guide teaching and learning such that students are mentored to construct knowledge by actually doing authentic science and engineering, is not the magic elixir to fix everything wrong with STEM education. Indeed, this framework did not suddenly appear and abruptly expect that students should do science. In fact, science educators have practiced inquiry strategies and used problem-based learning (PBL) models of teaching science for many years (AAAS, 1993; Barrows, 1986; Bransford et al., 2000; Gallagher et al., 1995; Norman & Schmidt, 1992; Zhang et al., 2010). For instance, books, articles, and entire journals (e.g., *Interdisciplinary Journal of Problem-Based Learning*) are devoted to PBL. Schools, institutes, and centers have been established to advance PBL instruction and research. Even some of the most successful medical schools pioneered PBL strategies decades ago (Barrows & Kelson, 1993). However, the three dimensions of the NGSS, consisting of disciplinary core ideas, science and engineering practices, and crosscutting concepts, moved the inquiry teaching strategy bar significantly. The NGSS paradigm is a novel attempt to combine theory and practice such that STEM education may align more closely to STEM practice; in other words, teachers and students learn science knowledge and sensemaking together by doing science together. Every performance expectation of the NGSS presents a practice common to scientists and/or engineers and aims for students to do science. Short explains the three dimensionality of the NGSS and further develops its relationship to phenomenon-based learning in the next chapter.

Suffice it to say science education stakeholders mostly agree, if the NGSS model is implemented efficiently and the praxis assessed sufficiently, educator and student both benefit as proficient practitioners of science (and engineering). This is part of the secret sauce for developing critical problem solvers within our teacher education programs and preparing these educators to think, act, and teach like scientists. Of course, beyond teacher preparation, authentic science literacy training must continue to be a key component of STEM teacher partnerships and professional development. Teachers are the most important element in advancing educational reform and essential for effectively producing a scientifically literate citizenry (Lederman et al., 2013; Liou et al., 2019).

Although consensus on a precise definition of scientific literacy is still lacking among researchers—let's credit this confusing fact to a diverse, healthy scientific mindset—most of us would agree that transferring scientific literacy into classroom practice and student learning is problematic for teachers (Smith et al., 2012; Vieira & Tenreiro-Vieira, 2016). Teacher preparation programs play an important role in addressing this problem and should provide preservice elementary teachers with a solid science education, which in turn will provide opportunities for students to develop scientific literacy (Al Sultan et al., 2021).

The need for teacher education programs to assess preservice teachers' scientific literacy is stated clearly in the current NGSS paradigm. Preservice teachers face serious challenges in future classrooms and may struggle to adopt science education reforms that require a scientific mindset and a pedagogical focus on scientific literacy (Autieri et al., 2016). As noted earlier, without a scientific mindset or understanding of the diverse aspects of scientific literacy, preservice teachers may enter the K–12 classrooms with misconceptions about scientific literacy or they may lack the skills to prepare students and support them to become scientifically literate citizens (NRC, 2012).

What is required to prepare teachers who possess a science mindset? In the spirit of teaching science as inquiry (Zhang et al., 2010), the challenging question presented above may perhaps best be answered with another round of questions: "What is the nature of science?"; "What is the nature of a scientist?"; "What is the scientific enterprise?"

THE SCIENTIFIC METHOD

No one method, no paradigm, will capture the process of science.
There is no such thing as the scientific method.

—Lewis Wolpert

Aristotle (325 BC), scientist, philosopher, and master of inference (Suter, 1939), is often credited with conceiving the "scientific method," but he would probably be dissatisfied with the notion. The scientific method is a purported methodical process of scientific discovery that scientists follow dutifully. This misnomer, unfortunately communicated at multiple educational levels, usually consists of six sequential steps: problem, hypothesis, research, experiment, procedure, and conclusion. Educators and scientists misuse and even disagree on the terminology and components of the so-called scientific method (Hammer & van Zee, 2006; McPherson, 2001; Rudolph, 2007; Russ et al., 2008).

It is essential for scientists to record their work accurately, meticulously take notes, systematically collect, analyze, and interpret data, establish validity of procedures, and ensure reliability of results, so the findings will be able to pass critical peer review and the experiment repeated later if necessary. However, scientists do not actually follow such cookie-cutter steps to explore and understand phenomena. As Richard Feynman (1998) lectured, science is often imprecise, unfinished, and does not come with a specific set of instructions. Science is indeed less precise in terms of methodology and much more dynamic, unsolidified, and assorted in the quest to acquire new knowledge pertaining to the natural world. I imagine the processes of science are quite possibly as profuse as the number of disciplines of science multiplied by all of the scientists practicing science and then added together with each of their collected interests in science. Suffice it to say, the *scientific process* is not *the* scientific method.

Consequently, it is a mistake to impress our preservice students, or any student, with such useless recipes for how the scientific enterprise is *not* accomplished. Likewise, educators should never limit students' exploration and discovery of the natural world to a set of simple formalities or teach recipes for science learning that mislead, bore, exclude, and antagonize young people toward the practice of real science. Educators and practitioners of science need to model the scientific enterprise to our students and fellow citizens. The expectation for teaching science in K–12 requires teaching science as inquiry-based with problem-solving (NRC, 2012), which are core practices of the scientific enterprise, and this proposition is applicable to teacher preparation in higher education.

NATURE OF SCIENTIFIC INFERENCE: WHAT IS SCIENCE?

The art and science of asking questions is the source of all knowledge.
—Thomas Berger

The scientific enterprise is a systematic approach to investigate and understand natural and physical phenomena through an organized process of evidence-based inquiry, practice, and application. As Carl Sagan said, "Science is a way of thinking much more than it is a body of knowledge." Ideally, people seek to understand the natural world; we marvel, observe, explore, question, and use what we learn to make informed decisions for positive societal and environmental outcomes. However, it is through education that we strive to develop a NOS culture (Lederman, 2014). Understanding that other ways of knowing undeniably exist is helpful; comparably the NOS episteme is an appropriate context to teach our students the knowledge enterprise, specifically scientific knowledge, is paradoxically comprehensive yet uncertain and unfinished. Scientists are not the only ones challenged with this; teachers and students struggle with this also (Lederman, 1992).

Developing a scientific mindset, especially among students and educators who often view science as just another set of concepts or facts, is challenging. Yet this skillset is crucial if everyone is to participate in sense-making (Rutherford & Ahlgren, 1991) and become part of the informed citizenry (Lederman, 2014). Inference does not move forward without information pertaining to the phenomenon or problem of interest.

Evidence, data, established facts, and the like are prerequisites that must be gathered, analyzed, and interpreted before meaning and/or application of the information is achieved. This process of forming conclusions or opinions requires reasoning and sensemaking of the information at hand, and this is precisely what scientists do. Asking 100 scientists how they go about this work would yield similar responses, and their methods of inquiry will certainly include the same general procedures of inference. Nevertheless, the details of their labor to learn and the sequence of their investigation will undoubtedly be varied and unique.

For instance, scientists argue and debate—this is expected and essential for several reasons to advance and review knowledge. As a young, naïve graduate student, I was somewhat aware of this component of the scientific enterprise. However, only later did I come to understand how important such deliberate and earnest debate helps to advance the science of important ideas. I remember presenting research on Precambrian volcanism and subsequent geologic structures that formed the Lake Superior basin at a well-attended geophysics conference in Montreal, Quebec. The enthusiastic questioning that arose at the end of my technical presentation caught me by surprise. The fervent discussion which continued after the session, into the hallway, and all during lunch provided a real experience of healthy scientific argumentation and was motivation that later resulted in successful peer review and publication of the research findings.

I always appreciate the look on my preservice teachers' faces, the first week of our science methods course, when I tell them that science, real science, as Feynman (1998) argued, is mostly wrong. Many of them are shocked and have no idea what scientific investigation, inference, and discovery entail. Of course, we discuss their dissatisfaction and disbelief in this statement, safely expose their faith in the unbelievable, and begin to build new skills for science practice such as claim, evidence, and reason. "Are you a scientist? Rate your response on a scale of 1 to 10 and please explain." As mentioned earlier, these questions cause the students to pause and reflect on the NOS, and the questioning helps them initiate the development of a scientific mindset. Success occurs when they learn how to ask critical questions and teach their students to ask meaningful questions.

PARADIGMS, EPISTEMOLOGY, INFERENCE, AND THOMAS S. KUHN

To raise new questions, new possibilities, to regard old problems from a new angle, requires creative imagination and marks real advance in science.

—Albert Einstein

Rather than being an interpreter, the scientist who embraces a new paradigm is like the man wearing inverting lenses.

—Thomas S. Kuhn

Most of my science colleagues are practitioners of science, meaning we essentially apply science processes to investigate, solve problems, and advance knowledge. However, some are philosophers of science, and a few occupy multiple spaces of theoretical, applied, and philosophical inquiry as Thomas Kuhn, arguably one of the most brilliant science philosophers of recent times, noted (Bird, 2018). The philosophy of knowing and the practice of theorizing the methodic essence and validity of scientific inquiry are imperative to the enterprise of inquiry and scientific investigation. Every scientist, perhaps every person, has a worldview, a particular outlook and philosophy of life, whether personal or entirely scientific. Conceivably, serious scientists and science educators appreciate the developed echelons of philosophy and epistemology which form the practical basis, connections, and elaborations necessary for scientific praxis, meaningful knowledge advancement, and evidence-based reasoning.

No doubt, the scientific enterprise is dynamic and on the move constantly. However, the rhythm of knowledge generation is not generally rapid, nor predictably advanced, even if the application of knowledge is swift and perhaps premature. Both knowledge construction and application exhibit a multifarious nature of minor and major fluctuations, an intricate combination of rarefactions and dilations in mindfulness, power, and belief which tend to oscillate the process of sensemaking over time. It seems also that knowledge generation and interpretation overlap in complex associations, and the convolutions of knowledge application are guided by societal, personal, political, and scientific paradigms. Further, a "mature" science, according to Kuhn, experiences alternating phases of "normal science" and revolutions of discovery and progression of knowledge (Bird, 2018). Kuhn argued that gradual accumulation of knowledge is not necessarily a catalyst for changes in accepted scientific thinking. However, Kuhn suggested large-scale "paradigm shifts" occur as radical phase changes in the structure of accepted scientific thinking and cause societal upheaval (Kuhn, 1970).

According to Kuhn (1970), big ideas, philosophical transitions, and scientific shifts in knowledge and practice have occurred many times in human history and mostly involved positive revolutionary change. These "paradigm shifts" occur when overwhelming evidence and information accumulate, such that scientists, practitioners, and public stakeholders generally reach consensus, share a unified viewpoint, commence to constructively make sense of the information, and assist society in the application and benefit of this new knowledge (Kuhn, 1970). Theoretically, this methodical knowledge progression situates the new paradigm at the forefront of scientific endeavor and is accompanied by new societal models of thinking and application. Ostensibly, a new intellectual recess is birthed, or unfortunately in some instances a worse period of knowledge paralysis is triggered, but inevitably another cycle of scientific thinking, knowledge progression, and possibly a revolution of inference is initiated.

However much epistemology is tested, expanded, or even reimagined, it is not entirely reinvented. Learning and scientific discovery do not cease. As discussed earlier by McConnell et al. (Chapter 1, this volume), data and information are piling up faster than ever before in human history. An exponential accumulation of knowledge linked to the formidable, yet exciting, challenges of rapidly evaluating, interpreting, and applying this new information signals a distinct anomaly, a paradigm shift, occurring today as we enter an Age of Inference.

Paradigms are the recognized epistemological models or frameworks of knowledge within which scientists gather and interpret evidence. According to Kuhn, the NOS is not just about the evidence; rather, it is also about how scientists interpret and make sense of the information (Bird, 2018). Knowledge acquisition is a complex activity, and sometimes scientific information is inaccurate, biased, rejected, or amended before science may advance. Additionally, the fruitful dissemination of this knowledge to public stakeholders is an often-neglected specialization. If we are honest, the volume of information that effectively reaches the general population is often diluted, exaggerated, or disappointing by another measure. Moreover, the important responsibility of knowledge generation and utilization is extremely limited if "scientists" are the only practitioners of inquiry and inference. Accordingly, how a community or society decides to apply or extend the information is critically important. In our present scientific, educational, and societal context, the Age of Inference signals an all-play, a paradigm shift that invites everyone, everywhere to participate in scientific sensemaking.

ART AND SCIENCE; SCIENTISTS AND ARTISTS

I am enough of the artist to draw freely upon my imagination. Imagination is more important than knowledge. Knowledge is limited. Imagination encircles the world.

—Albert Einstein

Years ago, after long hours of processing seismic reflection data until my eyes felt like they would fall out my sockets, I stared late one night at the squiggly lines arranged side-by-side into long sections of complex seismic wavelets, a series of troughs and colored-in peaks. These were the acoustic echoes off rock layers buried deep beneath the surface. The patterns in the seismic data mimicked stratigraphic boundaries and geologic structures from an ancient world buried, compressed, and now revisited as digital images. I marveled at how the digital data collected as discrete functions of acoustic impedance was numerically transformed to digital art, graphical visualizations of the ancient Earth. The results were artistic, expressive, and representative of the physical world, at least the world 300 million years ago during the Pennsylvanian Period (Henson & Sexton, 1991). As the caffeine kicked in, I felt creative, inventive, and decided to explore further if possible. I converted some of the seismic data to audible format by pushing the complex signal through an oscilloscope, hooked up an amplifier and speaker, and played the data as sound at various frequencies. The output was somewhat musical, out-of-this-world, and according to a fellow graduate student it sounded like several whales crying for help.

Scientists, like the seismologist described above, strive to understand the natural world by recording, processing, investigating, and observing data. Artists intend to understand and interpret the natural world and the abstract through representation, creation, practice, and storytelling. Fundamentally, these vocations are not so far from one another; both want to construct, understand, and communicate new information, and the outcomes are often quite useful, even if they originate from different strategies and mindsets. At the risk of hugely oversimplifying, art is as interesting and complex as the humans who construct it, and science is likewise challenging and beautiful as the world discovered and imagined. Each discipline is unique and simultaneously similar.

Continuing with the "art of seismology" theme, seismologists using "SeisSound" video and audio compilation techniques recently developed ingenious and more effective methods of converting seismic data, including earthquake events and volcanic eruptions, into audible files (Kilb et al., 2012). By pairing seismic sound with colorful spectrographic visualizations and animations, these innovative researchers dramatically enhanced STEM learning and engagement (Kilb et al., 2012; Peng et al., 2012). Victor "Hugo" Benioff, a pioneer of modern seismology, experimented with the intersections of science and music throughout his career, and he was among the first to use audible conversions of seismic data to differentiate earthquakes and seismic attributes recorded with his high sensitivity seismographs (Benioff, 1953, 1955). He developed long period seismometers that allowed geoscientists to record earthquakes worldwide and to begin acoustic imaging of the deep interior of the Earth. Additionally, during the following decades as the Cold War began to heat up, monitoring and correctly deciphering the magnitude and location of man made seismic events triggered when the Soviet Union and other nations tested nuclear weapons was of the utmost importance to U.S. and NATO security (Richards & Kim, 2009).

Subtle intersections between art and science serendipitously create interesting relationships and novel thinking which help to advance the success of humanity. At other times, these disciplines intentionally unite to confront environmental, pathological, or man-made threats. Such connected spaces for exploring, learning, and developing individual and social realism were the intent of atomic scientists who collaborated with artists to stem the global nuclear threat. After the bombings of Hiroshima and Nagasaki and the advent of this new Atomic Age, coalitions of scientists, artists, and advocates were codified in scholarship and forged in purpose. One of the important efforts created from this period was the organization founded by former Manhattan Project scientists, the *Bulletin of the Atomic Scientists* (2021). The "Doomsday Clock" (2021) has signified the nuclear threat since 1947, and today this emblem includes other global threats as part of an informative scientific and public forum on global security.

Interestingly, the February 1959 issue of the *Bulletin of the Atomic Scientists* featured several articles on science and art collaborations submitted by scientists and artists (Langsdorf & Smith, 2020). The special publication showcased scientific research and laboratory outcomes as visual art and experts commented on the creative intersections and aligned purposes of the two vocations. "It made artists aware of the visual and conceptual beauty of the scientist's world, and made scientists aware of the degree to which aesthetic enjoyment entered into their own activity" (Langsdorf & Smith, 2020, p. 363).

Indeed, scientists seek to know more than is understood, and artists express much more than they know. Literary, musical, and visual artists collaborate with scientists in many ways, and artists will continue to creatively extend the scientific exploration and research outcomes of scientists. Fiction and imagination morph foundationally into scientific investigation and discovery, and technological advances in media and digital art are increasingly utilized to elevate learning and enhance the scientific enterprise across nearly every discipline. Correspondingly, scientists, technicians, and engineers expand the availability of information, materials, and technology which increase opportunities of creativity and artistic expression (Langsdorf & Smith, 2020). Collaboration of artists and scientists is much more than "adding" arts or creative practices to science practice or science education, or using technology and systems of art to communicate new knowledge. Artists and scientists working and learning together can result in "new ways of seeing, hearing, experiencing, and knowing" the natural world (Ellison et al., 2018).

GEOLOGIC AGES OF INFERENCE

Rocks are records of events that took place at the time they formed. They are books. They have a different vocabulary, a different alphabet, but you learn how to read them.

—John McPhee

Geoscience is the systematic study of Earth history, how our planet changes, and how life occurs and reacts to tectonic, climatic, and human modifications as part of large-scale cyclical systems (Lenton, 2016). Geologists analyze the processes and structures that shape our dynamic Earth and study the association and composition of materials, such as minerals, rocks, sediments, and other remnants that comprise detailed stages and sequences of strata, to reconstruct the geologic ages (McPhee, 1982). Geologically speaking, an age is typically millions of years and characterizes a thematic collection of events in Earth history punctuated by distinct global changes, sometimes rapid and other times gradual.

When the great forethinkers of geoscience began making sense of the rocks and strata of the British Isles and elsewhere, they were confronted with the problem of organizing and categorizing their findings. They first had to develop a geologic sequencing of the events responsible for deposition, lithification, and positioning of the interesting strata they observed. James Hutton eloquently described patterns in the rocks he observed near his farm in Scotland, and his interpretations resulted in the modern science of geology. Subsequently, Charles Lyell, a lawyer who consumed the writings of Hutton and other scientists, stood on their shoulders to advance this new science further.

Lyell debated with his scientific peers and argued that contemporary natural phenomena shaping the Earth in the early 19th century occurred in the ancient past as well. He demonstrated how these natural processes explain the geologic record of Earth's history which he observed during his many travels around the globe (Rudwick, 1998). These farmers, lawyers, and laymen were no doubt well-studied scholars who dedicated themselves to meticulously gather and interpret the natural evidence available to them. They were able to transform the understanding of Earth history in their day by presenting evidence and reasoning for their claims, and in doing so established the foundations of geology and introduced a fresh paradigm for modern natural history and evolutionary thinking (McPhee, 1998).

Historically, as the founders of modern geology studied the history and nature of the Earth, they devised a simple time scale to systematically describe and record Earth events (Figure 2.1). On this scale, starting with an *age* and going from the smallest time unit to the largest, an *epoch* is a group of more than one age, a *period* of geologic time is more than one epoch, periods of time are gathered into an *era*, and more than one era combine to form an *eon* which consists of thousands of millions of years (Cohen et al., 2020). Geologists seem clever to sort and subdivide the vastness of deep time, especially when no observers, except God and the heavenly host, were around to keep the time. It is humbling and also helpful to remember that humans, including us geologists, have only been picking up, implementing,

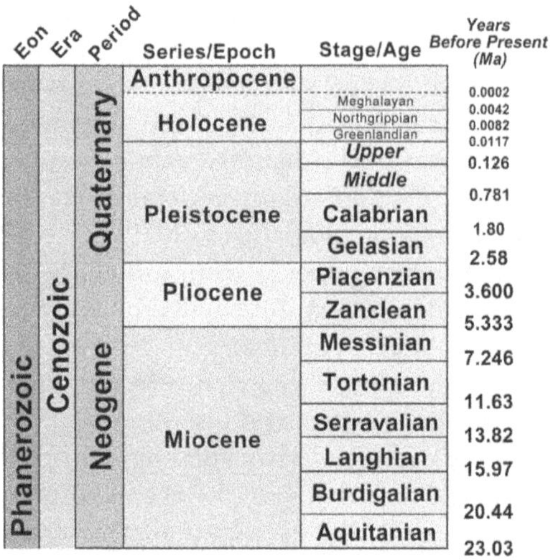

Figure 2.1 Ages, epochs, periods, eras, and eons of the geologic time scale.

and making sense of stones since the latter part of the Pleistocene Epoch, or about 0.035% of Earth history.

How do geologists decipher the ages of Earth's geologic history and account for the spectacular landscapes, formations, and deposits? Of course, geoscientists discover, measure, gather, and make sense of enormous amounts of evidence. However, this is particularly challenging because 4.6 billion years is tremendously long, and much of this time "appears" to be missing in the geologic record depending upon where we look. We'll come back to this dilemma. When geologists infer, we get excited about the big picture, and the abstract is often imagined before it is measured; but geologists just like other scientists are interested in discovering the evidence and sometimes deducing when information is missing (McPhee, 1982). However, the best geoscientists among us are quick to acknowledge the missing information, certain to offer an opinion on what is absent as well, able to distinguish between useful data and bosh, and dutifully go about gathering new data.

In 1912, Alfred Wegener developed a grand idea, a model of continents moving and joining as supercontinents that unified important geologic discoveries long before they were recognized or accepted. Wegener was mocked and his paradigm ridiculed by most scientists until 1968 when the theorists of plate tectonics organized enough evidence to build on his grand concept of "continental drift" (Le Pichon, 1968; Vine & Matthews, 1963; Wilson, 1968). Sometimes scientists are the opponents of good ideas until other scientists champion the revolution of a new paradigm (Kuhn, 1970).

In geologic time—you are probably wondering why I am babbling about eons, eras, and ages—well, this is what scientists do, especially geologists. We ponder, mentally meander as we explore, think aloud, and try to explain what we are thinking about to anyone who will listen. Heads up, you may not (or may) want to ride in my vehicle while traveling through rock exposures on the highway or in the canyons and mountain ranges of the Western United States. Geologists gaze at the colorful strata stacked and arranged like thick books in an old, dusty library, open up the volumes, read from pages, and visualize geologic time.

Good geologists are trained to think in pictures, describe things three-dimensionally, and imagine even more than what may be visible, which often includes significant intervals of time. As John McPhee (1998) declared, geologists tend to have "four-dimensional minds" and an "interdisciplinary ultraverbal way" (p. 611). As a geologist, naturally the first thought that occurred to me with regard to a book about the Age of Inference was how this particular age is positioned with respect to geologic time. Much like the way we teach our preservice teachers to use the K-W-L: "What I Know, What I Want to Learn, What I Learned" (Ogle, 1986), and similar strategies to construct and organize knowledge, I started thinking within the context of personal experience, scientific knowledge, and academic interest. I initially tried to use a personal context, and by default a scientific positionality and subjectivity grounded in the knowledge and extrapolations of as many colleagues as possible in order to better frame the topic of inference, especially in reference to the concept of time.

Present "ages" characterize human events and describe cultural and social phenomena, which come and go with much greater frequency than geologic ages. As McConnell et al. (Chapter 1, this volume) described, an age in civil terms is measured by marked references of human history. In this current Age of Inference, some of the world's greatest and most complex problems are, by nature, geologic and global environmental concerns that require efficient collection and collaborative analysis of enormous amounts of data.

Today, a broad spectrum of scientists and educators use an Earth systems approach to frame our discovery and understanding of how the earth dynamically changes over time (Lenton, 2016; Mayer et al., 1995; NRC, 1986). Earth system science (ESS) is a widely accepted geoscientific paradigm and application of systems science to describe how Earth's various subsystems interact within, on, and around the planet (Lenton, 2016). For example, fluctuations in the solid earth regions, such as the lithosphere, often activate or occur consequentially from interactions with other systems such as the biosphere, atmosphere, hydrosphere, and exosphere.

Obviously, studying the Earth and understanding these systematic relationships and intersections require collaborative efforts of natural and social scientists from many disciplines to employ global observation and sensemaking strategies. For example, a collection of scientists, with backgrounds in chemistry, atmospheric physics, environmentalism, geoscience, biology, oceanography, and ecology, recently highlighted importance of using the ESS framework to untangle current developments in human/nature interactions, to observe biophysical processes at global scale, and to develop more unified approaches to understanding and addressing anthropogenic phenomena (Steffen et al., 2020). Thankfully, such partnerships are increasing our understanding of our planet and promoting more effective and cooperative inference in dealing with our natural world.

CONSTRUCTING THE ANTHROPOCENE: DEVELOPING INFERENCE

Mr. McGuire: "I want to say one word to you. Just one word."
Benjamin: "Yes, sir."
Mr. McGuire: "Are you listening?"
Benjamin: "Yes, I am."
Mr. McGuire: "Plastics."
The Graduate, Nichols (1967)

In the 1967 movie, *The Graduate* (directed by Mike Nichols and written by Buck Henry), there is a conspicuous scene where Mr. McGuire, a family friend, gives Benjamin, the young graduate, seemingly important, one-word advice regarding the future... "Plastics." The concept of plastics seemed so obvious and forward thinking in the late 1960s, and so very modern and beneficial to everyone. Certainly, the plastics industry thrived and changed the world, figuratively and literally; however, there is quite a price for this success. Occasional unintended consequences to our human endeavors are part of human history, and unexpected outcomes to science and engineering enterprises are part of modern reality.

For instance, microplastics are present everywhere today, in every Earth subsystem, and a growing body of evidence regarding the negative and forthcoming environmental impact that the "genius" of plastics has wrought confronts us all (Zhang et al., 2020). Fortunately, scientists are working on solutions to this ecological disaster. Researchers are now engineering yeast to selectively degrade the harmful plastic polymers and upcycle (creating a higher-value product from the reclaimed plastic) to useful monomers (Dissanayake & Jayakody, 2021). Other scientists are discovering and creating designer bacteria purportedly to eat our way out of this problem (Yang et al., 2014). To avoid retrospect or worse, perhaps a less cavalier posture, tempered with a bit of healthy skepticism, and a more cautious approach toward promising technologies would be wise.

Perhaps, we should ask more questions and practice a more intense form of critical inquiry. In other words, what else might these engineered microorganisms want to eat after they devour the microplastics? Perhaps we should adjust our critical and scientific mindset with regard to new and future scientific endeavors, innovations, and technologies.

To say that humans have influenced our natural world is truly an understatement. Global climate change, human engineering of our natural world, resources mismanagement, rapid accumulation of our waste, among many other environmental concerns have rapidly become topics of scientific research. For nearly four decades, scientists have reported a profound, global disruption of the Earth systems caused by human activity that represents a distinct departure from the geologic time period known as the Holocene (or formerly Recent) epoch (Hamilton, 2016; Zalasiewicz et al., 2015). This anthropogenic demarcation, known as the Anthropocene epoch (Crutzen & Stoermer, 2000; Lewis & Maslin, 2015) and proposed by some to have originated in the 18th century (c. 1769–1784) with the invention of the steam engine by James Watts (Crutzen & Stoermer, 2000) at the onset of the Industrial Age (McConnell et al., Chapter 1, this volume), is now manifest as one the largest influences of Earth's history and natural systems. Concern for quality of human life as well as social equity, stability and balance in the natural world is quickly rising to the top of geopolitical importance in this modern era where the Anthropocene transcends well beyond national boundaries and agendas (Conversi, 2020). Scientists from a spectrum of disciplines gather and interpret data, disseminate results, advance our understanding, and collaborate with leaders and educators around the world to move this development to the forefront so that everyone can work to make sense of the human impact on our world, and if possible work together to mitigate the consequences.

Clearly, the present anthropological and ecological phenomenon confronting the Earth's systems is an all-play, especially in terms of education and scientific literacy (Moore & Miller, 2008). This present epoch of complex events and large-scale problems requires an Earth System Science approach that includes multidisciplinary problem-solving and sensemaking (Ehlers et al., 2006; Wysession, 2011). Collecting and making sense of enormous amounts of Earth systems evidence requires tedious examination, complicated analysis, and scientific collaboration that is beyond the scope and expertise of single individuals. For example, investigation of geologic records of recent sedimentation and correlation of that information to human data is like reading the pages of a very thick text written in several diverse languages, some ancient and/or extinct. Humans are the neogeological force constructing the layers of this new epoch. Decoding the very recent geological and environmental data, often buried in strata beneath deep lakes, locked within global marine sediments, or imprinted within organisms, ecosystems, and various reciprocals across the globe, is key to understanding this novel Anthropocene epoch and inferring the significance to society (Lane et al., 2019).

Most people would agree scientists intend goodwill—or at least to do no harm—as is the main principle of medicine and bioethics. Although scientists are not "social engineers," our aim is to participate and contribute to society as skilled practitioners who construct important knowledge and model sensemaking. We labor to increase knowledge and to make the world better. Scientists take heed of the data, trends, and signs that portend threatening conditions or warn of situations of potential disaster. Scientists study large, longitudinal data sets that summarize global changes due to human interference with the Earth's systems. Scientists not only research the natural systems and geologic processes, but we carefully decipher the cause and effect relationships and the interactions between humans and the Earth systems. Sometimes, we suggest strategies and interventions to mitigate potential negative outcomes.

However, human engineered projects to alter the surficial earth processes for the benefit of mankind have unknowingly resulted in more than geomorphological disturbances. For example, efforts over the last 250 years to master the watersheds, tributaries, and main channels of the Upper Rhine river in Germany by engineers like Johann Gottfried Tulla (1770–1828) successfully straightened the Rhine, improved navigation, and alleviated the effects of flooding (Blackbourn, 2011; Havinga & Smits, 2000; Pinter et al., 2006). Similar engineering feats, including locks, dams, channeling, and other planned human interventions of natural riverine systems have been accomplished all around the world and have affected nearly every waterway and river system. Of course, the vast Mississippi River system in the United States is among the most engineered features in the world (Remo et al., 2012).

Geologists, environmentalists, and other scientists have argued with engineers, bureaucracies, and policy makers about the detrimental environmental effects of human intervention along the Mississippi River from the headwaters in Minnesota to the distributaries of the delta at the Gulf of Mexico (Pinter, 2005; Pinter et al., 2008). The unforeseen costs of these human endeavors have emerged over the last century as environmental data have piled up, and concerns indicate the historical and recent human benefits now conflict with the natural environment and the quality of human life. This saga repeats at human and nature intersections around the globe far too frequently, and man's influence on the geologic systems and ecosystems is not always positive. In fact, these changes are measurably greater than natural or geologic processes in many instances (Steffen et al., 2007).

The Anthropocene is upon the entirety of humanity. We have constructed this new environmentally disruptive time period, and our coexistence with our world depends upon how quickly we make sense of our condition, purpose, and intervention in constructing this new epoch. Science can absolutely help, but a world full of scientifically literate people constructing knowledge together and building communities of shared interests on improving the human and environment condition will be of even greater benefit.

DIGITAL SENSEMAKING: THE COMPUTER

The inside of a computer is as dumb as hell but it goes like mad!
—Richard P. Feynman

When the problem [quantum chromodynamics] is finally solved, it will all be by imagination. Then there will be some big thing about the great way it was done. But it's simple—it will all be by imagination, and persistence.
—Richard P. Feynman

Arguably, one of the most transformative agents in the modern era of science and learning has been the computer. Computers, the electronic devices that digitally store and process all of our data, are everywhere and in all the various devices assisting us daily in every task and endeavor. Digitization of the world as we know it, or think we know it, is increasing all around us. Scientists and engineers create and use a seemingly endless source of digital technologies to guide our explorations, support discovery, drive innovation, foster invention, and advance understanding of the complex and dynamic natural world.

McConnell et al. (Chapter 1, this volume) pointed out that artificial intelligence (AI) is at the forefront of new ways in which scientists, engineers, analysts, and educators process data and create new information. Indeed, automation and AI regularly contribute to generating new knowledge, accomplishing the work, and educating our children; and, according to some experts, digital technology directly competes with humans in these activities (Herold, 2017; Klein, 2019). As AI, autonomous gadgets and vehicles, and digital computation become more ubiquitous, the citizenry will undoubtedly continue to benefit from these technological advances as well. However, everyone agrees that improved education and advanced training of a technically literate citizenry, consisting of more than digital consumers, is critically essential.

Additionally, critics of digital dependence and addiction caution us that computers and similar devices, which are sophisticated tools rather than experts with skills, may be causing other societal harms (Royakkers et al., 2018;

Rugai & Hamiliton-Ekeke, 2016; Van Rooij & Prause, 2014). Finding the appropriate balance to navigate, advance, and utilize digital technologies is a current challenge. Although machines and digital devices are dramatically more efficient at accomplishing some tasks or much faster processing calculations, at least for now these modern phenomena are insufficient and inappropriate substitutes for human critical thinking and sensemaking. We are not likely to be replaced soon (Autor, 2015; Jarrahi, 2018).

Beyond the realm of fiction, gaming, virtual reality, and edutainment, the human brain indubitably remains our most important tool for improving and making sense of the world. The interesting relationship between human cognition and the evolution of computer digital systems is a subject too involved for this chapter, and beyond the scope of this text. However, every scientist understands how the computer age and the present digital transition of almost everything have transformed discovery and dramatically influenced the creation of new knowledge. The digitization of personal and corporate information, currencies, art, and other valuables (think "non-fungible tokens"), and entire financial systems is creating radically new industries (Chowdhury, 2019). The science of cryptology and blockchain as a "science of it all" digitization is rapidly transforming our economies, inspiring personal prosperity, creating financial liberty, and producing virtual communities as well.

Additionally, what will the unseen digital euphoria or unimagined chaos of the coming quantum computing reality bring to our society? As quantum theory and harnessed computation edges closer to fruition, this technology promises to surge digital data processing speeds beyond imagination and to revolutionize our lives and communities (Feynman, 1985, 1996). The astonishing exponential capacity of these computer systems, which will be capable of performing in parallel many trillions of logical computations per second rather the mere billion operations per second of our present machines (Rieffel & Polak, 2000), will present an opportunity and a challenge for human inference required to make sense of and apply all the new knowledge generated and accessed.

Indeed, as education and everyday society experience a transformation from an age of information overload to a new reality of critical, adaptive, and big data analysis which progressively rely on augmented intelligence, artificial intelligence, and machine learning, basic and advanced skills of problem-solving and computational inference are increasingly essential. Teachers and educational technologists with such skills are already in critical demand and will absolutely be required to help our students learn and prepare for this new age (Klein, 2019).

The digital phenomenon influences nearly everyone, and accordingly human participation, endurance, and dependence within this digital world are equally validated. Humanity and the digital world are intensely connected; and this tethering to machines is assuredly evolving into a shared future of advances and failures. Inquiry, an important virtue of a free and democratic society, has the opportunity to prosper in this computational science environment where machines are learning along with humans. As with the scientific enterprise, there is some degree of uncertainty of the outcome, and there are other concerns especially regarding our privacy and freedoms in the digital future as well. We understand there are important questions that science can address well; however, there are some questions we currently are unable to answer (Feynman, 1998). Human imagination and persistence along with powerful computational partners will drive digital learning, progress us beyond our current abilities, and develop innovative applications to help solve our new global problems. Meanwhile, we humans have much to learn and benefit vis-à-vis the rapidly advancing world of digital technology, and researching all of the new human interactions and consequences that come with it will require advanced sensemaking and innovative application to find meaning and the best way forward.

NOISE AND NOISE REMOVAL

Progress is made by trial and failure; the failures are generally a hundred times more numerous than the successes; yet they are usually left unchronicled.

—William Ramsay

The objective in acquiring, processing, analyzing, and modeling scientific data is to enhance the signal and to decrease the noise. Noise is the undesirable component or unacceptable spectrum of the data. Taking careful measures to prevent or minimize background information, or noise, at the onset of data collection is good project design and avoids the "garbage in, garbage out" scenario during data processing. After gathering the information, whether quantitative or qualitative, analog or digital, visual or audio, the next step is the systematic removal of information that does not contribute to solving the problem, or does not help the investigator answer the research question. This seems rather straightforward, right?

Detection, filtering, suppression, and elimination of digital noise in disciplines like seismology, remote sensing, electrical engineering, mathematics, bioinformatics, and image processing require sophisticated computer algorithms. Increasing the signal-to-noise ratio, a measure of the amount of desired signal relative to the amount of background (undesirable) noise (Johnson, 2006), is necessary to produce the desired outcome. High-level image processing techniques remarkably reduce noise for a range of problems such as composite noise patterns in high-resolution geophysical data (Figure 2.2) used to image ancient Pueblo ruins (Henson et al., 2003),

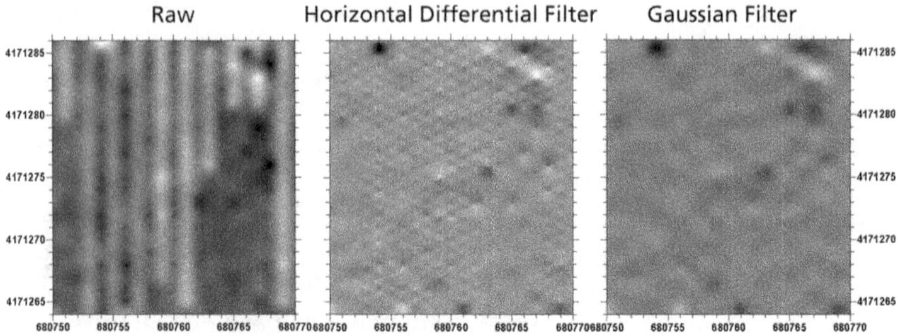

Figure 2.2 Noisy magnetic gradient data digitally filtered with a horizontal differential operator and a Gaussian filter to enhance magnetic signatures related to ancient Pueblo ruins.

signal striping (Chen et al., 2017) and impulse noise (Ajay & Kumar, 2014) in remote sensing and satellite data, and advanced iris detection (Amrita et al., 2013) and facial recognition/detection (Nagpal et al., 2010) developed for security applications. Document analysis techniques that eliminate impulse (Gaussian) noise common to poorly conserved or scanned manuscripts allow enhanced text recognition, improve fraud prevention, and rapidly detect important document features such as signatures (Haji et al., 2012). Experts in bioinformatics use noise removal to augment DNA sequencing processes and reduce error in large data sets during microbial diversity research (Quince et al., 2011).

How does one decide what is unacceptable or unimportant data? Quality control ensures through comparison the output meets the acceptable standard or desired specification. The better question may be: What is desirable? In science, much like art, the desirable depends largely upon the problem and the problem solver. Although Thomas Kuhn (1970) was not referring specifically to noisy data, he profoundly argued that scientists, and the scientific enterprise, do not always "proceed well," and consequently the data may become contaminated (i.e., noisy).

Kuhn's concept of paradigm calls for scientists, and I will humbly add all of us, to systematically construct ideas, establish and respect beliefs, and when necessary question and challenge the paradigm (Kuhn, 1970). Standards are desirable, and they establish reasonable and recognized certainty for a time; theories are prevalent, may be well-substantiated, and might withstand the scientific enterprise; however, laws of nature are uncommon and do not get replaced. Therefore, who decides what is desirable, needed, or best? How do we work collaboratively to filter out the noise in the enormous amount of information? Kuhn reminds us to challenge the paradigm.

The current epoch dominated by human activity, the Anthropocene, is a clarion call for making sense of the world full of information and reducing the noise pertaining to certain global events; for example, pandemics, civil injustice and tension, political unrest, violence, and other trials which threaten our freedom, democracy, and society. Epochs are comprised of ages, and it seems reasonable and practical that this current epoch should encompass a time of sensemaking, an Age of Inference. Scientists have answered the call many times to investigate and produce solutions, and most recently challenged the process with genetic technology to develop vaccines for COVID-19 in record time (Kim et al., 2020). Natural, social, and political scientists may collaborate magnificently to interpret the evidence and provide insight to guide society through such perils and unknowns. Of course scientists do not have all the answers, and an overwhelming accumulation of information still has to be processed and interpreted; and someone has to check for validity and reliability, evaluate the data, remove the bias, and remove the noise before the results are usable.

Noise and noise removal have always been an important part of the scientific enterprise. Adding additional noise during the debate and interpretation of the data is problematic. Respectful disagreement is expected and productive in science; however, disrespectful insults and name-calling are always inappropriate and unproductive (Edelman, 1893). As we argue and debate the meaning of knowledge, contemplate which is data and which is not, what is helpful and what is not useful, we must educate to promote critical scientific literacy and employ strategies of scientific enterprise to carefully construct, comprehend, and apply new knowledge.

REFLECTIVE QUESTIONS

1. While the difference in phrases may seem subtle and insignificant to many, describe ways in which quality instruction about the true nature of the scientific enterprise, rather than "the scientific method," could impact the interest in, acceptance of, critical thought about, and productive use of science by future cohorts of young citizens.
2. Thinking of the Age of Inference in relation to the geologic timescale, develop a cogent argument for other "ages" you would include in the current epoch. Give reasons for the inclusion and/or exclusion of other ages in this current epoch. If we are truly moving from the Information Age to the Age of Inference, provide evidence and reasoning for what may come next.
3. As we are propelled further into a world of digital sensemaking, will tools such as artificial intelligence and machine learning increase or decrease

the need for a broadly scientifically literate society? Reflecting on the intersections of art and science as well as the presence of noisy data, what uniquely human role in inferencing remains (if any) even as computer technologies continually breach limiting barriers?

CHAPTER 3

THE NATURE OF SCIENCE EDUCATION

Relativity of Theory

Philip C. Short

Le mal de prendre une hypallage pour une découverte, une métaphore pour une démonstration, un vomissement de mots pour un torrent de connaissances capitales, et soi-même pour un oracle, ce mal naît avec nous.

[The folly of mistaking a paradox for a discovery, a metaphor for a proof, a torrent of verbiage for a spring of capital truths, and oneself for an oracle, is inborn in us.]

—Ambroise-Paul-Toussaint-Jules Valéry

NO PLACE TO FLY

But before the understanding comes the wonder. Comes the delight.

—Simon Barnes

During an October, outdoor, biology lesson, a student's curiosity prevailed over her teacher's pontifications as she blurted out, "What's going on with

Age of Inference, pages 39–58

all of those blackbirds cackling and fluttering in the trees?" Just as the novice teacher began to redirect the girl back to his topic of predation, a louder cacophony demonstrated the Doppler effect as a dense flock of starlings appeared over a ridge. In awe, the students all pointed to the sky as those restless, perched birds began to rise and join the dance in convoluting waves across the horizon. Regaining control of the class, the instructor soon had all the students looking down, again, at the regurgitated owl pellet in hand for his well-prepared and structured lesson. This was no place nor time for flight.

Zugunruhe is a composite German word used by ecologists and, in particular, ornithologists when referring to a certain restlessness observed prior to impending, migratory departures (Kramer, 1951). The dated reference is offered to both credit the term's originator and, moreover, to illustrate how a well-established and researched concept in science may remain mysterious with fluid interpretations 7 decades later. As typically taught, specific climatic-hormonal cues serve to trigger individual changes resulting in group anxiety which initiates migratory flight. The phenomenon is often presented as though it is a precisely timed event to which students could nearly set their clocks.

Earlier studies do, indeed, clearly establish that photoperiod is a primary cue for initiating migratory restlessness (Gwinner, 1989, 1990); however, the influence of gonadal hormones has subsequently been found to play important roles in regulating overall migratory behavior (Ramenofsky & Wingfield, 2007). Further research by Owen et al. (2014) revealed that elevated testosterone levels can trigger the onset of migratory behavior even without normal photoperiod cues. Additionally, Doren et al. (2017) recently suggested the existence of higher evolutionary lability, than once thought, in the timing of zugunruhe with variance in the intensity and timing of restlessness among age groups as well as both inter- and intra-population variations. With decades of data collected on pre-migratory restlessness, the known and the uncertain tango together through time, challenging ecological researchers, in the most scientifically fascinating ways, to constantly reexamine their calculations and inferences.

Science classrooms, labs, and outdoor education centers are always sites where a semblance of zugunruhe is evident... or should be. The young teacher in the vignette above might have well been commended for both classroom management and lesson planning. Accolades might have been received for making his lesson more exciting and real in the outdoor setting. Nevertheless, the essence of science itself appears lacking as students were expected to simply catch authoritative, bolus facts hurled at them. Their attentiveness to the mentor's harangue belied an internal ferment to explore and soar.

SOLID STATE EDUCATION IN AN AMORPHOUS WORLD

If I'm concerned about what an electron does in an amorphous mass, then I become an electron. I try to have that picture in my mind and to behave like an electron, looking at the problem in all its dimensions and scales.

—James West

Diverse applications for modern life (including solar cells, thin-film transistors, light sensors, optical memory devices, x-ray image sensors, optical memory devices, laptop computers, and smartphones) are reliant on amorphous materials science (Dargar & Srivastava, 2019; Migliorato & Rahman, 2017; Morigaki & Ogihara, 2017). In the production of pharmaceuticals, the amorphous state is critical in determining the solid-state physical and chemical properties of many dosage forms (Hancock & Zografi, 1997). The new technological products of scientific applications are lauded by the general public. The investigatory processes, such as amorphous thin-film research, however, have had less appeal. Responding to a popular, social media site, Skylar (2013) claimed that people don't actually [explicative] love science. Reminding us that science is a hard, time-consuming, collective human endeavor, he argued that most people love the "residue" of science over the "process."

In P–20 schooling, students are too often passive consumers of science and technology rather than young researchers engaged in the processes of discovery and knowledge creation. In a solid-state, digital information age with teachers ill-prepared to guide inquiry into the amorphous, authentic data sets that could and should be compiled by their students, the easier default is to inculcate with the residue of science so readily available. Prime opportunities are often missed to encourage curiosity and capitalize on serendipity. When a proper scientific mindset is missing from even our science teachers, golden moments to help students develop the habits of mind necessary for critical questioning, repeated examination of data, and valid inferencing are lost as static, didactic instruction predominates over inquiry-based, constructivist approaches.

Although Short (2018–2019) posited that well-prepared science teachers, comfortable with constructivist and inquiry-based approaches to the national science education frameworks, are key to building national literacy in the sciences, Colburn (2017) stated that inductive reasoning, important to the framework, is rarely emphasized in schools. Teachers in science classrooms too often present material from a largely deductive approach with broadly assumed generalizations, if not an entirely modernist narrative. This traditional, and still common, content-oriented pedagogy stands counter to the National Framework for K–12 Science (National Research Council, 2012) and Next Generation Science Standards (NGSS Lead States,

2013) where a primary goal is for students to make sense of the natural and designed world through engagement in science and engineering practices (Schwarz et al., 2017). McComas (2016) argued that science teaching should focus on the goal of helping students understand how scientists develop, generate, test, and validate scientific knowledge, and that an appreciation for the strengths and limits of the scientific enterprise is essential. Simple dissemination of scientific dogmas not only falters in accomplishing the goals above, it effectively misdirects young people into a distinct paradigm of thought and actions inimical to scientific literacy.

Multiple, complex reasons exist for the poor status of science education today. Federal data has shown that every state in the United States experiences overall shortages of teachers, and most districts have struggled to find teachers for math and the sciences (Strauss, 2017). Science teacher shortages are not new but may be worsening. Inequities are evident as the dearth of qualified science teachers worsens in hard-to-staff schools such as urban and rural schools with concentrated poverty (Dee & Goldhaber, 2017).

Recent reports have revealed over 100,000 individuals teaching without having met certification standards (Sutcher et al., 2016), and just 36% of new science teachers are teaching only in their trained subject area (Christensen, 2017). Within the past decade, one of the most pressing concerns in education, according to Marginson et al. (2013), has been securing a sufficient force of highly qualified science teachers to staff public school classrooms, and Mentzer et al. (2019) indicated that students are negatively impacted by poor teaching quality as only a small fraction of science teachers hold degrees in their content fields.

Long-term trends have shown very limited institutional support and time for science education in elementary schools due to emphasizing priorities for performance on high-stakes testing (Banilower et al., 2015). A paucity of adequate science instruction is offered below Grade 4 in most schools in the United States. Smith and Nadelson (2017) reported a lack of proper training, deficient scientific culture, and resources for science teachers as parts of the problem, but did suggest teachers could become more effective in implementing NGSS practices if provided adequate professional development and modeling of inquiry strategies. Science educators are now encouraged to cover fewer topics in deeper, more meaningful ways; however, while the phrase "less is more" is frequently heard, it is less commonly implemented (Huff, 2016).

The gravity underlying efforts to curb the falling tide of educators who are proficient in both science content and pedagogical skills goes far beyond simply filling spaces in classrooms. Developing a broad base of P–20 teachers grounded in science content and equipped with student-centered strategies is essential for the changing scientific and technological needs of the nation and world. Students face a world where they will frequently be required to make important decisions on issues that range from health care to the environment (Huff, 2016).

The negative societal effect of teaching science as facts and products rather than a process to critique extant facts and improve products would be a stagnation in the support for basic research essential to the very benefits of science enjoyed by all. The populace needs to understand, through education, that solid-state advances rely on fluid, amorphous processes.

THE BORGESIAN MAZE IS NOT THE LUNCH LINE

The path to a scientifically illiterate society may begin with kindergarten classroom management.

—Philip Short

Stuart Firestein, neuroscientist, delivered a TEDTalk provocatively entitled "The Pursuit of Ignorance" (Firestein, 2013). In this primer on "what scientists do," he critiqued the similes of science being like an iceberg, puzzle, or peeling back the layers of an onion, clarifying that such examples incorrectly suggest that we can, theoretically, conquer all that is known with dedicated effort. Indeed, most metaphors and similes do fall short when attempting to illustrate the nature of science (NOS).

There is no intent here to disparage the daily efforts of primary school teachers in herding energetic bairns from classroom to lunchroom, no doubt a feat that, perhaps, breaches the boundaries of natural science to the realm of miraculous. Nevertheless, herd management of student populations that frequently exceed building and staffing capacity inadvertently encourages the early development of a Weltanschauung antithetical to establishing scientific habits of mind. Not unlike a Skinner box, the operant conditioning of young minds to follow authoritatively prescribed routes in lockstep, within the square tiles, to their nutritive rewards reinforces the idea that experts have determined the best and only path to their sustenance.

Likewise, back in the academic classroom, direct instruction too often mimics the lunch line in promoting inculcation over exploration. While modern classrooms allow for more discussion and open-ended responses during group work, a primary goal, dictated by the administration, is to prepare students for high-stakes testing which is assumed to be heavily content-based. In the span of the first few years of schooling, prior to most students experiencing any appreciable science instruction, children begin to internalize and comply with a conviction that knowledge is finite and that correct answers make them successful. In many science classes, exclusive use of lectures, textbooks, and rote activities lead to ritually compliant students quietly listening to a barrage of information but with no internal commitment to the topics (Chitman-Booker & Kopp, 2013).

A more realistic pathway to life's lunchroom or academic understandings would be the Borgesian maze (Borges, 1964). In this labyrinth, there is an entrance; however, as one thinks they have found their way to completion, another more complex maze emerges ahead, reducing the expert to novice on another level. Wilson (1998) compared Ariadne's thread in Borges myth to his concept of consilience among branches of learning needed to traverse the uncharted world of the maze (p. 67). He likens the champion of Athens, Theseus, as humanity in its search. The murderous Minotaur of deep, hidden passages is our dangerous irrationality inhibiting us. Wilson reminded us that it would be easier to retrace Ariadne's thread back to the gallery entrance of pure physics than to move forward into more complex and multidisciplinary problems ahead. Still, the only direction for humanity is, of course, forward. The only direction for fledgling scientists in school is deeper into the tangle.

It would be easy to dismiss the analogy of the Borgesian maze as impracticable for science education, that young learners need finite and concrete conclusions... even if this approach may not comport with the real world of science. A simple video game played by youngsters for 4 decades might suggest otherwise. Pac-Man, essentially a mouth chasing dots and fruits while avoiding ghosts in a kaleidoscope of changing colors, meanders through a maze until successful completion... only to find that another, more complicated labyrinth awaits. Wade (2015) further explored Pac-Man in the context of Borge's labyrinths and posits that the game "generates complex notions of space and time which are indicative of changing cultural, ethical and political considerations in wider society" (p. 248).

The modified scenes repeat over and over again, juvenile fingers guiding the round, yellow adventurer. During afternoon screen time, with no expected closure and infinite convolutions ahead, players are eager for the next challenge. They are subtly immersed in "complex notions of space and time where a range of ideas incorporating consumption, entertainment, play and gender are transmitted throughout" (Wade, 2015, p. 248). Kids fully understand the quest will never end. In school the next morning, however, students may again be subjected to promulgation with sharp edges on starting and stopping points, serving to limit rather than expand their horizons.

The first step toward cultivating a scientific mindset may be to redirect our youngest students from the straight and narrow lunch line to lifetimes of discovery in the Borgesian maze.

FROM SAGE TO ENGAGE

The sage belongs to the same obsolete repertory as the virtuous maiden and the enlightened monarch.

—Mason Cooley

Chitman-Booker and Kopp (2013) reported that students often sit in classrooms finding science boring, unengaging, and useless which can result in apathy and behavioral issues. Those who have had the good fortune of enjoying the true adventures in science, either as professionals or simply enthusiasts, would likely be disappointed if returning to such classes. Fortunately, current science education reforms offer the opportunity to change pedagogy for more meaning and effectiveness for learners (Nagle & Pecore, 2019).

Haverly et al. (2020) reported an emphasis on strategies to facilitate sensemaking in equitable ways among all students in the modern calls for science education reforms. They found that teachers who made space for sensemaking created opportunities for shared epistemic authority. These new reforms have culminated over decades of research leading to guiding documents from Project Synthesis (Harms & Yager, 1980), Project 2061—Science for All (American Association for the Advancement of Science, 1993), the National Science Education Standards (National Research Council, 1996), the National Framework for K–12 Science (National Resource Council, 2013), and the NGSS (NGSS Lead States, 2013). Resulting from the principles in these documents and accompanying NGSS is a conceptual and paradigmatic shift in approaches to science pedagogy (National Resource Council, 2013) outlined in Table 3.1 as adapted from the National Research Council (2015).

The required instructional shifts have not been embraced without skepticism and resistance. While Penuel et al. (2015) stated that the NGSS would result in better instruction, increased interest, and performance in science, adapting to these new frameworks for science education has not been easy for many educators. Quinlan (2018) noted that even curriculum stakeholders at a workshop hosted by the National Academies of Sciences, Engineering, and Medicine (2019) to address challenges of NGSS were baffled by some of the unique obstacles. The NGSS operationalizes shifts in science education by integrating instruction in three dimensions: (a) science and engineering practices (SEP), (b) disciplinary core ideas (DCI), and (c) cross-cutting concepts (CCC).

The importance of providing students with genuine practices of scientists has been well-established (Anderson, 2006; Driscoll, 2005; Schwarz et al., 2017).

TABLE 3.1 Instructional Shifts Required for 3D, Inquiry-Based Science Education

Science Education Will Involve Less	Science Education Will Involve More
• Rote memorization of facts and terminology	• Facts and terminology learned as needed while developing explanations and designing solutions supported by evidence-based arguments and reasoning
• Learning of ideas disconnected from questions about phenomena	• Systems thinking and modeling to explain phenomena and to give a context for the ideas to be learned
• Teachers providing information to the whole class	• Students conducting investigations, solving problems, and engaging in discussions with teachers' guidance
• Teachers posing questions with only one right answer	• Students discussing open-ended questions that focus on the strength of the evidence used to generate claims
• Students reading textbooks and answering questions at the end of the chapter	• Students reading multiple sources, including science-related magazine and journal articles and web-based resources; students developing summaries of information
• Preplanned outcomes for "cookbook" laboratories or hands-on activities	• Multiple investigations driven by students' questions with a range of possible outcomes that collectively lead to a deep understanding of established core scientific ideas
• Worksheets	• Student writing of journals, reports, posters, and media presentations that explain and argue
• Oversimplification of activities for students who are perceived to be less able to do science and engineering	• Provision of supports so that all students can engage in sophisticated science and engineering practices

As the focus in reforms has been on how in-service teachers must instruct to further student achievement in the emergence of NGSS, Hanuscin and Zangori (2016) contended that university teacher preparation programs must also be reflective in considering the courses and curriculum necessary to prepare teacher candidates. To be properly prepared for instruction under the new frameworks for science, new and seasoned teachers alike need to be open to shifting their teaching practice in a manner that reflects understanding and functional use of the content and structure of three-dimensional science standards (Reiser, 2013).

Adopting the 5-E instructional approach (Bybee, 2015) can help teachers in addressing the three dimensions of science education in modern reform efforts. Sequencing learning opportunities for students and introducing real-world, relevant phenomena in the initial engagement phase of the learning spiral assists in making the shift from teaching the residue (facts/products) of science to involving young minds in the process of the scientific enterprise. Intriguing but simple discrepant events are often employed in the engage phase by those attempting 5-E approaches. These are often potent presentations to stimulate students for specific, prescribed content activities. Employing relevant phenomena could expand the meaning for the engagement phase.

Shifting pedagogical strategies deeper into the new paradigm, teachers should consider tiers of initiating phenomena for different purposes. Three general categories of phenomena for science education (NGSS Lead States, 2013) are:

- Anchoring phenomena, where they are used to provide focus for a full unit of instruction;
- Investigative phenomena, which provide focus for a specific instructional sequence within a unit; and
- Everyday phenomena, which provide personal, relevant connections between anchoring and investigative phenomena to common experiences of students.

Use of phenomena needs not follow a single prescription. More than one phenomenon may be used at each categorical level, and one example may not sufficiently cover an entire learning segment. The use of some phenomena may be planned for students to figure out within a single class period. This can aid their grasp of a basic concept. Other phenomena may be complex and require weeks or even months of collaborative study, mastery of several different concepts, and clever integration of CCCs for students to resolve. The most complex, and arguably most important as students mature, are those phenomena that simply cannot be fully understood. Phenomena that lead students to more questions of increasing difficulty, as particular inferences made from student investigations are either rejected or supported by their data, best contribute to the development of critical thinking.

As stated in Chapter 1, information is now ubiquitous, but there is always more information to consider. While the access and dissemination of information are, indeed, expedient in this digital era, the post-Baconian scientific mindset has assumed our information sets and mastery of concepts to be incomplete for more than 3 centuries. A persistent and significant lag, however, has thwarted acceptance and implementation of this mindset in precollege education settings. Before 1900, science education was largely viewed as a body of facts learned through memorization and direct instruction. An inquiry-based rationale started appearing in classrooms by the 1950s and 1960s (Duran & Duran, 2004). These decades welcomed the Science Curriculum Improvement Study (Atkin & Karplus, 1962) for elementary schools. This project laid groundwork for the development of the 5Es in 1987 (BSCS Science Learning, 2019). The evolutionary events of modern science reforms, of course, have been complemented by ongoing implementations by practitioners.

Unanimity existing among studies has shown inquiry-based approaches to align with how people learn (Bransford et al., 1999; National Research Council, 2000). These studies suggested a considerable benefit to students. Supporting the idea above, that young learners are equipped to enter the academic Borgesian maze, Etheredge and Rudnitsky (2003) confirmed that even young children can learn through inquiry processes. Providing structure to open-ended inquiry is afforded by the 5-E instructional model with appropriate phenomena being introduced in the engagement phase. Passmore and Beauchamp (2017) contended that

> phenomena can act as a useful starting place for instruction, act as a springboard for curiosity, and ground instructional sequences . . . if we [instructors] harness the wonder in specific ways by asking appropriate questions to focus students on particular aspects of the phenomena. (p. 15)

In Figure 3.1, the student is squarely in the center of the learning process which begins with observations of phenomena guided by questions

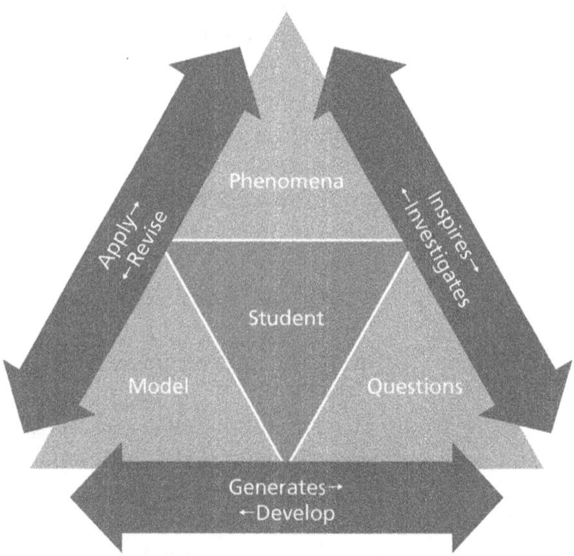

Figure 3.1 Phenomena–questions–models design for science instruction. *Source:* Adapted from Passmore & Beauchamp, 2017.

from the instructor who is facilitating the educational opportunity. Proper prompts inspire students to compose questions they have about the phenomena which, in turn, provide a basis for authentic investigations into the nature of the phenomena. As curiosity segues into focused inquiry, the students have organically moved into the exploration phase of the 5-E learning cycle. The process is not, necessarily, unidirectional as students may reengage with the phenomena as they are guided to design controlled tests of their hypotheses.

One of the more difficult parts of the 5-E approach for many teachers is the explanation phase. Feeling either external or internal pressure to cover more content, educators frequently find it more efficient to simply provide the "right" answers, whether or not they have actually allowed their students to generate the questions. As illustrated above, students should work collaboratively and equitably to develop their own explanations and models for better understanding of the phenomena in question. In this educative process, complete accuracy of student explanations is not required, but teachers typically struggle with flaws. In an empirical case study of the discursive language aspects of science education, Nygård Larsson and Jakobsson (2020) do caution, nevertheless, that students capable of transitioning between everyday and scientific languages are advantaged over those who only use colloquial language or relate the content to only everyday experiences. Their work suggests that language supports are important within the complex of school structures to maximize students' successes in an inquiry science class.

If science educators could truly adopt a scientific mindset, it would be obvious in their course planning that the professional, scientific community is constantly testing older models of the natural phenomena, confirming or revising explanations, and expecting new inferences to be tested by others in the field. It is, therefore, perplexing that we would expect young learners to "get it right" the first time using crude methods of investigation. It is equally baffling that teachers value conclusive answers over the process of sensemaking. Better understandings of the tentative NOS among teachers are imperative for improvements in science education.

Swapping the instructor with students at the center of the experience and allowing students to learn science more similar to the actual work of scientists could nurture an alternative worldview—one that should foster a grasp on the rigor of science, the difficulties in forming explanations and models, and the contingencies on which inferences are based. If teachers would transition from being a sage to a guide who will engage students, diverse populations would likely be empowered and granted a greater voice in creating their own knowledge as opposed to being uncoupled from concepts as passive consumers of information.

ISLANDS IN THE OKAVANGO

The educated do not share a common body of information, but a common state of mind.
—Mason Cooley

Typically, in late November, rains begin in the Angolan highlands and peak in January. Drops coalesce into converging rivulets to become the Rio Cuito, Cuanavale, and finally Cubango, the latter of which meanders along the Namibian border before dropping into the unique Okavango Delta of northern Botswana. The floodwaters will flow for 4 months over more than 1,200 kilometers to reach the lakes and marshes of the endorheic basin.

When the water of the delta boundaries is most restricted with exposed dry soil in the basin, fungus termites swarm, mate, and start building their iconic, massive mounds—the largest found anywhere in Africa. Uniquely built above the water table, the house built by termites becomes the foundation of homes for countless other animals. While hippopotamuses, elephants, and other large mammals create new channels through the marsh vegetation each year, the termite mounds have the greatest impact on the dynamic landscape as they dictate water flow, cause sediment deposition, and evolve into islands. Annually, the hydrology is altered as emergent terrestrial habitats trade places with submerged aquatic environs.

Scale is important. An aerial view makes the Okavango appear as a vast wetland dotted by separate islands... or, perhaps, it could be seen as terra firma generously sprinkled with parcels of water. Distinct herds and individuals within those groups can be seen while poling a *mokoro* (type of canoe) through canals. Closer examination on land might reveal individual termite workers collecting dried grass for their fungal farm. Giraffes, lions, buffaloes, storks, crocodiles, sausage trees, and, yes, the termites—all may be seen as "islands" in the Okavango. Nonetheless, all function together in an intra- and inter-specific dynamic driven by *stigmergy* (Grassé, 1959) where "individuals work as if they were alone while their collective activities appear to be coordinated" (Theraulaz & Bonabeau, 1999, p. 97). Lewis and Marsh (2016) defined the concept as "completed work that stimulates more work" (p. 1). Analysis of data from diverse studies of this alluvial fan encroaching on the Kalahari Desert, depending on scale of view, could yield quite different inferences for students of the Botswanan delta.

Whether immersed in curiosity about the functional dynamics of a vast wetland or trying to evaluate and improve interactions within science classrooms, it would seem important to adjust the focus of our scopes. Smith (1978), studying mud wasps, provided insights on the stigmergic behavioral mechanisms coordinating multiple, independent nest-building actions by showing that even solitary individuals are preadapted to social coordination. Studying a constructivist science education program is not entirely unlike observing other social species. Instead of a mud or paper nest, science students are building increasingly complex understandings.

A class can become an ecosystem of student interactions as individuals catalyze each other by identifying problems to explore, securing materials for investigation, generating products individually and collectively, developing inferences, and subsequently responding to those inferences. Borghini (2017) described this type of system as a

> cybernetic feedback loop where the action of one agent produces a modification in the environment that, in turn, stimulates the continued action of another agent... becoming a design engine that triggers and directs further actions in the correct sequence without need for top-down control. (p. 271)

An ideally planned 3-D, inquiry-based science course within a constructivist, 5-E approach might begin to approximate the stigmergy found in a pristine habitat. The top–down control of the teacher could give way to positive cybernetic feedback loops in the student population.

From the moment of birth, a child begins developing a stream of consciousness in the new world outside the womb. Individualized perceptions, understandings, and decisions will run, like rivers, through rapids and turbulence to loiter in recurring pools in which all input from the watershed of experiences is processed and sorted. From the purity of shallow headwaters to the sediments in brackish and deepening estuaries, the course inevitably changes over time... unless dredged, straightened, and channelized for singular purposes such as cheap transport of the basics from one place to another.

Educational institutions built upon the philosophies of essentialism or its close relative, perennialism, emphasize the transmission of core bodies of knowledge in disciplined and well-structured ways (Sadker & Zittleman, 2018). From these perspectives, learning should be focused on the objective, basic facts or assumed realities with a curriculum for preparing moral, functional, and productive members of society (generally defined by the dominant culture). Didactic, direct instruction can be sufficient for most goals in these educational archetypes and their associative, societal agendas.

In contrast, progressivism promotes hands-on or experiential learning opportunities in a student-centered, cooperative environment. John Dewey, often considered a founder of progressivism and one of the most influential educational philosophers to date (Williams, 2017), adapted and furthered ideas for education gleaned from the Baconian scientific enlightenment. Dewey deconstructed the wall between scientific processes and knowledge, promoting operationalism—the precept that knowledge *is* the scientific process in action (Clark, 1980). While experience was at the center of Dewey's philosophy, he did not grant equal value to every type of experience.

Those with negative, longer-term impacts on students, he assigned as *miseducative*, and those with lasting positive impacts as *educative* (Dewey, 1938). He deemed traditional education that stresses information transmission as often "restricting future experiences and rendering students callous to ideas, losing the impetus to learn" (pp. 25–26).

Certainly, Dewey's approach has had its detractors. Egan (2002) held child-centered, science-based, progressivist thought as responsible for what he called a catastrophic state of schooling. Egan lamented the lack of history, grammar, memory work, and rigor in modern education and made arguments for essential knowledge. Undoubtedly, Egan was influenced by Hirsch, one of the important voices for educational essentialism, the back-to-basics movement, and a common cultural literacy (Hirsch, 1996; Hirsch et al., 1988). Still, John Dewey remains a most influential educational philosopher, although he would surely find that adequate implementation of his principles has fallen short.

The intent should not be to place prejudiced values on the varied epistemological orientations in education; rather, the long-term effectiveness of approaches to curriculum and instruction merely needs frequent examination with respect to the ultimate goals of the discipline. Cartesian views that shaped Mortimer Adler's traditional and conservative essentialist models of education situate bodies of knowledge as static islands on which students stand alone to maintain and defend against the perennial floods of change inevitably reshaping natural and social landscapes around them. The *Paideia Proposal* of Adler (1984) would essentially treat students as "minds to be developed through immersion in and transmission of perennial and canonical works of high cultural significance" (Magrini, 2009, p. 4).

If, epistemologically, the goal is to sustain and perpetuate that which is familiar, comfortable, and presumably certain, a rational strategy, albeit blind to the larger realities sweeping around the shores of the classroom, might be to transfer islandic knowledge and skills from teacher to students who will successively assume the stationed posts. The essentialist ideology simply does not comport, however, with the goals and methods of science nor science instruction. Progressivism and constructivist models of education, building on instrumentalist views of knowledge, can be found emerging in the educational philosophies of Herbert Spencer, Charles Peirce, and William James, but is nowhere more evident and relevant for science education than in John Dewey's brand of pragmatism which values a path to knowledge and solutions comprised of experiences of human–environmental interactions that follow scientific protocols.

Magrini (2009), by invoking Dewey, provided clear contrasts between education that perpetuates traditional knowledge and that which constantly seeks to test old axioms while searching for new insights. Those who hold to the essentialist view of knowledge demand utter certainty to their knowledge, and further, believe they can achieve it. Conversely, those adopting the instrumentalist view believe that knowledge is always beyond categorical justification, for it is malleable, always in the process of being reworked, always in the process of evolving by means of our attempts to continually refine our theories about the world based on previous experience (Dewey, 1990).

A satellite snapshot of the Okavango Delta may suggest a majestic and ancient system of stable islands among still waters, one whose mysteries have been worked out by researchers of the past and can be shared across K–12 classrooms and university classes. Doing so, however, would ignore both the richness of this enigmatic, evolving basin as well as the collective scientific mindset that could have been cultivated through exciting and engaging pedagogy in those classrooms.

THE RELATIVITY OF THEORY

The world can only appear monochromatic to those who persist in interpreting what they experience through the lens of a single cultural paradigm, their own.

—Wade Davis

Any teacher of science can recall students who, on the first days of class, exclaim, "I don't like science." This is usually followed with, "I've just never been very 'good' at science." Similarly, science teacher educators in universities may sense apprehension and lack of self-efficacy among teacher candidates as they reflect on their abilities to adequately teach science lessons. While expected, perhaps, among future teachers of primary to upper elementary grade levels who only completed the required general education science courses, issues of self-confidence also afflict middle and high school science teachers who have completed more robust science courses. Elementary teachers often feel that they do not know enough about science concepts in general, even to address elementary student questions. Upper-level teachers from science majors often express insecurities about knowing enough on more complex, specific, science topics of their subject area to "stay ahead of the students." Interestingly, when drilling further into the sources of anxiety, a common cause of trepidation exists across the spectrum of grade levels taught. All of these teachers and teacher candidates are conflictingly trapped in an essentialist pedagogical view of a constructivist discipline.

In December of 2019, the report of a novel coronavirus in humans, SARS-CoV-2, began circulating. The virus appeared at the time to, sometimes, be the cause of significant respiratory issues. It became a newly described disease soon to be labeled COVID-19. By March of 2020, only a couple of months later, positive cases of and tragic impacts from SARS-CoV-2 were identified in countries around the world. Spreading through human populations, almost as rapidly as the virus itself, were assorted ideas about origins, diverse symptoms, purported cures, and stories of "where it all ends." Quite often, these ideas were reported as theories, from family gatherings to news outlets alike. Of course, 6 months later or 6 years later, there could be no real theory of COVID-19 as theories exist on another plane and timescale.

Both vignettes above of the teacher candidates and the brief history of COVID-19 illustrate that one of the more serious barriers to properly cultivating a scientific mindset is the relativity of theory. Admittedly, this provocatively invokes Albert Einstein's groundbreaking formulations on light, space, time, and gravity. No person, moderately educated to have heard rudimentary explanations of special and general relativity, rejects this theory. Those most unfamiliar with relativity still do not reject the daily conveniences only possible because of the theory—such as electricity from generators and transformers, GPS navigation to a new restaurant, and more. The term theory is accepted as a known, tested, and validated entity in this context. If adhering to Alder, we might include this knowledge in "canonical works of high cultural significance" to be transmitted.

Beginning teachers of science (and teacher candidates), having completed minimal requisite courses as well as those who have taken upper-level sciences, are likely to accept Einstein's theories as immutable laws of the universe. Therefore, they may become insecure about their personal comprehension to adequately convey the physical principles to their students. The teachers and candidates may also possess the same level of acceptance for cell theory, germ theory of disease, gene theory, atomic theory, kinetic theory of gases, molecular orbital theory, geological gradualism, and quantum mechanics... even with fragmentary knowledge of the concepts.

Simultaneously, being influenced by larger societal influences, the same teachers/candidates may very well subscribe, uncritically, to claims that SARS-CoV-2 originated from consumption of snakes, bats, or pangolins, that it was created in a lab for nefarious purposes, or that it is simply a nonexistent hoax concocted for governmental control. With little or no confirmatory data, or worse, confirmed data to the contrary, these truncated, unsubstantiated "explanations" are erroneously referred to as *theories.* The lack of consistency is further demonstrated by current and future teachers rejecting well-established scientific principles such as the big bang theory, theory of evolution by natural selection, the safety and efficacy of vaccines, and climate science.

The relativity of theory—or differential valuation and acceptance of established scientific findings—among too many extant populations is both a symptom and a source of deficient scientific literacy in society. The interpretation of language matters. Beyond the term *theory*, other commonly misused or misappropriated science expressions are *hypothesis, law, skeptic, nature versus nurture, significant,* and *natural.* Incorrect use of each grinds on the nerves of scientists in different ways. Rhett Allain, physicist, argued that we should do away entirely with the terms hypothesis, theory, and law in favor of *model* as a replacement (Ghose, 2013). In the same article, Michael Fayer, chemist, agreed that many people fail to understand the difference between the scientific use of theory—an explanation substantiated through vigorous repeated testing over time—and the common, layperson understanding of theory—*just an idea* that lives in someone's head. However, Fayer, finding similar problems with Allain's replacement term, model, contended that incorrect use should not change the language of science. Rather, better science education is warranted.

Srivastava (2018), in the article from which the subtitle of this section was adopted, posits that, in order to optimize the interpretation of data/information in scientific studies, observers must hold to two goals to: (a) explain the relative frequency of occurrence among different outcomes and (b) attempt predictions regarding the behavior of unobserved outcomes of the system based on his observation of past outcomes. "For either (or both) of these purposes, the observer must associate a level of certainty or uncertainty with each possible outcome of the system" (p. 3).

The relativity of theory is an obstacle to overcome at both ends of the spectrum if cultivating mindsets for functional science literacy is to be achieved. Many people experience cognitive disequilibrium when called upon to have confidence in inferences derived from empirical studies while, simultaneously, asked to recognize and be comfortable with a level of uncertainty, as healthy skepticism is embraced. Carl Sagan, popular astrophysicist as well as author and host of the *Cosmos* television series, described "true skepticism—not feeble or agenda-driven denial or contrarianism—as the 'self-correcting machinery' of science" (Ghose, 2013, para. 16).

Examining views on the place of NOS in science education and adapting elements identified by Lederman (2007), Kotter and Hammann (2017) composed six essential aspects of NOS that people should learn (p. 452).

1. a distinction exists between observation and inference,
2. a distinction exists between scientific laws and theories,
3. scientific knowledge involves human imagination and creativity (explanations are inventions),
4. scientific knowledge is subjective and/or theory-laden (background factors affect scientists' work),
5. science is practiced in the context of a larger culture (scientists are the product of that culture), and therefore,
6. scientific knowledge is tentative (*it is never absolute or certain*).

Likewise, eight aspects of NOS for K–12 education, identified by the NGSS (NGSS Lead States, 2013), comport well with the six elements above:

1. Scientific investigations use a variety of methods.
2. Scientific knowledge is based on empirical evidence.
3. Scientific knowledge is open to revision in light of new evidence.
4. Scientific models, laws, mechanisms, and theories explain natural phenomena.
5. Science is a way of knowing.
6. Scientific knowledge assumes an order and consistency in natural systems.
7. Science is a human endeavor.
8. Science addresses questions about the natural and material world.

An emphasis must be placed on the holistic internalization of the NOS by students and their teachers alike. The ability of people to make decisions as scientifically informed citizens is dependent on their personal views of NOS (Lederman & Lederman, 2014).

A most difficult hurdle to cross for teachers and their students is accepting a paradoxical confidence in the tentativeness of scientific data analysis. The misconception that science is fixed and absolute is common among K–12 students and preservice teachers (Lederman, 2007; Mesci & Schwartz, 2017). Students get a false impression that there is always a right or wrong answer whenever science teachers use the word *proof* rather than terms like *tentative conclusion* or *inference* in science courses. The accompanying anxiety in classrooms with dichotomous choices for success can create learning environments where students are less likely to take risks and try new ideas (Lederman, 2007).

This loops us back to the discussion of why epistemological considerations are vital in framing the foundation for science education. Dewey's advocacy for experience in education supports a modern constructivist approach for facilitating a mindset grounded in the NOS and which properly parses the relativity of theory in society. Essentialist classrooms dominated by direct instruction strategies tend to thwart the cultivation of the scientific mindset. Capps and Crawford (2013) argued that teachers must adhere to sets of knowledge and beliefs that engage students in answering science-oriented questions with data as evidence and with the understanding that inferences are tentative.

Even science professionals who have successful records tend to struggle. Every researcher would like to believe their experiments and models are accurate, but all complex systems are subject to failure, and some outliers are unavoidable. While good tools are available for estimating uncertainties, scientists are often hesitant to acknowledge long tails of uncertainty that produce outliers (Bailey, 2018). For scientists, teachers, and beginning students of science alike, developing and maintaining the proper scientific mindset is a perpetual and necessary requirement.

In the Age of Inference, as we become inundated with data from the explosive results of the information age, it will become increasingly essential for every member of society to acquire sufficient skills that enable the organization, assessment, and inference from the torrents of available evidence . . . as well as the unfortunate streams of misinformation. Fortunately, with reforms in science education, opportunities have blossomed to shift instructional approaches toward more meaningful and effective learning and teaching (Nagle & Pecore, 2019).

Using the 5-E approach to 3-D science, we can *engage* students in their empowered interests to look up and fly, as they join in the dance of the ever dynamic processes of science and engineering. Providing the security to *explore* in a messy, amorphous world of data/observations will help a future generation dismiss mistaken notions of rigid dichotomies. With thoughtful prompts for students to *explain* their findings through a maze of possible conclusions, they can deepen their understanding through additional levels of convolution that will both focus their attention on the data and reinforce the idea that there is always more data to collect and analyze. Moving from a sagacious teacher-centered role to a supportive student-centered one will aid students in making real-world connections with phenomena being studied so that they can *extend* their knowledge constructions for broader applications. Students, as well as the concepts they are learning, can appear isolated and disconnected just like islands in the Okavango. Refocusing the time allotted and scale of study, however, can produce a vibrant, dynamic stigmergy to their collaborative, open-ended learning environment. Interwoven throughout the inquiry process should be opportunities to formatively evaluate in a manner that provides a self-correcting mechanism for guiding the most educative experiences.

Although many publications and presentations beyond the scope of this text will address various questions more specifically, a grounded understanding of NOS and the relativity of theory in society is vital and prerequisite to the quality of all other discussions that follow.

> Science is not a bunch of facts. Scientists are not people trying to be prescriptive or authoritative. Science is simply the word we use to describe a method of organizing our curiosity. It's easier, at a dinner party, to say "science" than to say "the incremental acquisition of understanding through observation, humbled by an acute awareness of our tendency towards bias." (Tim Minchin)

REFLECTIVE QUESTIONS

This book addresses several topics from the perspectives of diverse authors. Fundamentally, the overarching theme is education or cultivation of a *Weltanschauung* for scientific decision-making and progress:

1. How do we educate (primary, middle grades, secondary, and postsecondary people) to embrace the blitz of information now available? Should it be all information? Who decides?
2. How can we help people of all ages develop the abilities to parse claims into categories of support that is substantial from that which is fragile? How is this accomplished in a world of specialization, where we all rely on "other experts?"
3. How will digital technologies like artificial intelligence (AI) and machine learning (ML) assist in answering the above question? How can (or should) we trust AI and ML? How can we educate to help a future generation both rely on assistive technologies while remaining alert to what cannot or should not be left to AI and ML?

CHAPTER 4

MATHEMATICS

Language, Modeling, and Comparison Assisting Inference

Mary Barone Martin, Tammy Jones, Dovie Kimmins, and Teresa Schmidt

The miracle of the appropriateness of the language of mathematics for the formulation of the laws of physics is a wonderful gift which we neither understand nor deserve.

—E. F. Winger

Recently a student in a graduate mathematics class I was teaching asked me after class, "Dr. Martin, what does math study?" I asked him to elaborate on what he was asking. (Actually, I said, "What?"). The student said, "Oh you know... botany studies plants and geology studies rocks, but what does math study?" I realized there were about six different ways to answer the question, all being true, and I needed to be careful with my answer.

The fact that the graduate student, with many years of experience studying mathematics, and a faculty member, with many years working/teaching as a mathematician, wanted to ponder this simple-sounding question speaks to the broadness and multifaceted nature of the mathematical enterprise. One can observe that over the years, many scientists and mathematicians

Age of Inference, pages 59–74

have exploited the connections between mathematics and science to further the development of both; physicist E. F. Winger, if not the first, then very eloquently expressed the amazing truth noted in this paper's introductory quote from Winger's paper entitled "The Unreasonable Effectiveness of Mathematics in the Natural Sciences" (Winger, 1960). Three years after this paper, Winger won the Nobel Prize in physics for his work in describing the nucleus of the atom (and coincidentally using algebraic group theory in the process). His paper is well-known for having generated controversy amongst scientists and the general public (who took turns arguing both sides of the premise that his observations supported the independence of science from mathematics and religion). In this chapter, as we attempt to answer this student's question, we will contemplate the nature of mathematics, the role mathematics can play in inference, distinguishing mathematics from/as a science, and some ideas regarding paradigm shifts. Our thoughts will develop as we examine how various tools and branches of mathematics have developed side-by-side with the progress of science; in particular, we will be exploring the distinctions that distinguish mathematics and science and yet make each a necessary companion to the other. For the purposes of this discussion on inference, science, and mathematics, we emphasize the connections between paradigm shifts and new knowledge.

NATURE OF MATHEMATICS, SCIENCE, AND INFERENCE, PART 1

Most academics would argue, broadly, that mathematics is a science. Carl Friedrich Gauss (1777–1855), who many consider the greatest mathematician since antiquity, called mathematics the queen of the sciences (Colyvan, 2012). So what is the difference, if any, between mathematics and science? Arguably, mathematics differs from the "physical sciences" in that mathematics most often deals with abstraction and abstract theory. The sciences most often deal with the concrete. However, the reverse is often true. Some philosophers argue that mathematics is "real," even when in its most abstract form. Others see the perfect, ideal existential circle as different from the imperfect, real-world circle that we can measure and manipulate. For the purposes of discussing the nature of mathematics as compared to science, we want to explore questions that sometimes connect mathematics to science and sometimes make them more distinctly separate. For purposes of this discussion, let us agree to use the terms "concrete" and "virtual" as opposites and proceed to seek some clear delineation between mathematics and science.

Invented or Discovered?

Mathematical knowledge is concerned with objects that are not located in time and space and do not participate in causal relationships, but rather are abstract. Some philosophers would argue mathematical objects are as real as objects in time and space; thus, philosophers on different sides of this fence have taken different views as to whether mathematical objects are discovered or invented. To address questions like this as well as arising paradoxes, the ancient Greeks established deductive inference as a major tool of mathematics (Colyvan, 2012; Linnebo, 2017); this contrasts with the tool of inductive inference that was being adopted by science. The Greek mathematician Euclid (ca. 500 B.C.E.) utilized an axiomatic method in which self-evident truths (called axioms) were identified and logic was applied to produce theorems. Over the course of time, this process was made more rigorous with more stringent criteria being placed on what qualified as an axiom and more formal language and logical methods employed, but the axiomatic method begun by the ancient Greeks, and utilizing deductive inference, is still an essential part of mathematical practice today (Linnebo, 2017).

Method of Reasoning

On the other hand, before stating strongly that inductive inference is *the* major tool of science and that deductive inference is *the* major tool of mathematics, it should be noted that mathematics is not devoid of inductive inference, nor is science devoid of deductive inference (Okasha, 2016). In fact, the overlap is considerable and sometimes only varies in the exact timing and order of how/when one switches between the two. Mathematicians working within the framework of the deductive method often use inductive reasoning to formulate conjectures upon which they apply logic to prove the conjectures (which they subsequently call theorems). Science also uses deduction, sometimes with induction starting the process—for example, when Kepler's laws of planetary motion were derived from the general laws of motion and the law of universal gravitation (Barberousse et al., 2018).

Fundamental Philosophy

We have seen that the tools used by mathematics and science do not seem to be a foolproof, distinguishing element between the two. The next approach might be to consider the philosophy of the discipline. The three major movements in the philosophy of mathematics, elucidated primarily in and after the early 20th century, shed more light on the multifaceted nature of mathematics. Designated as formalism, logicism, and intuitionism, the three movements/philosophies each emphasize a different role within the development of mathematical ideas. Mathematical notation and its manipulation are the main focus of formalism; logic is the main focus of logicism. The construction of mathematical objects and proofs concerning them is the major focus of intuitionism (Colyvan, 2012). Mathematicians define both mathematical objects and "operations" (actions) on the objects. Mathematicians employ notation to represent the objects and the operations. The notation is also used to represent actions performed on the objects. Mathematicians use logic in the construction of proofs regarding these objects. Taken as a whole, these philosophies reveal much about the nature of mathematics. Generally, these three movements represent the order in which the thinking of mathematical inference developed with respect to time; at the same time, they may represent the extraction of a virtual representation from the concrete examples that started the exact mathematical problem. From this perspective, formalism, logicism, and intuitionism represent the tools that allow the abstraction of meaning from concrete examples and, eventually, the dismissal of the concrete origins of mathematics. However, yet again, these early 20th century philosophies of mathematics do not give a complete distinguishing picture of the nature of mathematics nor of its use. Science has similar, yet distinctly different, ways of viewing its philosophy.

Learning/Teaching

Arguing that the learning/teaching process differs between any two disciplines is certainly a difficult and controversial road to travel. In addition, entire libraries of books are written about small pieces of each of the points which could be mentioned here. Leaving it to the reader to establish their own position on the broader question, it is yet appropriate here to point out some fundamental and established ideas in this realm that are common in both the world of mathematics and the world of science:

- Learning is experiential and developmental;
- learning requires vocabulary, notation, and communication;
- both fluency and conceptualization are necessary to allow the individual to progress from recitation of knowledge to application of knowledge;
- learning simultaneously represents understanding, common experience, creativity, and exploration; and

- building models (physical and conceptual) is core to learning. (National Council of Teachers of Mathematics, 2000, 2018; Willard, 2020).

Just as in arguing either the "nature" of science or in discussing the "learning" of mathematics, the value comes in the process of considering each question/trait individually. There are multiple perspectives from which to explore these questions thoroughly; multiple theories address the organization of individual knowledge, acquisition of knowledge, and principles of teaching, as well as curriculum and technological tools. A teaching practitioner needs to develop their individual perceptions and visions to become expert in the craft of teaching and learning science/mathematics using carefully crafted descriptions of core principles (National Council of Teachers of Mathematics, 2000, 2018; Tall, 2013; Willard, 2020). Suffice it to say that close examination of these descriptions of principles of teaching and learning, while worthy for many purposes, do not provide a clear, essential distinction between mathematics and science.

Process

Examination of the act of "performing science" to the act of "performing mathematics" leads to an aspect where the greatest similarity exists between science and mathematics. Both the mathematics and the science processes are iterative; that is, as one works, there exists constant checking, back-checking, testing, analysis, and comparisons. This is a self-correcting process in that the mathematician and/or the scientist is continuously observing, deducing, and making speculations about future developments. In each iteration of the process of "doing" mathematics and/or science, the core principle is to make sequential and incremental inferences that depend on what has already been accomplished and leading in the direction of new hypotheses or constructions. These inferences, along with the verification, revision, and certification of conclusions, propel the development of the process into the next phase. The essence of effective science and mathematics is the self-correcting and course-correcting nature embedded in the process. Arguably, the process of developing scientific/mathematical knowledge has "breaks" or "jumps" in the iterative process; the breaks most often correspond to a paradigm shift in perspective. More discussion of paradigm shifts follows later—suffice it to say here that paradigm shifts in science lead to new ideas in mathematics and vice versa. However, identity is not completely established by process (e.g., breathing is a process common to mammals).

Outcomes

Finally, let us consider the discussion of mathematics and science from the perspective of products, or outcomes. The purpose of science is "to explain, or perhaps to explain and predict" (Purtill, 1970). In other words, science applied to living objects is called biology; science applied to rocks and minerals is called geology. Could it be that mathematics has as its focus of study the processes that are used to explain and predict? Can one consider mathematics to be the discipline that creates explanation/prediction tools that are then used by science? This could lead back to understanding why Gauss referred to mathematics as the "queen of the sciences." Mathematics provides some of the language, context, rules of conduct, and tools of analysis (a sort of governance structure) that allow science itself to accomplish its purpose of explanation/prediction in a world of concrete objects. We need to note that inference is deeply embedded within the process of science as well as in the processes of mathematics. Inference is part of the "rules of conduct" and tools of analysis common to performance of both mathematics and science.

Returning to our question about what mathematics studies, we have difficulty arriving at a conclusion that fits a completely parallel structure with science. In other words, when comparing similarities, we get inconclusive results. Whether considering the nature of the development, the reasoning, the philosophy, or the outcomes, there are ways to argue each side of the question. In other words, sometimes mathematics acts like a science and sometimes it acts like something "other." Trying to directly answer the student's question from our beginning vignette has provided only a hint of a direction for a conclusion—so we will try a more indirect method.

MATHEMATICS AND SCIENCE—DOES FORM FOLLOW FUNCTION?

To indirectly approach the answer to the question "What does mathematics study?" (as in contrast to the answer for various sciences), it is appropriate to consider linkages between science and mathematics, especially taking note of the origin of the linkages. In other words, which comes first, mathematics or science? Whether the mathematics uses the science for inspiration or not, the two are intertwined throughout history. For example, Galileo Galilei (1564–1642), the first modern physicist, was the first to show that the language of mathematics could be used to describe behavior of physical objects such as falling bodies or projectiles (Okasha, 2016).

There are a surprising number of cases throughout history where mathematical objects, already developed purely from a mathematical viewpoint, have proved to model physical phenomena. Totally unmotivated by, and independent of, potential applications to science, mathematical objects have helped develop scientific theory. One example is in the area of quantum mechanics. Around 1925, German physicist Max Born observed that some rules of computation used in classical mechanics developed by the physicist Werner Heisenberg were identical to the rules of computation for mathematical objects called matrices. The term "matrix" was first used by the English mathematician Arthur Cayley, and rules of computation for matrices were developed by Cayley in 1857 (Andrews-Larson, 2015). Born, Heisenburg, and physicist Pascual Jordan decided to replace the variables representing position and momentum in the classical mechanics equations with matrices (Winger, 1960). The results agreed with previous experimental data. Wolfgang Pauli then applied the matrix model to a problem related to the hydrogen atom, and it again gave results that agreed with experimental data gathered. This was not surprising because Heisenburg's rules of computation were developed from theory applicable to a class to which the hydrogen atom belonged. However, matrix mechanics were then applied to problems for which Heisenburg's rules were thought to be meaningless, such as problems involving electrons of helium or heavier atoms. To everyone's surprise, the results agreed with experimental data (Winger, 1960). In this example, previously existing mathematics provided the language, order, and paradigm to understand principles that were already under study separately in the discipline of physics. Of course, once the linkage was discovered, mathematics also was able to provide tools needed for prediction.

From these examples, one can conclude that scientific theory does not always give rise to mathematics nor does mathematics always give rise to scientific theory. On the other hand, there are quite tight linkages between the kind of mathematics and the kind of science one is doing. Historically, for example, calculus was closely tied to classical mechanics in physics; geometry was closely connected to the science of mensuration (areas, volumes, and other measurements).

While we cannot say that there is an inviolate, or even usual, timing of scientific and mathematical development, we can argue that certain mathematical constructs are paired with particular paradigms of (scientific) thinking. As an example, it took many centuries of human thought to understand the need for a symbol (something) to represent emptiness (nothing). As soon as the concept of zero emerged, along with a concomitant notation, substantial progress was made in new areas of mathematics and science. Is it possible for humans who have ideas without the vocabulary and notation, to speak and write about them? In this chapter, we will have examined a very small selection of mathematical constructs that enlarged the dictionary/toolbox of paradigms available to mathematicians and scientists. For the teacher and the learner, the individual topics and connections are fun to think about. Can you find a missing construct that you would include or a science connection that is left out? On the macro-level, collectively these topics are strong indicators that new theoretical "organizers" or constructs develop in the presence of new notation and paradigms. A priori, you must invent a vocabulary and notation to discuss a new idea; some of these inventions end up being technically mathematical.

THE ROLE MATHEMATICS CAN PLAY

Once again, we have conflicting evidence—this time addressing the question regarding which comes first, science or mathematics. However, we have discovered a relatively tight connection between new scientific ideas and new mathematical ideas. Not only in the physical sciences, but in the life sciences as well, these connections are often very tight. For example, relatively new journals and societies demonstrate that life science employs mathematics, with mathematical biology, for example, becoming recognized as a field in the mid-20th century. The first research group in mathematical biology was formed around 1938, and the Society for Mathematical Biology was founded in 1973 (Society for Mathematical Biology, 2020). Can connections be described through examining the role that mathematics assumes within the individual examples?

Generally speaking, the *scientific mindset* includes the ideas of problem-solving, systematic approach, comfort with uncertainty, and making inferences. In educational circles, recent descriptions of a *learning mindset* include self-assessment and self-value, persistence, and even creativity. Arguably, whichever nuance or attribute of mindset is under consideration, the impact and power of science is its ability to abstract, analyze, describe, and predict the concrete world. Science aims to find patterns in reality. Perhaps mathematics plays a unique role in fostering invention/discovery, communication, and validation within the scientific process.

Our discussion has led us to the insight that mathematics is a tool for communication about, exploration of, and development of the interface between the concrete real world and the idealized abstract world of mathematics. The inferences, understanding, deductions, and predictions that one can make are bounded by how one can communicate, detect, and compare. Knowing if one is making "the right inferences" requires constantly developing and expanding vocabulary and communication tools.

Communication

Early in history, mathematics established a connection between the concrete world and the abstract world through counting. (*Note:* We are not committing to either side of the argument about whether abstractions are real or not. We just acknowledge their inability to be touched.) From number systems, to fractions, to mathematical notation, mathematics dedicated itself to perfecting methods of abstractly manipulating and discussing the concrete. From the ideas in the previous section, it is plausible that in the process of establishing the logic, guidelines, notation, and vocabulary to enable such a conversation, mathematics even assisted in the prediction and usefulness of concepts that could promote the development of future ideas. Examples range from a brief discussion of symbols for numbers, and the appropriate choice of base, to predictions that stretch and test the reality of experience: the square root of 2, imaginary numbers, parallel lines, and different sizes of infinity. Mathematical development in these areas begins with the concepts of construction and measurement to infer predictions about reality in the areas of electricity, architecture, chemistry, physics, and engineering; and sometimes mathematics, such as calculus, is invented and explored theoretically centuries before an actual measurable application is available to test the mathematics. Mathematics in this first case follows the photographic representation (mathematically speaking) of the world around us; this allows a greater depth of detailed observation to form the basis of inference. In the second case, mathematics creates a world of fantasy and waits for reality to populate it with objects. In both circumstances, mathematics facilitates these conversations.

Detection

As science continues to expand its questions, so does mathematics. Science and mathematics historically leapfrog over each other in different arenas while trying to make more and more advances. Rather than describing a moment in time, the mathematics of detection focuses on modeling change over time and hence predicting and/or explaining the future. Using functions and the idea of time as an independent variable, the mathematics of the detection process involves viewing the world over time (like a video) and allows the comparison between the expectation of the model and the observations of reality over time. Between developing a variety of models and methods of analyzing change, the mathematics of functions and calculus fills a role of assisting science in making inferences over time since it helps scientists detect differences over time and model them.

Comparison

With the development of large data sets and detailed measurements of populations comes the need to compare characteristics of a population. Alternately, for decision-making purposes, the scientist needs to know if two entities have slight characteristic differences due to individual variation in development or if the entities belong to different species. The entities in question do not have to be biological in nature; specifically, to address inferences in the context of variation of measurements, one uses statistics to "weed out" the noise to detect true relationships between concepts. Statistics aids inference by allowing one or two numbers to represent the information needed to draw an inference and/or to make a decision.

New Directions

Control theory, artificial intelligence, big data sets, and mathematical biology are developing areas today which are searching for new mathematical language concepts. In an attempt to manage decision options and a lack of perfection, fuzzy sets and fuzzy logic attempt to use imperfect measurements collected with great frequency to be analyzed and used for non-equation-based concrete decision-making. Fuzzy sets and fuzzy logic specifically detect the fuzzy nature of a boundary and allow the deduction of a reasonably distinct decision or inference. This area of mathematics and mathematical thinking leads into the new realms of automated decision-making, control theory, and artificial intelligence. Big data sets and mathematical biology are looking for new paradigms in linear algebra, fractals, and topology. Mathematics has a role in giving voice and description to the concepts developing in these areas. As science changes, evolves, and addresses different questions, mathematics evolves to meet the needs of these changing arenas; likewise, science pushes developments of new mathematics. So again, we come to a conclusion best described as intertwined: Sometimes the mathematics is developed and waiting for the science to catch up (as with a lot of applications of calculus); sometimes the science leads the way, and the mathematics develops in support of the science.

NATURE OF MATHEMATICS, SCIENCE, AND INFERENCE, PART 2

We started this chapter with a conversation involving "What does mathematics study?" We should return there to finish. A frequently cited and respected book about the nature of mathematics provides a "naïve definition of mathematics . . . the science of quantity and space" (Davis & Hersh, 1981, p. 6). While this is a good starting place, it may hide the true roles that the nature of mathematics plays in the act of doing science, and in inference. To "do" science, one must think, create, measure, approximate, compare, organize, and synthesize ideas along with data. While doing these things, one must describe, summarize, and compare. After that one continues to analyze, generalize, and communicate (to others and to oneself) the ideas under consideration. Science is not complete until *all* these activities have occurred.

The Role of Mathematics

The role of mathematics is that it supports the identification, analysis, and correction of flaws within the inference process. We have noted this role above in the previous sections discussing "method of reasoning" and "process." Furthermore, consider that the scientist is constructing two edifices when doing science: the real structure and the virtual structure. The connections between the real structure and the virtual structure allow the mathematics "rules, properties, and logic" to be used as tools for validating and comparing the real-world to the paradigm/model under construction.

Mathematics provides a succinct and precise language to express the ideas of science. Whether symbolic, diagrammatic, tabular (numeric), or verbal, mathematics supports the fluid movement between the communication method that most supports understanding and/or development of a new paradigm. The connections are there; the scientist just has to work at determining which mode supports improved understanding. While thinking, processing, and promoting the logic of the analysis, mathematics pares down all extraneous and ill-formed information. One can hone the precision of the mathematics and at the same time hone the train of scientific facts within the research. Once the scientific phenomenon is related to a mathematical model, the processes in the mathematical context take over; one can back-check, manipulate, and analyze an unknown science concept in the virtual playground of known mathematical logic and communications. The movement between the model (mathematics) and the physical world helps identify new ideas, flaws in logic, and predictions to verify. The mathematical knowledge provides points of correction that are a priori unbiased and even somewhat automatic; the mathematical validation provides points of validation in the real-world context. The confidence of the scientist in the mathematical world, where he or she has been before, translates into the ability to have confidence in the model that was so carefully constructed to be a precise parallel structure resting in the context of the unknown real world.

The Tools for Inference

Three tools that encourage, promote, and support all the activities mentioned in the previous paragraphs are ideation, communication, and mindset. Mathematics encourages and supports the entire process of science by making a context where these three tools become learnable, accessible, and effective. Specifically, *ideation*—the process of having/creating new ideas—is encouraged with vocabulary, notation, and processes that facilitate talking and writing about current knowledge and thoughts. The creation of radically new science requires the concomitant organization around a new paradigm. *Communication* is essential to solidify and understand one's own thoughts as well as to allow acquisition and merging with the thoughts and ideas of others. Mindset is the key to completing the process. Critically, a robust mindset—one that is able to tolerate both multiplicity of ideas and relativism instead of dualism—is promoted by the development of mathematics that allows one to abstract ideas, remove them from the subjective world, and let reality lead the researcher instead of their subjective preferences. The self-correcting nature of mathematics helps keep every project free of errors of all types if one will obey its rules of notation, calculation, and logic.

THE TOOLS FOR INFERENCE

The tools for inference are critical enough to consider just a moment longer. There is some value in considering three specific examples as context for understanding inference and the problems associated with inference. Presented in chronological order, these illustrations act as "dramatic presentations" in which the tools for inference play key roles. These examples tell fascinating stories of creativity, science, mathematics, and logic. While representing important outcomes and usage of scientific inquiry we observe the following:

- Even flawed science can be useful.
- Truth can be stranger than imagination.
- The self-correcting nature of scientific inquiry is most often seen in a repetitive process and is always ongoing.

Human Anatomy

One of the earliest recognized works of science was the work on anatomy written by Galen (Claudius Galenus), *On the Usefulness of the Parts of the Body* (Boorstin, 1986, pp. 347–349). Written somewhere around 165 A.D., this work, along with multiple other volumes, was passed along through the newly-forming medical community without question for more than 1,000 years—including the errors made from the fact that Galen never autopsied or examined a single human body! Galen drew his conclusions about human anatomy from studying monkeys and pigs. Two elements contributed to the long life of Galen's errors. During the relevant time in history, the citation of an authoritative source was more valued than any personal or eye-witness verification. Second, Roman custom forbade the dissection of the human body; Galen used monkeys and pigs for his studies of the human body due to his belief that the external and internal resemblance respectively to man would be sufficient to allow conclusions about human anatomy. Galen's work was not corrected until an accidental discovery of multiple deceased plague victims; this led to revelation that Galen's description of a human jaw (which included the wrong number of teeth for a human being) was incorrect. In other words, the simple mathematics involved in counting (swine teeth v. human teeth) provided the correction to a 1,000-year-old flawed model. It is interesting to note that some of the final corrections to Galen's work came from Leonardo da Vinci when a period of questioning authority, creativity, and exploration took hold of the Western world.

Cholera

Cholera is a devastating disease that breaks out in plague events, appearing at seemingly unpredictable times and places. An understanding of how these events occur, and even the nature of the cause of the plague, has been sought for centuries. A breakthrough in understanding came through an examination of an outbreak in the United States in the 1970s by Rita Colwell. First connecting the outbreaks to water, and then to bacteria, algae, and plankton, Colwell has accomplished 50 years of work that has progressed through finding the cause and discovering a hibernating state with vastly different physical characteristics; it is continuing in the formation of a predictive mathematical model (Colwell, 2014; Colwell & Huq, n.d.; University of Maryland, 2018). Colwell followed the most torturous, unbelievable series of changes, clues, and events in the propagation of the bacteria as it caused a plague. Her persistence in the face of unbelievable biological information as well as in the face of resistance in the scientific community is at the core of her success as a scientist.

COVID-19

The progression of COVID-19 in the United States and in the world has displayed science acting in real-time. All persons who could contribute are adding to the collection of knowledge and expertise in real time; multiple updates per day arrive at hospitals for critical care professionals to weigh and use in the most severe cases. One of the greatest and yet most frustrating tools has been the modeling to predict the need for supplies, ventilators, hospital beds, and, sadly, death rates (NCIRD, 2020). As this chapter is being written, there are 21 different models followed on a weekly basis and reported to the public at large; various assumptions regarding virus characteristics, impact of environment, and aspects of human behavior are adjusted in each model. Many of the models, and the modeling process itself, are criticized as being disconnected from reality. But a model is only as good as the equation selected, the parameters identified and measured, and the measurements and data used in the model. As this terrible pandemic progresses, scientists and mathematicians will work together on improving parameters, equations, and measurements to allow the modeling process to self-correct the models and refine the predictions to save lives now and in the future.

THE PROCESS OF MATHEMATICS, SCIENCE, AND INFERENCE

From the previous specific examples, it is clear that the challenges to inference in science can be varied. These challenges are encountered regardless of whether the scientific exploration is new to the world or new to the individual explorer. The tools to identify, combat, and overcome the inherent challenges embedded in "doing science" can be found in many places; synergistically, they are all found in the world of mathematics. The success of the inferential process depends on all the steps along the way in the search for conclusions. It is worth spending the time to explore one final example that illustrates the synergy between mathematics, science, and inference as well as the self-correcting and cyclical process involved in exploring scientific questions. While reviewing this example of developing a theory of astronomy, the reader is encouraged to look for instances of the following critical activities:

- Accurately identify assumptions (A).
- Validate logical progressions (L).
- Acquire confidence in unknown circumstances ©.
- Verify calculations and analysis (M).
- Tolerate corrections and uncertainty (U).
- Summarize & evaluate conclusions (S).
- Identify errors and take corrective steps (E).

As a university student, Johannes Kepler (1571–1630) was taught the geocentric astronomy of Ptolemy with its assumption that the other planets and the sun revolved around the earth (A); but he was also introduced to the heliocentric astronomy of Copernicus with its assumption that the earth and other planets revolved around the sun (A). Kepler initially believed the latter to be correct, largely since it was consistent with his cosmological theory. Kepler believed that the solar system was a system of nested spheres and Platonic solids (tetrahedron, octahedron, cube, icosahedron, dodecahedron) which governed planetary motion, a theory that seems bizarre to the modern reader. Had this cosmological theory been correct, the orbits of the planets would have to be circles (Field, 1999; L, M, E). In an effort to add credence to *his own* cosmological theory through the use of observational data, Kepler began working with the astronomer Tycho Brahe (L, M, S). Upon Brahe's death in 1601, Kepler inherited an unparalleled amount of data of the locations of planets at various times; using this data, Kepler created over 1000 sheets of arithmetic as he attempted to determine the precise orbit of Mars (L, S, M, U). Kepler finally concluded that the data were not consistent with a circular path, but rather with an elliptical path (U, E, C). Thus, Kepler had to abandon his false theory regarding the Platonic solids (Field, 1999; Levy, 2016; U, E, S). As noted before, even flawed science can be useful: Kepler's false theory had served him well in that his quest for its confirmation led him to new discoveries (L, U, S). His work also led, however not logically necessary in the process, to believe in the true Copernican theory. Newton later deductively proved what Kepler had inductively concluded, as the theory of gravitational motion yields the equation of an ellipse for the path (Barberousse et al., 2018; L, S). It is also interesting to note that prior to examining the observational data of Brahe, Kepler had found that his (incorrect) cosmological theory allowed him to predict the size of the paths of planets to within 10% using observational data available at that time; he believed at the time that these observational data supported the theory (Field, 1999; A, L, C, E). A final note of interest is that, in 1539, George Rheticus, a professor of mathematics and astronomy, wrote that Copernicus

> proceeds from the earliest observations to his own... [which] he then compares with the hypothesis of Ptolemy and the ancients... [and] he finds that astronomical proof requires their rejection; he assumes new hypotheses... by applying mathematics, he geometrically establishes the conclusions which can be drawn from them... and after performing all these operations he finally writes down the laws of astronomy.... (Levy, 2016, pp. 139–140)

In the scientific world, all of the challenges to inference occur daily. A scientist learns to deal with them from his/her scientific training. The nature of mathematics helps to make the scientist less likely to commit errors, more likely to catch errors when they inevitably occur, and totally able to deal with the chaos which unfolds in tandem with the progress of the project. This is what makes the mathematics/science pairing so effective and valuable in the realm of inference.

CLOSING VIGNETTE

So now my response to my student will be,

> Mathematics is the study of virtual model construction. It is the discipline that creates explanation/prediction tools and virtual realities which are either then used by science or can be studied in their own right. Specifically, it is the understanding of how to create and use language, logic, and analysis constructs that support the development of parallel, ordered, virtual depictions of reality. Mathematics is constructed to include its own self-correcting features, with the careful use of logic and principles, as well as to include characteristics that enable modeling and prediction. Science uses its connections to mathematics to import all the self-correcting features of mathematics into its realm of inquiry and process.

I look forward to seeing how the student responds to this description.

REFLECTIVE QUESTIONS

1. What do you consider to be the greatest paradigm shifts in your discipline? What way of thinking, communicating, or analyzing triggered that paradigm shift? Where did that shift lead?
2. Pick an arbitrary topic in your discipline. What tools and/or ideas help you develop clear thinking, logical concepts, and effective communication about that topic?
3. What role do definitions, theory/laws, experimentation, and mathematics play *in* either the teaching of or the historical development of a central topic in your discipline?

CHAPTER 5

STATISTICS

Developing Impactful Teaching and Learning

Mary Barone Martin, Tammy Jones, and Teresa Schmidt

You cannot be anything you want to be—but you can be a lot more of who you already are.

—Tom Rath

INTRODUCTION: CONNECTIONS BETWEEN STATISTICS AND SCIENTIFIC INFERENCE

The 21st century, even in its first decade, can be seen as a century of science. Various pundits make lists of the "most imminent" science and technology advances as well as argue for the "most important" outstanding questions in various areas of science. Looking in a crystal ball can be a lot of fun; for teachers and researchers, preparing the knowledge foundations to enable these breakthrough discoveries is our *business*. From biotechnology to artificial intelligence to space exploration to effective medical interventions, there are many tools needed in multiple disciplines.

Age of Inference, pages 75–89

As the development of "new science" shifted in the 1800s, scientists began to need the tools of calculus at an earlier time in a scientist's career; however, their lack of calculus paradigms caused this to be inaccessible to them even as they needed it most. There are interesting stories of scientists studying electricity, magnetism, and temperature who had to draft the help of mathematicians before the scientific world would accept their work (Stewart, 2018). The need for algebra and trigonometry, for example, did not disappear. However, the need for calculus was more urgent. If one agrees, even partially, with the discussions in previous chapters then one must recognize that science development will need a language of mathematics to enable/structure communications, processes, and conclusions.

Arguably, for the near future, statistics plays a role as the mathematical organizer central to the developments of science, perhaps more so even than calculus and algebra. In this chapter, the authors look at the structure of learning as it is exemplified in the context of learning statistics. The very nature of statistics encourages the teacher to re-envision the stages and scaffolding of the instruction/learning process. Since conducting a statistical analysis involves activities crossing a wide range of skill sets and cognitive levels, the stages of a learning cycle become more entwined with different skill sets and levels of learning. We want to examine some of those stages and processes. The ultimate goal of teaching/learning statistics is to present some of the paradigm shifts and communication tools of statistics so that they are ready when needed for scientists and mathematicians.

INTRODUCING TOPICS: TELLING THE STORY

The introduction of new paradigms and ways of thinking is the first step in beginning a new structure for communication and analysis; in this case, we are looking at introducing statistical ideas for the first time. One definition of statistics is that it is the science of gaining insight from data (Rossman et al., 2006). Fundamentally rooted in agriculture, statistics is a product of the 19th and early 20th centuries. Since the history of statistics is rooted in food production and quality control, the stories of statistics and statisticians are ones that can easily be told concretely to a variety of grade levels. For most students, the questions being asked are reasonable and realistic within their own time and place; they can even pose some of the questions regarding bias and implications as well as help set goals. Consequently, the teaching of statistics has a great advantage: Most of the ideas that concern you as a teacher can be presented through stories or scenarios. On the other hand, the intuitive acceptance (almost subconscious) and the necessary emphasis on complete, accurate statistical analysis requires exploration, experimentation, theory, calculations, analysis, and summarization—all of which must be written in the context of the original story or scenario. This crosses many areas of expertise—and the boundaries between the different skills are not clear.

Topics of statistics such as Fisher's *t*-test, pie charts, and bias can be viewed as synergistic and inevitable developments of perception and concept from within the context of the story. In other words, the story makes the statistical concepts seem natural and almost obvious. Using trade books, current news stories, and historically based stories can help develop interest and understanding. These stories can also be viable tools for differentiating the learning of statistics.

AMALGAMATION: READING, SCIENCE, CALCULATION, AND ANALYSIS

In its entirety, statistical analysis is a complex undertaking. It goes far beyond simply interpreting a situation, performing an experiment and/or calculation, and reporting results. It is a multidimensional process, which involves linkages between cognitive domains such as basic recall and analysis; additionally, it requires that information cross boundaries of multiple intelligence/skill sets such as from verbal into mathematical intelligence (Peck et al., 2019). Finally, it requires a quality of mindset that sustains multiple connections as well as relativistic outcomes. These transitions/lineages can be difficult for students and teachers; that difficulty is magnified when they happen repeatedly within the context of one learning cycle. Consider the following diagram as a representation of a learning cycle.

The teacher of statistics must make a point to accommodate (maximize the use of) the many different skill sets needed to complete a proper statistical analysis and the difficulty of blending the many parts into a whole. We can consider these pieces as parts of an entire process that requires multiple checkpoints to ensure successful progress.

At each stage of the process, and during the movement between stages, the learner must analyze progress, predict additional steps, and summarize developments. If the process has a unifying story, then these connections are more intensely important because the story is taking the role of encouraging the paradigm shift in the construction. Within a node, there is a particular type of activity happening—mathematical analysis, data collection, summarization, and so forth—which requires a particular set of skills. When there is a shift between nodes, there is an amalgamation or cross-fertilization between the different skills. This is not particularly unique to mathematics or science, although crossing these skill boundaries is required as often in the liberal arts, for example. The problem is that it is often too easy for the teacher and/or the practitioner to ignore these transitions (and even some of the nodes) and thus not complete the process.

Case in point: it is a fact that virtually all students will state with great fervor that they hate word problems, or at least they find them the most challenging. A few might be polite and say they are not good at them. However, no one can honestly deny that teachers and students alike wince when they get to word problems and often rush through them, or even worse, ignore them. One strategy that can be frequently (and regrettably witnessed) is that the teacher provides the equations and asks the students to answer prepared questions—hence, eliminating almost half of the purpose of the problem. Then there are the classrooms where time is running out and the teacher does not "cover" any "word problems." In statistics, neither of these options is available. The major requirement of statistics is to address the data/mathematics in the core scientific context, beginning with information.

If we summarize the actions taken in a statistical analysis, the implication of these statements become clearer. Statistical analysis, much like the scientific processes, includes certain well-recognized steps. These steps do not always proceed in a lock-step fashion; however, they are almost always present within the analysis when considered holistically. One must formulate an appropriate question from the scientific context—requiring reading comprehension and science knowledge. Decisions must be made about exactly what data should be collected in order to answer the question. Connected to these decisions is the method for collecting data (e.g., stratified sample, cluster sample, systematical sample, convenience sample, etc.). The data need to be selected in order to reduce bias, which requires science and math knowledge as well as analytic skills and knowledge. After collecting the data, the investigators must then rely on the computation skill set, technology, and/or analytical skills to complete the calculation and to assess the reasonableness of the outcomes. Ultimately, throughout the discovery process, the data and results must be analyzed and interpreted in order to arrive at a conclusion and to communicate the results to a wider audience.

Consequently, from the simple textbook statistical exercise to the more complicated "real world" circumstances, statistical analysis requires a myriad of knowledge, comprehension, application, analysis, and communication skills (depth of knowledge). Even more importantly, the level of ability of these skills must be available somewhat evenly in the different functional areas of science, mathematics, writing, and logical analysis (multiple intelligences). Finally, an individual must integrate, persist, and maintain a level of success in all of the functional areas in order to become proficient or to succeed at performing statistical analysis (mindset). The remaining sections of this chapter are to develop three ideas:

1. There are multiple skill sets needed to develop a statistical analysis; additionally, these skill sets are more evenly distributed in terms

of necessity. We will use three different measurements to develop teaching across skills sets.

2. Differentiation in statistics becomes critical because every human being has some weaknesses in one or more of these multiple skill sets. So, a computational whiz may need differentiated support in the area of writing the verbal analysis.
3. Organizing concepts and skills through repetition in different contexts is important. Two illustrations are provided.

BLOOM'S TAXONOMY, MULTIPLE INTELLIGENCES, AND PERRY'S SCHEME OF KNOWING

From the previous discussion, it can be seen that when learning or analyzing statistics and data, the actions are taking place simultaneously in a variety of contexts. The purpose here is to select goals, trajectories towards goals, and formative/summative assessments in order to guide the teaching within statistics, which requires that we consciously evaluate multiple areas/skills. Because of the different aspects of the process (depth of knowledge, multiple intelligences, and mindset), a quick overview of the scales/schemes is presented here which can help gauge progress in each area. There are other scales and schemes for understanding, and the teacher should feel free to change methodologies freely to match their preference. The areas that we want to examine are those of depth of knowledge, multiple intelligences, and mindsets. These organizational schemes can be used to orient instruction and assignments productively after understanding progress measures/benchmarks in each of these areas, then we will provide a contextual examination illustrating the design of a teaching plan.

Depth of Knowledge

Depth of knowledge refers to the level at which one can function in analyzing and understanding information in a particular discipline. Bloom's taxonomy is well established and widely used in the analysis of levels of learning. While Webb's depth of knowledge is a similar scheme, Bloom's taxonomy emphasizes "action" words to determine higher-level cognitive thinking. The structure of Bloom's can be represented as in Table 5.1 with higher-order thinking skills receiving a higher-level designation (Anderson et al., 2001; McDaniel, 2018). For example, if one is designing an activity for the second node, the teacher would want the student to be at least at Level 2–3 before moving on to the next node. In other words, for the activity of exploring the topic, the student needs to be able to understand and remember the basic

TABLE 5.1 Bloom's Taxonomy Levels

Bloom's Taxonomy Level	Action
6	Create
5	Evaluate
4	Analyze
3	Apply
2	Understand
1	Remember

terms and ideas of the calculation techniques. If the teacher is trying to move the student to an analytic level (4) in exploration of a topic, then the initial expertise in the introduction should most likely be at a capacity of evaluation (5). The key idea to consider is that when working on a statistics problem, the student has to move up the difficulty level in several areas simultaneously. For example, a student cannot be better talking about bias than they are in understanding and using the basic terminology.

Multiple Intelligences

Unlike learning styles, Howard Gardner's multiple intelligences represent a variety of intellectual abilities or skill sets. Generally speaking, educators are less widely accepting of the paradigm that there are a variety of intelligences and that individuals cross the spectrum of abilities; every individual operates at (usually unmeasured) levels in each spectrum and has some ability in each area. On the other hand, to properly teach statistics, it is necessary to acknowledge that there are different modalities of communication and reasoning that involve different skill sets. For example, some people are better at rhyming while others are better at drawing. Some individuals are better at calculations and others with a pictorial or verbal description. While intelligences may be a misnomer and may be out of favor, it is definitely true that this organizational conceptualization is a convenient way to recognize the different skill sets that the student/practitioner is accessing at different times in a statistical analysis. So, for these purposes, we will rely on the Gardner literature to benchmark the various ways of accessing and communicating material both in understanding the material and in assessing the material. This is important to help design effective communications and effective learning modalities. Finally, it has been recognized that working within an intelligence area improves one's ability to work with the tools in that intelligence area. Using the Gardner viewpoint,

TABLE 5.2 Gardner's Eight Multiple Intelligences

Intelligence	Attribute
Linguistic	strength in language arts, speaking, writing, listening, and reading
Logical—Mathematical	sequence learning logically, aptitude for reasoning, problem-solving, and numeracy
Musical	recognizes patterns and rhythms, learns well through songs and musical expressions
Bodily—Kinesthetic	activity and movement, hands-on tasks, games, building, and physical activities
Spatial	visual, organizing spatially, charts, graphs, tables, use of color, and drawing
Interpersonal	people oriented and outgoing, cooperative learning groups, partners, making comparisons, and sharing
Intrapersonal	work alone, in touch with one's own feelings, values, ideas, and doing observations
Naturalist	physical experiences, picks up on subtle differences, love of the outdoors, animals, field trips, and recording events

Source: Taylor, 2003.

Table 5.2 shows the intelligences that are currently considered appropriate; additions are considered regularly.

According to Gardner, students use these intelligences, individually and/or in conjunction with each other, when they engage in problem-solving and creating solutions (Gardner, 2008). Students, as well as educators, benefit when a student's primary multiple intelligences have been identified. Armstrong and the Association for Supervision and Curriculum Development (2018) used a different terminology for Gardner's basic eight intelligences, calling them "smarts." This appears to be more assessable to students and teachers. For example, linguistic intelligence becomes *word smart*, logical-mathematical is *number/logic smart*, bodily-kinesthetic becomes *body smart*, and spatial intelligence is *picture smart.*

Stanford (2003) suggested that these multiple intelligences/smarts can provide "a framework for teachers to reflect on their best teaching methods" (p. 82). Reflection includes what works and what does not as well as why. This reflection, coupled with the understanding of the intelligences and their students, provides teachers with a larger toolbox from which to choose more appropriate curriculum materials, strategies, and classroom structures in order to reach a more diverse population of learners. This framework shifts instruction and learning from the typical language-logic approach to one that allows students to have more agency. Taking things one step further, Karamikabir (2012) suggested a table "verifying the relation between recognition intelligence and Bloom's six levels of intelligence skill building" (p. 780). For example, when working with a regression function to make a prediction, a picture smart student might initially recall the overall graph of the function at a knowledge level, but, as the student's level of interaction and understanding with the concepts develop more deeply, they would move to actually drawing a diagram at the analysis level.

Mindset

In counterpoint to Bloom and Gardner, Perry's Scheme of Cognitive Development (Table 5.3) is more nuanced in a way that is particularly helpful when considering inference. Perry's Scheme has nine levels that describe an individual's response and understanding of a topic (Wilson, 2013).

Clearly, Perry's scheme has a more attitude-oriented measurement of learning and knowledge. It is less action-oriented and more focused on the attitudes and resistance/persistence of the learner. It can be argued that Perry's scheme possesses substantial value for STEM practitioners for two reasons.

1. Perry stated that when you enter a new discipline or even a new area within a familiar discipline, every single practitioner has to repeat the levels within the context of that area. This resonates wildly with every STEM learner since this is the nature of their experience every time they begin a new course in their collegiate career. For example, one's understanding of mechanics may overlap heat and thermodynamics only slightly; however, the ability to absorb and process nuanced ideas in mechanics makes one's progress in heat and thermodynamics more rapid. Sometimes this pseudo-transferability is referred to as a version of "disciplinary maturity."

TABLE 5.3 Perry's Levels

Level	Response and Understanding
9	Developing commitments—dealing with the choices
8	Consequences of commitments—seeing implications of imperfect
7	Initial commitments—deciding between imperfect choices
6	Commitment foreseen—decisions made, with resistance
5	Relativism correlate, competing or diffuse—knowledge must be contextual
4	Multiplicity—understanding ambiguity of knowledge
3	Multiplicity subordinate—no absolute authority
2	Multiplicity pre-legitimate—diversity must exist, uncomfortably
1	Basic duality—only black or white

2. Perry's levels help practitioners understand how to address the needs of the learner and to help them make progress. While they are not specifically action-oriented in terms of analyzing productive output, they are very helpful for the teacher and the learner to understand what is missing experientially in his/her work and what mindset is needed to move forward—which may or may not be connected to more concrete knowledge.

Finally, Perry maintains that a person's level can be a "4" in one area (e.g., math) and an "8" in another area (e.g., music). Every individual learns a variety of topics and can be at a different level in each area. However, Perry also believes that functioning at a Level 5–6 is a generally acceptable standard for areas in which you are not an expert. Dualism (Levels 1 & 2) are bad levels to remain at when one is trying to achieve quality learning and to make decisions as an adult. Sadly, Perry's research showed that most college graduates seldom move beyond a Level 4 or 5. Perry's insights are especially helpful for developing persistence and perspective with the metacognition of a struggling learner.

For the remainder of this chapter, we return to our cycle diagram as a critical organizer for constructing a cycle of teaching/learning for a particular concept. Developed by Martin and Jones (2019) to analyze a teaching/differentiation process, we want to look at each node/stage and use

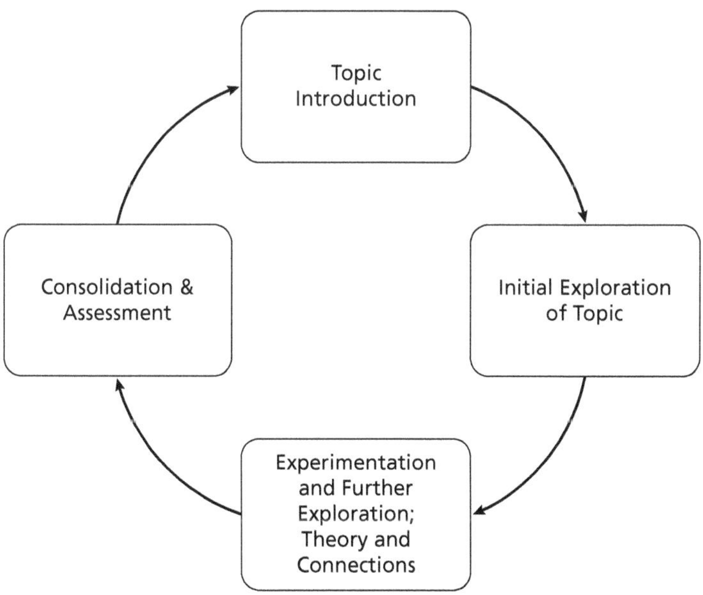

Figure 5.1 Representation of a learning cycle.

this paradigm to plan acceptable transitions within the process of learning a statistical concept. In Figure 5.1, each stage represents an insertion position for a differentiation action, a teaching point, an activity point, or an assessment point. From the perspective of *Understanding by Design* (Bowen, 2017), planning each of these stages completely can yield rich results. Similar to Perry's scheme, the repetition through the stages of the spiral may repeat several times before appropriate mastery of the concept as a whole is achieved. For the remainder of this chapter, we will examine activities/processes that facilitate moving around to the next stage of the cycle.

DIFFERENTIATION TOOLS

There is a "toolbox" of possible differentiation actions that can be used for various transitions described in our cycle. We mentioned one at the beginning of this chapter—historical stories and vignettes to introduce new concepts in an everyday context. Tomlinson (2014) provided a variety of strategies that educators can use to provide differentiation for the classroom. Incorporating stations, learning centers, tiered activities, complex instruction tasks, and tri-mind tasks are supports educators can offer students to support their learning needs. Tomlinson distinguished stations from centers where many educators see them being synonymous. Stations work in concert and are linked to provide a complete coverage for a topic or skill. Centers, on the other hand, are individual and are flexible to provide students support, review, or extension on a variety of topics that do not have to be connected.

Tiered activities, while usually quite successful, often provide the most challenges for educators to create. Teachers must consider the concept and/or skill being investigated as well as the readiness of the students in working with the concept. The activity being developed should also engage the students while offering the appropriate amount of complexity and skill level (Tomlinson, 2014). From first-hand experience, this is quite time-consuming for the individual teacher. However, in the world of today's professional learning communities (PLC), this task can be divided and conquered to provide a more accessible and meaningful learning experience to the student.

Complex instruction and tri-mind are both strategies that are focused on establishing equity of learning opportunities in the classroom, especially when more challenging material is being presented. Complex instruction tasks, according to Tomlinson, have many facets from students working in small, heterogeneous groupings, to being open-ended and involving real objects as well as being provided in multiple languages, as needed (Tomlinson, 2014). These types of tasks can be used as anchor tasks for introducing a new topic, proving to be most successful and beneficial to students of diverse and varying backgrounds, both socially and academically.

Tri-mind tasks are based upon the three forms of intelligence formulated by Sternberg in 1985 (Tomlinson, 2014). This theory states that intelligent behavior arises from a balance between analytical, creative, and practical abilities. These abilities, then, function as one to allow individuals to achieve success within a particular context, such as academics. These tasks are crested and focused around one of the three intelligences. The student then chooses one of the three and will gain the proper exposure to, experience with, and information about the concept being studied (Tomlinson, 2014).

Other strategies that Tomlinson says "invite differentiation" include compacting, choice boards, literature and discussion circles, and the use of Jigsaw (Tomlinson, 2014). These are more common types of differentiated instruction that many teachers are familiar with, but often forget to add to their daily, weekly, or topical instruction to provide variety as well as choice for the students. Teachers find facilitating discussion circles sometimes more challenging as many teachers need support with effective questioning (Jones & Texas, 2017). For this reason, integrating differentiation tools, such as the Q pyramid and overlay (Jones & Texas, 2017), allows not only the teachers to better facilitate discussion circles, but also allows the students to form their own questions as they engage in authentic discussion circles. The four faces of the pyramid mirror the four opportunities for effective questioning that are available when students are engaged in critical thinking and logical reasoning:

1. as they enter the conversation,
2. as they move through the conversation,
3. as they reflect on the conversation, and
4. as they extend the conversation.

The overlay provides a prompt where teachers, as well as students, can quickly form questions based upon the specific topic being discussed (Jones & Texas, 2017).

Another differentiation strategy that can easily be incorporated into the classroom is in regard to the artifacts that students create to show evidence of their securely holding the content they have been studying (Taylor, 2003). Taylor listed many options for artifacts on his Multiple Intelligences Product Grid (p. 2). These can be adapted for specific content as needed. For example, in statistics, verbal/linguistic students could write a series of typical story problems based upon a particular set of data, for other students to investigate. The logical/mathematical students could simply take a set of data and create a set of directions for how to use the statistical mode on a graphing calculator to determine specific statistical information about the data set. For the visual/spatial student, a visual display could be created based upon the results of a survey they created and implemented. The product grids offer educators the creative prompt they sometimes need to think of alternatives to the typical student artifacts, thus allowing more student agency.

This chapter concludes with two examples of constructing a plan to meet the needs of the learner. These are simply examples formed around the template of our learning cycle and include references to different skill sets and levels of learning. Note that the two figures include an additional "node" in the previously presented teaching/learning cycle to emphasize the paradigm construction aspect. In each illustration, please examine the table and the figure together to get a complete description of the process.

ILLUSTRATING THROUGH CLASSROOM EXAMPLES

Illustration 1: Consider a univariate example dealing with temperatures: An individual has a week of temperature data for a vacation destination. How should they pack for the trip? Provided is a table of data.

If we consider each stage of the cycle as supporting the development of univariate statistics, then we have a contextual goal for each stage and a differentiation tool to use to promote "leveling up" at each stage. Within the context, we also identify if this is primarily a gain in cognitive level, multiple intelligences access, or mindset.

The introductory context is the need to make a data set into one representative number to assist with decision-making. There is a differentiation tool at each stage, and the context of the story is identified (Table 5.4). The

TABLE 5.4 Details of Pairing Stages With Tools, Univariate Statistical Example

Stage	Context	Differentiation Tool
Introduction	The need for a representative statistic; *Bloom 2*	Story-telling or conversation[a]
Exploration	Mean, median, mode calculations; *MI: transition verbal to mathematical*	Authentic questioning[b]
Experimentation	Changing the data set/changes in the statistic; *Perry 4*	Technology; active modeling[c]
Theory & Connections	Reinforce Measures of Central Tendency; sensitivity to changes; *Perry 5 & Bloom 4*	Direct instruction[d]
Consolidation & Assessment	Conclusions and analysis; *MI: Logical—verbal, Bloom 5 & Perry 6*	Authentic writing[e]

[a] Lemonidis & Kaiafa, 2019
[b] Jones & Texas, 2016
[c] Lee, 2019
[d] Stein, 2006
[e] Ediger, 2006

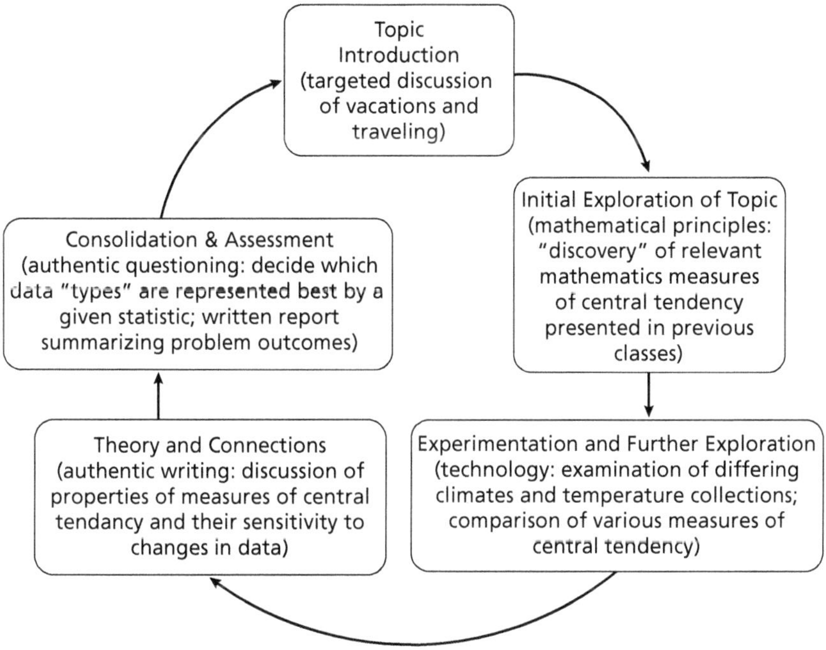

Figure 5.2 Illustration 2: Introduce the concepts of bias and experimental design.

teacher selects all the choices of tools, with the selection based upon which portion of the learning is new and which resources are available to support that particular skill. One could, in fact, also include the transition arrows as rows in the chart, which would emphasize moving information from one stage to the next. In the interest of simplicity, that was not done. The transitions are still important aspects of the cycle (see Figure 5.2). Note that in Chapter 6, the teacher can choose an assessment tool at each stage to address the success of the learning at that stage.

This second example centers around the concept of bias in experimental design (Table 5.5). The context and topic illustrate different choices and reflect the use of the book entitled *The Lady Tasting Tea* (Salsburg, 2002) to introduce the concept of bias and experimental design. Given the nature of the topic, multiple transits around the spiral could occur to support the development of more advanced analytic and logic skills.

CONCLUSION

The developments in current science are benefiting/pushing the paradigms that are best understood and described through the mathematics

TABLE 5.5 Details of Pairing Stages With Tools, Bias, and Experimental Design Example

Stage	Context	Differentiation Tool
Introduction	Bias in statistics; *Bloom 1–2*	Book and Video[a,f]
Exploration	Discovery and example of bias; *Bloom 4 & Perry 5*	Story-telling[b]
Experimentation	Changing the data set/detecting suspicious elements; *Bloom 4*	Direct instruction; Technology[c,f]
Theory & Connections	Measures of central tendency; sensitivity to changes; *Bloom 4–5 & Perry 4*	Direct instruction[d]
Consolidation & Assessment	Conclusions and analysis; *Bloom 5*	Authentic writing[e]

[a] ChangSchool, 2011
[b] Lemonidis & Kaiafa, 2019
[c] Lee, 2019;
[d] Stein, 2006
[e] Ediger, 2006
[f] Jones, 2014

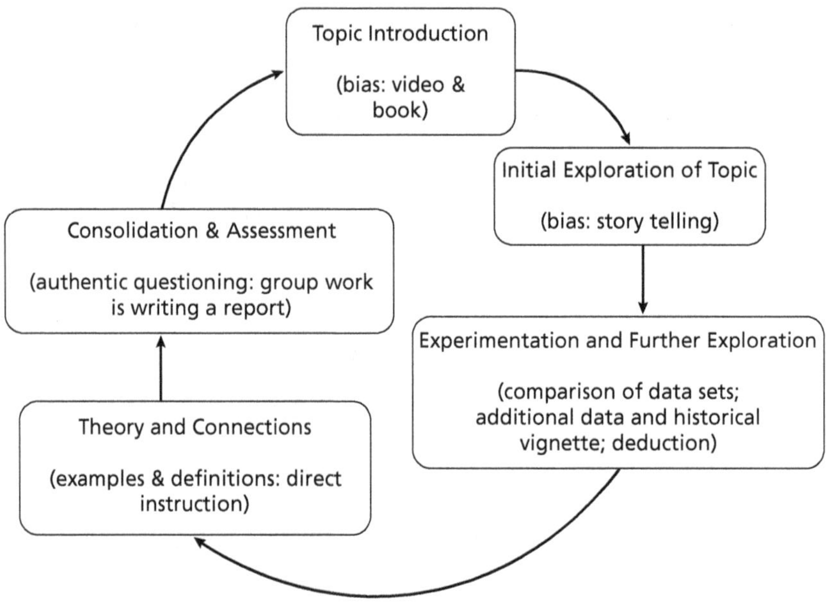

Figure 5.3 Sequence of learning, bias, and statistical design example.

found in statistics. Although not a branch of mathematics, statistics uses mathematical processes and modeling to describe scientific concepts. While it is appropriate for the educational community to recognize the forces that impel the teaching of statistics to newer and earlier grade levels, one must also recognize that the learning of statistics requires students to function in reading comprehension, mathematical calculation, and logical analysis simultaneously as well as to communicate the results. This brings with it considerable complications to the teaching and learning process. These are mostly found in the multiple transitions or focal points at each stage of the learning process. Analyzing these changes carefully will help make a more successful total learning experience.

In order to make the teaching and learning processes more effective, both the teacher and the student can benefit from understanding the nature of the processes, the level of the activity, and the need to connect segments of the material. Each stage of the process can be described in goals along with a level of cognition or a transition between intelligences. Arguably, if any of the three measures (cognitive level, multiple intelligences, and mindset) fall too far apart, the entire structure of learning is less successful. In the next chapter, the assessments can be chosen to support the learning goals at each stage. Understanding that there are multiple levels of learning in different areas of development is foundational; planning consciously for each area is critical to success. The more one believes that science and math construction go hand-in-hand with learning and inference, the more critical the need to address the learning cycle effectively.

REFLECTIVE QUESTIONS

1. How is statistics properly placed within the discipline of mathematics? What qualities argue against such a placement?
2. Can you identify more methods for differentiation and connect them to teaching particular statistical topics?
3. A famous and multi-ply reprinted book is entitled *How to Lie with Statistics* (Huff, 1954). How could you use this book to differentiate one or more statistics lessons? Are there other books or articles specific to statistics that you would recommend as useful differentiation tools?

CHAPTER 6

STATISTICS

Assessing Success in the Inference Process

Mary Barone Martin, Tammy Jones, and Teresa Schmidt

To know what you know and what you do not know, that is true knowledge.
—Confucius

Mathematics and science, taught and researched correctly, transcend and traverse the boundaries between language, mathematical, and analytical skills. The evidence for this statement consists of the dreaded, so-called "word problems." Too often, teachers and students can try to avoid such "applications" and stay with the routine, or even rote, selection of material. Statistics cross all sorts of boundaries, and usually in all problems if they are carried out with authenticity. Consequently, identifying specific areas of weakness and repairing them is more complicated and very critical. The source of the weakness can be within a skill area, within the intersection between content areas, or in the translation of information from one skill area into another skill area. The goal of this chapter is to propose a multistep process directing assessment choices. A brief survey of a variety of assessment tools is also provided in this chapter.

Age of Inference, pages 91–105

COMPREHENDING THE PROBLEM

While teaching any topic, it is important to check in on the progress of the learner. As was mentioned in Chapter 4, there are many scales, qualities, and activities involved in the teaching and the effective learning of statistics. In addition, there are multiple purposes for assessment:

1. to make adjustments in the next teaching/learning session or activity,
2. to quantify learning/benchmarks which have been achieved,
3. to ensure a mutual understanding between student and teacher about "What I know,"
4. to point toward necessary aspects of repair, and
5. to provide an environment in which to reinforce learning.

In the assessment world, these purposes fall into the broad categories of pre-assessment, formative assessment, and summative assessment. Within the discipline of statistics, the skills to be acquired can be classified in areas such as cognitive, technological, calculation, consolidation, ethics, mindset, fluency, communications, and analysis. We propose that a way to handle this kind of overlap, cross-influences, and multiple purposes is to consciously make decisions about assessment that are purposeful and intentional. In order to facilitate the various decisions that must be made, we once again organize the teaching/learning of statistics around the model developed by Martin and Jones (2019) to analyze a teaching/differentiation process. In Chapter 5, Figure 5.1 presented the stages in the learning cycle; Figures 6.1 and 6.2 are amendments to Figure 5.1 and include an additional stage to emphasize the paradigm construction and details of connections to assessments.

Movement through the stages of the spiral may repeat several times before appropriate mastery of the concept as a whole is achieved at an advanced level. Each stage represents an insertion position for a differentiation action, a teaching point, an activity point, or an assessment point. From the description of planning in *Understanding by Design* (Bowen, 2017), designing your teaching, in general, can yield rich results; using a model to organize the planning allows the assessment outcomes to be more targeted. The previous chapter explored the stages of learning, the interconnections of areas of expertise, and the prospects for differentiation; this chapter seeks to provide assessment techniques to help the instructor and the student as well as to provide a process that helps with the selection and interpretation of the assessment. The assessment techniques presented here are surprisingly robust for a wide range of skill levels and purposes. In the design of our lesson, the first cycle for learning a new topic could look like Figure 6.1; note that the parenthetical comment now represents the

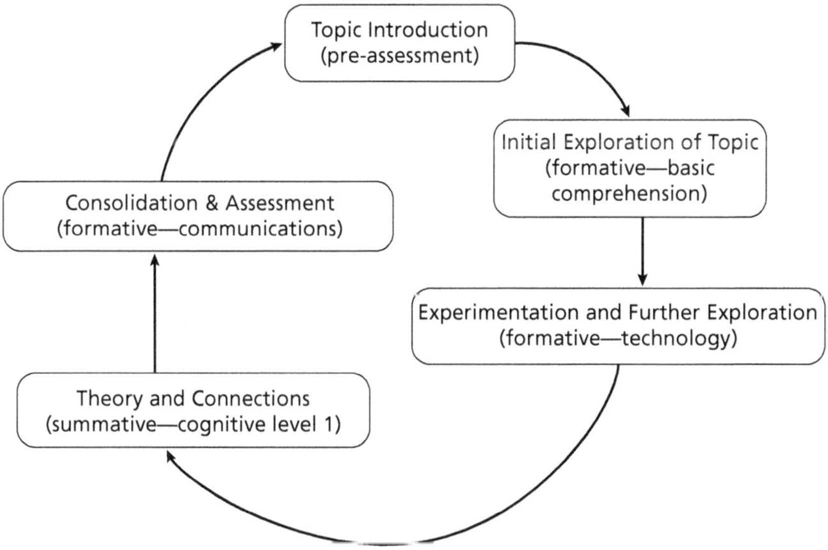

Figure 6.1 Learning cycle with assessment purposes.

purpose of assessment (instead of differentiation) that could be proposed for that stage of the cycle.

Based on the purpose of the assessment, one can choose the level or the time commitment for each particular stage. Needless to say, just as one cannot spend unreasonable amounts of class time assessing student learning, one can also not spend unreasonable amounts of planning time deciding upon assessment tools and plans. Planning the assessments around the learning cycle (Figure 6.1) can lead to organized and rapid planning.

1. Pick a stage of the learning cycle and choose the purpose of the cycle: pre-assessment, formative assessment, or summative assessment.
2. Choose the focus of the assessment: cognitive, technology, calculation, consolidation, fluency, communications, connections between intelligences, analysis, mindset, and so forth.
3. As appropriate, choose a preferred level of attainment for that focus. Level implies the scale (Bloom, multiple intelligence usage, Perry) and the level of performance expected with respect to that stage.
4. Select an assessment appropriate for the identified purpose, and focus, and stage. Using the previously selected contexts, pick an assessment that meets these criteria and is of the appropriate length.

Table 6.1 can serve as a tool to coordinate and/or clarify the process of assessment within one learning cycle.

TABLE 6.1 Planning Grid for Assessment Selection

Stage	Purpose	Focus	Level	Assessment
1				
2				
3				
4				
5				

TABLE 6.2 Example Row of Planning Grid

Stage	Purpose	Focus	Level	Assessment
4	Pre-assessment for Stage 5	Basic knowledge	1	Multiple choice

For example, suppose you are planning an assessment for Stage 4 of a learning cycle about calculating a measure of central tendency (Figure 6.1). You want to ensure students have the vocabulary and knowledge to start building an assessment of the use of central tendencies. Since you know that a multiple-choice test always addresses a Level 1–2 on the Bloom's scale and is quick, it would be useful as a pre-assessment before building towards additional theory or experimentation. The table entry would appear as shown in Table 6.2.

For the next sections of this chapter, we want to focus on information helpful in using the suggested chart as a planning tool.

PURPOSES, FOCUS, AND LEVEL OF ASSESSMENT

For our discussion, a successful assessment is one that helps the instructor accurately gauge student knowledge, assists the student in self-awareness of their learning, and provides information to modify or validate the learning activities of the class. In some cases, assessment is consolidated into knowledge used to evaluate in a larger aggregated group. At the ground level, though, assessment is all about student learning. This description of successful assessment leads to determining parameters and principles for the three columns in Table 6.1 that lead toward the selection of the exact assessment to be used.

Purpose

As previously noted, broadly speaking the teaching purposes for assessment can be categorized as pre-assessment, formative, or summative.

The teacher may have an intuitive idea in mind for the purpose of the assessment, or the teacher may systematically follow various inventories or recommendations. For example, Understanding by Design suggests addressing assessment evidence in the second stage of planning (Wiggins & McTighe, 2008). Barkley and Major (2016) argued that an instructor must first prioritize the learning goals for the class; one can formally assess this using a learning goal instrument. Ultimately, the choices are relatively narrow, with the National Research Council (2001) only recognizing three: assist learning, assess individual achievement, and program evaluation. The hierarchy for selecting an assessment would be first to consider the purpose of the assessment; the identification of the purpose will depend primarily upon the state of the learning cycle in which the assessment is to occur and the context of assessment. To illustrate the context of the assessment, consider the selection of a problem for an exam. One does not need to test a particular concept multiple times. Similarly, within a cycle, a pre-assessment might only need to occur once. So, the decision of "purpose" might be a combination of "what the teacher needs to know next" and "how long since the last time that was done." The practicalities define the guidelines for this choice.

Focus

After having determined your purpose, the next choice is the nature of the skill to be assessed; we will call that the "focus" of the assessment. It is tempting to over-emphasize "content knowledge," since most courses could be considered or construed to be "single goal" courses. However, with statistics, as discussed in Chapter 5, one must recognize that mastering the "content" means also mastering and fostering growth in areas such as analysis, information transfer, and communication. Essentially, this means assessing the three primary scales that we have recognized as major contributors to the construction of meaningful statistical information: (a) content, (b) multiple intelligence and transfer between intelligences, and (c) mindset/relativity as a perspective of the discipline. For the column headed "Focus," we would recommend selecting from one of these three options. This selection automatically makes a context for choosing the level of assessment in Column 4 of the planning table.

Before moving on to the selection of the level of assessment, it is worth discussing some related but slightly different choices for focus of assessment as presented by Barkley and Major (2016). The authors cited six domains within which to assess roughly corresponding to depth or level of learning in all three of the Perry schemes of knowing presented in Chapter 5. The six domains are somewhat combinations of focus and level: fundamental knowledge, application learning, integration, human dimension, caring dimension, and the study skills dimension. A teacher could use these six areas to have a combination Bloom/Perry scheme and then only need to add the multiple intelligence levels if that was of interest. Pursuing this plan would require the teacher to design their own leveling within each focus.

Level

The levels on the different scales for the focus were presented in Tables 5.1, 5.2, and 5.3 of the last chapter. Consideration of multiple intelligences must take a different path at this point. The level, as well as the focus, can change with each use of the learning cycles. For a particular topic, one might want to plan to repeat the learning cycle three times with a different purpose, focus, and level each time.

PLANNING ASSESSMENT

The last step in the process of assessment, for our purposes here, is to select a particular assessment that meets the needs that have been identified. This section provides some resources that can be customized for discipline and purpose; we have also included some examples of information that are useful for selecting a particular assessment. The assessments chosen here have the potential to work across multiple disciplines, have fairly descriptive titles, and are identified by source. Ideally, each teacher has a collection of assessments that serves regularly as a primary source for that individual. Alternatively, the teacher may have a list of five to eight assessments that are regularly used. Analysis of those assessments is another useful activity for planning purposes. This pre-classified list will be invaluable for speeding up the selection process. Readers will want to examine the assessment ideas in the following material to broaden their collection of assessments.

In Tables 6.3 and 6.4, please note that the columns have changed order and one column has been changed. The purpose column has been removed and the exact source reference has been included. The focus precedes the stage column since focus of assessments is the method of organization in most books.

Classroom Assessment Techniques

Angelo and Cross (2018) provided a variety of techniques that are oriented towards varieties of documentation. In most cases, the assessment

TABLE 6.3 Analysis of Selected Assessment Activities: Bloom

Focus	Stage	Activity	Level	Source
Knowledge Base	1	Focused Listing	1	A&C, 126–131
Critical Thinking	2	Pro & Con Grid	2	A&C, 168–171
Synthesis	2	Word Journal	1	A&C, 188–192
Problem Solving	3	Documented Solutions	2	A&C, 222–225
Application	4	Directed Paraphrasing	4	A&C, 232–235
Connections	5	Double-Entry Journals	5	A&C, 263–266

can be used in a variety of disciplines; they are also very easily adjusted for differentiation and different grade levels. In Table 6.3 are some activities suitable for a wide variety of assessment purposes and occasions.

Angelo and Cross (2016) provided detailed descriptions of each of the activities and examples of disciplinary contexts/suggestions for using the assessments. There were also suggestions regarding analysis and feedback from the results. For our purposes, the name of the activity is sufficiently descriptive to allow us to reach broad conclusions for discussion purposes about what the assessment would look like and the purpose of it. While almost any of these activities could be used at almost any stage, there are some ways of timing them so as to be more helpful. To illustrate, it would be generally problematic to ask someone, newly introduced to a topic, to work on a double-entry journal in order to compare and contrast two differing concepts. Generally, this is a higher-level ability, requiring more foundational material, and thus would generally come later in the learning and teaching cycle (although one could imagine settings in an early stage where it would be possible). We have added a general inferred learning level for each activity to help convey the intentions for the selection of that assessment.

Learning Assessment Techniques

Providing similar information for selected assessments from Barkley and Major (2016), we direct our attention to the second critical factor in choosing an assessment. These assessments focus more on the Perry levels of learning (Wilson, 2013), with the focus identifying more with the suggestions from Barkley and Major. The level is identifying with the Perry levels (see Table 6.4).

It is important to note that there is no intended nor actual correlation between focus and the knowledge level being assessed. Minor changes to an assessment can alter the level drastically higher or lower and the same is true of the focus. This is a critical underlying concept for understanding appropriate differentiation of learning and teaching.

TABLE 6.4 Analysis of Selected Assessment Activities: Perry

Focus	Stage	Activity	Level	Source
Fundamental Knowledge	4	Quick Write	1	B&M, 105–110
Application	3	Peer Problem Review	3	B&M, 185–190
Integration	5	Knowledge Grid	2	B&M, 208–213
Human Dimension	1	Editorial Review	4	B&M, 282–286
Caring Dimension	4	Briefing Paper	5–6	B&M, 353–357

This is but a sampling of alternative assessments that the authors have used in their own classrooms with students during a unit of study on statistical diagrams. These provide students with choices from which to select, one of the easiest forms of differentiation. Using a collection of assessments, such as these listed in Table 6.5, does create more work for the teacher when evaluating student responses and work. However, Gardner (2019) noted that "... many of the classes and schools claim that students are more likely to come to school, to like school, to complete school, and to do well in various assessments..." (p. 18) when the application of multiple intelligences theory is incorporated into schools. He also noted problems with the evidence since it is almost entirely based upon self-reporting by the schools. A final point to mention is that alternative forms of assessment do not replace the need to verify that core fundamental ideas are held securely by each student.

TABLE 6.5 Sample Statistics Assessment Activities: Gardner

Focus	Activity
Linguistic	Create a set of directions on how to create various statistical diagrams, including each diagram's purpose.
Logical—Mathematical	Develop a mind-map for statistical diagrams, including what each describes, and when to use each type.
Musical	Create a song, jingle, or rap that explains each type of statistical diagram and what each is used for.
Bodily—Kinesthetic	Create and act out a play in which the characters are the various statistical diagrams.
Spatial	Create a 3D example of each type of statistical diagram.
Interpersonal	Create a survey research project with your group and report the results using statistical diagrams.
Intrapersonal	Use guided imagery to see and solve a more complex statistical problem using statistical diagrams.
Naturalist	Research certain plant/animal traits and create a report using the various statistical diagrams.

PRINCIPLES FOR PRACTICAL ASSESSMENT

There are many pitfalls when it comes to assessment. In fact, there are probably as many pitfalls as there are reasons to accurately assess learning. With the purpose of offering inspirations and ideas for cultivating the proper mindset for the studying, teaching, and practicing of science, it is appropriate to provide some suggestions based upon the experience of the authors of this chapter. They are suggestions meant to be helpful rather than firm rules. Whether you use the process table provided in this chapter or not, the following ideas are good ideas to keep in mind.

1. Describe the purpose of the assessment and how the results will be reported. Do this *before* you administer the assessment. (*Note:* If you are not going to use the results of the assessment for teaching, then do not do it. If you do not have time to evaluate the assessment appropriately, then do not do it.)
2. Identify a skill, a level, and a stage for the assessment.
   a. What content and learning skill am I assessing?
   b. How advanced a learning level am I assessing?
   c. How early or late in the content topic is appropriate for this assessment?
3. Do not use 20 different assessment activities with one group of students. If you are truly looking for accurate results, you can use an unfamiliar assessment to get authentic initial responses; but, it takes a while for the students to learn how to think about the assessment. While you and the students are learning, pick two or three assessments for a course and use them the entire time. You can add a few as you go on to maintain freshness.
4. Do not invalidate the assessment process with threats and/or bribes ("If you do poorly on the test, you will have to..." or "I will give you extra credit if..."). This always corrupts your output data and you do not learn anything about what you were assessing. It also undermines good teaching and good ethical practices.
5. Keep the assessment simple and direct; you can modify the level without becoming confusing. You can get some variation by keeping the same actual assessment and editing it to raise or lower the level of performance.
6. Decide how you will report the aggregate results back to the class and how to make them useful in a timely manner. If you cannot give a generic, redacted report back to the class, then pick a different assessment or find another way to make the results valuable to the students. You must always complete the feedback loop.

7. Make a notecard for each assessment you use regularly and identify the purpose, focus, and level. As you add assessment techniques, make a notecard for each one. Now you have a pool from which you can quickly choose a new assessment for a new activity. It can also be sorted quickly by level, purpose, and so forth.
8. Remember to consider the assessment in terms of the level of knowledge. In other words, if you are assessing at a Level 5 for a skill and the class (students) is essentially at a Level 2, then the assessment will not serve the purpose of assessing student understanding. The students will not be able to perform adequately with that assessment tool and you will get back empty or meaningless responses. It is somewhat similar to trying to use a microscope to examine a planet. The wrong instrument is aimed at the target.

AUTHORS' RECOMMENDED ASSESSMENTS

Combined, the authors represent over 100 years of teaching experience; so, we decided that it would be appropriate for us to each add a comment that illustrates our view of assessment. One that is no-fuss, no-mess, multipurpose, easy to use, and with helpful outcomes. These ideas come from K–16 experiences and are presented with the hopes of being illustrative of a variety of views of assessment.

Martin

The assessment that serves multiple purposes for me, and that I use every class period except for an exam period, is a modification of "The Muddiest Point" (Angelo & Cross, 2018, pp. 154–158). I have been using this assessment for more than 25 years and it never fails to inform me. My use of it is so changed from the original that the name and the purpose often no longer matches with Angelo and Cross. Nevertheless, The Muddiest Point was my starting point. At the end of each class, every student turns in a 3x5 card with a notation of one or two starting places for the next class. In other words, what ideas/concepts do you want me to start with? Is there any major idea that needs revisiting? At the start of the next class, I summarize the requests and announce them. Usually, in a class of 40 students, there are no more than four to five requests, and there is almost always a clear "winner." I formulate the start of the next class (a math class, by the way) with a problem that incorporates a response to the question. I can usually handle all the requests with one or two examples. I always report the categories of requests and how many were in each category to the students. I also use these cards to take participation roll. So "None" is a lack of participation. I consider this assessment appropriate at any stage of learning but usually more helpful at the introductory stages. It is always a great pre-assessment for the next class and yet serves as a post-assessment for the day. It elicits questions mostly at early skill stages, I can ask for a focused list if I want a reality check, and yet I can modify the question some to move it to a higher learning level or a higher skill level. Students need practice with the higher levels.

Jones

The statistical concept to be presented is that of statistical diagrams. I assign the students to read a chapter or chapters from *The Lady Tasting Tea* (Salsburg, 2002). Using literature in the classroom supports students expanding their vocabulary skills and scientific reasoning (Hapgood & Palisncar, 2007). There is also evidence of students increasing their mathematical reasoning skills when trade books are incorporated in the classroom (McKinney & Hinton, 2010). As a pre-assessment and/or formative assessment, I would next ask the students to create a list of the types of statistical diagrams with which they are familiar. For students who are challenged by the material, this could be the initial assignment. Students who are more on target could also be asked to sketch an example of each type of diagram. To push students who are ready, the additional assignment might include describing a data set for each of the diagrams. Student responses will provide evidence of where the students are in readiness for the initial explorations of the topic.

For the next stage of the learning cycle, as students are beginning their initial explorations of the statistical diagrams, they will begin to experience the benefits and limitations of various data displays. Students should be asked to articulate these, both orally and verbally. Students who have difficulty organizing information will benefit from using graphic organizers (Fisher & Schumaker, 1995). In particular, students can create a table to show the benefits and limitations of each of the data displays. The creation of a concept map could also help students visualize and understand the various displays they are exploring.

In order for students to be able to apply and make use of the statistical diagrams in terms of a context, students will have to be able to transfer the information about when and why to use a display based upon its benefits and limitations to the actual creation of a display using technology, such as a TI-Nspire or TI-84 CE. At this point, the type of display being used is related to the level of the content being studied. As an entry point, teachers might choose to set up the data set themselves and simply transfer the file to the student's calculator so the student can explore the data set in order to observe patterns, trends, and/or relationships. I often use this process in order to cut down on nonmathematical time and at the same time ensure some comparability of student experiences. Other students will be able to choose the display type, input the data, and set up the display on their own. I ask each set of students to articulate why the display was chosen and what their initial study and analysis revealed about the data. Providing a list of scaffolded questions for the challenged student will guide them through the analysis reporting portion of the investigation, while a minimal list of things to include would be enough for other students.

According to Watson (2014), consolidation "plays a central role in becoming mathematical" (p. 21). She suggests that reflecting on an activity or task is an important part of the process for developing understanding of and meaning for the mathematics being studied. This consolidation needs to be planned carefully and deliberately. Authentic writing is one strategy for engaging students in consolidation. Here are a few examples of writing prompts and opportunities that could be used based upon quotes and ideas from *The Lady Tasting Tea* (Salsburg, 2002). They can be applied to a variety of statistical topics as needed.

- Journal: Complete the analogy: "A class in statistics is like ____________________."
- Write a meaningful paragraph using the terms in the section about...
- The author wrote *The Lady Tasting Tea* because he believed that the public is not fully aware of the degree to which recent developments in statistics have impacted the way we perceive the world. From your reading in his book and other sources, write in defense of his belief.
- While at Guinness, Stella Cunliffe did an analysis of the beer casks. The quality control worker, who at the time was a female, simply had to accept or reject the barrel. Discuss bias in light of Cunliffe's findings and how she de-biased the experiment (Salsburg, 2002).
- Fisher and Mackenzie (1923) argued that the analysis of variance is conditional on randomization. Write a defense of this statement.

Figure 6.2 shows a way to construct a learning cycle around the use of a tradebook.

Schmidt

Many of us teach the way we were taught; in some instances what has been referred to as "drill and kill," or in some other cases, modeling. Additionally, students often do not enter a statistics class with a solid background in elementary mathematics or well versed in the statistical method.

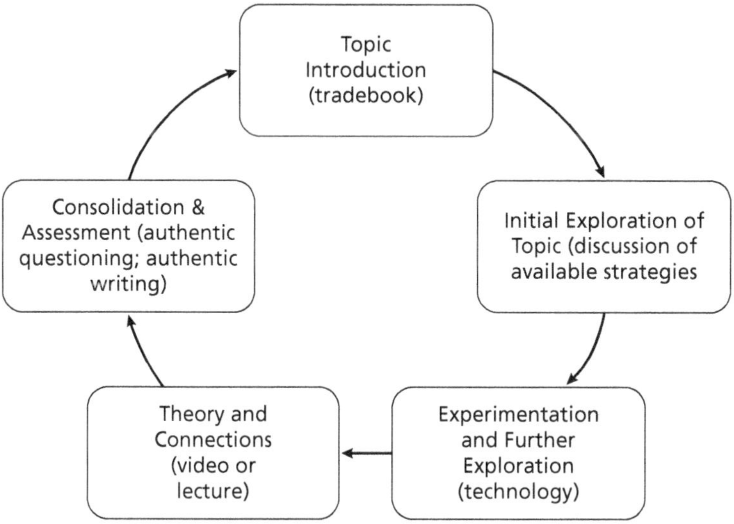

Figure 6.2 Learning cycle using a tradebook.

They come to class with the basics, such as measures of central tendency, but when asked, "Why are there different measures, and when do you use them," they may not know.

A majority of students may not have grown up with a culture of "cooperative or small group learning," even though such techniques have been around since the 1930s. Traditionally, statistics emphasized mathematical procedures and computational skills. However, with the proliferation of graphing calculators and personal computers, statistics education has grown beyond procedures and skills. The emphasis in statistics has now shifted to data collection, analyzing data, and communicating (or inferring) the results found through analyzing data.

By allowing students to work in small groups, teachers empower them to share, discuss, and brainstorm about how to address a situation, which can enhance both mathematical abilities and statistical reasoning (Curcio & Artzt, 1997). This has also created potential quandaries for educators; how does one assess group work? Group work assessment techniques should allow for both the process of problem-solving and the quality of the solution of the group and the individual.

Consider an example of a visual display of data. Visual displays are used for a myriad of reasons such as examining patterns, recognizing trends, and making predictions. When selecting a task, select one that invokes a higher-order thinking, open-ended, free-response task which allows the group to apply the statistical method in order to generate a response, and which will allow them to create a product. For this example, suppose that a student is given a random data set of passengers from the Titanic disaster and asked to summarize their data sets using a plan they themselves devise within small groups (i.e., focusing on what types of data they have, what type of display they want to make and how best to display it).

The group of students is then asked to create a product to be shared with the entire class that tells the story of their data (MTStatPal, 2016). Since many students already know the basic descriptive statistics and graphs, this gives the instructor a chance to see what they know, and how to help them think about using data and data displays in order to answer statistical questions.

The takeaway from the lesson goes beyond the basic application of descriptive statistics. Students can be expected to generate and read visual displays of data, organize both quantitative and qualitative data, and apply frequency and relative frequency distributions to construct a variety of visual displays, and identify the shape of a distribution. As an instructor, one is able to assess student work, both individually and collectively. According to Curcio and Artzt (1997), assessment should provide students with an accurate image of their capabilities and provide the teacher with a picture of what students can do.

By using small group activities and the creation of a final product, an instructor can assess the time spent talking and discussing the problem, planning a method for solving the problem, implementing the group's agreed-upon solution to the problem, and displaying/sharing the information with others. During the sharing of the information, the instructor can also ask probing questions to determine if students have reached a high level of cognitive performance, such as questioning them about the reasonableness of their conclusions they drew from their data.

CONCLUSION

From the previous short essays and comments, one can see a variety of concerns, areas of interest, and perspectives. Assessment carries with it a lot of confusion, chaos, valuable information, and high stakes. One of the greatest benefits from this chapter can be to provide the informed teacher with a template for building a rationale for educational decisions. It is our hope that we have been successful in encouraging a deliberative approach to teaching and its planning as well as engaging the reader through the presentation of a wide variety of valuable examples and contexts.

REFLECTIVE QUESTIONS

1. Examine your assessment practices. Do you repeatedly assess one type of skill or one particular level? What would serve your teaching purposes better?
2. How do you use your assessments to direct your teaching? Can this be improved?
3. Do your students have a good idea of what grade they will make on a test? Why or why not?
4. Is it possible to promote high-quality learning without assessment?

SECTION II

APPLICATION: FRAMEWORK FOR SCIENCE IN A DATA-RICH WORLD

This section of the book offers practical applications, inspirations, and ideas for cultivating the proper mindset for the studying, teaching, and practicing of science at all levels of education.

CHAPTER 7

CHILDREN'S LITERATURE RESOURCES TO SUPPORT AUTHENTIC SCIENCE PRACTICES AND ENVIRONMENTAL DECISION-MAKING

The *Conservation Tales* Series

Tom J. McConnell and Barbara Giorgio-Booher

In the end we will conserve only what we love; we will love only what we understand and we will understand only what we are taught.

—Babe Dioum

In our modern world, helping citizens develop a scientific mindset is critically important. News sources are filled with stories of issues that are based on science concepts, many of which are controversial. Examples include public debates over vaccinations, climate change, genetically-modified foods,

Age of Inference, pages 109–129

alternative energy, preventing infectious diseases, and the effectiveness of herbal supplements found in a variety of stores. In all these cases, the controversies are rooted in people's use (or disuse) of scientific information in making decisions. Claims from different groups may be based on opinion, marketing, or even deliberate misinformation. The public is often bombarded by conflicting ideas from many sources. This is not a new situation, but research has shown that the public's trust in scientific experts as a source of information has been declining (Gauchat, 2012; Krause et al., 2019).

Scientists and educators generally agree that this trend amplifies the importance of scientific literacy (Allison & Goldston, 2018; Bauer, 2004; Yacoubian, 2018). However, an emphasis on improving standardized test scores in mathematics and language arts has led to decreased time spent teaching science in developmentally critical years, such as elementary grades (Blank, 2013; Milner et al., 2011). A decrease in the time spent teaching science in elementary schools has been followed by falling scores on standardized science tests (Blank, 2013). This trend can only be expected to further erode the public's ability and willingness to use scientific reasoning when making important decisions. The need to improve science education with the goal of building a citizenry that is able to use scientific knowledge in daily life is increasingly urgent (Allison & Goldston, 2018; Kalman, 2010; Wieman, 2007; Yacoubian, 2018).

Emphasis on Dimensions of Scientific Literacy

Current standards for science education emphasize the importance of teaching the practices of science (Next Generation Science Standards Lead States, 2013). In the model presented by the Framework for K–12 Science Education (National Research Council, 2012) and the Next Generation Science Standards (NGSS Lead States, 2013), science is taught through three dimensions: core disciplinary ideas, practices, and crosscutting concepts. The practices embody the ways in which scientists do science. Recent literature argues that to help students develop both scientific literacy and a scientific mindset, we should teach learners *through* inquiry, not just about inquiry (Osborne, 2014; Wieman, 2007). The way we teach students science through inquiry is to engage them in authentic scientific activity—doing real science (Swarat et al., 2012). Examples of programs that accomplish this goal show that inquiry-based science teaching is effective in improving achievement scores on tests (Cotabish et al., 2013; Diamond et al., 2014; Heller et al., 2012; Slavin et al., 2014) and increasing student interest and motivation in science as a subject (Hiller & Kitsantas, 2014). All of these studies focus on inquiry STEM teaching as described in the NGSS. This modality of teaching helps students learn the processes of "doing science."

Students learn to question, make predictions, and design experiments. Students produce additional information for further analysis and practice pattern recognition skills used by scientists to generate inferences, theories, and laws about their world. In turn, the ways in which theories and laws inform our actions and choices are real-world connections that make up an important part of a scientific mindset.

We posit that helping children learn how scientists "know" about the world around us can help them develop a scientific mindset while gaining trust in the information scientists share with the public. Teaching children to think like scientists should begin in elementary grades to maximize the opportunity presented by children's curiosity about the world around them. Teaching inquiry-based science in early grades provides opportunities to establish a scientific mindset and habits of mind, reflecting the scientific practices that can allow a deeper level of content learning in middle and high school science courses. Isabelle (2017) summarized this goal clearly when he wrote, "For students to achieve the goals of the Next Generation Science Standards by Grade 12, thinking and acting like scientists and engineers must begin in the elementary grades" (p. 84). As described above, the accountability measures of standardized testing programs, mixed with initiatives at national, state, and local levels, have made it difficult for schools to prioritize science teaching reform (Johnson, 2013). As a result, schools often spend more time teaching mathematics and language arts at the expense of other subjects, including science (Blank, 2013; Isabelle, 2017; Milner et al., 2011).

Environmental Literacy as Part of the Science Curriculum

Environmental literacy is one of the domains of scientific knowledge that has been studied for many years. In the 1970s and 1980s, researchers examining patterns in children's views of wildlife and animals noticed that fewer young learners were familiar with living things in and around their own communities (More, 1979; Westervelt & Llewellyn, 1986). By the early 21st century, Richard Louv (2005) had coined the term "nature-deficit disorder" to describe the growing unfamiliarity of children with the environment in which they live.

The declining time spent teaching science in elementary grades presents a troubling contradiction between research on the value of inquiry-based science teaching and classroom practice. How do we bring more inquiry-based science into the classroom? Performance expectations emphasize the need to engage learners in real scientific phenomena (NGSS Lead States,

2013). Nevertheless, teachers are pressed to incorporate literacy and math in much of the curriculum.

One approach to integrating more authentic science into the elementary curriculum is to develop books that meet the needs of teachers while still presenting engaging scientific content and practices. For decades, studies have shown that books are one of the influences on children's ideas about animals (Eagles & Demare, 1999; Eagles & Muffitt, 1990; Huxham et al., 2006; More, 1979; Sousa et al., 2017). These books may lead to anthropomorphized views of animals (More, 1979) or limit children's understanding by appealing to emotional connections to a species rather than a scientific understanding. Kellert (1996) presented an argument that children's views about living things are based primarily on moralistic and aesthetic values than on scientific or ecological values. Moralistic values may lead children to "care" about animals, and aesthetic values can build an appreciation for the beauty and appeal of a species. However, without understanding the ecological role of an animal in its habitat, a child's ability to make informed choices about conservation is limited, or may even be misinformed. Even in older children and adults, research suggests our views of wildlife are primarily based on utility ("Is the animal useful to people?") and moralist values ("Animals have the right to exist, too"; Hunter & Bhrem, 2004; Reiter et al., 1999; Westervelt & Llewellyn, 1986) rather than on a scientific understanding. Teaching children to base their decision-making on "feelings" rather than evidence, putting emotional values above scientific knowledge (Monhardt & Monhardt, 2000), runs counter to what we hope to teach as a scientific mindset.

A New Plan for Designing Children's Science Books

These studies should inform the design of stories for children about wildlife if the goal is to build deeper scientific literacy about ecology, human impacts on the environment, and conservation biology. The design of such books should take into consideration the needs of teachers in the elementary grades. Most elementary teachers lack the depth of science content knowledge we expect for science educators in middle- and high-school grades (Trygstad et al., 2013). Teachers in younger grades are often less confident in their ability to teach science, especially inquiry-based science. But they are likely to find the teaching of science content more palatable when it is structured as children's literature (Milner et al., 2011). The challenge for authors and educators, then, is to find ways to develop books for elementary grades that present engaging stories while still maintaining scientific accuracy, depicting science as a process, and provoking questions and interests related to "doing" science.

If this goal can be achieved, books may offer resources that address the need for improving environmental literacy and action while at the same time contributing to the development of a scientific mindset among young children. To be most useful, books should actively engage readers in authentic inquiry. Research shows that engaging in activities involved in science leaves a more lasting impact on students than just learning about science (Swarat et al., 2012). If those activities focus on environmental science inquiries, evidence suggests that children will have much more scientifically accurate ideas that inform decisions they make with regard to environmental issues in their own communities (Dixon et al., 2005; Monhardt & Monhardt, 2000). By connecting scientific reasoning to environmental topics that are visible at home or in their own neighborhood, children can see a scientific mindset as easily accessible and clearly relevant to their own lives.

The design of books that help children see how science works in the real world is different than the traditional children's books about animals and science. In the following sections, we describe the Conservation Tales book series (Airway Publishing) as examples of features we propose should be included in children's books about science. We follow the examples with a list of recommendations for the design of new print resources for science teachers.

CONSERVATION TALES

The goal of developing quality children's literature that addresses wildlife conservation and the scientific process was the focus in our development of a series of books for children that engages young readers in authentic stories depicting human-generated effects on endangered and threatened species—both negative and positive. We planned the stories as a way to develop new habits, mindfulness, and behaviors in children that result in protecting and restoring natural habitats for both wildlife and humans. As the concept for the series developed, it became clear that such books could also teach children from diverse segments of the population to see themselves as potential scientists and citizens who use science in making everyday choices.

This seed of an idea evolved to become Conservation Tales, a collection of books that we will describe in this chapter. The series is a resource for teachers, parents, naturalists, informal educators, and others to help children learn about and practice authentic science as it relates to wildlife, including species in their communities. The books each feature a species listed as endangered, threatened, or "of concern" by state or federal governments. The main character in each story is a child who encounters the animal and wants to know more about it. The child meets researchers who study the animals. The researchers in the stories are real scientists who collaborated with the books' developers and are usually featured as characters in the stories. From the scientists, the child learns about the natural history of the animal, the factors that threaten its survival, and the scientific processes used by the researchers to learn more about the species.

The fictional children in the stories observe scientists at work and ask questions about what they are trying to learn, how they collect data, how the data are used, and the type of conservation actions suggested by the evidence. As the story unfolds, readers are exposed to authentic examples of how scientists collect and use data, find patterns that help them draw conclusions, and make sense of the patterns as they try to find ways to help protect a species or a habitat. The books lead readers to a collection of conservation actions they can implement at home and a set of inquiry learning activities that can help readers practice the scientific processes used by researchers in the story.

In this chapter, we will describe the features of the book and the ways they contribute to the development of a scientific mindset, including examples of how the books reflect the practices of the scientists shown in the stories. We will give examples of how the books are designed to be used in a variety of learning environments, with examples of educators' implementation of the books. We hope these descriptions will present a framework for planning and developing other science-based books for children.

HOW CONSERVATION RESEARCHERS "KNOW"

In the world of wildlife conservation, drawing inferences about populations of animals and environmental factors in their habitats is a crucial part of the process of understanding our impact on the environment and, more importantly, developing a plan of action to solve problems. For instance, researchers' decisions to list a plant or animal as "endangered" happen only after the community of scientists reviews census data collected using reliable sampling techniques, data from previous years, reproduction rates, and the presence of threats, both natural and man-made that pose a risk for the future of the species. Researchers who study wildlife rely on relatively simple methods of collecting data about population sizes, the movements of individual animals, changes in populations over time, and the health of animals as influenced by variables in their habitat such as availability of resources, climate, human impact, and the effects of introduced species.

In many studies on our environment, the body of evidence used by researchers begins as small samples of local observations and measurements that are compiled into large databases shared among the scientific community. We propose a model (see Figure 7.1) as a way to describe the patterns in practice we observed being used by many of the scientists depicted in

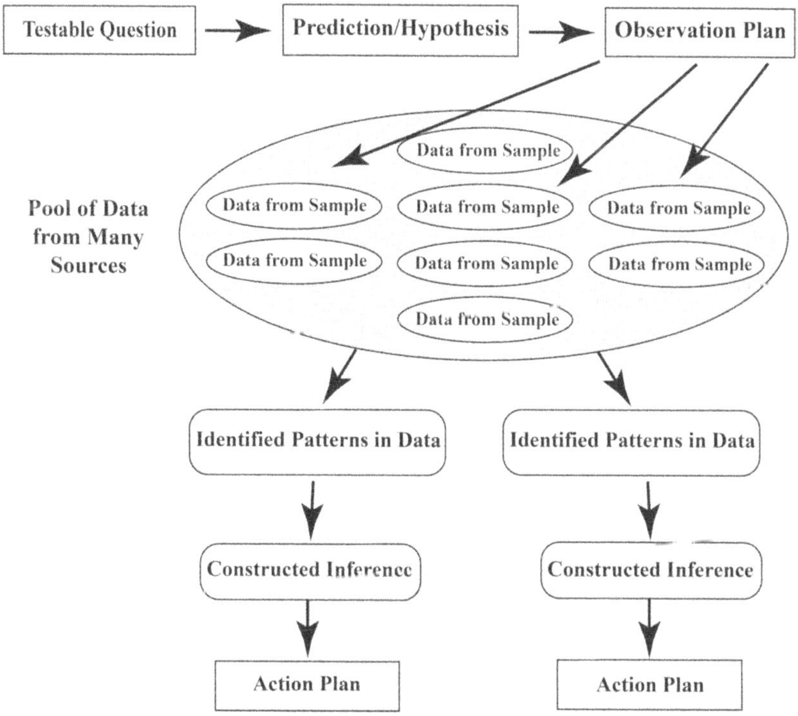

Figure 7.1 A common structure for conservation research.

the Conservation Tales series. Note that the data come from many samples, observed by many different researchers, over a span of time or across a wide geographic area. Data are shared by researchers who then try to identify patterns that can be used to support some type of action to protect the species and even to reduce a population size by controlled hunts, as happens with managed deer herds in some states.

One example of this approach is the research conducted by manatee researchers along the Atlantic and Gulf coasts of the United States and the surrounding waters in the Caribbean Sea. Observations focus on recording the environmental conditions and location of animals sighted, alive or dead, and identifying individual animals when possible. Many manatees have visible scars left by injuries from boat collisions and entanglements, so individuals are identifiable by those scars. Researchers record diagrams of the scar patterns and share them through an online database used by researchers. Census data are recorded by aerial photography and observations by scientists and volunteers on the ground. Additional data are collected through necropsies of deceased animals to understand their ages and cause of death.

All of the data from these smaller samples are compiled in databases shared by scientists from Virginia to Texas and throughout the Caribbean. Teams of researchers and government officials use data to identify trends in population changes, threats to the health of animals, habitat use, and seasonal patterns of movement. Inferences drawn from these data are used to enact local ordinances relating to manatee sanctuaries, boating speed limits, and even the use of fertilizers in areas adjacent to manatee habitats.

This is just one of many examples of the process described in Figure 7.1. As we consider ways to help learners think like scientists, it is important to present examples that are engaging, and that illustrate data collection and analysis methods they can replicate locally.

DEVELOPING A "CONSERVATION TALES" BOOK

The example of the manatee research is an excellent model of how many different scientists can contribute to a large body of data based on observations that can then inform practical decisions. This model is also a good example to describe features of a Conservation Tales book and the process used to develop the stories. In Spring 2018, a team of 12 undergraduate students and two faculty members at Ball State University began developing three books about endangered and threatened species found along the Gulf Coast of Florida. *Conservation Tales: Manatees* (McConnell & Stallard, 2018) was one of the volumes developed in that semester.

The student team included majors across a diverse set of disciplines. A pair of animation students illustrated the story, with help from a photography student, a graphic designer from the visual communication program, and an elementary education major. The students were part of an immersive learning program at the university that brings together interdisciplinary teams to create a tangible product for an external partner working with the course. The faculty mentors worked for nearly a year to establish a partnership with two teams of researchers and to secure funds to support the team's travel to meet with the researchers.

The external partners included manatee researchers from the U.S. Geological Survey's (USGS) Wetland and Aquatic Research Center in Gainesville, FL and Mote Marine Laboratory & Aquarium in Sarasota, FL. The USGS team permitted the group to observe and photograph a 2-day manatee health assessment study in Crystal River, FL, while Mote invited the team to spend 2 days observing and interviewing researchers at their facility. Both groups are identified in the *Conservation Tales: Manatees* (McConnell & Stallard, 2018) book as "content consultants," a term for researchers who partner with Conservation Tales book development teams and are often depicted in the stories. The project obtained permission to use images from visits to U.S. Fish & Wildlife Service's (USFWS) preserves in Crystal River and spent time snorkeling and kayaking in habitats where the manatees live, as well as exploring a nearby state park where manatees are found.

Team members observed the environment, scientists, animals, and the process of studying manatees in the wild and the aquarium during site visits. The students interviewed the scientists, using their notes to develop a storyline that is authentic and accurate. Photographs were taken to support the work of the illustrators and to include in the book. The illustrators sketched scenery, manatees, the aquatic environment, and scientists. The graphic designer contributed to sketches and stories and met with Mote's graphic designer to discuss how to work with the scientists and artists to develop layouts that are informative and engaging.

After the site visits, the team created a series of storyboards for the book, with text for the story guiding selection of illustrations and photographs. The team met twice a week to share the progress they were making, discuss the story and the need for illustrations, and plan for the development of learning activities.

Drafts of the story were sent to scientists at the USGS and Mote for their review. The scientists read the story and returned suggestions for revisions to text and illustrations. The scientists shared photographs with the designer to use in the story. The book was also reviewed by an elementary teacher who assessed the story's fit for the target age group (Grades 3–5). The student team used the feedback from scientists and the teacher to revise the book. After reviewing a proof copy from the print shop, the book was released to the public.

FEATURES OF THE "CONSERVATION TALES" BOOKS

The *Conservation Tales: Manatees* (McConnell & Stallard, 2018) volume of the Conservation Tales series represents a typical example of how the books are developed, but it also exemplifies certain elements that are consistent across all the books in the series. *Conservation Tales: Manatees* (McConnell & Stallard, 2018) features a main character who sees a manatee and wants to know more. He eventually meets some real scientists. The character observes research that the scientists are doing to study manatees and learns about things they can do to help protect the animals and their habitat. While this is the general framework that guides each of the stories, there are other characteristics that are common across the books, including diverse characters, a set of conservation actions, and a collection of inquiry learning activities. In this section, we will discuss each of the features as they relate to teaching a scientific mindset.

A Child's Curiosity

Children are naturally curious about the world (White, 2004). It is easy to imagine a child seeing an animal and wondering what it is or why it is there. For a scientist, that curiosity is an important driving force for any research. The Conservation Tales stories all begin with this element to help readers relate to the characters and hopefully share their curiosity. In Figure 7.1, we started the diagram with a question. This seems an essential part to include in our stories because it drives authentic science practices.

Authentic Scientists

Most children share a common stereotypical image of a scientist. You may have seen drawings made by children in a famous set of studies (Symington & Spurling, 1990)—a White male with "wild hair" and a white lab coat holding a flask in a laboratory. Other research has shown that students like *doing* science but cannot picture themselves *being* scientists because they do not want to be that stereotypical scientist (Archer et al., 2010). Perhaps one way to help students feel more comfortable expressing an interest in science is to show scientists that don't fit the stereotype. Field biologists can often break the stereotype, so Conservation Tales shows real scientists as characters in the stories.

The illustrators used those scientists as characters in the books. We used their real first names and included both photographs and illustrations. For *Conservation Tales: Manatees* (McConnell & Stallard, 2018), "Bob" the scientist is Robert Bonde, a well-known manatee researcher at the USGS who retired as we developed the book. He and his team of researchers and volunteers for the manatee health assessment can be seen in photographs throughout the book and in the illustrations created by the student team. This team includes students from the University of Florida who conducted blood tests and preserved specimens for further study in the laboratory. In the story, Bo asks questions of Maita, a character based on a doctoral student from Uruguay shown in the field lab in one of the photographs in the story. The goal was to help readers see real scientists at work. Figure 7.2 shows a photograph from the site visits with the USGS team and the illustration developed from the photograph as an example of the authentic representations in the book.

The choice to feature scientists as more than just fictional characters has provided a strong sense of authenticity in the stories. Children who have read the books commented about the story being "real." Parents, teachers, and scientists pointed to this element and the mix of illustrations

Figure 7.2 Comparison of photograph of scientists and illustrations.

and photos as an important feature that sends the message that the story is about "real science," not just a fictional story about animals or scientists.

Authentic Science Practices

Throughout the story, the main character, Bo, observes researchers at work. He helps the team on a spotting boat to locate manatees to be netted by a catch team, and watches as researchers take blood samples, measure exhaled CO_2, photograph the manatees, and record data about fat layer thickness, length, girth, and weight. He asks questions about diagrams on which scientists record scar patterns on individuals, and learns about aerial photography as a method to count manatee populations. All of these represent the variety of observations scientists do when studying manatees, and most are easy for children to understand. This presents an important example of one way in which scientists collect and compare data to help children learn to think like a scientist.

For each story, we worked to ensure that these processes are accurately represented. As we met with researchers, we paid close attention to how the teams measured animals, the observations they made, and the process for recording and storing data. Each book includes photographs and illustrations of these steps, and stories include details that may be important in helping readers understand what the scientists do. We gave attention to details like the clothing scientists wear, tools they use, and safety equipment they need. For instance, in *Conservation Tales: Salamanders* (McConnell, 2017c), researchers in the field were careful to clean their boots before and after going into the field. This helps prevent the spread of a fungal disease called chytrid (Chytridiomycosis) that can devastate amphibian populations. In the story, we showed the characters wearing boots and explained the reason for boot washing in the story. Our hope was to help children learn to be safe when practicing science—safe for themselves, and for the living things they study.

The key message in showing these authentic practices is that "anyone can be a scientist" if they learn to do what scientists do—ask questions, plan experiments, observe, collect data, look for patterns, draw conclusions that can lead to action. This theme—"anyone can be a scientist"—is also important in the next element of the Conservation Tales books.

Diverse Characters

During the development of characters for the first Conservation Tales book, an early discussion was about who the characters would be. What would they look like? What characteristics should they have? We became aware that this was an opportunity to show that "anyone can be a scientist." In the study mentioned above about children's image of a scientist (Symington & Spurling, 1990), nearly all the scientists drawn were Caucasian men. This is not surprising when most of the images of scientists in textbooks and other media at the time showed scientists as nearly all White, and nearly all male.

Despite a focus on this issue in the 1980s, textbooks still lack diversity in the way they represent scientists (Ceglie & Olivares, 2012; Lederman, 2003). It is still not common to find scientists depicted as non-White and female. This may be one of the reasons we see recent research confirming that students still perceive science as a "male" profession (Sikora & Pokropek, 2011). In a time when "diversity" means more than gender and ethnicity, there is still a need for examples of diverse scientists, and diverse children who have an interest in science. It is even harder to find representations of people with disabilities as scientists. It should be no wonder that 33% of a sample of children with disabilities expressed interest in science careers, but only 11% identified themselves as having the ability to be a scientist (Turner et al., 2011).

Conservation Tales makes a concerted effort to depict the children in our books as diverse and to include a diverse cast of scientists. It has been our experience that there is a growing diversity among the science community—women, people of color, people with disabilities, and individuals across the LGBTQ spectrum *are* scientists. Perhaps publishers and media sources have been less than effective in representing these characters. Since part of a scientific mindset should include the ability to see oneself as a scientist, we need more educational materials that include the entire diversity of human characteristics.

And so, we did in the *Conservation Tales: Manatees* (McConnell & Stallard, 2018) book. Bo, the lead character, uses a wheelchair. The story does not mention what kind of condition Bo has, but the illustrations show him in a wheelchair or using crutches when he is in a research boat. Our team was careful in researching how to represent a child in a wheelchair in the series. The illustrators shared sketches with the university's Office of Disability Services to get their feedback, and even sent drawings to a builder of custom wheelchairs for children. The feedback they received led to important changes in the illustrations. The team interviewed the crew of a charter dive service in Crystal River to find out what modifications are made for clients with limited mobility. The accuracy of the story is important in letting all readers know that "anyone can be a scientist."

In other books in the series, we included characters from mixed-race families, a range of ethnicities, a boy on the autism spectrum, a girl with a hearing impairment, and a child with same-sex parents. The diversity is not a major part of the story—we focus on the child's curiosity about an animal and the discovery of the scientific processes and conservation actions. But still, the message is apparent—if you develop a scientific mindset, you can be a scientist.

Even the scientists we featured in the stories reflect diversity. Many of the scientists we have included in the book are women, including women of color like Maita De Maria, the Florida doctoral student in *Conservation Tales: Manatees* (McConnell & Stallard, 2018), and Amanda Hodo, the researcher featured in *Conservation Tales: Seahorses* (McConnell & Brown, 2018). Readers see diversity both in the fictional characters and in the real scientists described in the stories. Our hope is that children in underrepresented populations will see the books as a source of models for "scientists who look like me."

Inquiry Activities

One of the last sections of each Conservation Tales book is a set of inquiry learning activities. Development of these activities was led by Dr. McConnell, a science teacher educator, who helps the development team reach an understanding of a definition of "inquiry-based learning." This definition is based on the National Research Council's (2000) description of the "elements of inquiry" (p. 25), and on the list of practices in the NGSS (NGSS Lead States, 2013). The facing page after the list of inquiry activities in each book displays a grid showing how the inquiry activities align with all three dimensions of the NGSS, as well as connected math and literacy standards. The goal of this section is to help parents and educators easily identify standards-aligned activities that reflect inquiry-based science teaching and learning.

In a sense, the inquiry activities are among the most important teaching tools in the series, at least when thinking about teaching a scientific mindset. Earlier discussions in this chapter mention the importance of helping children learn how scientists do science by collecting and analyzing evidence during an experiment or observations. Inquiry activities are an opportunity to not just learn about science, but to learn science by doing science. Each activity features at least one of the practices of science listed in the NGSS. The goal is to help learners practice making sense of evidence. This is not done by reading alone, but also by guiding readers to science activities that can take place online, at home, or in their community.

The page listing inquiry activities includes a URL for the Conservation Tales page where readers can find supporting materials for the activities. In most cases, links lead to websites for citizen science sites, PDF files with printable science investigations, or web-based learning activities that let students practice the same skills used by the scientists described in the books. In *Conservation Tales: Manatees* (McConnell & Stallard, 2018), the list includes four activities. The list represents a good sample of different types of activities readers can find in other Conservation Tales books.

The "Featured Activity" is "Manatee Match," a direct result of the development team's interactions with researchers at Mote Marine Laboratory & Aquarium. One team of manatee researchers at Mote travels to nearby waters each day, photographing manatees. When they return to the laboratory, they try to identify individual manatees in the images to accompany data about that animal's movements and health, and about the conditions and environment where it was photographed.

To identify an individual manatee, researchers use a shared database of the scar patterns seen on manatees. They compare photos to diagrams showing scars and any amputated limbs or tail seen in previous observations. In the story, Bo asks researchers about the diagrams and why they photograph the animals they capture, so the process is described in the story.

The Mote researchers developed a training tool to help new researchers and interns learn to use the database—a set of cards with photographs and diagrams showing individual animals. New researchers practice by matching cards. They use three sets with increasing difficulty, and only after mastering the third level can a researcher record a positive identification of manatees from photographs. The training activity helps teach scientists to observe specific details, and to understand the spatial relationships used to compare a diagram with a photograph that may show the animal from different angles. Figure 7.3 shows some examples of the photographs and their matching diagrams.

The students who created the *Conservation Tales: Manatees* (McConnell & Stallard, 2018) book and connected learning activities developed a similar

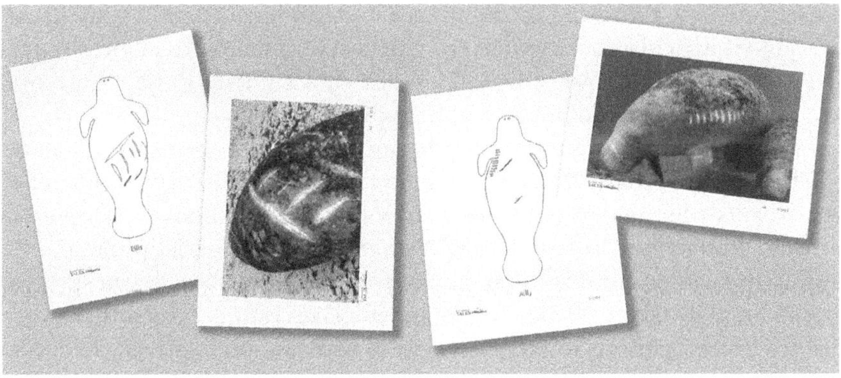

Figure 7.3 Diagrams and photographs of manatee scar patterns.

game for children. The team used images and artwork to develop the "Manatee Match Card Game" and an accompanying lesson plan. The lesson guides learners through the game and then prompts them to create their own cards for a different species that they may be interested in studying, like fish in a classroom aquarium, cattle on a farm, or monkeys in an exhibit at a local zoo. In the activity, students are practicing the very same skills as manatee researchers at Mote and experiencing the value and limitations of this type of photo-identification that scientists experience in the field.

Another activity, "Manatee Tracker," leads readers to an online site that allows them to view the movement of manatees on the Florida coast that have been released with GPS tracking devices. The lesson lets students ask questions that can be answered with tracking data, select some individual manatees, and record data and observations to answer those questions. Manatee researchers use the same process to study the animals. Data inform local decisions about manatee populations, like when to post seasonal boating speed limits in communities where manatees spend the winter.

Data in this activity do not exactly fit the definition of "citizen science" websites, but it has some similarities. In most citizen science projects, students and other "citizen scientists" can submit their own observations as data points. In the "Manatee Tracker" activity, this is not possible. But learners still get to experience the use of real data collected by other scientists to answer real questions. Sharing data is a practice that is growing in importance in the field of environmental science (Michener, 2015), and it is not always easy to replicate in a traditional classroom science lesson. Engaging learners in citizen science has been shown to be an effective way to help learners develop a scientific mindset while building a belief that they can be a scientist (Dickinson et al., 2012; Hiller & Kitsantas, 2014). Citizen science opportunities are growing in abundance and can be outstanding additions to science curricula when used in conjunction with standards-aligned plans. Other books in the Conservation Tales series link students to citizen science projects about birds, pollinators, and amphibians.

"Eye in the Sky" is another activity in the *Conservation Tales: Manatees* (McConnell & Stallard, 2018) volume that replicates skills used by manatee researchers who helped the Conservation Tales in the book development process. Researchers from the USFWS and Mote take aerial photographs during the winter months when manatees gather in shallow, warm springs. These images, taken during flights in small aircraft, are recorded every day for 2-week periods to take a census of manatee populations. They are not able to photograph every animal in the Gulf and Caribbean region, though, so the study serves as an excellent example of sampling techniques that are critical to the way scientists make sense of data (Sato et al., 2007). Readers use the lesson to download photographs of manatees that they can use to count individuals. During the activity, they experience the difficulties of counting individuals in varying water clarity, when individuals may be obscured by other manatees, and when overhead obstacles like trees make the sampling process more challenging. The activity prompts learners to discuss sampling procedures and to think about variables that may influence the degree to which samples represent the manatee population as a whole. As in other activities, this one helps children learn how scientists reach the conclusions they read about in books and in newspaper reports so they can better understand the trustworthiness of scientific information.

The last activity in Manatees is "What's Your Footprint." This activity is less directly tied to manatee research, but it connects readers to an evidence-driven view of a conservation action that affects manatees and many other species—climate change. In this activity, a link helps them estimate their own carbon footprint as they explore ways they can, as a child in a larger community, have some small impact on CO_2 levels. While some may question if this is true "inquiry" based science, the learners engage in a scientifically oriented question and formulate explanations based on evidence they collect. This aligns well with the National Research Council's (2000) definition of "inquiry." More importantly, learners practice making sense of evidence as they think about potential action plans. This is the essence of a scientific mindset.

Connecting students to inquiry-based activities after they read a book is an important way to extend the learning by helping students put the science process into practice. For teachers looking for resources to help them teach science more effectively, it is helpful if reading materials are closely associated with other learning activities. The inclusion of the inquiry activities in each book is our way to make it easier for teachers to integrate inquiry into their curriculum.

Conservation Actions

The final element we will discuss is included near the end of each story—a list of "conservation actions." This list, usually based on suggestions from content consultants for each book, are activities that readers can do at home, in their community, or with school groups to impact conservation of environments, the endangered species in the book, or similar species that may live in their community. The main goal of the books is to help children learn how they can have a positive impact on wildlife, so this section of each story is a critical component.

The actions range from habitat restoration, changing purchasing habits to avoid products made in ways that harm the wildlife, to simple activities that can help protect wildlife, like recycling plastics, placing reflective stickers on windows to avoid bird collisions, and avoiding insect repellent or sunscreen when handling amphibians because they have permeable skin. Some actions, like refusing to purchase ivory that may be related to elephant poaching, may not be practical for children—children do not typically buy ivory. But they can make other choices like looking for "green palm oil" logos when picking a brand of candy from the shelf or planting native wildflowers to support native bees and other pollinators.

The conservation actions are a step in the learning process when children move from learning about science to learning how to use scientific knowledge in ways that can make a difference in their communities. Children who read the books at home can put these actions into place in their own yards, but school groups, community centers, nature centers, and after-school groups like a Girl Scout troop or a library reading club can also adopt these activities as community service projects. In the next section, we will share a few of the stories about how Conservation Tales uses community outreach to help foster these kinds of activities.

IMPLEMENTATION OF CONSERVATION TALES

This chapter has described the design, and therefore the intent, of the Conservation Tales series. It is important to consider how the books are impacting learning when put into practice. A formal study of the outcomes of the book series is still in development, but we can share some examples of how educators in different settings have implemented the books and used them to lead to more inquiry-based learning.

The Conservation Tales team devotes time each year to planning and facilitating outreach activities in our community. These events include teacher professional development and children's learning activities in our community at venues like libraries, after-school reading programs, and public events sponsored by nature centers, a local Master Gardener's club, and other community-based groups.

One example of a community outreach event involved members of the Conservation Tales team visiting a local community center. The center hosts an after-school program for children across many grades, but most participants are in Grades 4–6. The activity we planned was a reading from the *Conservation Tales: Sea Turtles* (McConnell, 2018) book, followed by a group art activity to create a mural from recycled plastics. The director and staff of the community center then used the activity to begin a recycling program in the low-income neighborhood surrounding the center. Children in the program help collect plastics, record data about how much plastic they collect and recycle, and share the data with the entire community. While the outreach activity was not inquiry-based, the team used ideas from the book to extend the activity into a service project that continues to use evidence to report the impact on the community.

The books were used as part of a teacher professional development program at a zoo in a nearby city. Because several of the stories feature radio telemetry as a source of data used by researchers, the books led to the development of an activity in which teachers used radio transmitters and receivers packaged as the CatLocator™ (2020), a device to help pet owners track a lost cat. The devices work just like the telemetry units featured in the books about cerulean warblers and bats. The activity at the zoo involved placing transmitters on a variety of stuffed animals hidden in certain "habitats" in the zoo's botanical garden. Teachers in each of three teams "tracked" the animals, and recorded data about their habitats. Between each team's search, the animals were moved but were each placed in the same habitat as in the previous trial. The teams then shared their data and discussed conclusions about the habitats preferred by each "species" in the study.

One of the program participants, Tracy, teaches 6th-grade science. She adapted the activity to her school's setting and secured a grant to buy two CatLocators (2020) and five transmitters. She uses *Conservation Tales: The Cerulean Warbler* (McConnell, 2017d) and *Conservation Tales: Bats* (McConnell, 2017a) as a way to engage her students in a discussion of habitats and adaptations. Her students conduct their own "study" of habitats using the same practices as wildlife researchers in the field. This example demonstrates how activities described in the book can lead to practical ways for students to develop the same skills as scientists, including data collection and identifying patterns in data.

One last example involves a parochial elementary school located about an hour from the Conservation Tales team's university. The teachers at the school work closely with a nearby nature center located on a former farm along the banks of the White River. The nature center and the school requested a workshop about Conservation Tales, and the team decided to focus on *Bees.* After a workshop to discuss inquiry and conservation projects, the teachers purchased a classroom set of *Conservation Tales: Bees* (McConnell, 2017b), and used it to launch a long-term project. The project began with building native bee nest boxes to place near a garden plot at the nature center. At about the same time, students planted vegetables in the garden. Over the next year, groups from the school observed bees at the nature center, recording the different species they found and the locations of the species. The data led to a new experiment to see if planting wildflowers near the garden would affect bee diversity. This study is ongoing, but the students have harvested seeds from the first year's wildflowers and are expanding the project to send seeds to families of children in the school. The concept for studying wildflowers and bee diversity is a direct connection to the scientists featured in *Conservation Tales: Bees* (McConnell, 2017b). The project to share seeds with others in the community is an original idea generated by the children to expand the conservation actions of the class project.

IMPLICATIONS FOR SCIENCE EDUCATION

The use of children's books in the science classroom is already a part of the elementary school curriculum, in part because of teachers' comfort with books. Supporting authentic inquiry and an understanding of the scientific mindset needs to be an important feature of the elementary curriculum as well. For the science education community, one way to integrate these two issues to participate in the creation of more books that are accessible to teachers and children while also depicting science as the rigorous and systematic problem-solving method described in the NGSS.

Our team of faculty and students have learned that books designed to accomplish this goal are different from most of the traditional children's books used in classrooms, and even more different from the type of writing to which the science community is accustomed. We offer the Conservation Tales books as an example of some of the features that have helped teachers adopt the books as a part of the science curriculum. We propose that science educators should contribute to the production of other resources, both in print and in digital formats, that support the teaching of authentic science practices and a scientific mindset.

The examples from the Conservation Tales series described in this chapter help illustrate that if students can be engaged in stories about real science, the stories can support science learning that focuses on authentic practices and an understanding of how science works in their communities. We do not propose that books like Conservation Tales are the only way to help children understand the scientific processes, but we offer the features of the Conservation Tales series as a model that we suggest can work toward the goal of developing a scientific mindset in our children.

RECOMMENDATIONS FOR DEVELOPING CHILDREN'S BOOKS FOR SCIENCE TEACHING

Include Partners With Expertise in Science, Education, and Visual Communications

The type of books we described integrate content and communication methods from a diverse range of disciplines. Leveraging many different specialized skill sets will maximize the impact of the product.

Focus on Real Scientists, Using Photographs to Help Students to Relate to Scientists

If readers can clearly see that the characters are real, they may more easily perceive that they are capable of being a scientist, and accept that science has a real impact on their lives.

Emphasize the Practices of Science, Not Just Phenomena

A scientific mindset is not just about knowing science facts and concepts. It includes an understanding that science is a dynamic process done by groups of people. Children's books can include examples of how scientists collaborate to collect evidence and reach conclusions based on evidence. Our experiences suggest that children find these examples engaging and understandable.

Connect Science Ideas to Practical Decision-Making

We propose that learners are more likely to adopt a scientific mindset if they see that scientists' work is important to their daily lives. Children may struggle to relate to abstract examples, so these connections should be clear and apply to the target audience.

Feature Scientists Who Reflect a Wide Range of Diversity

The science community is diverse. We need to depict this diversity to send the important message that anyone can be a scientist. Our recommendation is to include diversity in our depiction of both diverse scientists and children.

Offer Opportunities for Students to Practice Science

Reading materials that lead to more exploration and investigation are ideal resources for teachers, especially those who are less comfortable designing inquiry science activities. Developers of materials for elementary science learners can extend the impact of books with hands-on activities, links to online resources, and examples of easy-to-implement science investigations.

If the community of scientists and educators produce a collection of engaging stories that help learners discover how scientists use science practices, we believe we can help teachers in elementary classrooms facilitate more and better science learning. With thought to the desired outcomes and the nature of science and science learning, we can help build curriculum resources that support the development of a scientific mindset.

REFLECTIVE QUESTIONS

1. In an age in which children engage with technology more than books, what limits and opportunities are presented if resources like Conservation Tales are presented in digital formats?
2. How do literature-based experiences influence children's understanding of and interest in science as a career or profession?
3. What strategies can teachers use to best implement the type of resources exemplified in Conservation Tales to move children to take action based on their science learning?

CHAPTER 8

SUPPORTING STATISTICAL LITERACIES IN THE CONTEXT OF A DATA VISUALIZATION PROJECT WITH ELEMENTARY STUDENTS

Lynn Hodge, Joy Bertling, and Shande King

In today's information age, representation, communication, and persuasion are increasingly connected (Kress, 2003). It is difficult to pick up a newspaper or browse a website without coming across a range of visualizations to read and understand. This data-intensive turn requires citizens who are able to understand, critique, and discuss quantitative concepts and arguments visually in a nimble fashion (Wolff et al., 2016). In addition, as Tufte (1983) and others have argued, good designers of visual graphics for mathematical relationships must be students of both mathematics and design. Thus, data visualizations bring together a consideration of context, mathematics, and design.

Age of Inference, pages 131–140

Engaging with data visualizations has the potential to highlight connections to students' cultural and linguistic resources given the creative and authoring practices that are embedded in this process. This chapter focuses on a pilot project that sought to understand how to support elementary students in engaging with data visualizations for the first time. Our purpose is to describe the project and to illustrate the different data visualizations, considering design and data analyses that students created as part of their participation in the 8-week learning experience.

DATA VISUALIZATIONS AS RESOURCES FOR STATISTICAL LEARNING

We drew on a theoretical framework that focuses on *sociocultural perspectives* which emphasize learning as a cultural accomplishment, dynamically connected to the identities, goals, relationships, and practices of individuals and their communities (Cole, 1998, 2008; Gutierrez & Rogoff, 2003; Lee, 2008; Nasir, 2012; Nasir & Hand, 2006). Through this theoretical lens, we view data visualizations as creative and productive ways to engage multiple communities with statistical observations. Through the expression involved with data visualizations, students can learn to think contextually and critically, develop multiple forms of expression for diverse audiences, and consider the roles of designers and mathematicians (Kotin et al., 2013). Additionally, visualizations can serve as a learning tool to help individuals integrate their ideas and reassess prior knowledge (Zhang & Linn, 2011). Within statistics, individuals have been shown to have an interest in data visualizations in specific contexts of museum learning, but their understanding was shown to be limited (Börner et al., 2016). This reinforces the idea that data visualizations can present data in an interesting manner; however, more support is needed to enhance individual competencies in making sense of data visualizations. The design of data visualizations has the potential to contribute to this kind of individual understanding.

Turning to statistical learning, a substantial body of research shows that inappropriate ideas about statistical concepts are widespread and persistent (Garfield & Ben-Zvi, 2007). Research studies reveal the complexities in and the importance of developing the notion of distribution (Cobb, 1999; Wild, 2006). An understanding of distribution means viewing a set of data as an aggregate with characteristics rather than as individual cases. Creating a foundation for statistics learning involves exploratory data analysis and the critical process of performing initial investigations on data to discover patterns, identify anomalies, test hypotheses, and check assumptions with the help of summaries and representations. This kind of statistical learning can also create opportunities for mathematical learning such as shifting from additive to multiplicative reasoning, which is a significant milestone in upper elementary and middle school mathematics.

While data visualizations emphasize the contextual nature of statistics, statistics and mathematics more broadly are often taught in a decontextualized way (Bajak, 2014, McGatha et al., 2002;). This point is particularly relevant to efforts that support the broadening of participation in STEM fields (Landivar, 2013). Many teachers and researchers are concerned that many students (and adults) dislike mathematics, feel incompetent at mathematics, and believe that being incompetent at mathematics is somehow acceptable (Gresalfi, 2009; Moses & Cobb, 2001). These challenges are further compounded by research that indicates STEM interests develop early and are relatively stable by eighth grade (Maltese & Tai, 2011). Approaches to supporting students from historically underrepresented groups in STEM tend to focus on one of two approaches: (a) developing curricula that build on the cultural assets and interests of students and their communities (Civil, 2007; Ladson-Billings, 2017) or (b) engaging students in the authentic practices of the discipline (Ball, 1993).

Mathematics, and statistics in particular, is often taught as a set of definitions without a deep understanding of the application of the concepts and the practices that make up statistical data analysis (Bajak, 2014; McGatha et al., 2002). Real-world phenomena presented to students often lack the connection to students' cultural and linguistic resources (Boaler, 1998). In addition, access to high-level mathematics courses where more complex statistics and visual representations may be encountered is far less likely for students from groups underrepresented in STEM fields (Adelman, 2006). To address diversity in STEM, access to both relevance and important mathematical or statistical ideas must be considered.

PROJECT BACKGROUND

As part of a pilot project, referred to hereafter as the *Data Viz* project, with the overarching goal of broadening STEM participation through creative practices and voice, we designed an elementary curriculum and approach emphasizing data visualization. From an initial meet with the STEM coach and principal, this project would engage students in their initial experience with data visualizations. Prior to this, students in the project collected data and created graphs that were determined by the textbook curriculum and the teachers. This data visualization project was implemented in a fourth-grade art class during a period of 8 weeks with weekly class sessions. The school that served as the context is a STEAM-focused (science, technology, engineering, art, and mathematics) magnet elementary school. The school is located within a mid-size city in the Southeast United States. The school student population is 84% students of color, and the project class participants are reflective of this statistic. Our cross-disciplinary project team included four members representing expertise in mathematics education, statistics education, art education, and science education. Members of this university-based team co-facilitated lessons and served as participant observers.

As mentioned previously, the purpose of the project was to introduce students to data visualization as a mode of communication, to engage them in processes of data analysis, and to provide an opportunity for them to communicate their findings to their school and local community. The 14 student participants, with 12 students participating throughout the project, adopted methods of social scientists and contemporary artists. In the Data Viz Project, we sought to design learning experiences that provided access to learning about data analysis and visualization.

EXPERIENCING DATA VISUALIZATION: A LEARNING TRAJECTORY

The learning trajectory we drew upon is described in the forthcoming paragraphs. We organize our discussion around the five segments of the trajectory. For the first segment, to introduce the concept of a data visualization, we engaged participants in an initial discussion and data visualization process inspired by contemporary artists Komar and Melamid (1997). In this first session, we began by questioning students about their previous experience with data. We worked together to define the term *data* as "information" and *data visualization* as "showing data." We continued by displaying two data visualizations: a traditional pie chart and an infographic depicting a population's distribution by gender, ethnicity, and age, using human symbols, differentiated by color and size. We asked questions such as, "Which visualization do you prefer? Why?" These prompts were designed to encourage students to make sense of the visualizations in discussion with each other. Many students responded that they preferred the more colorful and visually stimulating infographic, although a few students preferred the simplicity and familiarity of the pie chart. We then asked students to consider the question of why data visualization might be important. Students identified the importance of showing and remembering data, especially for the purposes of career readiness and professional advancement.

A second segment involved making connections between data visualizations and artistic practice. This was done to further emphasize the artistic aspect of data visualization by highlighting the broader context of art. In order to do this, we introduced students to Russian artists Komar and Melamid (1997), who worked with a professional marketing firm to poll people around the world about their preferences in paintings and then used these data to create most- and least-wanted paintings for each participating country. While their work playfully and ironically explores issues of taste and capitalist market research methods in Western culture (Govan, n.d.), it also served as a data visualization process that appeared concrete for and relatable to the students.

A third segment focused on furthering students' understanding of data visualization. Students were engaged in an adapted version of Komar and Melamid's (1997) artistic process. First, students individually completed a questionnaire by responding to 15 questions about their painting preferences. Next, these completed questionnaires were cut into question strips, sorted them by question, and distributed them to students in partner groups. Then, each group analyzed the preference data for their two assigned questions. While some items asked "either/or" questions, offering predetermined categories for a simpler analysis, other items were open-ended and required students to conduct an initial qualitative analysis to form the categories themselves. We used our knowledge of students' understanding of data analysis to determine which groups were ready for this more challenging task. After tallying the responses by item, students identified the strongest preferred characteristics for each question category and then shared their findings with the class. Following a class discussion on how such characteristics might be synthesized into a painting, students worked in groups to sketch ideas. In the subsequent class session, students took turns in groups drawing and then painting their class' preferences on a large paper. The resulting painting reflected their affinity for outdoor scenes, blue and red colors, sharp angles, and wild animals, among others. Upon the completion of this painting, students reflected upon their success in accurately representing the data. Throughout this process, we used statistical vocabulary, including *data, data collection, data analysis, data visualization, frequency, representation, typical,* and *majority*, to emphasize the learning of statistics by using terms during discussions. Therefore, the emphasis was not on memorizing definitions, but rather on making sense of ideas.

During a fourth segment of the learning trajectory, students were asked to engage in a more authentic data visualization activity. This activity presented a task that required students to engage in statistical thinking and to communicate both the patterns and context of a data set (Moore, 1998). To ensure the data set's relevance for students, we made the design decision to survey the fourth-grade students who attended the school on their interests and experiences. We involved the project participants in this process, by asking, "What are some things that you would like to know about the fourth-grade students at your school?" Using this feedback, we designed a questionnaire with 10 open-ended questions and asked the fourth-grade teachers to administer it to their students. In partners, students analyzed the data for their assigned question—determining the frequency of each response and developing categories as needed. To identify some strategies that might be helpful in their upcoming visualizations, we examined a few professional data visualizations. From an analysis of these works, we revisited the concepts of symbol, shape, proportion, color, and value as elements or strategies they might use to communicate data patterns and context. We displayed these terms on the board and encouraged students to consider them as they visualized the student interest data. In the upcoming section on insights, we focus on three student-created data visualizations to discuss the students' learning as reflected in their work.

A fifth segment of the learning trajectory involved the students developing final copies and titles of their data visualizations created in segment four. These were shared at a community event hosted by the school.

DATA COLLECTION AND ANALYSIS

The data collected during the Data Viz Project included video recordings of class sessions during the 8 weeks, field notes recording conversations with individual students and small groups, student work samples, and interview data collected at the conclusion of the pilot project. Thus far, we have analyzed the student work and field notes about small group conversations with attention paid to the rationale behind the data visualizations students created in segment four in particular. We have analyzed the student work using an approach that describes the student work and considers the relevant topics of conversation that emerged during the small group discussions. In this way, conjectures were tested as topics from students' discussions that were encountered in the notes. This back and forth process helped to ensure that the conjectures raised about the student-created data visualizations are grounded in the data (Strauss & Corbin, 1994). In the section below, we reflect on three work samples that reflected three ways that the project class approached the development of data visualizations. We do so to highlight the diversity in student strategies and considerations as they engaged with data and art.

INSIGHTS GAINED

The data visualizations created by students during segment four of the learning trajectory reflected a range of approaches in communicating patterns in the data and conveying the context of the data analyzed. We highlight three samples of student-created data visualizations from segment four that are representative of three ways of reasoning about data reflected in the class. The first example is shown in Figure 8.1.

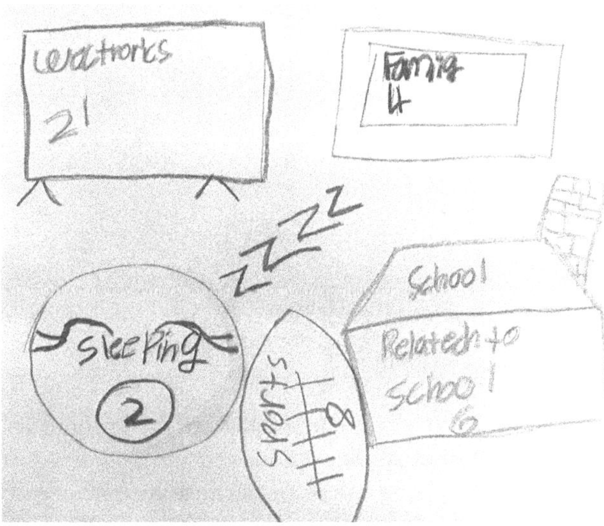

Figure 8.1 Example data visualization 1.

The data collected and analyzed by a small group of participants included responses to the question: What are your favorite things to do? In this first example, the students in the group discussed collapsing smaller categories such as watching shows/movies and playing video games into one broader category of electronics. It is interesting to note that the students focused on what the smaller categories had in common in arriving at their decision to use the name *electronics*. In addition to the category of electronics, represented by a monitor or television, the student group organized the responses into categories of family, sleeping, sports, and school (or related to school).

The observable features of the data visualization included an attention to the categories themselves with the sports category shown within a football and the sleeping category highlighted with a sleeping face. The group did not articulate a reason for the individual colors chosen but did make the point that they intentionally made each category a different color to highlight the individual categories. The pictures across categories were the same size with the number of responses written within each picture. This data visualization appears to reflect thinking that is more additive in nature in that the categories are shown separately, but no connections are visibly made across categories. The group emphasized the context of the responses by taking significant time to draw each of the pictures for the categories.

The second example (Figure 8.2) features data analyzed from fourth-grade responses to the question: What is your favorite color? This data visualization created by one student showed the colors in a linear arrangement

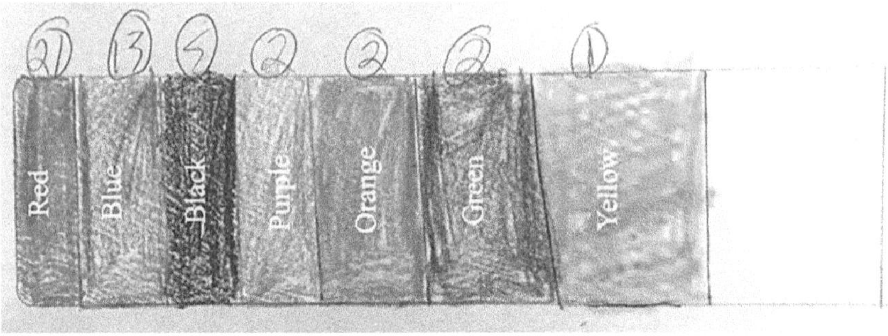

Figure 8.2 Example data visualization 2.

connected to each other. It was unclear whether the student created the visualization in this way because he/she viewed the responses as a collection of data, connected to each other, or because he/she considered the colors connected like that of a rainbow. Interestingly enough, the student included differences in the width of the color that seemed to be linked to the number of fourth-grade responses for each color. For example, one fourth-grader responded that his/her favorite color is yellow. This appeared to be the widest color band. Next were green, orange, and purple with two responses each. The differences in widths seemed to reflect differences in the number of responses, although there was not a strict adherence. Through a conversation with the student, it appeared that he/she was grappling with how to capture the differences in the number of responses in a way that was visually accurate.

In example three (Figure 8.3), the participant group analyzed fourth-grade data that answered the question: What is your favorite drink? In an approach blending pattern and context, the student group depicted fourth graders' favorite beverages in a drink diagram with the preferred types of drinks layered within the glass. Differentiated by color, the height of each layer loosely reflects the preference frequency. The notation to the right of the drawing indicated the number of responses for each category. The student group seemed to agree readily on collapsing the different sodas into one category. One participant in the group called attention to how only one student responded with water which was important because it is "the healthiest." The group's color choices seemed to be based on personal preferences. It appeared that the choice to use a beverage glass reflected a decision to both convey the context and to emphasize how the data were connected by the question of favorite drink, as evidenced by the small group discussion.

These three samples, though focusing on different questions, drew attention to the creativity that students employ when communicating their

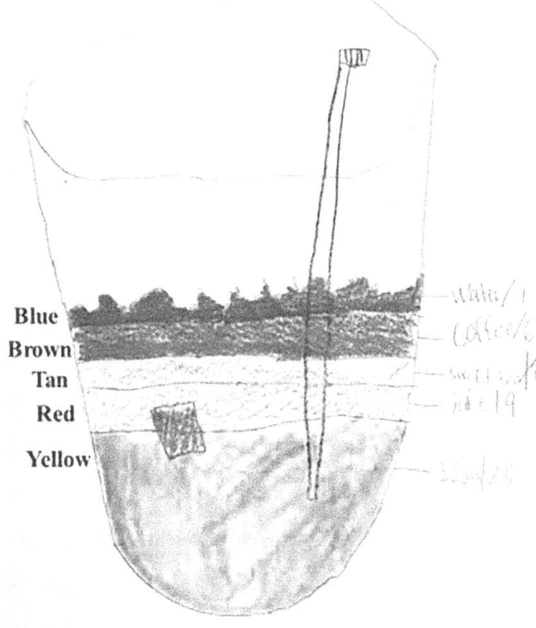

Figure 8.3 Example data visualization 3.

interpretation of data. In addition, the samples collectively pointed to the importance of students describing their rationales for a range of decisions about their data visualizations.

DISCUSSION AND CONCLUSION

Our findings, focusing more on student work and small group conversations, indicated a number of insights. First, students were able to explain the rationale behind their visualizations. Most of these explanations were grounded in students' data analyses and important consideration of defining the categories. More than one group engaged in collapsing smaller categories into broader categories when it made sense to do so. The decision-making seemed to hinge on finding something that was common across smaller categories and the need to be able to talk about the data more broadly. Second, students' visualizations possibly reflected a sense of data as a distribution or as individual entities. It is unclear whether the visualizations clearly reflected the idea of distribution, design features, or a combination of the two. Third, students' visualizations considered size, shape, and color primarily while considerations of density were more challenging.

In terms of research, it seems productive to explore students' identities in relation to analyzing data upon completion of a project or a unit related to the design of data visualizations. In terms of the Data Viz project, we were able to collect some data related to this in the post-interviews. Based on preliminary findings, the student participants enjoyed and could articulate the practices involved in analyzing and visualizing data. This does not speak to their identities per se, but this does say something concerning the practices they believe to be associated with data analysis. It would also be helpful to conduct a design research experiment that focuses on supporting elementary students' learning of data visualizations. In our pilot project, we conducted one iteration. It would be beneficial to collect data following two iterations of such a project in order to revise based on the initial iteration.

Related to instructional practice, we propose that this statistical design arts approach holds potential for supporting elementary students in making sense of data while valuing their creative decisions and voice. This also speaks to broader efforts to integrate subjects such as art into the core curriculum. Such efforts would draw on authoring and creative practices to develop a sense of affiliation for STEM. Clearly, more research and instructional wisdom are needed to fully explore the potential of such an approach.

REFLECTIVE QUESTIONS

1. How might use of data visualizations by all students from diverse backgrounds build on their prior knowledge and experiences to construct new understandings from data sets?
2. In what ways could creating data visualizations allow students to individually express their understandings of and connections to data, and how might this give teachers better insights into their struggles and successes with data?

CHAPTER 9

GREEN LITERACY K–5

Nurturing a Scientific Mindset

Jennifer Cullerton Johnson and Mary K. Gove

In the end we will conserve only what we love; we will love only what we understand, and we will understand only what we are taught.

—Babe Dioum, Senegalese environmentalist & poet

CREATING A GREEN LITERACY CLASSROOM

In the Age of Inference, Green Literacy offers ideas for nurturing the proper mindset for teaching critical thinking around scientific findings related to human impacts on the environment. Green Literacy is a constructivist practice of teaching that develops in-depth thinking, dialoguing, and responding to our relationship to the environment using literature and digital media as catalysts. Young people in K–5 become engaged in inference, drawing from evidence in these texts and digital media. Thus, in Green Literacy K–5 classrooms teachers begin the process of creating a scientific literate society capable of addressing pressing issues with a better grasp on how to view and infer from evidence. As you read this chapter, consider

Age of Inference, pages 141–156

specific ways Green Literacy's three cycles of comprehension resonate within the Age of Inference in a school's K–5 teaching practice. Also, think about how three cycles of comprehension facilitate engagement in inferential thinking as young people move from K to Grade 5. In addition, readers can reflect on how taking a critical stance in K–5 influences young people as they enter into middle and high school

Green Heroes: Read Write Act! (Johnson & Gove, 2017) is the first in a series of Green Literacy thematic teaching units. We introduced this series at a K–5 district-wide summer meeting. Teachers discussed two questions:

1. How can we as educators bring critical environmental issues into our classrooms?
2. What holds us back from adding inferential discussions about environmental challenges?

What struck us was the intention among teachers to take care of the living world and their sincere willingness to facilitate similar connections for students. Later, as we, the authors, culled the recorded dialogue, we found that even though there is teacher support for student environmental awareness, teachers face concerns, reasonable doubts, and significant challenges. Teachers shared the following challenges of teaching environmental issues in their classrooms.

Rachel: For me, this year is all about getting ready for standardized testing. I see the need for my students to get involved with environmental issues but I need to focus on literacy and math.

Nick: For me, I teach in the city. The neighborhood is a little dangerous so our school doesn't have a garden. We don't go outside much. What I need are ways that I can engage my urban students in environmental issues that are in the classroom and relate to their city life.

Sharia: Environmental issues are huge and scary. They are messy. I don't even know how to bring up something like climate change except in a superficial way. My students recycle. My students turn off the lights, but really, how do you start a deeper conversation? I wish I had a way to use something familiar with my fifth graders, something doable.

Henry: I've got a big concern. I want to talk about environmental problems with my students. But the environment and problems like fracking have become so politicized in the news that I am afraid to do so. Is there a way I can start this conversation so that it won't push the buttons of parents who have economic concerns?

Aziza: There are so many demands placed on me as a classroom teacher. I really believe in my third graders thinking about the environment. We created a classroom garden last year. But I want to start something where my students think deeper, I don't know if I have the time or know how to do it. If there was a way to add to what I am doing now, I might be interested in trying it.

From a place of shared concern, we began to explore formal ways of making a bridge between environmental awareness, literacy, and empowering young people. Through a decade-long process, we formulated and refined our bridge, which we call Green Literacy, a literacy-based practice anchored in our relationship with the earth and humanity, rooted in environmental justice and stemming from critical pedagogy.

Going into K–5 classrooms, we found that most language arts teachers felt confident in teaching literacy skills using Green Literacy's suggested readings and viewings, often using practices of Green Literacy as part of their social studies curriculum. Coming from a literacy-based subject area, teachers wanted to implement the literacy skills of their students to investigate environmental issues through familiar literature and nonfiction formats. Some, however, felt less assured about teaching scientific principles, including those in ecology and the natural sciences. These teachers considered what happens to the environment as imperative to student learning and wanted to use empowering literacy skills to talk about the environment.

We, the authors, value environmental education with its focus on teaching ecological science and its outgrowth of student excursions in nature. We believe that meaningful interactions with the living world often lead to student-initiated earth stewardship, as does Green Literacy practice. As we acknowledge the need for students to learn scientific principles focused on in the NGSS Framework for K–12, Green Literacy seeks to empower teachers and students through environmental justice.

Green Literacy thematic teaching units are fixed in critical pedagogy so that students examine social context of environmental justice issues, using literature and digital media as springboards. We created Green Literacy teaching units thematically so that students master how to use evidence to support their assertions and provide teachers with interdisciplinary ties to social studies and science. Green Literacy shares something with Ecoliteracy, which concerns understanding the principles of organization of ecosystems and their potential application to understanding how to build a sustainable human society. Both emphasize the importance of systemic thinking.

Next, we define three cycles of comprehension, the third of which involves engaging students in systemic thinking as well as other inferencing.

THREE CYCLES OF COMPREHENSION

Green Literacy thematic units use a tool we developed called three cycles of comprehension, which aligns with the Common Core State Standards. With the three cycles of comprehension, readers progress through knowing what the author wrote, making inferences and supporting their ideas about the text, and entering into scientific critical perspective-taking and systemic thinking. These three cycles of comprehension advance young people's critical thinking, talking, and responding, and are tools for teachers to develop their own Green Literacy thematic teaching units.

In Green Literacy practice, young people interact with text and digital media and engage deeply in the issues through conversations, role-play, readers' theatre, and other literacy-based perspective-changing activities that lead young people to actions toward earth stewardship. In Green Literacy young people and their teachers strive to unpack power relations in text and media as they relate to environmental justice. Green Literacy develops practices that assist readers to unlock and encounter meaning from text, as well as to understand what texts are doing to the reader and what the author of the text wants the reader to believe about the world. We believe authors and readers are influential people who have the capacity to perpetuate or challenge particular perceptions of the world, including issues of environmental justice.

Green Literacy Commentary

A unique feature of Green Literacy is the commentary. These commentaries are interpretations about an environmental theme that pose questions that often disrupt what is commonly assumed, investigate the credibility of writers and producers, and evaluate power relationships and the complexity of systemic thinking surrounding environmental dilemmas.

Our experiences working with teachers and students have shown us that teachers become more engaged with environmental themes and their complexity when they have access to supporting commentaries. Our commentaries question the credibility of what writers write and producers produce. We examine power relationships, leadership issues, and solutions that advocate systemic thinking. Our commentaries draw from sociology, ecology, and natural history. They reflect a critical stance, which can include ecocriticism, which takes an interdisciplinary point of view.

The purpose of our commentaries is to support teachers' thinking before they teach, while they teach, and when they reflect upon their teaching of a Green Literacy thematic teaching unit. Our commentaries supply rich background by asking questions that show a way of thinking emphasized by critical literacy theorists such as Shor (1992).

In order to illustrate how our commentaries support teachers, we offer a sample, which is exemplary of the ones found in *Green Heroes* (Johnson & Gove, 2017). This example is about a single text, Molly Bang's (1997) picture book, *Common Ground: Earth and Air We Share.* We chose this example because the theme is comprehensive and focuses on common natural resources that are shared by many and often polluted by a few. We provide context with a third-grade vignette on the environmental theme and book, *Common Ground* (Bang, 1997), showing how Albert, the teacher, used this commentary with his classroom.

Commentary on Common Ground

Common Ground: The Water, Earth, and Air We Share by Molly Bang (1997) gives credit for the inspiration for the book to Garrett Hardin's (1968) seminal paper, "The Tragedy of the Commons," published in *Science* magazine. Hardin's paper puts forth in a striking manner the problem faced by a group of New England landowners in managing the town commons. The commons provided grazing land for each landowner's sheep, but the number of sheep grazed needed to be limited or the grass would be ruined, destroying it for future use. As it is in the interest of each property owner to graze as many sheep as possible, the result, if the dilemma is unresolved, will lead to the "tragedy" of the destruction of the common resource. Drawing from this "big idea" of Hardin's, the picture book *Common Ground* introduces young readers to this concept of the commons, which is so central to our environmental dilemmas.

Through illustration and text, the book begins with the idea of the New England landowners sharing grazing land. *Common Ground* (Bang, 1997) then uses this concept to demonstrate how people and businesses benefit from the easy availability of oil, gas, and coal as fuel and to make products, and the seeming abundance of water for all our needs, at least "in the short run."

The book shows how the water, earth, and air we share are endangered, and unless the predicament of overuse of these environmental resources is resolved by society, they will no longer be available. A good question that propels critical thinking concerning this issue is "What should we keep and preserve for the common good?" and "What should be made private and for profit?" Each person, rich and poor, needs air to breathe, water to drink and bathe, food to eat, and some form of energy to move about. For example, consider, can someone own the air we all breathe? Can anyone fish in the ocean or should someone own it?

Using this commentary about *Common Ground* (Bang, 1997) as support, a third-grade teacher, Albert, began to think about ways to engage his students in understanding the idea of the commons. Since he was not an environmental scientist, this commentary instilled in him a confidence to begin teaching about the commons to his students. After reading the commentary, Albert was motivated to do his own research on the topic of the commons. He found Hardin's (1968) scientific paper difficult to read, but was captivated by reviews of Hardin's thoughts. After considering the importance of the idea of the commons, Albert located and mapped out local examples of commons near his school such as a park and the public school where he taught. Albert thought about what were common spaces and other spaces were private. For example, Albert recognized a nearby lake was used in common for swimming and boating, even for his community's water supply. He also thought about how he and his family owned their home on the lake, which included private beach access.

How did Albert incorporate the Green Literacy commentary into his teaching of the book *Common Ground* (Bang, 1997)? How did his students gain understanding of common ground through the classroom discussions? We follow the thinking of one student, Mia.

Exploring the Commons in a Third-Grade Vignette

Before reading the book *Common Ground: The Water, Earth, and Air We Share* by Molly Bang aloud to his students, Albert wanted them to be aware of the concept of common ground. He planned 2 consecutive days for discussion before reading the book aloud. During the first discussion, the students wavered in their understanding about common ground and the importance of preserving their environment. Many could not articulate what common ground looked like. One student, Mia, commented that common ground belonged "everywhere but nowhere." Along with the rest of her classmates, she had heard the word pollution and said, "smoking stinks!" but did not connect how pollution played a big factor in her urban life or in the preservation of the commons.

The second day's discussion began with brainstorming things that could be shared in their homes, their classroom, their school, and their neighborhoods. Mia offered several suggestions, including shared sidewalks, and in her case a shared courtyard at her apartment complex. While students came up with examples of shared resources, Albert emphasized the idea of sharing and supporting resources for the "common ground." The concept began to click in the students' minds. They could understand the need for a shared, common supply of pencils available when a student needed one. With Albert's guidance, the students came up with other examples of sharing toys and books as well as the streets and drinking fountains outside. Mia came up with the idea that "common ground must be like a park. Everyone can go there and no one owns it."

For the third and final day's discussion, Albert read aloud *Common Ground: The Water, Earth, and Air We Share.* The class debated the importance of taking care of their shared or common environment, and the implications of pollution in their homes, classrooms, and school. Another discussion took place. This time Mia remembered being at the park where a strong smell came from water in a small pond. The water was green and slimy. "That pond isn't for the common good! Nobody can use it!" Mia's response led the way for other students to consider how commons can be polluted by the few while affecting the many.

Next, we will provide an example from *Green Heroes* of what Green Literacy looks like in a K–2 setting. The springboard for the constructionist teaching unit is *The Mangrove Tree: Planting Trees to Feed Families* by Roth and Trumbore. This picture book is a powerful example of a community coming together to change environmental problems into an environmental possibility.

"THE MANGROVE TREE: PLANTING TREES TO FEED FAMILIES"

Commentary: Biography of a Project

Cell biologist Dr. Gordon Sato started a project growing mangrove trees by the shore of the salty Red Sea so that the local herds of sheep and goats could eat the leaves as a new food source. *The Mangrove Tree* (Roth & Trumbore, 2018) focuses on Dr. Gordon's project and makes the book an important resource on sustainability. Behind the scenes of this book, years of conflict, economic stagnation, and famine devastated the people of the Eritrean village, Hargigo. They suffered from malnutrition and struggled with their well-being. They were stuck in "environmental problems" until an innovative idea of "environmental possibility" led to dramatic changes in the local food chain.

Through Dr. Sato's influence, women who planted and tended the seedlings received training in fertilizing the young trees with special nutrients that would allow the trees to grow in salt water. Shepherds learned how to complement the mangrove leaves with seeds and fish so the herds would produce healthier milk. Local fishermen brought home larger catches because the mangrove roots served as homes for small sea creatures that attracted bigger fish.

TABLE 9.1 Grades K–2 Thematic Teaching: Environmental Leaders	
Suggested Text	**Teaching Components Leading to In-Depth Dialogue**
The Mangrove Tree: Planting Trees to Feed Families by Susan L. Roth and Cindy Trumbore	Teacher reads aloud, with students' wonderings, questions, and thoughts about the author's ideas, writing, and illustrations.

Notes: Grade Level CCSS Standards: RI K.1, RI 1.1, RI 2.1, SL K, 1, 2SL K,.1,SL1.1, 2.1, SL K.2, 1.2, 2.2

Dr. Sato and the townspeople made changes by planting and fertilizing mangrove trees, which provided food for the herds of sheep and goats as well as firewood. Feeding the herds then provided food for the people of Hargigo, Eritrea.

The authors employed a motivating technique: On the left side of the page, the young person finds a "House That Jack Built"-type summary of the story as it unfolds. Most young readers know this step-by-step format. They recall how the story unfolds and predict what happens next. This format also helps young people keep track of what has happened in the previous part of the story. It cleverly illustrates how everything links together, from the planting of seedlings to the people who tend to them, so the seedlings may become the trees that provide sustenance for so many.

The detailed description of the implementation of Dr. Sato's vision on the right side of the page entices more experienced readers. The text style, the message, and the collage illustrations engage and extend young readers' concept of storytelling.

Second Grade Vignette

Katie, a second-grade Green Literacy teacher at an International Baccalaureate school in an urban area of Colorado, read *The Mangrove Tree: Planting Trees to Feed Families* to her class. She began the lesson with a map that displayed South America and Africa.

"Why do places far away from each other have things in common?" Katie asked.

One student replied, "They both have much heat." Katie told the class to keep "the heat" in mind.

After she read the book's title, she showed her students the cover. "What observations can you make about the cover?"

Jasmine said, "Maybe they have seeds to plant."

Katie said, "Yes, maybe so," and then posed, "What about their clothes?"

"Most of them dressed like the people in the rainforest," said Terrell.

"The man in the blue suit looks like our clothes," said Victor, and made a connection between the man's clothes and where his father works.

As Katie began reading the book, she wondered aloud, "How could a tree make families not hungry anymore?"

Students responded with different ideas, including "growing food" and "animals living in the trees." To these and other answers, Katie said, "Great ideas."

In a similar fashion, Katie guided her students with questions about the text as she read. Periodically, students made observations about the collages. Other students offered wonderings such as, "What do they use the tree trunk for?" Another student concluded, "Houses and boats." Students built a text-to-text connection with another book about the rainforest in which animals made their homes in trees as they did in the mangrove trees.

Supportive of all observations, Katie encouraged connections, observations, and wonderings her students made throughout the book. On two occasions she asked, "What is your evidence? Why do you think so?" At another point, a student made an observation that *The Mangrove Tree* occurred in the rainforest. Katie did not judge the answer as incorrect. Instead, she asked the student if this book occurred in the rainforest and the student said, "Sort of." Katie moved on with reading the next page of the book. She would come back later to this student's confusion about Eritrea being in the rainforest.

After the discussion, students took out their Wonder Journals, a technique often used in inquiry learning, where young people are asked to write any questions that went through their minds as they listened to the story. She said,

> Also, write about changes that happened in the village Hargigo because of the planting of the mangrove trees. Tomorrow we will get out our iPads and see if we find answers to our wonderings. Plus, we will share changes that occurred to Hargigo because of the mangrove trees.

One girl said, "I don't have any wonderings."

Katie said, "No wonders? Here, look at the book to help you." The girl got her journal, looked at the book, and began writing.

The next day, Katie and her students talked about the questions they had written in their Wonder Journals. Then Katie asked the students, "Do you think after reading and talking about *The Mangrove Tree*, we need to write a new Green Literacy Ideal?"

Some students agreed. Others were not so sure.

"I think we can add something about food sources," Katie said. "What do we notice about the changes that happened in the Hargigo community once the mangrove trees grew?"

"The mangrove leaves were fed to the goats," said Lucy.

"Branches of the trees were used to build fires," offered Tyson.

"Because they had more goats they had more meat to eat," said Hunter.

"And more milk to drink," chimed in Alice.

Katie entered in, "What could we write as a Green Literacy Ideal?"

"You have to have new ideas to get better," said Nico.

"I agree with Nico. Class, what's the new idea Dr. Sato brought to Hargigo? Let's discuss." Katie said. After the discussion, the class created a Green Literacy ideal, building on Nico's contribution: Often new ideas can be worked on and bring about many good things. In this case, the new idea was growing mangrove trees and the good things were more food and firewood.

This second-grade example of *The Mangrove Tree* shows how Katie engaged with the K–2 age level where the children came up with their wonderings, questions, and thoughts about the author's ideas, writing, and illustrations. Using this open-ended, supportive dialogue, the class also developed a Green Literacy Ideal concerning the mindset needed for new ways of doing that bring about new food sources.

Next, we will provide a part of a Green Literacy unit in which teachers and students in Grades 3, 4, and beyond use the *Seeds of Change* by Jen Cullerton Johnson as the catalyst for a critical discussion examining the motivations of differing factions that often form when environmental actions such as planting a large number of trees occurs. This is a part of a larger teaching unit in *Green Heroes* on "How Do Young People Become Green Heroes or environmental leaders?"

"SEEDS OF CHANGE," COMMENTARY, BIOGRAPHY OF A MOVEMENT

The picture book, *Seeds of Change* by Jen Cullerton Johnson (2010) exemplifies a biography of both a person and a movement. One storyline centers on the leader and the catalyst of the movement. The other parallel storyline focuses on the movement and the people who supported and shared the leader's vision. These perspectives blend together, creating a whole story.

Seeds of Change (Johnson, 2010) tells the life story of Wangari Maathai, who became the first African woman, and environmentalist, to win a Nobel Peace Prize. She blazed a trail across Kenya, using her knowledge and compassion to promote the rights of her countrywomen and help save the land, one tree at a time, through the Green Belt Movement. In many ways, Wangari's life story mirrors the Green Belt Movement, an organization she founded. Wangari's vision became a mutual mission with others in the Green Belt Movement. The Green Belt's message was simple: Work together and results will come.

Students take the Green Belt's message one step further and interpret its meaning as evidence that when people work together, collective results have a domino effect, inviting others' participation. When students evaluate Wangari's life and the lives of those within the Green Belt Movement, they realize that biography is more than one person's life and is rather many lives woven together; they move from the problem of deforestation and poverty to the possibility of financial independence and rebuilding an ecosystem.

"SEEDS OF CHANGE"—OVERVIEW OF TEACHING STRATEGIES

Cycle 1: Simple Comprehension
  Free response strategy
Cycle 2: Criteria Comprehension
  Think–pair–share
Cycle 3: Critical Comprehension
  Engagement Strategy: Step 1—Finding the voices; Step 2—Enacting to solve an issue

Cycle 1: Simple Comprehension *Seeds of Change*

During simple comprehension, the class arrives at a mutual understanding about what took place in the story and in the life of the main character and those people who helped her vision. To do this, the Green Literacy teacher uses the *free response strategy* as she reads each book aloud. Free response strategy is when the teacher stops at preselected spots within the story and asks comprehension questions.

Green Literacy teachers use a free response strategy by reading the book aloud, stopping at preselected places. The young people write their comments and later share them with the class. The free response strategy gives students time for response through comments in writing/discussing the story, plot, or characters which reveal their perceptions and preoccupations about the story. All responses ring correctly as long as the responses relate to the text in some way. These perspectives blend together to create a whole story.

Cycle 2: Criteria Comprehension *Seeds of Change*

In this learning activity, young people make personal connections to *Seeds of Change* using the *think–pair–share.* Think–pair–share (Lyman, 1981) is a useful engagement tool for all students; even the shyest student will be involved.

Think–Pair–Share

Think: Start with a question/prompt that gets the students thinking about the story. Students are given a short amount of time to reflect on the question.

Pair: Students pair up with a partner and share their responses. The goal is for the partners to compare their information and come up with the most complete response to the question.

Share: Each pair shares their responses with the whole class.

Students explain why their connection is pertinent. For example, suppose after reading about the protagonist Wangari Maathai, one student says his connection is that he saw a bulldozer take down a grove of trees for a condominium development in his neighborhood. The student then elaborates on how this is connected to Wangari's life.

Come back together in the larger group at the end of the think–pair–share and continue the discussion using the following questions:

- What did Wangari do when she saw that trees had been cut down in Kenya?
- What happened with the people who supported Wangari's vision?
- What evidence is there about the importance of how the community supports the individual? Students cite evidence in the text.
- Focus on the reasons, rationale, and criteria students provide. Emphasize these in the discussion, especially where students differ. For example, a student could say the condo is needed so more people could live in the neighborhood. Another may say, but green space is needed for play and provides oxygen to decrease greenhouse gasses.

Cycle 3: Critical Perspective Comprehension
Seeds of Change

Lead the young people into an engagement strategy (Long & Gove, 2003), a dramatic two-step strategy that promotes critical thinking concerning what differing characters think and feel. We have found this teaching strategy helpful in supporting students to think through ambiguous situations in which there are different points of view in play.

Step 1: Finding the Voices

In this example, we choose four voices or "points of view": the Green Belt women who listen to Wangari and plant 30 million trees in Kenya; Wangari's friends at the university in Kenya; the wealthy businessmen who pay corrupt police officers to arrest Wangari; and Wangari, herself, freed from jail. The class forms four groups. Each group brainstorms about what these people think and say. Then the groups share their ideas with the class as a whole.

Step 2: Enacting to Solve an Issue

The class then reenacts the trial of Wangari. The students act out Wangari herself, her Kenyan university friends, the Green Belt women who worked with her to plant trees, and the wealthy businessmen who worked with police to put Wangari behind bars. The teacher plays the part of the judge. She asks the class to make their case, drawing from the ideas developed in Step 1. To stage this enactment, the teacher explains what is occurring and then turns around. When the teacher faces the class again, she is the judge. Class participants present to the judge their beliefs about why Wangari should or should not be freed. The judge may then rule that Wangari should be freed or that some other action is necessary. Upon the conclusion of the enactment, one person plays Wangari and describes what she plans to do next and why. Through this process, young people think deeply about the issues surrounding Wangari's imprisonment and her feelings and ideas concerning what she may decide to do after her sentence.

Finally, we share a constructivist teaching unit from *Green Heroes: Read Write Think!* for 5th grade and beyond using a film *Jane's Journey* by Lorenz Knauer (2011).

JANE'S JOURNEY, COMMENTARY, BIOGRAPHY OF A HUMAN AND PRIMATE FRIENDSHIP

Knauer's (2011) 1-hour and 51-minute film, *Jane's Journey*, focuses on primatologist and environmental activist Jane Goodall. Goodall dedicates her life to the natural world and its preservation. In particular, Jane particularly focuses a majority of her time and research on primates, such as chimpanzees, believing in human and primate friendship. This biography is a subtle call to arms for animal and human rights, a biography of human and primate friendship. As the film tells the story of Jane Goodall, so the story of primates unfolds. Also, in this film, readers are introduced to Jane's Roots and Shoots organization, which connects people and their advocacy for a sustainable planet.

The film starts with the 75-year-old Goodall reflecting on her life. Through her recollections and film footage, we meet the girl who went to Tanzania to commune with the chimpanzees. These brief glimpses paint a fascinating portrait of Goodall's early career, marriages, and motherhood. The film describes a major life shift when Jane, in 1986, opened the Jane

Goodall Institute, which empowers people to make positive differences in the lives of all living beings, including primates. Watching the film builds up young people's awareness toward different organizations connecting through the theme of helping the planet.

Our final vignette uses the digital film, *Jane's Journey* (Knauer, 2011), as a springboard for a critical conversation. This is an illustration of Green Literacy teaching in Grades 5 and beyond.

JANE'S JOURNEY—OVERVIEW OF TEACHING STRATEGIES

Cycles 1 and 2: Simple comprehension and criteria comprehension. While watching *Jane's Journey*, take notes on what Jane did, how others supported her, and the projects she talked about.

Cycle 3: Critical perspective comprehension Jane's Journey. Free write on connections to *Jane's Journey*

Cycles 1 and 2: Simple comprehension and criteria comprehension: Jane's Journey. While watching the DVD, *Jane's Journey*, young people jot responses to the following open-ended questions about Jane Goodall, her projects, and the people who supported her:

- What does Jane do?
- Who are the people in the different parts of Jane's life that supported her as a child, when she went to Tanzania to study chimpanzees in her 20s, as she conducted the many studies of the chimpanzees, and finally during her life as an activist?
- List projects that she talked about.

After watching the film, young people discuss their responses. Then in small groups, students complete the chart below. Afterward, they engage in large group discussion centering on how each of the projects helped people or the natural world or both. In the next class, students will come back to their ideas. Students gather again in small groups. Students discuss what led Jane later in her life to devote herself to activism. Groups make a list of reasons, then compare their lists in the whole group.

Jane's life and people who supported her.

- What happened in Jane's life? Events in Jane Goodall's life
- Who helped Jane? People who supported Jane
- Results of Jane Goodall's efforts and the people who supported her

Cycle 3: Critical perspective comprehension: Jane's Journey. Building on prior activities and knowledge, students integrate their ideas through the strategy called: free write. Students free write on the following:

- What personal connections do you make to the ideas in *Jane's Journey*?
- How do you connect with animals?
- In what ways do you share with Jane and her friendship with animals?
- What are some animal friendship ideas and projects you might like to try?

Free write tips: Free writing is a simple process that is the basis for other discovery techniques. Basic free writing follows these student guidelines:

- Write nonstop for a set period of time (5–15 minutes).
- Do not make corrections as you write.
- Keep writing, even if you have to write something like, "I don't know what to write."
- Write whatever comes into your mind.
- Do not judge or censor what you are writing.

Using free writing in conjunction with group discussion on a single text and/or digital media and then later adding ideas drawn from additional texts and/or digital media is one way students integrate their big picture ideas. It is also another way to hone in on skills set within the Common Core State Standards (CCSS). Teachers who use free write often remark that student ideas jell over time. Many times, with the aid of free write, students articulate their ideas and feelings more clearly.

TAKE-AWAYS: GREEN LITERACY K–5 AS NURTURING A SCIENTIFIC MINDSET

Our goal in developing Green Literacy thematic teaching units is to impact young people's perspective and critical thinking. As classroom teachers in urban areas, we have witnessed young people participate in Green Literacy practice and amplify their point of view, a great way to work through the ambiguity of complex situations. In the picture book, *Duck! Rabbit!* (Krouse Rosenthal & Linchtenfield, 2009), author Amy Krouse Rosenthal invites the readers to decide if the image on the page is a duck or a rabbit. She uses the lure of optical illusion to reel in the reader's curiosity. "Is this a duck? Is this a rabbit?" The reader shifts her perspective and the images change. Yet when the reader pulls back, she can see the image is both a duck and a rabbit. This is true with environmental issues.

We see teachers and young people developing a continuing shift in view, a magnification of thought, a deeper compassion for the natural world, an ability to grasp and respect our connections to each other and all living things. We believe future generations will need to have the ability to see many sides and the big picture if they want to solve environmental justice challenges.

In short, using the Green Literacy tools of three levels of comprehension and commentaries on environmental issues, teachers create classroom conversations around environmental issues invoking critical thinking and fair assessment of data/evidence/valid information, which lead to constructing rational resolutions to these issues. Green Literacy engages young people and their teachers in argument from evidence found in real-life environmental situations found in young people's literature and digital media. This chapter provides many illustrations of how nurturing a scientific mindset can look in practice in K–5 classrooms. Also, Green Literacy, as a longer-range goal, aims to not simply produce scientists, but a scientific literate society capable of addressing pressing issues with a better grasp on how to view and infer from evidence.

REFLECTIVE QUESTIONS

1. How do you think the three cycles of comprehension resonate within the Age of Inference in a school's K–5 teaching practice?
2. How will these three cycles of comprehension facilitate engagement in inferential thinking as young people move from K to Grade 5? How would taking a critical stance influence them as they enter into middle and high school?
3. A unique feature of Green Literacy is the commentary. These commentaries are interpretations about an environmental theme that pose questions that often disrupt what is commonly assumed, investigate the credibility of writers and producers, and evaluate power relationships and the complexity of systemic thinking surrounding environmental dilemmas. Explain how these commentaries can be supportive to teachers as they engage young people in discussions concerning environmental issues.
4. Environmental social justice issues are complex. Their solutions draw from many disciplines. In what ways can a Green Literacy mindset support young people as they grapple with this complexity?
5. How does a Green Literacy mindset help produce a scientific literate society capable of addressing pressing environmental issues with a grasp of how to view and infer from evidence?

CHAPTER 10

COMPLEX MULTIMODAL TEXT SETS TO SUPPORT SCIENCE LITERACY

William Romine, Amy Lannin, Torrey Palmer, Delinda van Garderen, Rachel Juergensen, Cassandra M. Smith, and William Folk

Reasoning draws a conclusion, but does not make the conclusion certain, unless the mind discovers it by the path of experience.

—Roger Bacon

The need to develop a scientific mindset, exemplified by applying inferential reasoning toward making evidence-based claims, is now a central element of the Common Core State Standards (CCSS) and the Next Generation Science Standards (NGSS Lead States, 2013). Balancing the need to evaluate information systematically with the need to accept complexity and uncertainty is difficult for students (Sadler et al., 2007), but essential for attainment of science literacy (Norris & Phillips, 2003). Linking Science and Literacy for All Learners is designed to help learners navigate fundamental and derived aspects of literacy through use of complex texts. This chapter presents a multiple case study documenting similarities and differences for

Age of Inference, pages 157–181

how the teachers implemented and integrated multimodal text sets into their instruction and the comparative impact this had on students' ability to make and evaluate arguments using the claim-evidence-reasoning (CER) framework (Gotwals & Songer, 2010).

THEORETICAL UNDERPINNINGS

Literacy in reading and writing is central to argumentation and inference, and to development of a scientific mindset in general. Multimodal text sets are a resource by which students have the opportunity to learn and apply argumentation and inferential reasoning which is framed in terms of CER. Toward achieving the performance expectations of the NGSS, use of text sets in science classrooms helps ensure that students are able to participate regardless of their backgrounds and abilities.

Students bring a range of vocabulary and language backgrounds that affect their learning (Hart & Risley, 2003; Gilkerson et al., 2017; Sperry et al., 2019). Further, these early language differences matter in later reading performance. When followed into secondary grades, students with lower levels of literacy early in their lives were specifically found to be at a disadvantage in reading abilities in later years (Golinkoff et al., 2018; Hart & Risley, 2003).

Readers who have prior knowledge and experience with particular topics can more readily make connections between what they are reading and what they know (Cervetti & Hiebert, 2015; Mclaughlin & Overturf, 2012; Pearson et al., 1979). In two past studies, students with knowledge of a subject (either from direct instruction or from background experience) demonstrated greater comprehension than students with lesser expertise, despite differences in reading ability (Pearson et al., 1979; Recht & Leslie, 1988). Considering the importance of vocabulary and knowledge in reading comprehension, utilizing effective strategies to shore up and accelerate language stores, particularly for diverse learners, continues to be essential.

Students' knowledge funds or schemata provide a framework for classifying information within a text; the more the individual knows about something, the stronger the framework or schemata for classifying new information (Pearson et al., 1979). Reading or listening to a series of texts on the same topic can yield as much as four times the vocabulary growth in comparison to reading discordant pieces (Landauer & Dumais, 1997). This sequencing of texts to build vocabulary and knowledge on a topic draws from schema theory, which highlights the importance of domain knowledge to enhance reading comprehension (Spiro et al., 2003). This allows the reader to connect old words to new, and develop nuanced understandings based on these connections.

Cervetti et al. (2016) studied the impact of text sets with fourth-grade students, exploring whether knowledge building through the reading of a conceptually coherent set of texts supported comprehension of related texts and increased students' interest in the focus topic. They found that students who read a series of texts on a topic demonstrated better comprehension of the new text on the topic, as compared to students who read a series of disconnected texts.

Work with text sets has drawn increased attention since the advent of the CCSS, particularly with the increased text complexity expectations outlined in Reading Standard 10. The challenge of supporting students in reading even more complex texts, when there are already few students reading at grade level (NCES, 2019a), is real and concerning considering that reading is a component of the scientific practices described in the NGSS. Using these considerations, text sets are defined as collections of resources from different genres, media, and levels of reading difficulty, strategically sequenced to build vocabulary and knowledge.

Text sets can be used across content areas and literacy instruction, to provide students with rich opportunities to build knowledge and vocabulary (student achievement partners).

There are many ways of organizing multimodal text sets. For the Linking Science and Literacy for All Learners program, the line of inquiry of a text set is determined by an anchor text. The anchor text is the focus of a close reading with instructional supports. The number of subsidiary texts and materials in a set, called *supplementary texts* or *content scaffolds*, can vary depending on purpose and resource availability around a given topic. What is important is that the materials in the set are connected meaningfully to each other to build knowledge and vocabulary to support understanding of the anchor text. In a sense, the texts and materials "talk to one another" so that in reading the set, students build a coherent body of knowledge around a topic.

Through the construction of a strong multimodal text set, CER is the primary strategy used for synthesizing and reasoning around the core scientific concepts. Argumentation is a key practice both in the NGSS and the CCSS. It is argued in the NGSS that scientific argumentation is critical for development of civic and cultural awareness. Students are thereby expected to use argumentation to comprehend and evaluate competing ideas and methods based on their relative merits (NGSS Lead States, 2013). CER is a framework for developing and critiquing scientific explanations that not only helps students learn the science content but also prepares them to be scientifically literate adults (McNeill & Krajcik, 2012).

PROFESSIONAL DEVELOPMENT PROGRAM: CONTEXT AND IMPLEMENTATION

The Linking Science and Literacy for All Learners program is a collaboration among faculty and professionals from different backgrounds and experiences including biochemistry, science education, literacy education, and special education as well as sixth–eighth grade teachers in either science, English, or special education. Teachers from districts and schools with varied needs throughout the state apply and participate in a year-long program.

The primary aims of the program, guided by teachers' input about content, include:

Aim 1

Developing sixth to eighth grade STEM multimodal text sets and linked inquiry activities to address commonalities in science and English language arts practices delineated by Missouri Learning Standards (MLS), NGSS, and Common Core English Language Arts Standards.

Aim 2

Providing instructional support for using the STEM multimodal text sets and linked inquiry activities, with special attention to the needs of diverse learners.

FLIGHT OF THE BUMBLEBEE STEM MULTIMODAL TEXT SET

The *Flight of the Bumblebee* multimodal text set (Folk et al., 2020) addresses NGSS MS-PS4-1 Waves and Their Applications in Technologies for Information Transfer and MS-LS2-1 Ecosystems: Interactions, Energy, and Dynamics. The anchor text is adapted from recent primary literature describing the use of sound waves to monitor bumblebee *pollinator* activities (Miller-Struttman et al., 2017). The anchor text's quantitative complexity ranges from Lexile 900-1105 for various sections and Flesch Kincaid grade level is 8.3. Anchor text qualitative demands include the multiple dimensions of science and engineering content; technical language and text structure; and experimental data from which claims, evidence, and reasoning are developed. Reader and task considerations for diverse learners are addressed by scaffolds including multi-genre texts, audiovisual resources, and three-dimensional science learning (Table 10.1).

TABLE 10.1 Instructional Sequence of the "Flight of the Bumblebee" Multimodal Text Set

Stage in 5E Cycle[a]	Scaffolds Used (Title and URL)
Engage (Audio-videos)	"The Beauty of Pollination-Moving Art™" (Louie Schwartzberg) https://www.youtube.com/watch?v=MQiszdkOwuU https://www.youtube.com/watch?v=MT-tMyUbijY Bee Buzzes: https://www.youtube.com/watch?v=MT-tMyUbijY
Engage (Poetry)	"To Make a Prairie" and/or "The Bee" (Emily Dickinson) https://poets.org/poem/make-prairie-1755 https://www.scottishpoetrylibrary.org.uk/poem/bee/
Engage (Audio-text)	"A Sting in the Tale" (Dave Goulson) read by Tim McKinnery on BBC Radio 4. http://www.sussex.ac.uk/lifesci/goulsonlab/astinginthetale
Explore	SpectrumView™ https://oxfordwaveresearch.com/products/spectrumviewapp/ or other similar app/program (Anderson, Minshew, et al., 2015)
Explain	Sections of textbooks used in classrooms as well as any of the following: Sound Waves: https://www.ck12.org/physics/sound-waves/ Frequency and Pitch of Sound: https://www.ck12.org/Physics/Frequency-and-Pitch-of- Sound/ Mechanical Waves: https://www.ck12.org/physics/mechanical- wave/lesson/Mechanical-Wave-MS-PS/?referrer=concept_details Wave Model: https://www.ck12.org/physics/wave-frequency/lesson/Wave-Frequency-MS-PS/ What is Sound? https://exploresound.org/explore-sound-home/what-is-acoustics/ Sound: https://www.readworks.org/article/Sound/8aa4414c-ed23-463c-963c-e9dfada69297#!articleTab:content/contentSection:2bf83852-84fd-4d7f-9742- de8ef7245205/ Characteristics of Sound: https://www.ck12.org/book/CK-12-Fourth-Grade- Science/section/1.2/ What are waves? https://betterlesson.com/lesson/628342/what-are-waves Music: https://www.brainson.org/shows/2013/08/01/music

(continued)

TABLE 10.1 Instructional Sequence of the "Flight of the Bumblebee" Multimodal Text Set (continued)

Stage in 5E Cycle[a]	Scaffolds Used (Title and URL)
Elaborate	North American Bees: https://3.bp.blogspot.com/qCCTKiZ5vcA/WKaNR56wIGI/AAAAAAAAB_M/ueipGGcepRECI8jgORySRZcZQJDcqvv QCLcB/s1600/backyard%2Bbees%2Bof%2Bnorth%2Bamerica%2Bposter.jpg Bird Sounds:How to learn about bird songs and calls, and Bird Song Hero: The Song Learning Game for Everyone: https://www.allaboutbirds.org/news/how-to-learn-bird-songs-and-calls
Evaluate	Elements of NGSS MS-PS4-1 and CCSS-ELA.RST pertinent to the lesson e.g., (McNeill, Katsh-Singer, et al., 2015) Student discourse, journals, posters, and presentations addressing MS PS4 Performance Expectations https://ngss.nsta.org/DisplayStandard.aspx?view=topic&id=28

[a] Choice of content scaffolds used in a particular 5E Learning Cycle lesson depends upon the NGSS and CCSS-ELA performance expectation/competencies being targeted and the learners' capabilities. The content scaffolds listed here were used in lessons targeting MS-PS4

MAJOR FEATURES OF THE PROGRAM

The Linking Science and Literacy for All Learners was a year-long professional development (PD) program that began with a 1-day orientation session followed by a weeklong summer workshop and four follow-up sessions during the academic year. All activities were held on the University of Missouri campus. The PD was focused on the following: (a) developing teacher knowledge about complex text, multimodal text sets, CER, and life sciences content; and (b) development and implementation of the text set along with linked inquiry activities. An overview of the year-long program can be found in Table 10.2.

During the orientation session, several critical concepts that served as the "pillars" and rationale for the program were presented. The pillars included: (a) three-dimensional teaching and learning (previously referred to as "scientific inquiry"), (b) disciplinary literacy, (c) text complexity, and (d) instructional scaffolding. These concepts were reintroduced within the summer workshop session but extended to the development and implementation of multimodal text sets with diverse learners.

Three-dimensional teaching and learning ("scientific inquiry") includes the use of science and engineering practices to engage learners in science learning (e.g., sensemaking of phenomena) that could be implemented via various instructional models. For the purpose of our program, we used the 5E Learning Cycle (Bybee, 2015). This inquiry-based approach frames how

TABLE 10.2 Major Features of the PD Program: Linking Science and Science Literacy for All Learners

Summer Professional Development		Academic Year
Orientation Session (1 day)	**Summer Workshop (5 days)**	**Follow-Up Workdays (4)**
Focus of orientation: • Meet participants and introduce goals of PD. • Introduce target content area for inquiry activities and text set. • Identify and learn about key concepts the PD is built on. • Assign tasks for 5-day workshop (e.g., readings about content area, locating resources).	*Focus of workshop:* • Experience lessons that address the targeted standards and model text set implementation. • Identify materials and develop text set. • Identify and develop linked inquiry activities. • Develop implementation plans. • Identify and learn about instructional practices to support diverse learners.	*Focus of follow-ups:* • Share implementation practices, challenges, and solutions; identify additional practices. • Refine text sets and linked inquiry activities.

teachers engage with the learning throughout the week, and also the design of specific lessons they take back to their classrooms. Second, disciplinary literacy is strongly present in both the CCSS and the NGSS practices. The CCSS take an interdisciplinary approach to literacy, specifically highlighting that literacy must be a shared responsibility within the school. In Grades 6–12, there are domain-specific reading and writing standards for reading in English and language arts (ELA), social studies/history, and science and technical subjects.

The standards for science and technical subjects place a premium on evidence-based argumentative writing and analysis of grade-appropriate complex scientific texts. Likewise, the NGSS practice obtaining, evaluating, and communicating information highlights that students should have ample opportunity to participate in reading, analyzing, writing, and otherwise communicating science so that they can deeply engage with disciplinary core ideas and crosscutting concepts (Bell et al., 2012).

Text complexity was the third pillar that informed the program's text set design and implementation. Text complexity is written into the CCSS through Reading Standard 10, which specifically calls for students to read and comprehend grade-level literary and informational texts independently and proficiently. Text complexity emerged as a priority in the standards because of evidence of a steady decline over time across Grades K–12 in the complexity of textbooks while, at the same time, writing in college texts and science journals had become increasingly complex. Further, the 2006 ACT Reading Between the Lines study (ACT, Inc., 2006) revealed that the complexity of the text, instead of question type, was the greatest differentiator in student performance on the standardized ACT assessment.

Text complexity is important because it sets the bar for what students are expected to read at the end of each grade level and because complexity analyses are essential to understanding what barriers may impede comprehension. This, in turn, informs instructional planning, or the selection of subsidiary texts (content scaffolds) for text sets. The fourth pillar comprises ensuring appropriate support is provided for diverse learners in meeting these aims. Too often scaffolding dilutes the task so that students are not working at grade level expectations. However, the goal is to scaffold to grade-level expectations, or in this case, the anchor text.

This project drew on the work of Bunch et al. (2012) in that scaffolding was carefully and strategically designed to "induce students' development and increase autonomy" (p. 9). The subsidiary texts were sequenced so that students begin by reading simpler texts that build knowledge and vocabulary and through the sequence, move through increasingly complex texts and concepts. The expectation was that all students read the anchor text, though even within it, some scaffolds may be provided.

During the summer workshop, each session was designed to provide an opportunity to develop knowledge of the content of the multimodal text set, learn about pedagogical practices for implementing the multimodal text set with diverse learners, and develop the multimodal text set to be implemented by each teacher participant with their learners. The typical daily structure involved a lesson demonstration (where teachers assumed the role of the learner) and debrief in the morning followed by learning and planning (role of teacher) in the afternoons.

METHODS

Evaluation of the Program

Rather than a prescribed set of lessons, this program allowed for flexible and contextual implementation. Every teacher's interest and instructional environment are different, so it is reasonable to expect that no teacher's text set and implementation style will be exactly alike. Nonetheless, strategies for making complex text both accessible and beneficial to students are likely to cut across different types of content and learning environments. As a result, understanding the ways that teachers engaged with and implemented the materials dependent on their learners, curriculum, and standards, was a central focus. Key outcomes were evaluated using mixed methods as part of a multistage evaluation design of a multiple-case study (Creswell & Plano Clark, 2007; Merriam, 1998; Yin, 2003).

The case studies included a pairing of quantitative and qualitative data, facilitating a deeper analysis of two teacher participants' implementation. Data collected and analyzed included artifacts such as lesson plans and instructional logs, transcripts of semi-structured interviews, and measures derived from scenario-based assessments (SBA). By looking carefully at data from the two teachers, themes and trends emerged, elucidating how they implemented the text sets, what instructional strategies they used, and what they noticed about student engagement and learning. A mixed methods approach facilitated connection of qualitative findings with the quantitative analysis of students' writing on the SBA. The quantitative analysis informed how the implementation of program materials and strategies impacted student argumentation.

Teacher Participants

Five teachers participated in the first year of the program. Two of the teachers provided the most complete implementation plans, and so they were the focus for this multiple case study. Demographic data for the students in the two classes are presented in Table 10.3.

Jane, a middle school science teacher (female, Caucasian), started the program with 13 years of science teaching experience. She was working on a master's degree and was certified to teach middle school mathematics, science, and language arts. Her teaching position was at a rural school as the eighth grade science teacher. The middle school's total enrollment was 186 students, 96% Caucasian and free-or-reduced lunch (FRL) at 48%.

TABLE 10.3 Demographic Data for the Students in Laura's and Jane's Classes

Teacher	Total Students	Gender	Ethnicity	ELL	SPED
Ms. Laura	129	55% F 45% M	Asian: 2% Black: 5% Multiracial: 5% American Indian/Alaska Native: 1% Hispanic: 2% White: 85%	5%	0%
Ms. Jane	61	52% F 48% M	Asian: 0% Black: 0% Multiracial: 3% American Indian/Alaska Native: 5% Hispanic: 3% Persian: 2% White: 87%	3%	8%

Laura, a middle school English and language arts (ELA) teacher (female, Caucasian), had completed a master's degree and was certified to teach elementary, middle school, gifted K–12, and English 6–12, at the time of the program. She was teaching in seventh and eighth general education classrooms at a rural school with an enrollment of 534 students. At the start of the program, she had 17 years of teaching experience and 4 years in ELA classrooms.

DATA COLLECTION AND ANALYSIS

Qualitative Data

Qualitative data included the teachers' instructional materials (the NGSS three-dimensional learning), instructional logs kept during the implementation of the text set and lessons, and semi-structured interviews. These are discussed in turn.

Instructional Materials

As a part of the PD and prior to implementation with their students, the teachers developed a multimodal text set (anchor + scaffolds; see Figure 10.1) using the *Flight of the Bumblebee* (Folk et al., 2020) as the anchor. From the anchor, they identified the Missouri state standards (ELA and/or science) that they were going to teach at some point during the academic year. Using the standards as a guide, the teachers selected scaffolds (various

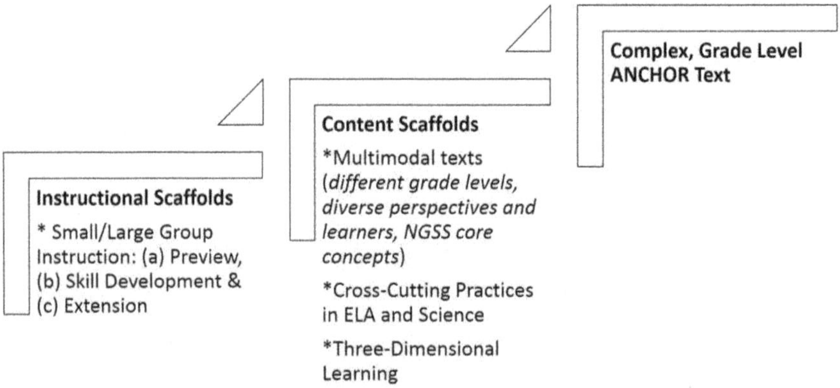

Figure 10.1 Structural elements of a multimodal text set which support mastery of the anchor text and promote three-dimensional learning.

multimodal texts primarily provided by the program) and compiled these into a multimodal text set. Instructional materials (i.e., lesson plans, resources, and worksheets—NGSS three-dimensional learning opportunities) were created.

These instructional materials often integrate various multimodal texts used to scaffold learning. Following implementation of the instruction, the teachers were asked to format their instructional materials using a template provided by the program. Any improvements or modifications to the materials were also made at that point. The instructional materials were collected from the teachers at the end of the year-long program.

Instructional Logs

As the teachers implemented their lessons using the instructional materials they developed, they were asked to keep a log of what they did with one of their classes for each time they taught from the materials. The log was online and solicited the following information: date of lesson, class minutes spent on lesson, multimodal text set focus (scaffold or anchor), lesson phase (introducing lesson, continuing lesson, closing lesson), and an open-ended response where they were encouraged to write about: (a) something that worked, something that didn't work, something that surprised you, something you learned; (b) diverse learners' engagement; (c) CER skill development; and (d) text set involvement in the lesson.

Semi-Structured Interviews

Semi-structured interviews were designed to generate a rich understanding of how the teachers formed and rationalized implementation decisions as well as their reflections on what worked and did not work. These were carried out after the completion of the year-long PD and conducted by the external evaluator and a graduate research assistant.

Qualitative Data Analysis

The data gathered from the instructional materials and instructional logs were used to develop a narrative description (Stake, 1995) of what each of the teachers focused on and how they implemented the text sets in their classrooms. Narratives and interviews demonstrate how the teachers were similar and different in their implementation. The transcripts from the semi-structured interviews were analyzed to determine themes for teacher implementation, and student engagement and learning. Parts of the transcripts were highlighted and used to connect certain information in the interviews to the overarching topic. Then, quotes were grouped to identify patterned regularities indicating key themes which were then contextualized within the framework from the literature (Creswell & Poth, 2018).

Quantitative Data

Quantitative data came from a SBA (adapted from the work of Womack et al., 2017, 2018) designed to measure students' argumentation ability in the form of CER. The SBA was designed as a 1–2 page complex text that presented a scenario or problem that needed a solution. Data in the form of graphs, tables, and figures were incorporated into the text which allowed students to use inferential reasoning to come up with their claim. These data were also used in the evidence students provided to support their claims.

The SBA asked students to read a scenario, and then to complete a series of argumentation tasks: (a) making a claim, (b) providing evidence, and (c) giving reasons that connect the claim with the evidence. In addition, students were evaluated on their writing ability and use of discipline-specific vocabulary. Finally, students were given a holistic score reflective of the evaluator's appraisal of the student's ability to construct an argument. These tasks comprised six related measures which were combined to provide an estimate of a student's CER (inter-rater reliability > 0.8; internal consistency > 0.9).

Toward making a causal inference on the effect of the instruction on CER, our experimental context for evaluating the effect of the lessons was limited by the fact that there was no comparison group. Therefore, the differential impact of the text sets on CER was assessed using the double pretest design (95% confidence, 2-tailed; Knapp, 2016). The motivation behind this design is that students can serve as their own control. Specifically, the SBA was given 2 weeks before the implementation (pre-pretest), and then directly before the implementation (pre-test), and again after the implementation (post-test). The change in CER between the first two testings (pre minus pre-pre) represents the expected effect of normal classroom activities. The change between the second testing and the final testing (post minus pre) represents the expected effect of the text sets.

The intervention effect, then, was derived from a comparison of the change before the intervention and that during the intervention. Given the focus on teachers as individual cases, this was done using separate paired samples *t*-tests for each of the two teachers under the null hypothesis that there were no significant differences in the change in CER before and during the implementation. In addition to evaluating statistical significance (2-tailed $\alpha = 0.05$ level), we used Hedges *G* corrected for small sample sizes (Hedges, 1981) as a measure of practical significance. Hedges *G* quantifies the magnitude of the change on a scale of standard deviations; Cohen (1992) suggests that $G < 0.2$ implies a negligible effect; $0.2 < G < 0.5$ implies a small effect, $0.5 < G < 0.8$ implies a moderate effect, and $G > 0.8$ implies a large effect.

RESULTS AND DISCUSSION

Qualitative Results

Ms. Jane implemented the text set in life sciences classes ($N = 61$), and Ms. Laura in ELA classes ($N = 129$). This section describes their implementation of the texts, and how this impacted student learning. Readers interested in the specific transcripts aligned with these findings are encouraged to contact the authors.

Ms. Jane

Ms. Jane's text set was designed for use during a unit on ecosystems. She implemented this text set with four of her eighth grade life science classes. The classes ranged from 7–23 students with a range of abilities. Ms. Jane used the *Flight of the Bumblebee* (Folk et al., 2020) anchor text as her complex text and thoughtfully designed her text set with texts of different modalities in order to scaffold her students' engagement with the anchor text. Table 10.4 details important elements of the unit she designed and implemented over five lessons.

Ms. Jane used the 5E instructional model (Bybee, 2014) to design all five lessons in her unit (Table 10.5). Within each lesson, she intentionally included scaffolds that were multimodal in order to engage her learners. She placed a heavy emphasis on students using the readings to construct their own knowledge. She did this by planning meaningful opportunities for her students to engage in the topic she was teaching. For example, when teaching her first lesson about scientific writing, she chose several types of scientific articles and laid them out for her students to explore.

Ms. Jane was careful to select articles with topics that would be of interest to her students. She posed the question, "In what ways is scientific writing organized? Do you see similarities/differences between these pieces of writing?" and asked her students to write down their thoughts so they could

TABLE 10.4 Outline of Ms. Jane's Implementation With the "Flight of the Bumblebee" Anchor Text

Outcomes	Guiding Questions	Length of Implementation	Examples of Scaffolds
Analyze how scientific writing is organized and how the structure contributes to its meaning. Visualize sound so as to determine its properties and features of the source. Specialized plant structures affect the probability of plant reproduction. Discover that flowers are adapted to specific pollinators. Practice constructing explanations grounded in scientific data. Learn that many plants depend on animals for pollination and many pollinators depend on plants for food. Understand the basic elements that need to be addressed in a "problem-solving" process. Identify claims and cite evidence to support claims. Identify a potential solution that considers the complexity of the ecosystem as a way to address the declining crop productivity. Evaluate and critique a solution in response to the problem of declining crop productivity.	How is scientific writing organized? How does the organization of scientific writing help us to understand the content? How can computers be used to understand sound and its source? How can sound waves be used to identify animals? What is the purpose and function of plants? Are they important? What is the purpose and function of flowers? Are they important? How are flowers adapted to attract specific pollinators? What is the relationship between pollinators and plants? How do you solve a design problem?	559 instructional minutes 7 weeks	Fiction Text Non-fiction Text Text with videos Videos Articles Text with audio Inquiry activity

TABLE 10.5 Outline of Ms. Laura's Implementation With the "Flight of the Bumblebee" Anchor Text

Outcomes	Guiding Questions	Length of Implementation	Examples of Scaffolds
Students will identify key vocabulary words in informational text. Students will explain the main ideas in informational text. Students will analyze properties of sound using a spectrogram. Read and interpret a poem. Students will explain the main idea and key vocabulary from informational text. Students will analyze parts of the flower to better understand pollination. Students will learn that flowers are adapted to attract specific pollinators. Students will recognize and construct claims based on evidence grounded in scientific data. Students will offer explanation/commentary that shows the relationship of the evidence to the claim. Students will evaluate the work of peers.	What is sound and how is it used? Are bees (or other pollinators) important to the environment? Why are pollinators important to the environment?	372 instructional minutes 2 weeks	Fiction Text Non-fiction Text Poetry Text with videos Videos Articles Text with audio Audio Inquiry activity

share them later with the class. After getting engaged in the topic, exploring the different scientific articles, and explaining what they noticed, Ms. Jane asked the students to analyze a complex scientific article and look for text features that might give them a sense of what the article is about.

This lesson ended with students elaborating on what they learned about how scientists write. This lesson served as a scaffold to help students as they worked with the anchor text, which was also written in the form of a scientific article. Additionally, this lesson scaffolded the use of CER, which she indicated was useful for getting the discussion going.

An inquiry activity connected to three-dimensional learning was also used as a scaffold in Ms. Jane's unit. In the inquiry activity, Ms. Jane wanted to guide students to think about the questions: "Why do we need pollinators?" and "Why are pollinators important?" To accomplish this, she had a variety of snacks out on a table in front of the classroom. She asked her students what they thought these snacks had in common. Her use of snacks was a way to engage the students in the topic.

After a class discussion about the questions, the students figured out that the snacks on display would not exist without pollinators. In order to explore this topic further, Ms. Jane asked her students, "Do you think all flowers are trying to attract the same pollinators? Why are there so many types of flowers?" before watching a quick video titled *Trading Food for Fertilization* (Rayor & Jennings, 2016). Students were asked to jot down facts they learned while watching the video to share later, and she gave them the opportunity to revise their earlier thinking about pollinators based on any new information learned from the video.

To wrap up the exploration, Ms. Jane assigned small groups a pollinator and asked them to analyze a data sheet about pollinators and types of flowers they visit to list three traits that might attract their groups' pollinator. To further students' explanation of what attracts certain pollinators, the students were asked to use the data sheet along with additional information from pollinator cards to document evidence to support their claim. She continued to elaborate on this topic by introducing an illustrated picture book text, *The Flowers are Calling* (Gray & Pak, 2015). This text has beautiful illustrations of different flowers and the different pollinators that visit the flowers. A unique feature of this text is that it provides facts about flowers and pollinators sprinkled throughout the book.

To evaluate student learning in this inquiry lesson, Ms. Jane glued images of different flowers to plastic straws. Students were able to explore this "flower garden" and crystalize their thinking about the initial questions posed in this lesson. The students created presentations to explain to the class why their pollinator is attracted to that flower. Overall, this lesson engaged students in a meaningful topic and guided them to explore pollinators and flowers, use evidence to support claims they were making about pollinators, and use multiple modes of expression to show what they learned.

The focus on CER was woven throughout all of Ms. Jane's lessons. In the previous explanation of the inquiry activity, she asked her students to find evidence about their pollinator and flower to support their claims. In other lessons, Ms. Jane was more explicit about CER. She would take time to define each of the elements in CER, look at examples of each of the elements, and then identify each within a scientific article. All of the opportunities students were given to see examples, explore, identify, and come up with their own CER served as scaffolds to support them in working with the anchor text in the following lessons.

Ms. Laura

Ms. Laura's text set was designed as an interdisciplinary unit emphasizing use of background knowledge and vocabulary to engage in complex, scientific text. She implemented this text set in two sections of eighth grade English. Each section consisted of a diverse group of students with a variety of needs and abilities. Ms. Laura used the *Flight of the Bumblebee* (Folk et al., 2020) anchor text over three lessons as a complex text and purposely designed a text set that integrated multimodal scaffolds to support students' engagement with the complex anchor text. The scaffolds were designed to strengthen students' background knowledge, vocabulary, and literacy skills.

Ms. Laura designed each lesson using the 5E instructional model (Bybee, 2014). Within each lesson, scaffolds were integrated to support students' individual learning needs. Ms. Laura's text set emphasized the development of students' background knowledge and text analysis skills. She did this by providing scaffolded activities for students to practice text analysis and build background knowledge. For example, Ms. Laura had students utilize a rolling journal when reading a variety of informational texts relating to sound and pollination. In groups, students read texts, identified vocabulary, and summarized the main idea. The rolling journals scaffolded students' vocabulary formation and textual analysis skills.

The journals guided students through the process of identifying the main idea in each text, comparing the main ideas between the texts, and summarizing the main ideas among the texts. Through this analysis, students were able to deepen their understanding of sound and pollination. Students were provided an opportunity to share their new learning with their classmates. This enabled students to make connections between their and other students' perceptions of the new material. This lesson served as a scaffold to build background knowledge, vocabulary, and literacy skills needed when engaging with the anchor text. The rolling journal provided an ongoing collection of students' thinking and a place to organize the notes from their reading. This journal allowed students to go back to look at evidence and information they had written down and to guide them in making claims.

Ms. Laura observed many benefits of the scaffolded text set, including development of speaking and writing skills, and making sense of complex ideas through discussion and note taking. Ms. Laura implemented inquiry activities to scaffold new learning. The inquiry lesson began with students reading the picture book described earlier, *The Flowers are Calling* (Gray & Pak, 2015). Then, students participated in an activity that prompted the exploration of the relationships between flower adaptations and specific pollinators. The activity began with students dissecting flowers using a flower diagram as a guide. While dissecting, students created their own flower diagrams that labeled the parts of the flower. Once their flower diagrams were completed, students created a claim that expressed the pollinators they believed would be attracted to their dissected flower using evidence from the book.

Creating claims based on scientific evidence from the inquiry activity provided students an opportunity to practice CER. To further explore the relationship between flower adaptations and specific pollinators, students participated in an additional inquiry activity. Students were assigned an unidentified pollinator and given pollinator observation data sheets and a pollinator profile that corresponded with their pollinator. The pollinator observation sheet described seven flowers' traits and number of pollination visits per pollinator. Students examined their pollinator observation sheet and pollinator profile to determine the flower traits that attracted their assigned pollinator. Then, students described three flower traits that attracted their pollinator using evidence from their observation sheet and pollinator profile. This provided students with another opportunity to practice CER with scientific evidence.

Lastly, students examined all seven flowers from the observation sheet to identify one flower their pollinator may be attracted to. Overall, these activities scaffolded students' understanding of the relationship between pollinators and flowers, as well as the utilization of CER with scientific evidence.

Ms. Laura embedded CER throughout the text set. CER was integrated into rolling journals, inquiry activities, and class discussions. Students created a claim regarding why bees are important utilizing their rolling journals for evidence. At the end of the activities, students presented their flowers and explained why their flower is matched to a certain pollinator.

During a fishbowl discussion, students read a text about honeybees and discussed their claims and evidence regarding which bees are important. To scaffold students' use of CER, Ms. Laura provided a mnemonic framework—RACE (*restate* and *answer* to create a *claim*, cite evidence, and *explain* how the evidence supports the claim). Overall, the integration of CER throughout the text set provided students opportunities to practice CER within a science context. This practice scaffolded students' CER skill development and prepared them to engage with the anchor text.

IMPACT OF THE LESSONS ON CER

Both classes experienced growth in CER through the course of evaluation (Figure 10.2). Readers interested in the specific outcomes from the statistical tests are encouraged to contact the authors. Ms. Laura's students actually experienced the greatest growth before the main implementation of the multimodal texts. Based on follow-up, this can be explained by her efforts to prepare students for the text sets prior to the official start of the intervention. Hence, Ms. Laura showed a small but significant negative intervention effect due to the small but significant increase in the SBA score before the intervention started and a nonsignificant increase during the course of the intervention. In contrast, Ms. Jane experienced a large positive intervention effect due to a nonsignificant increase in the SBA score before the intervention and a large increase in SBA score during the intervention.

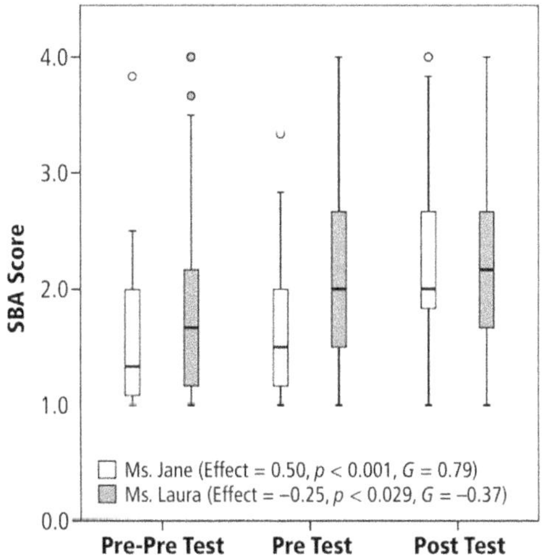

Figure 10.2

Although gains were experienced at different points during the evaluation for Ms. Jane and Ms. Laura, an important message to take from this is that the data provide support for the efficacy of improving middle school students' CER through integration of complex texts.

WHAT WE LEARNED FROM THE TEACHERS

What were the teachers' own perspectives on: (a) what their students gained from the instruction, and (b) what they themselves learned through the PD?

The curriculum helped students by fostering inclusiveness and support for all learners and by improving students' stamina and confidence with respect to the writing process. During the PD, the teachers described their own learning, and how they integrated science and literacy into their classrooms to help students achieve the above outcomes. They also offered perspectives on ways to make these efforts sustainable and applicable beyond the scope of a single program, the most important of which was collaboration with teachers across disciplines.

Stamina and Confidence of Learners

Reading and writing are difficult, especially with new content and types of text. This presents a challenging cycle for students who must navigate reading the text, writing about the text, and learning content from the text simultaneously. Rather than avoiding complex texts and writing opportunities, teachers can provide regular, scaffolded writing and reading in the content areas (Graham & Perrin, 2007; Lattimer, 2014).

We found that as the teachers engaged their students in regular writing and working with a range of text towards a complex anchor text, students' stamina and confidence increased. Both Ms. Jane and Ms. Laura described their own surprise at the engagement of their learners, which they saw created confidence and stamina as the students worked with challenging reading and writing tasks.

In the context of the quantitative evaluation, at the beginning and ending of the instructional cycle for the text set, students completed a reading and writing SBA. Ms. Jane shared with us her amazement at how much students' depth of reasoning improved, even in the lower-level kids. Although spelling and grammatical errors existed, she emphasized how important it was that her students now had the confidence to get their thoughts on paper.

Ms. Laura also noted the development of students' belief in their ability to complete the tasks as part of the text set instruction. In particular, she emphasized how her use of scaffolding helped one of her high-needs students gain confidence and blossom.

Support for All Learners

The characteristics of science and engineering texts, including text and sentence structure, technical vocabulary, use of background knowledge, evidence, and argumentation, can be especially significant barriers for diverse learners (Mason & Hedin, 2011). Too often, as a result, these learners are not given opportunities to engage in complex text. However, research findings suggest that even students who struggle in reading need to engage in complex reading material (Fisher & Frey, 2014). It was exciting to see that the teachers also described the positive learning experiences for their diverse range of learners, including English language learners (ELL) and students who were not confident in their reading and writing or may have generally read texts at levels below Grades 6–8. Ms. Jane emphasized how the scaffolded texts eased the students into the topic, and so by the time they got to the anchor text, the content was no longer difficult for them. Ms. Laura indicated that the scaffold texts were especially useful for ELL students who did not have discipline-specific vocabulary. The process of working up to the anchor text offered not only appropriate vocabulary but also increased confidence and accountability.

Teachers as Learners

As part of the PD program and supported by research on effective PD, it was expected that teachers would design instruction and adapt the text sets to meet the unique needs of their learners and curriculum requirements (Koba et al., 2013; Loucks-Horsley et al., 2009). Both teachers described their own learning in seeing ways to use different types and levels of texts to support their learners, and in the importance (and fun) in finding new materials to add to their text sets. Ms. Jane was most impressed by the fact that she could pull multiple articles at multiple different reading levels and use them in the same class. Ms. Laura lauded the fact that this type of structure also made learning more spontaneous and fun since the scaffold texts could be drawn from many sources.

Integration of Science and Literacy

The integration of literacy practices as part of scientific learning is key to the Linking Science and Literacy for All Learners program. Reading, writing, and all forms of making meaning of any text are essential to science (Norris & Phillips, 2003). This larger view of literacy helps cultivate a scientific mindset as teachers and students approach reading and writing tasks within science. For instance, scaffolded instruction guides the reading of complex texts in order to not just comprehend but to analyze how texts use evidence to make and support claims.

The teachers describe adding more texts and scaffolding the texts as part of their instruction. One of the scaffolds was the use of rolling journals to guide students in locating and analyzing concepts in several texts and to synthesize ideas across texts. The idea of rolling journals was new to both teachers, and both described creative methods for engaging the students in this practice. Ms. Jane utilized an electronic format by putting them on Google Docs. The integration of content areas, science and ELA, provided a challenge for Ms. Laura, an English teacher, because she did not have the content background. Ms. Laura's subsequent effort to implement some of the scientific practices to help herself and the students engage with the content not only facilitated deep thought and discussion about pollinators but was also well-received by her students.

Collaboration of Teachers Within and Beyond the Program

As Transcript 11 shows, the teachers within the program benefited from collaborating with one another, such as using model lessons that were presented within the PD days. The literacy skills that are critical to building knowledge in science (Cervetti et al., 2012; Norris & Phillips 2003; Pearson et al., 2010; NGSS Lead States, 2013) are a shared responsibility of middle school ELA and science teachers, but substantive collaboration in their teaching rarely occurs (Rhodes & Feder, 2014). The collaborations also reached beyond program days and into schools. Both teachers described sharing with colleagues what they were learning in the program, and as Ms. Jane describes in Transcript 12, adopting a common language to talk about claim, evidence, and reasoning within argument reading and writing.

Ms. Laura sought out the science teacher in her grade level to collaborate on text set implementation. This teacher, Mr. Daniel, helped garner the support of their department head, and even attended one of the follow-up days of the professional development.

However, collaborations are not always embraced, and Ms. Laura was aware of the potential challenges from both the administrative side as well as student perspective. In particular, she expressed the reluctance of school administrators to allow crossover between disciplines as well as resistance from students themselves when a teacher tries something new and unfamiliar.

Expansion and Sustainability of Program Practices

Concern regarding sustainability of practice, where teachers continue to use program components in their professional practice over time while maintaining the core beliefs and values of the program components (Clements et al., 2015), has been of focus for a significant period of time (e.g., Klingner et al., 2001). Both teachers described planning for continued use of text sets including adaptations to the *Flight of the Bumblebee* (Folk et al., 2020) text set as well as additional text sets to develop. The model of using literacy practices as part of a scaffolded text set towards reading and understanding a complex anchor text became a practice that the teachers wanted to expand and continue. For example, Ms. Jane expressed interest in designing a text set centered on the theory of evolution.

CONCLUDING COMMENTS

Multimodal complex text sets are a way to structure a science curriculum that places value on argumentation and critical discourse. In doing so, a cross-disciplinary approach helps students see the complexity of scientific problems and look at them from multiple points of view. This helps students develop literacy skills that are central to the process of inferential reasoning and a scientific mindset in general. Although both teachers used the same anchor text, they created multimodal text sets using different scaffolds to connect to the standards they focused on within their respective disciplines. They implemented scaffolds in different ways with their learners and used different instructional practices. Despite the differences, they were both committed to developing learners' abilities to use CER as a practice and way of thinking about the content. It is interesting that despite the different ways they enacted the multimodal text sets, their reflections on their implementation and the impact on their learners were very similar. This indicates important commonalities in challenges and best practices associated with using complex texts which not only apply across classrooms, but also across content, curricula, and programs.

The process of reading complex texts and putting arguments in writing, while initially uncomfortable for many of the students, benefitted even the lowest-performing students. In both classes, the multiple scaffolds helped make the lessons inclusive for all learners, thereby giving students of all ability levels the opportunity to participate in meaningful critical discourse around the anchor text. This brings home the importance of choosing appropriate scaffolds in efforts to help students comprehend and critically evaluate complex texts.

Both teachers emphasized that their implementation of complex texts were efficacious in making scientific readings accessible to students at a variety of reading levels including English language learners, increasing students' confidence and stamina with respect to reading and writing, and helping make a diverse student body see science as interesting and fun. In order to achieve these outcomes, certain best practices had to be kept in mind. For a teacher who wishes to develop and use complex multi-model text sets, perhaps the most important factor to consider is choosing scaffold texts. Choosing appropriate scaffold texts which are tailored to a variety of interests and reading levels is essential for engaging a diverse classroom, and thereby helping all students work up to the anchor text. Next, it is important to have activities that help turn students into active readers. Namely, students should be encouraged to write about what they are reading and apply what they are learning in class. Both of the teachers in this study found rolling journals to be an effective strategy for getting students to write about what they were reading. In addition, inquiry activities and class discussions helped the students apply what they were reading in an active social context. The process of choosing an appropriate anchor text, a diverse set of scaffold texts, and strategies for helping students become active readers, requires considerable effort but is time well spent given ever-increasing emphasis on the value of argumentation and critical discourse in science classes. Cross-disciplinary collaboration with other teachers in the school may help with the sustainability of these types of efforts. Collaborating teachers can offer complementary content expertise and espouse the benefits to skeptical students, parents, and administrators who have been taught that science is a collection of facts to be memorized, and that subjects like science, language, and the arts should not be allowed to mingle. This case study shows that students begin experiencing measurable benefits after a single multimodal text set. This warrants optimism that schools placing value on argumentation and critical discourse will also see the benefits in the course of a semester or school year.

ACKNOWLEDGMENTS

We thank members of the Linking Science and Literacy for All Learners team, and especially Jeannie Sneller, Lori Pinkston, Anna Scharnagle, and Sarah Hill for their input. We acknowledge financial support by NIH/SEPA award #8R25GM129228 and the University of Missouri. This publication is solely the responsibility of the authors and does not necessarily represent the official views of the NIH or the University of Missouri.

REFLECTIVE QUESTIONS

1. How can one support higher-order thinking skills like argumentation, inferential reasoning, and acceptance of complexity while also making learning inclusive for students of varying levels of literacy?
2. What strategies can be employed to make learning more authentic and interdisciplinary within a system that positions various disciplines as separate entities?
3. What are best practices for efforts to introduce and sustain creativity and communication literacy into science classes? What are best practices for introducing and sustaining science concepts into "nonscience" areas like language arts, art, music, and history?
4. What types of attitudes do teachers need to have in order to help students develop a scientific mindset?
5. What strategies can be employed to help students become more confident in their reading and writing abilities, and more comfortable with reading and writing in general?

CHAPTER 11

POWER UP OR PUT AWAY?

Using Mobile Phones for Authentic Student Investigations

Kristin T. Rearden and Blanche O'Bannon

Leave the beaten track behind occasionally and dive into the woods. Every time you do, you will be certain to find something you have never seen before.

—Alexander Graham Bell

SCIENCE STANDARDS: A BRIEF OVERVIEW

From the 1990s through the early 2000s, the National Science Education Standards (NSES; National Research Council, 1996) and Benchmarks for Science Literacy (American Association for the Advancement of Science, 1993) were the two primary documents used for K–12 science education curricular development across the United States. The majority of state education departments in the United States framed their guidelines for science education around what the NSES deemed as most valuable for K–12 students to know (Hollweg & Hill, 2003). The intent behind the NSES was to create a coherent, comprehensive resource that provided a consensus of

Age of Inference, pages 183–193

what science content was important to know in school, and what methods should be used to deliver it (Hollweg & Hill, 2003). The NSES described learning science as an "active process," meaning that "science is something that students do, not something that is done to them" (National Research Council, 1996, p. 20). However, while the NSES was strongly influential on many fronts, it did not escape from detractors.

Critics of the NSES claimed that the standards were "overstuffed but undernourishing," noting that although the content to be taught was significant in size, it did not promote a depth of understanding (Raizen, 1998, p. 12). Educators argued that the time for students to investigate, explore, and participate in a meaningful discourse—in other words, the practices which are important to the development of a student's understanding—was sacrificed in order to cover the breadth of required content.

Most state programs required elementary teachers to cover an immense amount of subject matter over several science disciplines in just one school year (i.e., Earth/space, physical science, life science, nature of science). Coupled with an increased emphasis on reading and math in the elementary schools, and a corresponding decrease of time spent in science instruction, this "mile wide and an inch deep" coverage of scientific concepts left students with incomplete conceptual knowledge (Schmidt et al., 1997).

UPDATING THE SCIENCE STANDARDS FOR THE NEW CENTURY

In response to a national demand for the NSES to be revised and to include fewer, higher, and clearer standards, the Committee on the Conceptual Framework for New Science Education Standards (CCF-NSES) became responsible for creating a framework that shifted the focus of science content from wide and shallow to narrow and deep (National Research Council, 2012). The first resulting document was the *Framework for K–12 Science Education* (National Research Council, 2012); this was followed by the Next Generation Science Standards (NGSS Lead States, 2013). "The *Framework* provides a sound, evidence-based foundation for standards by drawing on current scientific research—including research on the ways students learn science effectively—and identifies the science all K–12 students should know" (NGSS Lead States, 2013, para. 2, emphasis in original). The NGSS has been adopted by the District of Columbia and 20 states, and 24 states have standards based on the *Framework* (National Science Teachers Association, 2020, emphasis in original). One unique feature of these new standards that sets it apart from the NSES is the emphasis on three-dimensional learning. By organizing the standards into learning progressions that interweave disciplinary core ideas, science and engineering practices, and crosscutting concepts, students are provided the opportunity to develop a deeper understanding of the presented material.

Consistently embedding science and engineering practices in the standards, as opposed to separating out an "inquiry-based science" component, shifts the focus from portraying active engagement in science in isolation to engaging students in a more authentic representation of how science and engineering work. The eight essential practices for K–12 education include:

1. asking questions (for science) and defining problems (for engineering)
2. developing and using models
3. planning and carrying out investigations
4. analyzing and interpreting data
5. using mathematics and computational thinking
6. constructing explanations (for science) and designing solutions (for engineering)
7. engaging in argument from evidence
8. obtaining, evaluating, and communicating information

By engaging in these practices, students will better understand how scientific knowledge develops and evolves over time. Exposure to these standards gives students an appreciation of the various ways the world is explored, modeled, and explained. As the *Framework* and NGSS have been introduced nationwide, the goal of engaging students in authentic science exploration must still be pursued. Students must have the opportunity for engagement with data. One strategy for supporting students with this engagement is through the use of mobile phones.

MEETING THE NEW SCIENCE STANDARDS WITH MOBILE PHONES

In the past decade, mobile phones have transitioned from devices primarily used for voice-based communication and limited applications to ubiquitous tools for countless tasks, both utilitarian and recreational. The rise in popularity of mobile phone ownership is due to the decreasing cost and increased capabilities, thereby making an item once coveted by the business world into an item owned by the majority of U.S. teenagers. Texting surpasses other forms of communication for teens (Lenhart, 2012). Nearly 84% of U.S. teenagers have their own mobile phone, with the average teenager spending nearly 3 hours a day viewing videos (Kamenetz, 2019). The utilization of mobile phones for instructional purposes in science must be looked at from a holistic perspective in which both challenges and benefits are analyzed.

MOBILE PHONES IN CLASSROOMS: DRAWBACKS AND CHALLENGES

As mobile phones began increasing in popularity among teenagers, many schools chose to "treat mobile phones as a distraction that must be managed and often excluded from the school and classroom" (Lenhart et al., 2010, p. 4). Early implementation barriers associated with fully integrating technology into instruction included lack of personal use, lack of training, and fear of change (e.g., Bitner & Bitner, 2002). A more persistent concern is the use of mobile phones for cheating which has been confirmed by studies (Common Sense Media, 2010; Tindell & Bohlander, 2012). Studies by multiple researchers (e.g., Dietz & Henrich, 2014; Kuznekoff & Titsworth, 2013; Ravizza et al., 2014; Rosen et al., 2011) on the influence of texting during instruction suggest, perhaps unsurprisingly, that academic performance decreases when students text during class.

Using phones for cyberbullying is a concern of educators, particularly those who work with middle school students. Research by Holfeld and Grabe (2012) found that over 40% of bullying incidents in middle school occurred through the use of phone-based methods. Another drawback is when students are using the phones for noninstructional purposes, such as sending and reading text messages or email messages (Baker et al., 2012; McCoy, 2013). Although implementing classroom management strategies to promote on-task behavior with mobile phones with strategies such as the "Good Behavior Game" may mitigate occurrences of misuse, off-task use of mobile phones remains a persistent concern (Hernan et al., 2018).

MOBILE PHONES IN CLASSROOMS: BENEFITS FOR SCIENCE

Despite these challenges and potentially negative influences, mobile phones are also viewed by many educators as essential tools for learning. A primary advantage of mobile phones in the classroom is that users can access information in any location and at any time (Alley, 2009). Access to information on the Internet for research is one of the more prominent uses of mobile phones (Purcell et al., 2013). Preston et al. (2015) noted that mobile phones have the potential for student-directed learning when used for purposeful and constructive tasks. Similarly, student-centered learning can be supported through differentiation strategies (Kukulska-Hulme, 2007).

Mobile phones offer a platform through which students can engage in science and engineering practices, whether through Internet-based explorations, phone-based tools, or apps. For example, the practice of developing and using models reflects the real-world experiences of scientists and engineers who use models, including simulations, to make predictions about system behaviors (National Research Council, 2012, p. 46). Apps such as NASA NeMO-Net support this practice. Through this app, users participate in a coral reef classification project by coloring 3D models of actual coral reefs to distinguish between substrate and biotic features (see Table 11.1 for a review of each app and Internet site). Similarly, the app PictureThis–Plant Identification could be used for planning and carrying out investigations, such as comparing plant species in different areas around the school campus and students' residences. The *Physics Toolbox Sensor Suite* includes a g-force meter, light meter, and other sensors that can be used for collecting and analyzing data as well as supporting mathematical and computational thinking. Additional science-based apps are discussed later in the chapter.

In addition to content-based apps, assessment apps also provide new ways for monitoring student progress. Assessment apps provide real-time data for both teachers and students to determine next steps in a lesson, and can also be used to foster a collaborative effort among students who work in teams on crafting responses, thereby promoting the science and engineering practice of obtaining, evaluating, and communicating information. These experiences promote the science and engineering practices articulated in the *Framework*, and research suggests that student academic achievement is positively impacted through engagement with mobile phones (e.g., Zhai et al., 2019).

PROMOTING MOBILE PHONE UTILIZATION IN SCIENCE: ONE STUDY

Recent research conducted by the authors on the use of mobile phones in classroom settings focused on examining middle students' and teachers' perceptions of the use of mobile phones for instructional purposes after the teachers engaged in a series of content-based professional development sessions (O'Bannon et al., 2017). A team of educational researchers was specifically recruited to support 15 teachers at a private school in Mumbai, India in four content areas, including science. These initial teachers would ultimately support additional teachers within the school and eventually the 80-school organization. The team created and synchronously delivered a series of professional development workshops for the teachers over a 3-year period. An overarching goal of the workshops was to provide the teachers with resources and strategies for effectively incorporating mobile phones as

TABLE 11.1 Apps Suggested for Science Lessons

Name of App	Purpose	Compatibility	Price	Access	Updated
KidWings http://kidwings.com/virtual-pellet	Science	All devices with Internet & browser	Free	Web-based	2017
NASA	Science	iOS 12 up; Android 5 up	Free	App Store Google Play	2020
NASA NeMO-Net	Science	iOS 11.0 up	Free	App Store	2020
Night Sky	Science	iOS 11.0 up	Free Premium: $19.99/yr	App Store	2020
PictureThis: Plant Identification	Science	iOS 10.0 up	Free	App Store	2020
Physics Toolbox Sensor Suite	Science	Android 5.0 up	Free	Google Play	2020
Simple Machines	Science	Android 4.0.3. up	Free	Google Play	2015
Formative goformative.com	Assessment	All devices with Internet & browser	Basic: Free Premium: $12 Site: Quote	Web-based	2020
Google Forms www.google.com	Assessment	All devices with Internet & browser	Free	Web-based	2020
Kahoot kahott.com	Assessment	iOS 9.3 up; Android 5.0 up	Basic: Free	App Store Google Play	2020
Quizlet quizlet.com	Assessment	iOS 11 up, Android 5.0 up	Basic: Free Plus: $23.49 Teacher: $35.99	App Store Google Play	2020
Quizizz quizizz.com	Assessment	iOS 9 up; Android 4.4 up	Free	iOS Google Play	2020
Seesaw web.seesaw.me	Assessment	iOS 9 up, Android 5.0 up, Chromebook	Basic: Free Plus: $120/yr. Site: Quote	App Store Google Play Chrome	2020

content-area learning tools. All students owned a mobile phone, with the most common being an Android. Similar to situations common across the United States, teachers were seeking ways to integrate 1:1 technology in a manner that promoted student academic progress.

Promoting Student-Centered Science Instruction Using Mobile Phones

During the science-based professional development sessions, the focus involved supporting teachers with strategies for garnering student-generated data obtained through mobile phone capabilities such as free apps, phone-based cameras, and phone-based audio recorders. The goal was to introduce teachers to mobile phone features that could support meaningful opportunities for authentic science investigations. The first step of the professional development series was to modify the school science curriculum to more precisely identify student outcomes. For example, suggestions for clarifying the eighth grade physical science standard "To enable the students to understand the terms related to simple machines" included "To identify types of simple machines" and "To compare the uses of different types of simple machines." Following the clarification of student goals and rewriting them to include measurable outcomes, strategies for using mobile phones to support student-centered instruction were shared. The teachers were highly receptive to apps such as the NASA apps and Simple Machines see Table 11.1) as well as some apps that are no longer available. They were also very receptive to Internet-based resources such as the Kidwings virtual owl pellet dissection (see Table 11.1). The Kidwings website has an interactive activity in which students can "dissect" a virtual owl pellet. This activity could be used to promote the *Framework* standard "LS1.C: Organization for Matter and Energy Flow in Organisms" (National Research Council, 2012, p. 147). Additionally, the activity could support the science practice of using models. Understanding the interaction among organisms in an environment with additional species or the withdrawal of species in an energy food web would promote the consideration of the negative impacts of species extinction and invasive species.

Additionally, teachers were supported with using built-in phone features for gathering student-generated data. One example of how to enhance a phone-based feature was modifying the camera to take high magnification pictures. Using the lens from a laser pointer, a phone camera magnifier can be made for under $10 in just a few simple steps (Taylor, 2013). Using the magnifiers, students can capture magnified images of both abiotic (such as fabric) and biotic (such as insect specimens) items to describe, compare/contrast, and evaluate aspects.

Similarly, phone cameras without magnifiers could be used to capture near-space images, such as moon phases. With sequential pictures, students could determine shape patterns during the lunar cycle over a period of 4 weeks. Noting the directional location, areas of illumination, and relative position of the moon throughout the lunar cycle can lead students to inferences about how these aspects vary in a predictable manner. This activity could be used to support "ESS.1.B, Earth and the Solar System." A key question noted in the *Framework* for this standard is "What are the predicable patterns caused by the Earth's movement in the solar system?" (National Research Council, 2012, p. 175).

Focusing on Assessment

Assessment was another aspect of lesson design provided during the professional development. Apps that were introduced to the teachers had at least a cost-free basic version, were practical to use with large (over 20 students) classes, and provided formative feedback in a meaningful manner. Based on the feedback from participating teachers, the most popular assessment app from the professional development sessions was Formative (see Table 11.1). Formative allows teachers to create multiple choice, short answer, true/false, or "show your work" questions. Advantages of Formative included many question types and ease of use by teachers.

Another positively rated assessment app that was shared was Seesaw. This app, while requiring more time on the part of the teacher to set up, could be used with young learners and allows for differentiation of assignments. A third popular assessment app was Quizizz. Similar to the well-known app Kahoot, Quizizz has the teacher set up the quiz and students join with a code. One difference is that this app has a self-paced feature, so unlike Kahoot, students can progress individually rather than as a whole group. This is an advantage for students who work at different paces; however, they do not receive immediate feedback on their responses comparable with Kahoot. Quizizz has an extended time feature for each question (up to 5 minutes), thereby accommodating students who need a longer time to process the information and respond. With Quizizz, students see the answer choices on their own device rather than the whole-group display of Kahoot.

In addition to the previously discussed apps, Quizlet and Google Forms were also presented as assessment alternatives. Both of these apps have unique features that previously discussed apps lack. Quizlet is a flash card creator which is ultimately used as a study tool. Information is organized in *study sets* that students use to master concepts. Google Forms is a part of the Google Suite of tools and is used for creating surveys or quizzes that are used to collect information in a spreadsheet. Advantages of Google Forms include more question types than other applications and quizzes can be graded by the software. All of these assessment apps provide teachers with alternatives to traditional paper-and-pencil testing and provide teachers with real-time formative feedback on their students' progress.

Teacher and Student Perceptions

In addition to sharing potential uses of mobile phones as learning tools, training also had to support teachers with mitigating the challenges and perceived barriers for implementing student-led learning endeavors. Survey data was collected from all 15 teachers and 103 students regarding their perceptions of using mobile phones as instructional tools. The teachers tended to have slightly more concerns about using mobile phones for instruction when compared with students. The main challenge noted by teachers was the potential for students' accessing inappropriate content on the Internet. For students, the main challenge was having access to a mobile phone. Disruption of class was rated a low concern by both students and teachers. For a full description of the study, see O'Bannon et al. (2017).

Mobile Phones in the Science Classroom: "How?" Instead of "Yes or No?"

It is hard to imagine that, just over 10 years ago, the use of iPods by students was heatedly debated by school officials because of their potential for distraction (see Callahan, 2007). With iPod technology essentially outdated, the new dilemma for school administrators is whether to allow or ban the use of mobile phones by students. The prevalence of mobile phones continues to expand on an exponential basis, thereby increasing their potential for instructional uses at an explosive rate but also rendering difficult situations for teachers and administrators regarding policies about use. Similar to the mid-2000s debates about iPods, the use of mobile phones for instructional purposes has been questioned (Beland & Murphy, 2016). States such as California have proposed restricting or banning smartphones from K–12 classrooms (McGreevy, 2019).

Specific Advantages for Science Education

For science instruction, mobile phones can provide teachers with a low-cost alternative to expensive laboratory equipment, thereby increasing opportunities for students to engage in authentic science and engineering practices. In the science classroom, multiple mobile phone features can augment typical laboratory tools. In particular, digital cameras on phones have immense potential, as demonstrated in the previous section. Additionally, recording steps of a procedure and outcomes of experiments can be easily implemented with the use of mobile phone cameras. Other mobile phone features that can be utilized for science-based instruction include the calculator and clock (Thomas et al., 2014).

In particular, physics instruction is well-suited to utilizing smartphone technology. Çoban and Erol (2019) described how smartphones can be used to determine the kinetic friction coefficient in secondary science physics classes. In their rationale for designing smartphone-based laboratory activities, they note that sensors to "measure physical quantities such as acceleration, position, angle, magnetic field, loudness (and) light intensity" make smartphones an alternative to the cost of setting up an expensive laboratory (p. 1). In their description of how to use smartphone technology to calculate the coefficient, they provide two different approaches to setting up the experiment and collecting data, thereby further expanding the potential of phone-based instrumentation to cultivate a scientific mindset.

Similarly, a physics-based activity by Tho et al. (2018) utilized an accelerometer feature which can be found in the Physics Toolbox Sensor Suite app. Using this sensor, students can conduct investigations to explore simple harmonic motion of playground swings and calculate acceleration due to gravity. Investigations such as this can address physical science core ideas in areas such as motion and stability, energy, and waves. In addition to the ease of use, Tao et al. (2018) noted that using smartphones as instructional tools opens up possibilities for learning outside of the school day and beyond the classroom, stating that "the innovative use of smartphones enables greater flexible delivery (anytime, e.g., after school or during holidays), different learning environments (anyplace, e.g., playgrounds and parks) and new visualization possibilities (interactivity, e.g., real-time graph plotting)" (p. 28).

EXPLORING BEYOND THE BEATEN TRACK

The impact of any teaching resource on student achievement is a paramount consideration. Zhai et al. (2019) noted that phones used to augment existing instruction positively impacted student academic outcomes. However, merely using phones in a substitution capacity by replacing traditional instruction failed to yield the same positive outcomes. This demonstrates that the implementation of mobile phones in and of themselves will not necessarily lead to increased student achievement. Like any other instructional tool, a clear purpose with well-designed implementation strategies will support the realization of potential benefits.

Teachers can continue to explore options for using these ubiquitous technology devices to enhance instruction or suppress their use. Based on the potential of mobile phones in science instruction, the authors advocate for "powering up" rather than "putting away" in order to maximize students' opportunities to engage in the type of instruction espoused by the NGSS (NGSS Lead States, 2013). Personal research conducted by the authors, as well as the current status of research-based outcomes, speak to the potential of mobile phones in a classroom setting to support student-generated data collection, analysis, and reporting. Apps and Internet-based science education tools will continue to evolve, and it is likely that resources mentioned here will continue to be enhanced, updated, and even replaced. The authors encourage teachers to continue exploring mobile phones as educational tools and seek additional websites and apps that support student learning in science. Engaging in real-world explorations and taking ownership of learning through self-driven learning experiences can promote authentic science experiences that reflect a scientific mindset. As stated in the introductory quote by Alexander Graham Bell, inventor of the telephone, educators can leave the well-beaten path of traditional instruction and assessment formats and explore the vast opportunities afforded by phone-based tools.

REFLECTIVE QUESTIONS

1. To what extent do your school district's cell phone use policies promote the use of mobile phones for instructional purposes?
2. How frequently do you engage your students with using their mobile phones during science instruction?
3. What are some other technology resources that you could use to support the cultivation of a scientific mindset by your students?

CHAPTER 12

SELF-REGULATED LEARNING THEORY TO BUILD SCIENTIFIC MINDSETS FOR DIVERSITY IN STEM

Giuseppina Mattietti and Erin E. Peters-Burton

"Omnia Mirari, etiam tritissima"
(find wonders in all things, even the most commonplace)
—Linnaeus

Views about science, technology, engineering, and mathematics (STEM) indicate that there is a general consensus about the importance of science to society and that the development of STEM initiatives should be a national priority (Rainie & Funk, 2015). Indeed, by the numbers only, the K–16 education efforts aimed at the development of a strong STEM workforce have been successful. Since the early 1990s, the STEM workforce has increased by almost 80% (Fayer et al., 2017).

Notwithstanding the nationwide consensus on the importance of STEM and the availability of STEM learning opportunities, those who choose a STEM career are still fewer with respect to the projected needed numbers

Age of Inference, pages 195–212

and their percentages do not reflect the actual diversity of the population (Funk & Parker, 2018). For example, most women employed in STEM are in the health care system, whereas women are underrepresented in computer sciences, by far the fastest-growing STEM field. African Americans (11% of U.S. workforce) constitute only 9% of the STEM workforce, and only 7% of STEM workers are Hispanic (16% of U.S. workforce). The percentages regarding women and Black, Indigenous, and people of color (BIPOC) drop further when considering STEM careers for those with BS or higher degrees (Funk & Parker, 2018). These numbers indicate that STEM careers are not equally accessed by representatives of the population diversity, an unbalance that might reside in the way in which science as a discipline is perceived by the public.

In a broad sense, there are two purposes for K–16 STEM education:

1. to prepare students for future STEM workforce; and
2. to develop STEM-related thinking skills such as logic and computation for a literate citizenry.

K–16 science education promises to prepare citizens who are:

1. aware of the importance of science,
2. able to evaluate general scientific discourse, and
3. able to use basic scientific reasoning process of observations-inference.

Adapting to the ways of the Information Age, science education has found a way to popularize STEM knowledge through media. For example: within hours of its publication, a news agency/TV network with competent science writers on their staff can turn a newly published, highly technical peer-reviewed paper into a well-written piece to be distributed through the media. Governmental agencies dealing with science (e.g., NASA, USGS, DOE) constantly update web pages targeting to educate nonscientists of all ages. If the availability of free, high-quality science content and the variety of tools in aid to teaching science (educational products targeting people as young as toddlers) were enough to achieve a scientific mindset, we would have millions of minds potentially able to work incessantly at solving STEM problems, but currently we do not.

Confining our discourse to the K–16 population, students of science should be able to make inferences from information and to make claims of scientific arguments that they can apply when reasonable, relative to their level of education.

At the undergraduate level, students majoring in non-STEM disciplines make up a large majority of those enrolled in lower-level STEM classes;

most take science courses because these fulfill their general education requirements. Many declare themselves as not "STEM-minded"; they are conservative in taking learning risks because of a concern that scoring a low grade in a science class will hinder their opportunities for keeping or obtaining scholarships in their major field of study. Some students in the non-STEM group report that dealing with science classes gives them anxiety (Kastrup & Mallow, 2016), the opposite effect to the joy of science, which is primarily the ability of "finding wonders" auspicated by Linnaeus, whose quote inspired us in the writing of this chapter.

Beyond the reaches of K–16 education, often college-educated people refer to science as a system of beliefs. For example, frequently, people claim that they do/don't believe in climate change. What long-term benefit is there for science courses in the education system if there is no building an appreciation, if not even a mindset for appreciating science as a way of knowing? Beyond winning the science category at trivia night, one of the greatest values in learning science is the ability to think rationally and systematically to solve problems, which is helpful in seeing through the so called validity sales of products with pseudoscientific claims of which we are all very familiar. At the root of the problem is that while science content is readily available, the process guiding a STEM discipline's mindset remains hidden for as long as the focus on science education is keeping up with content for the final test.

Although there are still many barriers to be broken regarding equity in the STEM fields (Espinosa, 2011), we argue there are problematic equity issues in the K–16 system regarding the most basic level of understanding STEM ways of knowing. This chapter analyzes and summarizes evidence from empirical studies that use interventions based on self-regulated learning theory to make the nature and purpose of a scientific mindset transparent, offering one approach to creating environments that support successful experiences in scientific ways of learning for all students.

Many students in the K–16 education system deselect opportunities to engage in STEM learning because they genuinely feel excluded; even though they have funds of knowledge—academic and accumulated life experiences—that connect to STEM ways of thinking (Gonzalez et al., 2005; Velez-Ibanez & Greenberg, 1992). They view science as a "culture" disengaged from their life experience, their personal "subculture" (Aikenhead, 1996).

Teachers who do not share the same cultural background and experiences as their students may struggle to communicate effectively (Atwater et al., 2010). We posit that teachers who embrace a scientific mindset, but do not explicitly communicate it, fail to connect with students who are unaware of the nature and purpose of the field of science or of STEM. Drawing on the idea of border crossing (Giroux, 1992), we examine the use of self-regulated learning to unlock disciplinary thinking strategies to engage students who think they are not "STEM-minded."

TEACHING SCIENCE PRACTICES

One approach to building a scientific mindset in students is to explicitly teach science practices. Science practices are not only skills involved in investigation, science practices also include knowing when and how the skills should be employed and the rationale for using the skills to produce valid and reliable knowledge. When students are mindful of not only what to do but why they are doing a particular practice in science, they develop a scientific mindset.

The Next Generation Science Standards (NGSS; NGSS Lead States, 2013) defines science practices as these eight areas:

- asking questions
- developing and using models
- planning and carrying out investigations
- analyzing and interpreting data
- using mathematics and computational thinking
- constructing explanations
- engaging in argument from evidence
- obtaining, evaluating, and communicating information

The NGSS defines and sets standards for engineering practices as well, but for the purposes of this chapter, we will focus only on science practices. NGSS also defines science practices as both the skills and knowledge of the nature of the skills that help build and verify knowledge in science. For example, one of the science practices is asking questions. One must possess skills to ask questions, but to understand that science practice, one must also understand that only testable questions about the natural world are valid questions in science. A student who previously felt disengaged with science can learn important underpinnings of the discipline in a tangible way by focusing on science practices to develop content knowledge.

There is a distinct difference between teaching science content knowledge (facts and concepts) and teaching science practices (investigation skills). Science content knowledge is declarative knowledge. Students and teachers can easily see when students have acquired content knowledge because often science content knowledge has agreed upon, convergent conceptions of the natural world. Students can demonstrate their understanding of content knowledge by stating the facts that they have learned, and teachers can mark them correct, partially correct, or entirely incorrect. Teaching science practices involve skills and procedural knowledge that does not have a static or set end point. Planning and carrying out an investigation can be done correctly in a variety of ways, and incorrectly in a variety of ways. To add to the difficulty, teaching students process knowledge is more difficult than teaching outcome knowledge, such as factual knowledge. Because teachers must evaluate students' performances of science practices while they are happening, it is logistically difficult, as compared to assessing outcome knowledge on tests of multiple choice questions.

To assist students in developing a scientific mindset, teachers can give students consistent, timely feedback about their performance of science practices, because the more a student understands how to use science practices, the more developed their scientific mindset can be. A template to assess (or self-assess) practices when they occur is one way of reducing the logistic difficulties with providing immediate feedback about student learning when engaged in scientific practices. An example of such a template, easily customizable to appropriate K–12 grades and other STEM discipline-specific practices, can be found in Figure 12.1.

In our own teaching practice, we saw this need of emphasizing the connection between science practices and mindset and we turned to a learning theory based on observing cognition and metacognition related to a learning performance to help us assess and give feedback to students on their scientific mindset. The theory we chose was self-regulated learning (SRL) theory (Zimmerman, 2000) because it can be a template to understand how students are approaching learning, monitoring their learning, and reflecting on their learning when involved in science practices.

Student Task: Use a microscope to examine an unknown culture. (9 pts).

Microscope Use Checklist

Observed	Skill
	Wipes slide with lens paper.
	Places drop of two of culture on slide.
	Adds a few drops of water.
	Places slide on stage.
	Turns to low power.
	Looks through eye piece with one eye.
	Adjusts mirror.
	Turns to high power.
	Adjusts for maximum enlargement and resolution.

Score: ____ /9 pts.

Figure 12.1 Sample template to assess students accomplish the task.

SRL THEORY

SRL theory provides a framework and language for students to explain their own approaches to understanding STEM disciplinary skills (Zimmerman, 2002). The use of SRL theory in curriculum provides guideposts for student epistemic thinking in science by supplying scientific mindset cues and tactics to scaffold learners new to thinking like scientists (Peters-Burton, 2015). SRL is useful as a support tool because of its direct alignment with student scientific mindset practices and the mechanisms that govern scientific thinking, such as logic, reason, abstraction, and generalization. SRL principles embedded within classroom instruction can help students understand their own learning processes in science while concurrently revealing student learning processes to teachers, creating a third space where both teacher and student share understandings about thinking processes.

Further, SRL processes are aligned to the phases of the 5E curriculum model (Bybee, 2004) which is a highly recommended format for designing authentic problem- and project-based learning curriculum for integrated STEM lessons (Peters-Burton & Botov, 2017). SRL prompts integrated into science learning, especially when learning is focused on accomplishing an investigation, has positively impacted school-aged students: Equipped with SRL scientific mindset supports, students are able to use STEM ways of knowing in problem-solving as well as discussing the rationale for making decisions (c.f. Cleary & Labuhn, 2013; Peters, 2012; Peters-Burton, 2015; Peters & Kitsantas, 2010). Students using SRL to reveal their learning strategies are able to cross borders where they no longer think that the processes guiding the discipline are hidden, effectively providing new opportunities for students to use STEM skills in the classroom and beyond.

SUPPORTING A SCIENTIFIC MINDSET THROUGH SRL

Students from kindergarten to undergraduate levels who feel overwhelmed or disconnected when learning science can be helped with additional support that breaks down the tasks they are working on and makes the details explicit to them (Peters & Kitsantas, 2010). SRL theory is one template that teachers can use to help students become more aware of their learning in science and promote good learning habits to develop a scientific mindset. A learner who is self-regulated is metacognitive and can be self-motivated to behave in ways to promote their own learning (Zimmerman, 2000).

We have found that students who do not consider themselves science-minded can develop a scientific mindset with some external support by instructors using the cycle of SRL to support student processes (Peters & Kitsantas, 2010; Peters-Burton, 2015). By being aware of learning the

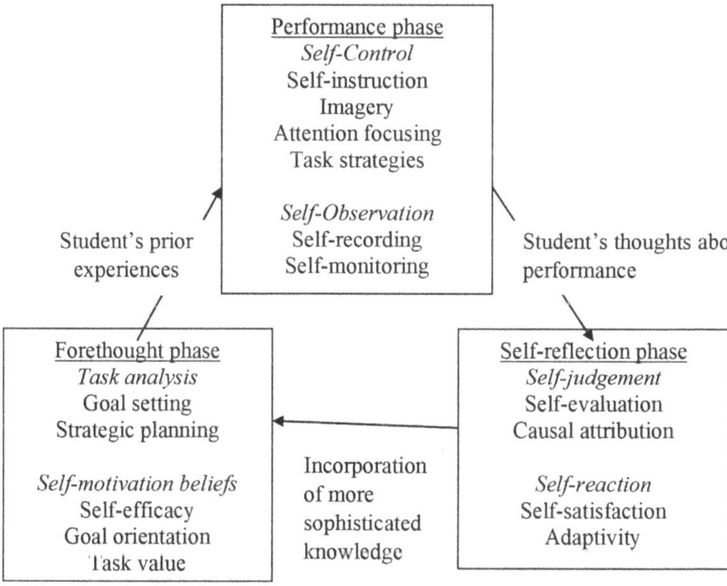

Figure 12.2 Self-regulated learning for developing a scientific mindset.

underpinnings of science practices, students understand the purpose and rationale for the practice, promoting their scientific mindset. Learner processes are categorized in SRL in three phases of a cyclical model, forethought, performance, and self-reflection as seen in Figure 12.2.

Forethought Phase in SRL

The processes in the forethought phase occur prior to learning science practices and consist of self-motivation beliefs and analysis of the science task-at-hand. The self-motivation beliefs consist of self-efficacy for the task, intrinsic value for the task, outcome expectations, and goal orientation (Zimmerman, 2000). Learners approach a task, such as learning how to perform a science practice such as planning and carrying out an investigation, with a particular level of self-efficacy (Bandura, 1986). If the learner has a high self-efficacy for planning and carrying out investigations, they will be willing to take risks and challenge themselves in the upcoming task (Bandura, 1986), possibly leading to improved science mindset. If a learner has a low self-efficacy for planning and carrying out investigations, they will most likely follow a prior familiar routine without extending their scientific mindset.

There are four sources of self-efficacy: prior experiences, positive encouragement, vicarious experiences, and physiological effects (Bandura,

1986). The most influential source is prior experiences. If learners have successfully planned and carried out a scientific investigation, then even if the task-at-hand is a different type of investigation, the learner will be motivated to succeed. Positive encouragement is a less influential source, but encouragement that includes positive feedback, such as "you are looking at this investigation in terms of variables, and that is a logical way to do it," could raise learner self-efficacy towards a task. When a learner sees someone they consider a peer, successfully do the science practices, the learner will tend to have a higher self-efficacy towards the practice. Finally, the weakest influence for self-efficacy is a feeling of excitement or some other type of physiological effect such as sweating or feeling anxious.

Instructors can help student self-efficacy in science practices by starting the instruction with a science practice in which all students can be successful, providing positive prior experiences in the practice. The next time the instructor asks learners to use this science practice, they should refer to the success of the learners to encourage self-efficacy for the new task. Additionally, instructors can encourage students through specific constructive feedback for the science practice. In these ways, instructors can give all students, even those who have little experience with science, a chance to develop a scientific mindset.

Even if a learner has a low self-efficacy towards a task, once they find value in the task, they will most likely be motivated to have perseverance to learn the skill (Peters-Burton & Botov, 2017). For example, if a learner sees that valuable information can be obtained using a scientific investigation, then they are more likely to be motivated to conduct the scientific investigation to the best of their ability. They may be prepared to ask questions when they get stalled in their learning or they may be thinking about ways they have done an investigation in the past and remember how that skill helped them learn science. Similarly, students who have positive outcome expectations and goal orientation can visualize their success in science and begin to feel more science-minded.

Positive self-motivation beliefs are not the only things needed to be successful when approaching science practices. Self-regulated learners also analyze the learning task, which consists of setting appropriate goals and strategically planning to meet the goals (Locke & Latham, 1990). Productive goals for learners tend to be goals that help them learn the processes involved in meeting the goal rather than merely what the outcome should be (Kitsantas & Zimmerman, 2002). This means that new learners need guidance from instructors that help break down the steps to be proficient in the science practice, rather than focusing on only the end-product. For example, learners who are attempting to plan an investigation need to know that they should understand the phenomena they are examining so that they understand the possibilities for the variance in variables. They will then be able to choose appropriate variables to manipulate and test, along with choosing appropriate tools to measure the variables and recording the measurements in an organized way. Understanding the types of self-motivation beliefs and task analysis processes that learners have when approaching a learning task such as science practices is a way that teachers can guide students to develop a scientific mindset.

Performance Phase in SRL

The performance phase of SRL occurs when a learner is engaged in learning the science practice. During this phase, learners who metacognitively monitor their progress tend to be able to change their practice flexibly if they are not being successful (Cleary, 2011). On the other hand, a learner who is not metacognitively monitoring their progress will not be mindful of their practices and may "go through the motions" of that science practice without mastering the skill.

A skillful learner will make periodic self-observations and compare these observations with the goals and strategic plans they have set. Instructors can help learners with their self-observations by providing reminders throughout the learning task to compare their skill in the science practice with their goals and strategic plans. Skillful learners also focus their attention on the most important features of a practice, which is developed through experience with the science practice. However, learners who do not have much experience in the field of science will not understand where to focus their attention and may be spending their time investigating unrelated variables or measuring inconsistently. This is an opportunity for instructors to intervene and point out to the learners the areas in which to focus for an improved scientific mindset.

Self-Reflection Phase in SRL

The self-reflection phase occurs after the learner receives feedback about their performance. Feedback can be from an instructor, the physical environment, or self-generated feedback. There are two parts to self-reflection, which are self-judgment and self-reaction (Zimmerman, 2000). When a skillful student receives feedback, they will assess the reliability of the feedback and attribute their success or failure to a specific reason. Assuming the feedback comes from a reliable source such as an instructor or expert and is accepted as such, the learner then attributes success or failure to a source. If the source is external from the learner such as some innate talent, genetics, or "the instructor just does not like me," then the learner perceives that there is no way to change their learning process, and the learner will most likely not approach the next learning experience of a science practice with high motivation or perception of ability to accomplish the learning. However, if a learner attributes their failure or success to an internal source, such as their process for learning, then the next time the learner approaches a learning context with a science practice, they will likely have high motivation to learn.

Self-reflection phase also includes the ability of a learner to have a self-reaction to their self-judgment. This entails the learner being satisfied or dissatisfied with their performance, based on the feedback. When skillful learners are dissatisfied with their performance during the self-reflection phase, they find ways to adapt. This may be in the form of trying a new learning process for the task or asking for help from a reliable source. In most cases, the instructor is the readily available and reliable resource, able to provide guidance tailored to the individual. Alternatively, the learners may rely on peers, social media, and in general web-based resources.

The next sections present various SRL experiences that resulted in an improved scientific mindset for students from middle school to undergraduate instruction.

SUPPORTING FORETHOUGHT PROCESSES OF SCIENTIFIC MINDSET AND INFERENTIAL REASONING

Student self-efficacy for a scientific mindset is key in helping all students improve the way they think about science. In one study, we examined undergraduate students' self-efficacy for ways of communicating scientific knowledge (Peters-Burton & Mattietti, 2011). These students were not majoring in science and were taking an introductory geology course only to fulfill the natural science course load requirement. The study focused on the students' understanding of stratigraphy principles, key principles guiding inferential reasoning about the meaning of time in earth sciences. Students were asked to identify and explain the geologic history of an area by using stratigraphic principles to explain evidence from stratigraphic columns, technical diagrams widely used in the discipline. Students were asked to mark the key elements on the drawing (diagram form) and answer a few related questions in a narrative form. Additionally, students were asked to rate how confident they were about their answer being correct. Statistical analysis of the data indicated several areas of the required knowledge where the correct answer and self-efficacy were negatively correlated, especially for answers provided in narrative form. Conversely, students felt less confident about their answers in the diagram form, but their answers were correct in that form. (Peters-Burton & Mattietti, 2011). From this information, the instructor was able to identify where interventions were needed to support the self-efficacy building effort. Two interventions were adopted to improve students' self-efficacy: (a) assuring the students that they were knowledgeable about explaining their work in a diagram and (b) guiding students in identification of the key words in their writings that constitute the necessary and sufficient elements to provide a correct answer.

Opportunities to support forethought with level entry undergraduates are readily available in the classroom environment where the instructor can model the forethought steps, especially when it comes to task analysis and strategic planning. These do not require expert content knowledge and can be carried out as exercises in their own right. With younger students, metacognitive prompting can support students in setting goals to engage in science practices (Peters & Kitsantas, 2010). We conducted an educational experiment when 14- and 15-year-olds were studying about permanent magnets with guided inquiry lessons. Before starting to learn about magnets, students wrote down everything they knew about magnets. However, in the treatment group, we provided some prompts to help the students think about how their prior knowledge connected with the research questions they were about to explore. The prompts were short sentences encouraging the students to develop a scientific mindset, such as: "My observations are clear to other people who are not performing this lab" and "My observations are not judgments about what I thought would happen before I did the investigation." The control group was given extra content material to read to be sure the time on task was the same for both groups.

At the end of the 8-week series of investigations, we found a significant difference from pre- to posttest for the treatment group on their content knowledge of magnets, even though the control group had more time reading about magnets. We believe that the difference happened because students were given guidance from their teacher about how to develop a scientific mindset from the prompts. The prompts cued students into the most important practices when doing an inquiry investigation, and helped students develop inferential skills by modeling what they should be doing in small increments. We were also successful in using these types of prompts in the other phases of SRL: performance and self-reflection.

SUPPORTING PERFORMANCE PROCESSES OF SCIENTIFIC MINDSET AND INFERENTIAL REASONING

Students who are self-regulated learners tend to monitor their progress in the performance phase, which helps them notice if they are doing the science practice in the way that is intended, in other words, are they keeping their scientific mindset as they are performing the science practice. In our work with providing eighth grade students metacognitive prompts, we gave guiding advice on how to make measurements that were scientifically valid. In doing so, we provided students a list of statements that explain key characteristics of making measurements and students checked off the statements as they performed them. For example, "My observations are made up of measurements that other people can agree upon when possible. For example, instead of saying, 'It is big,' I say, 'The blue car is 20 cm long.'"

We provided students prompts over the 8 weeks of the educational experiment, focusing on different areas of scientific practices, such as making empirical observations, taking measurements in an accurate and precise way, and having respect for evidence (Peters, 2012). For each type of science practice, we provided a different set of prompts and we took away the previous prompts so that students could focus their attention on only one science practice at a time. We saw that not only did the students use the prompts that were given them, but they also used the prompts that we took away, showing that they were developing a scientific mindset and orientation to inferential reasoning (Peters & Kitsantas, 2010).

Metacognitive prompts, when used in a variety of science practices, can help students form a multifaceted scientific mindset. We have started to look at how metacognitive prompts can help students in high school develop computational thinking practices when they engage in data during a science investigation. For example, when students are generating data from observations, we ask them to break it down by asking: "What do we already know about this problem?" "What data are we generating?"; "What are the key types/sources of data that we might use to answer the essential question?"; "How will we generate this data?"; and "What metrics can we use?" (Peters-Burton et al., 2020).

In this project, we have identified prompts to help students create, collect, manipulate, visualize, and analyze data with computational thinking practices of decomposition, pattern recognition, algorithmic thinking, abstraction, and automation. Modeling scientific practices for students helps all students develop an understanding of how to make inferences that are valid, reliable, and empirical.

An upper-level undergraduate final course project in igneous petrology used the same approach. During the semester, by analyzing peer-reviewed literature and textbook examples, students learned about the ways in which sets of chemical analysis of rocks could be used to make inferences about the origin and evolution of magma from various areas of the world. Rather than constraining the application of chemical petrology to content knowledge to be tested in a traditional exam, we designed a project in which the students use their knowledge to perform a similar investigation, based on selecting, manipulating, visualizing, and analyzing data.

Each student selected a raw dataset of chemical analysis from an area of the world of their choosing (we used the GEOROC database, an open-source database, available from the Max Plank Institute for Chemistry, in Mainz, Germany). Students were asked to formulate a testable question to be answered using the datasets they selected. Students were asked to produce visualizations in the form of bivariate, ternary, and normalized graphs to make inferences about the nature and evolution of the rocks represented by the set of data of their choice.

We are currently analyzing the data collected during this study, however, some direct evidence of the outcomes, based on the student scores of the project (based on the quality of the work and the student insights on the report) indicates that first, not all the students who earned higher scores in content-based tests were the same who performed the highest scores in the project. Secondly, students adopted a variety of behaviors in strategic tasking, time management, help-seeking, and use of self-instruction.

In journals that students were asked to keep, a range of metacognitive awareness was revealed. Some students simply reported a list of tasks completed, while others dwelled on the reason why they were carrying out a certain task, probing new ways, unaware that they were performing a self-regulating learning cycle in its entirety. Students who became involved in this study (not just completed the task of it) developed not only an increased awareness of the process of performing the process of "doing" science, but developed a sense of ownership of their work, as they were the ones trying to ask their own questions, they crossed the border into the doing of science.

SUPPORTING SELF-REFLECTION PROCESSES OF SCIENTIFIC MINDSET AND INFERENTIAL REASONING

When students have experience planning for valid science practices and have some model to compare their performance against, then they are ready to self-reflect on their performance, especially if they have been provided feedback from an expert. We have supported student self-reflection on science practices by asking students to justify why they do a specific science practice. By asking for a rationale of a science practice rather than just asking how a student did a science practice, students provide evidence about their scientific mindset development. If we only ask how they did the science practice, we get the procedure they did, but if they do not know why they did a science practice, then the student may not have evidence of a scientific mindset. To help students make their scientific mindset explicit, we ask them questions such as:

- "Other people can understand my observation out of context." (Explain.)
- "My observation is free of any judgment." (Justify your answer.)
- "My observations are relevant to the purpose of the investigation." (How so?) (Peters, 2012).

Asking students these questions helps them to see how much they progressed their scientific mindset. We have had some excellent outcomes with supporting students' self-reflection processes by asking these questions. In interviews with 14- and 15-year-old students during our educational experiments, students have said "I knew we were supposed to do something differently in science, but I didn't know how to do that until I read the prompts." Students using the prompts even went back to gather more data to be sure that their conclusions were accurate: These behaviors show that students are adopting a scientific mindset.

Metavisualization through concept mapping is a powerful tool for the building of a scientific mindset. The validity of concept mapping is shown in several studies as a learning tool for students and as a powerful assessment tool for the instructors (Angelo & Cross, 1993).

A study carried out in a large general education introductory geology class (on average 100 students per lecture class) indicated that the practice of concept mapping can offer the students and the instructor a powerful tool for self-reflection (Mattietti & Peters-Burton, 2015). Students enrolled in large general education introductory science classes have very little opportunity to engage in the practice of self-reflection. Reasons for this are the large amount of discipline content matter that the instructor is contractually bound to deliver, and the reality that providing the opportunity for self-reflection requires a prompt from the instructor; a step almost impossible for the large general education science classes.

In addition, geology is traditionally perceived as the go-to class that "nonscience" minded students can take to easily fulfill the natural science requirement; the class' only challenge is considered to be memorization of course content rather than the understanding of the synthetic nature of the discipline. Concept mapping can be used to overcome this barrier as demonstrated by this study based on data collected over a time span of 5 years. Students were asked to build a concept map as a way to prepare for a midterm exam. Each student chose which geologic concepts to use and how to link them to make causal inferences among concepts. Each student received feedback specifically targeting inferences that tied the concepts. Later in the semester students were offered to produce a second concept map in preparation of the final exam.

While it is hard to demonstrate a direct relationship between the concept mapping intervention and the final grade, the study indicated that a fourth of the students who participated in this project showed evidence of increased involvement with the process of mapping their knowledge. Evidence was mostly the improved ability to draw causal attribution (better defined links and spatial organization), in others it was simply an increased care in the design of the map, indicating a personal connection with the task. Most notably, the average score of poorly performing students who showed evidence of being engaged with the exercise of concept mapping increased on average by 15 to 20 points. In some of these cases, maps were accompanied by unsolicited spontaneous declarations of feeling more confident about the discipline, adding an affective element to their learning experience (Mattietti & Peters-Burton, 2015). The concept mapping practice, in addition to its usefulness as a formative assessment tool, can be used in the self-reflection process to strengthen inferential reasoning. For students not engaged with the discipline, it can provide an opportunity to begin building a bridge into the subculture of science (Aikenhead, 1996).

CROSSING BORDERS HELPS STUDENTS DEVELOP A SCIENTIFIC MINDSET

As science educators, our primary concern is for students to learn not just the discipline content, but become familiar with the process of doing science, the scientific mindset, the ability to ask testable questions, and to make causal inferences from observations. The explicit teaching of science practices ideally promotes the development of the scientific mindset; there is the risk that the practices become but a list of procedures, unless there is a significant engagement of the educators in continuously monitoring and providing feedback to the students, a tall order to add to the demands of the disciplinary curriculum.

We found that SRL theory (Zimmerman, 2000) gives us an effective framework to help students develop a scientific mindset. Inferential reasoning guides the three steps: approaching learning (forethought phase), making and monitoring progress (performance phase), reflecting on their learning (self-reflection), and thus coming to the opportunity to repeat the cycle as needed. Our studies have highlighted how the mindful approach to SRL results in successful learning and personal growth for diverse student populations.

Teaching to develop a mindset, rather than simply providing discipline content and procedures, requires dealing with individual subcultures that have been shaping the students' personal ways of knowing since infancy. In a way, as we consider the mindset of science, we are saying that science is a type of culture in its own right, and we seek students to become acculturated to it. In order to do that, students have to "cross borders" (Giroux, 1992). The mindset of science is embraced when science makes sense to those who study it; however, students from diverse social and cultural backgrounds may arrive to the study of science from a great variety of mindsets, so if a science mindset harmonizes with a student's life–world culture, then science will make sense with little to no effort. Contrariwise, if science is at odds with a student's view of the world, then the self-declared nonscience student will feel at odds with the scientific mindset (Aikenhead, 1996). Therefore, depending on the nature of the relationship between students' personal world and their success in school science, the level of effort required to cross the border into the scientific mindset can range from smooth to manageable to hazardous to virtually impossible (Costa, 1995; Phelan et al., 1991).

As the results of our studies suggest, all the students benefited from the SRL approach to some extent. To some, the step of the SRL came naturally, either because they had already embraced the scientific mindset or were able to cross personal borders into the mindset with minor guidance. Others for whom the crossing could be defined hazardous to "virtually impossible" needed more prompts and guidance (the "tour guide" model of Aikenhead) but were still able to make progress at least in considering how scientific inferences are made and what a scientific mindset would look like. In a sense, use of SRL to create a scientific mindset helps provide a reliable bridge for all those who want to cross the border into the land of scientific mindset.

Many barriers need to be overcome before the opportunity to develop a scientific mindset is an opportunity for all. In addition to sociopolitical issues regarding the equitable opportunity for all to access science education and succeed in it, there are other intrinsic barriers mostly related to the culture of science. The availability of science content in many ready-to-use formats clogs K–16 curricula with facts leaving little room to work on mindsets. Often, overwhelmed by the amount of content knowledge and technical vocabulary accompanying the science disciplines, students across the spectrum of age and culture, become turned off or intimidated by the culture of science. The same overwhelming feeling is perceived by the educators pressured to cover the material required by the school curriculum. There is also the risk of turning the purposeful teaching science practices aimed to enhance the science curricula into a set of procedures, where the focus is the procedure rather than the inferences that guide the steps.

Sometimes students report they place a great deal of effort into studying but still receive poor results on exams. Most students are not aware that there are diverse forms of studying; among these, self-reflection does not come naturally to most people unless they are guided into SRL by an instructor experienced in doing the process themselves. SRL is a powerful tool on which to build science educational opportunity for all to cross bridges into a mindset of science, but it is not a deus ex machina that will appear by itself to solve all issues regarding the successful establishment of a scientific mindset in all those who study science at any level.

SRL requires practice, it is guided by metacognition, strategic actions, and reflective practices that are mastered in time; moving up the learning curve might happen at a different pace for each individual but requires effort and dedication by all. For this reason, it is important that educators become aware of the nature of SRL for themselves before they promote this way of learning to their students.

There are strategies used in all level classrooms to develop SRL but often due to logistic and time constraints, the process stops short at the self-reflection, thus cutting out the cyclical aspect of the experience, which embodies the constructivist nature of the scientific mindset. Our own experience indicates that the best results are obtained on new iterations of the SRL cycle, that is where the borders are finally crossed for those who never thought science could work for them.

Ideally, all humans have the ability to cross the border into science. We all are born with inquisitive minds; as children, the sense of wonder about natural science is more aesthetic than scientific. Growing up, the human ability to grasp abstraction and unsolved questions increase, however, the science taught is a mostly body of facts, typically reducing complexity and concealing inconsistencies for ease of delivery and assessment. By the time people reach adulthood, many have lost the grasp on the nature of science, lost the curiosity and the joy of it, lost the sense of wonder, which is what drives minds to science (Lindholm, 2018).

Those who became scientists have learned to be at ease with complexity and inconsistencies; attracted to science, they leaped across the border into the science mindset. Once there, they continue to make inferences from what they learn, and undaunted by setbacks, take on the cycle of forethought, performance, and self-reflection. Science education could successfully tap into greater diversity by offering opportunity to cross the border of the scientific mindset, let young minds check it out, and then decide if they want to stay a bit or forever!

REFLECTIVE QUESTIONS

As we reflect on our own experience with our quest to help students crossing borders into the scientific mindset, we have developed a few questions to guide our own evolution as scientists and educators.

1. How would you define a scientific mindset in your classroom context?
2. How might you support student goal setting to foster student development of a scientific mindset?

3. How can you help students think scientifically as they monitor their work during an investigation?
4. What features of a scientific mindset and inferential thinking can help students self-reflect on their own scientific mindset and inferential reasoning?

CHAPTER 13

A CASE FOR THE MODEL-BASED REASONING CLASSROOM

Arthur Beauchamp and Cynthia Passmore

Model-based reasoning is, inherently, an inference making endeavor where the strength or rationality of those inferences is improved when thinking is shared, made public, critiqued, and revised.

—Arthur Beauchamp and Cynthia Passmore

As human beings, we are driven to make sense of the world around us. This sense-making endeavor takes on different forms for different purposes, but it is ultimately about seeking patterns, predicting what might happen next, and explaining why certain things happen. This drive is one that humans are born with and it is what makes us such amazing learning machines in early childhood (Gopnick et al., 1999). Too often, unfortunately, school experiences squander rather than capitalize on this innate drive. However, science provides an ideal venue to take advantage of these reasoning patterns and inclinations for sensemaking as the progress of science is much like the sensemaking children do. Children, like scientists, use what they know to build new knowledge; they revise and extend

Age of Inference, pages 213–221

their knowledge as new information becomes available. This fundamental aspect of science, that it builds on and extends what came before, is central to understanding and reasoning in this field (Nersessian, 2008). Merely telling students what they should memorize about particular ideas and/or concepts is, at the core, a violation of what science is all about and deprives students of key opportunities to harness their innate sensemaking drive. Instead, students should experience something in the world that is worth their time to figure out, a phenomenon or class of phenomena that is recognizable from the real world. Students should be steeped in potential explanatory ideas and develop and refine their own ideas that can be used to make sense of phenomena. Ideally, students should then be placed in a context in which ideas need to be expanded upon or revised based on new evidence. In sum, they should be asked to make inferences from prior knowledge and evidence to figure out how aspects of the natural and designed world operate.

This description of what students should be doing in science classrooms is consistent with calls in the *Framework for K–12 Science Education* (National Research Council, 2012) that teachers shift their instructional practices from didactic modes to methods that engage students more actively and authentically in the endeavors of science. Students, too, must change their role in the science classroom from predominantly recipients of information to that of participating critical thinkers using information and scientific practices to figure out relationships, solve problems, construct explanations, and make sophisticated conclusions based on evidence. Over the last 2 decades, there has been significant work in the development of new tools, strategies, methods, and approaches to science instruction (e.g., Schwarz et al., 2017; Windschitl et al., 2018.). Here, we focus on the model-based reasoning approach (see Gouvea & Passmore, 2017; Passmore et al., 2017 for one view of this approach). The role of developing and using models is recognized as one of the key science practices in the *Framework* and *Next Generation Science Standards.* Indeed, the writers of the *Framework* state that scientists use models "to represent their current understanding of a system (or parts of a system) under study, to aid in the development of questions and explanations, and to communicate ideas to others" (National Research Council, 2012, p. 57). Many educators agree that bringing the practice of developing and using models into the classroom is important, but supporting students in this work takes a new set of structures and techniques that can assist teachers in creating classroom cultures and processes that promote the flow and expression of thoughts, ideas, and conclusions.

MODEL-BASED REASONING AND INTEGRATING INTELLECTUAL WORK WITH LITERACY-BASED TASK STRUCTURES

Model-based reasoning is, inherently, an inference-making endeavor where the strength or rationality of those inferences is improved when thinking is shared, made public, critiqued, and revised. We have instantiated these views in an approach centered on integrating opportunities for model-based reasoning with literacy strategies in the classroom as a way to bring the inference making that students do in the modeling classroom into the public space. We have operationalized the essence of modeling in the classroom by identifying three key elements and the connections between them (see Figure 13.1). This tool is alternately called the reasoning triangle or simply PQM. We represent this epistemic tool as a triangle formed by the words phenomena, questions, and model. The arrows represent the interconnectedness of phenomena, questions, and model, and serve to illustrate that multiple pathways and iterations can be taken in designing, sequencing, and teaching lessons that are built to support students in developing models for answering questions about phenomena in the natural or designed world (Gouvea & Passmore, 2017). Most often, we depict this tool with a person, the cognitive agent, in the middle as a reminder that all the work of sense-making in science is done by humans with specific purposes in mind.

The reasoning triangle can be used to connect the work being done in the classroom from one day to the next and situate knowledge building as an ongoing endeavor. Moreover, the English language arts processes of dialogue, reading, and writing are the means by which we access, consider, explore, share thinking, debate, and make decisions about the structure and details of scientific ideas and inferences. Each of these processes requires that the listener, reader, or writer consider data, weigh evidence, make inferences, make decisions, and draw conclusions, and when done in conjunction with a modeling approach these cognitive processes are done with regard to a phenomenon under investigation. That is, reading, writing, and

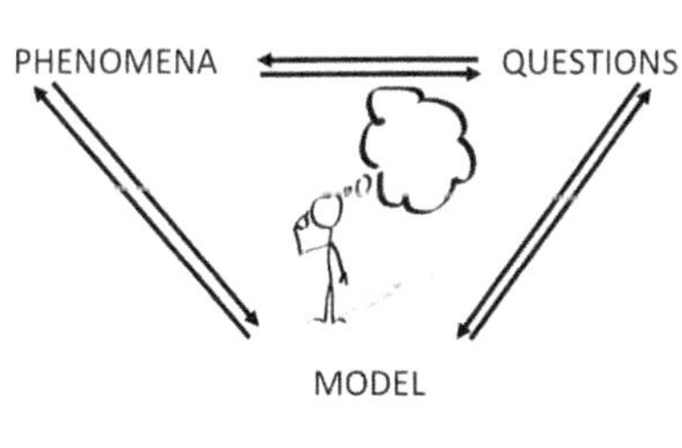

Figure 13.1 The reasoning triangle (P, Q, M).

dialogue are essential to the endeavor of science. The individual thinking that goes into idea formation and scientific explanation building is crucial, however, the public sharing, and discourse that follows moves scientific knowledge building forward. When the processes of dialogue, reading, and writing are structured in pedagogically effective ways in the science classroom, student learning benefits (Beauchamp et al., 2011.).

EXAMPLE LESSON: SEABIRD DEATHS

Below we describe a lesson sequence that was designed and delivered using the PQM frame with attending literacy supports. Key mappings of this approach to the PQM triangle and the role of reading, writing, and dialogue are summarized in Table 13.1. The lesson opens with the teacher talking with her students about a phenomenon—a large-scale die-off of ocean-going seabirds in Alaska. She explains that *The New York Times* reported on the common murre population and the fact that the birds were dying in large numbers from apparent starvation. To date, scientists had not figured out the underlying cause of this die-off. As in this case, a teacher may introduce an interesting phenomenon, but if students do not engage in a dialogue about what they observe and build a common understanding about what they are witnessing, then the opportunity for further intellectual engagement is limited. It is important that student observations, ideas, and thinking drive the instruction. This does not mean that teachers relinquish their role in guiding the learning, it means that the teacher has to employ skills and techniques to shepherd the expression and exchange of ideas in productive directions.

In this classroom, students watched a video of a typical common murre colony and after viewing and recording observations the students engaged in small group dialogue about what they had observed. They also received information about another episode of seabird die-off that had happened several years before in the North Atlantic as well as excerpts from a scientific article on the problem that occurred in the North Atlantic. At this point, the class discussed what they knew and came to agreement about what the phenomenon was and began thinking about questions they had about what was happening.

Next, the class worked on developing and stating a driving question for their investigation. The question ends up being something like this: What are the major factors leading to the die-off of common murre populations in Alaska? Once they had a driving question, they also developed ancillary questions, such as, "What do common murres need to survive and successfully reproduce?"

At this point, the class engaged in reading several articles on murre biology (feeding, reproduction, and migration). They used a "jigsaw" technique

TABLE 13.1 Representation of PQM in Relation to Intellectual Work and Literacy Aspects

Substance of the Science: PQM	Intellectual Work	Literacy Aspects: Use of Dialogue, Reading, and Writing
Phenomenon Vertex 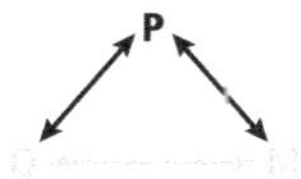 Looking for patterns, bounding the issue, observe and describe, sorting out what is relevant/irrelevant, what am I wondering about, what do I already know about this thing/what do I know that might be relevant or applicable, accessing prior or intuitive ideas, data collection	Students make sense of the phenomenon itself (common murre die-off) coming to a collective statement of a description of the problem. They also observe common murres (via video) and are exposed to scientific information about common murres—they build background knowledge. The students work on bounding the problem—sorting out what might be relevant or important and what might be less important. They begin to wonder more deeply about the phenomenon and are starting to think about what data might be useful in developing an explanation for the die-off.	R: Reading portions of a scientific article on common murre populations as a way of understanding murre ecology. W: Creating a list of observations from a video on a common murre colony. Writing a statement that describes the problem with common murres. D: Partner dialogue about observations from video and how to state the common murre problem.
Question Vertex 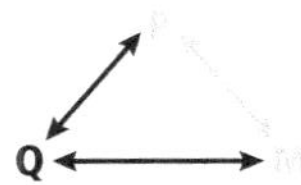 Brainstorming, formulating specific questions based on a broad wondering, harnessing curiosity, going below the surface/dig deeper (5 whys), deciding on importance of questions/tractability of them, sequence to answer them	Students consider the information they have on common murres and brainstorm ways to state a driving question for their investigation. They engage in dialogue that leads to the crafting of an agreed-upon driving question.	R: None W: Constructing questions to help in developing answers to reasons behind the common murre decline. Writing out the reasoning as to why a piece of information might help explain the phenomenon. D: Group dialogue about ideas and questions relating to the decline in the common murre population. Use paraphrase passport technique for sharing information and ideas.

(continued)

TABLE 13.1 Representation of PQM in Relation to Intellectual Work and Literacy Aspects (continued)

Substance of the Science: PQM	Intellectual Work	Literacy Aspects: Use of Dialogue, Reading, and Writing
Model Vertex 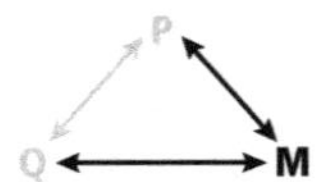 Figuring out mechanisms, connecting ideas/facts, making inferences, distinguishing facts from concepts, making deductions, interpreting data, sensemaking, running/applying/activating the model to original or new phenomenon, refining/simplifying the model, making decisions about efficacy/black-boxing	Students make sense of information from scientific articles on common murres and dialogue with classmates about their understanding. They interpret data from more than one source and connect facts with inferences and ideas about various factors that influence common murre survival. Students make decisions about what is more important and what is less important in developing an answer to the driving question. They consider abiotic and biotic factors that can influence seabird populations and they construct a food web to show energy relationships in the ecosystem under consideration. Students, with the help of the teacher, develop "model statements" (agreed on ideas, constructs, or concepts relevant to the phenomenon). They use a food web to help them in developing a scientific explanation for the large-scale die-off of common murres.	R: Jigsaw reading activity with articles on murre feeding, reproduction, and migration. Use Focused Reading Protocol to process text. Reviewing available information on food chains and building a food web that illuminates relationships and incorporates information on common murre food sources.
		W: Recording group ideas and building a representation of a food web. Writing out a "scientific" explanation that provides reasoning and the evidence for that reasoning as to why common murre populations are declining. Writing task—You are a scientist explaining to the legislature why minimizing impacts to the ocean environment is important and how the common murres are a symptom of a larger challenge.
		D: Brainstorming activity to generate explanatory ideas, then small group dialogue to build common understanding, make explanatory ideas public and connect ideas to evidence. Students use paraphrase passport as a dialogue structure to increase understanding of differing viewpoints and ideas.

to read and process the text-based information. In the jigsaw technique students individually process information that is divided among a group from various sources and share what they have learned with peers. Scientific work often rests on the transfer of large amounts of information and much of that transfer takes place through text. Reading, being a set of process skills that facilitate the accessing of knowledge, facts, data, and ideas via text, requires readers to make inferences, decide between competing ideas, construct connections, and make decisions. Effective science instruction utilizes reading structures and supports that assist students in processing textual information and make use of that information in constructing their own understanding of science. A central task when reading textual information revolves around identifying various levels of importance in the material to synthesize a coherent and congruent scientific understanding or explanation.

Robust dialogue ensued as students made decisions about the relative importance and implications of information and data. Next, they viewed a video on oceanic food webs and learned about murre food sources. Dialogue is a commonly used process to vet scientific ideas, debate the merits of evidence, share information, exchange points of view, and formulate scientific ideas and explanations. Instructors can leverage the power of dialogue by having students engage in productive dialogue through the means of structured protocols that support idea development, critical thinking, and explanation construction. In this classroom, they used the dialogue protocol *paraphrase passport*. This protocol sets up a structure in which each speaker paraphrases the speaker who immediately preceded them. This helps the group build on one another's ideas in a deliberate way. Using this protocol, the students worked together to construct a food web for common murres which they used to help them make decisions about factors that influence food source availability

Finally, they came to consensus on a mechanism and explanatory model for why the common murre population in Alaska experienced such a severe die-off. In arriving at an explanatory mechanism or model, the students explored murre biology involving breeding, reproduction, migration, and movement, as well as feeding and the dynamics in the oceanic food web of common murres. They examined nutritional value of food sources, ocean currents, and temperature data for the regions inhabited by the murres. In the end, their models revolved around changes in ocean temperatures as a cause of distributional changes in the food sources of the murres. This left the murres with less nutritious prey organisms, which lead to undernourished birds less capable of breeding or raising chicks successfully.

The final individual task for students was to take on the role of a scientist explaining to the Alaskan legislature the reasons the common murre die-off occurred and why minimizing impacts to the ocean environment is important. The task of writing in science requires the writer to not only convey information but also to defend their ideas or conclusions with evidence. This is not a trivial task. Therefore, using techniques that encourage students to reveal their thinking when writing is important in promoting good science writing. Frequently, the writing produced in science classrooms is regurgitative in nature, meaning that students are often simply repeating in writing information they have been exposed to or are copying information from another source and transposing it onto their document. Providing students with a structure for writing often increases the quality of the writing. Effective practices include giving the student a role to write from, that of a scientist in this case, and an audience to write to, as in members of the Alaskan legislature for this example. Providing these aspects bounds the writing task, gives it meaning, and provides a framework to write from.

This example illustrates how the model-based reasoning approach espouses a systematic approach to having students take in and process information and make inferences in the process of model development. It requires a mindset that allows for a degree of comfort with uncertainty and elevates student thinking in the science classroom. Indeed, the model-based reasoning approach relies on these characteristics as essential features of student learning.

CONCLUSION

In this example of how one set of lessons using the modeling approach was structured, we illustrate how teachers can create conditions in the classroom that make it possible for students to engage in robust reasoning about scientific problems. By structuring the work around the reasoning triangle with explicit attention to phenomena, questions, and model development, the unit of study is focused on the utility of knowledge building in an explanatory context. That is, the knowledge-building work is done with the express purpose of figuring out how or why something happens; it is a means to an end where both the means and the ends are important. As the lessons take students between the vertices of the triangle they engage in iterative knowledge building work based on inferential reasoning. They have the opportunity to see how they must zero in on what it is they are trying to figure out, work to harness their own and others' ideas to propose key mechanisms and patterns, and then return to see if their ideas work to answer their initial questions. These processes require that students continually assess and revise their thinking about the specific context. Once that is explained then they can turn to an even more important task: determining what it is about their ideas that might be generalizable to other phenomena. Thus, the reasoning triangle provides a template to guide a spiral of knowledge building that often moves from specific phenomena through the development of models with broad explanatory power. Providing students with opportunities to actually engage in intellectual work in the science classrooms that mirrors important aspects of science as it is practiced in the professional sphere is a powerful way to support their learning of the science content and has the potential to cultivate a scientific mindset with lasting impact.

REFLECTIVE QUESTIONS

1. In the classroom, the reasoning triangle is a pedagogical tool used to structure and support scientific thinking. In what ways might this tool be an advancement over other instructional approaches?
2. Reflecting on the writing that you have students engage in within your classroom, what might be some ways to increase the frequency of explanatory writing as a tool for learning?
3. In the context of your curriculum, what might be some useful phenomena to have students explore and work to explain? How could those phenomena inspire questions that would lead to model development?

CHAPTER 14

CULTIVATING A SCIENTIFIC MINDSET THROUGH INQUIRY-BASED SCIENCE LEARNING UTILIZING NASA RESOURCES FOR EDUCATORS

Leslie Huling and Virginia Resta

By partnering with NASA, both formal and informal educators can play a critical role in helping students learn to think critically and to cultivate the scientific mindset necessary to confront the many challenges of today and in the future.

—Leslie Huling and Virginia Resta

In the coming years, the United States will need more STEM workers than ever before. It is estimated by the President's Council of Advisors of Science and Technology (PCAST, 2012) that the United States needs to produce one million additional STEM professionals in the next decade in order to retain its historical preeminence in science and technology. The National Academies of Sciences, Engineering, and Medicine, (2017) report predicted a shortfall of nearly 3.4 million skilled technical workers by 2022. The

Age of Inference, pages 223–237

computer occupational group alone is projected to yield over 1 million job openings from 2014 to 2024 (United States Bureau of Labor Statistics, 2017).

Further, specific groups (minorities, women, special needs individuals, and those from economically disadvantaged backgrounds) have traditionally been underrepresented in STEM fields, resulting in tremendous untapped potential that is critically needed if the United States is to maintain its position as a global leader in STEM innovation (Enriquez et al., 2014; Kleist, 2015). In order to achieve these goals, it will be necessary to attract larger numbers of students from all backgrounds in STEM. Alone, these needs would be sufficient to merit increased STEM education opportunities for all students and the implementation of specific targeted efforts to promote the development of scientific mindset among students. These skills are important in developing understanding around complex ideas. Additionally, these skills are essential for living in a complex society. This holds true for professional scientists or citizens going about daily life.

DEVELOPING A SCIENTIFIC MINDSET: NOT JUST FOR SCIENTISTS

While there are many ways to conceptualize the scientific mindset, one approach is to use the analogy of the three-legged stool. In this analogy, the three legs of the scientific mindset stool include (a) a reliance on data for decision-making, (b) collaboration and communication skills, and (c) dispositions for a scientific mindset. Each of the three supports is critical to the integrity of the scientific mindset structure which collectively is comprised of both concrete, specific skills and "habits of mind" that combine intellectual curiosity and openness to evolving understandings. The absence of any one of the three supports depicted in the scientific mindset three-legged stool can destabilize the entire enterprise (see Figure 14.1).

One of the primary foundations of the scientific mindset is *a reliance on data for decision-making* (Slavin, 2007). Scientists aspire to be objective, make their decisions based upon an analysis of data, and judge the quality of data by applying a set of agreed-upon scientific principles related to study design, sample selection, and data collection procedures (Fraenkel et al., 2019; Schreiber & Asner-Self, 2011). Most often, scientists rely on multiple data sources and frequently engage in a triangulation process (McMillan, 2012) through which they consider findings from multiple data sources to verify whether the findings are generally consistent with those of other respected researchers or rather is an outlier that should be further scrutinized. Scientists typically give additional credence to research that has been peer reviewed and replicated by those who are considered to have expertise in the field of study (McMillan, 2012). This process of verifying the

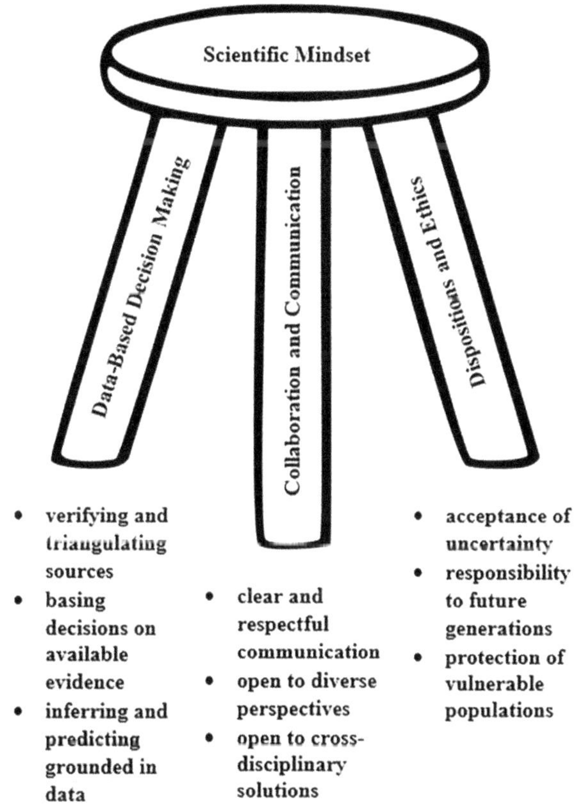

Figure 14.1 Scientific mindset three-legged stool.

reliability of sources of data is certainly necessary for scientists but is also a general good practice for all information consumers as they consider the sources from which their data emanates. In today's information-saturated society, critical thinking skills, coupled with a healthy dose of skepticism, are needed as one judges the merits of various arguments and assertions.

Other important data-based factors for the scientist include the skill set of being able to both interpret and to create data visualization tools to aid in data sensemaking procedures (Fraenkel et al., 2019). These skills are important in developing understanding around complex ideas. Additionally, these skills are essential for living in a complex society. This is true whether one is a professional scientist, or a citizen going about daily life. Finally, scientific inferences and predictions are developed by extrapolating from the available data, taking into consideration relevant factors shown to be related to the phenomena under consideration (Johnson, 2002).

Collaboration and communication skills are also integral to the scientific mindset. A commitment to healthy, informed, respectful debate is also a critical component of the scientific mindset. Clear communication skills are necessary to develop logical arguments that are supported by evidence. Multiple perspectives elevate the discussion and frequently lead to an improved outcome (Fraenkel et al., 2019), and therefore, the ability to collaborate and work together toward a common goal in spite of personal differences is crucial both in the sciences and general day-to-day living. Many problems are so complex that a multidisciplinary approach is not only desirable but is also essential in weighing the costs and benefits of various solutions on different aspects of society.

Dispositions for a scientific mindset is the third leg that supports the critical work of scientists. A natural part of the scientific process is acceptance of uncertainty (Schroeder et al., 2019), the embracing of the fact that as additional data become available conclusions and recommendations may change. This evolution of understanding, in the view of the scientist, represents progress rather than failure on the part of previous investigators. In other words, uncertainty is a natural part of the scientific process and is to be embraced rather than denied.

Another critical aspect of the dispositions for scientific mindset is ethical in nature. A strong sense of ethics is vitally important to the scientific mindset. Scientists have an ethical responsibility to be truthful in reporting findings, to protect public health, and to preserve the quality of life of future generations (Slavin, 2007). Science and humankind will be better served if educators can help students develop the practice of ethical decision-making, a commitment to global well-being, and a sense of responsibility to protect vulnerable populations.

The collective skill set that comprises the scientific mindset is essential for work in scientific disciplines, but they are equally helpful to the average citizen. Whether a teenager is trying to judge the truthfulness of an online claim, or a homemaker is deciding whether to buy organic produce, or a voter is trying to understand a drainage project included as a part of a community bond package, scientific mindset along with analysis and inferencing will be a useful approach.

This being the case, investments made as a society in preparing the next generation of scientists will also pay dividends in preparing the next generation of responsible global citizens. Given the importance of this undertaking toward collective well-being, the authors propose that it be a shared responsibility rather than relegating it solely to classroom teachers. Although teachers are the front-line providers in helping students develop a scientific mindset, there are also many other opportunities for learners to benefit from STEM engagement experiences through after-school programs, summer camps, community events, and other programming offered through public venues such as museums and libraries. Informal educators working in these settings are continuously seeking STEM-related activities that are educationally worthwhile, engaging, and enjoyable for students.

The NASA STEM Engagement and Educator Professional Development Collaborative (EPDC) is a valuable resource for both formal and informal educators providing a wealth of well-designed, inquiry-based, Next Generation Science Standards (NGSS) aligned, NASA classroom activities, free materials, and resources to support student learning targeted at cultivating a scientific mindset.

In order to illustrate examples of cultivating scientific mindsets utilizing NASA education resources, three case examples are presented: Case Example 1 with preservice teachers and their university professors, Case Example 2 with practicing teachers, and Case Example 3 with community organizations. Each case example illustrates how NASA EPDC provided professional development plus the teaching resources for educators to help guide students through investigations of real-life issues such as global climate change, engineering design challenges, rocket forces, water studies, and so forth, while simultaneously assisting students in developing their scientific mindset through inquiry-based learning. The specific links that educators can use to access these free NASA resources are included in tables below. The chapter concludes with a general discussion of the advantages of the inquiry-based instructional approach utilized in the NASA activities and ways in which these activities incorporate specific tasks that help learners develop a scientific mindset.

THREE CASE EXAMPLES UTILIZING NASA RESOURCES

In each of the following three examples, NASA instructional resources provided the bulk of the STEM content that was included in the professional development and STEM engagement events. NASA has an abundance of educational resources from which event organizers can select and combine into an event tailored to meet the needs of their participants, along with the suggested amount of time available, and the specific learning objectives being addressed. In the examples, the event organizers integrated some of their own activities combined with NASA activities to create the professional development event. The examples presented below are not intended to be prepackaged stand-alone events, rather they are offered as sample events of differing durations and for different audiences to demonstrate the flexibility and utility of NASA activities and resources in planning and delivering professional development for educators and STEM engagement events for students. For each case presented, a sample agenda or activity list is provided to supplement the description and links to available NASA resources. Following a brief description of three case examples, there is a discussion of how specific activities support the development of the STEM skills that comprise the scientific mindset.

Case 1: Professional Development for Preservice Teachers and University Faculty

NASA has made a unique professional development opportunity, Minority University Research and Education Project (MUREP) educator institutes or Minority Education Institute (MEI), available to university students enrolled in teacher preparation programs and their faculty sponsors from minority serving institutions (MSIs) across the nation. MSIs are designated by the United States Department of Education and typically serve a student population that is comprised of at least 25% of a specific underserved population. Among the types of MSI classifications are historically Black colleges and universities (HBCUs), Hispanic serving institutions (HSIs), tribal colleges and Native American serving non-tribal colleges, and various other classifications involving Asian American and Pacific Islander student populations.

MEIs were conducted during the summers of 2016, 2017, and 2018 to leverage existing resources in place through the 10 NASA Centers and the NASA EPDC. MEIs capitalized upon the existing infrastructure to ensure that the resources invested in the institutes generate the greatest benefits possible for the professional learning of preservice teachers and their faculty sponsors across the United States. A total of 36 MEIs were conducted during this 3-year period, serving 1,077 preservice teachers and 236 faculty sponsors. One of the goals of MEI was to familiarize participants with the work occurring within each of NASA's four mission directorates (science, space technology, aeronautics, and human exploration). Several activities representing each mission directorate were included in the 5-day professional development institute.

The MEI experience consisted of a 1-week onsite experience at one of the nation's 10 NASA Centers, coupled with 8 hours of online professional development prior to the Institute and 8 hours of post-Institute online professional development. MSIs eligible to attend MEI were invited to send a team of up to five participants, accompanied by a STEM education faculty member from the institution.

The 1-week institute experience was grounded in research-based principles of teacher development and provided rich inquiry-based science learning experiences upon which teachers could scaffold their content knowledge and further develop their content-specific pedagogical practices, and develop their scientific mindset. MEI learning experiences were fully integrated with tours of center facilities and opportunities for participants to interact with the center content specialists. Prior to coming to the institute, participants were introduced via webinar, to the center, the center's EPDC educational specialist who helped facilitate the on-site experience, and to various other NASA EPDC resources. The institute covered the costs of four nights of lodging, and daily breakfasts and lunches. Upon successful completion of the institute experiences and follow-up activities, student participants and their faculty sponsors earned a $500 stipend.

Table 14.1 shows a 5-day agenda from one MEI and the weblinks where many of the activities can be accessed. An explanation of how these activities contributed to the development of specific skills that comprise the scientific mindset can be found after the case studies in this chapter.

TABLE 14.1 NASA MEI Institute Sample 5-Day Agenda

Activity	Duration	Source
Day 1 Afternoon		
Welcome, Introductions, & Logistics	45 mins.	Facilitator Training Guide Developed and Arranged by Center Instructional Team
How NASA Fits Into STEM Education and What Participants Can Expect From This Institute	45 mins.	Instructional Team Developed Activity
State and National STEM Curriculum Standards	1 hr.	Instructional Team Developed Activity
Making STEM Relevant for Diverse Student Populations: Factors to Consider	45 hr.	Instructional Team Developed Activity and Resources From Facilitator Training Guide
Center Immersion Activity	45 mins.	Instructional Team Developed Activity
Day 2 Morning		
Center Immersion Activity	1.25 hrs.	Developed and Arranged by Center Instructional Team
Marsbound!	1.5 hrs.	http://marsed.asu.edu/lesson_plans/marsbound
Field Trip to the Moon	1.25 hrs.	https://www.nasa.gov/audience/foreducators/topnav/materials/listbytype/Field_Trip_to_the_Moon_Educator_Guide.html
Day 2 Afternoon		
Solar System in My Neighborhood	1.5 hr.	http://www.lpi.usra.edu/education/explore/solar_system
Center Immersion Activity Debrief, Teacher Insights, and Reflections	2 hrs.	Developed and Arranged by Center Instructional Team

(continued)

TABLE 14.1 NASA MEI Institute Sample 5-Day Agenda (continued)

Activity	Duration	Source
Day 3 Morning		
Science and Engineering Practices: "Planning & Carrying Out Investigations"	1 hr.	Instructional Team Developed Activity
Mass vs. Weight	1 hrs.	http://education.ssc.nasa.gov/massvsweight.asp
Field Trip to NASA Visitor Center	2.5 hrs.	Developed and Arranged by Center Instructional Team
Day 3 Afternoon		
Maker Mars	1.5 hrs.	http://marsed.asu.edu/lesson-plans/makermars
NASA's BEST Students Debrief, Teacher Insights, and Reflections	2 hrs.	http://www.nasa.gov/audience/foreducators/best/index.html
Day 4 Morning		
Science and Engineering Practices: "Analyzing and Interpreting Data Using Mathematics and Computational Thinking"	1 hr.	Instructional Team Developed Activity
Smart Skies	1 hr.	http://smartskies.nasa.gov/flyby/
Learning to Fly: The Wright Brothers Adventure	1 hr.	http://www.nasa.gov/audience/foreducators/topnav/materials/listbytype/Learning.to.Fly-The.Wright.Brothers.Adventure.html
Demonstration Lesson Planning	1 hr.	Developed and Arranged by Center Instructional Team
Day 4 Afternoon		
Mission Geography	1 hr.	http://missiongeography.org/
Astroventure Biology Training	1.5 hrs.	http://astroventure.arc.nasa.gov/teachers/bio_train.html
Presentation From Space Grant Consortium Debrief, Teacher Insights, and Reflections	1.5 hrs.	Developed and Arranged by Center Instructional Team
Day 5 Morning		
Center Immersion Activity	1.5 hrs.	Developed and Arranged by Center Instructional Team
Human Body in Space	2 hrs.	http://www.nasa.gov/audience/foreducators/spacelife/topics/humans/index.html

(continued)

TABLE 14.1 NASA MEI Institute Sample 5-Day Agenda (continued)

Activity	Duration	Source
Looking Ahead: The Post-Institute Experience Debrief, Teacher Insights, and Reflections	1 hr.	Facilitator Training Guide

Case 2: Professional Development for K–8 Teachers

In this example, EPDC collaborated with an urban area university to provide a 5-hour professional development event for K–8 teachers and administrators. Such an event allows additional time during the day for educators to tour or visit a related facility or to engage in collaborative planning about how to integrate and utilize the content and resources included in the event. In this particular collaboration, the university provided the facility and communicated with area school districts to advertise the event and recruit educator participants. EPDC staffed the event, provided facilitators and materials for training, and contributed NASA promotional materials that were given to participating educators.

The opening keynote at this particular university was presented by several of their nationally recognized scholars who presented their work in studying the process that children progress through in developing their identity as emerging mathematicians and scientists. This topic integrated well with EPDC's focus on culturally relevant pedagogy and its commitment to serving disadvantaged student populations that have typically been underrepresented in STEM fields. The remainder of the morning was devoted to two NASA-based hands-on inquiry activities—one related to science and engineering practices focused on the earth science content of the importance of soil and water, and a second activity using an engineering design challenge related to NASA's missions of returning to the Moon and traveling to Mars. Lunch was served as a part of the event, followed by a third activity involving a NASA-provided activity that entailed an entry, descent, and landing engineering design challenge.

Table 14.2 depicts the list of activities delivered at the various learning stations included in the Community STEM Day and weblinks where the activities can be accessed. After the case studies in this chapter, an explanation is provided illustrating how these activities contribute to the development of specific skills that comprise the scientific mindset and equip educators to promote the development of these skills in their students.

TABLE 14.2 A 5-Hour PD Event for K–8 Educators

Time	Topic	Resource Link
8:30	Registration	
9:00	Welcome and Introductions	
9:15	Opening Address: Identity Construction in Mathematics and Science	
10:00	NASA STEM Earth Science: The Importance of Soil and Water	https://www.globe.gov/web/elementary-globe
11:00	NASA Best (Beginning Engineering, Science, and Technology) Moon to Mars: Engineering Design Challenge	https://www.nasa.gov/audience/foreducators/best/activities.html
12:00	Group Discussion and Lunch	
12:30	Apollo to Orion, Small Steps to Giant Leaps, Entry, Descent, and Landing Engineering Design Challenge	https://www.nasa.gov/stem-ed-resources/on-the-moon-guide.html
1:30	Group Discussion and Close	

Case 3: STEM Engagement Through a Community-Based Organization

A Saturday Community STEM Day event was co-sponsored by the Chicago Pre-College Science and Engineering (ChiS&E) Program and the NASA STEM EPDC. In this particular collaboration, ChiS&E worked with the school district to provide the facility, to advertise the event, and recruit students, parents, and community members to attend. EPDC staffed the event, provided facilitators and materials for the learning stations, and contributed NASA promotional materials that were provided to attendees free of charge. The event, held from 9:00 a.m. to 3:00 p.m. at a local elementary school, was organized into seven hands-on learning stations, each staffed by 1–3 adult facilitators. Learning stations were set up in the school's gymnasium, library, and the sport-court area of the playground.

As students and parents checked in to the event, they were greeted by event organizers and were given a "passport" that listed all of the stations. Students could complete the activities in any order and at their own pace, allowing them to spend additional time at the station(s) in which they were most interested. Most students spent between 3–5 hours at the event.

As students completed each activity, the station facilitator stamped the passport indicating that the student had participated in that learning activity. After students had participated in each activity, they returned to the registration desk with their completed passports, and event organizers checked the passport and gave the student a clear plastic NASA backpack that had been

TABLE 14.3 NASA Community STEM Day

Activity Stations	Resource Link
Humans in Space: The Radiation Challenge With UV Beads	https://sdo.gsfc.nasa.gov/assets/docs/uv_beads_museum.pdf
Moon to Mars: Design a Stomp Rocket	https://www.jpl.nasa.gov/edu/teach/activity/stomp-rockets/
Engineering Design: Simply Circuits	https://www.nasa.gov/stem-ed-resources/paper-circuits-light-up-exploded-stars-and-constellations.html
Aerospace Engineering: Design an Aircraft	https://www.nasa.gov/glenn-edcs-spacecraft-safety
Mars Exploration: Make a Model of the Orion: Launch Abort System	https://www.popularmechanics.com/space/a11639/build-this-paper-model-of-nasas-next-spacecraft-17392321/
Rocket Science: SLS Art Activities	https://informal.jpl.nasa.gov/museum/content/space-launch-system-activity-sheets
High School Engineering Design Challenge: Return to the Moon	https://www.nasa.gov/pdf/473107main_MoonMod%20Teach.pdf

donated by EPDC. Students and their parents were also able to choose a free NASA poster and were given other NASA and space-related promotional materials such as stickers, bookmarks, and pamphlets featuring other NASA opportunities such as engineering design challenges and internships.

Table 14.3 lists the Community STEM Day learning station activities and weblinks.

The following section provides a rationale for the inquiry-based approach utilized in activities provided by NASA. In addition, specific examples are used from the activities to explain how they contribute to the development of specific skills that comprise the scientific mindset.

INQUIRY-BASED LEARNING APPROACH AND DEVELOPING SCIENTIFIC MINDSET SKILLS

Developing a scientific mindset requires a shift from instruction focusing on students' ability to recall content toward instructional approaches that provide opportunities for students to solve real-world problems and participate in tasks reflective of work engaged in by professionals in STEM fields (Friesen & Scott, 2013). The constructivist inquiry-based learning approach fits well into a learning sequence designed to cultivate and sustain the developing scientific mindset. This approach can be especially helpful in meeting diverse learning needs of students who can benefit greatly from authentic learning experiences.

Inquiry-based science challenges students' thinking by engaging them in investigating scientifically oriented questions where they learn to give priority to evidence, evaluate explanations in the light of alternative explanations, and learn to communicate and justify their decisions. Inquiry-based science adopts an investigative approach to teaching and learning where students are provided with opportunities to investigate a problem, search for possible solutions, make observations, ask questions, test out ideas, think creatively, and use their intuition. (Cairns, 2019).

In order to analyze specific NASA activities and how they contribute to skill development, it is helpful to review the three components, and their requisite skills, that collectively comprise the scientific mindset. Recall that *data-based decision-making* encompasses the reliance on data-based evidence for purposes of making decisions, inferences, and predictions, as well as skills related to the triangulation of data, judging the accuracy and validity of data sources, and the ability to interpret and create graphic representations that enhance data sensemaking. *Collaboration and communication skills* include the ability to work with others, respectful communication, acceptance of diverse viewpoints, and recognition of the value of multidisciplinary approaches to problem-solving. *Dispositions for scientific mindset* encompass the acceptances of uncertainty as a part of the scientific process, an understanding that science is advanced by both successful and unsuccessful experiments, openness to changing understandings and conclusions as new findings emerge, and the embracing of the ethical responsibilities associated with scientific work.

The majority of NASA activities are aligned with NGSS and are presented in a 5E format (engagement, exploration, explanation, extension/elaboration, evaluation) that promotes hands-on learning and engages students in critical thinking and analysis (Chen, 2018; Susilowati & Anam, 2017). Additionally, the vast majority of the activities are structured to allow students to work in groups to collaboratively problem solve and provide them with opportunities to develop group and communication skills. NASA's engineering design challenges (Case Examples 1, 2, & 3) advocate the use of the engineering design cycle (Baker & Reeve, 2019). Briefly, this cycle consists of: (a) Ask—"What are the problems and constraints?"; (b) Imagine—Brainstorm ideas and chose the best one; (c) Plan—Draw a diagram and gather needed materials; (d) Create—Follow the plan and test it out; and (e) Improve—Evaluate results and make plans to repeat Steps 1–5. For example, the activity "Moon to Mars: Design a Stomp Rocket" (Case Example 3) allows students to design a rocket, test it, make modifications, and retest it until they perfect their design.

Many of NASA's earth science activities such as "Mission Geography" (Case Example 1) and "The Importance of Soil and Water" (Case Example 2) engage students in discussions about the conservation of natural resources, climate change issues, and the responsibilities each generation has to the well-being of future generations. Many NASA activities integrate numerous skills that cut across data-based decision-making, collaboration and communication, and dispositions for the scientific mindset. For example, "Maker Mars" (Case Example 1) asks students to brainstorm the requirements that humans will need to live and work on Mars and to identify one specific issue to address. They begin by researching this issue, identifying whether their sources are primary or secondary sources, and then judging the credibility of the source using rubrics that specify criteria for credible and non-credible sources. Students then work as a group to develop a design and sketch it for presentation to their classmates. Based on feedback they get from the group, they refine their design and build the prototype using materials from the classroom such as pipe cleaners, soda can, foil, plastic cups, cardboard, and so forth. The groups then peer evaluate the projects using a rubric focused on the engineering design cycle including, prototyping the description, designing reflection, and thinking reflection.

Many of the NASA activities are single lessons from a collection of lessons focused on a central theme. For example, the "Human Body in Space" (Case Example 1) is from a learning module titled "Mission X: Train Like an Astronaut." All of the activities in this module are hands-on explorations designed to help the student understand more about how physical activity and nutrition affect the human body. Because the module relates in many ways to the International Space Station, it is, interestingly, available in 19 languages. There are 26 activities in this learning module, each of which has its own lesson plans and student materials. As one example, in the activity titled Energy of an Astronaut, students use the science processing skills of predicting, observing, comparing, gathering, and recording data while they investigate the food pyramid and the basic foods that make up a balanced diet and their daily energy needs. They examine "Nutrition Facts" labels for serving size, calories, protein, calcium, and vitamins and determine their own daily energy needs. As a culminating activity, students create a 5-day menu based on Food Pyramid recommendations and their own dietary needs.

"Field Trip to the Moon" (Case Example 1) is a similar type of learning module that consists of six different investigations focused on ecosystem, geology, habitat, engineering, navigation, and medical. The "Field Trip to the Moon" program uses an inquiry-based learning approach that fosters team building and introduces students to careers in science and engineering. The educator can select which investigations are best suited for their students and learning context, knowing that each activity will provide students with the opportunity to use their cooperative learning skills to design a self-sufficient lunar station. Working in teams, students develop critical thinking skills, problem-solving techniques, and an understanding of complex systems as they discuss solutions to the essential questions they are presented.

Both formal and informal educators can explore a wealth of other NASA educational resources grouped by topic area and by grade level at https://www.nasa.gov/stem/foreducators. For educators wishing to host an event featuring NASA resources, and depending upon the audience to be served and the length of the event, one could start with one of the agendas provided in Tables 14.1–14.3. These agendas could then be adapted either by removing or replacing certain activities with other selected activities depending upon the preferences of the service provider. All NASA educational resources are free and activities can easily be tailored for specific student groups and learning contexts. When it comes to NASA educational resources, literally "the sky is the limit."

CONCLUDING THOUGHTS

Both formal and informal educators play a critical role in helping to prepare the next generation of STEM professionals that the United States will need in the next decade in order to continue to be a global leader in the fields of science and technology. Further, these educators will be the ones to help curtail the shortfall of nearly 3.4 million skilled technical workers by 2022 as predicted by The National Academies of Sciences, Engineering, and Medicine, (2017). Achieving this goal will necessitate that educators provide rich STEM experiences that will actively engage and inspire students from all groups, especially those from groups who have traditionally been underrepresented in STEM fields (minorities, women, special needs individuals, and those from economically disadvantaged backgrounds).

By making STEM educational resources readily available to educators for use with learners in multiple settings, NASA is helping to build a diverse future STEM workforce. In addition, by providing the resources needed to engage students in authentic learning experiences, NASA is helping form more responsible citizens who are better prepared to function effectively in the 21st century, information-rich environment. The use of these readily available NASA resources can greatly reduce the amount of time that classroom teachers and informal educators typically spend researching and planning authentic STEM learning activities thus providing additional time to prepare for delivery of high-quality instruction.

By partnering with NASA, both formal and informal educators can play a critical role in helping students learn to think critically and to cultivate the scientific mindset necessary to confront the many challenges of today and in the future. By making these resources readily available, NASA has not only strengthened public understanding and appreciation of the value of STEM, they are also helping to build the future by engaging students in authentic learning experiences with NASA people, content, and facilities that extend far beyond the classroom walls.

ACKNOWLEDGMENTS

This material is based upon work supported by NASA cooperative agreement award number NNX14AQ30A. Any opinions, findings, conclusions, or recommendations expressed in this material are those of the author(s) and do not necessarily reflect the views of the National Aeronautics and Space Administration.

REFLECTIVE QUESTIONS

1. In which of the types of formal and informal learning settings (e.g., K–12 classrooms, after-school programs, summer camps, community events, or other programming offered through public venues such as museums and libraries) do you anticipate that you are most likely to use inquiry-based authentic learning activities and what challenges can be anticipated in implementing inquiry-based instruction in each type of setting?
2. What challenges can be anticipated in partnering with an outside entity and how might these challenges be mitigated?
3. In what ways can educators empower and inspire students to envision a STEM career as a viable option in their futures?
4. How might an educator respond to parent or administrator concerns about using an inquiry-based approach as opposed to a traditional direct instructional approach?

CHAPTER 15

BRIDGING THE DISCONNECT BETWEEN HOW WE DO AND TEACH SCIENCE

Cultivating a Scientific Mindset in an Era of Data-Driven Education

Jana Bouwma-Gearhart

The quote–unquote "data" I get about my teaching from my university's student evaluations are worthless.

My intuition serves me well; I can tell when my students are getting it, when they're looking at me and nodding.

Everything there is to know about teaching and learning has already been discovered.

I AM the expert about my teaching, and teaching in my discipline. Others' data is not applicable.

I can barely get my lecture together, just in time for class.

—Comments overheard in the postsecondary environment

The above are sentiments heard over years of researching postsecondary education improvement. All reflect, in one way or another, educators' suspicion of using instruction-related data to improve curriculum, instruction,

Age of Inference, pages 239–263

and programming. Policy makers, education leaders and researchers, and parents and students alike may be discouraged by what may appear to be educators dismissing this cornerstone of good teaching practice. Indeed, past research indicates that most postsecondary educators may not consider the collection of or reflection on instructional data to be their responsibility (Blaich & Wise, 2010). As well, these educators may not have access to meaningful instructional data (Blaich & Wise, 2010; Jenkins & Kerrigan, 2008), may not possess competencies to analyze it (Jenkins & Kerrigan, 2008), or may not have the time to engage in data-driven decision-making concerning teaching practice (Anderson, 2006; Julian & Ofori-Dankwa, 2006). Even those trained in the STEM disciplines (science, technology, engineering, and mathematics), assumed to possess requisite data-related abilities and commitments per their disciplinary training, have shown limited instructional data use (Bouwma-Gearhart & Hora, 2016).

If educators with strong scientific skills and persuasions struggle with this, how can we effectively and efficiently ensure these critical analytical and responsive practices among postsecondary educators in this Age of Inference? This question is quite timely. While requirements for postsecondary educators' systemic use of instructional data do not rival those applying to K–12, multiple indicators point to these accountability measures becoming ever more prevalent; these include state performance-based institutional funding models; national, regional, and disciplinary accreditation policies; and improvement consortium frameworks and requirements (Bouwma-Gearhart & Hora, 2016; Hora et al., 2017).

The push for all educators' data-driven decision-making concerning their instructional practice is well-founded. Research spanning the 20th and 21st centuries confirms positive associations between educators' systematic, data-based monitoring and modification of their teaching and enhanced student learning and achievement (McClenney et al., 2007). Inspired by these findings, policies and other interventions are increasingly prevalent across formal K–20 education, that encourage educators' systemic collection, analysis, and use of data, to document student learning outcomes and guide revisions to teaching practice (Bouwma & Collins, 2015; Coburn & Turner, 2012; Spillane, 2012). These interventions include strategies meant to challenge more typical methods educators use to make their teaching-related decisions—including intuition and anecdote—towards more rigorous assessment of how their students are faring (Mandinach, 2012).

Considering the plethora of these interventions, however, we have limited knowledge about educators' response to them. What we do know largely concerns K–12 systems (see Coburn et al., 2009, for some review). And what we know from this research is largely the degree to which K–12 educators and their organizations implement policy interventions with fidelity (Meyer & Rowan, 1977; Spillane et al., 2002). With an overall answer of "not much," this research provides little helpful information for those wanting to promote postsecondary educators' instructional data-use practices.

A growing body of practice-based research considers the realities of educators, their unique contexts, and their agency and capacity to select and adapt data-use interventions (e.g., Achinstein & Rodney, 2006; Burch, 2007; Coburn, 2004; Halverson & Halverson, 2011; Spillane et al., 2002). This is progress. From this research we have more nuanced insight about why and how instructional data-use interventions are effective and, too often, not. For instance, we now know that instruction-related data must be translated as information that educators find relevant and meaningful for their contexts in order for them to change practice in light of data (Spillane, 2012). More specifically, we know that instructional data-use interventions are filtered by educators' noticing and interpreting them in relation to other contextual affordances (Coburn & Turner, 2012; Spillane, 2012), including organizational routines and norms, educators' social networks, and their individual proclivities and information-processing tools (Halverson et al., 2007). As with other interventions targeting practitioners, we know from this research that the impact of those promoting educators' instructional data use is positively correlated with their awareness of educators' contexts (Coburn & Turner, 2012; Spillane et al., 2001).

Yet, a limited amount of research has explored the specific *design* of instructional data-use-related interventions as affordances for actual practice outcomes (Coburn & Turner, 2011). Indeed, we are in need of more rigorous explorations of educators' instructional data use in light of interventions, especially within postsecondary systems. Overall, little is known still about how postsecondary educators make teaching decisions (Bouwma-Gearhart et al., 2018), including how their decisions are informed by teaching-related data (Bouwma-Gearhart & Hora, 2016; Hora et al., 2017). Much of the scholarship in this area translates into case studies and advocacy pieces, limiting generalizability of findings (Bouwma-Gearhart & Collins, 2015). As well, we lack insight into disciplinary influence on educators' data-driven decision-making, and how this intersects with interventions' designs (Ahren et al., 2008; Bouwma-Gearhart et al., 2019). Of unique focus are factors influencing postsecondary STEM educators, a target of many current postsecondary education improvement efforts (Bouwma-Gearhart et al., 2016), including those promoting educators' instructional data use. STEM educators present an interesting case of practitioners who should know well the critical importance of decision-making based on data, and often operate from a scientific mindset, but who, like other educators, may still largely operate from inference with respect to their instructional practice.

This chapter details postsecondary STEM educators' instructional data-use practices and explores the affordances they perceive as assisting them in these, including relevant interventions. In light of findings, intervention design is explored, toward informing how to cultivate postsecondary STEM educators' scientific mindsets regarding teaching (improvement), better aligned with how they approach and view their disciplines.

STUDY FOCI AND METHODS

This chapter details findings from a field-based research study that investigated the degree to which postsecondary STEM educators may be exhibiting scientific mindsets for teaching, and what might strengthen these. Specifically,

- What are postsecondary STEM educators' instructional data-use practices to inform their instruction?
- Why do they engage in these practices—what affords them? Specifically, to what degree do interventions that explicitly promote instructional data use serve as affordances for educators' instructional data-use practices?

Semi-structured interviews were conducted with postsecondary science and engineering faculty at three public research universities in the United States and Canada. The interviews included both *instructors* actively teaching courses ($n = 59$; teaching at the 400 level and below) as well as departmental and program *administrators* ($n = 20$). Nonprobability sampling yielded a frame consisting of all potential faculty from four disciplines (biology, earth science, physics, and mechanical engineering) serving undergraduate students. Interviewees included administrators, such as departmental chair and deans, and tenure line and nontenure line instructors. Given the potential influence of targeted interventions on educators' instructional data-use practices, roughly one-half of the sample were those affiliated with some campus-based undergraduate STEM education improvement effort; the other half was not.

During interviews, faculty participants were asked about practices, norms of, and affordances for their instruction-related data use and decision-making. Given a practice-based framework to uncover educators' notions and realities, interviewees were allowed to conceptualize instructional data and data-use practices broadly (see Hora et al., 2017 for a more detailed discussion of interviewees' conceptions of these). Interviews were transcribed verbatim and analyzed via a structured approach to grounded theory (Corbin & Strauss, 2008). As the codebook emerged and was revised, at multiple time points, analysts established inter-rater reliability across at least 10% of transcripts.

FRAMEWORKS

The study assumed the premises of *perceived affordance theory* (Greeno, 1998; Norman, 1999). *Affordances* are conceptualized as contextual factors that an educator perceives as allowing them to shape/take action with respect to a situation-specific task in light of their self-perceived ability to attend to that task (Bouwma-Gearhart et al., 2019). For instance, affordances can be objects educators use to teach; an educator might perceive a computer simulation as helping them better convey knowledge about the process of cellular mitosis. Affordances can also be a compilation of physical objects and activities (e.g., a lab experiment utilizing gel electrophoresis to test the presence of a gene), or a social (e.g., a professional position) or organizational structure (e.g., a workshop on backwards design that helps educators develop course curriculum). Within a *systems-of-practice* perspective (Halverson, 2003), educators' social and organizational structures (including instructional data-use interventions) were explored as contextual affordances for educators' instructional data-use practices.

Towards informing instructional data-use-related intervention design, findings are additionally situated in a model from Halverson and Halverson (2011) that explored interventions design comprised of features that, via educators' sensemaking, allow interventions to be perceived as affordances for specific outcomes (in this case, educators' instructional data-use practices). In Figure 15.1, note the interchange of the theorists' term, *artifacts*, and this chapter's focus on *interventions*.

FINDINGS

Postsecondary STEM Educators' Instructional Data-Use Practices

Faculty indicated being engaged in diverse instructional data-use practices. Overall, 79 interviewees made 260 mentions of their instructional data-use practices, grouped into five types of data/information and 10 practices varied by the source of data, timing of data analysis, and the nature of the subsequent action (see Table 15.1 for summary, including prevalence of

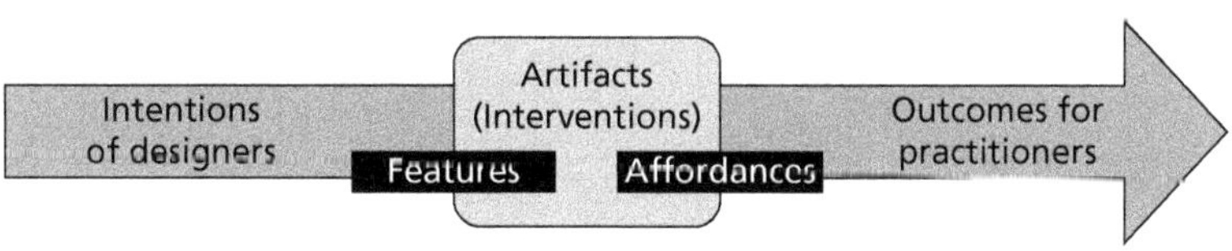

Figure 15.1 Reproduction of Halverson and Halverson's (2011) artifact analysis model.

TABLE 15.1 Instructional Data-Use Practices Linked to Five Types of Interventions

Main Data Type	Source of Data	Timing/ Purpose of Analysis	Faculty Total Practice Claims (n = 79), (Inst/Admin) (n = 59/n = 20)	Total Number Practice Instances Across Faculty (Inst/Admin)	Total Mentioned Practices Not Linked to Any Intervention (Inst/Admin)	Total Number Claims Practice–Intervention Links Across Faculty						Instructor Claims Practice–Intervention Link						Admin Claims Practice–Intervention Link					
						Total	SET	SERI	CRP	DPRev	EngP	Total	SET	SERI	CRP	DPRev	EngP	Total	SET	SERI	CRP	DPRev	EngP
Narrative, Curricular artifacts	Past syllabi, lecture notes	Post course/ Planning for class or course	40 (38/2)	40 (38/2)	35 (34/1)	5	0	0	3	0	2	4	0	0	3	0	1	1	0	0	0	0	1
Numeric, Summative assessment	Student responses via exams, quizzes, clickers	Post-class or post-course/Planning for class or course	36 (25/11)	41 (27/14)	13 (11/2)	28	1	12	6	5	4	16	1	8	4	2	1	12	0	4	2	3	3
Numeric, Evaluative	Student responses on teach/course evals	Post-course/ Planning for class or course	32 (16/16)	35 (16/19)	9 (2/7)	26	14	3	2	5	2	14	12	1	0	1	0	12	2	2	2	4	2
Verbal, Student	Conversations with Students	During course/ Planning for class	29 (15/14)	33 (15/18)	19 (13/6)	14	1	3	3	5	2	2	1	1	0	0	0	12	0	2	3	5	2
Verbal, Colleagues	Conversations with Colleagues	Ongoing/Planning for class or course	29 (19/10)	29 (20/9)	19 (13/6)	9	0	3	2	4	0	6	0	3	0	3	0	3	0	0	2	1	0
Personal Memory-based	Educators' mental constructs	During class to inform immediate practice; Post course/class planning for course	24 (23/1)	26 (23/3)	22 (22/0)	4	0	0	1	1	2	1	0	0	0	0	1	3	0	0	1	1	1

(continued)

TABLE 15.1 Instructional Data-Use Practices Linked to Five Types of Interventions (continued)

Main Data Type	Source of Data	Timing/ Purpose of Analysis	Faculty Total Practice Claims (n = 79), (Inst/Admin) (n = 59/n = 20)	Total Number Practice Instances Across Faculty (Inst/Admin)	Total Mentioned Practices Not Linked to Any Intervention (Inst/Admin)	Total Number Claims Practice–Intervention Links Across Faculty						Instructor Claims Practice–Intervention Link						Admin Claims Practice–Intervention Link					
						Total	SET	SERI	CRP	DPRev	EngP	Total	SET	SERI	CRP	DPRev	EngP	Total	SET	SERI	CRP	DPRev	EngP
Numeric, Formative assessment	Student responses via clickers, quizzes, worksheets	During class to guide immediate practice	20 (15/5)	20 (15/5)	9 (9/0)	11	1	8	2	0	0	6	0	4	2	0	0	5	1	4	0	0	0
Education Research, Data and Implications	Research articles	Ongoing/ Planning for class or course	15 (9/6)	15 (9/6)	13 (7/6)	2	1	1	0	0	0	2	1	1	0	0	0	0	0	0	0	0	0
Narrative, Notes to self	Notes on lecture notes, paper scraps, Powerpoint	Post course/ Planning for class or course	10 (8/2)	12 (8/4)	8 (8/0)	4	0	0	0	2	2	0	0	0	0	0	0	4	0	0	0	2	2
Narrative, Formal qualitative	Student survey, Focus Group Report, Peer Observ Data	Post course/ Planning for course	8 (6/2)	10 (6/4)	1 (1/0)	9	3	0	1	1	4	5	3	0	0	0	2	4	0	0	1	1	2
Totals				260 (177/84)	148 (120/28)	112	21	30	20	23	18	56	18	18	9	6	5	56	3	12	11	17	13

Note: SETs = Student Evaluations of Teaching (n = 52/79 faculty recognized); SERI = Science Reform Initiative (n = 46/79 faculty); CEP = Course Curriculum Policy (n = 44/79 faculty); DPRev = Department/Program Review (n = 35/79 faculty); EngP = Engineering Accreditation Policy (n = 27/79 faculty) practices for both instructors and administrators). Further detail and analyses concerning the nature of these data use practices, and related implications, are discussed in two other publications, (Bouwma-Gearhart & Hora, 2016; Hora et al., 2017).

Numeric Data Practices

Numeric data were utilized by interviewees across three different practices:

1. formative-data about student learning collected via assessments (e.g., clicker questions) and analyzed in-class to guide on-the-spot practice decisions;
2. summative-data about student learning collected via assessments (e.g., exams) and analyzed post-class or post-semester to guide decisions about teaching and/or course design; and
3. evaluative-data about student experiences collected via student evaluations and analyzed post-semester to guide later decisions about course design.

Verbal Data Practices

Verbal data was utilized by interviewees across two different practices, talking to

1. students or
2. colleagues about their experiences.

Both types of data were recalled intermittently when making decisions about teaching and/or course design.

Narrative Data Practices

Narrative data was utilized by interviewees across three different practices, examination of

1. curricular artifacts, concerning course structure and content, intermittently collected to guide decisions about course design;
2. notes to self on curricular artifacts, concerning success/failure of class activities, used to guide decisions about course design; and
3. qualitative information that was formally collected (e.g., via class "exit slips") about student experiences to inform decisions about teaching approach and/or class design.

Personal Memory-Based Practices

Faculty retrieved and considered their memories, most frequently pertaining to course content or student misconceptions about content, to guide decisions about teaching/course design.

Education Research

Faculty considered information from educational research articles, both research data, and accompanying narrative/implications for teaching, recalled intermittently to guide decisions about teaching/course design.

Certain data practices were more typical across the sample, such as numeric data gathered for summative assessment. Both instructors and administrators engaged in verbal data and narrative data practices as well, and practices that were arguably more formative with respect to their teaching. Some differences were noted regarding the prevalence of data use practices when comparing instructors and administrators (Table 15.1).

AFFORDANCES FOR EDUCATORS' INSTRUCTIONAL DATA-USE PRACTICES

Educators claimed that most of their instructional data-use practices (148/260, or about 57%) were often performed without link to an intervention. Most notably, common formative and qualitative data-based practices in which they engaged were seldom linked to interventions, including reflections on verbal data from students and colleagues, notes they had made to themselves about teaching, and their review of previously used curricular artifacts. A less common but relevant practice for 20% of faculty, the use of education research for class/course programming, was also almost never linked to an intervention.

Regardless, educators claimed to engage in these instructional data-use practices somewhat regularly to inform their teaching practices. In fact, educators told us they often engaged in practices of their own design, per a lack of otherwise available, meaningful instruction-related data and systems to inform their teaching (for further exploration of this, see Bouwma-Gearhart & Hora, 2016; Hora et al, 2017).

Still, faculty attributed a fair share of their instructional data-use practices to interventions promoting this. Forty-three percent of instructional data-use practices (or 112/260 mentions) were linked to five types of interventions (see Table 15.1), including:

1. a voluntary campus-wide STEM education reform initiative (on 2/3 campuses),
2. an engineering program accreditation policy (on all three campuses),
3. institutionally mandated student evaluations of teaching (on all three campuses),
4. institution- and discipline-mandated departmental/programmatic review processes (on all three campuses), and
5. various institutional curriculum policies (on all three campuses).

Faculty most often linked to interventions their quantitative and summative data use practices, especially use of post-course assessment and student evaluation data.

Instructors indicated that the STEM education reform initiative (absent on one campus) and institutionally mandated student evaluations of teaching were the interventions that most influenced their data use practices, in comparison to curricular policy, departmental or program review, or accreditation policy. On the other hand, administrators regarded departmental, program, or curriculum review as the intervention type most influential of their instructional data-use practices, and linked their practices relatively often with accreditation policy, the STEM education reform initiative, and curricular policy. Across institutions, administrators linked their data-use practices twice as often to accreditation policy than instructors. Administrators scarcely spoke of student evaluations of teaching as connected with their data use practices.

Intervention-Specific Features as Affordances

Specific intervention features were credited as affordances by faculty, most new to using instructional data as affordances. Detailed below are two cases of instructional data-use interventions, an engineering program accreditation policy (EngP) at Institution B and C, and a campus-wide STEM education reform initiative (SERI) at Institutions A and B. These are highlighted per their mention by both instructors and administrators as informing data-use practice, as well as relevance across campuses, largely due to their origin from forces outside the postsecondary institution, allowing more robust analysis in relation to intervention design.

Interventions Organize Practice Around Learning Outcomes

Regardless of the type of data-practice inspired, interviewees spoke of a critical associated framework/conceptual tool advanced by both SERI and

EngP around which to organize data-use practice, that being the concept of learning outcomes. One geologist noted about SERI:

> I've seen a tremendous amount of change... knowing that there are goals that I need to achieve, and [that] these goals can be measured in terms of achievement... Without the SERI there wouldn't have been a way for us to be very aware about it... really methodically including or using those concepts in order to teach.

Administrators and instructors in mechanical engineering reported that instructors are mandated by EngP to clarify the general learning outcomes that are suggested by EngP, and to measure their meeting of them. Overall, interviewees were complimentary of the learning outcomes mandated by EngP, and the data-use practices associated with them. An instructor stated, "We are becoming more conscious of what we are really trying to achieve. What are the attributes, what do students go out with?" Another instructor in mechanical engineering noted an appreciated change to EngP policy a few years back that equated to EngP reports being less of the "bureaucratic, bean-counting types" to those requiring examination, documentation, and response to data concerning more meaningful "12 attributes-oriented" learning outcomes via diverse data with educator oversight.

Interventions Prescribe Continuous Instructional Data Use

Interviewees spoke of SERI and EngP also prescribing continuous processes of instructional data use. One geologist noted, "From that SERI structure comes the methods of how learning has to go, and from that methods comes assessment on how that learning went, and then repeat several times." An administrator stated, "As a result of participating in the SERI, instant feedback systems were created by departments that afforded huge amounts of information, including data allowing for just-in-time teaching in response to student data." While instructors' collection of numeric data for in-the-moment analysis (in-class) was a fairly typical practice in response to SERI participation ($n = 8$), largely via instructors' use of clickers in the classroom to gather student learning data, SERI was credited as affording processes of instructional data-use practices spanning minutes to entire class periods to terms and years. An administrator in biology detailed how the initiative also encouraged formative feedback to students including via use of "clickers as a way of reinforcing learning as students go along."

Interviewees claimed EngP inspired regularly occurring inquiry cycles meant to include continuous improvement to instruction/curriculum. Administrators in mechanical engineering reported that instructors would present evidence not only of "collecting data" but also showing a continuous "feedback process" concerning their teaching practices in response to these data. An engineering instructor reported that EngP policy motivated the creation of reports that served as and indicated instructor reflection on the "discoveries" from previous EngP reviews, including how to modify courses in response to identified problems of practice, also for "the next person who teaches it."

Interventions Promote the Use of Diverse Data and Processes

Additionally, and regardless of actual data type or practice, interviewees spoke of SERI and EngP features promoting the use of diverse data, and related procedures, in their decision-making concerning instruction. One administrator in mechanical engineering reported that EngP promoted instructors to draw upon student evaluations, exams, work samples, student exit interview, and personal reflection to get a more complete read on how their program and courses were meeting the requirements. While EngP mandated course and program learning objectives and gathering of data to assess these, EngP did not mandate the means for this data. In response to EngP, educators were motivated to draw upon both quantitative and qualitative data from students about their program experiences. For instance, at Institution B, in addition to quantitative data, faculty also collected student focus group interview data. An administrator in mechanical engineering elaborated:

> Every 3 years, we run focus groups... we'd show one of the learning objectives to the students... They write down strengths of the class and weaknesses of the class. And they write them as a statement... And then we use these for the following semester for what's called a task force [for program improvement].

Student work samples were another qualitative type of data collected by engineering instructors to demonstrate EngP learning objectives. Another administrator in mechanical engineering noted that accreditation facilitated the use of verbal data, inspiring program personnel to collect student exit interview data to ascertain program impact. An instructor stated that the EngP's focus on learning outcomes allowed him to expand his instructional data-use practices to include "personal" data stored in his memory.

While types of instruction-related data and processes around its use were suggested by the SERI, faculty claimed that initiative leaders did not prescribe these. Many credited SERI personnel for providing instruction on how to gather various types of data via the use of automated response system ("clicker") technology. Yet both instructors and administrators had significant autonomy to collect and respond to data of their interest. Alongside promoting diverse instructional data types and practices, the SERI helped to remedy the constraints to collect diverse data. Beyond clickers, an administrator in physics stated that SERI-provided postdoctoral fellows to create materials to align with learning goals, helped instructors build assessment systems, and implemented these systems. One biologist indicated that the SERI supported instructors to use student survey data to design a course and a first-year course sequence.

Interventions Provide Motivators Regarding Instructional Data Use

Interviewees also spoke of EngP and SERI features that served as motivations to engage in instructional data-use practices. Individuals credited the SERI with, as one instructor put it, providing "alleviations for human capacity constraints to engage in instructional data-use practices," and these features were most credited towards helping to secure individuals' engagement with the intervention. Engagement with the SERI was voluntary at the level of individual educators. Impediments remedied by SERI included including time, expertise/experience, and physical resources to engage in instructional data use. Financial support from the initiative facilitated the supply of human capacity with expertise in instructional data use and data management. A biologist emphasized the significance of the SERI personnel afforded by the initiative (largely in postdoctoral positions) in helping to connect instructors to pertinent knowledge regarding data collection, analysis, and relevant response. Instructors both valued and respected this expertise which they sometimes claimed not to have themselves. Said one:

> They have time and abilities that instructors do not have in terms of dealing more directly with the research, the material that's out there, and bringing to our attention things that we wouldn't have known about, helping us master certain techniques that we would not have been able to do on our own.

Departments and programs were collectively motivated to participate in the instructional data-use practices encouraged by SERI per these same resources. Even individual educators who had not originally desired to be part of SERI often ended up being so. A biologist noted, "We have money from the initiative. As a consequence of that, we have basically roped a bunch of people in and they're catching the bug."

In contrast to the SERI, EngP's influence on instructional data-use practices, including continuous improvement of offerings in response to data, was compulsory in nature. The nature of the impact of EngP, as accreditation policy, could be summed up as threats to program legitimization. The impact of the EngP intervention, more than any other intervention, was rooted in anxiety, namely concern for what one administrator summed up as "a program could lose accreditation on the basis of not meeting the required outcome and that would be catastrophic."

Interventions Help Build a Climate of Support for Instructional Improvement

Lastly, regardless of actual data type or practice, interviewees spoke of SERI promoting a climate of educators working together to improve teaching and learning via instructional data-use practices. As noted above, postdoctoral experts financed by the initiative, aided faculty in both collecting and analyzing data, including surveys and verbal data regarding student satisfaction. A biologist noted the influence of one of these postdoctoral experts in motivating regular meetings to "talk about teaching practices." More than any other intervention discussed, the initiative was credited in helping instructors to communicate with other colleagues about instruction (including data to inform it). A biologist claimed that regular conversations between colleagues, fostered by the initiative, focused on:

> What did we do that worked well? What didn't work well? What could we change? So, we had that conversation separate from talking about the curriculum and what, you know, specific content, how's it going, what do we need to change?

Another biologist noted "the people from the initiative are really good" in helping to create and maintain this climate.

The SERI even promoted instructors interacting with students explicitly about issues of teaching and learning. For instance, the SERI promoted discussions between educators and instructors about the rationale for data collection. One instructor said:

> I'll tell my class that... I need the feedback from them because what that's telling me is not that there's been a failure to learn but there's been a failure to teach and that's my responsibility. I need to understand what I did wrong.

Contextual-Intervention Nexus of Affordances for Instructional Data-Use Practices

Overall, while interventions, and their features, often served as affordances for faculty members' instructional data-use practices, they were not for many of the most common data-use practices claimed across faculty, nor the ones faculty deemed most meaningful, including their use of data as more immediate formative feedback regarding their teaching. While some affordances for educators' instructional data use were attributed to interventions design, we found that the extent to which instructional data-use interventions, overall, impacted faculty instructional data-use practices turned largely on interventions' features being perceived as affordances by educators in relation to other individual/positional characteristics and organizational norms and structures. These factors were also affordances for their instructional data use irrespective of any interventions.

Commitment to Practices and Other Professionally Situated Factors per Position

Instructors' professional interests regarding the scholarship and improvement of teaching and learning, related to position type and time to promotion, were contextual affordances impacting educators' instructional data-use practices, including the impact of data-use interventions. A physicist reported, "At that point in time [when I was affiliating with the SERI] I was very interested in teaching and learning already." A biologist said, "If I wanna go up for promotion in the lecturer track... they will look at my evaluations... my goal is definitely to raise my average student evaluation score, because it will have an impact on my promotion."

Dissatisfaction With Typical Institutionalized Instructional Data Collection

Instructors' dissatisfaction with institutionalized instructional data collection, namely the ubiquitous end-of-term student evaluations of teaching, was a contextual affordance impacting instructors' other data-use practices. Institutionalized student evaluations were claimed to yield low response rates and less-than-meaningful data, partially per assumed student biases and of enough time for students to reflect on the course impacts. These dissatisfactions encouraged instructors' other instructional data-use practices, including those intervention-inspired. A biologist said, "We're doing the electronics [institutionalized student evaluations of teaching] and I never get information worth anything. So now... I can get a lot of feedback from [other sources]."

Multiple Instructional Data-Use Interventions on Campus

Instructors we interviewed claimed to collect, analyze, and respond to data in response to diverse interventions active on their campuses, such as the EngP accreditation policy, the SERI STEM education reform initiative, and departmental, programmatic or curricular review. Felt synergies from their participation in these seemed to afford reduced trepidation regarding the "burdens" implicated by the instructional data-use interventions. It seemed that participation in one intervention reduced resistance to participating in another, and the practices promoted by it. As one administrator from Institution C put it, instead of having to collect "two sets [of data] I just have to put a different title on it."

Novelty of Course or Sequence Offering

Another contextual affordance for instructional data-use practices for instructors was the need to provide data regarding a new course or course sequence offerings regarding impact on student learning.

Committee/Administrative Oversight

This was closely related to a novel course or sequence offering, as when a department head encouraged data-driven review of a new program. While discussing a teaching evaluation policy and related data-use practices, a biologist said, "This was a newly designed course... really pushed [instructors] to give me feedback of how it went for them."

The cases of SERI and EngP illustrate how intervention features intersected with contextual ones as affordances for instructional data use. Features of SERI recognized as affordances for instructional data use notably capitalized on contextual affordances that interviewees claimed largely impeded their instructional data use, including time, expertise/experience, and physical resources, as well as professional commitments and positions, and dissatisfaction with other instructional data collection routines.

Importantly, clicker use was already somewhat institutionalized where the initiative was linked to practice, highlighting the impact of institutional-supported data-gathering and analysis technological tools, and norms for their use, as contextual affordances. Similarly, while a pre-standing collegial environment was noted as a contextual affordance at one institution, the SERI initiative was credited for strengthening this contextual affordance that, in turn, became an ever-stronger influence on educators' instructional data-use practices. Still, providing alleviation from contextual constraints concerning human capacity may be the ultimate explanation for its link to the greater number of instructors' data use practices.

General limits to time and experience with instructional data-use practices, including data collection, analysis, management, relevant reflection, and practice changes were the most significant, and often intertwined, contextual affordances influencing educators' data use practices. Time constraints were a major impediment to educators collecting, analyzing, and responding to instruction-related data. The SERI intervention's features were recognized as alleviations to these instructional data-use practice constraints.

In comparison, the design aspects of EngP recognized as affordances for instructional data-use intersected with other contextual affordances for instructional data use ultimately concerned threats of accreditation loss. Given this, and that administrators linked EngP and their instructional data use twice as often as instructors, administrators may have felt the EngP policy as more intertwined with other context-related affordances for instructional data use.

DISCUSSION AND RECOMMENDATIONS

More structures that mandate postsecondary educators' collection, analysis, response, and distribution of instructional data are surely coming down the pike. The envisioned impact is well-founded. As at the K–12 level, educators' reflection in light of valid and reliable instruction-related data is a documented must for continuous improvement to practice. As a result of these realities, interventions that promote postsecondary educators' use of instructional data to improve practice are becoming more numerous. This is to be commended. Postsecondary educators, too, must come to understand teaching and learning as a science (something to be rigorously and continuously investigated) and instructional practice as improvable per its methods. One is not "born" a teacher (or not). Good practice is not made solely on experience, unquestioned without rigor.

A growing array of interventions promoting instructional data use intend to develop these understandings among postsecondary educators. Still, these interventions have largely been launched without guiding knowledge of the extent to which, how, and why postsecondary educators use instructional data. This is a missed opportunity. Like all professionals, postsecondary educators are complex, as are the contexts in which they practice. Without rigorous investigation of such, how are we to know how to best help these practitioners use instruction-related data to improve their teaching practice? What data might they find meaningful? What data, and related processes, may actually allow for meaningful improvements? Do these practitioners have the knowledge and skills to ascertain the validity and reliability of data, how to analyze instruction-related data, and how to make changes to practice in light of it? Put another way, how do we create strategy to help educators discover the right information for instruction-related problems and solutions?

And how might we do all of this given the added complexity that some postsecondary educators may not even recognize the existence of problems that instruction-related data could uncover? Or see the need to truly investigate their teaching practice, via inquiry, requiring acknowledging uncertainty and potential room-for-growth with respect to their practice? How do we help educators, including those who understand the worth of rigorous inquiry to exploring other complex phenomena (in this case faculty trained in the STEM disciplines), understand the phenomena of teaching and learning as complex as any others, demanding of evidence beyond the anecdotal and inferential? Put another way, how do we help postsecondary educators foster a scientific mindset with respect to teaching?

This chapter detailed a study of postsecondary STEM educators' instructional data-use practices, and the affordances they perceive as assisting these, including relevant interventions. Findings indicated that educators' data-use practices are at the intersection of intervention features and individual/professional- and organizational-contexts, and that certain intervention features are especially helpful to educators' instructional data use. In light of the findings shared in this paper, we now consider how to design instructional data-use interventions to better serve as affordances for educators' instructional data-use practices.

Design Instructional Data-Use Interventions With Acknowledgment of Educators' Focal Practices, Associated Timely Needs, Desires, and Commitments

Proponents of continuous improvement of postsecondary offerings may be pleased to note our finding that some educators, at research universities and in the STEM disciplines, recognize the power of data-driven decision-making regarding their practice. The postsecondary STEM faculty detailed in our study were engaged in diverse practices of instructional data use. Data-use practices differed in the type of data collected (e.g., numeric, verbal, etc.), the timing of data use (e.g., in class, after class), and the nature of subsequent decisions (e.g., immediate decision-making concerning practice, future course planning). Having lamented limitations to acquiring meaningful data to inform practice, faculty we spoke to worked to remedy these limitations, sometimes creating their own instruction-related data-driven decision-making systems (Bouwma-Gearhart & Hora, 2016; Hora et al., 2017). As we have noted elsewhere, STEM faculty, including those at research universities, show significant interest, motivation, and agency in improving instruction, curriculum, and programming (Bouwma-Gearhart, 2008; 2012a). In essence, some seem committed to and ready to implement scientific methods with respect to their teaching.

Notably, faculty engagement in instructional data-use practices was largely voluntary and performed by educators irrespective of instructional data-use interventions. In fact, most faculty claimed instructional data-use practices were usually not linked to any specific data-use intervention, even as they recognized multiple data-use interventions active on their campuses. Taken per their initiative, intentionally to meet most significant teaching practice needs, faculty interviewees' instructional data-use practices seemed to exist as what Borgmann (1987) termed *focal practices.* These actions reflect certain underlying beliefs, commitments, and strategies of postsecondary STEM educators in terms of improving their teaching practice, arguably indicative of an emerging scientific mindset regarding instruction, including:

- beliefs that instruction can be improved;
- recognition of their significant practice needs, that are not being adequately attended to;
- a tenacity to address/remedy their practice needs;
- commitment to improving practice via use of instruction-related data and data-driven decision-making;
- willingness to engage in instructional data-use practices (e.g., use of qualitative data, consultation of education research), including types not always privileged by formal instructional data-use interventions, such as institution policies;
- privileging of certain instructional data-use practices that demonstrate both summative and formative desires, including using qualitative and verbal data (from students and colleagues) to inform their more immediate and in-the-moment practice decisions; and
- ultimate intentions similar to designers of instructional-data use interventions.

Engage Postsecondary Educators as Partners in Intervention Design Around Their Realities

Diagnosis of postsecondary educators' instructional data-use practices as focal practices, and related implications regarding their beliefs and commitments, is important to proponents of improving postsecondary (STEM) education writ large, and via instructional data use, specifically. First, as we have argued elsewhere (Bouwma-Gearhart, 2012a, 2012b;

Bouwma-Gearhart et al., 2012), the realities documented here argue for a revision to the common assumptions that faculty (including STEM faculty at research universities) do not believe in, care about, or know anything about how to improve their teaching, and with respect to engaging in scientific practices to improve instructional practice specifically. Advocates for postsecondary (STEM) education improvement are well served in recognizing faculty as partners in these endeavors.

Faculty partners, and their realities, should be consulted in the creation of interventions meant to support improvements to practice via instructional data use. Researchers studying the instructional data-use practices of K–12 educators have argued similarly. The focal practices of practitioners implicate more specific and targeted designs of "systems that support intentional work" of practitioners (Halverson & Halverson, 2011, p. 15), including "how to redesign data use interventions so as to increase their impact to practice" (Coburn & Turner, 2012, p. 101). As we have argued elsewhere (Bouwma-Gearhart et al., 2019), focal practices demonstrate key, timely realities of postsecondary educators, where problems of practice intersect with their competencies and needs, indicating potential for impact on and entry into their attempts for practice improvements. Educators' focal practices concerning instructional data-use practice can serve as *meditational means* (Wertsch, 1993) in both the design and implementation phase for interventions being perceived as affordances. In this study's case, STEM faculty may be especially well-positioned, per their disciplinary training, to work with education experts on developing strategies meant to foster instructional data use to improve practice.

Design Inventions to Meet Educators' Desires for Diverse Data to Inform Their Diverse Practice Needs and Motivate Their Participation

Although most of the instructional data-use practices reported by the faculty in this study were not linked to an intervention, many were. When a link between practices and instructional data-use interventions was noted, analysis revealed that interventions often served as affordances for summative, numeric data use. Links were less likely for many of the other common data-use practices of faculty, such as the use of qualitative data or verbal data from students and colleagues, formative data use to guide in-the-moment instruction, and the use of education research.

Thus, it seems faculty may also see value and desire to engage in instructional data-use practices less likely to be a focus of interventions. Intervention designers should consider uncovering and supporting educators' needs and desires around *specific* instructional data-use practices, allowing for exploration of the relative worth of practices, including those involving data potentially to more formative for practice (e.g., data informing in-the-moment action or planning in the near future, as for the next class), richer per the experiences of key stakeholders (e.g., via conversations with students), and based on more systematic and rigorous inquiry (e.g., the products of peer-reviewed education research).

Overall, the extent to which instructional data-use interventions impacted faculty instructional data-use practices seemed to largely turn on interventions' features being perceived as affordances by educators in relation to other contextual features they were noticing. The five data-use interventions explored were seen as impactful per educators' desire for professional collaborations or pedagogical commitments via position, dissatisfaction with typical institutional data-collection systems and routines (such as student evaluations of teaching, somewhat ubiquitous across U.S. institutions of higher education) and a related need for more meaningful instructional data for promotion bids to demonstrate teaching efficacy.

Other organizational norms and structures acting as contextual affordances included synergies of multiple instructional data-use interventions, systems, and tools leading to lowered resistance concerning data-use practices, and the novelty of a course or course sequence inspiring exploration of its efficacy via data. These realities reflect additional factors for intervention designers to uncover/be made aware of and attempt to support via intervention design, all of which strengthen the possibilities of educators strengthening their scientific mindsets informing their practice. Alongside educators' focal practices of instructional data use, they also indicate potential motivators for educators' participation in interventions that intervention implementers may want to take advantage of during recruiting intervention participants.

Center Instructional Data-Use Interventions on the Important, Intertwined Concepts of Learning Outcomes and Continuous Instructional Data-Use Practices

Case analysis of two interventions, a voluntary interdisciplinary STEM education initiative (SERI) and mandatory engineering program accreditation policy (EngP) further illuminated the extent to which interventions impacted faculty practices; namely, per interventions' specific design features encouraging enhanced or specific, instructional data-use practices. These findings confirmed some of those already described previously in this chapter, such as the fact that interventions perceived as affordances featured promotion of diverse data and processes. These analyses also identified the impact of these two interventions' features, those being a prescription of continuous instructional data use and the organization of instructional data-use practices around the concept of learning outcomes. These features were intertwined as affordances.

The concept of learning outcomes provided a foundation for educators' continuous instructional data use. Educators planned curriculum and instruction around the learning goals they had for students, and created and implemented tools and processes that could assess the degree to which these goals were attained via student learning data. Given the meaningfulness of these intertwined concepts and a plethora of research indicating the importance of them with respect to effective teaching practice, designers and implementers of future interventions may want to make sure to engage educators around these intertwined concepts, as central instructional data-use practices on which to build all others. As such, they may serve as a conceptual backbone for educators' scientific mindsets regarding teaching, a backbone that centers a main focus of inquiry, students mastering learning outcomes, and a process around them that is iterative in design.

Consider Goals and Tradeoffs of Consequences for Implementation: Build Collegial Climates and Diverse Activities for Educators' Instructional Data-Use Collaborations

An additional feature of both EngP and SERI, noted by educators as affordances, ultimately concerned what Halverson and Halverson (2011) termed *consequences for implementation.* For EngP, consequences for NOT implementing mandated instructional data use were potential loss of accreditation from an international body certifying university-level engineering programs. In comparison, consequences for not engaging with the SERI were missed resources to alleviate teaching barriers (professional development activities, data experts, and data technologies) that could help improve instruction, including via instructional data.

When compared to the mandated EngP intervention, SERI also helped build a climate of commitment and support for instructional data-use practices, and teaching improvement more generally. At the K–12 level, ongoing, collegial collaboration and communication between educators about instructional data-use practices have been shown to motivate systemic data use, serving as both lever and indicator of individual and organizational learning with respect to teaching (Frank et al., 2004; Marsh, 2012). Based on the data from this study, intervention implementers should focus efforts to build collegial environments for postsecondary educators' collective work to improve teaching, and specifically those promoting instructional data-use practices as part of the scientific mindset to make the most important and effective improvements.

Even instructors potentially impacted by the accreditation policy of EngP linked the voluntary SERI initiative to their data-use practices much more often. This was the case even as EngP was recognized as promoting a framework of teaching and continuously assessing learning outcomes aligned with attributes-oriented outcomes and data types (e.g., numeric and student work data) that were valued by our educator sample. The impact of the EngP on helping to foster frameworks and methods for a scientific mindset regarding teaching should not be undervalued.

While the EngP was mostly perceived by our interviewee sample as less directly impactful on a wider array of faculty members' instructional data-use practices (largely to meet accreditation bid requirements), it still motivated important practices and commitments important to a scientific mindset for teaching and related teaching improvements. Given its affordances, and the synergies interviewees noted between interventions as affordances for their instructional data-use practices, policy interventions like EngP may have important parts to play in a system of interventions promoting postsecondary educators' instructional data use, in both motivating and helping to appropriately frame the foci of scientific investigations of teaching and learning.

CONCLUSIONS

This chapter adds to a growing body of research (largely concerning K–12) educators' instructional data use, including its relationship with contextual constraints/affordances (Coburn et al., 2009). Such research is practical, towards informing the design of interventions promoting instructional data-use practices, more aligned with the preexisting norms and needs of educators (Fullan, 2010; Slavin, 2002; Spillane et al., 2001). In light of data presented here, deliberate planning and processes seem necessary, on the part of education leaders and intervention designers, towards realizing meaningful and widespread postsecondary educator instructional data use to improve practice. Figure 15.2, from the findings within "Halverson and Halverson's Artifact Analysis Framework," summarizes potential means for deliberate and informed intervention design and implementation towards postsecondary educators' instructional data use, including considerations of contextual and educators' focal practice-based affordances.

Designers can sync with and capitalize on contextual and educators' focal practice-based affordances to strengthen the possibility of intervention features, such as practice prescriptions, suggestions for organizing practice, consequences for implementation, and conceptual and physical resources, also being perceived as affordances for instructional data use.

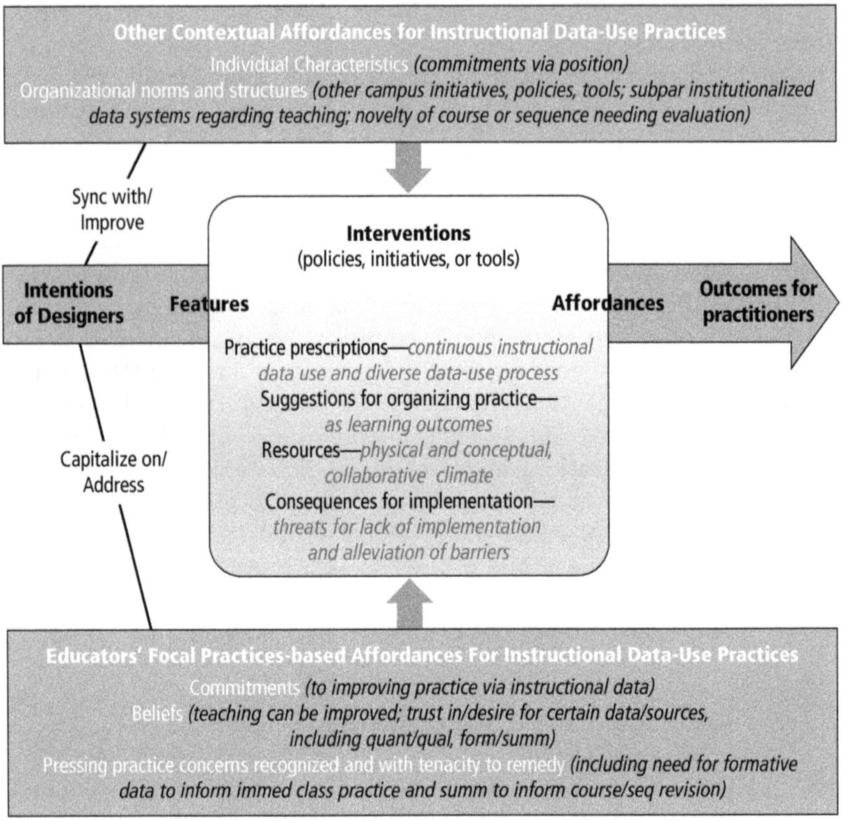

Figure 15.2 Affordances for science and engineering faculty instructional data-use practices with intervention design implications.

This is especially key at a time given "the tendency for colleges and universities to not engage faculty in continuous improvement systems regarding educational change" (Hora et al., 2017, p. 393). Policy makers and postsecondary education leaders proposing, creating, and implementing instructional data-use interventions must uncover and attend to postsecondary educators' realities (needs and interests) within their organizational and professional contexts if they wish their intervention strategies to be considered as affording educators' data-use practices.

Additionally, researchers should continue to explore postsecondary educators' focal practices and other contextual affordances that impact their instruction and activities and commitments regarding improvement. The current and privileged instructional data-use practices of postsecondary educators, specifically, can inform the design of future initiatives (across the voluntary-mandated spectrum) to be better perceived as affordances for practice improvements.

Via both acknowledging their realities and promoting that postsecondary educators, themselves, have "a seat at the table," we can better realize instructional data-use interventions as affordances for educators' scientific mindsets for teaching.

ACKNOWLEDGMENTS

This work is based on work supported, in part, by the NSF under grants #1347817 and #1224624. Any opinions, findings, conclusions, or recommendations expressed in this material are those of the authors and do not necessarily reflect the views of the NSF.

REFLECTIVE QUESTIONS

1. What data might practitioners in your organization find meaningful?
2. What data do they have the knowledge and skills to use meaningfully?
3. How do answers to these questions compare to data practices promoted or mandated by your organization, and how they may inform related improvements to practice?
4. What other contextual and practitioner-based factors may be relevant to uncover or consider in designing structures and processes promoting practitioners' data-based decision-making around their practice?

CHAPTER 16

THE SCIENTIFIC METHOD CARD GAME

Applications for Any Educational Context

Kallina M. Dunkle

I am shocked by how upset students get when they realize nature doesn't always provide an answer.

—Kallina Dunkle

Utilizing active learning greatly enhances the cultivation of a scientific mindset, as it better represents the true nature of scientific problem-solving. This is especially true for addressing and understanding uncertainty as it allows for the learner to truly experience uncertainty versus only passively learning about it during lectures. The ability to immediately obtain answers on the internet and expectations that there is typically one "right" answer means that uncertainty can be an incredibly difficult concept for students to comprehend. Furthermore, because uncertainty is a key component of inferential reasoning and a scientific mindset, activities that address uncertainty are especially beneficial to the learner. Finally, interdisciplinary

Age of Inference, pages 265–277

activities or those that can be broadly applied in multiple fields allow for the learner to gain insight into the working aspects of modern science, which requires the integration of various disciplines for problem-solving.

The Scientific Method Card Game was adapted, with permission, from a K–12 activity, "Nature vs. Science: The Hypothesis Card Game" (http://icedrill-education.org/portfolio/nature-vs-science-the-hypothesis-card-game/). The Scientific Method Card Game is a low-cost activity that employs group work, critical thinking skills, and competition to allow learners an opportunity to experience uncertainty as a "scientist" or create and observe this uncertainty as "nature" following one of its laws.

Additionally, learners investigate how scientists develop hypotheses through observation and prior knowledge. Overall, this activity helps to foster both an understanding of and comfort with uncertainty, as well as a scientific mindset and inferential reasoning. Although initially implemented in an introductory science course at a university, the game can be adapted for use at all educational levels, as well as with scientific practitioners. Specifically, it can function as an introductory activity to the scientific mindset where not knowing is the key driving factor. Students need opportunities to publicly display uncertainty to overcome the typical classroom mindset of not knowing being a liability and overall improve a class' scientific engagement (Watkins et al., 2017). Furthermore, this generic game can be used in any scientific setting and can easily incorporate discussions of interdisciplinary research.

SCIENTIFIC METHOD CARD GAME OVERVIEW

The Scientific Method Card Game, as discussed in the introduction, is a low-cost game that is easily adaptable to any educational level or science course, as well as different groups of science practitioners. The directions and materials discussed in this section will include all aspects of the game for the collegiate level, however, later sections in this chapter will discuss modification and implementation suggestions to scale the activity up or down for different educational settings.

The general setup for the game is for learners to work in groups of 3–4, with one person acting as "nature," and the remaining persons as "scientists." Nature will receive a "law" that must be followed, if possible, and the scientists make observations to test their hypotheses of the law. The law may be something simple, such as "always play a red card on a red card" or more complex, such as "always add one to the number in red and always subtract one from the number in black." The scientists and nature each receive a deck of playing cards so that a test and result can be made.

The following materials are required for the Scientific Method Card Game: (a) a handout for learners that needs to include key concepts, rules/

directions, a table for observations, and questions to analyze their learning; (b) two decks of playing cards for each group of students; (c) Nature's Law Cards; and (d) Scientist Grant Cards. The following paragraphs will describe each of these materials in detail. Note that all of these materials are or can be items printed on paper or card stock, which makes this a low-cost activity.

The handout for learners is the most important aspect of the game, especially in large classrooms where it may be difficult to provide one-on-one instruction with every group. In particular, the rules/directions need to be easy to follow. The first section of the handout needs to be the key concepts the game addresses so the learners are aware of the concepts the game is addressing. These could also be modified to read as learning outcomes or goals. Figure 16.1 includes examples of the four major concepts addressed through the game play written as bullet points, which can be used as written or modified. The second section of the handout needs to be the rules of the game or directions so the learners know how to play the game and help them avoid making errors in game play.

The example rules in Figure 16.2 include what cards are used for the game, the importance of nature not telling them the law, and details for how to play. This is particularly important for nature who has to follow the law without looking through their deck and has to respond with "no data" if there is not a card that fits the law. For example, if the law is "always add one to a card," since 10 is the largest number in nature, there would not be

Key Concepts

- A scientific hypothesis is a statement based on prior knowledge and observation. It is often stated as an "If…then" sentence. It has to be a testable statement.
- A scientific theory summarizes a hypothesis or a group of hypotheses that have been supported by repeated testing. This differs from how the word *theory* is often used in the media. It is not just a "hunch" but a way that facts are interpreted based on a large body of observable evidence (i.e., gravity or evolution)
- Whether something is a hypothesis or a theory, there is always some degree of uncertainty, as scientists cannot speak to nature to ask for verification.
- Scientists often work together on problems, and often in interdisciplinary groups, as many of our scientific problems require insights from a variety of expertise, which no one person could acquire on their own.

Figure 16.1 Examples of key concepts.

Rules

1. Each group will get two different sets of cards. Make sure you have 40 cards in total (aces count as 1).
2. If you are "NATURE," you must shuffle your deck of cards and obtain a "Nature's Law Card" from your instructor.
   a. Do **not** show the "SCIENTISTS" the card and **never** tell the "SCIENTISTS" what the "Nature's Law Card" says. This is part of the fun of the game and after all, nature cannot talk!
   b. Make sure as "NATURE" you understand the "Law" before starting.
3. Each "SCIENTIST," beginning with #1, will perform the number of tests indicated on their grant card.
   a. To perform one test, the "SCIENTIST" may look through his/her deck and play any card he/she wishes. "NATURE" should respond by playing a card that follows the pattern on the "Nature's Law Card." Nature must play the first card from the top of her/his deck that follows "Nature's Law."
      i. "NATURE" should always hold her/his cards, shuffled and face-up in her/his hand. She/he must always play the first card in the deck that fits the "Nature's Law" pattern. Those cards that do not fit the pattern should go into the bottom of the deck. "NATURE" may not create false patterns in order to confuse the "SCIENTIST" more.
      ii. If "NATURE" cannot play a card that fits the pattern, she/he should play a card face-down to indicate "NO DATA."
   b. Continue this process to perform the additional number of tests. Do not forget that "NATURE" can only respond by following the pattern on the "Nature's Law Card" and should **never** tell the "SCIENTIST" anything about the pattern.
      i. "NATURE" may re-play a card from the table if she/he runs out of cards that fit the pattern.
      ii. Play your cards in an organized fashion so a pattern is easier to see, but make sure not to mix the decks of cards:

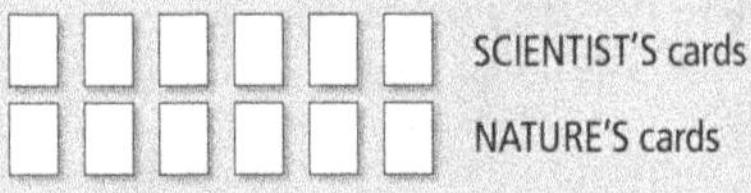

Figure 16.2 Examples of game rules.

any data if a scientist tests a number 10 card. Note that visuals of game play can be helpful, and an example is included in Figure 16.2.

The record observations section of the handout is next, with an example table in Figure 16.3. It works best if this is the only item on this page, with 15–16 rows for observations to be recorded. Additionally, make sure there is enough space in each cell for learners to record. Half-inch row height

SCIENTIST #	TEST #	SCIENTIST'S Card	NATURE'S Card	Hypotheses (SCIENTIST = yours; NATURE = guess at SCIENTIST'S

Figure 16.3 Record of observations.

generally allows for enough space and 16 rows on one page; however, this row size could be increased and the table split over two pages. Finally, the last section should include critical-thinking questions that allow the students to make connections to the real world. In my handout, this section is titled "Analysis and Conclusions."

Figure 16.4 includes a list of questions that could be used either in the handout or as follow-up discussion questions for the class. The number of questions selected is going to depend on the amount of time available for

Analysis and Conclusions

1. If you were a "SCIENTIST," did your hypothesis change as you did your own tests and/or watched the other tests? Why or why not? Conversely, if you were "NATURE," could you tell what hypotheses the "SCIENTISTS" were testing? Why or why not?
2. Is a wrong hypothesis of any value to a scientist? Explain.
3. Why does "NATURE" never tell the "SCIENTIST" whether they are correct?
4. How is the card game similar to a scientist solving a problem in real-life? Explain and give examples.
5. Why does the "SCIENTIST" have to start the game by playing cards and how does this relate to real-world problem solving?
6. In what ways is it beneficial to have multiple "SCIENTISTS" working on testing hypotheses for the same "law"?
7. Determine an example real-world problem where it would be beneficial for scientists from different disciplines to work together.
8. What would need to occur for the "SCIENTIST'S" hypotheses to become theories?

Figure 16.4 Analysis and conclusions.

the activity. The first four questions are those that I typically use on the handout for the introductory college science courses.

Each group of students will need two decks of playing cards, one for nature and one for the scientists. As listed in Figure 16.2, if using decks of regular playing cards, only aces (ones) and numbers 2 through 10 of each of the four suits (hearts, diamonds, clubs, spades) were used to avoid the complication of having jacks, queens, and kings having to be assigned different numbers. However, full decks could be used with jacks as elevens, queens as twelves, and kings as thirteens. Another option is to utilize the jacks only and count them as zeros. I would strongly recommend purchasing cards with two different colored backs so if the scientists and nature accidentally mix up their cards it is easier for them to sort back out. In place of purchasing decks of playing cards, an educator could create their own deck of 40 (or more) cards using simple text boxes and shapes in any number of readily available programs (see examples of these in Figure 16.5).

These could be printed on card stock and even laminated if they will be regularly used. In this case, cards could be printed on two different colors of card stock or stickers could be put on the backs of only one of the decks. If color printing is not available, the red-colored suits could become gray-colored suits. One benefit of creating your own is if only a handful of cards are damaged or lost, it is much cheaper to reprint a few cards than to have to purchase new decks. Another benefit is it allows for the option of having zeros, or numbers 11, 12, and so forth printed as numerals instead of using face cards, or gives the overall option of having a larger deck.

The Nature's Law Cards are all of the possible laws that each person acting as nature could receive. At a minimum, you will want to have enough for one per group, but ideally two or three per group if they are simple or if you plan to have the learners take turns being nature. These laws could be typed and printed on strips of paper or card stock, or handwritten on note cards. A list of potential laws of varying difficulties is in Figure 16.6, but any pattern that can be followed with a deck of cards could be created as a law.

Each group receives a set of Scientist Grant Cards, so that each scientist in the group receives a grant that specifies the number of tests they can

Figure 16.5 Example cards to create your own deck.

Examples of Nature's Laws

- Play a diamond on any card.
- Play a spade on any card.
- Always add one to the number in any color.
- Always add three to the number in any color.
- Always add three to the number in the opposite color.
- Always play a red card on a red card.
- Always play a black card on a black card.
- Always play an odd card.
- Always play an odd card that is less than the card the scientist plays.
- Always play a card that when added to the scientist's card will result in an odd number.
- Always subtract one from the number in any color.
- Always play a heart on even cards.
- Always play an even card on spades and diamonds.
- Always play a card that when added to the scientist's card will result in an even number.
- Always add one to the number in red and always subtract one from the number in black.
- Always play the opposite color.

Figure 16.6 Examples of nature's laws.

perform, as well as the order of testing. For example, one group may receive the following sets of grants:

- Scientist 1: Great job, your <insert name of appropriate state agency> grant will allow you to run four tests.
- Scientist 2: Congratulations, your National Science Foundation grant will allow you to run seven tests.
- Scientist 3: Good work, your internal grant will allow you to run two tests.

Overall, I would recommend creating at least a few differences in the set of grants that the groups receive. This could include variations in the numbers of tests and types of grants. For example, one group could have two state agency grants and one internal grant. The only key for these is to make sure the total number of tests for each group is similar. Finally, I printed these on card stock and put each set in an envelope so they could be used in the future, but these could be printed on paper and paper clipped together.

IMPLEMENTATION IN COLLEGIATE INTRODUCTORY COURSES

This activity was incorporated in the first week of classes in an introductory physical geology course at a large, comprehensive, public, regional university. This is a freshman-level course requirement for geoscience majors and also a university general education course option, which means the student population is a mix of majors and nonmajors from first-semester freshman to graduating seniors. In physical geology, a number of topics include uncertainty, which stresses students. This is especially true with relative dating, which involves using clues in the rock record to determine the order of events such as rock deposition, erosion, and faults.

Even simplified real-world examples do not have one exact order of events as there is always at least a couple of events where not enough evidence is available to determine which of these two happened first. This is further complicated by the difficulties of understanding the relative dating principles and in essence thinking in four dimensions. To combat this problem, I utilized the "Geo-Sleuth Murder Mystery" activity from Lesson 3 of the U.S. Geological Survey's School Yard Geology resources (available from https://d32ogoqmya1dw8.cloudfront.net/files/NAGTWorkshops/urban/activities/GeoSleuth.doc). However, students were incredibly stressed when they discovered there was not an answer to the mystery of what happened to the person lying facedown on a rug with a stain on their shirt, but rather only possible hypotheses they determined based on their observations. I should note these hypotheses ranged from someone spilling their coffee on their shirt and taking a nap on the rug because they were upset, to someone being murdered as they interrupted a robbery.

While this "geo-sleuthing" improved their understanding of relative dating principles, they seemed more upset by uncertainty than previously, which is why I implemented the Scientific Method Card Game the first week of classes. This gave students the opportunity to face uncertainty early on in the course, and provided a concrete reminder for later in the semester as they continued to deal with uncertainty in physical geology. At least anecdotally, students seemed less upset by the lack of answers later in the semester as they had already handled this challenge and were likely adopting a more scientific mindset. Additionally, as an instructor, I found myself pointing out uncertainty more regularly than in previous semesters of teaching the same course. This also seemed to encourage more questions from students in which my answer included "excellent question, but no one can fully answer that at this point as it is still an active area of research."

The implementation will vary to some extent with class size and scheduling, but the key aspect is walking the entire class through an example before splitting them into groups. I made the mistake of doing the example after getting into groups and most of the groups were not paying attention, which led to confusion, so the order is important! After a short (~5 mins) lecture and discussion of what the scientific method is, I incorporated a slide within my lecture that demonstrated the scientist playing a card to make a test, followed by nature's response. Then a second test was shown, followed by a class discussion of what their hypothesis was for this law. Three more test examples were shown, each followed by a hypothesis discussion, and one including a "no data" result to clarify that part of the game. I then had a second slide that told them to get into groups of four and send one person to collect material (handouts, two decks of cards, and an envelope with their Scientist Grant Cards for the group). With 40–50 students in the course, there were a few groups of three. In these instances, I instructed that one of the scientists would receive the two smaller grants in the envelope. Finally, this slide instructed, "Whoever is best at keeping secrets should be nature."

After all of the groups had their materials as listed above, I asked all of the nature participants to meet in the hallway. I reminded them that nature cannot talk or give any indication if the scientists hypotheses are correct, and must always follow their law. Then I randomly gave each of them their law, and told them to ask me if they had any questions about how to interpret it before they went back to their groups to begin testing. The only comments or questions I had were concerning having to "do math" for some of the laws.

As students were beginning their tests, I quickly walked around all of the groups to check that they were understanding the process, then I worked to spend some time with each group to ask how they were forming their hypotheses and if there were any surprising results. I also spent time observing groups and the process. It was interesting how incredibly frustrated the scientists were that they could never check to know if they had figured it out, which was compounded by only being allowed a certain number of tests.

I found nature generally taking their job of secret-keeping very seriously, overhearing one student commenting that I had instructed them to "take it to their grave," although that was not even close to the wording I used. As groups were starting to finish, I encouraged the class to spend some time completing the questions and reflect with their group. Once all groups were finished, we had a very short (~3 mins) conversation as a class to consider the questions. Ideally, closer to 10 mins would have been better, and in the case of this course we did continue the discussion at the start of the next class period, but that was 2 days later.

From an overall timing perspective, with class sizes of 50 or less and proper implementation, this activity can be completed within a 50–60 minute class. However, the introduction to the scientific method needs to be kept short (~5 mins) and there is no time to lecture on any other materials, which was another error I made the first time implementing this activity. Larger classes should be able to complete the game, but the discussion would have to move to the next class period. This timing was based on 13–15 tests per group, so a reduction to 8–10 tests per group would help with timing in larger classes without affecting the ability of groups to get a sense of testing their hypotheses and uncertainty. Additionally, it should be noted that playing cards with only aces (ones) and 2 through 10 were used, so if incorporating face cards for zeros or other numbers, allow for additional time for explanation.

Providing an opportunity for class discussion at the end of the class period, or beginning of the next, is a way to provide feedback to question responses without having to grade the activity, which can be cumbersome in a large class. More importantly, it helps correct any misconceptions, ensures learning goals are met and allows for perspectives that contribute especially to the interdisciplinary nature of science. In particular, questions that ask about relating to real-world problems and determining examples get a broad range of responses from multiple disciplines, and often as an instructor I can relate some aspect of an example to geology.

A useful method for being able to facilitate this type of discussion, especially for catching misconceptions, is talking to the small groups or casually looking over their written responses as you circulate during the game. It should be noted that although not all of the potential questions are explicitly listed in the activity, these can be utilized in the discussion and can further highlight uncertainty and the interdisciplinary nature of science.

Finally, this activity could easily be applied to other scientific disciplines as it broadly looks at the scientific method and encourages the learner to create hypotheses while facing uncertainty. As with introductory physical geology, this would likely fit well within the first week of classes in other disciplines. I typically spend the first class day discussing expectations, the course syllabus, and an overview of what is geology and why it is beneficial to society. Then the second class day is the scientific method with this card game. This provides an early opportunity for a discussion of uncertainty, which can lead to a better understanding of scientific thinking. Additionally, this sets the tone for my class that we will have active learning and encourages discussion, questions, and group work, which is beneficial for building a community of learners (Evans & Nicholson, 2003; Kim et al., 2014; Willems & Gonzalez-DeHass, 2012).

SUGGESTIONS FOR ADAPTING TO K–12

The Scientific Method Card Game could easily be adapted for use in K–12, as it was adapted from a K–12 activity (http://icedrill-education.org/

portfolio/nature-vs-science-the-hypothesis-card-game/). Adaptations can be made to the laws used in the game, set-up of numbers of scientists and "grant" testing guidelines, who act as nature, reflections questions, methods of implementation, and even the decks of cards. The numbers and types of adaptations will vary with grade level, with some suggestions described in the following paragraphs.

For Grades 9–12, it is possible that little to no adaptation will be needed for the game. However, there are some simple changes that could be made to reduce the complexity of the activity. One option would be to avoid more complicated laws that involve different changes by suits or colors. Another possibility would be to keep the number of questions on the handout to a minimum and spend more time discussing in small groups and as a class. Additionally, it should be noted that if using playing cards, it would be easier to avoid using face cards to represent numbers as this can add too much confusion. Finally, if it is a smaller class, it might be possible to play a round of the game together to demonstrate how it works. This would be similar to the example placed in the slides at the college level course but allow for more interaction.

For Grades 6–8, here are several simple adaptations that could be used to adapt the card game. First, the grant aspect could be removed entirely and students can work in pairs where there is only one scientist and nature. Second, it would help to do an example as a class where the teacher is nature and all of the students work together as the scientist to understand how the game works. Third, avoid the complicated laws with multiple rules or those with changes by suit or color.

For Grades 3–5, in addition to removing the grant aspect and complicated laws, and working a class example as described for Grades 6–8, students could work in groups of three, where there is one student as nature and the other two working together as a scientist team. For Grades K–2, the game could be further modified to have the whole class act as a scientific group and the teacher be nature. Additionally, you could create your own cards with shapes or colors instead of suits, and potentially only use two or three options instead of four.

SCALE IT UP: AN EXAMPLE WITH UNIVERSITY DEPARTMENT CHAIRS

The Scientific Method Card Game could also be adapted for use by practitioners, such as for in-service training or faculty meetings. As an example, the game was utilized during a pre-semester retreat for department chairs in a college of science, technology, engineering, and mathematics as an introduction to a discussion of how we can improve learning in introductory courses and overall retention. Few changes were made to the game play relative to the full version utilized in introductory collegiate courses.

The main changes were the removal of the simplest laws that only involved an addition or always playing a certain suit, encouraging groups that finished early to choose someone else to be nature and run the game again with a new law, and focusing the discussion on how and why these types of activities could be beneficial for students. Anecdotal observations indicated that not only did this allow for a robust discussion and brainstorming session, but also increased camaraderie and acted as a team-building exercise as the department chairs played the game. Unexpectedly, the department chairs did not just participate, but really got into the game and had several takeaways from it. One chair's explanation highlights these takeaways and some of the postgame play discussion:

> I found playing the scientific method card game intriguing. As long-time scientists, we may have mostly forgotten what it is like to be a student who has not done a deep dive into thinking about the scientific method. Playing this game helped me think about ways I could improve teaching the scientific method in my introductory science courses. I was particularly fascinated by the part of the game where the correct answer was never given "because nature does not reveal its answers." Of course, this is obviously true, but we tend to forget this fact. It is important to emphasize to students that science is dynamic—there are still plenty of things about nature that we do not understand, and by using the scientific method we will be able to better understand nature. Conversely, there may be things that we think we understand, but because nature does not reveal its answers, we may discover only through careful testing and observation that our current understanding of a phenomenon is not completely correct, and we need to rethink the problem and design new scientific tests to come up with an improved understanding of nature.

The dean of the college also noted, "One of the things that were very apparent was the frustration level of not knowing the answer." This is especially telling given that as practitioners we know and understand uncertainty, but can still find dealing with uncertainty a challenge. Finally, reiterating the importance of understanding what our students are going through, the dean of the college also noted, "It's always good to have individuals actually do the exercise that you are having students do, because that process allows for better implementation."

CONCLUSION

The Scientific Method Card Game is a low-cost activity that can be adapted for use at all educational levels and with practitioners. The activity provides an opportunity for the learner to experience the challenges of uncertainty, either helping develop a scientific mindset or reminding practitioners of both the difficulties and importance of teaching uncertainty. Whether utilized for a class or for practitioners, the Scientific Method Card Game is best applied as an introductory activity to begin the discussion and application, or teaching of uncertainty.

ACKNOWLEDGMENTS

The original activity from which this was adapted was produced by the Ice Drilling Program for the IDP School of Ice under NSF grant 1836328 and adapted with permission from John Chamberlain and Laura Cox (unpublished).

REFLECTIVE QUESTIONS

1. What key concepts can your learners gain from utilizing the Scientific Method Card Game in your class? How could you incorporate other activities or discussions to build on these concepts?
2. Why is understanding and accepting uncertainty a challenge for learners? What are ways you can help your learners improve their understanding and comfort with uncertainty?
3. How can the nature of interdisciplinary work in science be applied to the Scientific Method Card Game? What follow-up activities could you utilize to build on the importance of interdisciplinary work?

CHAPTER 17

TOWARD A DESIGN-CENTERED SCIENTIFIC MINDSET

Closing the Opportunity Gaps via 3D Design and Printing in STEM Teacher Education

Lingguo Bu, Harvey Henson, and Euginia Nyirenda

Thinking with a model—in our heads, on paper, out of clay, on computer displays, or innumerable other ways—is one of our basic tactics of understanding.

—Perkins, 1986

Maker technologies such as 3D design and printing provide unprecedented opportunities for STEM teacher educators to incorporate design-based STEM learning experiences in a teacher education program to transform the nature of STEM education and further empower preservice teachers as problem solvers and agents for educational change. Under the framework of design thinking and the Next Generation Science Standards (NGSS) expectation of using and developing models, this chapter reflects on the

Age of Inference, pages 279–295

authors' own making experiences in 3D design and printing as teacher educators in elementary preservice teacher education, and reports on the initial research findings using stories, evaluation data, and voices of our preservice teachers. Further, an invitation is extended to all STEM educators to consider the affordances of maker technologies in curricular development and research to close the opportunity gaps and address equity issues in STEM education under a design-centered scientific mindset.

Kayla (pseudonym) is a preservice teacher in elementary education, passionate about teaching, student engagement, and the well-being of children. Like many of her fellow preservice teachers, however, she has a narrow perspective, through no fault of her own, on mathematics and STEM in general, where rules, formulas, procedures, and facts have stood in the way of her professional growth. To break from a largely rule-bound mathematical mindset (Zazkis & Campbell, 1996), Kayla will need to relearn, unlearn, and extend her mathematical knowledge and experience toward an inquiry-rich approach to mathematics teaching and learning for schoolchildren (Ball, 1988, 1990; Ball et al., 2005). It is evidently a long journey that is full of serious challenges in terms of both mathematical content and personal feelings, considering the realities of K–12 schooling and STEM education (Banilower et al., 2013). Indeed, teacher educators frequently encounter questions from preservice teachers about the nature of STEM and STEM teaching and learning.

Preservice teachers struggle with fostering genuine sensemaking in their classrooms, and they lack the skills and tools to stimulate analysis and inference of STEM information for their students. One preservice teacher may ask, "If we do not teach rules and procedures, what do we teach in a math class, especially to students with special needs?" Another may follow, "If 'invert and multiply' for fraction division is not mathematically meaningful, why was it taught to me in the first place?"

These questions touch on the very nature of mathematics or STEM, the pedagogy of STEM education and teacher education, and eventually lead us to critique our own practices and search for innovative solutions. In recent years, 3D design and printing (or making) were strategically integrated into mathematics methods courses at Southern Illinois University Carbondale in response to the dynamic and diverse needs of teacher candidates in elementary education and in recognition of the central role of models and modeling in the current framework for STEM education. In particular, design was adopted as an approach to sensemaking, problem-solving, and creative data inference in the context of STEM teacher education.

Recently, Kayla was a participant in one of the classes. During one teaching experiment, the class built cubes with polyhedrons and explored the 11 nets that fold into a cube (Figure 17.1).

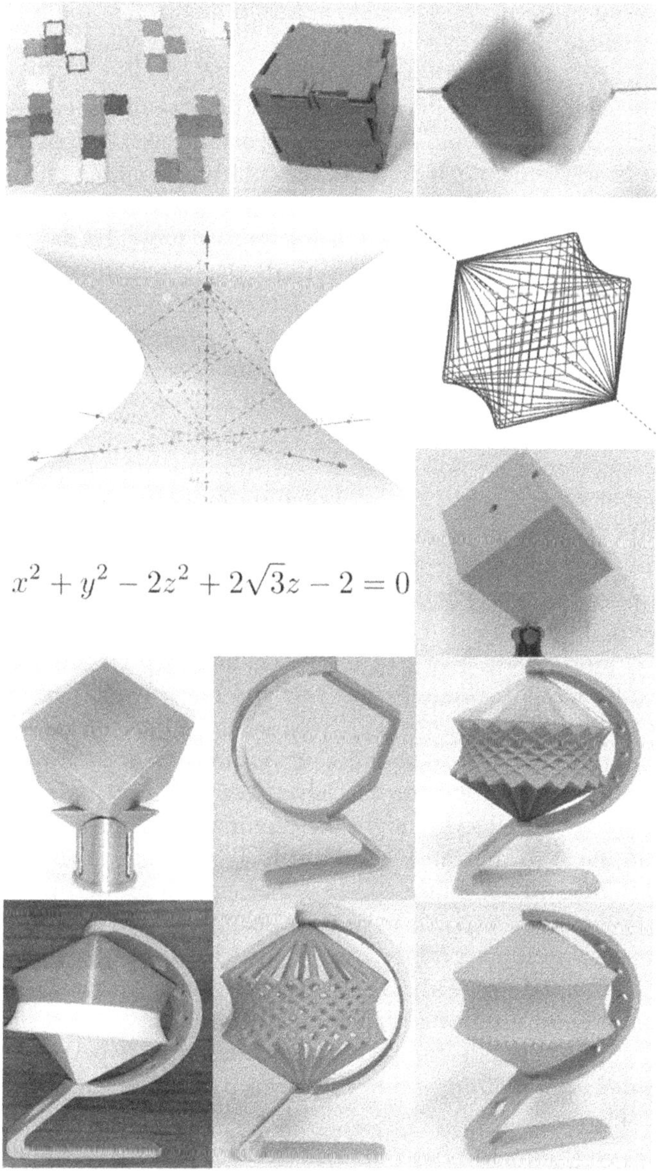

Figure 17.1 The story of cube spinning, to be read clockwise from the upper left.

Readers are invited to visit https://www.thingiverse.com/thing:4410543 for a sample cube net and 3D-printable polyhedrons. Out of spontaneous curiosity, the instructor suggested the class spin their cubes, without fully knowing the consequences. Kayla tried several times and was able to get the cube spinning smoothly on a vertex, which immediately caught the attention of the whole class. "It is such a surprisingly pretty shape! But what is it mathematically?"

The class mentioned several shapes—diamond, hourglass, cylinder, cone, circle—each suggestion captured part of the 3D surface swept out by a spinning cube. In subsequent explorations, the cube was mounted on a string for easy spinning, which further demonstrated the appeal of a spinning cube. The problem, posed in an unexpected pedagogical move, became more and more interesting. In subsequent class periods, the class mathematically simulated the spinning cube using GeoGebra 3D (http://www.geogebra.org) and further resorted to 3D design and printing for open-ended inquiries.

At first, the class designed a cube with three axes (holes through the cube), which could be mounted on a small screwdriver. Then, the class made several versions of the spinning cube to showcase the 3D solid at various resolutions. The printed cube was subsequently taken to a STEM night event at a local elementary school and caught the attention of an art teacher who asked to showcase the design in an art classroom. This is one example of using and developing models to spark real learning for teachers and students—a spinning cube found its way to an art teacher and elementary students (Bu, 2019).

There is more to the story. In the weeks after the classroom episode, further explorations were conducted into the history and mathematics of the spinning cube and unveiled the hyperboloid nature of the 3D surface and its algebraic equations. These discoveries were shared with the class in a playful demonstration. Meanwhile, several different versions of the spinning cube were created to highlight the essential elements of the problem, as shown in the visual narrative in Figure 17.1. Spinning cubes with a bearing mount and another spinning cube that can be printed in one piece were also designed in response to student imaginations. The spinning cube thus became an exemplary design story in the STEM teacher education program and resonated well with STEM faculty, teacher educators, classroom teachers, and children. Kayla became an advocate for and practitioner in design-minded STEM education and helped design a hyperboloid-shaped pencil holder personalized with her name as part of the cube spinning experiment (Figure 17.2).

Celebration of Kayla's professional growth led to the recognition of the reflexive nature of design-oriented exploration and collaboration. Without Kayla's inspiring spin, her classmates would not have paid much attention to the art and STEM richness of the spinning cube, which would not have entertained, in a STEM sense, so many preservice teachers, teacher educators, and even mathematicians. The cube spinning experiment was truly an art-rich STEM integration project, during which a host of worthwhile artifacts were created that probably had not been in existence before Kayla's class.

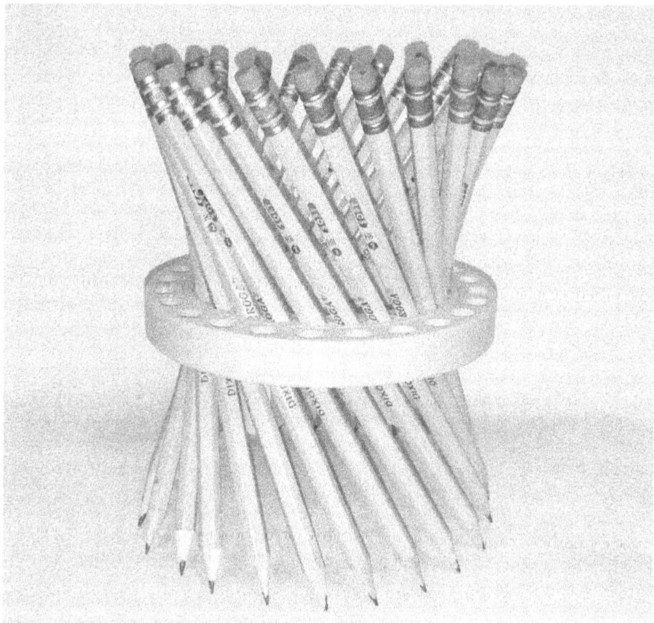

Figure 17.2 A hyperboloid pencil holder was designed after the cube-spinning episode.

The project has been replicated since Kayla's class with similar successes among elementary preservice teachers; the algebraic analysis has been implemented with secondary preservice teachers. In addition to the spinning cube, experimentation with dozens of design activities in the context of elementary STEM teacher education has emerged. The overarching goal is, on one hand, to provide preservice teachers with rich resources and pedagogical models for their future teaching, and on the other hand, to enable and support their first-hand experiences with STEM to fill the existing gaps in their expertise toward a scientific mindset with design as a central aspect.

DESIGN MINDSET IN STEM TEACHER EDUCATION

Knowledge is essentially developed through a process of designing and redesigning under the constructivist perspective on teaching and learning (Cope & Kalantzis, 2011, 2015; Perkins, 1986, 2009). The aim of design is to cultivate appreciation for the purpose, structure, models, complexity, and argumentation associated with a STEM phenomenon while developing a sense of agency in problem-solving and scientific inquiry (Agency by Design [AbD], 2015). With mathematics education, in particular, guided reinvention has been widely recognized as an empowering way of teaching and learning (Freudenthal, 1973; Gravemeijer & van Galen, 2003; Treffers, 1987; Van den Heuvel-Panhuizen, 2003), where students mathematize realistic problems horizontally and vertically, developing increasingly complex models for related mathematical inferences and insights.

Addressing the dynamic meanings of the term "design," Cope and Kalantzis (2011) argued that while design tends to speak for the structures and patterns of things around in a traditional sense, it has shifted, in the context of drastic social and cultural changes, toward "an act of conception and an agenda for construction" (p. 47). In other words, design has increasingly taken on the meaning of "a fluid and dynamic process of agency" (p. 47), leaving "space for identity, subjectivity, and situational specificity" (p. 48). Accordingly, teacher educators live in a world of designs, constantly engaged in the process of designing, and producing the redesigned to transform the world around them albeit on a small scale, only to have the existing designs reinvented iteratively in the future (AbD, 2015; Cope & Kalantzis, 2011, 2015).

This semantic shift of design toward agency further resonates well with the emerging maker movement and design thinking in STEM education (AbD, 2015; Carroll, 2015). As a theoretical framework, design thinking recognizes the central roles of human learners in problem definition and problem-solving, giving prominence to prototyping and testing in its iterative approach to STEM teaching and learning. Within design thinking, learners and teachers are constantly empathetic to each other in light of the human nature of STEM education, focusing on the process of problem-solving, while generating ideas and taking actions to address the emerging disciplinary and pedagogical issues in teaching and learning.

Retrospectively, the cube spinning teaching experiment stands as an exemplar of design thinking in the practice of teacher education. Teacher candidates desire and desperately need hands-on and meaningful mathematical explorations because of their lack of rigorous prior STEM experience. Educators must empathize and respond to their calls for action with meaningful STEM activities. Specifically, the cube spinning experiment starts with teacher candidates' open explorations, defines the tentative problems, comes up with some initial ideas, creates both abstract and concrete prototypes, tests designs, and uses the information to launch more in-depth explorations.

Along this journey, preservice teachers will witness the transformative nature of design thinking on the part of the problem, the learners, and the teachers. In a sense, the cube spinning activity has become a "model case" (Perkins, 1986) for design-oriented pedagogical re-imagination. Along with the spinning cube episode, numerous similarly generative topics (Ritchhart, 1999) exist in school mathematics and sciences that are equally worth replicating or tinkering in the search for a transformative pedagogy in STEM teacher education.

Therefore, design thinking stands as a "model of thinking" for STEM education (Li et al., 2019), although it has not been traditionally emphasized in school mathematics and science education. However, as teachers and teacher educators come to empathize with their audience and especially their inequitable STEM experiences, we come to see the transformative and agentive affordances of design-based activities. In a compelling editorial on design thinking in STEM education, Li and colleagues (2019) argued that everyone is a designer, and

> it is imperative that school curricula and instruction integrate design in students' subject content learning, not just in engineering and technology but also in other STEM subjects and beyond, and also help foster their design intuition and thinking early on. (p. 94)

Such a design mindset is equally desirable in the STEM education of K–12 preservice teachers, perhaps more urgent in light of their limited prior STEM experience and the growing demands of their future teaching positions.

In summary, a design mindset in STEM education recognizes the transformative and generative nature of design and design-based reflections and actions in the process of STEM teaching and learning and uses design as a model for content articulation, pedagogical planning, student engagement, and knowledge and identity development. While design goes far beyond 3D design and printing in STEM teacher education, the focus here is on the increasing presence of 3D design and printing in K–12 schools and teacher education programs. Insight into STEM teacher candidates' enriched experiences is needed as they unlearn, relearn, and deepen their understanding of mathematics and science for the purpose of teaching schoolchildren.

DESIGN THINKING IN ACTION FOR TEACHER EDUCATION

Maker technologies, such as 3D design and printing, have matured and become affordable for educators. This presents enticing opportunities for STEM teacher educators and K–12 teachers to explore the design space for its pedagogical values and to advance implementation of design-based educational experiences for their respective audiences. A growing number of schools and local libraries have invested in 3D printers (AbD, 2015; Ali & Khine, 2020; Ysoft, 2016). Meanwhile, 3D design software environments, such as TinkerCAD®, Fusion 360®, BlocksCAD®, and OpenSCAD®, have become openly accessible to STEM educators at all levels. These technologies are finding their way into K–12 classrooms and households, inviting educators to reflect on traditional models of education and to craft innovative approaches to STEM teaching and learning.

In light of the growing popularity of 3D design and printing in education, integration of 3D design and printing into the STEM methods courses has occurred in teacher education program in recent years (Bu, 2019; Maloy et al., 2017; Novak & Wisdom, 2018, 2020; Sullivan & McCartney, 2017). Moreover, STEM design labs have been widely established for design-based modeling, pedagogical explorations, and STEM outreach in local school districts and learning communities (AbD, 2015; Ali & Khine, 2020; Bu, 2017, 2019). Integration and scaled-up 3D design and printing activities have promoted research and pedagogical collaboration with both in-service teachers and preservice teacher candidates. Because of the generative nature of maker technologies, there are indeed diverse paradigms to tap into 3D design and printing in STEM teacher education.

First, teachers at all levels could print and use ready-made designs to support their curricular experimentation. Second, teachers, along with teacher educators, could design completely new models or tinker with existing ones to suit the specific needs of their curricula and students. Third, STEM educators could engage their students in reimagining innovative pathways of STEM teaching and learning, using design as a model of thinking and making, toward design-based STEM education. In collaborations with preservice STEM teachers, teacher educators are discovering new ways of engagement in helping teacher candidates blend multiple modes of design integration in response to their diverse needs, preferences, and attitudes (Ali & Khine, 2020; Bu, 2019; Novak & Wisdom, 2018).

In particular, the essential principles and processes of design thinking (Carroll, 2015) can be implemented in the context of elementary STEM teacher education—empathizing, defining, ideating, prototyping, and testing. In *empathizing* with preservice teachers, and through close interactions and observations, it becomes obvious that the vast majority of them are passionate about working with young children in spite of their strong procedural view of and experience with mathematics and science. They believe in the use of concrete hands-on and visual activities, although the actual effectiveness of these manipulatives is largely a matter of pedagogical decision-making (Ball, 1990; Willingham, 2017). However, hands-on modeling meets the social and emotional needs of preservice teachers as they develop their own identities as STEM educators.

In the long run, such concrete experiences may provide the cognitive foundations for their understanding and teaching of mathematics and science. This stands as an equity issue because most preservice teachers did not experience mathematics or science content in the depths and breadths laid out in the new professional standards (Banilower et al., 2013). Therefore, preservice teachers may benefit from rich and hands-on opportunities to explore 3D design and printing under a collaborative mindset. Indeed, in the context of design technologies and model-based STEM engagement, teacher educators can seize on preservice teachers' inquisitiveness and inspire them to start with their own ideas to create new designs, develop innovative teaching strategies, and accordingly increase their content competencies.

With an empathetic understanding of the STEM learning needs of preservice teachers, it makes sense to further *define* this collaborative exploration as an effort to foster design-based learning and teaching in the community of teacher educators and preservice teachers. As a community, they seek to co-create and recreate a growing library of design-based STEM models that are flexible and responsive to K–12 STEM education. The designs should be flexible in that they are not tied to any specific topic but are rather open in terms of curricular integration. The NGSS promotes this curricular integration through its alignment with the Common Core State Standards (CCSS) for mathematics and English language arts (NGSS Lead States, 2013). The designs should be responsive and generative, and the source codes and processes can be readily customized or extended in response to preservice teachers' suggestions and their specific needs.

Regarding the specific designs during *ideation*, initial focus can be on some classic models (e.g., tangrams and base-10 blocks at https://www.thingiverse.com/thing:2599132 or 3083201) and their immediate reimaginations (e.g., customized tangrams and hard-to-find base-7 or base-6 blocks at https://www.thingiverse.com/thing:3083238 or 3959422). Later on, the design space can be extended to a wide variety of puzzles, mathematical and mechanical toys, arts, and even utility tools. The design space can grow to cover a host of K–12 STEM, art, and literacy ideas and continue to be energized by the curiosity and creativity of children, preservice teachers, and teacher educators.

Prototyping is a characteristic dimension of design thinking. 3D design and printing technologies enable educators to make prototypes of STEM models, including those created by preservice teachers, in a timely manner, to satisfy their teaching, learning, and emotional needs. While most models take a few hours to prototype, printing scaled-down models can occur in a single class period. As ideas are transformed into tangible and playful models for critique and further iterative design, preservice teachers can experience the transformative power of STEM learning to develop a kind of ownership, responsibility, and mindset for the STEM education of children (Allen, 2010). Whenever possible, preservice teachers are permitted to keep the prototypes, including the imperfect and failed ones. Interestingly, a former preservice teacher visited our design lab long after her methods class and asked for a flexible cube. She noticed one with some printing flaws. A promise was offered to make a better model in the coming days, but she insisted on keeping the imperfect cube because the one with flaws felt more real. Indeed, a prototype does not need to be perfect but it must be meaningful, personal (individually or collectively), and engaging.

Finally, *testing* is the phase of design thinking when reality, reflection, and evaluation converge before the launch of yet another round of design thinking. As far as 3D design and printing are concerned, testing is a process of integrated STEM learning. First of all, did the model print well on the printer? If so, does the printed model function as expected? Frequently, problems and issues of printing and design manifest themselves. For example, to print a spinner, there needs to be an appropriate amount of space left between the parts. But how much is too much or too little? Further, assuming the model prints well, does it work in accordance with our pedagogical anticipations?

In most cases, designers go back to the drawing board to start another round of design and making. Since the source codes and the prototypes are readily available, testing allows the designer to showcase the iterative nature of STEM learning, which is full of trouble-shooting, frustration, and exciting discoveries. In the cube-spinning project, for example, the iterations of design and redesign produced more than a dozen different versions, each with its limitations and affordances (Figure 17.1). For teacher educators, finding the perfect design is not necessarily the goal; instead, appreciating the complexity of numerous design problems and, most importantly, the creativity and diverse preferences of our preservice teachers is more beneficial and satisfying.

UNDERSTANDING PRESERVICE TEACHERS' EXPERIENCES WITH 3D DESIGN AND PRINTING

Preservice teachers are generally positive about integrating 3D design technologies in their STEM methods classes where they explore and experiment with the pedagogical promises of design and making for their K–12 classrooms. In preparation for systematic integration, a pilot study was conducted with a group of 23 preservice teachers enrolled in a mathematics methods course in order to hear their voices and make sense of their experiences with design and making in elementary teacher education. The study was carried out during the second half of the fall semester. Based on prior 3D designs, a diverse collection of over 50 models related to elementary mathematics, ranging from fraction circles, 2D and 3D geometric puzzles, to probability games were printed in advance. More models were added along the progress of the study with input from preservice teachers.

In the beginning of the study, each preservice teacher took one 3D design of their choice and kept it for that week of the class. They were informed of the purpose of the study and were encouraged to share the design with their friends or roommates. When the class met the following week, the preservice teachers were each given an evaluation sheet, which was anonymous and completely voluntary, and asked to rate their design in multiple dimensions on a 10-point Likert scale and to provide optional comments or suggestions (Table 17.1).

The evaluation, they traded their models with other classmates or picked up a new model from the class collection. It was explained to the preservice teachers that they would not be responsible for any lost or damaged models since new ones could be easily replaced. However, they were explicitly asked to play with their models as a teacher and a STEM learner.

The study continued until the week before the final exam as new designs were gradually added to the pool of choices. During the final exam week, the preservice teachers were informed that they could keep their models if they wanted, and they could access any of the designs for their clinical experiences or future teaching. By the end of the semester, the class interacted with more than 80 designs, all of which are openly accessible at www.thingiverse.com/lgbu/designs and other online portals.

Meanwhile, 127 evaluation sheets were collected. Because of the nature of the study, one individual student could have submitted multiple evaluation sheets addressing different 3D designs, and the same design could have been reviewed by multiple participants. However, each evaluation sheet represented the relationship between a unique pair of a design and a participant. Together, these evaluation data provided insight into the

TABLE 17.1 The 3D Design Evaluation Form

Brief Description or Drawing of Design Reviewed											
Items	**Rating (Please Circle a Number (1 = Lowest—10 = Highest)**										**Notes**
Mathematical Content	1	2	3	4	5	6	7	8	9	10	
Pedagogical Value (Supporting Teaching)	1	2	3	4	5	6	7	8	9	10	
Artistic Value	1	2	3	4	5	6	7	8	9	10	
Playfulness	1	2	3	4	5	6	7	8	9	10	
Value for Teaching Math Literacy	1	2	3	4	5	6	7	8	9	10	
Teacher Friendliness	1	2	3	4	5	6	7	8	9	10	
Child Friendliness	1	2	3	4	5	6	7	8	9	10	
STEM Integration	1	2	3	4	5	6	7	8	9	10	
Value for Parental Involvement	1	2	3	4	5	6	7	8	9	10	
I Wanted to Keep One	1	2	3	4	5	6	7	8	9	10	
Overall Value	1	2	3	4	5	6	7	8	9	10	
Comments/Suggestions (Please Use the Reverse Side If More Space is Needed)											

experiences of preservice teachers with a new kind of design-based STEM engagement. It is worth noting that the library of 3D designs has grown substantially since this experiment.

The evaluation questionnaire consists of 10 primary items in the context of design-based STEM education, grounded in literature and current professional standards (AbD, 2015; Martinez & Stager, 2013), including mathematics content, pedagogical value, artistic value, playfulness, literacy, teacher-friendliness, child-friendliness, STEM integration, parental involvement, and personal attachment (Table 17.2). Across the 10 items, the mean ranges from 7.91 to 9.21 on a scale of 1 to 10, with the standard deviation ranging from 1.43 to 2.85 (as shown in Table 17.2), representing a high range of ratings across the evaluation questions. An additional item asks about the overall value of a 3D design under review. It has a mean score of 9.01 out of 10, indicating that the preservice teachers had an overall positive feeling toward the designs and their potential values in the context of STEM education.

Since all the 10 evaluation items had a high mean, the interconnections among the items are interesting: Are there any major dimensions (or clusters) in the data? There are certain limitations due to the small sample size

TABLE 17.2 Descriptive Statistics and Exploratory Factor Analysis for Preservice Teacher's Experience with 3D Designs and Making

				Loadings			
Evaluation Items	***M***	***SD***	***n***	**Factor 1**	**Factor 2**	**Factor 3**	**Factor 4**
Content	8.66	1.68	127	.002	.330	.700	.454
Pedagogical Value	8.61	1.80	127	.215	.227	.817	.261
Artistic Value	8.95	1.76	127	.517	.611	.163	.202
Playfulness	8.76	2.12	127	.735	.495	–.004	.241
Mathematical Literacy	8.48	1.83	126	.329	.135	.849	–.063
Teacher Friendliness	9.13	1.75	127	.134	.838	.381	.133
Child Friendliness	9.21	1.54	127	.300	.841	.164	.154
STEM Integration	8.62	1.99	125	.380	.243	.233	.811
Parental Involvement	8.63	1.93	127	.794	.136	.335	.119
Keep One	7.91	2.85	127	.843	.210	.218	.154
Overall Value[a]	9.01	1.43	126				
Eigenvalue				2.555	2.328	2.291	1.114
% of variance				25.551	23.278	22.910	11.138

Note: Each item is rated on a Likert scale of 1 to 10. Extraction Method is principal component analysis. Rotation method is varimax with Kaiser normalization. Rotation converged in 8 iterations.

[a] Overall value is not considered in factor analysis.

($n = 23$). However, because of the unique method of data collection, there are 127 unique responses in terms of design-participant pairs. Exploratory factor analysis with varimax rotation was applied to make sense of the data within the boundaries of this case study. As shown in Table 17.2, there is indeed strong evidence of clustering among the 10 evaluation questions.

Four factors contribute approximately 26%, 23%, 23%, and 11%, respectively, to the total variance in the data. There is a moderate overlap between Factor 1 and Factor 2, as illustrated by the shaded coefficients. Upon thematic examination, Factor 1 is strongly related to the cluster of artistic value, playfulness, parental involvement, and personal attachment ("I wanted to keep one"), which is tentatively labeled as "Attractiveness." Factor 2 correlates with artistic value, teacher- and child-friendliness, and is thus labeled as "Friendliness."

Factor 3 correlates with content, pedagogical value, and mathematical literacy, which are important curricular issues. Accordingly, Factor 3 is tentatively labeled as "Curricular Values." Finally, Factor 4 is strongly connected to the idea of STEM integration, referring to the potential uses of a 3D design in tackling multiple STEM ideas. Naturally, Factor 4 is labeled as "STEM Integration." These four factors account for 83% of the total variance. There are certainly other ways to make sense of the data for different clusters and purposes. However, for the purpose of this pilot study, these four factors provide a meaningful set of lenses to make sense of the nature of the educational practices of using 3D design and making in support of STEM teacher education as shown in Figure 17.3.

In summary, to an elementary preservice teacher, the 3D designs, in the context of STEM education, are playful and appealing not only to themselves but also to children and parents. They also hold pedagogical potentials to address a variety of content and literacy strands in STEM teaching and learning.

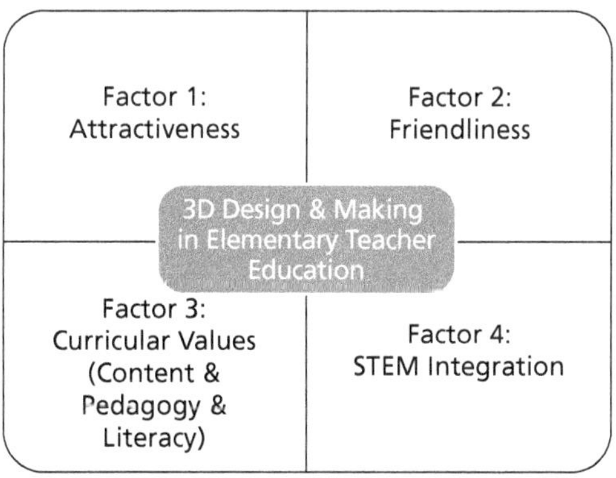

Figure 17.3 There are four principal factors underlying preservice teachers' experience with 3D design.

These findings are not surprising in terms of teacher educators' empathetic observations of preservice teachers, who are striving to fill the gaps in their prior knowledge base and experience, especially regarding the very nature of STEM learning as inquiry, problem-solving, and identity development.

IN THE WORDS OF PRESERVICE TEACHERS

The preservice teacher participants also left more than 70 comments totaling 1137 words. To complement our analysis of the numeric evaluation data, the comments were examined for evidence of recurring ideas. A Wordart® visual captures the primary themes of preservice teachers' thoughts, resonating well with the four factors discussed above (Figure 17.4): The

Figure 17.4 A Wordart® visual illustrates the major themes of preservice teachers' comments (generated at www.wordart.com; word sizes are related to their frequencies).

responses indicated the designs were playful, toy-like, fun, and cool to feel and manipulate, which also prompted them to think about STEM teaching to children and parents. For example, one preservice teacher wrote, "[The design] takes engineering, a great way to connect art and math, everyone loved it, a good project for parents and children to collaborate, loved it. Please make more!!!"

Another teacher said, "I really feel like this is a good hands-on way to discuss Pascal's Triangle patterns (https://www.thingiverse.com/thing:3066732). The students will be able to see the pattern and make the pattern, which will really help the idea stick." A third teacher, apparently referring to the abacus model, mentioned that "[the instructor] had a lecture over an abacus, and I was blown away by the practicality, playfulness, and visual representation. I love this toy! The way it represents the mathematical concepts and teaches how to deconstruct numbers was phenomenal." Similar comments included "I played with this obsessively"; "Love that it's fractions, colorful, 21-year-old roommate entertained"; "I liked how this design is a great visualization of a sometimes difficult concept for young minds to grasp"; "It was really entertaining and I didn't put it down. My favorite one, love this toy! I liked this, didn't know if all pieces were supposed to fit inside, but it was playful and promoted thinking"; and "This toy was fun to play with and is a good way to teach students how shapes change."

In short, responses of the preservice teachers in the mathematics methods class were overwhelmingly positive. The preservice teachers approached a variety of STEM ideas in a manner that resonated with reform-based practices such as exploration, playful inquiry, problem-solving, communication, sensemaking, and making connections. Incorporating the feedback from these preservice teachers and scaling up our design-to-teach project, the design lab has created more than 200 3D designs, with on-site source codes, to meet the growing needs of our elementary preservice teachers. These designs cover a wide spectrum of K–12 STEM topics and can be quickly prototyped or re-prototyped for on-campus instruction and off-campus STEM outreach. More than 3,000 artifacts (3D printed models) have been distributed to preservice teachers, in-service teachers, parents and guardians, and other members in the community at various STEM events.

CONCLUDING REMARKS

The STEM education of elementary preservice teachers is at a crossroads today. While the new curricular and assessment standards are in place to deliver meaningful and rigorous STEM and literacy experiences to K–12 students, the majority of elementary preservice teachers enroll in a teacher education program (TEP) without the same level of STEM knowledge or mindset as conceptualized in the new standards. However, they will be expected to teach STEM, model problem-solving, and set up high expectations for young children, according to the new standards (Council of Chief State School Officers [CCSSO], 2010; National Council of Teachers of Mathematics [NCTM], 2000; NGSS Lead States, 2013). This is truly a dilemma in teacher education, because, without substantial intervention, teachers tend to teach in the way they were taught (Ball, 1988, 1990; Wilson et al., 2005). On the one hand, teaching is a highly complex endeavor, involving multiple levels of social and cognitive processes; on the other hand, a great many preservice teachers are less experienced in STEM areas, holding a persistent rule-based and decontextualized view of STEM.

There exist wide achievement gaps among elementary preservice teachers in terms of STEM sensemaking and problem-solving. Upon close examination, however, the achievement gaps are indeed opportunity gaps—too many preservice teachers have not experienced STEM as genuine sensemaking, problem-solving or inquiry, productive struggle, a tool of communication, a form of art, or a source of intellectual pleasure. Recent maker technologies provide a unique modeling environment, with meaningful cognitive tools, for teacher educators to reconsider STEM teacher education from the mindset of design thinking and making.

Maker technologies and maker-based activities in K–12 STEM education hold exciting promises for STEM teachers and students to recognize and further appreciate the design nature of the products and processes in the real world, including various instructional models (AbD, 2015; Ali & Khine, 2020). With the cognitive tools and a scientific mindset, educators, along with their students, can shape and reshape their STEM experiences as they seek to build, tinker, or redesign a variety of models and artifacts, realizing their potentials as problem solvers, sense makers, and model makers in a community of shared practices of design and making (Lee & Hannafin, 2016). In STEM teacher education, maker-based activities hold promise in filling the experience gaps and addressing equity issues in STEM education. As preservice teachers build their sense of personal agency, ownership, efficacy, and community, they will no doubt redesign rich STEM learning experiences for schoolchildren.

As STEM teacher educators apply the primary principles of design thinking onto their own practices in teacher education, there are opportunities to ignite the passion and empower the capacity of preservice teachers as they reshape their STEM experiences and mindsets. While engaging in making and remaking a variety of STEM instructional models, teacher educators can not only fill a gap in their own STEM educational experiences but also cultivate a mindset for design-based or maker-centered STEM teacher education. With genuine support of preservice teachers and the STEM education community, the authors have co-designed more than 200

3D models, openly accessible at www.thingiverse.com/lgbu/designs, which will certainly be tinkered or redesigned in the very spirit of design thinking. Looking into the future, teacher educators have exciting opportunities to explore the curricular implications of design and making in STEM teacher education. In particular, teacher educators can engage preservice and in-service teachers in adopting design and co-design as the means of sensemaking, problem-solving, and creative data inference, seeking to see what has been seen in STEM education from fresh and diverse angles and thus blending teacher education and K–12 STEM education through iterative design research.

ACKNOWLEDGMENTS

The authors would like to thank the Southern Illinois University Foundation and the STEM Education Research Center for their financial and material support for our design-to-teach project. We are indebted to our preservice teachers and other members of our community for their passion for and insight into STEM teaching and learning. All mistakes belong to the authors.

REFLECTIVE QUESTIONS

1. Is there an instructional model or an everyday object you would like to design or have redesigned for STEM education?
2. In what ways does design thinking empower your teacher candidates and schoolchildren in STEM learning?
3. What concerns do you have about introducing design and making technologies into STEM teacher education?
4. How do you think design can support the development of STEM partnerships in teacher education and the community at large?
5. To what extent does design enable multimodal teaching and learning?

SECTION III

CONCLUSION: THE FUTURE FOR INFERENCES AND ACTIONS

This section of the book ponders what the Age of Inference holds for the many aspects of our society, from its diverse constituents to the fields in which they will work and the environment that we all share.

CHAPTER 18

DEVELOPING CRITICAL LITERACY SKILLS AMONG DIVERSE LEARNERS DURING THE AGE OF INFERENCE

Laveria F. Hutchison

Tell me and I forget. Teach me and I remember. Involve me and I learn.
—Benjamin Franklin

告诉我，我会忘记。教我，我记得。参与我，我学习。
—Confucius

Eighth Grade Science Teacher:

> Next month is our virtual field trip to the National Aeronautics and Space Administration (NASA) space center. During this field trip, my students will learn about the sequence of events that assisted NASA in developing the scientific and technological achievements that resulted in successful human spaceflights. I will encourage my students to take notes and to ask the presenter questions at appropriate times about information provided during the virtual field trip. My instructional path is to prepare my students to enjoy a successful

Age of Inference, pages 299–316

> field trip. This preparation will begin with establishing a background that explains NASA and incorporating disciplinary literacy skills into my instruction that will include an exposure to vocabulary terms, visual NASA space images, text sources that will provide contextual information, and peer conversations that will give my students the opportunity to discuss new information. This overview is important because my students are from diverse backgrounds and several of my students are English learners. Therefore, I need to be sure my students understand the language and concepts that will allow them to enjoy a meaningful experience.

The vignette above describes a science teacher's intentional desire to find ways to assist students in acquiring, understanding, and applying the concepts presented during their virtual NASA field trip experience. The vignette gives readers of this chapter a peek into instructional strategies the teacher will consider to assist students, who have varied educational and language backgrounds, to acquire information presented in this science class. As readers of this chapter, you are encouraged to consider the following guiding questions:

- How can I develop a creative way to introduce new information to my students?
- After I assist my students in identifying new information about a topic, what are some disciplinary literacy strategies I could use to assist them in acquiring a process for developing oral and written products?

As you read this chapter, three disciplinary literacy strategies are presented to assist readers in providing instruction that enhances critical thinking among students.

INTRODUCTION

Teachers today are expected to use state standards that will assist in the preparation of their students to become linguistically, cognitively, and scientifically ready to function in a global society. For decades, teachers and other stakeholders have held the belief that all racial and ethnic populations should receive a quality education (Lloyd et al., 2001). According to Rittle-Johnson et al. (2021), educators continue to believe that a quality education is a priority; however, the attainment of educational skills through effective STEM instruction continues to lag among marginalized students in classroom settings. During and after the historical span of slavery, educational opportunities and access for marginalized students have seen both an increase and a decrease. Although the *Brown v. Board of Education* 1954 Supreme Court decision mandated educational equality and the elimination of separation of Black students from their White peers in public schools, there continues to be an academic separation from their White and Asian peers. According to the report on the National Assessment of Education Progress (NCES, 2019b), eighth grade minority students in this country continue to show below grade-level scores in reading and mathematics. In 2017, Carnoy and Garcia reported that Black students in eighth grade scored 0.71 standard deviations lower in mathematics and 0.55 standard deviations lower in reading than their White peers. In the same report, Carnoy and Garcia (2017) found that Hispanic students scored 0.30 standard deviations lower in mathematics and 0.27 standard deviations lower in reading than their White peers. This lack of educational achievement growth combined with the change in the demographic landscape presents academic challenges for K–12 educators. To be more specific regarding the demographic change in school settings, NCES in 2019 found that, of the 50.7 million students enrolled in public schools, 24.1 million were White, 7.7 million were Black, 13.6 million were Hispanic, and 2.8 million were Asian/Pacific Islander. These statistics reflect a 17-year decrease from 61% to 48% among White students and an increase from 16% to 27% among Hispanic students. Considering the growth of English learners in schools in the United States, the conversation regarding marginalized students has expanded to include instructional practices to enhance their academic achievement. It is important to note that some states, like Texas, refer to the approximate 10.1% of the total K–12 grade population in the United States learning to speak/write English as English learners and *not* as English language learners. The Texas Education Agency (2019) and Rafa et al. (2020) from the Education Commission of the States refer to this student population as English learners.

As educators consider the changing demographics among students in K–12 classrooms, the education system in the United States struggles with a certified teacher shortage. According to Sutcher et al. (2016), this teacher shortage increased from approximately 64,000 teachers needed from 2012–2013 to approximately 110,000 teachers needed by the 2017–2018 school year with the projected gap continuing to increase over the following years. Educators continue to express concern regarding the complex worldwide issues students will face due to the knowledge and skills they will need to become successful future workforce participants. These skills will require content knowledge along with the ability to be problem solvers who can respond to current and future situations as scientific innovators, critical thinkers, and global workforce contributors. As educators grapple to identify ideas to increase educational opportunities among students during a time of demographic change and teacher shortage, it is important to identify an effective instructional intersection that connects students' content knowledge with their development of critical cognitive skills.

The teacher shortage occurring in K–12 educational settings has caused concern among school leaders and community stakeholders. This concern is based on states needing to reduce certification requirements to fill teacher vacancies. Academic excellence depends on the types of classes students take and on their access to highly qualified teachers who are equipped to provide quality instruction. Quality instruction for K–12 students is a result of teachers having effective content knowledge, access to continuous professional development, access to campus leaders who support teachers' initiatives, and suitable workplace conditions. Currently, the COVID-19 crisis is causing concern among the K–12 education workforce. EdWeek (2020) reported that 66% of teachers, principals, and district leaders indicated concern regarding in-person teaching and 36% of the same population reported personal physical conditions related to the virus. This concern poses difficulties for students, including marginalized students, to have the capacity to receive effective instruction by qualified teachers. In addition to health concerns among K–12 educators, highly qualified STEM teachers are less likely to be teachers of minority students in high-poverty schools compared to schools with wealthier student families.

THEORETICAL PERSPECTIVES

The theory-based perspectives to promote critical literacy skills should consider student engagement with social contextual interactions and meaningful discussions. Classroom research on student learning has provided a lens into the benefit of directed and meaningful social interactions used to impact cognitive development. Bull et al. (2000) indicated that effective learning connects an individual with others in a dialogical exchange to acquire a deeper understanding of concepts acquired using speech, visual cues, and feedback from peers and linguistically responsive exchanges from the teacher. Vygotsky (1986) suggested that learning occurs in a sociocultural environment that allows various forms of language to give and provide understanding. Both theories connect learning to cooperative interactions by enabling and encouraging students to respond to prompts that require critical thinking responses provided through various types of student-produced products. For example, consider the instructional scenario, as shown in Figure 18.1, presented to students by a middle school mathematics teacher. The teacher provided the students with the time to work collaboratively in groups to discuss and plan the steps needed to solve each mathematical

- One student volunteers to read the problem to the group.
- Students discuss the information and steps needed to solve the problem.
- Students write the steps needed to solve the problem, draw the steps needed to solve the problem, write a description of the process used to solve the problem, and provide the answer to the problem.
- Each group presents to the teacher and peers the steps used to solve the problem and provides the answer to the mathematical problem.

Figure 18.1 The teacher assigns a different mathematical problem to groups of five students.

problem. This type of collaboration encourages dialogical exchanges that promote language acquisition and content skill development.

As educational systems consider the instruction of marginalized students, including students-of-color, it is incorrectly believed that scripted and drilled delivered instruction at a lower level of cognitive inquiry and without social interactions is all that is needed to provide learning that will meet the requirements of standards-based assessments. However, Vygotsky (1978) and Krashen (1985) indicated that meaningful and teacher-guided collaborative interactions are important factors in acquiring and learning concepts. As the education system embraces theories recommending processes for providing spaces for students to learn and apply scientific concepts, educators should consider the following: (a) teachers will need to provide conceptual information that leads students into discussions that promote critical thinking, (b) teachers will need to assist students in learning to respond to items that elicit responses at a higher level of thinking, (c) teachers will need to provide instructional spaces that allow students to interact with peers in discussion formats that may promote constructive *noise*, and (d) teachers will need to encourage students to use rich language during oral interactions and in written products. The capacity for teachers to promote this type of learning will require a process to be in place that gives students the tools to explore learning that leads to a documented record of progress that can be presented to educators and other stakeholders in a variety of statistical dashboards. Therefore, disciplinary literacy strategies and critical literacy instructional ideas educators can use are critical to support the acquisition of scientific content through meaningful social engagement and dialogic discussions among middle-level and secondary-level students.

TEACHER EXPECTATIONS FOR DEVELOPING DISCIPLINARY AND CRITICAL LITERACY

The education system in this country expects teachers to offer their instruction through the application of text sources, visual presentations, oral lectures, multimedia outlets, and other formats. However, this instructional expectation generally no longer requires teachers to only expect students to memorize information for test purposes. Today, teachers are expected to provide instruction that allows for a variety of products to demonstrate student learning. The instruction in STEM subjects should give students the opportunity to investigate relatable problems, demonstrate their learning in a variety of contexts, and apply their learning in a variety of forms such as written responses, group presentations, art and musical presentations, and technology-enhanced products. The question then becomes how we give teachers the academic permission to get to this instructional position. The process begins by permitting these professionals to select instructional sources and processes, to engage in curriculum development, to design academic products that highlight student learning, and to use assessments that move students from learning and memorizing facts to deeper understanding.

Most educators desire a comprehensive suite of assessment tools to determine achievement growth among K–12 students. A process that educators find effective for implementation in K–12 classrooms is using the 2013 Next Generation Science Standards (NGSS) to investigate science knowledge through three-dimensional assessments. Results from assessments emphasizing these standards have moved educators' thinking from no longer "just knowing facts" to using assessments that involve three-dimensional discipline-connected core ideas, science and engineering practices, and crosscutting concepts. These performance assessments require students to demonstrate knowledge and understanding of their learning by solving real-world problems in engaged collaborative classroom settings. Teachers use the results of these assessments to guide instruction and to provide feedback to students, parents, and stakeholders.

Teachers should also become innovators in designing daily informal assessments that determine effective student learning. Teacher constructed informal assessments used to determine the acquisition of learning could be items such as: (a) asking students to write a song that provides a response to a question, (b) asking students to produce an illustration that depicts a response to a question, and (c) asking students to develop a media product that responds to a question. Teachers must have the capacity to immerse their students into practices that promote reading, writing, critical thinking, and social discussions of ideas with their peers that will produce constructive *noise* as they respond to statements/questions prompted by their teachers. This constructive noise includes group discussions, student movements around the classroom to locate resources to seek new information, cross-group discussions that may engage two or more students exchanging ideas, and standing in small groups to plan and complete a project. Constructive noise removes the outdated notion of students sitting in rows listening only to the teacher without any student interactions. Teachers are encouraged to monitor this noise to ensure students are remaining on task and not just engaging in social talk. Teachers' instructional delivery needs to be comprehensible, even with complex content, especially when teaching students with limited content backgrounds, language considerations, and other academic needs. The disciplinary literacy strategies and assessments teachers use with students should be ones that will complement any type of content (Echevarria et al., 2000; Hutchison, 2020).

Teacher Presentation Approach

Teachers can assist with the delivery of instruction for all levels of content difficulty for students, including marginalized students and English learners, by:

- slowing the rate of instruction to build students' background for learning new information;
- introducing key vocabulary terms with background-related definitions, sentences using each new term embedded into a description, and placement of new terms on a classroom content wall with the definition for students to use in oral and written products (these vocabulary introductions offered by the teacher provide exposure for students to observe an expert modeling academic language);
- providing frequent opportunities for students to rephrase, repeat, clarify, and discuss (with peers) responses to statements and questions posed by the teacher; and
- providing various forms of informal assessments to gain insight into students' retention of both new information and information previously taught by the teacher; then, using the results of these assessments to determine the concepts that need reteaching for additional clarification.

Teacher to Student Demonstrations

Teachers can model various processes. For example, teachers can model the steps for solving a mathematical word problem or the steps for conducting a scientific experiment by:

- presenting the various steps by using clear speech, oral and visual representations of concepts, posting of the steps in a visible location in the classroom, and asking students to restate the information in a variety of formats; and
- providing students with authentic tasks to practice and demonstrate their learning and understanding of new concepts.

Teacher Provides Space for Student Engagement

A benefit of heterogeneous student grouping for interaction and engagement can support English language proficiency, skill development, and the ability for students to use their native language to clarify ideas and concepts during group discussions prompted by:

- asking students to respond to statements and questions at various levels of comprehension;
- visiting small group discussions to check for students' understanding of concepts, to respond to students' questions, and to clarify misunderstood and inaccurate student understanding; and
- providing students with a rich variety of resources beyond textbooks such as newspapers, videos, novels, and other meaningful materials that provide opportunities to discuss in small group settings the information found in these resources.

Teacher Identifies Reading Characteristics for Critical Reading Thinkers

Scientific reading requires investigations and understandings that go beyond printed words, and teachers will need to develop critical scientific thinking by:

- identifying and using instructional objectives that provide sequential steps for acquiring information;
- providing students with a process to answer statements and questions at higher levels of thinking that goes beyond just factual gathering of information;
- using data to evaluate information that lead to oral and written responses;

- understanding how to define academic vocabulary in a variety of contexts that include oral and written products gained through both individual and group responses;
- allowing students to collaborate with peers when experiencing difficult tasks (English learners could use their first language to communicate the understanding of ideas before translating information into English); and
- assisting students with using a variety of formats, such as illustrations and graphic presentations, to demonstrate understanding and learning.

As teachers prepare students to become critical thinkers and creative problem solvers in the Age of Inference, using a strategic set of discipline-specific instructional strategies can assist students in learning to acquire, retain, and apply information. Educators for decades have realized students who appropriately use strategically selected instructional strategies are usually more successful in school settings than their peers who do not apply instructional strategies (Biemiller & Meichenbaum, 1992). Instructional strategies for classroom and content use were introduced in 1946 with Robinson's description of the survey, question, read, recite, review (SQ3R) method. This method was teacher-directed with little mention of dialogic discussion, peer engagement, or consideration for diverse learners. The focus currently is on disciplinary literacy strategies that emphasize critical thinking at higher levels of inquiry and encourages students to apply knowledge through peer discussions, written products, visual representations, and other forms of demonstrated learning (Shanahan & Shanahan, 2012). Currently, teachers are encouraged to consider instructional formats that embrace students' funds of knowledge they bring with them into classroom settings from their cultures and home environments (Moll et al., 1992). What follows are three examples of disciplinary literacy instructional strategies: the cognitive process dimension, the revoicing procedure, and note-taking.

Disciplinary Literacy Instructional Strategies

Disciplinary literacy is based on encouraging students to engage with text sources that enhance learning by analyzing information, critiquing information, and questioning information presented in both printed and visual sources. The Age of Inference calls for an instructional space for teachers to assist their students in acquiring and utilizing skills that demonstrate a capacity to be creative and critical thinkers. This capacity needs development among all students, including students with diverse backgrounds, through the introduction and implementation of cognitive inquiry. As educators, we understand that instruction should be crafted and differentiated to meet the instructional capacity of all students. Differentiated instruction reflects a growth mindset that establishes another dimension of effective teaching. This type of instruction enables teachers to be flexible in responding to the varied instructional levels and styles of students in classroom settings. It is important to realize that students need to develop higher-level thinking skills and academic vocabulary understanding to ensure that successful learning is acquired by all students. A widely used framework for inquiry is Bloom's taxonomy, which is currently called the cognitive process dimension (Walsh & Sattes, 2005). Teachers today realize their students represent different cultures and will often be English learners; thus, they need to identify strategies that will encourage discussion. The revoicing strategy will provide an instructional space to promote students talking to reinforce their learning of new concepts. As teachers assist students in learning to provide inquiry-based oral and written responses, students will need to have a process for recording information acquired from reading and discussing text sources to gain new information to review multiple times. Designing a note-taking process would assist students with this task. The passage in Figure 18.2 will provide a context to explain and demonstrate examples of the cognitive process dimension, a revoicing discussion, a note-taking process, and examples of practices that will incorporate differentiated flexible instructional ideas for classroom implementation.

Engineers at NASA are now experimenting with the development of a spacesuit that is dustproof because dust in a spacesuit can limit movement. It is also important to design a spacesuit that will keep dust from entering the oxygen system because this can start a fire. Did you know NASA plans to send astronauts to the Red Planet, Mars, some time during the 2030s? When astronauts spent time on the surface of the moon, they were outside of their spacecraft for a few hours, while on Mars, astronauts will stay there for about 500 days and will be out of their spacecraft for longer periods of time. Engineers are considering designing modular spacesuits with sections that can be changed when these sections become damaged. The modular design is being considered because spacesuits will need to fit different body types. The Z-2 is NASA's newest spacesuit. Mars has gravity. Therefore, for the exploration of Mars to be successful, and for identifying and collecting interesting artifacts, the spacesuits will need to be lighter. The design team is trying to get the weight of the Z-2 for travel to Mars to be less than 250 pounds. NASA engineers are considering all sources for innovative ideas to design this new spacesuit.

Figure 18.2 NASA spacesuits for exploring Mars.

The Cognitive Process Dimension (Bloom's Taxonomy)

The categories of the cognitive process dimension use verbs to assist teachers in moving students from rote learning and memorization to active learning by assisting them to develop inquiry prompts that promote this type of learning (Walsh & Sattes, 2005). The six classifications of this resource are defined along with a list of verbs and examples to consider when developing inquiry items.

- *Remember:* Statements or questions request students to recall or recognize information from a text source. Although the remember level is the lowest form of comprehension, this level is the building block that assists students in making cognitive text connections to the other parts of the text (Figure 18.3). A sample list of verbs: define, label, recall, show, and tell.
- *Understand:* Statements or questions that request students to transfer memorized information to new information by seeking responses that go beyond memorized facts (Figure 18.4). A sample list of verbs: classify, discuss, illustrate, rephrase, and summarize.
- *Apply:* Statements or questions that request students to apply, transfer, or use data to complete a procedure or task, with minimum di-

Example: Can you **state** another name for Mars?

Differentiation Examples (Students):

- Read the selection and provide the response in a sentence.
- Listen to a peer read the passage to provide an oral response.

Figure 18.3 Remember.

Example: Explain the difference between the spacesuit used for travel to the moon and the spacesuit that will be used for travel to Mars.

Differentiation Examples (Students):

- Write a paragraph that provides a contrast between the two spacesuits.
- Draw illustrations that contrast the two spacesuits.

Figure 18.4 Understand.

rections, of either a familiar task or an unfamiliar task (Figure 18.5). A sample list of verbs: build, construct, model, plan, and solve.

- *Analyze:* Statements or questions that request students to break apart, classify, or make assumptions about information showing how the parts are related (Figure 18.6). The following components connect to analysis: distinguishing fact from opinion, finding evidence to support the author's purpose for providing specific information, and connecting conclusions with supporting information. A sample list of verbs: categorize, contrast, demonstrate, and show.
- *Evaluate:* Statements or questions that request students to make an assessment, critique, or judgment based on a set of standards or criteria (Figure 18.7). A sample list of verbs: assess, compare, interpret, justify, and summarize.
- *Create:* Statements or questions that request students to consider all components of a text to create or to design a new pattern that defines the students' prior knowledge and understanding of the information (Figure 18.8). A sample list of verbs: build, combine, discuss, plan, and solve.

Using the components of this taxonomy benefits the teacher by providing guidelines for constructing statements and questions for students to use as

Example: Predict the reason, or reasons, NASA engineers are considering designing a modular spacesuit.

Differentiation Examples (Students):

- Write a letter to NASA requesting sample drawings of a modular spacesuit.
- Create an analogy between the previous and new modular spacesuits.

Figure 18.5 Apply.

Example: Show the impact a lighter spacesuit would have on travel to Mars

Differentiation Examples (Students):

- Investigate tasks astronauts can perform wearing a modular spacesuit.
- Use the information identifying what astronauts can do wearning the modular spacesuit to develop a chart providing this information to the class.

Figure 18.6 Analyze.

Example: Can you **conclude** from the information in the text if NASA engineers have already designed a spacesuit for travel to Mars?

Differentiation Examples (Students):

- Design a flowchart that outlines the development of the modular spacesuit.
- Write a set of steps used to develop the modular spacesuit.

Figure 18.7 Evaluate.

Example: Using the information learned from the text, **describe** and construct your version of a spacesuit NASA could use for travel to Mars. You may work in a group and you may use a variety of materials to complete your spacesuit.

Differentiation Examples (Students):

- Design an illustration of the modular spacesuit developed for travel to Mars.
- Compose a rhyme, poem, or rap to advertise the modular spacesuit for travel to Mars.

Figure 18.8 Create.

they provide oral and written responses. Teachers benefit by having a tool that provides information for responding to the inclusion of state standards and learning objectives in daily instruction, for lesson planning, for instructional activities that provide a platform for language development, for constructing comprehension statements and questions, and for having a process to conduct informal student assessments. The students benefit by having the ability to construct language-based responses individually, in small group settings, and by having an opportunity to develop critical thinking skills.

The Revoicing Procedure

This instructional procedure allows the teacher to engage students, including English learners, by focusing on reciprocal oral exchanges that promote deep understanding of contextual concepts. Teachers can also restructure student responses so that students can hear their ideas expressed using grammatical accuracy, accurate academic language, and accurate content responses. The example shown in Figure 18.9 uses the content from the NASA spacesuit text to demonstrate this procedure.

Teacher: May I have a volunteer to explain the reason NASA engineers are planning to design a new type of spacesuit for travel to Mars?

Student One: NASA engineers need to find a way to keep dust from entering a spacesuit when astronauts travel to Mars.

Teacher: So, you are saying the newly designed spacesuit should keep dust from entering the inside of the spacesuit?

Student One: Yes, that is what I am saying because the dust can cause damage to the oxygen system in the spacesuit.

An extended Conversation to Include a Different Student (Student Two)

Teacher speaks to Student Two: Restate in your own words your classmate's reason for NASA designing a new spacesuit for travel to Mars.

Student Two: NASA engineers found that dust can be harmful to a spacesuit and can cause damage to the oxygen system. It is important for the engineers to design a new type of spacesuit before astronauts travel to Mars.

Teacher: To add to your response, do you think the spacesuit will be designed by next year? What information from the text helps you respond to my question?

Figure 18.9 The revoicing procedure.

Note: The dialog can continue between the teacher and the students and has the potential for including other students in this exchange (Figure 18.10).

The additional contribution from Student 2, along with the consideration for differentiated student activities, gives the teacher an opportunity to assess the students' understanding of the text. To promote more teacher

- The teacher uses an extended text for students to read about NASA, space orbiters, spacesuits, and minority astronauts.
- The teacher assigns products such as a collaborative assignment to investigate and write a report about the life and contributions of minority astronauts.
- The teacher assigns students to create art designs that show the progression and changes in spacecraft over a 20-year period.

Note: The differentiation examples use a variety of student-generated products that include reading printed material, writing reports, and providing illustrations. Therefore, they account for the differing learning styles and academic levels of students.

Figure 18.10 Differentiation examples.

engagement with students, the teacher could continue rephrasing the concepts as well as asking different statements and questions regarding the text. Revoicing allows other students in the class to hear their classmates' thinking and use of language. This procedure allows practice of language skills that can assist English learners with using language patterns, and it allows students to think about other ways to respond to a teacher's statements or questions.

Note-Taking

Students read text sources, listen to teachers' lectures, and listen to their peers' oral speech for a significant part of the school day. This information is often forgotten if there is not a procedure in place to record the information. The two-column note-taking guide includes an informational header, a listing of academic vocabulary terms, a column for writing notes, and a section for writing a detailed summary of the notes (Figure 18.11). The example

Student's Name: Date:

Subject: Pages Covered:

Topic Covered:

Academic Vocabulary:

Instructions: Academic vocabulary terms should be defined and discussed before reading and discussing text information.

Note: This discussion of academic vocabulary provides sheltered instructional consideration for English Learners.

Statements and Questions (Provided by the Teacher)	**Student Responses to the Statements and Questions Provided by the Teacher**
Provide Mars' other name. What impact would a lighter spacesuit have on travel to Mars?	

Summary: Students are encouraged to use the responses presented in the response column on the right side of the note-taking guide to provide a written summary that captures the most significant information related to the topic.

Figure 18.11 Note-taking.

provided in this section uses the content from the NASA spacesuit text to demonstrate this procedure and show how a teacher-scaffolded and guided note-taking process can assist novice note-takers in learning to collect information as they either listen to a teacher-led lecture or read a text source.

As students become expert note-takers, the note-taking guide presented below changes to a note-taking sheet that does not have as many guided scaffolds provided by the teacher for students to use. Students take notes by writing directly on the form to record information from either a text source or a lecture, determine the topics to identify on the left side of the form following their note-taking, and generate a summary from their notes (Figure 18.12). As teachers continue to differentiate instruction and encourage students to become critical users of information, students could form groups to compare and enhance their notes with additional information.

Note-taking provides the teacher with an opportunity to establish a discussion platform for students to engage in group settings that provide time to evaluate their notes, to add new information to their response section, to clarify information provided in the response section, and to compare summary statements. Note-taking discussions also allow students a safe space to practice oral and written language (Hutchison, 2020).

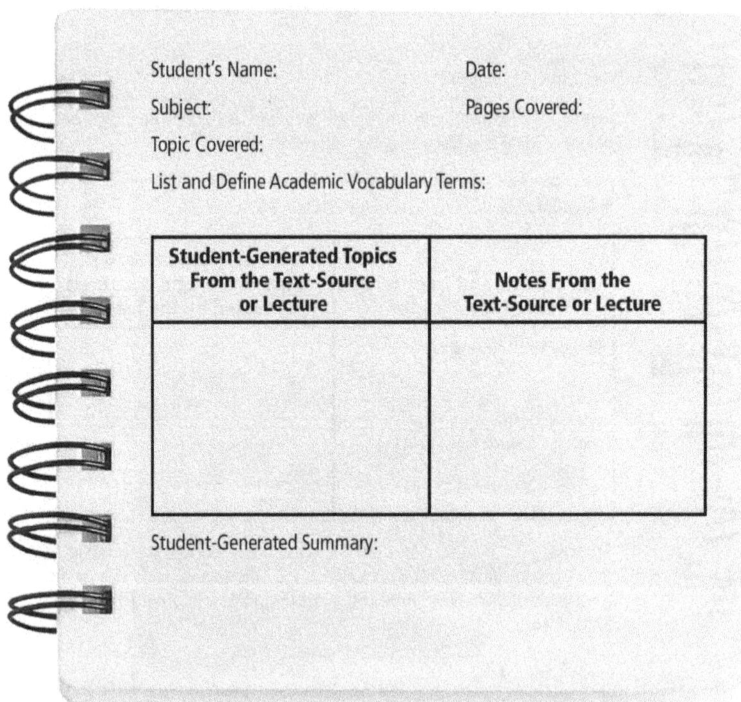
Student's Name: Date:
Subject: Pages Covered:
Topic Covered:
List and Define Academic Vocabulary Terms:

Student-Generated Topics From the Text-Source or Lecture	**Notes From the Text-Source or Lecture**

Student-Generated Summary:

Figure 18.12 Note-taking guide.

SUGGESTIONS FROM A NASA ENGINEER

The following list was provided by a 15-year employed NASA engineer after being asked to provide recommendations for students to consider as they advance through their STEM classes:

- Read a variety of printed sources to broaden your vocabulary.
- Try solving difficult problems that surface beyond your classes to broaden your higher-level thinking skills.
- Join extracurricular school activities that promote scientific creativity.
- Be very concerned about learning while documenting a profile of high academic achievement, awards, grades, and teacher comments that document exemplary performance in school settings and community organizations.
- Seek out summer experiences such as volunteering at science venues, summer science camps, and other experiences to document for later use on various types of applications.
- Talk to neighbors and other adults about scientific-related workplace positions.
- Research STEM-related careers and seek out professionals who are willing to provide additional information related to workplace opportunities.
- Attend tutoring sessions even when you are earning high grades in school.
- Above all, have fun learning!

SUMMARY

The capacity to acquire critical thinking skills through disciplinary literacy practices can be difficult for students, especially for English learners. As noted by Carnoy and Garcia (2017), Black and Hispanic students continue to academically lag behind their White peers. Therefore, it is important for teachers to provide and demonstrate strategic instruction that will engage all learners in effective and meaningful instruction. Researchers, such as Bull et al. (2000), stressed the importance of teachers providing opportunities for students to engage in dialogical exchanges to demonstrate their conceptual understanding of all types of information. The instructional disciplinary literacy strategies in this chapter provide examples that can advance engaged, collaborative, and differentiated ideas to enhance the achievement growth for all learners. These strategies are important because they provide students with opportunities to gain information in multiple ways and spark their interest in reaching the right inferences from multiple data sources. Teachers are encouraged to include disciplinary literacy strategies with their instruction to provide a path for their students to perform as an academic expert in their classroom settings and community. As teachers consider what is important for students to be able to know and do in the Age of Inference, it will become apparent that students benefit from having the capacity to learn in a collaborative, creative, and nurturing environment that provides space for becoming critical thinkers.

REFLECTIVE QUESTIONS

1. After reading this chapter, are you of the opinion that the eighth-grade science teacher can plan instruction that will spark interest among the students as they venture on their virtual field trip to NASA?
2. If so, how do you think the science teacher will design and sustain instruction to address the different backgrounds and achievement levels among the students that include English learners?
3. As you reflect on the quote by Benjamin Franklin and Confucius—"Tell me and I forget. Teach me and I remember. Involve me and I learn"—what other disciplinary literacy strategies might you apply in your instruction to *involve* your students?

CHAPTER 19

CONTENT AND PEDAGOGICAL KNOWLEDGE FOR TEACHING CONFIDENCE INTERVALS IN A POST $p < 0.05$ WORLD

Jennifer J. Kaplan and Kristen E. Roland

A one size-fits-all approach to statistical inference is an inappropriate expectation: accept uncertainty. Variation, one of the causes of uncertainty, is everywhere. Be thoughtful, open, and modest. Be thoughtful and clear about the level of confidence or credibility that is present in statistical results. Be open in your reporting. Be modest about the role of statistical inference in scientific inference.

—Wasserstein et al., 2019

The term, inference, as used by statisticians, describes the set of statistical techniques through which conclusions about a population are made from information provided by a sample selected from that population. Unlike scientific inferencing, frequentist statistical inference, especially as taught in the statistics and probability strand of the Common Core State Standards, is quite formulaic with a well-defined series of steps:

Age of Inference, pages 317–346

1. Define the population of interest.
2. Select or create samples in a way that allows the statistician to use statistical inferential procedures to infer conclusions from the sample back to the population.
3. Verify the conditions underlying the statistical inferential procedure for the context and/or data collected.
4. Apply the statistical inferential procedure to the sample data.
5. Interpret the findings and draw a conclusion about the population.

In contrast to statistical inference, scientific inference cannot be reduced to a "series of allegedly neat and tidy methodological steps whose dutiful observance renders the output 'science'" (Hubbard et al., 2019, p. 95). Hubbard and colleagues (2019) described scientific inferencing as the development of the best explanation for the available facts: Scientists study observable behavior and propose theories about the causal mechanisms that generate the observed behavior. The frequentist statistical methods use the information limited to the sample collected and provide only probabilistic conclusions about the population. As Wild (2009) said in his plenary talk at the U.S. Conference on Teaching Statistics, using a sample to make conclusions about a population is like viewing reality through wavy glass and guessing what is on the other side. In contrast, Bayesian statistical methods, which have become more popular as access to computational power has increased, use all available information to continually update probability distributions used to model the population.

Despite the differences between scientific and frequentist statistical inference, the scientific community has come to rely on frequentist statistical inference to move the field forward (Goodman, 2019). The two main frequentist statistical inference techniques are hypothesis testing and confidence intervals. Of these, hypothesis testing and in particular, the use of the *p*-value cutoff, $p < 0.05$, for publication of scientific results, is ubiquitous (Hubbard, 2016, 2019). Both the American Statistical Association (ASA) and the American Psychological Association (APA) have issued statements cautioning against the overreliance on *p*-values in scientific research (see Wasserstein & Lazar, 2016; Wilkinson, 1999). Wasserstein et al. (2019) imagined a "world where researchers are free to treat '$p = 0.051$' and '$p = 0.049$' as not being categorically different, where authors no longer find themselves constrained to selectively publish their results based on a single magic number" (p. 1). By reducing scientific decisions to cut off values, such as $p < 0.05$, or use asterisks indicating other cutoffs for *p*-values, users of statistics are in essence denying the uncertainty associated with inferential results. A first step to help the scientific community (and more globally, users of statistics) accept uncertainty is to make the reporting of point and interval estimates and/or effect sizes routine and to be sure that all reported point estimates are accompanied by a measure of uncertainty, such as a standard error or interval (Wasserstein et al., 2019). Accepting uncertainty in this way will also lead to thoughtfulness, openness, and modesty in the reporting and communication of statistical results (Wasserstein et al., 2019).

If the statistics and science communities can no longer report *p*-values as cut scores, they will have to be more thoughtful about communication, which starts in how inferential results are discussed in the K–12 curriculum. Statisticians have no doubt the transition from the use of the $p < 0.05$ cut point will be difficult, requiring education at all levels of scientific training. Statistics educators realize this change will require collaboration with science reform movements in various scientific disciplines, providing new curricula designed to help students develop understanding of statistical reasoning and uncertainty (Steel et al., 2019), and examples of good communication of the same aspects of statistical inference (Goodman, 2019).

At present, most recommendations for increased acceptance of uncertainty, thoughtfulness, openness, and modesty in presentation of inferential results have been directed at researchers. For instance, Anderson (2019) proposed three questions that researchers should address to be thoughtful in their communication of inferential results: "What are the practical implications of the estimate? How precise is the estimate? And is the model correctly specified?" (Wasserstein et al., 2019, p. 3). These questions can easily be incorporated in K–12 discussions of inferential results. In describing openness of communication, specifically about *p* values, Wasserstein et al. (2019), reminded us that *p* values are continuous, rather than dichotomous, and should be interpreted in the context of sample size, effect size, and practical significance.

The exhortation to be modest served as a reminder that inferential findings cannot prove a hypothesis correct. Each study adds to a body of evidence and the combined results of replications should be used to summarize the level of evidence for or against a hypothesis. As the presentation of results attends to the uncertainty and are thoughtful and open about communication, they should also become modest and not overstate the claims made from data (Wasserstein et al., 2019). In sum, the recommendations being made by the statistics community, for example, the reporting of interval estimates (Fricker et al., 2019; Matthews, 2019; Wasserstein et al., 2019), should lead to an increased use of confidence intervals in scientific research. It is, therefore, imperative that K–12 curricula rise to the call of communicating inferential results, in particular interval estimation, with instruction focused on thoughtfulness, openness, and modesty.

Scientists already use interval estimates in reporting of modeling: For example, in predictions about the path and intensity of a storm or the spread of a disease or a contaminant spilled into a water source. Many citizens have seen predicted storm path figures in media coverage of major storms. In a

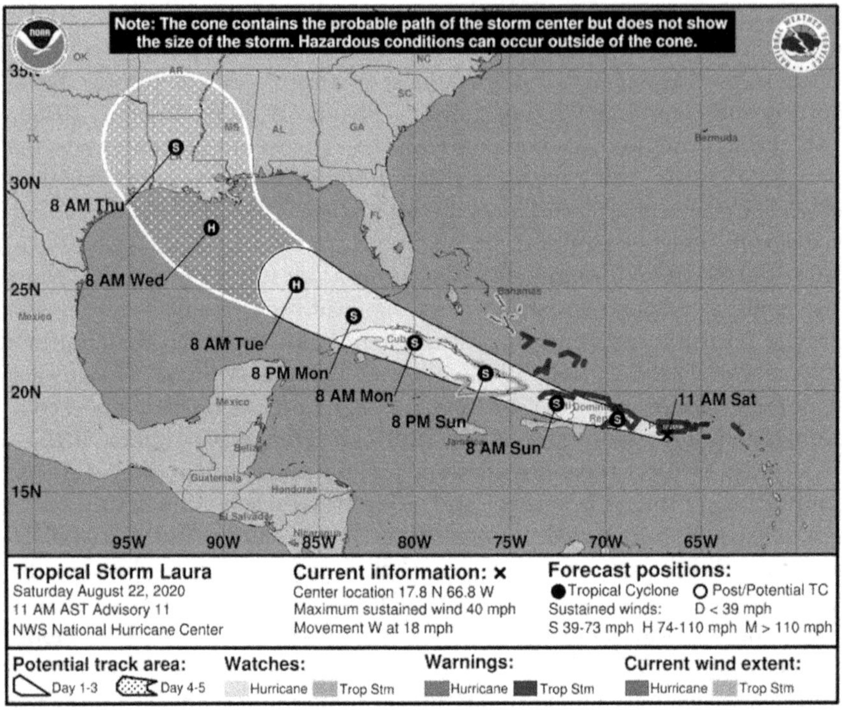

Figure 19.1 Warnings/cone static image of tropical storm Laura on August 22, 2020.

warnings/cone static image (Figure 19.1) for a tropical storm, the National Hurricane Center showed a predicted location of a storm over time as well as a band within which a storm might be. The predicted location could be considered the point estimate for the parameter, defined in this case as the actual path the storm will take, and the bands could be considered the confidence interval, representing the plausible locations for the storm. When citizens can use such figures to make decisions, for example, about evacuation, rather than arguing about the correctness of the prediction when a storm deviates from the center of the predicted path (despite staying within the reported confidence bands), they are exhibiting an understanding of an interval estimate or confidence interval.

This chapter is designed to address the suggestions for promoting better communication of uncertainty with the use of confidence intervals by discussing requisite content and pedagogical knowledge for teaching confidence intervals, with a focus on what confidence intervals represent rather than the procedures to create them (Steel et al., 2019). The chapter begins with a description of a confidence interval and an explanation of the meaning of the confidence level from the standpoint of statistical theory to help the reader build content knowledge (Groth, 2007) of confidence intervals. This section is followed by a synthesis of the existing research results on student and researchers' understanding of confidence intervals to illustrate the potential pitfalls that may result during instruction, building pedagogical knowledge (Groth, 2007) for teaching confidence intervals.

The chapter finishes with implications and suggestions for instruction based on the literature discussed. While statistical inference may have been a topic traditionally reserved for undergraduate courses in statistics, both the *Framework for K–12 Science Education: Practices, Crosscutting Concepts, and Core Ideas* (National Research Council, 2012) and the Common Core State Standards for Mathematics (National Governors Association Center for Best Practices, 2010) contain competencies associated with statistical inference. As a result, ideas surrounding inferential methods are likely to be taught starting in middle school, with prerequisite skills taught earlier. This chapter can be used as a primer to meet the needs of any instructor who teaches the ideas associated with statistical inference. Those who work with pre- and in-service teachers are encouraged to supplement the ideas in this chapter with several excellent resources for such work, The Statistics Education of Teachers (Franklin et al., 2015) and the Developing Essential Understandings of Statistics for Teaching series (Kader & Jacobbe, 2013; Peck et al., 2013).

WHAT IS A CONFIDENCE INTERVAL?

At its core, a confidence interval is a range of plausible values for a particular summary value associated with a population: the parameter. For simplicity, two potential parameters considered here are a population proportion and a population mean, but a parameter may be any value that summarizes a quantitative aspect of the population, such as the maximum or minimum value or the standard deviation. Imagine we are ecologists set out to study the prevalence of a disease among fish in a lake. To measure the effect of the disease on fish in a particular lake, we might want to know what proportion of all of the fish in the lake have the disease, the population proportion, or if the disease affects the size of the fish, we might want to estimate the mean size of all of the fish in the lake, the population mean. Harvesting and testing and measuring all of the fish in the lake would provide us with the exact values we seek, but taking measurements from every member of a population is rarely feasible. Instead, we select a sample of fish from the lake, and for each fish we record the presence or absence of the disease and the size of the fish. We use these data to create confidence intervals, ranges that contain the plausible values for the actual proportion of fish in the lake that have the disease and for the mean length if we considered all of the fish in the lake.

Before we take the sample, we may have no prior knowledge about the fish in the lake. That is to say, the plausible values for the prevalence of the disease may be from 0–100%. It is less likely that we would have no information about the size of the fish in the lake. For example, a typical size for a yellow perch is 7.5 inches, with a typical range from 4 to 11 inches, but yellow perch can be as long as 19.7 inches (U.S. Fish and Wildlife Services, n.d.; "Yellow Perch," 2019). If the fish in the lake are diseased, we might expect a mean length for the population to be closer to the smaller end of the range, but we are unlikely to have a mean length larger than 11 inches as this would require every fish in the lake to be unusually large. Thus, before we start our study, we have some sense of the plausible values for the mean length of all of the fish in the lake. The process of creating a confidence interval further narrows the range of plausible values from our initial pre-data information.

How do we do this? The short answer is mathematics, or to be more precise, probability. The mathematics underlying frequentist statistical inference is theoretically independent of the sample selected and based only on the population. An understanding of mathematics requires an understanding of two related statistical ideas: sampling variability and sampling distributions. Sampling variability is the idea that two different samples are unlikely to be identical. In this example, if we go to the lake on two different days and each day take a sample of fish, even if the samples are the same size and we have put the fish from the first day back after taking the measurements, we are unlikely either to select the exact same fish or to select fish that lead to the same data and/or calculated values. Statisticians like to say "samples vary," by which we acknowledge that we know that the sample we have is only one of many possible samples and that the values associated with our sample are unlikely to match the value for the entire population.

If samples vary and are unlikely to be exact reflections of the population, how can we use them to learn about (infer back to) the population? The answer to this question is sampling distributions, and this is the part of the process Wild (2009) referred to as wavy glass. A sampling distribution is the expected distribution of a value calculated from a sample if we imagine taking many samples and calculating the same value from each one. This value is called the statistic. In our example, we would calculate the proportion of fish in the sample that have the disease, the sample proportion, and the mean length of fish in the sample, the sample mean, but as we mentioned above, we could be interested in other aspects of the population, such as the maximum size of the fish, in which case we would consider the size of the largest fish in our sample, the sample maximum.

Sampling distributions model the expected behavior of a statistic. In order for something to exhibit behavior, we must imagine that it happens many times. Take, for example, the game show Jeopardy! If you watch the show over time, you might start to know where to expect or not expect the daily double clues. Similarly, if we took many samples from a population and calculated and graphed a statistic from the sample, we might develop knowledge of typical values of that statistic. In general, however, a scientist only takes one sample from a population and not many samples. Mathematics does the job for scientists describing the behavior of statistics that watching many episodes of Jeopardy! does for fans describing the behavior of the location of the daily doubles. While sampling distributions for many common parameters have been calculated empirically, those that do not have a theoretical calculation may be generated by simulation (for textbooks that develop inferential ideas through simulation, see Lock et al., 2013; Tintle et al., 2014). Regardless of the method of generation of sampling distributions, by mathematical theory or simulation, their use in statistical inference, once generated, is similar.

In our example, behavior of the sample proportion, the proportion of fish in the sample who have the disease, will be well modeled by a binomial distribution, and the only information needed to specify this distribution is the proportion of fish in the population (all of the fish in the lake) that have the disease and the intended size of the sample. It has already been stipulated that we have no prior knowledge of the prevalence of the disease among the fish in the lake, but for each potential proportion of diseased fish, a sampling distribution can be created. Figure 19.2a shows five sampling distributions for disease prevalence in the population corresponding to 10%, 30%, 50%, 70%, and 90% for samples of size $n = 50$ fish. The leftmost distribution, corresponding to a population prevalence of 10%, or $p = 0.1$, has its tallest bar at the value 0.1. This means the most probable value of the sample statistic is 0.1, which means 10% of the fish in the sample having the disease. Note, however, that there are samples that will have as few as 0% or as many as 24% of the fish in the sample that are diseased.

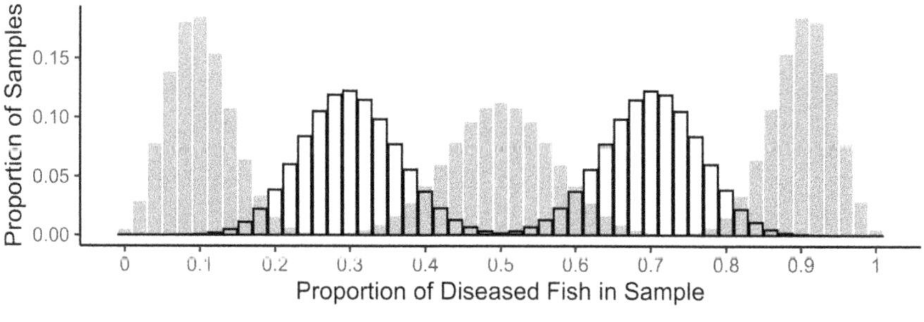

Figure 19.2a Sampling distributions for $p = 0.1$, $p = 0.3$, $p = 0.5$, $p = 0.7$, $p = 0.9$ with $n = 50$.

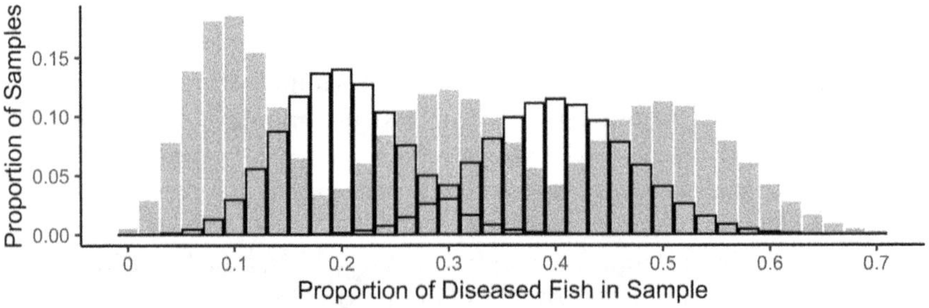

Figure 19.2b Sampling distributions for $p = 0.1$, $p = 0.2$, $p = 0.3$, $p = 0.4$, $p = 0.5$ with $n = 50$.

Figure 19.2b zooms in and shows the sampling distributions for disease prevalence in the population of 10%, 20%, 30%, 40%, 50%, again with a sample size, $n = 50$. In Figure 19.2b, the sampling distributions start to overlap, which helps to explain the need for confidence intervals. If 10% of the fish in the sample are diseased, it might be that 10% of the fish in the lake are diseased, but looking at the second distribution in Figure 19.2b, corresponding to a disease prevalence in the population of $p = 0.2$, some of the samples are expected to have a disease prevalence of 10% as well.

Calculating theoretical sampling distributions for a sample mean, in our case the mean length of the fish in the sample, is a bit more complicated as it relies on the knowledge of the standard deviation of the lengths of the fish in the population and the sample size. For the sake of simplicity, the standard deviation of the lengths of the fish in the lake is set to 1.75 inches and a sample size of $n = 50$ fish is used. Figure 19.3a shows the nine sampling distributions for the mean length of the fish in the sample for fish populations with population mean lengths from 3 inches to 11 inches in 1-inch increments. Figure 19.3b, zooms in to show the sampling distributions for population means from 4 inches to 9 inches, at 0.5-inch intervals. In both figures, 19.3a and 19.3b, there is overlap between the sampling

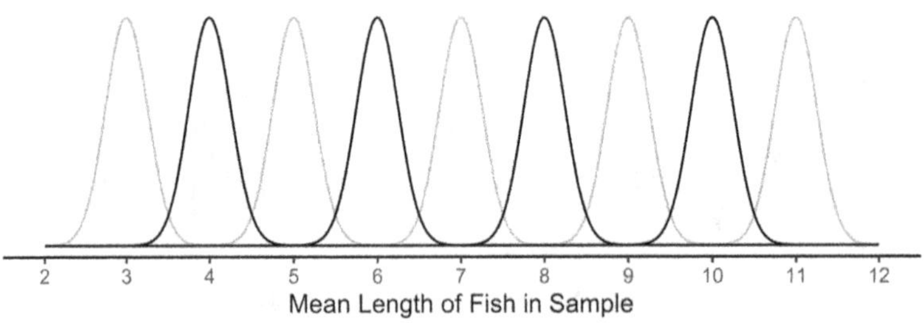

Figure 19.3a Sampling distributions for $\mu = 3$, $\mu = 4$, $\mu = 5$, $\mu = 6$, $\mu = 7$, $\mu = 8$, $\mu = 9$, $\mu = 10$, $\mu = 11$, $\mu = 12$, $\mu = 13$, with $\sigma = 1.75$ and $n = 50$.

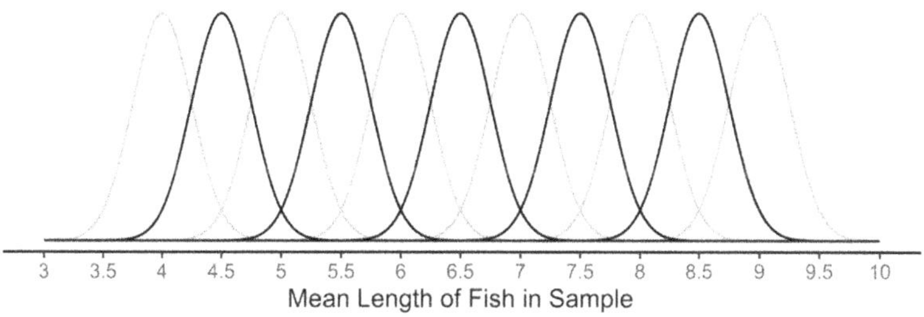

Figure 19.3b Sampling distributions for $\mu = 4$, $\mu = 4.5$, $\mu = 5$, $\mu = 5.5$, $\mu = 6$, $\mu = 6.5$, $\mu = 7$, $\mu = 7.5$, $\mu = 8$, $\mu = 8.5$, $\mu = 9$, $\mu = 9.5$, with $\sigma = 1.75$ and $n = 50$.

distributions, meaning that the same value of a sample statistic could have come from different populations with different values of its parameter.

Now imagine that 26% of the 50 fish in our sample are diseased. This value, 26% or $\hat{p} = 0.26$, is a point estimate and current best guess at the proportion of all fish in the lake with the disease. Because we understand sampling variability, however, we know that this value is unlikely to be the actual value and that a different sample is likely to produce a different value. Because we know about sampling distributions, we can use the value from our sample to decide from which sampling distribution our value was likely to have come and, more importantly, from which it was unlikely to have come. When we eliminate the sampling distributions from which the value was unlikely to have come, we are reducing the range of plausible values for the parameter, the proportion of all fish in the lake that have the disease. This new reduced range is our confidence interval.

Figure 19.4 shows the sampling distributions shown previously in Figure 19.2b with a vertical line at the value of our sample statistic. That line passes through bars associated with the sampling distributions corresponding to the parameter values, $p = 0.2$, $p = 0.3$, and $p = 0.4$, but not those corresponding to $p = 0.1$ or $p = 0.5$. We would, therefore, eliminate the values

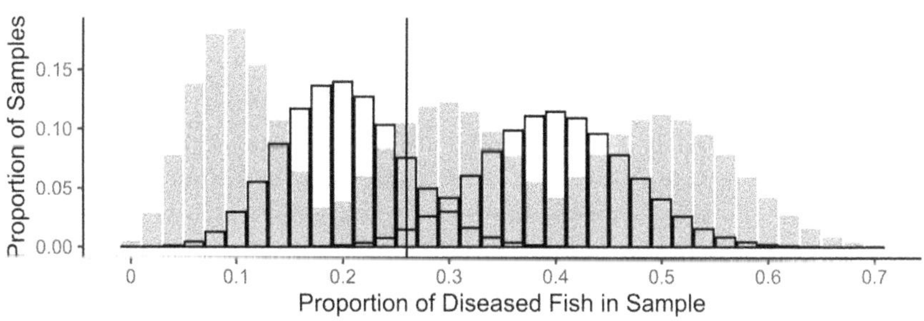

Figure 19.4 Sampling distributions for $p = 0.1$, $p = 0.2$, $p = 0.3$, $p = 0.4$, $p = 0.5$ with $n = 50$, Marked at $\hat{p} = 0.26$.

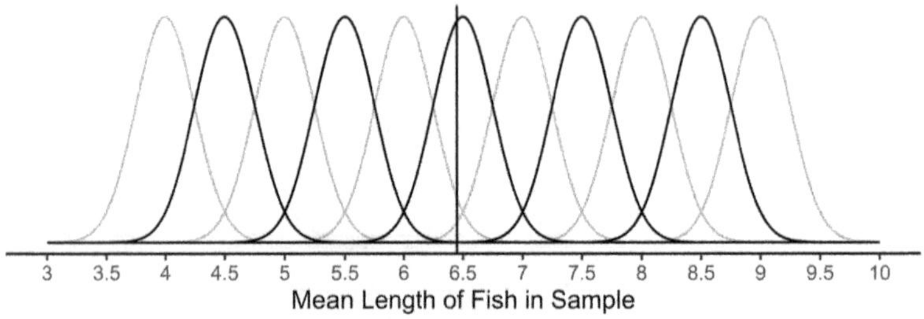

Figure 19.5 Sampling distributions for $\mu = 4$, $\mu = 4.5$, $\mu = 5$, $\mu = 5.5$, $\mu = 6$, $\mu = 6.5$, $\mu = 7$, $\mu = 7.5$, $\mu = 8$, $\mu = 8.5$, $\mu = 9$, $\mu = 9.5$, with $\sigma = 1.75$, and $n = 50$, marked at $\bar{x} = 6.45$.

of 10% and 50% as plausible values for the prevalence of disease in the fish in the lake and retain the values from 20% to 40%. The graphics provided are insufficient to find an exact boundary, but the reader should imagine zooming in on the distributions to find the boundaries. The authors did and found that the bar corresponding to 13 diseased fish in the samples, or = 0.26, was visible on the sampling distributions from populations with disease prevalence from 11% and 49%.

Similarly, if the mean length of the sample of $n = 50$ fish is 6.45 inches (Figure 19.5), from the distributions shown, we would retain those corresponding to $\mu = 6.0$ inches, $\mu = 6.5$ inches, and $\mu = 7.0$ inches, because the vertical line passes through the sampling distributions associated with these values, indicating that the value from our sample is plausible for those distributions and eliminate the others, because the vertical line does not pass through the sampling distributions associated with these values, indicating that the value from the sample should not have come from those distributions.

WHAT IS THE CONFIDENCE LEVEL?

Typically, a 95% confidence interval is reported, where the 95% is what statisticians call the *confidence level.* While a confidence interval may be calculated for any confidence level (such as 90% or 99%), when no level is specified, the level is generally understood to be 95%. In the example above, plausible values of parameters were eliminated if the statistic from our sample was unlikely to have come from the sampling distribution associated with the value of the parameter. The values of the parameter for which the value of the statistic was a value likely to occur in the sampling distribution were retained as plausible values of the parameter. The confidence level provides a numeric quantity for the cut off between likely and unlikely.

In the construction of a 95% confidence interval, for example, values of the parameter retained as plausible are those values for which the statistic is in the middle 95% of the corresponding sampling distribution, and values of the parameter that were eliminated corresponded to those sampling distributions for which the statistic is in the lower or upper 2.5% of the distribution. Similarly, to construct a 90% confidence interval, the retained plausible values of the parameter correspond to the sampling distributions from which the statistic is in the middle 90% of the distribution, and the eliminated plausible values of the parameter corresponding to the sampling distribution from which the statistic is in the lower or upper 5% of the distribution. To construct a 99% confidence interval, the values of the parameter for those values for which the statistic is in the middle 99% of the corresponding sampling distribution are retained as plausible and the values of the parameter for those values for which the statistic is in the lower or upper 0.5% of the corresponding sampling distribution are eliminated.

By selecting the range of plausible values for the parameter as those values for which the value of the statistic lies in the middle C% of the sampling distribution, a process has been used that will be successful for C% of all samples associated with the actual value of the parameter. Another way to think about the process is to imagine the sampling distribution for the actual value of the parameter, the value we hope to capture in our confidence interval. Consider the example of the mean length of the fish in the lake and denote the actual value of the parameter with the Greek character, μ. Figure 19.6 shows the sampling distribution for sample means of samples of size, $n = 50$, if the actual value of the parameter is μ. Without going into the mathematics, the mean length of the fish in the sample should fall within two standard errors of the value of μ for roughly 95% of possible samples and the standard error of the distribution is 0.25 inches. It is important to keep in mind that the value of μ, the mean length of all fish in the lake, is fixed, but unknown. In other words, it may be any one of the potential sampling distributions (Figure 19.3). What is known is the value of the statistic, the mean length of the fish in the sample. Instead of comparing the value of the statistic to all

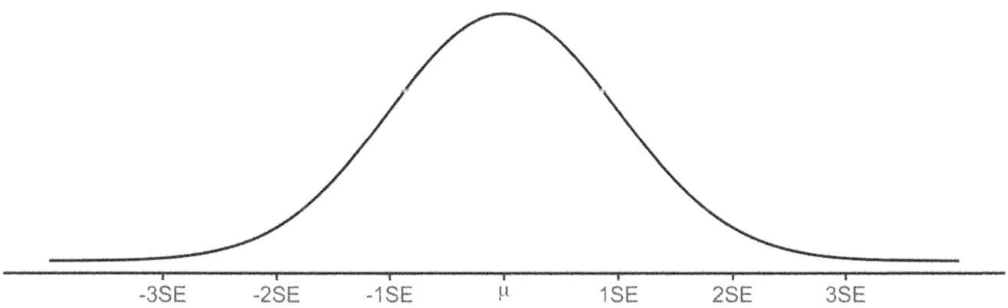

Figure 19.6 Sampling distribution of a sample mean.

of the sampling distributions for retention or elimination, the same range of plausible values can be determined by thinking about where on the actual sampling distribution the value of the statistic might lie.

For a 95% confidence interval, we assume our sample mean resides in the middle 95% of the sampling distribution of the actual value of the parameter. It could be 1 standard error above the value of the parameter. In this case, the value of the parameter would be 6.45 – 0.25 = 6.2 inches (Figure 19.7a). It could be 1.5 standard errors below the value of the parameter. In this case, the value of the parameter would be 6.45 + 0.375 = 6.825 inches (Figure 19.7b). At the upper end, it could be 2 standard errors above the value of the parameter. In this case, the value of the parameter would be 6.45 – 0.5 = 5.95 inches (Figure 19.7c). At the lower end, it could be 2 standard errors below the value of the parameter. In this case, the value of the parameter would be 6.45 + 0.5 = 6.95 inches (Figure 19.7d). These last two values encompass all possible values of μ if we imagine that our sample mean is in the middle 95% of the sampling distribution.

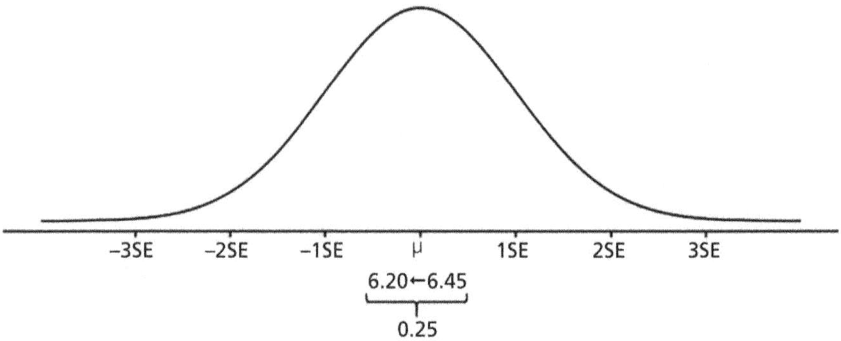

Figure 19.7a Value of μ if $\bar{x}$ is 1 standard error above the value of μ.

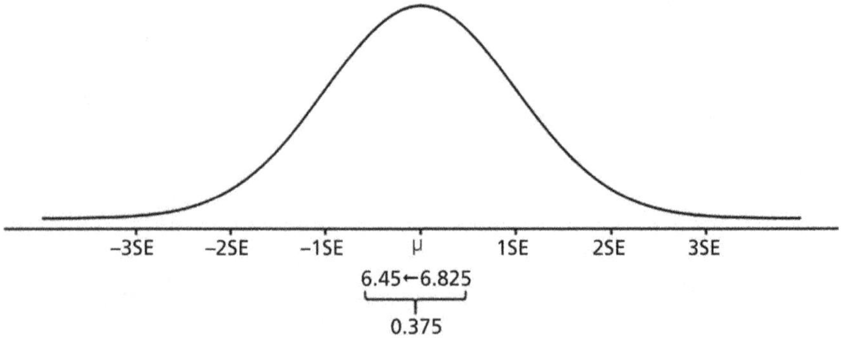

Figure 19.7b Value of μ if $\bar{x}$ is 1.5 standard error below the value of μ.

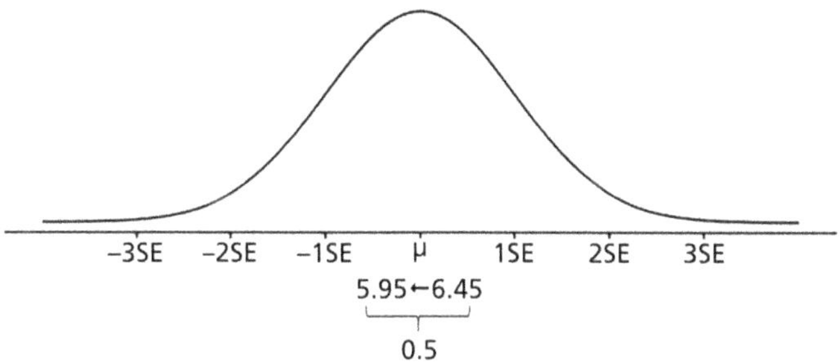

Figure 19.7c Value of μ if $\bar{x}$ is 2 standard error above the value of μ.

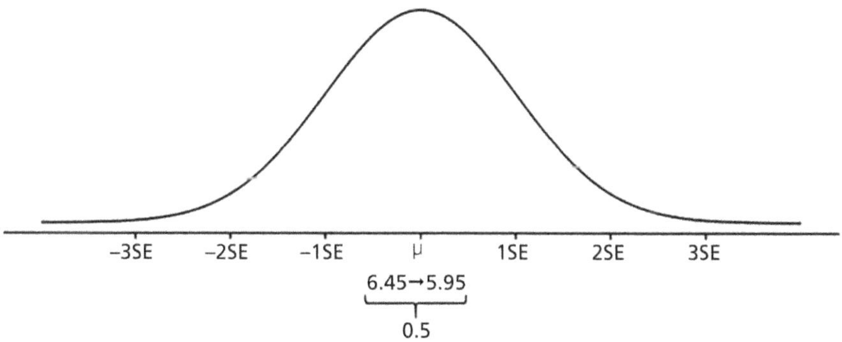

Figure 19.7d Value of μ if x is 2 standard error below the value of μ.

As long as we have one of those samples, we will have captured the actual value of μ. If we have one of the other samples, a sample with a value of the statistic in the tail of the sampling distribution, our interval will not contain the actual value of the parameter. What should be clear is that this process, for 95% of all possible samples, will lead to a confidence interval that contains the actual value of the parameter. This leads to the statistical interpretation of the confidence level: When statisticians say they have created a C% confidence interval, they mean they have used a procedure that is expected to be successful for C% of all possible samples.

INTERPRETATION OF THE CONFIDENCE INTERVALS

The typical textbook interpretation of a confidence interval applied to the example of fish length is, "We are 95% confident that the mean length of all the fish in the lake is between 5.95 inches and 6.95 inches" (see Agresti et al., 2017; De Veaux et al., 2018; Larson & Farber, 2019; McClave & Sincich, 2017; Triola & Iossi, 2018). This statement of 95% confidence is NOT equivalent to there being a 95% probability that the actual mean length of all of the fish is between the two values. To understand the difference between the use of the word confidence in describing the intervals rather than probability, imagine flipping a coin. Before the coin is flipped, there is a 50% chance of flipping a head. Similarly, before a sample is taken, there is a 95% percent chance of selecting a sample that will lead to a confidence interval that captures the true value of the parameter. The probability describes the process: flipping a coin or taking a sample and creating the interval. Once the coin has been flipped it either is or is not a head, so the probability of having flipped a head is either 1 or 0. Similarly, once the sample has been taken and the interval has been created, the interval either does or does not contain the actual value of the parameter, so the probability of containing the actual value of the parameter is either 1 or 0, and not 95%. In summary, the probability describes the process. Once the process is complete, we have a confidence in the results of the process, without a probability.

Common Non-Normative Reasoning About Confidence Intervals and Levels

The idea that the confidence level is also the probability that the confidence interval contains the actual value of the parameter is just one of the issues in understanding confidence intervals that appears in the education research literature. This section will focus on the known non-normative reasoning about confidence intervals, in particular, those identified in the literature as definitional. Types of *definitional* reasoning are those based on the definitional knowledge required to understand confidence intervals (Fidler, 2005). Definitional characteristics of confidence intervals can be categorized as: (a) procedurally computing the confidence interval (see Henriques, 2016), (b) interpreting the confidence level, and (c) interpreting the confidence interval. The discussion in this chapter is restricted to the interpretations of confidence intervals and levels, with the notion that the confidence level is the probability that a computed confidence interval contains the actual value of the parameter being one example of a definitional non-normative reasoning.

The non-normative reasoning about interpretations of confidence intervals and levels identified in the research literature stems from issues differentiating between populations and samples and parameters and statistics, and knowing which values are fixed and which values vary. In order for the reader to recognize the normative interpretations of confidence intervals and levels, these terms are redefined briefly. In the example, the population consists of all of the fish in the lake and, in general, the population is made up of every element or subject in the target group. The parameter is the quantitative value of the population being estimated. In the example, the parameters are the proportion of fish in the lake that are diseased and the mean length of all the fish in the lake. In frequentist statistics, the value of the parameter is taken as fixed. That is to say, there is an actual prevalence of disease and mean length of all fish in the lake and those values are not changing. The sample is comprised of the selected elements of the population from which the measurements have been collected. In the example, 50 fish are selected. These 50 fish are the sample. The statistic is the value calculated from the data produced from the sample: in this case, the proportion of fish in the sample that are diseased and the mean length of the fish in the sample. Since samples vary and each sample provides a potentially different statistic value, it is the samples and the statistics that vary (i.e., are not fixed). Similarly, since sampling distributions are created from population values, they are fixed. Confidence intervals, created from samples/statistics, vary and are not fixed as a collective.

Interpreting a Confidence Interval

The literature reports that roughly half of all undergraduate and graduate students and researchers can identify a correct interpretation of a confidence interval (delMas et al., 2007; Hoekstra et al., 2014): The statement, "We are 95% confident that the actual value of the parameter is between the lower and upper values calculated." This proportion may be as high as 75% for undergraduate students at the end of an introductory statistics course (delMas et al., 2007). While the percentage of people who correctly identify valid interpretations of confidence intervals increased after instruction, many subjects indicated both valid and invalid interpretations of confidence intervals were valid interpretations (delMas et al., 2007).

Fidler (2005) addressed most of the non-normative reasoning around the *interpretation of a confidence interval* defining the interval to be the range of plausible values for the parameter. While nearly one-quarter of the participants correctly identified the confidence interval as the range of plausible values for the population parameter, more subjects identified the confidence interval as the range of plausible values for the sample statistic. Another incorrect interpretation of the confidence interval is that it is the range of plausible values for individual observations (Fidler, 2005; Kalinowski et al., 2018).

Grant and Nathan (2008) extended Fidler's findings using the theory of conceptual metaphors to identify productive and nonproductive conceptual metaphors about confidence intervals. The authors used metaphors to determine participants' understanding of *fixed interval.* The authors defined the productive metaphor to be *changing ring metaphor*, which implies that the confidence intervals are changing rings around a fixed point: In other words, confidence intervals are not fixed, but are located and moving along an interval near the actual and fixed value of the parameter. Students who hold the nonproductive, *fixed disk metaphor*, believe the confidence intervals are of a fixed size but the parameter is moving. This is a nonproductive metaphor because it leads students to develop the conception that the confidence interval, instead of the parameter, is fixed. Grant and Nathan (2008) found these two metaphors to exist and often existed together in the minds of the participants.

Foster (2014) made the point in his discussion of the interpretations of confidence intervals that the language of the interpretation is rather precise and can be lexically ambiguous. He uses the two statements: "the population mean lies within the confidence interval" and "the confidence interval contains the population mean" to demonstrate one possible confusion. In the first statement, there is implied action on the population mean—indicating that the population mean is not a fixed, but unknown, quantity. The second statement removes the action of the population mean. It is generally accepted that the first statement indicates that a student thinks the interval is fixed, but the parameter is changing. The second statement is considered correct. Foster likens these statements to "the milk is in the fridge" and "the fridge contains the milk," which are equivalent statements in English, and argues that language needs to be more precise.

Callaert (2007) commented on the difficulty surrounding the use of the word *confident* in interpreting the confidence interval. From his experiences at AP readings, he found that students had learned that confident was the correct word to use, but questioned whether students knew what this word meant. Kaplan et al. (2010), in a more rigorous study of lexically ambiguous statistical terms, reported that the most frequent category contained student responses that "mentioned a level of certainty or surety" (p. 10), which was broken into several sub-themes: (a) about the location of a value, (b) of something vague or unspecified, and (c) that something is correct. The authors reported that a large proportion of students defined confident using a response classified as a level of surety or certainty and a smaller proportion defined confident implying a high level of certainty. Kaplan et al. (2010) were troubled by the large proportion of students with incoherent meanings. From these three studies, the interpretation of a confidence interval and the meaning of the word confident are not as straightforward as it would appear.

Interpreting the Confidence Level

Some of the non-normative interpretations of the *confidence level* of a confidence interval documented in the literature are: (a) the proportion of the population data that is contained within the interval (Canal & Gutiérrez, 2010; delMas et al., 2007), (b) the proportion of sample statistics that are in the interval (delMas et al., 2007; Kalinowski et al., 2018), (c) the probability the parameter is in the interval (Andrade et al., 2014; Andrade & Fernández, 2016; Foster, 2014; Hoekstra et al., 2014), and (d) the probability the statistic is in the interval (Canal & Gutiérrez, 2010).

Some of the non-normative interpretations of the confidence level are linked to non-normative interpretations of the confidence interval. Someone who identifies the confidence interval as the range of plausible values for individual observations might believe the confidence level is the proportion of the population data that falls in the calculated range. Similarly, someone who identifies the confidence interval as the range of plausible values for the sample statistic might believe that the confidence level is the proportion of sample statistics that will fall in the calculated range.

A normative interpretation of the confidence level is something like, if the same process was repeated many times, the confidence level represents the proportion of all the intervals created that are expected to contain the actual value of the parameter. Canal and Gutiérrez (2010) found that only half of the experts they studied and one-third of students correctly identify the normative interpretation of the confidence level. Published studies indicate that one-third to one-half of students incorrectly identify the interpretation of the confidence level as the proportion of the population that is contained in the interval even after instruction (Canal and Gutiérrez, 2010; delMas et al., 2007). An example of such a statement in our context is, "We expect about 95% of the fish in the lake to be of length between the endpoints of the confidence interval." An example of a non-normative statement that might be made by someone who thinks the confidence level is the proportion of samples with statistics lying in the interval is, "We expect about 95% of all the samples of 50 fish from the lake to produce mean lengths within the calculated interval." A majority of students indicate that this is a valid interpretation of the confidence level after instruction (delMas et al., 2007).

The non-normative reasoning about probability and confidence level may be related to the issues raised by Callaert (2007) and the lexical ambiguities of the words *confident* and *probability*. In a number of studies, including novices and experts, at least 50% of subjects identify statements such as "the probability that the true population mean is within the confidence interval is 95%" as normative (Canal & Gutiérrez, 2010; Foster, 2014; Hoekstra et al., 2014), exhibiting the non-normative idea that the confidence level is the probability that the interval captured the parameter value. Recall that the probability is on the process of selecting the sample and calculating the interval. Once the sample has been collected and the interval calculated, there is no probability associated with that interval much like there is no probability about the outcome of a coin toss after the coin has been observed.

The non-normative idea that the confidence level is the probability that the interval contains the statistic incorporates the non-normative reasoning about what is fixed and what varies as well as issues with the notion of probability. When building a confidence interval, a range of plausible values, for a parameter, the statistic is the best guess at the actual value of the parameter. It is, therefore, by definition a plausible value and under no circumstances would it not be contained in the confidence interval. In other words, there is a 100% probability (i.e., it is certain) that the value of the statistic will be in the confidence interval regardless of the level used. Andrade and colleagues (2014, 2016) tried to disrupt this non-normative reasoning using instructional tasks with preservice teachers (PSTs) designed to use the students' understanding of probability and sample space. In both studies, the authors found that the PSTs did not view the confidence interval as an event that was part of a larger sample space and the instructional tasks were unable to change the PSTs assumptions that the confidence level was the probability the parameter was in the interval.

IMPLICATIONS FOR TEACHING

The calls by professional societies for increased use of confidence intervals require changes in instruction in statistical methods (Steel et al., 2019). Using the results found in the literature, instruction around confidence intervals should be designed to encourage students to develop correct notions about what is fixed (the value of the parameter and the associated sampling distribution) and what varies (samples and their statistics) as well as correct conceptions about how the process leads to a range of plausible values for the parameter for a certain percentage of all possible samples. Strong understanding of confidence intervals and levels requires foundational knowledge: knowledge of distributions; the definitions and differences between parameters, statistics, populations, and samples; and sampling distributions. While the topic of statistical inference was once reserved for undergraduate or graduate statistical methods courses, these ideas are now included in curricula starting in middle school and prerequisite knowledge is included in elementary school standards (Bargagliotti et al., 2020; Franklin et al., 2007; National Governors Association Center for Best Practices, 2010; National Research Council, 2013b).

The Guidelines for Assessment and Instruction in Statistics Education (GAISE) Report: A Curriculum Framework (Franklin et al., 2007) and the updated *GAISE II Report* (Bargagliotti et al., 2020) are the most comprehensive curriculum frameworks for statistics instruction at the K–12 level. The GAISE documents are grounded in the statistical problem-solving process in which students are expected to learn statistics through a cyclic approach involving four components (investigative cycle): formulating statistical investigative questions, collecting and considering data, analyzing data, and interpreting results. A similar framework is implied in the "Practices for K–12 Science Classrooms" in *A Framework for K–12 Science Education: Practices, Crosscutting Concepts, and Core Ideas* (National Research Council, 2012). The science framework includes in the list of practices: asking questions, planning and carrying out investigations, analyzing and interpreting data, and engaging in argument from evidence.

The GAISE provides three developmental levels for each step of the investigative cycle through which K–12 students should progress to reach statistical literacy. Called Levels A, B, and C in the documentation, these levels are roughly equivalent to elementary, middle, and high school, respectively, but are mainly used to identify a student's level of statistical thinking. Similarly, the science frameworks provide a progression for students for each scientific practice. In particular, these documents suggest that elementary school students should recognize the need to record data and use data to make predictions and decisions. Middle school students should distinguish between samples and populations and embark on informal statistical inferencing, and high school students should learn formal statistical inference, including margins of errors and confidence intervals.

The remainder of the chapter is organized around the three K–12 school levels and is intended to support teachers in designing instruction that helps students build normative reasoning and avoid non-normative reasoning about confidence intervals. Many publications were developed because of the perceived need for training and support for K–12 mathematics teachers to teach statistical ideas and all have as their primary intended audience K–12 teachers and/or teacher educators (Batanero et al., 2011; Franklin et al., 2015; Franklin et al., 2007; Garfield & Ben-Zvi, 2008a; Garfield & Ben-Zvi, 2008b; Garfield et al., 2008; Harradine et al., 2011; Kader & Jacobbe, 2013; Peck et al., 2013).

Elementary School: Variability in Data and Predictions

The GAISE Reports (Bargagliotti et al., 2020; Franklin et al., 2007) at Level A and the scientific frameworks and Common Core Mathematics Standards for Elementary School Students suggest that students should recognize the need to record observations to answer scientific questions and collect, display, and summarize categorical and quantitative variables. Students at this level should be able to describe key features of distributions including variability and make conclusions or predictions using their data. There is no mention in the standards documents at this level about populations or samples. The suggested approach in elementary school is to treat data as a population without seeming to infer from our data to a larger population.

Given this approach, we turn away from the example of the yellow perch to a scientific topic found in the science frameworks that lends itself to data collection in an elementary classroom, around which one can easily make or find predictions that have been made, and for which the population is difficult to imagine: weather and climate. In particular, the science framework specifies that by the end of Grade 2, students should measure weather conditions to describe patterns over time, and by the end of Grade 5, students should record patterns across time and area to make predictions about weather in the future. In elementary classrooms, students can collect daily measurements on at least one categorical variable, for example, whether or not it rained, and one quantitative variable, for example, temperature or humidity at a certain time of day or amount of rainfall in the previous 24 hours, potentially from two instruments placed at different locations. Having more than one instrument would allow students to develop the idea of measurement variability. Collecting both categorical and quantitative data allows students to develop ideas around distribution of each type of variable: measurements of centers and variability as well as appropriate displays of each variable type.

By Grade 5, the science frameworks suggest that students should work with larger data sets, those potentially available online. Students in upper elementary school could find or be provided with historical weather data, which they could use to make predictions. For example, at the start of the school year, students could be given historical weather data for some month in the future. They could be tasked with analyzing the data to predict a weather event in that upcoming month, for example, the highest temperature, the amount of rainfall, or the number of days above or below a certain temperature. Again, at least one categorical and one quantitative variable be used in such an investigation so students can develop statistical techniques for summarizing distributions for both variable types. This activity lays the groundwork for two ideas necessary to understand formal statistical inference: understanding of the distribution of a variable and understanding of variability in predictions.

A robust understanding of sampling distributions and formal statistical inference requires coordination of ideas associated with three distributions: the distribution of the population, the distribution of the sample, and the sampling distribution of the sample statistic (Saldanha & Thompson, 2002). When estimating a proportion, such as the proportion of days in a month on which it is likely to rain or prevalence of diseased fish in a lake, the distributions of the categorical variable in the population and in the sample are visualized as bar graphs with two bars (rain/no rain or disease/no disease). When estimating a population mean, such as the mean temperature for the days in a month or the mean length of the fish in a lake, the distribution of quantitative variables (the temperature or the length) in the population and sample are typically displayed in a dot plot or histogram. In both cases, estimating the proportion or the mean, the sampling distribution of the statistic, is generally visualized as a histogram or a dotplot. The weather data activities should provide students early opportunities to develop language and graph skills associated with describing distributions of both categorical and quantitative variables used in informal and formal inference.

When students are asked to use data analysis to make predictions about weather at some time in the future, their predictions can be used to lay a foundation for thinking about variability associated with predictions. Imagine that students made predictions about the highest temperature that would be recorded in October. At the beginning of November, the predictions could be tested against the actual data from October. It is unlikely that any one prediction will be correct (although that is certainly possible), but it is likely that the actual value will fall in the range created by the predictions. In other words, the predictions will act as a prediction interval, helping students to anticipate the incorporation of variability in estimating necessary to understand confidence intervals (this is called a prediction interval to distinguish from a confidence interval due to the lack of confidence level associated with the task).

Another potential weather-related activity that could be conducted with upper elementary school students or middle school students to develop understanding about uncertainty in modeling and predictions uses hurricane modeling as a context. Teachers could provide students a warnings/cone static image, such as that seen in Figure 19.1, at the beginning of a storm. Students could track the actual path of the storm on the original image to see how close the storm stayed to the central path and whether it stayed within the probabilistic path model. As new maps are produced, those could be compared to the original map. It would be particularly salient to discuss the difference in the width of the probabilistic path over the time of the prediction. In particular, there is less variability in the near term, closer to the current location of the storm, and more variability as the predictions are further into the future. Such a discussion should lay a foundation for students to think critically in the future about factors that control the width of a confidence interval, such as the confidence level or the sample size.

Middle School: Sampling Variability and Informal Statistical Inference

Confidence intervals, along with the use of methods recognized by the statistics and research community to make generalizations about a population from a sample, are formal inferential reasoning (FIR) as discussed in the statistics education literature (Makar & Rubin, 2009). The GAISE Reports and Standards documents do not suggest that Level B/ middle school students learn FIR. Instead, these students should recognize uncertainty due to sample-to-sample variability, use the knowledge of sampling variability to generalize beyond the sample, and state limitations from using sample data to make such generalizations: aspects of informal inferential reasoning (IIR; Tobias-Lara & Gomez-Blancarte, 2019). IIR requires statistical evidence and should employ probabilistic language, but is more open to the use of descriptive and exploratory analyses, rather than formal notions of sampling distributions (Tobias-Lara & Gomez-Blancarte, 2019).

Turning back to the making of inferences about a population from data provided by a sample means returning to the example of the yellow perch as the context of weather does not provide a clear and meaningful population/sample dichotomy. In middle school, students should develop informal notions of sampling variability. The literature around this level of IIR is focused mostly on testing hypotheses informally and not constructing plausible intervals (see Bakker & Derry, 2011; Ben-Zvi et al., 2012; Nilsson, 2020). Nevertheless, the suggested activity is based on a classroom game described by Nilsson (2020). In the described game, students in a mathematics class select repeated samples from a known population with a uniform distribution of colored balls to develop informal notions about the way samples vary. The students then use these informal notions to decide which of a number of unknown populations do not have a uniform distribution of colored balls. A similar activity can be enacted in a science class using variables representing the characteristics of fish.

If the activity set begins with a categorical variable of interest, such as whether a fish is healthy or diseased, two different colored balls or pellets can be used: one color representing a diseased fish and the other a healthy fish. The pellets can be put in a large-mouth plastic bottle in the correct proportion and students can sample the "fish" by tipping the pellets out of the bottle. The activity should start with the use of clear bottles, as was done by Nilsson (2020), so the students can see the distribution of the population and estimate the parameter of interest, the proportion of fish that are diseased, by looking at the bottles. The activity should start with populations (lakes represented by bottles) at two extremes: relatively healthy lakes with 80–90% healthy fish and relatively diseased lakes with 80–90% diseased fish. Students should collect repeated samples of the same number of fish and record the number (or proportion) of diseased fish in a histogram or dot plot. As they collect more samples and add data to the dot plot, they are growing a simulated sampling distribution. Teachers can help students develop strong reasoning about sampling distributions by asking questions such as, "Did every sample have the same number of diseased fish?"; "What was the lowest/highest number of diseased fish in any of the samples?"; and "What was the median number of diseased fish in the sample?"

Once students can reason about sampling variability, they can move on to play "Guess My Parameter," a game designed to develop IIR around confidence intervals. Using colored bottles or paper so the students cannot see the contents of the bottle, the teacher can create a number of "lakes" with different proportions of diseased fish. Students can work in groups to take one sample of fish from each lake and then work as a group to order the lakes from most healthy to most diseased. They can also provide a range of values for each lake representing the smallest and largest proportion of fish in each lake that they would believe are diseased. Students should be encouraged to justify their ranges using the data compiled in the previous activity about how much samples are expected to vary.

After each group has completed the ordering and IIR confidence interval generation, the groups can pool their samples as a class. The teacher can use this opportunity to explain that these samples can be considered replication studies: Each group is one team of researchers who have replicated the findings of the other groups of researchers. The groups or class should then be given time to revise their responses and reasoning about the levels of diseased fish in the lake. This activity should help students develop informal notions of sampling variability, that samples will not all be the same and will not all be exact representations of the population, while also learning that samples vary in a predictable way, and that the predictability can be used to make informal inferences from a sample back to the population. Similar activities for quantitative variables, such as the length of fish, are more complicated to enact, the Visual Inference Tools (VIT) modules (https://www.stat.auckland.ac.nz/~wild/VITonline/index.html) associated with the iNZight Project (https://www.stat.auckland.ac.nz/~wild/iNZight_2016-08/index.php) have a number of excellent resources and visualizations that can be used with middle school students.

High School: Sampling Distributions and Randomization-Based Statistical Inference

The GAISE II Report (Bargagliotti et al., 2020) specified that students at Level C (high school) should use simulations to determine sampling distributions of statistics, use the simulated sampling distributions or other simulation techniques to construct confidence intervals for a population characteristic, and interpret the confidence interval and margin of error in terms of plausibility of and variability around estimates and predictions. The Common Core State Standards for Mathematics (National Governors Association Center for Best Practices, 2010) contains similar suggestions.

The call to use simulations to introduce sampling distributions is widespread in the literature, but research has shown that guidance must be provided to focus student attention on the important aspects of the technology for such activities to be efficacious (McDaniel & Green, 2012). Attention to two critical ideas are recommended as students move from the informal ideas associated with sampling variability to the formal idea of the sampling distribution: (a) the unit of observation in the sampling distribution is different from the unit of measurement in the distribution of the sample or the population and (b) students may need a hands-on experience before using computer-generated simulations.

As discussed previously, a robust understanding of sampling distributions and formal statistical inference requires coordination of ideas associated with three distributions: the distribution of the population, the distribution of the sample, and the sampling distribution of the sample statistic (Saldanha & Thompson, 2002). When estimating the prevalence of disease in the fish in the lake, the unit of observation for the distribution of the population is a fish. Similarly, the unit of observation for the distribution of the sample is a fish. The unit of observation for the sampling distribution of the statistic, the proportion of fish in the sample that has the disease, is a sample of fish. The distributions of the population and the sample are displayed in bar charts with two bars, one showing the number of diseased fish and one the number of healthy fish. The sampling distribution of the statistic is typically displayed as a histogram (Figure 19.2) showing the number of samples of fish with a particular proportion of diseased fish. In estimating the mean length of the fish in the lake, all three distributions can be visualized using a histogram, but as in the case of the sample proportion the unit of observation in the distributions of the population and sample are individual fish, but the unit of observation in the sampling distribution of the sample mean is a sample of fish. In other words, the sampling distribution of the sample mean shows the means of potential samples of fish. It is important to make this point salient while working through the suggested activities below.

Instruction should start with a hands-on simulation activity prior to using computer-based simulations. The hands-on simulation is meant to help students understand what is being done by the computer program. To simulate the prevalence of disease in the fish in the lake, the pellet set-up described in the previous section could be used, or two different colors of paper could be cut into pieces of the same size and then put in a box. A teacher could choose the proportions and could make different boxes with different proportions (using unique colors in each box so the "fish" do not become mixed up, changing the underlying proportions). While samples of size $n = 50$ may be unreasonable to select and count, a class should be able to generate a reasonable number of samples of a smaller size, for example, $n = 10$, so the general pattern can be seen in a sampling distribution. Similarly, an instructor could generate 1,000 fish lengths with a given mean and standard deviation and then print them in a way that the paper could be cut into equal size squares each with one fish length (and if you want to get fancy, you can print the lengths and the outline of a fish). Again, students could take samples of 10 fish, find and graph the sample means, and see the sampling distribution take shape.

Once students have created sampling distributions by hand for small samples, they should move on to an applet to generate sampling distributions more quickly to learn about the factors that change sampling distributions, for example, the value of the parameter and the size of the sample. The Rossman-Chance Applet Collection is an excellent resource, partly because these applets display clearly the three distributions: the distribution of the population, the distribution of the last sample selected, and the sampling distribution of the sample statistic (see http://www.rossmanchance.com/applets/; for the Reeses Pieces applet, http://www.rossmanchance.com/applets/OneProp/OneProp.htm?candy=1 [Figure 19.8]; for proportions and the Sampling Words applet, http://www.rossmanchance.com/applets/OneSample.html?population=gettysburg [Figure 19.9] for means).

In the Reeses Pieces applet, the dispenser shows the distribution of the population and the proportion of orange candies in the dispenser is equivalent to the prevalence of disease in the fish in the lake. In Figure 19.8, the proportion of orange/diseased fish is set to 30% and have selected 10,000 samples of size $n = 50$, recording the proportion of orange candies/diseased fish in each of the 10,000 samples. Using the *population model* option in the Sampling Words applet allows the user to set the mean and standard deviation for the lengths of fish in the lake, defining the distribution of the population. In Figure 19.9, the mean fish length is set to 7.5 inches, the standard deviation to 1.75 inches, and assumed a normal model for fish lengths. Then 10,000 samples of $n = 50$ fish were selected and the mean length of the 50 fish for each sample was recorded.

In using applets, it is important to connect the parts of the applet to the hands-on simulation. In other words, where is the applet taking the sample or calculating the statistic from the sample? It is also important to ensure students can find the population and its distribution, the sample and its distribution, the sampling distribution of the statistic, and the values of both the population parameter and the statistics from the last sample collected. If you ask students to create sampling distributions for samples of different sizes from the same population and record the mean and standard deviation of the population, last sample selected, and the sampling distribution, students should see that the population parameters are fixed, while values from the samples are varying and that the sampling distribution is centered on the parameter value.

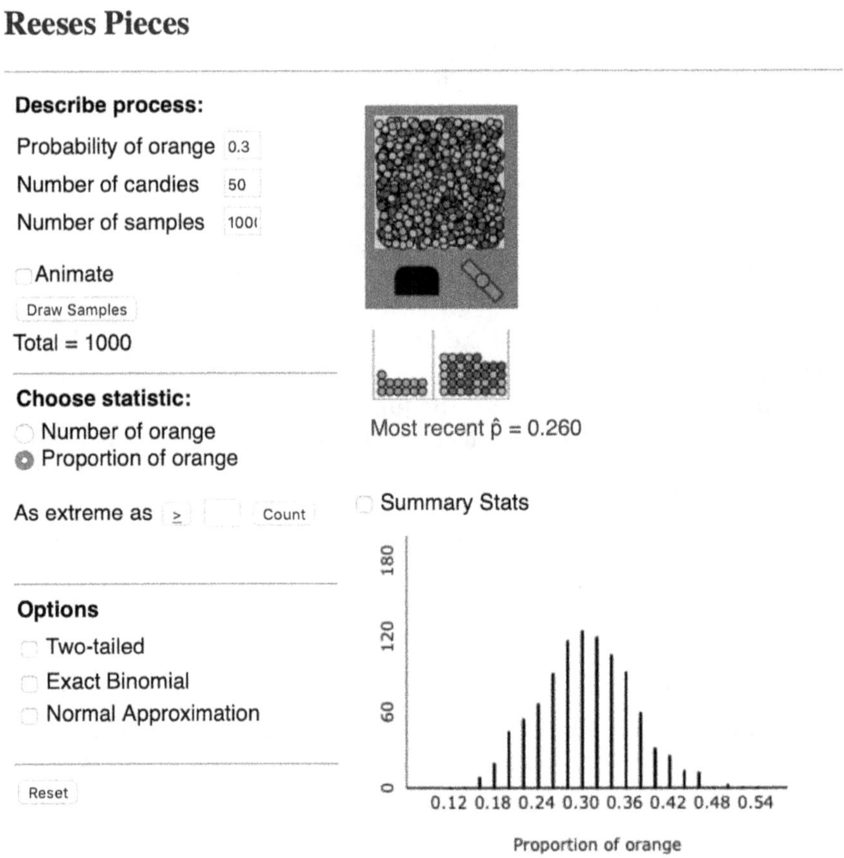

Figure 19.8 Reese's pieces applet set for $p = 0.3$, $n = 50$, 10,000 samples.

Once students have mastered sampling distributions, confidence intervals can be introduced as using a sample to create a range of plausible values for the population parameter. Students could take a sample from a population with an unknown parameter value and use the applets to find plausible and implausible values of the parameter. This is akin to "guess and check" as students would have to guess at the parameter value and check whether their statistic was in the plausible part of the sampling distribution for that value of the parameter. They would have to estimate the boundary values. For this activity, starting with the population proportion (Reeses Pieces applet) is recommended because the only information necessary to complete the task are the proportion and the sample size. Doing this activity for other parameters would be more complicated because of the amount of information needed to set up the populations.

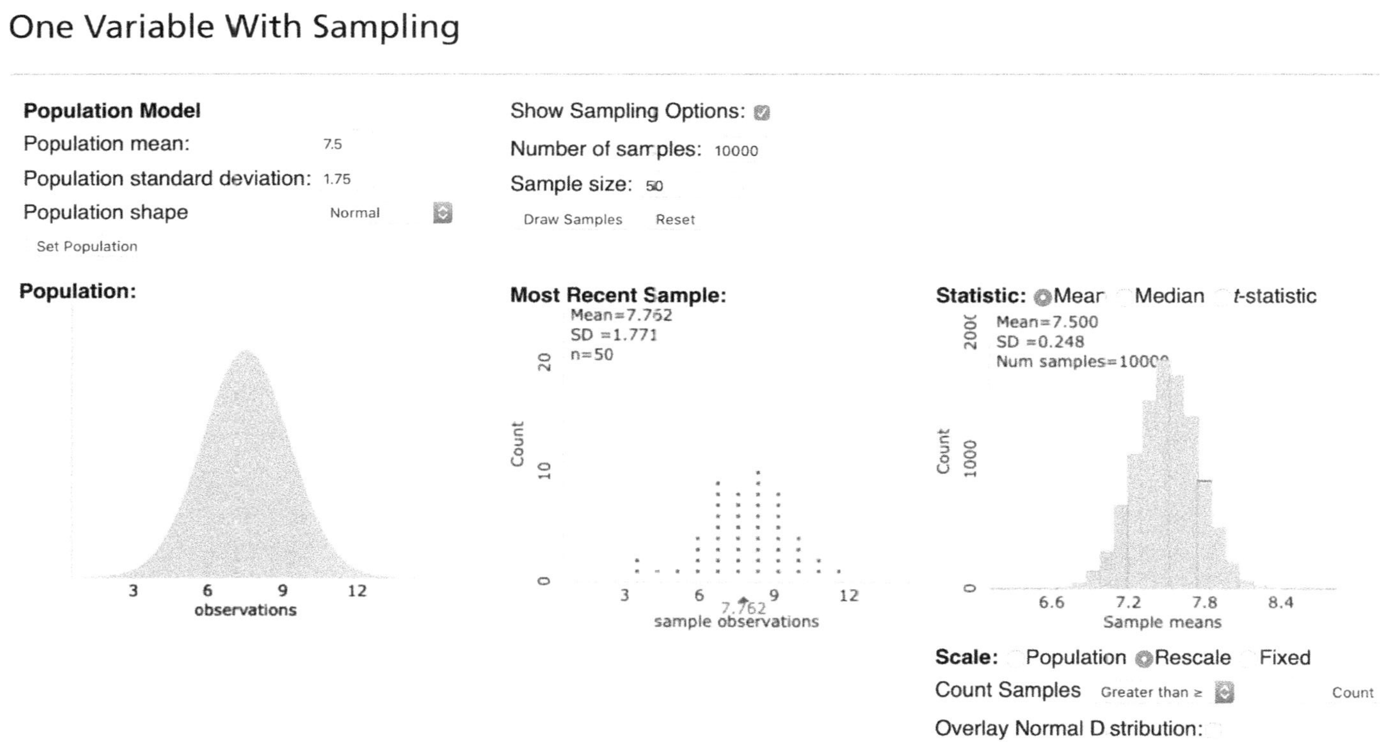

Figure 19.9 Sampling words applet set for $\mu = 7.5$, $\sigma = 1.75$, $n = 50$, 10,000 samples.

When students have learned to calculate confidence intervals, it might be useful to address directly the non-normative reasoning about the confidence levels. There are a number of applets that demonstrate the idea that C% of samples will generate confidence intervals that capture the actual value of the parameter. See, for example, the Simulating Confidence Intervals applet (http://www.rossmanchance.com/applets/ConfSim.html), shown in Figure 19.10, in which 96 of the 100 samples drawn create 95% confidence intervals that contain the actual value of the parameter set to be $p = 0.3$. Instruction should also address the non-normative ideas that the confidence level is the proportion of the sample, the proportion of the population, or the proportion of the sample statistics that have values in the confidence intervals directly. This could be done by having students select a sample from a known population and calculate the 95% confidence interval from that sample. The students could then test the three propositions, that 95% of the sample values, the population values, or the sampling distribution, are in the calculated range. While for some samples this may be true, with a reasonably sized class, there should be counterexamples.

The chapter began with an exhortation for the use of confidence intervals to replace reliance on hypothesis testing to advance science in a post

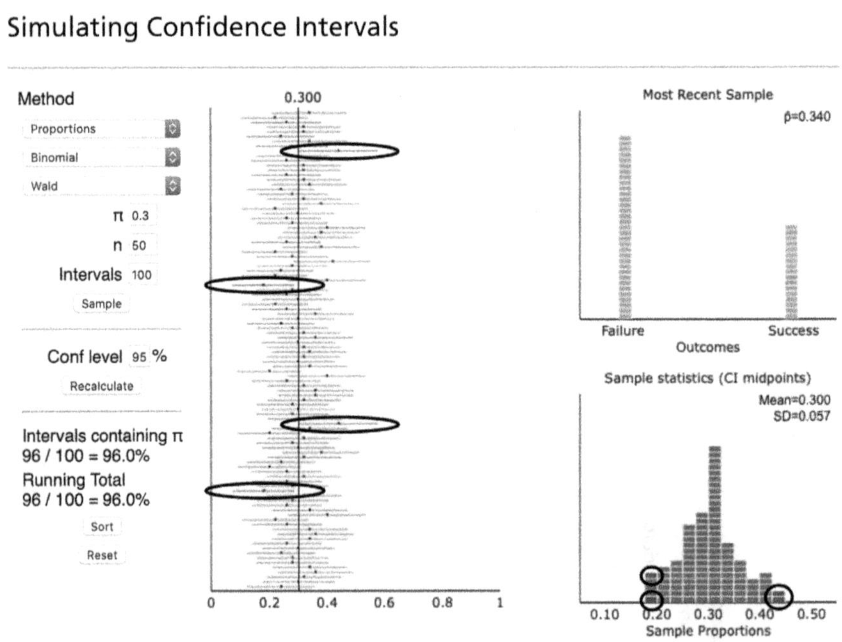

Figure 19.10 Simulating confidence intervals with $p = 0.3$, $n = 50$, creating 100 intervals.

$p < 0.05$ world. While errors in reasoning about confidence intervals have been enumerated, Hoekstra et al. (2012) found that participants made fewer inferential mistakes, fewer references to significance, and more references to effect size when presented with confidence intervals over hypothesis testing. There is, however, the same danger with confidence intervals as with hypothesis testing if a confidence interval is used to make decisions about particular values. From personal experience, it is not uncommon for statistics instructors to tell their students that if a value is not contained in a 95% confidence interval, they should reject that value as if they were testing it in a two-sided hypothesis test. Instruction on reasoning with confidence intervals should, therefore, focus on plausibility and compatibility rather than significance and rejection (Amrhein et al., 2019; Greenland, 2019).

The intent of this chapter is to provide instructors with the background to teach the statistical inference technique of confidence intervals in a way that will help students build a strong understanding of what testing and estimation can tell us, as suggested by Steel et al. (2019) and become thoughtful researchers in a post $p < 0.05$ world. This was done embedded in a real scientific context to model some of the other suggestions made by Steel et al. (2019). As teachers design instruction around data analysis and statistical inferencing, they are encouraged to follow as many of suggestions by Steel et al.: For example, to teach statistical communication explicitly, including communication about the benefits and limitations of statistical conclusions and to encourage students to create analyses based on the scientific question at hand. Scientists, science and mathematics educators, and teacher educators in STEM fields are encouraged to learn more about statisticians' visions for statistical inferencing in a post $p < 0.05$ starting with the excellent summary by Wasserstein et al. (2019).

REFLECTIVE QUESTIONS

A group of statisticians and statistics educators was having dinner at a restaurant while traveling on business. Just before the bill came, one of the statisticians asked the server for pens and paper. He distributed slips of paper to everyone at the table and asked us to write our guess for the total amount of the bill. All of the dinner guests began arguing, claiming they hadn't looked at the prices or didn't know what people at the other end of the table had ordered. The statistician who suggested the game told everyone else not to worry, that the range covered by our guesses would be a 95% confidence interval for the total amount of the bill. This statement immediately calmed the group, and everyone submitted their guess (which did indeed contain the actual bill amount between the lowest and highest guess).

1. Why do you think the information that our guesses would be a 95% confidence interval alleviate the reluctance to submit guesses?
2. What did the statistician mean when he said the guesses would be a 95% confidence interval for the total amount of the bill?

CHAPTER 20

THE MULTIDIMENSIONAL LEARNING GOALS FOR MAKING INFERENCES WITH DATA

Ryan Seth Jones, Anna Strimaitis Grinath, and Fonya Scott

Interdisciplinary thinking is rapidly becoming an integral feature of research.
—National Academies of Sciences, Engineering, & Medicine, Facilitating Interdisciplinary Research

Teaching data analysis is not easy, and the time allowed is always far from sufficient.
—John Tukey

In the Age of Inference, making inferences with data requires a diverse set of ideas and practices. Data, data visualizations, and models make use of mathematical and statistical ideas related to quantity, variability, space, and chance. Nevertheless, these ideas are never independent of context. Data are generated to inform a question about *something* (Cobb & Moore, 1997; Wild et al., 2018). This means that knowledge of the investigation context must be knit with the mathematical and statistical knowledge in order to make inferences with data, which is always an interdisciplinary act.

Age of Inference, pages 347–354

Schools, though, are often organized around disciplinary boundaries, such as mathematics and science. Students go to one class to learn math, another to learn science, and another to learn about communicating with an audience. As they move across these boundaries, it is common for students to see the various classes as disconnected from each other. This creates significant challenges for supporting the development of the ideas and practices necessary for making inferences with data because students must develop an integrated, coherent set of interdisciplinary ideas and practices across multiple years of schooling (Lehrer & English, 2018). How will students be able to do this without support to see connections across disciplinary boundaries?

Teachers and school leaders will need to think creatively in order to develop innovative strategies for supporting this type of interdisciplinary learning. However, there is still very little known about how to productively integrate concepts and practices across diverse STEM disciplines (Honey et al., 2014). Conceptualizations of integrated STEM vary widely and, at times, are poorly defined (Martin-Paez et al., 2019). Integration alone does not necessarily create better opportunities for students to learn and can, at times, impede learning because of the complexity of a given set of concepts or practices.

One of the key challenges in integrating across mathematics and science education is to coordinate developmental trajectories for disciplinary knowledge while also supporting students to engage in practices that leverage knowledge from separate disciplines (Honey et al., 2014). To date, research on integrated STEM teaching and learning has overwhelmingly focused on engineering design as a practice to organize the integration of STEM disciplines (Honey et al., 2014; Martin-Paez et al., 2019). Although much less attention has been given to making inferences with data as an organizing framework for integrated STEM learning, there is evidence that careful integration across STEM disciplines can support students to better understand how to leverage tools from different disciplines to generate and revise knowledge (e.g., Lehrer & Schauble 2004; Schuchardt & Schunn, 2016).

LEARNING TO MAKE INFERENCES WITH DATA MAKER SCIENCE

Data modeling and argumentation knowledge explorations to rethink science (Data MAKER Science) is a framework we have developed to organize interdisciplinary mathematics and science learning around the practice of making inferences with data. The Data MAKER Science framework (Figure 20.1) coordinates data learning goals and appropriate scientific phenomena that evoke data forms, representations, and models that are consistent with the data learning goals. It also guides the design of learning

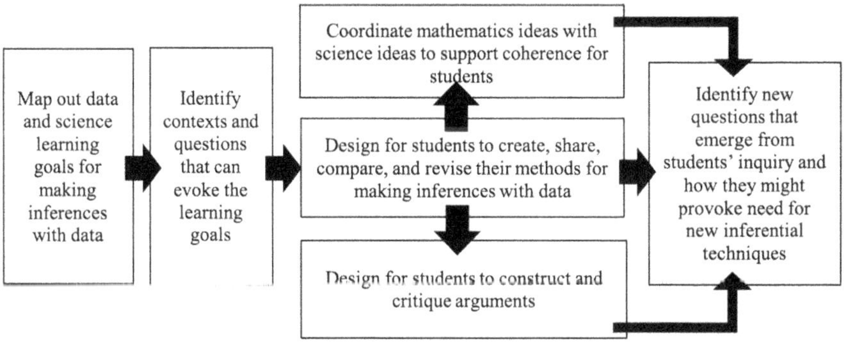

Figure 20.1 Data MAKER science framework.

environments where students have agency to create novel approaches to making inferences with data models and to construct and critique arguments based on these models. Lastly, it guides the coordination of learning environments that will support the different disciplinary learning goals. This may happen across different math or science classes, or it could happen within one interdisciplinary STEM learning environment.

Making Data and Inferences About Sponge Form and Function (Phylum: Porifera)

Here we illustrate the Data MAKER Science framework by describing how it informed the development of an investigation of form and function relationships of organisms in marine ecosystems. This investigation provides an example of the ways the Data MAKER Science framework can guide the work of designing for the interdisciplinarity of making inferences with data about the natural world.

The Data MAKER Science approach begins with mapping out data and science learning goals associated with the kinds of inferences students will be making with data. For this illustration, we mapped middle school mathematics standards related to statistics and probability with middle school life science learning goals for the core idea of structure and function (Figure 20.2). In this Data MAKER Science module, students develop and apply their understanding of foundational mathematical and statistical concepts in the context of investigating the relationship between the feeding structures of a sponge and the function of filter-feeding on a coral reef. We chose the sponge filter-feeding context to provoke a need for making an inferential claim about sponge volume in the midst of measurement variability. Although measurement is often not treated as an inferential activity,

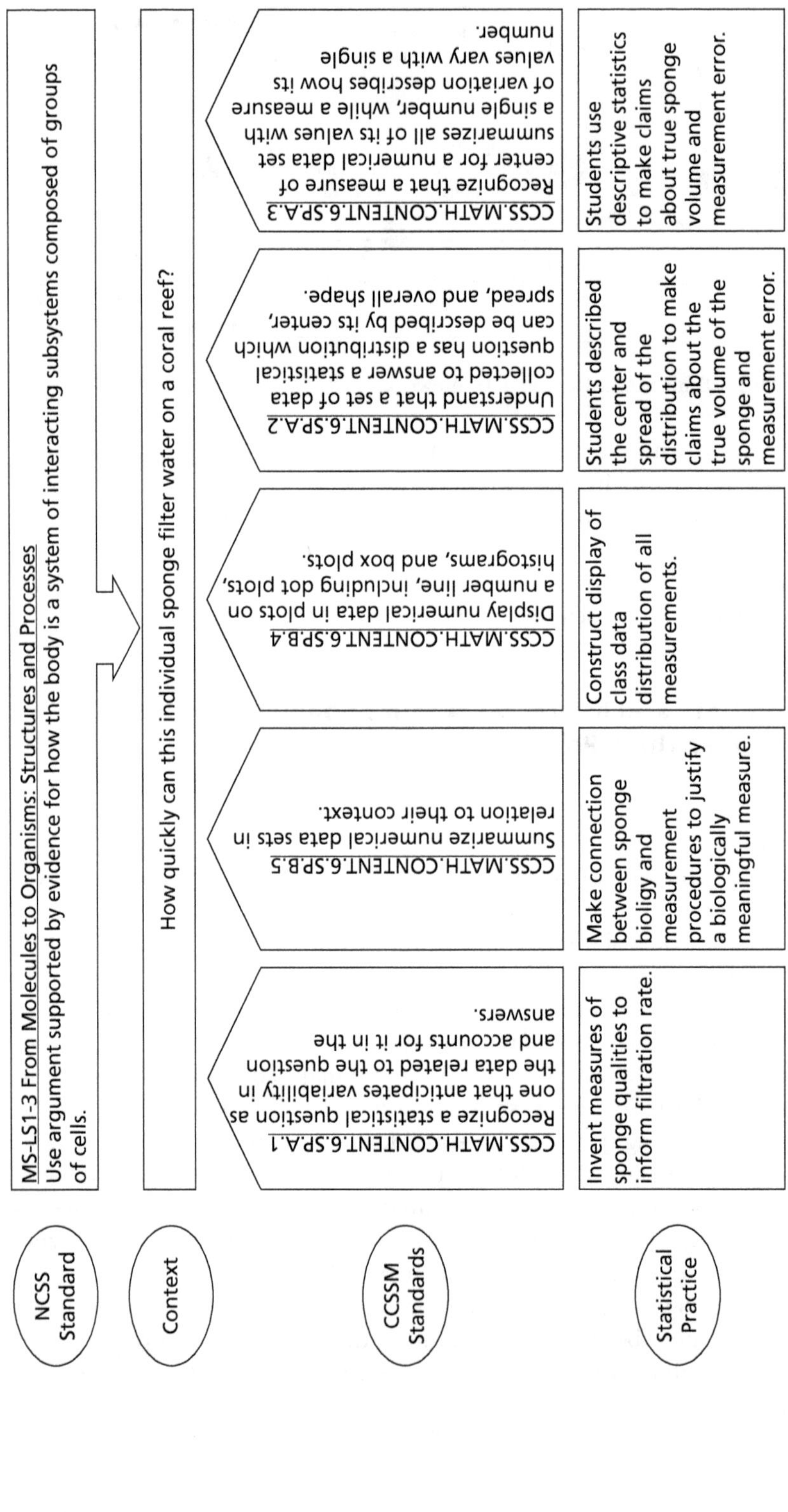

Figure 20.2 Coordination of mathematics and science standards and practices.

our approach emphasizes that measurement is always inferential because of measurement error. An individual sponge is an irregularly shaped organism that is difficult to measure precisely. Thus, when many students measure the same individual sponge, the measurements will vary, creating a need for distribution and statistics to describe the collection of repeated measurements. Students engaged in this investigation address the driving question: How quickly can this individual sponge filter water on a coral reef?

Students began by watching a video that makes sponge filtration power visible by squirting dye at the base of the sponge and waiting for the dye to flow out after being filtered through the sponge body. Students examined sponge specimens and diagrams (top left of Figure 20.2) and explored their initial ideas of how sponge structures were related to filter-feeding function (NGSS MS.LS1.3). We then leveraged this discussion to motivate a need to quantify our qualitative descriptions of sponge form that would be important to understand the individual sponge's filtration rate (CCSS Math 6.SP.A1). Student groups invented and negotiated measurement methods, and used their group's methods to independently measure the volume of identical 3D printed sponge individuals (bottom left of Figure 20.3). Although students invented a variety of measurement procedures, this provided the opportunity to compare the approaches and to discuss which were most biologically meaningful to make inferences about filtration rate (CCSS Math 6.SP.B.5).

The identical 3D printed organisms proved to be an important piece of infrastructure for students to consider repeated measures of an object within the context of a large class. Although students measured identical sponges, these measures were highly variable due to the irregular shape of the sponge and variation in the methods students used to take the measurements. This variability, though, provided a ripe context for students to grapple with the practice of measurement and the role of variability in quantifying biological qualities of an organism. For example, many students

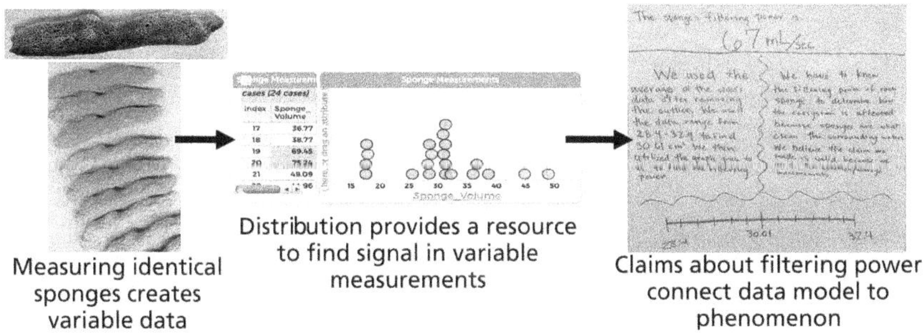

Figure 20.3 Designed infrastructure to support students to grapple with making claims with variable data.

anticipated that everyone should measure the "exact same value," and were troubled by the variable measurements.

The class collaboratively constructed a data distribution (center of Figure 20.2; CCSS Math 6.SP.B4), leading some students to claim that the variability in measures made the true sponge volume unknowable because "the data are way too widespread to make a conclusion that that's the true size." However, during the class discussion of the data, other students noticed that some measurements were similar or identical. This gives the center and spread of the distribution an epistemic role by informing the students' claims about "true" size and the extent of measurement error (Lehrer & Schauble, 2007; CCSS Math 6.SP.A.2). We then asked students to use descriptive statistics to make a claim about the true volume of the sponge model and measurement error (CCSS Math 6 SP.A.3). Students were also asked to justify how they used the data model (e.g., statistics describing characteristics of the class data distribution; CCSS Math 6 SP.A.3) and biological concepts (e.g., the relationship between sponge structure and function; NGSS MS.LS1.3) to support their claim. Students collaboratively constructed one argument per group (right of Figure 20.3) and negotiated what claim to make and how to support it.

After each group constructed their argument on chart paper, they critiqued arguments constructed by students in another class. These arguments were from a different class; therefore, students did not have access to the data distribution generated by the other class and had to rely on the evidence and justification provided in the arguments to judge whether the claims made by the other class were supported by the data. This allowed students to recognize the critical role of communicating a clear justification of the statistical and biological reasoning they used to draw inferences from the data model. This critical role is difficult to recognize when students only focus on articulating their reasoning for their argument because students are very familiar with the inferences underlying their claims and may have not considered other plausible inferences. By critiquing arguments generated in a different class, students are forced to consider the validity of other plausible inferences.

In these lessons, we have observed that students often move from thinking of measurement as the act of finding exact values to the practice of making inferences in the midst of variation. For example, many students initially stated that "we all gotta have the same numbers" when discussing what will happen if they all measure the identically printed 3D sponge. Others, though, expected that the measurements would not be identical, but "should be around the same area." Many of the students who once thought of measurement as the search for exact values came to use distributional characteristics, such as center, for making inferences about sponge volume. By the end of the investigation, we saw some students beginning to account for variability in their claims about the filtering rate. This is an important shift in developing a scientific mindset towards inference because inferences about measurement in the sciences always account for variability from measurement error.

DISCUSSION

It is challenging work to design activities to support students in making meaningful inferences from data that correspond to disciplinary practice. School structures that separate disciplines can unintentionally undermine the development of inferential practices because inference is interdisciplinary by nature. The Data MAKER Science design framework informs both the interdisciplinary design in classrooms and the infrastructure to support student learning. We think this has the potential to contribute to a deliberate approach to creating interdisciplinary STEM learning environments that engage students with making inferences with data about disciplinary specific phenomena.

However, this framework also has the potential to illuminate tensions and challenges in supporting students to develop interdisciplinary inferential practices. Teachers may realize they need to coordinate their instruction with colleagues from different disciplines to ensure that the diverse disciplinary ideas necessary for making inferences with data are treated with sufficient depth. For example, science teachers may need to identify times when math teachers are discussing properties of different measures of center so these ideas can be sufficiently developed before they are expected in the science class investigations. Likewise, mathematics teachers may need to collaborate with science colleagues to identify when students will discuss ecology if they are supporting students with a task using data about plant growth. In the illustration provided, it is likely that middle grades math and science teachers would need to collaborate to discuss the parts of the lessons on which each class would focus. This will often require new opportunities to collaboratively plan and reflect on instruction together. However, this effort is necessary to support students in the interdisciplinary practice of making inferences with data.

The framework also can help to illuminate tension between developmental trajectories for learning about data and learning about science. For example, often biology learning trajectories can develop ideas about genetics early in the semester in order to provide a powerful mechanism to describe organisms, variation, and inheritance. However, the measures and data required to make inferences about genetics are much more difficult to think about than measures and data about visible organisms in ecological settings. So, although the genetics may provide a mechanism for explaining observations in ecological settings, suggesting genetics should be studied first, the data students collect in ecological settings are much more accessible to students which suggests ecology may be a better fit for early investigations to develop students' competencies in making inferences with data. Our framework privileges the data learning trajectory, but this will certainly be a regular tension for teachers to negotiate. We see the illumination of these challenges as a main goal for this framework. If left hidden, these tensions can create invisible barriers to student learning. Although the challenges may not be simple to resolve, they are important to be considered.

The implications for this framework can stretch beyond middle grades. For example, we have also used this framework to design undergraduate science classes because students in those classes are often asked to engage with and make sense of complex inferential models. Without appropriate support from earlier grades and careful design at the undergraduate level, this can often become little more than an exercise in following procedures and reporting findings based on given criteria. And while working to support more coherent interdisciplinary learning environments in K–12 is critically important, undergraduate instructors will have students for many years that have yet to learn about making inferences with data in meaningful ways. Our aim is to support instructors across diverse grades and disciplines to coordinate learning goals related to data with the learning goals in their discipline so that students can understand both what scientists know, and also how they know (Talanquer & Pollard, 2010).

In both K–12 classrooms and undergraduate settings, there are significant challenges to supporting the development of inferential reasoning with data because of the interdisciplinary nature of the act, and the disciplinary boundaries in organized schooling. Although the Data MAKER framework can inform this challenging work, it will take the careful thought, work, and resources of teachers, school leaders, and researchers to develop innovative approaches to supporting students to learn to make inferences with data. However, this careful work is necessary in order to support a more coherent approach to making inferences with data in the Age of Inference.

REFLECTIVE QUESTIONS

1. What additional challenges are associated with supporting students to develop a scientific mindset towards making inferences with data?
2. How might the Data MAKER Science framework inform instruction in other science disciplines, such as chemistry or physics?

CHAPTER 21

EXPECTATIONS AND DISCIPLINARY BLENDS

L. Jeneva Clark, R. Alexander Bentley, Nicholas N. Nagle, and Vasileios Maroulas

Sometimes the job of a data scientist is to know when you don't know enough.
—Cathy O'Neil

In K–12 and higher education math and science courses, students encounter and experience evidence-based conclusions (NGSS, 2013) and these encounters and experiences nurture their inferential reasoning (Makar et al., 2011). At the undergraduate level, in particular, course content is chosen and designed to prepare students for their vocation, for future coursework, and/or for informed citizenry (Commission on the Future of Undergraduate Education—American Academy of the Arts and Sciences, 2017). To this end, professional organizations, such as the Mathematical Association of America (MAA), have attempted to standardize course content of math "service courses," which support students' knowledge for their work in non-math disciplines (e.g., Saxe & Braddy, 2015). Calculus I may be a service course for students majoring in biology, while Statistics I may be a service course for students majoring in psychology.

Age of Inference, pages 355–367

The MAA Committee on Curriculum Renewal Across the First Two Years (CRAFTY) maintains curricular recommendations and leads national initiatives related to math service courses (maa.org). One such initiative, featured in this chapter, is *SUMMIT-P: A National Consortium for Synergistic Undergraduate Mathematics via Multi-institutional Inter-disciplinary Teaching Partnerships* (https://www.summit-p.com/resources), funded by the National Science Foundation (grant DUE-1625557). The authors of this chapter are principal investigators in this *SUMMIT-P* multi-institutional consortium, which actively redesigns math service courses using a *Listen First* model of partnership with those from other academic disciplines.

WHAT DO WE MEAN BY "LISTEN FIRST"?

Many recipes (e.g., Dick & Carey, 1985; Wiggins & McTighe, 1998) for instructional design begin with the identification of course objectives; however, we want to pitch an idea for a prequel. Before composing outcomes, there must be an assessment of needs. Coining a phrase, we advocate for a Listen First approach, a radically intentional effort to create course content descriptively, rather than prescriptively. Often, undergraduate mathematics courses are designed by mathematicians, who believe they have some notions about what mathematical topics students need to know; however, we introduce the SUMMIT-P "fishbowl protocol" (https://www.summit-p.com/resources/collaboration-tools), which initiates math course development with extra-disciplinary insight. In this protocol, experts in nonmath areas are invited to describe what mathematical content they think is most essential for students majoring in their programs.

The name "fishbowl" was adopted to emphasize that math teachers are only there to listen and observe. For example, geography faculty could discuss prompts such as, "What do you want your geography students to understand about data science or about mathematics?" During this discussion, mathematics faculty only observe, take notes, pose clarifying questions, and try to listen with comprehension. Following this process can lead to a geographer's wish list of mathematical content. The SUMMIT-P consortium is dedicated to listening first and beginning course design with these wish lists from partnering disciplines, rather than beginning with mathematicians' preconceptions or mass-production textbooks. By intentionally blending disciplines in this way, we can more appropriately prepare students for their future studies, but also bring more relevance to their learning.

"Can you hear me now? . . . Can you hear me now?" This repeated inquiry echoes frustrations of low-quality phone calls but also strikes a familiar resonance with faculty who collaborate across disciplinary borders. There can be static and interference on the lines of cross-disciplinary communication, stemming from differences in substantive content, differences in research methodologies, and differences in academic language. When experts from kindred fields communicate, their jargon is familiar, and this facilitates a shared understanding. However, listening to colleagues who work outside one's own area of expertise takes more effort. "Can you hear me now?" and other checks for understanding, such as "What is your interpretation of this?" become essential to progress in disciplinary blends.

WHAT DO WE MEAN BY "DISCIPLINARY BLENDS"?

"That's not chicken salad! That's a chicken smoothie!" In a marital quibble, a couple bickers about their ingredients' isotropy. When does a collection of groceries become a sandwich, a salad, a smoothie, or a soup? Through discussion, they attempt to discretize a continuum with agreed-upon typological vocabulary for their lunch. Similarly, disciplines can be blended to varying degrees of homogeneity. Toward a meeting-of-the-minds about terminology for such blends, Stember (1991) described a spectrum from *intra-* to *trans-*disciplinarity, and Huutoniemi et al. (2010) further developed a typology (see Figure 21.1).

The least disputable definition is that of *intra-disciplinarity*, in which traditional insular disciplines live in separate worlds, with methodologies, practices, and paradigms not informed by other disciplines. In our analogy, each ingredient lives on a designated aisle of a segregated supermarket. Cross-disciplinarity, however, is more like a bag of groceries; experts working cross-disciplinarily are more aware of other disciplines' work. Next, multidisciplinary work may be cooperatively solving problems, while still approaching those problems from separate disciplinary perspectives. Such multi-disciplinary collaborations can lead to inter-disciplinarity, in which experts maintain the vantage point of their own expertise but can also peer through the lenses of

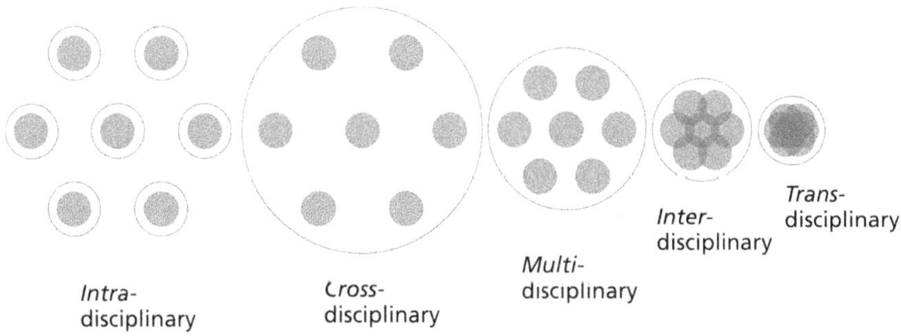

Figure 21.1 Disciplinary blends. *Note:* Our typology is derived from Stember (1991) and Huutoniemi et al. (2010).

others. Finally, trans-disciplinarity, the elusive academic smoothie, is a homogeneous and isotropic blend that takes on new methods and practices, making it unable to be easily decomposed into its disciplinary ingredients.

We do not view trans-disciplinarity as the coveted top echelon of a hierarchy or as the end goal of an academic pilgrimage, no more than we view chicken smoothies as the epitome of taste. We do, however, believe that movement toward disciplinary integration and attempts to relandscape a siloed terrain are usually enriching and rewarding. Furthermore, as we describe our work in this chapter, we do not envision a discrete system of buttons or switches for each prefix (intra-, cross-, multi-, inter-, or trans-); instead, our described work continually slides side to side on a scrollbar, with an ever-changing level of blend.

COULD DISCIPLINARY BLENDS FACILITATE INFERENTIAL REASONING?

The National Academies of Science, Engineering, and Medicine (NASEM, 2018) recommended that all U.S. undergraduate students should develop a basic understanding of data science to prepare them adequately for the workforce. Fueled by supply and demand, and propelled by promising career options, data science is a young, but foreseeably robust, academic field. Social media and remote sensing have sent data stores surging, offering opportunities for informed decision-making practices about transportation, crime, health, and business locations (NASEM, 2018). Data science utilizes mathematics, computing, statistics, and domain sciences. Surpassing this intrinsic disciplinary blend, we acknowledge the need to design data science courses in a way that is guided by non-mathematics domain disciplines like anthropology and geography, with expectations of rich real-world relevance resulting from these partnerships.

WHAT HAPPENED WHEN WE LISTENED FIRST?

Drawing on the ideas from the SUMMIT-P consortium, the authors conducted a Listen First meeting in which geography faculty were asked to respond to the following questions:

- What do you want geography majors to understand about data science?
- What math topics should one of your department's graduates know?
- If there were an introductory course in data science offered by the Department of Mathematics, what topics or contexts would increase relevance for geography majors?

- What would be an ideal balance between mathematical theory, algorithms, and conceptual understanding?
- How do you perceive that certain mathematical topics are currently taught? Is that what you want your students to experience? Is it more than your students need? Less? Different?
- Can you think of any assignments that you would like to give to students, but you are unable to because of your students' incomplete background in data science or math?
- What topics do your students regularly struggle with because of their incomplete math background?

Our meeting was attended by seven geography faculty, all engaged in math-intensive teaching and research. One of the authors, also a member of the geography faculty, served as a moderator for this discussion. In keeping with SUMMIT-P's fishbowl protocol, three mathematics representatives observed, listened, and took notes.

As we wrestled with big curricular questions of "What should be taught?"; "How should it be taught?"; and "When should it be taught?" one emergent question focused on sequencing. Students could learn math first and applied data science subsequently, or students could become immersed in data science first and then learn the underlying mathematics and statistics. In the former instance, if ideally enacted, students develop strong foundational knowledge of mathematical theory before manipulating any data sets themselves. In the latter, like learning a foreign language by cultural immersion, students' first-hand experiences with data work feed their motivation to learn math. This immersion approach may seem unnerving to mathematicians, as students can learn to code in a programming language to perform simple operations, like correlation tests, or even complex operations, like fast Fourier transforms, without necessarily knowing their theoretical underpinnings. On the other hand, students can learn what the analyses effectively tell them and how the results can be used as evidence in real-world scenarios.

We recognized the forced dichotomy in this cart-before-the-horse question and discussed alternative ways to sequence content. In recent attempts to make STEM programs more accessible for students, mathematics departments have begun using more corequisite courses. Traditionally, certain classes precede other classes, creating an uninviting obstacle course of prerequisites; however, in a more integrated curriculum, prerequisite knowledge can be introduced when it is needed, just in time and not sooner. Instead of requiring a trigonometry course to precede a calculus course, trigonometry can be learned concurrently with a calculus course via modules assigned at precise curricular moments when trigonometry is essential to calculus problem-solving (Burn et al., 2018). Could this just-in-time approach be useful within our intentional disciplinary blends of data science?

Faculty attested to having observed a similar dynamic. Students sometimes take entry-level classes in data science because of perceived career relevance. Then, thanks to the accessibility of coding environments and a wealth of real-world data, students are surprised by their own enjoyment of data science, enthused by relevance to their own interests. This momentum carries the student to creatively use tools (e.g., mapping tools, text mining tools, topic models, database interfaces) to develop inferential reasoning. Later, students enroll in math courses to gain the fundamental knowledge needed to truly understand their tools. Although this may sound backward, in some ways it mimics how real problem-solving often works. Often, a scientist's work begins with an anchor problem, like global warming or poverty, and then the scientist asks, "What knowledge/skills/data are needed to solve this? What needs to be done or learned to get there?" This then motivates the learning, the experiments, and the development of disciplinarily blended teams.

We also found, when we listened, that faculty from various disciplines wanted students to develop certain habits or ways of responding to data. We collected a list of these habits, reminiscent of Goldenberg's (1996) "Habits of Mind," but tailored for data science. The faculty described this as a "data science reflex," consisting of:

- thinking creatively and constructively about data;
- approaching data sets of any size and complexity;
- choosing data models pertinent to the problem;
- algorithmic implementation using data via reproducible code;
- evaluating approaches taken by other data scientists;
- articulating findings about the data via clear visualizations and language;
- examining ethics, bias, and privacy of data; and
- transferring data knowledge to other data-driven disciplines.

A more content-oriented list was also formed. From the fishbowl protocol, we collected a wish list of topics that geography faculty would include in a quantitative service course. In Table 21.1, we have loosely categorized these topics into groups that could form separate units of such a course.

Next, we deliberated over these wish-list items and gathered ways in which overarching themes meaningfully underpin our respective disciplines and motivate inferential reasoning. In this chapter, we have chosen *expected value* as an example, and we include descriptions of expected value's role in inference.

TABLE 21.1 Categorized Wishlist From Geography Fishbowl

Numbers and Functions	Shape and Form	Data and Decision-Making
matrices, vectors, interpreting eigenvectors, multiplying matrices and vectors together, sigma notation for summation, sine, cosine, logarithms, exponentials, solving linear algebra systems, permutations and combinations, continuous v. discontinuous variables	spatial data, geometry, polar coordinates, distance measure, different ways to measure distance, different scales of measure, graph theory, thinking about data visually and in different dimensions, networking problems that can be represented as graphs or matrices	formal logic used in coding, maximizing the likelihood of something by using calculus and probability, probability distributions, mean, standard deviation, reading graphs and histograms, data ethics, expected value, Bayesian statistics, fuzziness, different ways of measuring uncertainty in contexts such as poverty

Note: We arranged the topics into categories that could facilitate course development.

WHAT IS OUR PERSPECTIVE ON EXPECTED VALUE?

In a positivistic paradigm, science educators often emphasize that data do not discriminate and empirical evidence does not show favoritism (Gil-Pérez et al., 2005; Niaz, 2018). Before recent reform in science education (NGSS, 2013), elementary school bulletin boards often showed the scientific method as a linear string of steps. Steps could include (a) make an observation, (b) form a hypothesis, (c) collect data, (d) analyze data, and (e) draw a conclusion (Lastrucci, 1963). However, we envision a map that shows layered constructs and comparisons to stimulate students' critical thinking, rather than recipe following. In Figure 21.2, curiosity is shown as the impetus for experimentation, and the expectation–observation duo is even-handedly held in contrast, while an experiment is framed by a scientist's purposely selected system of controls and conditions.

Expected Value and Ethics

When humans make decisions, both small scale and large scale, they must consider what constructs they deem important and allowable to influence their decisions. Although an ethicist might call these essential constructs "values," we think of these as variables, functions, or parameters, in our quantitative mindset. In a complex system, we may want to maximize justice, while minimizing health risk, and while maximizing emotional well-being. These constructs are not static but instead may undulate with fluctuating volatility. We not only want students to think about what constructs

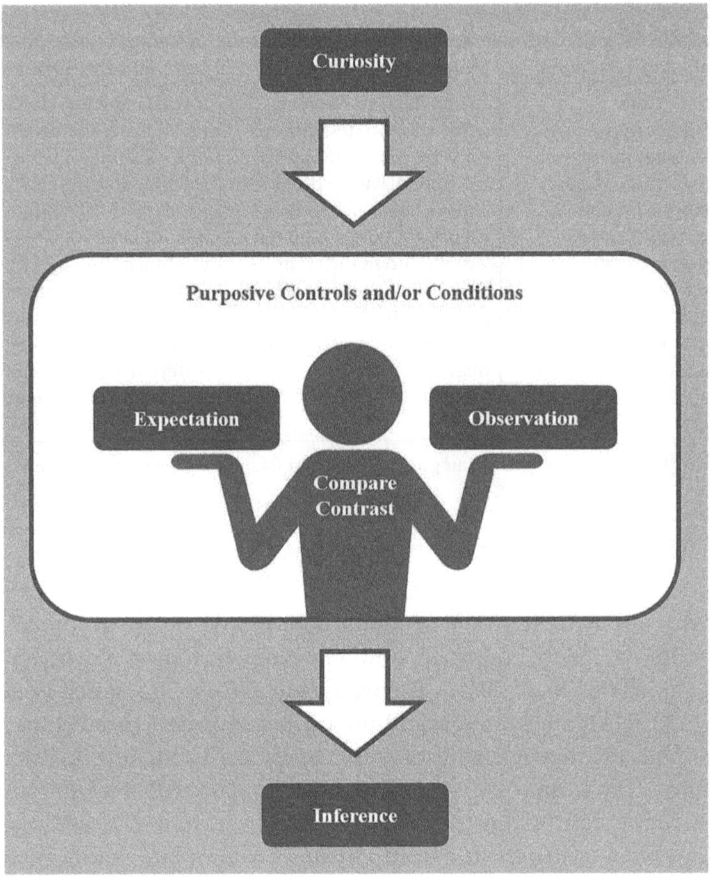

Figure 21.2 A schematic for scientific inference. *Note:* Expectation and observation are even-handedly held in contrast during an experiment.

are important in decision-making, but we want them to appreciate the complexities of ethical systems and to feel the connections of data-based decision-making and real, living and breathing, humans.

In one of our lessons from a math service course, the instructor first asks students to briefly think about the ethics of healthcare decisions. "This lesson looks at a serious and real topic. Before we begin, take a moment to reflect about what you think might be the most important values to consider when making healthcare decisions." Students are asked to circle four words they think we should consider most when making decisions about healthcare.

Constructs are provided such as politics, finances, safety, science, ethics, happiness, economics, freedom, and justice. Then, a fictional scenario is set up for students to consider. "The island of Imaginopolis has exactly five inhabitants. You are their insurance provider. Each person has different risk factors for the G.U.N.K. (Gross Unsanitary Nasty Killer) virus, which can be treated for $2,000." Each person's name and photo are presented, accompanied by individual likelihoods of needing the G.U.N.K. treatment within the year. The five probability values are: 50%, 25%, 20%, 10%, and 1%.

The inhabitant with the highest G.U.N.K. risk is William, who has a 50% chance of needing the $2,000 G.U.N.K. virus treatment this year. Students are asked to figure out what the average risk is to have William as a policyholder for a G.U.N.K. coverage policy. What would a typical William cost in a typical year? To conceptualize this, students imagine having more than one of William. If they had six Williams, they could expect that three would need the treatment this year. Three sick Williams would mean the insurer would need to have 3($2,000) = $6,000 in the fund for the year. Recalling that insurance funds provide a way for all the policyholders to share the risk, students then calculate what dollar amount each of the six Williams would need to contribute into the fund in order to have the needed $6,000. Each of the six Williams would have to pay in $1,000 so that the fund would have enough.

The thought experiment of cloning William allows students to imagine what a typical, or average, William would cost the insurance fund. This is the expected value for the amount William will cost the fund. It may sound strange to students to say that we "expect" William will cost $1,000 in claims this year, when, in fact, we know that there is no way William will cost exactly $1,000. He will either cost $2,000 or he will cost $0, each with 50% likelihood. However, the expected value, the average value after running many trials of an experiment, would still be helpful. Although we cannot put William into a life simulator and calculate an average after many trials of the upcoming year, it is still useful for a fund manager to calculate expected values. With this simple example, students then notice the formula that simplifies calculations, and they can then calculate the expected values for each of their five Imaginopolis inhabitants and sum them to find an expected need for the fund's total.

"Now you know how much you need to collect from your five clients for the year. How do you want to do that? Do you want to charge the same price to each policyholder? What would be the pros and cons?" Students often surmise that the character with the lowest risk, and an expected value of only $20, may not want to pay the same price as William. Students recalculate the costs if the low-risk client chooses to go uninsured and there are only four policyholders. The calculations are simple, and the students see the policy price climb up. Then, a fictional character named Madeline objects. "I don't want to buy a policy for $525. I know my risk for the G.U.N.K. virus isn't that high." Before running calculations, students can predict what will happen if Madeline opts out. The fund would be deficient, prices would need to adjust, and the premium would cost more for others.

In reality, countries usually have more than only five citizens. Often, the low-risk citizens outnumber the high-risk. After scaling up the example to an island with 90 inhabitants, 60 of which have a low risk of 1%, only 1 of which has a high risk of 50%, and with a given distribution of other risk-level characters, students calculate that G.U.N.K. coverage could be funded by charging approximately $100 each. Denying coverage to William would bring the price down for everyone else. Students can calculate the amount of the difference. However, the likelihood that G.U.N.K. could claim an uninsured victim in Imaginopolis is 50%. What would happen if the lowest risk citizens opt out of coverage? How much would the policy price change? If all 60 with low-risk chose not to purchase coverage, the price of the policy would almost triple. In this case, the likelihood that G.U.N.K. could claim an uninsured victim in Imaginopolis would be 45%. By calculating simple expected values, students begin to see that shared decisions can be complicated and can profoundly impact human well-being. In decision-making, risks and benefits commonly tug against each other. However, in addition to the quantifiable factors like expected value, there are also ethical dimensions to problems, such as autonomy, freedom, justice, beneficence, and human rights. Limited access to healthcare is a problem we all share. Understanding these dynamics, both quantifiable and ethically, helps us make shared decisions about shared risks and the policies that influence our shared well-being.

Expected Value and Bayes' Formula

To discuss how expected value is related to Bayes' formula, we again invite students to Imaginopolis, whose population has grown to 1,000 residents. The infamous G.U.N.K. (Gross Unsanitary Nasty Killer) virus has infiltrated the island and has infected approximately 5% of the population. The residents are interested in sharing the costs via an insurance policy. To help calculate the risk of each resident, you offer free G.U.N.K. screenings to everyone. The test advertises 90% accuracy for patients who have the virus and 80% accuracy for patients who do not. A resident named Sadie tests positive. Sadie panics and assumes she probably has the G.U.N.K. What is the likelihood that Sadie actually has the virus? Figure 21.3 helps students visualize the implications of these statements. All 1,000 residents are shown. The 5%, or 50 residents, with the virus are in the shaded region. The dotted loop contains all those who test positive for the virus, both the 90% of infected residents and the 20% of those noninfected but who receive false positives.

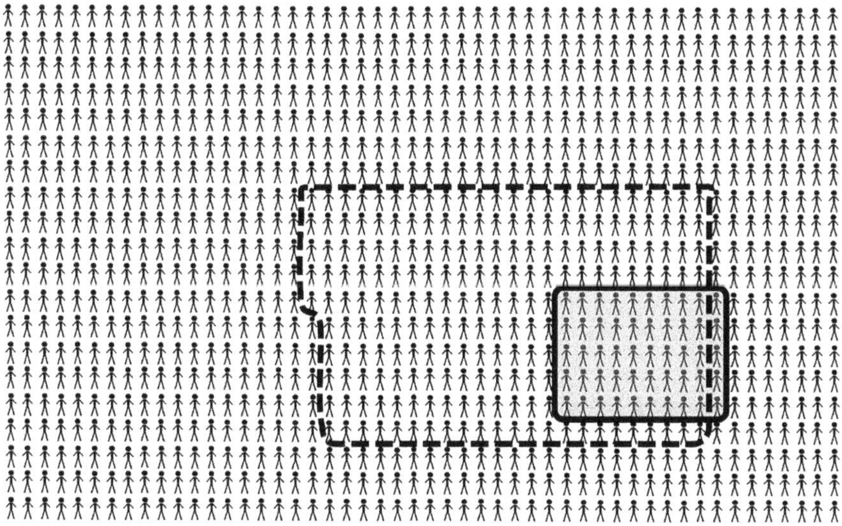

Figure 21.3 A visualization of Bayes' formula. *Note:* Residents with the virus are inside the shaded region, and those inside the dotted line loop tested positive.

Sadie's foreboding test result has placed her somewhere inside the dotted loop in Figure 21.3. One can crop the diagram to only include those 235 who receive positive results, delimiting the sample space. Her knee-jerk assumption that she "probably" has the virus was incorrect. This scenario shows the utility of Bayes formula. While the diagram allows a brute-force calculation of

$$\frac{45}{235} = 19.15\%,$$

Bayes' formula

$$P(H|E) = \frac{P(E|H)}{P(E)} \cdot P(H),$$

where H represents a hypothesis and E represents evidence, more expediently quantifies Sadie's chances.

In this case, let H represent the hypothesis that Sadie has the G.U.N.K. virus, and let E represent the evidence of a positive test result. Bayes' formula would yield the following:

$$P(H|E) = \frac{P(E|H)}{P(E)} \cdot P(H) = \frac{.90}{.0010(.20(950) + .90(50))} \cdot (.050) \approx 19\%.$$

The probability that Sadie does not have the virus is 81%, a likelihood 4.2 times higher than the likelihood that she does have the virus, given the condition that Sadie tested positive. The Bayes factor is 4.2. From this example, some students fail to see a connection of Bayesian calculations to expected value, which is contrastingly apparent in traditional hypothesis testing. However, another way to arrive at the Bayes factor in this situation would be to divide the expected number of false positives by the expected number of true positives, and arrive at

$$\frac{(.20)(.95)}{(.90)(.050)} \approx 4.2.$$

If two opposing hypotheses (e.g., *have* vs. *do not have* a virus) happen to be equally likely, then this ratio would be one. Students might think that such a state of neutrality would be entirely uninteresting, especially if they are accustomed to traditional hypothesis testing, which focuses on sufficiency of evidence and dichotomous rejection verdicts. However, the implications of unitary odds in Bayesian inference can offer insights, such as which pieces of evidence are influencing odds the most and also allow room for researchers to see how hypotheses' likelihoods change. After all, as conditions change, more evidence is uncovered, and as more evidence is uncovered, our expectations and the strengths of those expectations adjust.

WHAT DID WE LEARN?

Naturally keen on quantitative evidence, the authors of this chapter are largely data scientists at heart, hardwired to seek robust replicable results. However, this chapter proudly presents qualitative information about our journey, which we contend is essential for propagating large-scale change. Integration of STEM domains may or may not be successful on grand scales, but unless a preservice teacher can see what inter-disciplinary partnerships look like in practice, or unless a department head can confidently implement a cross-disciplinary collaboration model, then movement toward disciplinary blends will be tentative at best. Partnerships can begin with intentionally and systematically crossing disciplinary borders and listening first. Partnerships must be fluid and flexible, rather than rigid. We tout freedom to respectfully blend disciplinary methodologies and paradigms from multiple domains, from sandwich to smoothie levels, to fit the needs of the work at hand. We offer this example of how a team might work together to build a service course curriculum from the ground up, based on authentic local learning needs. Lastly, we seize an opportunity to synthesize expected value, pedagogical approaches to it, and how expected value relates to inferential reasoning.

REFLECTION QUESTIONS

1. In what scenarios might it be appropriate to move from one degree of disciplinary blend to another? What aspects would change in such a transition?
2. "Fishbowl" meetings are not always possible to conduct. What are other ways to assess learners' needs and develop objectives?
3. What uses of expected values could be unethical or harmful?
4. What are the differences, if any, between prejudice and expectation?

CHAPTER 22

MACHINE LEARNING

A New Lens for Integrating Computational Thinking and Science in the High School Classroom

Michael Daley, Zhen Bai, Raffaella Borasi, and Dave Miller

The goal is to promote a revolution in scientific discovery and to enable the fastest-possible expansion in the knowledge base of mankind. The development of AI systems with such a level of intelligence would have a profound impact on the future of humanity.

—Hiroaki Kitano, 2016

ARTIFICIAL INTELLIGENCE AND MACHINE LEARNING IN THE AGE OF INFERENCE

The capabilities of artificial intelligence (AI) and machine learning (ML) have advanced tremendously in the past decade, and the transformative power of this technology is increasingly being recognized. Applications of AI and ML are affecting all sectors of our economy including health care, retail, education, manufacturing, and energy. For example, in the banking

Age of Inference, pages 369–384

industry, AI and ML are leveraged to make decisions about potential fraudulent financial transactions, such as fraudulent credit card transactions, via intelligent analysis of vast amounts of data collected by companies to identify fraudulent activity as well as activity that requires additional investigation. In the transportation sector, AI and ML are used to analyze vast data from inputs such as cameras and sensors integrated into automobiles along with geographic positioning data to allow autonomous vehicles to make decisions including speed, lane location, and collision avoidance.

The advancement of AI and ML has widespread implications for K–12 schools, particularly when the future of work is considered. AI advances have created a vast demand for new STEM jobs that did not previously exist. As a recent report estimated, there will be a shortfall of up to 250,000 data scientists in the United States in a decade (Henke et al., 2016). However, data scientists do not operate in isolation within an organization. In the same report, Henke et al. (2016) estimated that the demand for "business translators" will be two to four million jobs in the next decade. "Business translators" are individuals who can move between working with data scientists and the daily functions of the organization, are able to articulate questions that can be addressed through AI and ML, as well as to interpret the meaning for management and clients. The report highlights the growing demand for not only people with the analytical skills of a data scientist but also for people in the field with enough background and knowledge of AI and ML to be able to ask questions that can be addressed by these technologies. The need for basic literacy in AI and ML is becoming more apparent, and today's K–12 schools need to take these transformations in the workplace into account.

Equally important, though, is preparing today's K–12 students to embrace the opportunities and challenges presented by the use of AI in their everyday life. As more children learn from their AI toys that can understand words and facial expressions and talk back to them in everyday play, it becomes critical for all members of society to learn how to navigate in this increasingly technical and intelligent world—which in turn calls for providing a solid foundation for AI literacy for all K–12 students.

WHAT ARE AI AND ML, REALLY?

AI is an interdisciplinary field with primary pillars in philosophy, mathematics, psychology, neuroscience, economics, and computer science. AI allows computer systems to fulfill intellectual goals and tasks through rational thinking and acting (Russell & Norvig, 2016). It has many subfields including reasoning, planning, learning, computer vision, natural language processing, and robotics. AI pioneer and Nobel Laureate Herbert A. Simon and colleagues spent decades of research on placing AI research in the philosophy of science through the computational model of scientific discovery (Newell & Simon, 1976).

ML was coined by Arthur Samuel (1959) to describe the field of study that gives computers the ability to learn without being explicitly programmed. ML trains computers to automatically identify patterns and make predictions from existing data (Alpaydin, 2014). As the data-processing power of computers continues to grow, exponentially, the explosion of big data sets is driving the advancement of this field, and with this the development and proliferation of pattern-recognizing algorithms.

ML algorithms are essentially one of four basic types: clustering, association, classification, and regression (Witten et al., 2016). Clustering divides data sets into natural groups of "similar" items (i.e., items that share a stronger resemblance to each other than those in other groups). Clustering can be very helpful to obtain insights about data, suggest hypotheses to be explored, and help with building prediction models. It is widely used by ecosystem scientists in studying freshwater ecology (Céréghino et al., 2008), forest ecology (Kupfer et al., 2012), and conservation biology (Bonn & Gaston, 2005). Association learning tries to find meaningful relationships among co-occurring features of a data set. Some common examples include shopping behaviors (Kaur & Kang, 2016), relevant associations among genes (Anandhavalli et al., 2010), and understanding traffic accidents (Li et al., 2017). Classification and regression are supervised learning methods to fit unseen examples into discrete classes (classification) or numerical values (regression) based on a set of pre-labeled examples. Some common applications include facial recognition, disease diagnosis, predicting academic performance, and stock market analysis, among others.

TRANSFORMATIVE POTENTIAL OF ML FOR THE PROCESS OF SCIENTIFIC DISCOVERY

ML algorithms and tools are increasingly used by scientists and engineers to analyze, manipulate, and represent increasingly large data sets. Indeed, in the Age of Inference, ML is considered the new engine that revolutionizes practices of knowledge discovery for major STEM domains such as biomedicine, chemistry, ecology, geophysics, and beyond (Gil et al., 2014; Kitano, 2016). The availability of massive data sets, obtained through the use of new technology including data-logging probes and sensors, is leading to a mindset shift in how many scientists approach problems in their fields. While there are many pathways to discovery in science, a traditional approach may involve generating a hypothesis based on observations and then collecting data in an attempt to reject or not reject the hypothesis (see Column A in

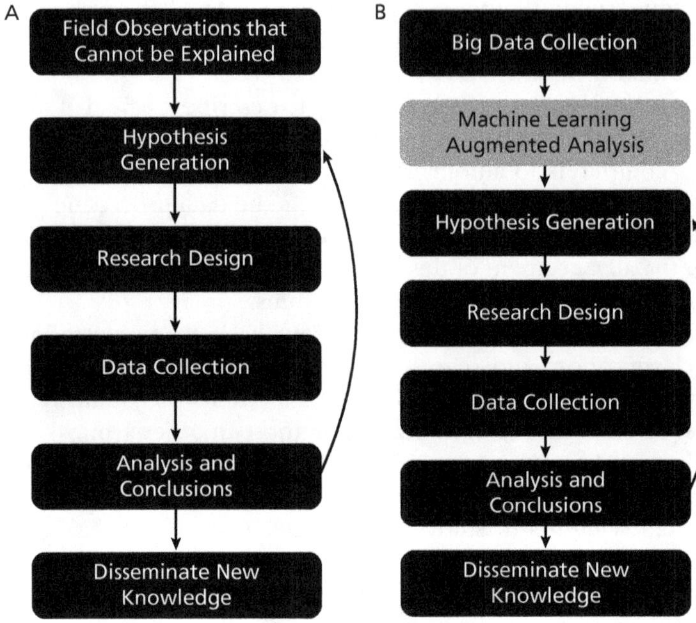

Figure 22.1 A comparison of traditional and ML discovery approaches.

Figure 22.1). Data are collected based on the research design surrounding the hypothesis and can be limiting. Statistical tests were developed to support this type of methodology such as linear regression models, *t*-tests, and chi-square tests. However, the combination of increased computational processing speed along with the development of ML algorithms is resulting in a new wave of science. Now, one approach to discovery using ML might have scientists starting with a big data set and applying ML algorithms to identify patterns (see Column B in Figure 22.1). In other words, scientists can use ML algorithms to identify patterns and develop hypotheses, which constitutes the initial step to uncover scientific phenomena in reference to prior domain knowledge.

ML approaches allow scientists new venues for solving highly complex and global problems in their fields. Some interesting examples of this new approach to science are now being published in the literature. For example, in conservation biology, Pelletier et al. (2018) used ML to predict what plant species are threatened across the globe. The researchers were not only able to use ML to classify the conservation status of plant species, but they were also able to identify hotspots to target conservation efforts and funding. This ML approach replaces more traditional and time-consuming approaches to species conservation and will likely result in the conservation of more plant species globally.

The examples from the medical literature are also exciting. One area that is gaining attention is in disease prediction. Doctors have access to many health markers that can be used to help make a diagnosis. Typically, doctors are using summary data in making decisions. ML algorithms have the ability to identify deeper patterns and signals in the data that humans cannot detect. Now, studies are reporting the power of ML to predict premature death (Juarez-Orozco et al., 2020; Weng et al., 2019). This predictive data might be able to provide doctors the additional insights needed to provide patients appropriate care and preventative medicine. Advanced ML algorithms have been playing a critical role in supporting a fast, global response to the unprecedented health emergency caused by COVID-19, through rapid diagnosis (Mei et al., 2020), early triage (Liang et al., 2020), mortality prediction (Yan et al., 2020), and drug discovery (ul Qamar et al., 2020).

NEW K–12 STANDARDS INVOLVING ML

The importance of developing ML literacy for K–12 students, to enable them to navigate and participate successfully in this age of inference, has been recognized by several professional organizations, as well as state departments of education, and has resulted in the creation of new standards related to AI and ML.

Most notably, the Association for the Advancement of Artificial Intelligence (AAAI) and the Computer Science Teachers Association (CSTA) have recently created a joint working group to define the big ideas for K–12 students in AI, in preparation for developing new AI-specific K–12 standards. The AI4K12 initiative is developing the first national guideline for teaching AI for K–12 students (Touretzky et al., 2019). The guideline specifies five big ideas in AI education for K–12 learners, including (a) computers perceive the world using sensors, (b) agents maintain models/representations of the world and use them for reasoning, (c) computers can learn from data, (d) making agents interact comfortably with humans is a substantial challenge for AI developers, and (e) AI applications can impact society in both positive and negative ways. Agents in the context of AI are commonly described as intelligent systems that "perceive and represent the world, deliberate, and produce outputs that affect the world" (Touretzky et al., 2019, p. 9797).

CSTA K–12 Computer Science Standards (Computer Science Teachers Association, 2017) explain computer science (CS) as a core discipline that supports and links to other sciences and contributes to the training of future scientists using AI fields such as pattern recognition, image processing, and data-based modeling across subjects. The most recent CSTA K–12 Computer Science Standards include AI concept learning under algorithm and programming at Grades 11–12, which requires students to "implement an artificial intelligence algorithm to play a game against a human opponent or solve a problem" and "describe how artificial intelligence drives many software and physical systems" (CSTA, 2017, paras. 109–110).

POTENTIAL FOR CONNECTIONS AND SYNERGIES WITH SCIENCE EDUCATION

ML and AI open up new opportunities to strengthen the integration between CS and science education in two complementary ways. First, AI and ML may enhance students' understanding of science by providing new tools to study specific phenomena as part of the scientific knowledge discovery process (see Exhibit 22.1). The technology can support students' engagement in many of

EXHIBIT 22.1
The Owl Pellet Lab Transformed

The owl pellet lab is a very common activity completed in science classrooms across the country. In this hands-on activity, students are provided an owl pellet to dissect. Owl pellets are the undigested components of prey such as fur, bones, claws, and teeth that are packaged and regurgitated by the organism. Students dissect the owl pellet and sort the bones, teeth, and claws to identify the biodiversity of the organisms consumed by the owl. In sorting, students engage in a classifying activity as they search for similarities in features. Students then use a key to identify different prey consumed. Often, these include rodents, shrews, moles, and bird.

To extend digital literacy, students could train a computer to recognize images of the bones they take. For example, students might train a computer to answer the question, "Is this skull a bird, mouse, shrew, or mole?" To complete this exercise, students first need to train the computer by correctly identifying shrew skulls, taking images from multiple angles, and input this information into the system. With enough training, the computer will be able to assess if an uploaded unknown image of a skull from an owl pellet is a shrew. The machine will report probabilities which will provide the teacher the opportunity to address the requirements and limitations of image recognition technology. The process is repeated for bones of the other organisms.

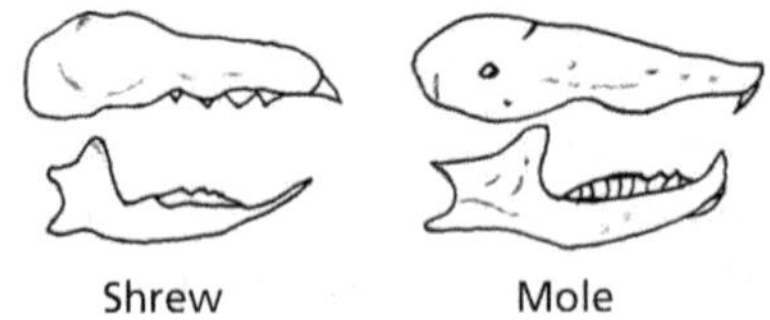

the science practices highlighted in the Next Generation Science Standards (NGSS Lead States, 2013), most notably analyzing and interpreting data, engaging in argument from evidence, and obtaining, evaluating, and communicating information. Second, science activities may enhance AI and ML learning by providing meaningful contexts to study AI and ML concepts and methods (see Exhibit 22.2). As previous research shows, meaningful STEM contexts motivate participation in computational thinking through a sense of authenticity and real-world applicability (Weintrop et al., 2016).

EXHIBIT 22.2
Species Identification Using ML

Camera traps are used in biodiversity research to capture observations of organisms. Typically, cameras are fitted with a motion detector that will trigger a photo to be captured when organisms cross in the path. Camera traps have been used in ecosystems across the world and have been incorporated into many citizen science projects such as Snapshot Serengeti and Wildcam Gorongosa. In these projects, citizens are tasked with examining and classifying the organisms captured by the camera traps. By engaging citizens, the researchers are able to obtain much larger datasets than if they needed to classify the organisms alone. In this AI activity, teachers will extend Snapshot Serengeti to explore how image classification technology could be applied. In this introductory activity, teachers will use the Microsoft Species Classification API and uploaded student images to expand understanding of image classification. The Species Classification API returns results with multiple possibilities and probabilities. The output provides the teacher the opportunity to explore issues with image classification and the concepts of probability used in AI.

The classification results using the Microsoft Species Classification API Demo

Latin Name	Common Name	Probability
Tamias striatus	Eastern Chipmunk	71.81%
Callospermophilus lateralis	Golden-mantled Ground Squirrel	6.34%
Sciurus carolinensis	Eastern Gray Squirrel	3.06%
Ochotona princeps	American Pika	2.20%
Sylvilagus floridanus	Eastern Cottontail	1.95%

This position is supported by the large overlap of practices and core concepts in curriculum standards in the K–12 CS framework and NGSS with respect to data collection, visualization, model and inference, and developing and using abstractions and computational artifacts. Both standards also emphasize the importance of sensemaking and problem-solving of computing and scientific phenomena through real-world problems. Among the eight practices identified in NGSS as essential for learning science and engineering, of particular relevance is the use of mathematical and computational thinking, which is an essential practice utilized in both science and engineering to represent physical variables and their relationships. The accessibility of many ML algorithms and tools, coupled with publicly available real-time data sets, creates opportunities for high school students to become aware of ML advances and their implications for scientific discovery through authentic inquiry experiences.

These examples illustrate how ML can shed light on new methods to identify evidence and promote scientific investigation in K–12 education, which aligns with how AI and ML are revolutionizing knowledge discovery for major STEM domains such as biomedicine, chemistry, ecology, geophysics, and beyond.

Using ML tools may be especially important to help students interpret patterns and construct models from data, as research showed that students tend to struggle with this practice and then often prefer to use personal experience instead of empirical evidence to make explanations and support claims (Kelly et al., 2017). Furthermore, given concerns about an already overextended K–12 curriculum, the inclusion of foundational ML concepts and processes in K–12 schools may be more likely to happen if integrated in the existing STEM curriculum, rather than by imposing new requirements for separate CS courses—a point revisited later in the chapter.

KEY CHALLENGES OF INTEGRATING AI/ML INTO THE K–12 SCIENCE CURRICULUM

Although there is potential and value in integrating the teaching of AI/ML into the K–12 science curriculum, there are also some major challenges faced when integrating these areas in K–12 science classrooms.

First, there is the concern of how AI/ML can be made accessible to students with limited mathematical and computational backgrounds. AI/ML is abstract and complex, with connections to logic, probability, statistics, algorithms, and programming. As a result, AI/ML is traditionally only taught in college-level CS programs, which largely eliminates education opportunities for non-STEM undergraduate majors, K–12 students, as well as educators, decision makers, and the general public. Thanks to emerging learning technologies, young students have more opportunities to experiment with key AI/ML technologies such as text understanding, image and speech recognition, robot control, and model training through block-based visual programming languages (see Touretzky et al., 2019). Obstacles remain, however, as recent studies show that students with limited programming experience (Kahn et al., 2018), especially those from low and medium socioeconomic schools (Druga et al., 2019), struggle to advance their AI/ML understanding due to lack of prior knowledge with these programming environments.

Second, even if AI/ML standards become part of graduation requirements moving forward and we figure out how to make AI/ML concepts more accessible to young students, the concern remains about how such a complex topic could be added to an already overcrowded K–12 science curriculum—thus raising the question of how AI/ML can be integrated in the science curriculum.

Third, resistance from K–12 science teachers may create a major impediment to introducing AI/ML in the K–12 science curriculum. Unlike college faculty teaching AI/ML, the training of K–12 science teachers rarely includes AI/ML. This is likely to make most science teachers question their ability to include AI/ML in their teaching—and indeed, without some basic understanding of AI/ML, it will be difficult for them to effectively implement learning experiences involving AI/ML, even when created by experts. Perhaps even more important, lack of knowledge of AI/ML may impede science teachers' appreciation of its potential value to K–12 science students, which in turn will inform their instructional decisions. Therefore, it will also be important to consider how science teachers can be prepared to effectively engage in AI/ML activities with their students.

These are not easily solvable challenges, but what follows are some initial ideas about how we could begin to address them.

ADDRESSING THE CHALLENGE OF MAKING AI/ML ACCESSIBLE TO K–12 STUDENTS

We are surrounded by the products of AI/ML, often with little to no awareness of the role AI/ML has played. Initiatives such as AI4ALL are calling for increased ML and AI literacy. However, promoting AI/ML literacy requires making the technology more accessible for all K–12 learners in an equitable way across diverse student populations. Researchers are working on this challenge and have started to develop engaging activities such as gameplay, robot construction, and interactive visualization (Burgsteiner et al., 2016; Sintov et al., 2016; Touretzky et al., 2019). The authors of this chapter are also working to develop tools and activities to help make ML accessible. Not only do we want students to learn ML concepts, but we want students using ML actively in authentic science inquiries.

ML combined with data visualization has the potential to enhance knowledge discovery and sensemaking of large and multidimensional real-life data sets through the use of user-friendly graphical representations such as maps, charts, diagrams, and glyphs for efficient visual reasoning (De Oliveira & Levkowitz, 2003; Friendly, 2008; McCosker & Wilken, 2014). Data visualization has long been used in STEM classrooms, where students learn to use diagrams such as bar charts and pictographs to analyze and interpret data (NGSS Lead States, 2013). In addition, it has shown promise in engaging general audiences and younger learners when communicating scientific discovery (Ma et al., 2012; Segel & Heer, 2010). Although its ease of interpretation makes data visualization a common method for presenting machine-mined knowledge (De Oliveira & Levkowitz, 2003), novel learning environments with accessible and interactive data visualization have not been explored as a means of learning ML concepts, and scientific knowledge discovery powered by ML.

In this section, we illustrate the potential learning benefits of glyph-based data visualization to support the integration of ML and scientific discovery in high school science classrooms. This illustration, called the "Beetle Inquiry," is based on an ongoing research project initiated by an interdisciplinary research team with researchers from the Department of Computer Science and the Warner School of Education at the University of Rochester.

Glyph-based data visualization methods map individual data points to familiar graphical representations like cartoon faces, stars, stick figures, leaves, bugs, or weathervanes (Fuchs et al., 2015; Ward et al., 2010). Figure 22.2.a provides an example of a novel emoji-based glyph visualization learning environment named SmileyCluster (Wan et al., 2020), which is developed by the authors' research team that maps individual data features to facial features. Glyph-based visualization mitigates the loss of multidimension information better than other methods, enabling investigators to not only inspect machine learned patterns, but to also get detailed insights of features of data points and underlying relationships among data points. The high accessibility of the data may provide specific learning benefits for young learners to help them acquire a straightforward understanding of basic concepts in ML, as well as eliciting inquisitive learning activities for these learners through hands-on and collaborative exploration leading to productive scientific discoveries.

Imagine the following learning scenario in which a high school science teacher guides students to carry out a scientific investigation of ecosystems through a novel glyph-based learning environment. The activity starts with students brainstorming variables that may have an effect on beetle abundance. Following the brainstorming session, the teacher provides students

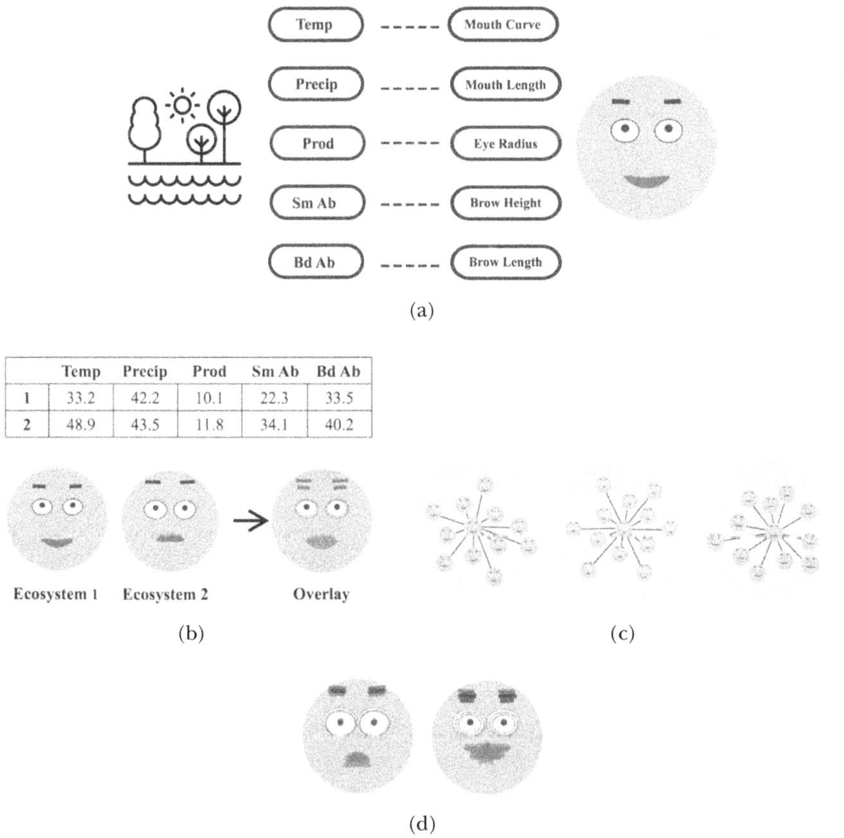

Figure 22.2 Illustration of "emoji face exploration": (a) data mapping to emoji face; (b) illustration of "emoji face exploration"—pairwise similarity comparison; (c) illustration of "emoji face exploration"—cluster of emoji faces; (d) groupwise similarity comparison.

with real-life data from the Central Plains and Massachusetts NEON field stations to allow them to discover empirical evidence to explain their initial questions and hypotheses.

Such a data set will inevitably be difficult for students to work with using the data driven scientific practices commonly used in today's scientific community.

- First, like other real-world phenomena, this data set requires a multidimensional feature space involving many related attributes such as temperature, annual precipitation, plant productivity, small mammal abundance, and breeding bird abundance. The statistics and probability curriculum in common core high school mathematics only covers patterns of association in bivariate data (Council of Chief State School Officers, 2010) leaving the students ill-equipped to handle the data set.

- Second, Euclidean distance on a multidimensional feature space is a basic similarity computation approach, but high school students are only introduced to two-dimensional (plane) Euclidean geometry (Council of Chief State School Officers, 2010).
- Third, it is often difficult for young students to develop a global understanding of a group of data as a whole. As one example, research has shown that middle school math students are inclined to perform local comparison of pairwise differences of data, but need additional scaffoldings to build a global view of the data set (Ben-Zvi & Arcavi, 2001).

Returning to our scenario, to make the sensemaking of multidimensional data more accessible, the teacher has students use SmileyCluster (Wan et al., 2020) to convert each data point into a visual glyph. In this case, the glyph is an emoji face (Figure 22.2a) and is created by mapping individual variables to a visual feature such as eye radius and brow height. The visual encoding of individual and groups of data points provides an inviting reasoning space for students to link the visual representation with various features and patterns. Students can examine characteristics of multiple ecosystems by leveraging their natural skills of visual comparison. For example, a student may observe that the mouth curve is different and thus conclude that the temperature must be different between the ecosystems (Figure 22.2b). In particular, the visual encoding transfers the computational similarity of data points to overt visual similarities that are more familiar for young learners.

After initial discoveries with the individual data point comparison, students realize that they need more data from different sites to develop a global explanation of their primary question. The teacher provides more data from the NEON data set with additional ecosystems. The learning environment generates visual representations for each ecosystem supporting students' analysis of the data to construct explanations. For example, the student might apply the clustering method to divide the emoji glyphs into some number of groups (Figure 22.4c).

Students experiment with different clustering results to discover the most appropriate number of groups by comparing the similarity of glyphs within the same cluster and also how they differ from glyphs in other clusters. These intuitive visual inspections align with common clustering analysis methods and concepts such as intragroup cohesion and intergroup separation (Figure 22.2d; Tan et al., 2013).

As this scenario demonstrates, the learning environment provides exploration scaffoldings to help students establish global similarity comparison between clusters. For example, by identifying shared features of glyphs in one cluster, the student can trace them back to shared features of the corresponding ecosystems. A student can also engage in what-if exploration. For instance, they can remove an individual glyph visual feature (e.g., eye) to see how it impacts the group. These exploratory learning behaviors may lead to new hypotheses and productive discussions with other students.

Additionally, the flexible nature of visual representation allows students and teachers to create their own glyphs and to define their own mappings of data to visual features. This process may further motivate students to engage in scientific discovery to deepen their understanding of relationships and patterns of the data set, as well as fundamental concepts of ML such as multidimensional feature space, similarity, k-means clustering, and cluster analysis. A preliminary research study with high school students in a precollege summer program (Wan et al., 2020) confirmed that SmileyCluster can lead to positive change in learning ML concepts and methods, and engage students with basic pattern interpretation in a meaningful way relating to the scientific contexts.

ADDRESSING THE CHALLENGE OF HOW TO INTEGRATE AI/ML IN THE SCIENCE CURRICULUM

A major concern of all science teachers today is "How do I find the time to meaningfully address the many topics I'm expected to include in my course?" Given this situation, integrating ML in the K–12 science curriculum will require being able to reassure science teachers that ML will not be another topic they are asked to "add on."

First of all, given the recent adoption of NGSS by many states and the radical changes in curriculum and teaching practices required by these new standards, it will be important to demonstrate that AI/ML learning can support the achievement of specific NGSS goals. We believe that indeed this is the case, as illustrated by the "Beetles Inquiry" example presented earlier. In this specific case, the unit will enable students to address a number of NGSS expectations about *ecosystems*, as well as contribute to the students' long-term development of key scientific practices—as identified in Table 22.1.

Recognizing the importance of showing connections with NGSS also suggests the value of creating several sample units of study informed by NGSS that integrate AI/ML with science curriculum topics and then documenting the learning gains resulting from these experiences.

Even showing how using ML may help address the NGSS standards, though, may not be enough—as indeed the current science curriculum is already overcrowded. Rather, we hope that the implementation of new CS standards will provide the opportunity for policy makers and K–12 schools

TABLE 22.1 Selected NGSS Performance Expectations and NGSS Practices Supported in the Beetles Inquiry Unit

NGSS performance expectations supported by the "Beetles Inquiry" unit include:

- HS-LS2-2. Use mathematical representations to support and revise explanations based on evidence about factors affecting biodiversity and populations in ecosystems of different scales.
- HS-LS2-5. Develop a model to illustrate the role of photosynthesis and cellular respiration in the cycling of carbon among the biosphere, atmosphere, hydrosphere, and geosphere.
- HS-LS2-1. Use mathematical and/or computational representations to support explanations of factors that affect carrying capacity of ecosystems at different scales.
- HS-ESS2-6. Develop a quantitative model to describe the cycling of carbon among the hydrosphere, atmosphere, geosphere, and biosphere.
- HS-ESS3-6. Use a computational representation to illustrate the relationships among Earth systems and how those relationships are being modified due to human activity.

The unit also supports the long-term development of the following scientific practices:

- Asking Questions and Defining Problems
- Analyzing and Interpreting Data
- Using Mathematics and Computational Thinking
- Engaging in Argument from Evidence

to make a disciplined evaluation of the current content covered in the K–12 science curriculum, and make decisions about what could be eliminated.

Exploring the most appropriate way to include AI/ML in the K–12 curriculum, therefore, can be seen not just as a challenge, but also as an opportunity to reimagine what integrated STEM instruction could look like and the place it may have in the K–12 curriculum.

ADDRESSING THE CHALLENGE OF PREPARING SCIENCE TEACHERS TO USE AI/ML

As mentioned earlier, current science teachers' lack of AI/ML knowledge may be a major impediment to their willingness and ability to leverage AI/ML in their science courses. Simply adding an introductory CS course as a licensure requirement for all science teachers, however, will not provide a solution to this challenge. Science teachers will need to develop an appreciation for the potential uses of AI/ML in scientific inquiry and an awareness of the tools available to leverage this potential with their students.

A robust way to empower science teachers to learn about AI/ML, while at the same time developing their appreciation for the role AI/ML can play in scientific discovery, is to engage them in "experiences as learners" in which they, themselves, will use AI/ML in the context of authentic scientific inquiry on a topic new to them—such as an adaptation of the "Beetles Inquiry" shared earlier. There is a rich tradition in the STEM teacher education literature for engaging teachers in "experiences as learners" when asked to consider innovative teaching practices and/or content (e.g., Borasi & Fonzi, 2002; Luehmann, 2007; Windschitl, 2002). Theoretical support for this approach can be found in both a *cognitive apprenticeship* model of learning complex practices (e.g., Collins et al., 2019)—as "experiences as learners" can be considered a specialized form of modeling—as well as identity theory (e.g., Luehmann, 2007), as they represent a form of participation in practices at the core of the community of practice one aspires to belong. This approach was piloted using SmileyCluster with master teachers in the Robert Noyce Teacher Scholarship Program at the University of Rochester in the Spring of 2020.

We also believe it would be very valuable to engage science teachers in co-designing learning experiences that integrate AI/ML within a course they are currently teaching with an expert. This will help science teachers better appreciate the potential of AI/ML to support specific NGSS standards, figure out how to best "fit" their curriculum constraints, as well as increase self-efficacy for AI and ML.

CONCLUSIONS

In this chapter, we present an argument for the integration of AI/ML into science education. AI/ML offers a new way of knowing for scientists in many fields. With all the power and promise and application-in-practice that AI/ML will seemingly provide, many questions arise for leaders and K–12 administrators to ponder; in particular:

- Are we providing appropriate pathways for learners to transition into AI/ML-driven science?
- The traditional scientific method is still the overwhelming paradigm in K–12 science education, but this is changing; is the integration of AI/ML into science enough to prepare learners for the future?
- Do we need more explicit coding, AI, and ML type courses?
- Would time be more wisely spent teaching random forest classification compared to mitosis?

These questions do cause pause and demand we reflect on what STEM we are teaching in K–12 schools and why. Learners in today's K–12 classroom will be entering a highly digital society. How are we preparing them for this world? The integration of AI/ML into the science curriculum is an opportunity to start this preparation.

Unless connections of AI/ML to NGSS are demonstrated, it will be challenging to advance literacy in AI/ML. The curriculum in schools has a rooted history and is difficult to change. It is highly unlikely that states will adjust the curriculum to provide all students with instruction in AI/ML in the next decade. However, the significance of AI/ML for society is rapidly increasing, and the importance of AI/ML literacy is growing. Connecting AI/ML to NGSS provides a pathway for all students to gain some literacy in AI/ML. Most students will not go into careers that require technical knowledge of AI/ML, but all students will use the products of AI/ML in their lives. It is important to find opportunities to increase literacy in AI/ML and connect to science instruction to provide such a path.

REFLECTIVE QUESTIONS

1. What are the implications of machine learning for the development of scientific mindsets and practices in today's students?
2. What should high school students know about machine learning and its applications to their lives?
3. How can we best introduce foundational concepts of artificial intelligence and machine learning to students without advanced mathematics and computer science preparation, and enable them to benefit from machine learning in their scientific investigations?

CHAPTER 23

BECOMING A POSTMODERN STEM TEACHER LEADER IN THE AGE OF INFERENCE

Rebekah Hammack

The time is now to blur the lines of distinction between those who teach in schools and those who lead them.

—Barnett Berry

It is doubtful anyone, even the legislators who are proponents of accountability and standardized testing, would argue that a single assessment given at the end of the school year is an accurate measurement of what a student knows. However, the current accountability era in which we live has placed a great emphasis on standardized assessments that are too narrow in scope to assess complex indicators of student knowledge and skill development. Teachers are being evaluated and schools are receiving funding based on these test scores, resulting in a "teaching to the test" culture that detracts from the rich, meaningful, learning experiences described by Dewey (1938) in *Experience and Education*. The question then becomes how we, as educators, can guarantee equitable education and create meaningful learning experiences for all students while still working within accountability mandates. This is a question with which teachers and scholars have been

Age of Inference, pages 385–392

struggling for some time now. If finding such an answer was simple, the U.S. education system would not be struggling as it is today. One solution that can be proposed is to empower teachers through leadership, such as mentoring, sharing best practices, and conducting action research. In his book, *Five Minds for the Future,* Gardner (2008) asks, "What are my obligations as a scientific researcher, a writer, a manager, a leader?" (p. 8). Reading those words, one can begin to question their own role as a STEM educator in the Postmodern Era in which we now live.

According to Handler (2010), effective curriculum leadership requires advanced knowledge of the political, historical, philosophical, and sociocultural aspects of education. Most educator preparation programs, however, do not address these issues in depth and should be adjusted to provide preservice teachers with more background in curriculum theory, allowing them to understand "curriculum at the deeper level necessary to make decisions beyond the classroom level" (Handler, 2010, p. 38). To further complicate matters, many of the curriculum theories that are valuable to teachers are often laden with jargon that is difficult to navigate, making interpreting the theories an arduous task. This chapter attempts to interpret the verbiage and apply what the author thinks are the core values of post-structuralism to STEM education. While the chapter attempts to break down post-structuralism into its simplest tenets, providing a very basic background that will be required for those who wish to become teacher leaders, it must be stressed that this is a very limited definition meant only to provide an introduction to the concept, and anyone wishing to read in more depth should do so.

POST-STRUCTURALISM

The postmodern era refers to the period of time following the modern era, and spans from the 1950s to the present day, overlapping the Information Age. During this time period, many theorists were dissatisfied with structuralist theories, which stated that all social phenomena could be explained by formal systems or structures. According to post-structuralists, underlying social structures could not map the human condition, which was continuously in flux—as are all facets of human society. The three basic tenets of post-structuralism: discourse, crisis of representation (différance), and subjectivity are rooted in linguistics (Slattery, 2013).

Post-structuralism posits that a person's ways of thinking are discursively constructed based on what language is used and how, when, and under which circumstances that language is spoken. The choice of language can be used to elicit very different responses to the same situation. For example, consider the phrases *fat as a hog* and *pleasantly plump.* Each could be used to describe the same overweight person, but one has a very negative connotation, while the other is more positive. Additionally, post-structuralists consider the meaning of written language to be deferred from the time when it was written until the time it is read, because readers interpret what they read based on their own experiences and not those of the writer. Reading Shakespeare is a great example of this because today's readers are living in different times than during Shakespeare's life, making the interpretation of the writing different today than it was in the 1600s. Jacques Derrida coined the term différance to describe this deferred meaning of text. Not only is language used to give meaning to written and spoken words, but it is also used to discursively construct individual identity through subjectivity.

The third tenet of post-structuralism, subjectivity, posits that there can be no objective reality because reality is constantly shifting based on an individual's beliefs about the ever-changing sociopolitical context in which they live. Students come into the classroom from very diverse backgrounds, and teachers witness the different ways in which they construct their own meanings and interpret text. Beyond this individual level of meaning making, subjectivity suggests that a person's identity is socially constructed. We live in an age when we are labeled from the time we are born. Societal norms place us into categories based on the labels to which we are given by society. Are we gendered/nongendered, heterosexual/LGBTQI, White/a person of color, able-bodied/disabled, and so forth? A major problem with this categorization, though, is that the categories are socially constructed. How do intersex or transgender individuals identify themselves when asked about their gender? What constitutes White or Black or LatinX? Do the answers to these questions depend on whom you ask and when you ask them? These socially constructed categories create hegemonic binaries that can result in a dominant group and an oppressed *other* group. Post-structural theorists try to shed light on the ways that language functions to create these oppressive categories. They recognize that the implementation of any recommendations or action steps, no matter how well-intended, would act to leave some group oppressed.

As science educators, we should strive to identify programs and strategies that will benefit all students. While there is no program that will equally benefit every child, if educators do not try to identify positive steps for change, then we will continue to perpetuate the broken, oppressive system that exists and progress will never be made. We must go beyond simply identifying examples of *diverse* scientists (e.g., women, people of color) to examine how the culture of traditional western science places Eurocentric views in a place of authority, resulting in the exclusion of those whose identities do not align with Eurocentrism. A specific example of this can be seen in the binary of traditional western science and traditional knowledge (TK) of indigenous peoples. TK and traditional western science are often constructed as opposing worldviews (Guillory & Wolverton, 2016) with TK being viewed as less valuable than western science (Menzies & Butler, 2006). This *othering* of traditional ways of knowing can alienate students who do not come from the dominant culture and prevent them from engaging in science learning experiences.

When teachers recognize that the traditional ways in which science has been presented can devalue TK, and thus oppress indigenous students, they can take steps to learn about TK and the ways it can be coupled with traditional western science to emphasize the common ground between the two (Aikenhead & Ogawa, 2007), such as the use of empirical data to understand natural phenomena (e.g., making observations, identifying of patterns, revising based on new observations). Steps teachers could take to do this work might include visiting students' homes and communities, speaking with community members and elders, reading about the culture, or visiting museums devoted to the culture and then reflecting on what they have learned and contrasting it with the culture of traditional western science (Aikenhead, 1996). After this reflection, teachers can consciously move back and forth between both TK and traditional science, using the language conventions of both to develop cross-cultural science teaching practices (Aikenhead, 1996) that place constructivist meaning making based on observations of data at the center of learning. By doing so, students from different cultures can examine data to make evidence-based claims that align with their personal identities and enhance their understanding of the world.

We currently live in the Age of Inference, when scientific interpretations of data impact daily life and dictate what technology is developed and for what purposes. Understanding the impact of language, context, and subjectivity on inference generation is important for highlighting the oppressive functions of language that we all unknowingly disseminate and for making informed inferences that minimize hegemony. If teachers are aware of the creation of *others,* such as the indigenous example provided above, they can make conscious decisions about the actions and language they use in their classrooms. Just as the tenet of différance suggests there is deferred meaning in interpreting a written text, there will also be deferred meaning in the ways students interpret data based on current societal language construction, their prior experiences, and exposure to various sociopolitical contexts. Keeping différance in mind, teachers can explicitly talk with students about ways to identify any noise that may be present in their data that could influence their inferences. This could be something as simple as having students observe a particular phenomenon or data set and record their observations. Then, the class can go through the list of observations and discuss each one to identify any that might actually be inferences rather than observations. An example of such a lesson can be found in the *Science Scope* article "Making a Leap Toward Concrete Inferences" (Scribner-Mclean, 2009).

TEACHER LEADERSHIP

Teachers can also take steps to empower themselves and those around them in the fight to provide all students with equitable, high-quality, engaging STEM learning experiences. Lewthwaite (2006) stated:

> The factors influencing science teacher-leader development cannot be generalized but, instead, are unique to each individual; their personal attributes; the context in which their development takes place; the time (life-span) at which development is occurring; and the process each person experienced during development. (p. 333)

While each teacher leader's experiences and path will be unique, there are some general practices that should prove beneficial to teachers in the STEM field, including broadening the definition of teacher leadership, the use of role models, and teacher reflection. York-Barr and Duke (2004) defined teacher leadership as "the process by which teachers, individually or collectively, influence their colleagues, principals, and other members of school communities to improve teaching and learning practices with the aim of increased student learning and achievement" (pp. 287–288).

Further, they identified seven dimensions of teacher leadership: (a) coordination and management, (b) preservice teacher education, (c) contributions to the profession, (d) school and district curriculum work, (e) parent and community involvement, (f) professional development of colleagues, and (g) participation in school change and improvement. Many teachers engage in multiple leadership dimensions but often dismiss the value of their daily experiences as they consign leadership to formal positions outside of classroom teaching (Hanuscin et al., 2012). Akert and Martin (2012) found that principals viewed the impact of their teachers' leadership higher than the teachers themselves did, indicating that teachers may not be seeing the leadership capacities they take on. Empowering teachers as leaders will require broadening their definition of leadership to include both formal and informal activities that fall within the seven dimensions of teacher leadership described by York-Barr and Duke (2004). This will allow teachers to identify the many ways they engage in leadership and enhance their self-confidence in their abilities to be leaders and effect change.

Expanding teachers' definition of what a STEM teacher is will also be required. In particular, we must target elementary teachers who do not instinctively view themselves as the STEM teachers they are. National and state organizations, as well as district-level professional development coordinators, will need to provide resources for elementary teachers to enhance their STEM teaching practices and develop master STEM teachers at the elementary level. Waiting until middle or high school to invest in STEM teachers and programs will result in students entering secondary schools with deficits in STEM knowledge and skills that are too great to reverse during the time they are at the secondary level.

According to Fishman and Krajcik (2003), teachers lack the influence needed to produce change within their building and beyond. However, research on the effectiveness of professional learning communities and teacher leadership suggests otherwise (Akert & Martin, 2012; Vescio et al., 2008). As more teachers become empowered as leaders and are viewed as respected, accomplished role models by their colleagues, the amount of influence they have at the local, state, and national levels will increase. The key to this will be to engage in leadership through the position of role model. When STEM teachers engage in activities such as actively participating in professional organizations, building partnerships with community organizations, encouraging parent participation, and modeling reflective practice, they are leading by example and extending their STEM knowledge and skills to others (York-Barr & Duke, 2004). For instance, a teacher in a southern state received a grant to start an engineering program at her school that offered students the opportunity to engage in rigorous problem-based learning activities.

When starting this program, she formed an advisory board of local stakeholders, including parents, university faculty, and industry members to help inform the program's development. By actively engaging with local stakeholders, word of the successful new program quickly spread throughout the community. After the first year, there was an article highlighting the program in the local paper, and, a year after that, the teacher was asked to bring her students to the capitol to share the program with the state's board of education. By year three, the state superintendent was visiting the classroom to view the program in action. This led to other local schools adopting similar programs. This is just one instance of a teacher leading by example, empowering others to do the same, and thus creating a domino effect of change throughout the profession.

Teacher leadership is a socially distributed phenomenon (Szczesiul & Huizenga, 2015). Teachers need mastery experiences to gain efficacy (Bandura, 1977) and multiple opportunities to reflect on that mastery within the social context (Szczesiul & Huizenga, 2015). Teachers who are involved in leadership decisions have been reported to be more invested in schoolwide programmatic outcomes (Barth, 2001). "Teachers have front-line knowledge of classroom issues... and they understand the support they need to do their jobs well" (Paulu & Winters, 1998, p. 7). When asked to share this knowledge and expertise with their colleagues, teacher leaders have reported feeling a sense of gratification (Akert & Martin, 2012), and teachers are supportive of participating in professional learning communities (PLCs) that offer teachers opportunities to take the lead of their professional learning (Vescio et al., 2008).

Research suggests that when schools institute strong PLCs, there is a shift in school culture that results in increased focus on student learning, teacher empowerment, collaboration, and continuous teacher learning (Vescio et al., 2008). Further, it has been reported that students who attend schools with higher levels of teacher instructional leadership have higher levels of engagement (Leithwood & Jantzi, 1998) and increased performance on state-mandated assessments (Ingersoll et al., 2017; Hollins et al., 2004). School administrators need to rethink the way principals and teachers work together to ensure that teacher leaders are trusted by their administrators and given a prominent voice. Further, school schedules need to be adjusted to allow teacher leaders time to collaborate with each other (Berry, 2019) and institute PLCs.

REFLECTIVE PRACTICE

One way for STEM teachers to empower themselves as leaders is through self-reflection. Dewey (1933) wrote about the importance of reflective thinking in education. Drawing upon Dewey's work, Spaulding and Wilson (2002) described reflective thinking as "essential to identifying, analyzing, and solving the complex problems that characterize classroom teaching" (p. 1394). Even the best teacher leaders can improve but only if they know how what they are currently doing is impacting student learning, the teaching profession, and the broader community. This can only be accomplished through reflection. I went through the National Board Certification process a few years ago, which required me to reflect on all aspects of my teaching practice. I critiqued videos of my teaching; examined my lessons and student work to determine the level of my students' learning; and reflected on my outreach and involvement with parents, community members, and other educators. This self-reflection changed the way that I approach my teaching practice and helped me grow as a practitioner and a leader.

Through this reflective practice, I noticed that I was allowing a few students to dominate classroom discourse, so I incorporated a number of different classroom discussion techniques to allow for more voices to be shared. I also noticed that I was not offering students enough opportunities to engage with primary data sources and practice making the evidence-based claims that are critical in today's Age of Inference. This realization resulted in an immediate shift in my pedagogy in which I placed more deliberate emphasis on three-dimensional instruction (National Research Council, 2012).

Daily questions that reflective practitioners might ask themselves include: "What worked well today?"; "What didn't work so well?"; "What can I do differently to reach more students?"; "How might my actions today have been viewed by others?"; "What do I need to do next to make sure my students are having valuable learning experiences?"; "What steps can I take to help my colleagues improve?" After answering questions like these and personally dissecting how they teach and serve as a leader, teachers can begin to understand the impact they have on their students and the greater STEM community. Through reflection, they can identify the strengths and weaknesses in their teaching, as well as any hegemonic language they may unknowingly be using, and work to improve. Good teachers use a variety of different teaching strategies to reach all of their students, but teacher leaders reflect on those strategies and continually modify what they are doing to not only reach every student, but to identify ways to serve as practiced role models and enhance the profession. All teachers are encouraged to take these steps toward self-reflective practice and take the steps to become teacher leaders.

This chapter concludes with a call to action for all those interested in improving the quality of STEM education in this country. The author challenges each reader to reflect on their daily practices and identify the hidden ways (words, body language, textbook choices) in which they unknowingly disseminate socially constructed hegemonic norms. Then, they can take steps to correct these practices, leading by example so others can learn from their practices. Finally, readers, please recognize that you, as educators, parents, students, or community members, have the ability to become leaders and bring about change. You do not need to be in a formal leadership role in order to be a leader; all you have to do is step up to the plate and accept the challenge.

REFLECTIVE QUESTIONS

1. As mentioned above, teachers often have a narrow definition of leadership, failing to classify the activities in which they engage as leadership, despite their principals viewing them as such. What is your definition of leadership? How might you expand your definition of leadership to be inclusive of your own practice? What steps can you take to engage in reflective practice? How can you be a role model and lead by example?
2. Going back to the Howard Gardner quote shared at the beginning of this chapter, we should each ask ourselves "What are my obligations as a scientific researcher, a writer, a manager, a leader?" What steps can we take to lead and empower other teachers to lead for change?

CHAPTER 24

SEEKING HOMEOSTASIS IN A HETEROSCEDASTIC WORLD

A Sense of the Stakes in the Age of Inference

Philip C. Short, Donna F. Short, and John R. McConnell

If the end does not justify the means, what can?
—Edward Abbey

"Why is the sky blue?" was the prompt given by a mother to her 10-year-old son during a home-schooling session necessitated by the COVID-19 pandemic in 2020. The boy, an advanced student with a high level of interest in science, promptly spouted off, "It's because blue light from the sun gets scattered in the atmosphere." His younger sister interjects from the next room, "I thought it was just blue being reflected from all the oceans."

A minor battle of the wits ensued until mom, the instructor, redirected them both. "So, you both seem to have different answers, but I am not sure either of you has answered my question. What do you think I meant by 'why'

Age of Inference, pages 393–409

in my question? Was I asking, 'How is it that the sky appears blue?' Is either of your answers complete for that question? What evidence did you give me? Was I asking, 'What does it matter that the sky is blue?' Neither of you even tried to answer that question.

"When I ask you a question and you think you have the answer for *it*, I want you to think a little deeper about what *it* actually is. The most important questions should cause you to think, '...but now, so what?' I want you to stop all of your other studies for today. Use all of your resources as well as all of your reasoning skills to bring me a consensus answer tomorrow, with data and evidence, for the following questions: 'If you think blue light is being scattered, where did the blue light come from and what is causing it to be scattered?'; 'Why isn't red or yellow or green being scattered like the blue?'; 'If you think that the oceans are reflecting the blue to the sky, explain how the oceans are blue'; and 'Why don't the oceans appear red?' Those are the easier questions.

"By the end of the week, I want both of you to have either a joint answer (or different responses) to these more important questions: 'Why does it matter that the sky is blue?'; 'What does a blue sky mean for our life on earth?'; and 'What do you think would happen if more or less blue light reached the earth's surface?' When I ask you a question, kids, don't think you know *it* until you are sure which *it* is important. Remember, the answers to the most important questions are not simply copied from your textbooks."

The brother and sister replied in agreement, "Your assignments are a lot harder than our regular teachers' work!"

EPISTEMOLOGY AND THE COMFORTABLE DELUSION IN KNOWING

Evolving as a social species, we have needed assurances. There is good reason that organismal traits, behaviors, cultures, and institutions, from schools to governments to religions, are slow to evolve, even when changes in surrounding conditions appear to outpace the adaptations. Krebs (1978) best described life's conflicting pressures with the statement, "The distribution and abundance of organisms are fixed by the evolutionary processes of the past impinging on the changing environments of the present" (p. 16).

Humans must certainly promote traits suited for survival under the current circumstances. A drive to also predict behaviors and innovate for future success is uniquely innate in our self-aware and intelligent species. Nevertheless, our cleverness for invention often appears to surpass the wisdom of its proper utility for long-term benefit. Even as new discoveries and developments have grown exponentially over the past few centuries, societies have been reluctant to discard older ideas that have had apparent benefit throughout our known verbal or written history. Embedded in this reluctance seems to be an aversion to being wrong or, equally, to permit wrong (as the dominant group may define it) in others. Science and society have long been at odds over this resistance to change, sometimes with deadly consequences.

> All new knowledge is heresy, and when one's new findings are significant and important, in a long-term sense, the expression of those ideas may be perceived as lunacy by static forces in the population—the societal norm—as innovative thinking is always, by definition, an outlier. (Short, 2007, p. 148)

Given that survival of our species and quality of life should come through public discourse attended in plenary fashion, a primary goal of educational institutions must be the development of critically thinking participants in democracy who have the knowledge and tools to make decisions for the long-term benefit and sustainability of humans. Determining the appropriate knowledge and tools becomes the point of contention. In the satirical parable of *The Saber-Tooth Curriculum,* Benjamin (1939) illustrated the gap existing between "essential knowledge" that schools transmitted and the knowledge future generations needed to survive in a changing world. The hypothetical, stone-age curriculum taught children how to grab fish, club woolly horses, and scare saber-tooth tigers as skills needed to sustain themselves. Over time, conditions changed, and new, different skills were needed; however, the school leaders, resistant to change, continued teaching the original curriculum, believing it to be foundational for traditional community values.

Naturally, this tension between the knowledge and skills that have served us in the past versus new insights for tomorrow's challenges extends beyond the scope of the scientific focus in this tome. *Cultural Literacy: What Every American Should Know* (Hirsch et al., 1988) was a celebrated academic work illustrating this tension and the tendency toward social inertia and adherence to the interpretations and products of a dominant culture. Hirsh's actual progressive intentions in service of social justice and equality were, apparently, lost in interpretation by those stoking a culture war and defending a Western canon; therefore, it is important to consider decoding context around any proposed cultural core and to continually reimagine what is of value in that core if moving society forward is the goal (Liu, 2015).

The tensions within the scientific enterprise, in an increasingly data-rich world, do not differ terribly from those of a broader social and cultural context. While evidence continues to guide us in this burgeoning Age of Inference (see Chapter 1, this volume), a fundamental understanding of epistemological foundations in science is needed among the citizenry. The seeds for understanding the nature of science (NOS) should be sown in fertile ground among the youngest of our citizenry.

The 10-year-old boy in the opening vignette is a representative product of his previous 4 years in the school system which is, after all, an operationalized expression of societal values. Limited science knowledge and low self-efficacy among elementary teachers have long been known factors in avoidance of science instruction or reluctance to shift to more inquiry-based approaches (Appleton, 2003; Blank, 2013; Nollmeyer & Bangert, 2017; Sowder & Harward, 2011). Students learn early, in a system of binary responses, that rewards lie with correct recall of facts predetermined as valuable by the curriculum holders. Rudolph (2020) reminded us that scientific communities had long outgrown naïve beliefs concerning absolute truths and cited Feinstein and Waddington (2020) in noting that science education has been harmed by giving the impression of scientific findings as absolute rather than approximated truths.

In the first 2 decades of the 21st century, the emphasis on knowledge recitation has grown due to pressures on teachers to cover a breadth of content. This pressure has been applied even while science education reform initiatives have deemphasized facts and endorsed teaching NOS and scientific process through inquiry (Hout & Elliott, 2011; Kind & Osborne, 2017; Next Generation Science Standards [NGSS] Lead States, 2013). Plank and Condliffe (2013) posited that the reasoning for highlighting performance on high-stake assessments is that this emphasis holds teachers and schools accountable and would make teachers align to the standards and push for content mastery (Cherbow et al., 2020; Smith & Nadelson, 2017). The relationship between accountability pressures and classroom quality appears to be an inverse one, however, as higher pressures on student test performance actually lowers classroom quality and time for subjects such as science (Judson, 2013; Lidar et al., 2020).

It is perplexing that we should impress upon a 10-year-old child that certitude is attainable and the prioritized goal. As those children become adults embedded with delusions of truths, this misconception becomes stagnating at best and dangerously divisive when adherence to inflexible narratives predominate. A surprise would come to many upon discovering that, after centuries, even a fundamental agreement on what constitutes scientific progress eludes us.

Preceding even the seminal work of Kuhn (1962/1996), definitions of science and corresponding progress have varied. In recent decades, Bird (2007, 2008) has argued from an epistemic approach, met with rebuttals from Rowbottom (2010, 2015) for a semantic account of progress who, in turn, has been met with counter-arguments by Niiniluoto (2014).

Mizrahi (2013) joined the philosophical polemic with a case for broadening the conception of progress. Beyond the epistemic and semantic, he suggested looking to scientific practice. In his view, progress is made when scientific discoveries contribute to the increase of empirical, theoretical, practical, and methodological scientific knowledge. This approach has support as it has been employed by the scientific community to reward groundbreaking work.

Following decades of the riveting, point-counterpoint discussions of science history and philosophy may stimulate some readers. The point made here, however, is that expectations not shouldered by working scientists are too often placed on very young people. The high stakes in summative assessments demand from students a level of definitive knowing not recognized in the global scientific community. Generations of young people, steeped in a discomfort with uncertainty and stifled in classrooms burdened by *fixed-mindset triggers* (Dweck, 2015), grow up but never mature past the artifacts or residue emerging from scientific endeavors as limited by current technologies and analytical methods.

Epistemology—in this context, the meaning and scope of knowledge in science and the methods of validation in an increasingly data-rich, information-saturated world—is central to cultivating mindsets for lifelong learning from proper inferencing. The Information Age swept in with blistering velocity, inundating the populace sans a well-structured mechanism to process the constant stream of data. Multiple generations who have been influenced by direct, didactic instruction have been left nomadic in a rainforest of diverse, confounding information but a desert of analytical prowess.

The positive contributions of the Information Age have been emphasized, but negative ramifications have also been noted for 2 decades. Rogerson (2003) related the potential issues of his (then current) period to red flags raised by Karl Polanyi in the 1940s. Substituting information for materials, Rogerson signaled concern over the tension between two dynamics: (a) the tendency of information to be free-flowing and not to lose its value as it moves, and (b) the tendency to want to control that flow of information in order to profit from its value. A decade later, the National Assessment Governing Board (2014) echoed and codified similar concerns in the National Assessment of Educational Progress. Along with holding students accountable for functional skills and for describing the benefits of information technologies, the additional expectations for understanding are that (a) the problems can be caused by using digital information without verifying quality; (b) the potential disadvantages of uncritical use of the technologies; and (c) the ubiquitous use of information communication and dissemination affects governments, news, and other organizations as well as individuals. Recent political discourse and violent actions, understanding and acceptance of public health protocols, volatilization in climate policy discussions, and many other examples exemplify the effect of an unplumbed proliferation of commoditized information.

The beginning quote for this chapter is not to be interpreted as "every end justifies every means." Rather, it suggests there is really no other way to evaluate a means/action (i.e., instruction, technology, decision-making) other than to know the target objective(s) upfront and to have an assessment plan for the end results. The world has likely been immersed in the Information Age for sufficient time to begin gauging whether the societal effects at this current endpoint do or do not justify the means thrust upon us. A corollary question would be whether this evaluation might have yielded different results had we produced a more scientifically literate citizenry over the past several decades.

In the cases to follow, consider the potential impacts on cohorts of students and, ultimately, societies that may be influenced by essentialist educational philosophies demanding simple acceptance of authoritative knowledge as compared to more fluid instructional methodologies that Al-abdulkareem (2012) contended would help students explore and evaluate their views and beliefs about the essential terms of science, fact, and absolute truth. Consider why large swaths of the population are reluctant to change ideas and behaviors when new evidence has long moved scientists to do so (in nutrition, medicine, chemistry, ecology, and many other fields).

BREAD, BUTTER, AND EGGS: WRAPPED IN PLASTICITY

From 1916 through 2011, the U.S. Department of Agriculture (USDA) provided publications on science-based dietary guidance from eight somewhat different approaches, and newer guidelines have been made available (USDA, 2011; U.S. Department of Health and Human Services and U.S. Department of Agriculture, 2015; Willett & Stampfer, 2006). Sidestepping, but not entirely dismissing, issues of influence from agribusiness (Berge, 2008; Brusie, 2017; Karlan-Mason & Shi, 2021), the focus here is on the very legitimate nature of change in science. A common refrain of those unfamiliar with scientific processes has been, "I don't believe the scientists know what they're talking about. They tell us to eat more breads and cereal grains, and then tell us to cut carbs. They tell us eggs are bad, but later suggest otherwise." The fault should lie less with these individuals than on a systemic failure to properly teach NOS and data inference.

Bread Science in Society

At the base of the original 1992 USDA food pyramid (modeled after an earlier 1974 Swedish pyramid) were breads, pastas, and cereal grains. When the public followed what they believed to be science-based guidelines, heart disease and obesity actually *increased.* Diabetes nearly quadrupled since the early 1970s in the wake of food guidelines with carbohydrates at the base of the pyramid (Centers for Disease Control Division of Diabetes Translation,

2017). Critical to the themes of this book, it is important to acknowledge that one factor cannot be assumed to tell the entire story behind the increase of Type II diabetes, as multiple variables may be teased from additional data sets. Nevertheless, current science does depict the prominent dietary habit from the 1970s, and particularly after the 1992 distribution of the USDA Food Pyramid, as a causal factor in the epidemic. As data showed the pyramid to be counterproductive, and a 2011 MyPlate model, influenced by former first lady Michelle Obama, was introduced to the public, many people balked. Again, they doubted that science was any more reliable than political whimsy.

While dietary science has progressed and improved upon older findings, much of the issue rested on the inferences made by developers of the earlier dietary guides as well as the public to which it was presented. The message people received was broad and general in terms of carbohydrates as well as the suggested choices for other food groups. There was no clear differentiation among simple, complex, and processed carbohydrates. The recommendations assumed that most people needed more caloric intake, and carbohydrates were cost-effective in providing this. Another issue stemmed from a public conflation of "servings per day" and "portion size per plate." It would be inaccurate to state that the data were nonexistent in 1992, but it is important to remember that information accessibility was considerably different than presently available. Brusie (2017) revealed that a little known, and less understood, booklet accompanied the original USDA pyramid which explained quantified "servings." As an example, a single bagel would account for 6–11 servings of processed carbohydrates, rather than one as many would infer. A scientifically illiterate society would naturally bristle at the skepticism or guilt suddenly induced by restrictions on a favorite brunch snack.

Part of the impetus for people to increase carbohydrate intake (without discretion for the *type* of carbs) was the erroneous equating of *low-fat* as *healthy* (becoming a widely accepted ideology for all Americans in the 1980s) and the push to replace high-fat foods with highly processed foods (Berge, 2008; Brusie, 2017). Butter became a casualty as did human health.

Butter Science in Society

From a mid-1800s challenge by Napolean, wanting an inexpensive butter substitute (Cardiologists Kitchen, 2015) for the military, French Chemist, Hippolyte Mège-Mouriès, invented oleomargarine (later shortened to margarine—although some, perhaps, remember grandparents using oleo as an abbreviation). Improvements in the chemical process through the early part of the 20th century led to hydrogenated vegetable oils resulting in the formation of trans fatty acids products (Sellami et al., 2012) and in butter giving way to a cheap replacement (Chrysam, 1996). It was a popular campaign in the 1980s promoting margarine and trans fats as "healthier alternatives" to saturated fats, however, that caused a great increase in use. Globally, based on the available evidence of the time, this transition was also advocated by medical guidelines (Cardiologists Kitchen, 2015). Reports over the following decades identifying the multiple diseases linked to trans fat (Holt et al., 2015; Institute of Medicine, 2005) led to changes in the production of margarines (Israel, 2015) with state bans and eventual changes in U.S. Food and Drug Administration recommendations and labeling policies. Real butter seemed to be coming back into vogue, with more moderation being stressed.

Egg Science in Society

For much of the 20th century, a reflection of public dietary sentiment could be characterized by a line from a 1906 novel, where P. G. Wodehouse wrote "The good old egg is the foundation of daily life." By 1980, however, many in the medical profession contributed to the public's fear of fat by acknowledging that accumulated cholesterol in our cardiovascular systems, assumed to be associated with consumption of certain foods like butter and eggs, was likely detrimental to our bodies (Eilat-Adar et al., 2013; Miranda et al., 2015; Stetka, 2017). By 2013, questions about methodologies in earlier studies led the American College of Cardiology and American Heart Association to issue new guidelines suggesting more individualized rather than blanket targets for low-density lipoprotein (LDL) cholesterol levels should be sought (Lopez-Jimenez et al., 2014).

The public had been warned against frequent egg consumption for 40 years based on the assumption that high dietary cholesterol consumption is associated with high blood cholesterol levels and cardiovascular diseases (CVD), but subsequent research suggested that dietary cholesterol in general and cholesterol in eggs, in particular, had limited effects on the blood cholesterol level and on CVD (Eilat-Adar et al., 2013; Miranda et al., 2015). Reenter the incredible, edible egg! Still, the new report was met with skepticism by some dietary and cardiovascular researchers who contended that individuals with atherosclerotic vascular disease, high LDL levels, and those with diabetes limit intake to provide protections from further deterioration (Ades, 2014).

Wrapped in Plasticity

How can there be so much scientific data over such long periods of time without full consensus on the implications of the available information?

The packaging in which food arrives to our tables will further illustrate this paradox. How can original, innovative, science-based ideas to solve pressing problems become much bigger problems than those originally addressed?

In the 1800s, as demands for ivory drove the slaughter of elephants and threatened their populations, John Hyatt developed the first synthetic polymer in response to a $10,000 business offer to find a substitute for natural substances like tortoiseshell, horn, and ivory (Science History Institute, n.d.). It seemed, at the time, that plastics could help protect the natural world from the demands of human consumption. The first, fully, synthetic plastic was invented by Leo Baekeland in 1907 with many more variants and uses to follow so that, by World War II where plastics became important to military successes (Nicholson & Leighton, 1942), a massive production increase had set the stage for what would become a postwar economic boon. The annual plastics production increased from 0.5 million tons to 260 million tons between 1950 and 2007. Numerous markets opened to replace more expensive, natural materials in limited supply, including the changeover to plastics from paper and glass in packaging (Freinkel, 2011).

Growing environmental awareness in the 1960s created public concern about plastic products, despite their many benefits, through the 1980s when recycling became available—by the plastics industry itself. The public remained, perhaps justifiably, skeptical as it confronted a dilemma between ameliorating the known detrimental effects from the variety of polymer plastics on the natural environment and essential uses to modern life from construction materials, to medical advances, and components in digital devices of the Information Age. Of 140 million tons of plastics produced annually, about 37% are used for one-use packaging (Plastics Europe, 2008) with considerable amounts of waste entering the global ecosystems with deleterious effects (Dey et al., 2012; Gu, 2017; Hassan & Haq, 2019; Kumar et al., 2017; Sarmah & Rout, 2019; Worm et al., 2017).

It would be simplistic to suggest that bread, butter, eggs, and other products started arriving in our homes wrapped in plastics merely as a result of a century of industrial and economic evolution. The entire science underlying the production, roles, and evaluation of polymer uses for human and environmental welfare has been "wrapped in plasticity." Joel (1995) presented the Greek origin, *plastikos*, as having the characteristic of molded into different shapes or forms. This very fluidity of science, inference, and application is the essence of what can be lost on another cohort each time a teacher posts and teaches from an elementary chart showing the steps of the scientific method (as though one exists). Interestingly, Karl Popper (1983), an influential 20th century philosopher of science noted:

> As a rule, I begin my lectures on Scientific Method by telling my students that scientific method does not exist, and I ought to know... having been, for a time, the one and only professor of this nonexistent subject... my subject

> does not exist because subject matters in general do not exist...there are only problems, and the urge to solve them. (p. 5)

Of course, there are standard protocols and consistent methods of analysis in the various branches of science. Stringent peer review and consensus in the global scientific community should (but does not always) drive the enterprise. An issue for general scientific literacy arises, however, when the impression of a rigid, linear process leading to both accurate and beneficial solutions is given to learners. Of these two outcomes, accuracy in collecting and analyzing scientific data, while still fraught with opportunities for error, is more likely achievable than determining long-term benefit.

Throughout the chapters in this book are discussions of how to better equip a citizenry with a fundamental understanding of NOS and use data sets appropriately for rational inferencing. Included are the roles of newer technologies to assist in cultivating proper mindsets for the Age of Inference. The efficiency and effectiveness of actions in a scientifically literate society assisted by information technologies can, ultimately, only be measured at some determined endpoint and on the basis of valuation input of the original target goals. As values and priorities change, an end is experienced while a new beginning is ushered in. Sound science supported by faster data processing are merely tools for the uniquely, perennial, human tasks of deciding and acting.

FROM PAUL MULLER'S PRIZE TO ALLIGATOR PHALLUSES: THE BIG "SO WHAT?"

Sixty-six years after p,p'dichlorodiphenyltrichloroethane (DDT) was first synthesized, it was Paul Muller who discovered the insecticidal effectiveness of DDT for which he was later awarded the Nobel Prize (Klaassen, 1996; Mangochi, 2010; World Health Organization, 1979). From the 1940s through the next few decades, many viewed DDT as something of a miracle chemical, being successful for an array of uses from controlling typhus and malaria vectors to agricultural pests (Attaran & Maharaj, 2000; Mangochi, 2010; Roberts et al., 1997). Educational campaigns to promote DDT reflected this view with slogans such as: "DDT is Good for Me," "Use DDT to Control Household Pests," "Protect Your Victory Garden with DDT," and "Protect Your Children from Insects with Trimz DDT Children's Wallpaper." Once again, science and the best analytical tools of the day resulted in revolutionary discoveries and cutting-edge applications for priority problems of the day.

Although still in wide use at the time, questions about the safety of DDT emerged in the 1960s environmental awakening prompted, in no small part, by Rachel Carson's (1962) classic, "Silent Spring." DDT was shown to quickly degrade to p,p'-dichlorodiphenyldichloroethylene DDE with a significantly long half-life, allowing it to bioaccumulate in fatty tissues and present long-term toxic effects in human and natural environments (Agency for Toxic Substances and Disease Registry, 2002; Aylward et al., 2014; Grandjean et al., 2008; La Merrill et al., 2013; Plouffe et al., 2020; Whitehead et al., 2015; You et al., 1999). Some of the first alarms about the hazards of DDT rang out as shell thinning of bird eggs was noted in studies that accompanied significant declines in a number of species. DDT and its metabolites in the environment have long since been documented to negatively impact bird reproduction (Blus, 1982; Cooper, 1991; De Kock & Randall, 1984; Douthwaite, 1989; Hartley et al., 1995; Lundholm, 1997; Peakall et al., 1973; Snelling et al., 1984; U.S. Department of the Interio, 1998). The effects on bird populations continue to be a subject of study, particularly in countries where DDT use is still permitted for malarial control (Bouwman et al., 2019; Plouffe et al., 2020).

The estrogenic effect of DDT and DDE in disrupting male sexual development was later reported in many studies (De Jager et al., 2006; Guillette et al., 1995; Kelce et al., 1997; Mangochi, 2010; Rhouma et al., 2001; Sonnenschein & Soto, 1998; Turusov et al., 2002; You et al., 2002). One particular researcher studying alligators in Florida's Lake Apopka began noting ambiguous gonads and a 25% reduction in male penis size over a couple of years (Guillette et al., 1994, 1996). A chemical company's waste pond overflowed in 1980 and, even 10 years after the spill, high levels of DDE were present in alligator tissue samples and eggs. Phallus size is testosterone dependent, and abnormal levels of the sex hormones were noted; however, correlation does not, necessarily, mean causation. The relationship between penis size and sex hormones was not found to be a simple one, but subsequent, experimental, laboratory work did show that DDE could cause endocrine disruption whereby testosterone levels were depressed (Guillette et al., 1995; Guillette et al., 2000; Pérez & Wise, 2018).

As the mother/teacher in the opening vignette suggested to her young students, the "So what?" question is, arguably, more difficult to answer than the direct scientific questions regarding whether data support a specific hypothesis. In this example, what does it matter that DDT caused shell thinning in many bird species? Who really cares about the penis size in alligators? These are questions of value that every society must answer and where science is limited; nevertheless, improved scientific literacy and abilities to draw valid inferences from data should produce more informed resolutions to the many socioscientific questions.

Scientists were, in fact, alarmed at Guillette's reports of the shrinking alligator penises being linked to endocrine disruption by DDE. A dramatic reduction in fertility placed the population at risk, especially in their ability to recover from a natural disaster or outbreak of disease. A collapsing alligator population may, in itself, be met with the "So what?" question among some stakeholders involved in the issue. Once more, additional science helped inform the issue and reveal its complexity as researchers have shown alligators to be keystone species in ecosystems (Elsey et al., 2016; Elsey et al., 2013; Kushlan, 1974; Kushlan & Kushlan, 1980; Nifong & Silliman; 2013; Palmer & Mazzotti 2004) although some still have called for more evidence linking the importance of crocodilians to the broader ecosystem viability (Somaweera et al., 2020).

Beyond alligators and their swampy environs, environmental studies of DDT/DDE have led to other research findings of altered androgen expression and reproductive toxicity in mammals, including humans (De Jager et al., 2006; Kelce et al., 1997; Rhouma et al., 2001; Sonnenschein & Soto, 1998; Turusov et al., 2002; You et al., 2002). While the scientific protocols, data analyses, and inferencing processes are essentially the same through all of the studies, it is the societal value placed on the findings that ultimately determines the support for continued research as well as the resulting behaviors and actions on individual and collective scales. The likely answers to "So what?" changes as the data appear more relevant, as humans are directly affected.

SCIENCE EDUCATION IN A DATA-RICH SOCIETY

Verma et al. (2020) suggested that future leaders and citizens will struggle to use tools of science for decision-making unless explicit connections are made between activities of the science classroom and pressing societal phenomena and problems. They further called for providing sensemaking experiences that would be societally relevant to all learners. Lee (2020) proposed, especially for students who have been disconnected from science, that making sense of phenomena may be the most important instructional shift necessary in three-dimensional (3D) science classrooms. He continued with the suggestion that failing to select appropriate phenomena that help students access science in relatable ways to their homes and communities will further marginalize students by alienating them further from science. Lee and Campbell (2020) found that STEM learning could be more compelling for students when data science and computer science are integrated into investigations of current, relevant phenomena and complex societal problems.

The challenges of a citizenry confronted with newly emerging scientific data are well illustrated in the previous examples of this chapter. While academic inertia exists, societal inertia is entrenched. This is particularly true in populations where education has been suffused with authoritative absolutism, an artifact of teacher-centered instructional approaches dominated by direct, didactic methods. There is no reason that educational institutions should be moribund with symptoms of irrelevancy; however, to resuscitate, priorities must shift to holistic views of the learning environment where authentic investigations of place-based phenomena initiate engagement. The teachers' roles subsequently serve students in constructing new knowledge based on prior foundations (Fairbanks, 2011) while eliminating damaging misconceptions (Sewell, 2002) through open dialogue about discoveries from the investigations.

As Lee and Campbell (2020) recognized, integrating explorations of real-world phenomena with data science is important to authentic STEM learning. The inundation of data in the Information Age complicates the interactions of students with data if using traditional means of calculation in schools. Many technological opportunities to assist students in organizing large datasets exist and continue to be developed (Luckin et al., 2016). Nevertheless, much of the intrigue with artificial intelligence (AI) and machine learning (ML) in education has centered on data-mining, the extracting and analyzing of data from students and teachers for purposes of what has been termed *datafication of education* (Andrejevic & Selwyn, 2019; Bradbury, 2019; Domínguez, 2020; Johal et al., 2018; Kim et al., 2020; Luckin et al., 2016; McStay, 2018; Williamson, 2020a, 2020b; Williamson & Eynon, 2020; Williamson et al., 2020). The pace at which AI and ML have found their ways into schooling processes has both excited and concerned scholars.

While Sellar and Gulson (2019) revealed how AI techniques enable new thinking that shapes human decision-making that can influence educational policy making and practices, Perrotta and Selwyn (2019) highlight the risks of restrictive understandings of learning and the potential for biological discrimination (Martschenko et al., 2019). Academic debates over the use of robots in instruction (Javaheri et al., 2019) have divided those who have advocated for human instructors in the classroom (Li, 2015), and others have emphasized the positive outcomes of robotics in education (Belpaeme et al., 2018; Edwards et al., 2016; Park et al., 2011). Brown (2020) noted that technologies such as learning analytic platforms impose limits that can result in pedagogic reductionism. Further, Gilliard and Culik (2016) contended that certain social and minority groups are systemically disadvantaged through *digital redlining* as algorithmic decision-making automates inequalities and discrimination, while Hayes and Cheng (2020) argued that datafied and metricized systems make a positive move toward equity. Banja (2019) maintained that AI technologies are held to an unfairly high bar while acknowledging a real problem of algorithmic fairness found in biased predictive models.

Regardless, computer-assisted instruction and evaluations are likely to increase in prominence as reports show that significant gains in knowledge recall among students are realized with robot delivery (Li et al., 2015). The important question lies in the a priori goals and objectives we set for education. Assessing the effectiveness of instructional technologies would seem to need a broader basis than simple knowledge recall if ultimate educational goals include decision-making skills for fluid science-related social issues. Zeide (2019) expressed concerns that teachers' discretion and judgment can be reduced with AI and robotic technologies in the classroom, and similar questions about the effectiveness of AI and ML in promoting higher-order learning could reasonably be raised. The automated analysis and feedback provided by data systems depend on how those systems are trained to learn as AI must be socialized to learn human subjects, but it is important to note that quantifying and analyzing all forms of learning may not be possible (Knox et al., 2020; Williamson et al., 2020). Jasanoff (2017) posited that data are constructions about the world for specific purposes and not simply representations of reality independent from human thought.

VALUE-LADEN, EVIDENCE-BASED ACTIONS IN THE AGE OF INFERENCE: ENDPOINTS

We shake with joy, we shake with grief. What a time they have, these two, housed as they are, in the same body.

—Mary Oliver

When one ponders the scientific enterprise and the Weltanschauung with which it must be conducted, it brings both excitement and trepidation to think that the same process may result in either acceptance or rejection of our best ideas. It humbles us, or should, that a revolutionary discovery promising amelioration of today's issues may very well be the source of tomorrow's ills. Housed in the same body is joy and grief from evidence. The difference is found neither in the process nor the data; rather, it lies in the capricious values held by a society of people.

In examples from this chapter, the tandem evolution of both science and societal values revealed the manner in which a singular problem can yield varying inferences and, ultimately, human actions over time. Attention to this point must not be lost at the conclusion of this tome. Upon entering the Age of Inference (see Chapter 1, this volume) in a data-saturated world, a prudent reminder is offered that even the best tools for data analysis only partially complete the tasks involved in sentient inferencing. What then, one may ask, may ultimately evaluate the success and usefulness of our inferencing attempts? This question, too, is subject to individual and sociocultural, prejudiced subtleties. Successes in discovery, technical application, convenience, economic gain, and even (sometimes) a medical breakthrough are not, necessarily, indicators of long-term survival value for either humans or their sustaining environment. Granted, it may be easier to calculate success within the framework of shorter-term goals such as convenience or economic gain, but these goals constrain the paradigm of what is good and useful. Environmental sciences and environmental education (EE) serve us well to illustrate the complexities in inferencing as data become more accessible and as AI /ML make processing more accurate and efficient.

Odum and Odum (2000) suggested that ecosystems of the world are threatened because market values are inverse to contributions. They further stated that economic valuation can never be used appropriately to evaluate environmental capital because soils, forests, fisheries, and other environmental products contribute the most when they are abundant although the market value is small. When the resources become scarce, they contribute less, but the market value is high.

Attempts to evaluate long-term effects may risk falling prey to either the *Sin of Synecdoche* (Gorss, 2003) and/or the *Metonymy of Matrices* (Lamb, 2018) where, respectively, a part is used to represent the whole to which it belongs, and where a word, phrase, or notation is used in substitution of a concept that is more complex in a way that renders the substitution insufficient. Robust data analyses and emerging inferences can, conceivably, lead to erroneous conclusions if those analyses are conducted on data sets extracted from a synecdoche or metonymy rather than a sample more representative of the real, complete system. Apart from specific objections, such as those of Odum and Odum (2003), to valuations based on accurate data analysis but within a limited scope, the scientific community has been harangued by societal challenges that call into question the very legitimacy of the scientific process itself.

An idea that scientific knowledge was merely a social construct and not based on some objective reality has had tangible implications in the postmodern era (Rudolph, 2020). The trends toward anti-intellectualism and science denial of recent years hint at something fatidic in the revelation by Zammito (2004) that some socioscientific philosophers were eager to claim that truth in and about the world was less dependent on natural forces than the whims of culture, politics, or human psychology. Ethereal, academic discourse can have potent implications as seen in disturbingly, regressive, anti-science advocacy in the 21st century. Rudolph (2020) provided a retort in suggesting that sociological factors may, indeed, color our thinking about how the world functions, but these recognized influences do not allow for "just any expression" to be considered valid when discussing topics about the nature of the world such as climate change, the safety and efficacy of vaccines, whether face masks are effective in slowing the spread of COVID-19, or many other topics. He continues with a critique of NGSS stating that, while the newer science education framework contains the needed goals of improving science skills and cognitive abilities among the citizenry, it falls short by failing to provide adequate contexts for the importance of science skills in areas of public policies (Rudolph & Horibe, 2016; Zucker & Noyce, 2020). Rudolph (2020) followed by suggesting a civic argument can be made for an emphasis in science teaching that reinforces the ideas of trusting science (Oreskes, 2019; Pennock, 2019) as a valid and reliable source of knowledge (Slater et al., 2019) that can help us live better and more humanely with one another.

Undoubtedly, the pursuit of scientific answers is an outgrowth and maturation of our youthful curiosities. Inquiries into the behavior of light energy by the likes of James Maxwell were, in part, probably initiated by the same questions every child asks. Why is the sky blue? What makes up a rainbow? Through grounded theory laid down by predecessors, experimentation, data analysis, and innovative inferencing, great mysteries of the universe are solved. Yet, like this chapter's opening vignette with the 10-year-old child, the end goal of a question may not be clear or may not be the same for every purpose. To be certain, the context of this book has been to advocate for greater scientific literacy in this expanding Age of Inference where data/information inundates the citizenry. Knowledge of the standards, protocols, and tools available for proper scientific analysis and rational inferencing is essential for informing and guiding the more important personal behaviors, policies, and actions. To assess the success or effectiveness of learning and applying these skills, however, requires that the end is considered in the beginning. What are the ultimate, endpoint objectives? Is it enough to simply equip people with knowledge and skills? Can data inferencing be accomplished if divorced from values clarification? Would evaluations of the usefulness of margarine, DDT, or plastic at the end of 1955 yield a different inference than assessments today?

The scientific revolution was hard to achieve and is difficult to maintain. Realizing benefits from the Age of Inference may come at a slower pace than those from the Information Age, and these are likely to be shared less equitably under the status quo of educational systems. Computer-assisted handling of big data will obviously be required. More emphasis on some basic level of statistical knowledge and inferencing skills will be necessary. Societal values will, undoubtedly, shift though. Utilizing better technologies to process the data and equipping the public to properly interpret and infer from the data should be a goal. Moreover, achieving a level of scientific literacy in society that balances confidence and acceptance of the scientific enterprise with healthy, academic skepticism, rather than baseless and dangerous conspiratorial ideas, is a must for humanity's advancement. This balance should take us far toward personal and public actions that are, indeed, value-laden but richly informed and which bend in the direction of progress for the equitable welfare of all. The end evaluation will either justify or reprove the means, and, arriving at this end, another chapter will start with eyes sharpened eagerly toward a presumably more enlightened terminal. After all, one view holds that science is merely seeing what has been seen for a thousand years but in a different way.

Every new beginning comes from some other beginning's end.
—"Closing Time," Semisonic, 1998
(Original quote from Lucius Annaeus Seneca in 54 BC)

REFLECTIVE QUESTIONS

1. Is there any knowledge that would be better not to have? Should all populations have access to all available knowledge? Defend your thoughts with attention to end results.
2. If the scientific community has reached a tentative consensus based on current findings but the new theory is not exactly right, can it still be useful? Explain.
3. Fritz Haber discovered a process that allowed fertilizers to be made, making farming more efficient. However, overuse of chemical fertilizers has resulted in devastating effects on aquatic systems including a hypoxic dead zone in the Northern Gulf of Mexico measuring up to 22,000 square kilometers. Who should be responsible for the use of a scientific discovery and its consequences on society? Do the benefits offset the costs?
4. Are there any scientific inferences that scientists should not share? For instance, if a physicist spotted a comet that would cause imminent, unavoidable destruction heading to Earth, should the news be made public? If a virologist identified a pathogen that could infect and potentially kill all of humanity but is also needed for investigating its cure (in case, say, someone else develops the same pathogen), should it ever be disclosed?
5. Is a hypothesis always just true or false or are there other possible outcomes? How should research state their conclusions/inferences about hypotheses upon analyzing data?
6. Humanity has advanced through time as a response to various problems it has encountered. For instance, current advancements in scientific inference were necessary to cope with the abundance of information that we now have. What problems might these "solutions" cause? What problems do you foresee as being important to solve in the future? What's next as we progress beyond the Age of Inference?

REFERENCES

Abd-El-Khalick, F., & Lederman, N. G. (2000). Improving science teachers' conceptions of nature of science: A critical review of the literature. *International Journal of Science Education, 22*(7), 665–701. https://doi.org/10.1080/09NCE S500690050044044

Achinstein, B., & Ogawa, R. T. (2006). (In)Fidelity: What the resistance of new teachers reveals about professional principles and prescriptive educational policies. *Harvard Educational Review, 76*(1) 30–63.

ACT, Inc. (2006). *Reading between the lines: What the ACT reveals about college readiness in reading.* https://www.act.org/content/dam/act/unsecured/documents/reading_summary.pdf

Adelman, C. (2006). *The toolbox revisited: Paths to degree completion from high school through college.* US Department of Education.

Ades, P. (2014). A controversial step forward: A commentary on the 2013 ACC/AHA guideline on the treatment of blood cholesterol to reduce atherosclerotic cardiovascular risk in adults. *Coronary Artery Disease, 25*(4), 360–363.

Adler, M. (1984). *The Paideia proposal.* Macmillan Publishing.

Agency by Design. (2015). *Maker-centered learning and the development of self: Preliminary findings of the Agency by Design Project.* http://www.pz.harvard.edu/sites/default/files/Maker-Centered-Learning-and-the-Development-of-Self_AbD_Jan-2015.pdf

Agency for Toxic Substances and Disease Registry. (2002). *Toxicological profile for DDT/DDE/DDD* (Update). U.S. Department of Health and Human Services, Public Health Service.

Agresti, A., Franklin, C., & Klingenberg, B. (2017). *Statistics: The art and science of learning from data* (4th ed.). Pearson.

Age of Inference, pages 411–460

Ahren, C., Ryan, H. G., & Massa-McKinley, R. (2008). Assessment matters: The why and how of cracking open and using assessment results. *About Campus, 13*(2), 29–32.

Aikenhead, G. S. (1996). Science education: Border crossing into the subculture of science. *Studies in Science Education, 27*(1), 1–52. https://doi.org/10.1080/03057269608560077

Aikenhead, G. S., & Ogawa, M. (2007). Indigenous knowledge and science revisited. *Cultural Studies of Science Education, 2*, 539–620. https://doi.org/10.1007/s11422-007-9067-8

Ajay, T., & Kumar, G. A. (2014). Removal of impulse noise from remote sensing images using wavelets based on image fusion algorithm. *The International Journal of Advanced Research in Electrical, Electronics and Instrumentation Engineering, 3*(9), 2320–3765.

Akert, N., & Martin, B. N. (2012). The role of teacher leaders in school improvement through the perceptions of principals and teachers. *International Journal of Education, 4*(4), 284–299.

Alabdulkareem, S. (2012). Science, fact, and absolute truth: Critical views of learning. *Social and Behavioral Sciences, 93*, 2100–2108.

Ali, N., & Khine, M. S. (Eds.). (2020). *Integrating 3D printing into teaching and learning: Practitioners' perspectives.* Brill.

Allen, R. H. (2010). *High-impact teaching strategies for the 'XYZ' era of education.* Allyn and Bacon.

Alley, M. (2009). *Mobile learning: Transforming the delivery of education and training.* Athabasca Press.

Allison, E., & Goldston, M. J. (2018). Modern scientific literacy: A case study of multiliteracies and scientific practices in a fifth grade classroom. *Journal of Science Education and Technology, 27*(3), 270–283.

Alpaydin, E. (2014). *Introduction to machine learning* (3rd ed.). MIT Press.

Al Sultan, A., Henson, H., & Fadde, P. (2018). Pre-service elementary teachers' scientific literacy and self-efficacy in teaching science. *International Academic Forum Journal of Education, 6*(1), 25–42. https://doi.org/10.22492/ije.6.1.02

Al Sultan, A., Henson, H., & Lickteig, D. (2021). Assessing preservice elementary teachers' conceptual understanding of scientific literacy. *Teaching and Teacher Education, 102*(2021), 1–10. https://doi.org/10.1016/j.tate.2021.103327

American Association for the Advancement of Science. (1993). *Benchmarks for science literacy.* Oxford University Press.

Amirshokoohi, A. (2016). Impact of STS issue oriented instruction on pre-service elementary teachers' views and perceptions of science, technology, and society. *International Journal of Environmental & Science Education, 11*(4), 359–387.

Amrhein, V., Greenland, S., & McShane, B. (2019). Retire statistical significance. *Nature, 567*, 305–307.

Amrita, Cheema, J. S., & Neeru, N. (2013). Detection and removal of noises in iris recognition system- A review. *International Journal of Engineering Research & Technology, 2*(4), 463–471.

Anandhavalli, M., Ghose, M. K., & Gauthaman, K. (2010). Association rule mining in genomics. *International Journal of Computer Theory and Engineering, 2*(2), 269–273.

Anderson, A. A. (2019). Assessing statistical results: Magnitude, precision, and model uncertainty. *American Statistician, 73,* 118–121. https://doi-org.ezproxy.lib.apsu.edu/10.1080/00031305.2018.1537889

Anderson, G. (2006). Assuring quality/resisting quality assurance: Academics' responses to 'quality' in some Australian universities. *Quality in Higher Education, 12*(2), 161–173.

Anderson, J., Minshew, L., & Brown, S. (2015). Exploring sound! *Science Scope, 38*(8), 18.

Anderson, L. W. (Ed.), Krathwohl, D. R. (Ed.), Airasian, P. W., Cruikshank, K. A., Mayer, R. E., Pintrich, P. R., Raths, J., & Wittrock, M. C. (2001). *A taxonomy for learning, teaching, and assessing: A revision of Bloom's taxonomy of educational objectives.* Longman.

Andrade, L., & Fernández, F. (2016). Interpretation of confidence interval facing the conflict. *Universal Journal of Educational Research, 4*(12), 2687–2700.

Andrade, L., Fernández, F., & Álvarez, I. (2014). Fostering changes in confidence intervals interpretation. In K. Makar & R. Gould (Eds.), *Proceedings of the Ninth International Conference on Teaching Statistics* (p. 4). International Statistical Institute.

Andrejevic, M., & Selwyn, N. (2019). Facial recognition technology in schools: Critical questions and concerns. *Learning, Media and Technology.* https://doi.org/10.1080/17439884.2020.1686014

Andrews-Larson, C. (2015). Roots of linear algebra: An historical exploration of linear systems. *PRIMUS, 25*(6), 507–528.

Angelo, T. A., & Cross, K. P. (1993). *Classroom assessment techniques: A handbook for college teachers.* Jossey-Bass Publishers.

Angelo, T. A., & Cross, K. P. (2018). *Classroom assessment techniques: A handbook for college teachers.* Langara College.

Appleton, K. (2003). How do beginning primary school teachers cope with science? *Research in Science Education, 33*(1), 1–25.

Archer, L., Dewitt, J., Osborne, J., Dillon, J., Willis, B., & Wong, B. (2010). "Doing" science versus "being" a scientist: Examining 10/11-year-old schoolchildren's constructions through the lens of identity. *Science Education, 94*(4), 617–639.

Armstrong, T., & Association for Supervision and Curriculum Development. (2018). *Multiple intelligences in the classroom* (4th ed.).

Atkin, J. M., & Karplus, R. (1962). Discovery or invention? *The Science Teacher, 29*(5), 45–51.

Attaran, A., & Maharaj, R. (2000). Ethical debate—Doctoring malaria, badly: The global campaign to ban DDT. *British Medical Journal, 321*(7273), 1403–1405.

Atwater, M. M., Freeman, T. B., Butler, M. B., & Draper-Morris, J. (2010). A case study of science teacher candidates' understandings and actions related to the culturally responsive teaching of 'other' students. *International Journal of Environmental and Science Education, 5*(3), 287–318.

Autieri, S. M., Amirshokoohi, A., & Kazempour, M. (2016). The science-technology society framework for achieving scientific literacy: An overview of the existing literature. *European Journal of Science and Mathematics Education, 4*(1), 75–89.

Autor, D. H. (2015). Why are there still so many jobs? The history and future of workplace automation. *Journal of Economic Perspectives, 29*(3), 3–30.

Aylward, L., Hays, S., Kirman, C., Marchitti, S., Kenneke, J., English, C., Mattison, D. R., & Becker, R. A. (2014). Relationships of chemical concentrations in maternal and cord blood: A review of available data. *Journal of Toxicological Environmental Health B: Critical Reviews, 17*(3), 175–203.

Bailey, D. (2018). Why outliers are good for science. *Significance, 15*(1), 14–19.

Bajak, A. (2014). Lectures aren't just boring, they're ineffective, too, study finds. *Science, 12.*

Baker, J. M., & Reeve, E. M. (2019). Engineering design on display: Using an engineering design process to bring the local community into the technology and engineering education classroom. *Technology & Engineering Teacher, 79*(1), 1–8.

Baker, W. M., Lusk, E. J., & Neuhauser, K. L. (2012). On the use of cell phones and other devices in the classroom: Evidence from a survey of faculty and students. *Journal of Education for Business, 87*(5), 275–289. https://doi.org/10.1080/08832323.2011.622814

Bakker, A., & Derry, J. (2011). Lessons from inferentialism for statistics education. *Mathematical Thinking and Learning, 13*(1–2), 5–26. https://doi.org/10.1080/10986065.2011.538293

Ball, D. L. (1988). Unlearning to teach mathematics. *For the Learning of Mathematics, 8*(1), 40–48.

Ball, D. L. (1990). The mathematical understandings that prospective teachers bring to teacher education. *The Elementary School Journal, 90*(4), 449–466.

Ball, D. L. (1993). With an eye on the mathematical horizon: Dilemmas of teaching elementary school mathematics. *The Elementary School Journal, 93*(4), 373–397.

Ball, D. L., Hill, H. C., & Bass, H. (2005, Fall). Knowing mathematics for teaching: Who knows mathematics well enough to teach third grade, and how can we decide? *American Educator, 29*(1), 14–17, 20–22, 43–46.

Bandura, A. (1986). Fearful expectations and avoidant actions as coeffects of perceived self-inefficacy. *American Psychologist, 41,* 1389–1391.

Bang, M. (1997). *Common ground: The water, earth, and air we share.* The Blue Sky Press.

Banilower, E. R., Smith, P. S., Weis, I. R., Malzahn, K. A., Campbell, K. M., & Weis, A. M. (2013). *Report of the 2012 national survey of science and mathematics education.* Horizon Research.

Banilower, E. R., Trygstad, P. J., & Smith, P. S. (2015). The first five years: What the 2012 national survey of science and mathematics education reveals about novice science teachers and their teaching. In J. A. Luft & S. Dubois (Eds.), *Newly hired teachers of science: A better beginning* (pp. 3–29). Sense.

Banja, J. (2019). Welcoming the "intel-ethicist." *Hastings Center Report, 49*(1), 33–36. https://doi.org/10.1002/hast.976

Barberousse, A., Bonney, D., & Cozic, M. (2018). *The philosophy of science: A companion.* Oxford University Press.

Bargagliotti, A., Franklin, C., Arnold, P., Gould, R., Johnson, S., Perez, L., & Spangler, D. (2020). *Pre-K–12 guidelines for assessment and instruction in statistics education (GAISE) report II.* American Statistical Association and National Council of Teachers of Mathematics.

Barkley, E. F., & Major, C. H. (2016). *Learning assessment techniques: A handbook for college faculty.* Jossey-Bass.

Barr, A., & Feigenbaum, E. A. (Eds.). (1981). *The handbook of artificial intelligence.* Heuristech Press.

Barrows, H. S. (1986). A taxonomy of problem-based learning methods. *Medical Education, 20*(6), 481–486. https://doi.org/10.1111/j.1365-2923.1986.tb01386.x

Barrows, H. S., & Kelson, A. (1993). *Problem-based learning in secondary education and the Problem-based Learning Institute (Monograph).* Southern Illinois University School of Medicine.

Barth, R. S. (2001). Teacher leader. *Phi Delta Kappan, 82,* 443–449.

Batanero, C., Burrill, G., & Reading, C. (Eds.). (2011). *Teaching statistics in school mathematics: Challenges for teachers and teacher education.* Springer.

Bauer, M. W. (2004, April 3–4). The vicissitudes of 'public understanding of science': From 'literacy' to 'science in society'. In *Science meets society* [Symposium]. Conference held at Calouste Gulbenkian Foundation.

Beauchamp, A., Kusnick, J., & McCallum, R. (2011). *Success in science through dialogue, reading, and writing.* Regents of the University of California, Davis.

Beland, L. P., & Murphy, R. (2016). Communication: Technology, distraction and student performance. *Labour Economics, 41,* 61–76. https://doi.org/10.1016/j.labeco.2016.04.004

Bell, P., Bricker, L., Tzou, C., Lee, T., & Van Horne, K. (2012). Exploring the science framework: Engaging learners in scientific practices related to obtaining, evaluating, and communicating information. *Science Scope, 36*(3), 17.

Belpaeme, T., Kennedy, J., Ramachandran, A., Scassellati, B., & Tanaka, F. (2018). Social robots for education: A review. *Science Robotics, 3*(21), eaat5954. https://doi.org/10.1126/scirobotics.aat5954

Benioff, H. (1953). Earthquakes around the world [Song]. On *Out of This World.* Cook Laboratories.

Benioff, H. (1955). Earthquake seismographs and associated instruments. In H. E. Landsberg (Ed.), *Advances in geophysics* (Vol. 2; pp. 219–275). Academic Press.

Benjamin, H. R. (1939). *Saber-tooth curriculum, including other lectures in the history of paleolithic education.* McGraw-Hill.

Ben-Zvi, D., & Arcavi, A. (2001). Junior high school students' construction of global views of data and data representations. *Educational Studies in Mathematics, 45*(1–3), 35–65.

Ben-Zvi, D., Aridor, K., Makar, K., & Bakker, A. (2012). Students' emergent articulations of uncertainty while making informal statistical inferences ZDM. *The International Journal on Mathematics Education, 44*(7), 913–925. https://doi.org/10.1007/s11858-012-0420-3

Berge, A. (2008). How the ideology of low fat conquered America. *Journal of the History of Medicine and Allied Sciences, 63*(2), 139–177.

Berry, B. (2019). Teacher leadership: Prospects and promises. *Phi Delta Kappan, 100*(7), 49–55.

Bi, B. (2019, January 16). *What will come after the information age?* Forbes. https://www.forbes.com/sites/quora/2019/01/16/what-will-come-after-the-information-age/#773eb43d3d7d

Biemiller, A., & Meichenbaum, D. (1992). The nature and nurture of the self-directed learner. *Educational Leadership, 50*(2), 75–80.

Bird, A. (2007). What is scientific progress? *Noûs, 41*(1), 64–89.

Bird, A. (2008). Scientific progress as accumulation of knowledge: A reply to Rowbottom. *Studies in History and Philosophy of Science, 39*(2), 279–281.

Bird, A. (2018, Winter). Thomas Kuhn. In E. N. Zalta (Ed.), *The Stanford Encyclopedia of Philosophy.* https://plato.stanford.edu/archives/win2018/entries/thomas-kuhn/

Bitner, N., & Bitner, J. (2002). Integrating technology into the classroom: Eight keys to success. *Journal of Technology and Teacher Education, 10*(1), 95–100. https://www.learntechlib.org/p/9304

Blackbourn, D. (2011). *The conquest of nature: Water, landscape, and the making of modern Germany.* Random House.

Blaich, C. F., & Wise, K. S. (2010). Moving from assessment to institutional improvement. *New Directions for Institutional Research, 2010*(S2), 67–78. https://doi.org/10.1002/ir.373

Blank, R. K. (2013). Science instructional time is declining in elementary schools: What are the implications for student achievement and closing the gap? *Science Education, 97*(6), 830–847.

Blus, L. J. (1982). Further interpretation of the relation of organochlorine residues in brown pelican eggs to reproductive success. *Environmental Pollution Series A, Ecological and Biological, 28*(1), 15–33.

Boaler, J. (1998). Open and closed mathematics: Student experiences and understandings. *Journal for Research in Mathematics Education, 29*(1), 41–62.

Bonn, A., & Gaston, K. J. (2005). Capturing biodiversity: Selecting priority areas for conservation using different criteria. *Biodiversity and Conservation, 14*(5), 1083–1100.

Boorstin, D. J. (1986). *The discoverers: A history of man's search to know his world and himself.* Penguin Books.

Borasi, R., & Fonzi, J. (2002). Professional development that supports school mathematics reform. In *Foundations: A monograph for professionals in science, mathematics and technology education* (Vol. 3). Directorate for Education and Human Resources, National Science Foundation.

Borges, J. L. (1964). *Labyrinths: Selected stories & other writings.* A New Directions Book.

Borghini, S. (2017). Stigmergy in the design of social environments. *European Physical Journal: Special Topics, 226*(2), 269–281. https://doi.org/10.1140/epjst/e2016-60361-4

Borgmann, A. (1987). *Technology and the character of contemporary life: A philosophical inquiry.* University of Chicago Press.

Bouwma-Gearhart, J. (2008). *Teaching professional development of science and engineering professors at a research-extensive university: Motivations, meaningfulness, obstacles, and effects.* Oregon State University.

Bouwma-Gearhart, J. (2012a). Research university STEM faculty members' motivation to engage in teaching professional development: Building the choir through an appeal to extrinsic motivation and ego. *Journal of Science Education and Technology, 21*(5), 558–570.

Bouwma-Gearhart, J. (2012b). Engaging STEM faculty while attending to professional realities: An exploration of successful postsecondary STEM education reform at five SMTI institutions. *APLU/SMTI Paper, 5.*

Bouwma-Gearhart, J., & Collins, J. (2015). What we know about data-driven decision making in higher education: Informing educational policy and practice. In *Proceedings of the 19th international academic conference, Florence* (pp. 89–131). International Institute of Social and Economic Sciences. http://www.iises.net/proceedings/19th-international-academic-conference-florence/front-page

Bouwma-Gearhart, J., & Hora, M. (2016). Supporting faculty in the era of accountability: Facilitating the use of instructional data for continuous improvement to teaching and learning. *The Journal of Higher Education Management, 31*(1), 44–56.

Bouwma-Gearhart, J., Ivanovitch, J. D., Aster, E. M., & Bouwma, A. M. (2018). Exploring postsecondary biology educators' planning for teaching to advance meaningful education improvement initiatives. *CBE-Life Sciences Education, 17*(3), 1–12. https://doi.org/10.1187/cbe.17-06-0101

Bouwma-Gearhart, J., Lenz, A., & Ivanovitch, J. D. (2019). The interplay of postsecondary science educators' problems of practice and competencies: Informing better intervention designs. *Journal of Biological Education, 53*(4), 365–377.

Bouwma-Gearhart, J., Perry, K., & Presley, J. B. (2012). Improving postsecondary STEM education: Strategies for successful interdisciplinary collaborations and brokering engagement with education research and theory. *Journal of College Science Teaching, 44*(1), 40–47.

Bouwma-Gearhart, J., Sitomer, A., Fisher, K. Q., Smith, C., & Koretsky, M. (2016). Studying organizational change: Rigorous attention to complex systems via a multi-theoretical research model. In *Proceedings of the 2016 ASEE Annual Conference & Exposition.*

Bouwman, H., Yohannes, Y., Nakayama, S., Motohira, K., Ishizuka, M., Humphries, M., van der Schyff, V., du Preez, M., Dinkelmann, A., & Ikenaka Y. (2019). Evidence of impacts from DDT in pelican, cormorant, stork, and egret eggs from KwaZulu-Natal, South Africa. *Chemosphere, 225*, 647–658.

Bowen, R. S. (2017). *Understanding by design.* Vanderbilt University Center for Teaching. https://cft.vanderbilt.edu/understanding-by-design

Bradbury, A. (2019). Datafied at four: The role of data in the "schoolification" of early childhood education in England. *Learning, Media & Technology, 44*(1), 7–21. https://doi.org/10.1080/17439884.2018.1511577

Bransford, J. D., Brown, A. L., & Cocking, R. (Eds.). (1999). *How people learn: Brain, mind, experience, and school.* National Academy Press.

Bransford, J. D., Brown, A. L., & Cocking, R. R. (Eds.). (2000). *How people learn: Brain, mind, experience, and school.* National Academy Press.

Brown, M. (2020). Seeing students at scale: How faculty in large lecture courses act upon learning analytics dashboard data. *Teaching in Higher Education, 25*(4), 384–400. https://doi.org/10.1080/13562517.2019.1698540

Brusie, C. (2017, October 3). *How did the government get the food pyramid so terribly wrong?* https://www.healthyway.com/content/how-did-the-government-get-the-food-pyramid-so-terribly-wrong/

BSCS Science Learning. (2019). BSCS 5E instructional model. *BSCS.* https://bscs.org/bscs-5e-instructional-model/

Bu, L. (2017). Exploring Liu Hui's cube puzzle: From paper folding to 3-D design. *Convergence, 14.* https://doi.org/10.4169/convergence20170102

Bu, L. (2019). Spinning the cube with technologies. *The Mathematics Teacher, 112*(7), 551–554.

Bull, K. S., Kimball, S. L., & Montgomery, D. L. (2000). Designing instructional content: Constructivist instructional design. In K. S. Bull, S. L. Kimball, & D. L. Montgomery (Eds.), *Quality university instruction online: An advanced teaching effectiveness training program—An instructional hypertext.* Oklahoma State University Press.

Bulletin of the Atomic Scientists. (2021). *About us.* https://thebulletin.org/about-us/

Bunch, G. C., Walqui, A., & Kibler, A. (2012). Attending to language, engaging in practice: Scaffolding English language learners' apprenticeship into the common core English language arts standards. In *Understanding language: Language, literacy and learning in the content areas* (pp. 5–23). Stanford University.

Burch, P. (2007). Educational policy and practice from the perspective of institutional theory: Crafting a wider lens. *Educational Researcher, 36*(2), 84–95.

Burgsteiner, H., Kandlhofer, M., & Steinbauer, G. (2016). IRobot: Teaching the basics of artificial intelligence in high schools. In *30th AAAI conference on artificial intelligence, AAAI 2016* (pp. 4126–4127). AAAI Press.

Burn, H. E., Mesa, V., Wood, J. L., & Zamani-Gallaher, E. (2018). *National survey of community college mathematics chairs: Technical report and summary.* University of Illinois at Urbana-Champaign Office of Community College Research and Leadership.

Bybee, R. W. (2004). Scientific inquiry and science teaching. In L. B. Flick & N. G. Lederman (Eds.), *Scientific inquiry and nature of science* (pp. 1–14). Academic Publishers.

Bybee, R. W. (2014). The BSCS 5E instructional model: Personal reflections and contemporary implications. *Science and Children, 51*(8), 10–13.

Bybee, R. W. (2015). *The BSCS 5E instructional model: Creating teachable moments.* NSTA Press.

Cairns, D. (2019). Investigating the relationship between instructional practices and science achievement in an inquiry-based learning environment. *International Journal of Science Education, 41*(15), 2113–2135.

Callaert, H. (2007). Understanding confidence intervals. In D. Pitta-Pantazi & G. Philippou (Eds.), *Proceedings of the fifth congress of the European society for research in mathematics education* (pp. 692–702). University of Cyprus and ERM.

Callahan, J. (2007, April 11). School officials consider banning iPods, electronics. *Ocala Star Banner.* https://www.ocala.com/article/LK/20070411/News/604228371/OS

Campbell, D. T. (1976). *Assessing the impact of planned social change. Occasional Paper Series, #8.* Public Affairs Center, Dartmouth College.

Canal, G. Y., & Gutiérrez, R. B. (2010, July). The confidence intervals: A difficult matter, even for experts [Conference session]. In C. Reading (Ed.), *Data and context in statistics education: Towards an evidence-based society. Proceedings of the Eighth International Conference on Teaching Statistics* (ICOTS8, July, 2010). International Statistical Institute. http://iase-web.org/documents/papers/icots8/ICOTS8_C143_CANAL.pdf?1402524973

Capps, D. K., & Crawford, B. A. (2013). Inquiry-based professional development: What does it take to support teachers in learning about inquiry and nature of science? *International Journal of Science Education, 35*(12), 1947–1978. https://doi.org/10.1080/09500693.2012.760209

Cardiologists Kitchen. (2015, February 23). *A brief history of margarine and trans fat.* https://medium.com/TheCardiologistsKitchen/a-brief-history-of-margarine-and-trans-fat-220a3add28c6

Carlini, N., & Wagner, D. (2017). Towards evaluating the robustness of neural networks. In *Proceedings of the IEEE Symposium on Security and Privacy* (pp. 39–57). IEEE.

Carnoy, M., & García, E. (2017). *Five key trends in U.S. student performance: Progress by Blacks and Hispanics, the takeoff of Asians, the stall of non-English speakers, the persistence of socioeconomic gaps, and the damaging effect of highly segregated schools.* Economic Policy Institute.

Carroll, M. P. (2015). Stretch, dream, and do-A 21st century design thinking and STEM journey. *Journal of Research in STEM Education, 1*(1), 59–70.

Carson, R. (1962). *Silent spring.* Houghton Mifflin.

CatLocator. (2020). *The CatLocator pet tracking system.* http://www.thecatlocator.com/

Ceglie, R., & Olivares, V. (2012). Representation of diversity in science textbooks. In H. Hickman & B. J. Porfilio (Eds.), *The new politics of the textbook* (pp. 49–68). Sense Publishers.

Centers for Disease Control Division of Diabetes Translation. (2017, April). *Long-term trends in diabetes.* https://www.cdc.gov/diabetes/statistics/slides/long_term_trends.pdf

Céréghino, R., Biggs, J., Oertli, B., & Declerck, S. (2008). The ecology of European ponds: Defining the characteristics of a neglected freshwater habitat. *Hydrobiologia, 597,* 1–6. https://doi.org/10.1007/s10750-007-9225-8

Cervetti, G. N., Barber, J., Dorph, R., Pearson, P. D., & Goldschmidt, P. G. (2012). The impact of an integrated approach to science and literacy in elementary school classrooms. *Journal of Research in Science Teaching, 49*(5), 631–658.

Cervetti, G. N., & Hiebert, E. H. (2015). The sixth pillar of reading instruction: Knowledge development. *Reading Teacher, 68*(7), 548–551.

Cervetti, G. N., Wright, T. S., & Hwang, H. (2016). Conceptual coherence, comprehension, and vocabulary acquisition: A knowledge effect? *Reading and Writing, 29*(4), 761–779.

ChangSchool. (2011, May 25). Lady tasting tea-inferential statistics and experimental design. *YouTube.* https://www.youtube.com/watch?v=lgs7d5saFFc

Chen, Y. (2018). Connecting argumentation to 5E inquiry for preservice teachers. *Journal of College Science Teaching, 47*(5), 22–28. https://doi.org/10.2505/4/jcst18_047_05_22

Chen, Y., Huang, T. Z., Zhao, X. L., Deng, L. J., & Huang, J. (2017). Stripe noise removal of remote sensing images by total variation regularization and group sparsity constraint. *Remote Sensing, 9*(6), 559. https://doi.org/10.3390/rs9060559

Cherbow, K., McKinley, M. T., McNeill, K. L., & Lowenhaupt, R. (2020). An analysis of science instruction for the science practices: Examining coherence across system levels and components in current systems of science education in K–8 schools. *Science Education, 104*(3), 446–478.

Chitman-Booker, L., & Kopp, K. (2013). *The 5 Es of inquiry-based science.* Shell Education.

Chowdhury, N. (2019). *Inside blockchain, Bitcoin, and cryptocurrencies.* CRC Press.

Christensen, A. (2017, July 19). Research shows that just 36 percent of new science teachers are teaching only in their trained subject. *Phys.org.* https://phys.org/news/2017-07-percent-science-teachers-subject.html

Chrysam, M. (1996). *Margarines and spreads.* John Wiley and Sons.

Civil, M. (2007). Building on community knowledge: An avenue to equity in mathematics education. In N. Nasir & P. Cobb (Eds.), *Improving access to mathematics: Diversity and equity in the classroom* (pp. 105–117). Teachers College Press.

Clark, G. H. (1980). *Thales to Dewey: A history of philosophy.* Baker Book House.

Cleary, T. J. (2011). Shifting towards self-regulation microanalytic assessment: Historical overview, essential features, and implications for research and practice. In B. J. Zimmerman & D. H. Schunk (Eds.), *Handbook of self-regulation of learning and performance* (pp. 329–345). Routledge.

Cleary, T. J., & Labuhn, H. (2013). Application of cyclical self-regulation interventions in science-based contexts. In H. Bembenutty, T. J. Cleary, & A. Kitsantas (Eds.), *Applications of self-regulated learning across diverse disciplines: A tribute to Barry J. Zimmerman* (pp. 89–124). Information Age Publishing.

Clements, D. H., Sarama, J., Wolfe, C. B., & Spitler, M. E. (2015). Sustainability of a scale-up intervention in early mathematics: A longitudinal evaluation of implementation fidelity. *Early Education and Development, 26*(3), 427–449.

Coban, A., & Erol, M. (2019). Teaching and determination of kinetic friction coefficient using smartphones. *Physics Education, 54*(2), 1–5. https://iopscience.iop.org/article/10.1088/1361-6552/aaff84/pdf

Cobb, G. W., & Moore, D. S. (1997). Mathematics, statistics, and teaching. *The American Mathematical Monthly, 104*(9), 801–823.

Cobb, P. (1999). Individual and collective mathematical development: The case of statistical data analysis. *Mathematical Thinking and Learning, 1*(1), 5–43.

Coburn, C. E. (2004). Beyond decoupling: Rethinking the relationship between the institutional environment and the classroom. *Sociology of Education, 77*(3), 211–244.

Coburn, C. E., & Turner, E. O. (2011). Research on data use: A framework and analysis. *Measurement: Interdisciplinary Research & Perspective, 9*(4), 173–206.

Coburn, C. E., & Turner, E. O. (2012). The practice of data use: An introduction. *American Journal of Education, 118*(2), 99–111.

Coburn, C. E., Honig, M. I., & Stein, M. K. (2009). What's the evidence on districts' use of evidence? In J. Bransford, D. J. Stipek, N. J. Vye, L. Gomez, & D. Lam (Eds.), *Educational improvement: What makes it happen and why?* (pp. 67–86). Harvard Educational Press.

Cohen, J. (1992). A power primer. *Psychological Bulletin, 112*(1), 155–159.

Cohen, K. M., Finney, S., Gibbard, P. L., & Fan, J. (2020). International chronostratigraphic chart. *International Commission on Stratigraphy.* https://stratigraphy.org/ICSchart/ChronostratChart2020-03.pdf

Colburn, A. (2017). *Learning science by doing science.* Corwin Publishing.

Cole, M. (1998). *Cultural psychology: A once and future discipline.* The Belknap Press.

Cole, M. (2008). Cultural and cognitive development in phylogenetic, historical, and ontological perspective. In W. Damon & R. M. Lerner (Eds.), *Child and adolescent development: An advanced course* (pp. 593–646). John Wiley and Sons.

Collins, A., Brown, J. S., & Newman, S. E. (2019). Cognitive apprenticeship: Teaching the crafts of reading, writing, and mathematics. In L. B. Resnick (Ed.), *Knowing, learning, and instruction* (pp. 453–494). Laurence Erlbaum Associates.

Colwell, R. (2014). Cholera and the environment: A classic model for human pathogens in the environment. In *From outside to inside: Environmental microorganisms as human pathogens* [Symposium]. American Association for the Advancement of Science Annual Meeting. https://www.nsf.gov/news/speeches/colwell/rc040214aaascholera.htm

Colwell, R., & Huq, A. (n.d.). *Cholera-carrying copepod.* https://www.nsf.gov/news/speeches/colwell/rc01_anatlesson/tsld024.htm

Colyvan, M. (2012). *An introduction to the philosophy of mathematics.* Cambridge University Press.

Commission on the Future of Undergraduate Education—American Academy of the Arts and Sciences. (2017). *The future of undergraduate education, the future of America.* American Academy of Arts and Sciences. https://www.amacad.org/publication/future-undergraduate-education

Common Sense Media. (2010). *Hi-tech cheating: Cell phones and cheating in schools: A national poll.* https://docplayer.net/15777428-Hi-tech-cheating-cell-phones-and-cheating-in-schools-a-national-poll.html

Computer Science Teachers Association. (2017). *CSTA K–12 computer science standards.* ACM Publications. https://www.csteachers.org/page/standards

Conversi, D. (2020). The ultimate challenge: Nationalism and climate change. *Nationalities Papers, 48*(4), 625–636. https://doi.org/10.1017/nps.2020.18

Cooper, K. (1991). Effects of pesticides on wildlife. In W. J. Hayes & E. R. Laws (Eds.), *Handbook of pesticide toxicology* (pp. 463–496). Academic Press.

Cope, B., & Kalantzis, M. (2011). 'Design' in principle and practice: A reconsideration of the terms of design engagement. *The Design Journal, 14*(1), 45–63.

Cope, B., & Kalantzis, M. (2015). The things you do to know: An introduction to the pedagogy of multiliteracies. In B. Cope & M. Kalantzis (Eds.), *A pedagogy of multiliteracies: Learning by design* (pp. 1–36). Palgrave Macmillan.

Corbin, J., & Strauss, A. (2008). Strategies for qualitative data analysis. In J. Corbin & A. Strauss (Eds.), *Basics of qualitative research: Techniques and procedures for developing grounded theory* (3rd ed.; pp. 65–86). SAGE Publications. https://doi.org/10.4135/9781452230153

Costa, V. B. (1995). When science is "another world": Relationships between worlds of family, friends, school, and science. *Science Education, 79*(3), 313–333.

Cotabish, A., Dailey, D., Robinson, A., & Hughes, G. (2013). The effects of a STEM intervention on elementary students' science knowledge and skills. *School Science and Mathematics, 113*(5), 215–226.

Council of Chief State School Officers. (2010). *Common core state standards for mathematics.* National Governors Association Center for Best Practices, Council of Chief State School Officers. http://www.corestandards.org/math

Creswell, J. W., & Plano Clark, V. L. (2007). *Designing and conducting mixed methods research.* SAGE Publications.

Creswell, J. W., & Poth, C. N. (2018). *Qualitative inquiry and research design choosing among five approaches* (4th ed.). SAGE Publications, Inc.

Crutzen, P. J., & Stoermer, E. F. (2000). The "Anthropocene." *IGBP Newsletter, 41,* 17–18.

Curcio, F. R., & Artzt, A. F. (1997). Assessing students' statistical problem-solving behaviors in a small-group setting. In I. Gal & J. B. Garfield (Eds.), *The assessment challenge in statistics education* (pp. 123–138). https://www.stat.auckland.ac.nz/~iase/publications/assessbk/chapter10.pdf

Dargar, S. K., & Srivastava, V. M. (2019, June). Double-gate tri-active layer channel amorphous-IGZO thin film transistor for AMLCD pixel circuit. In *2019 PhotonIcs & Electromagnetics Research Symposium-Spring* (pp. 2448–2453). IEEE.

Davis, P. J., & Hersh, R. (1981). *The mathematical experience.* Birkhauser.

De Jager, C., Farias, P., Barraza-Villarreal, A., Avila, M. H., Ayotte, P., Dewailly, E., & Bailey, J. L. (2006). Reduced seminal parameters associated with environmental DDT exposure and *p, p'*-DDE concentrations in men in Chiapas, Mexico: A cross-sectional study. *Journal of Andrology, 27*(1), 16–27.

De Kock, A. C., & Randall, R. M. (1984). Organochlorine insecticide and polychlorinated biphenyl residues in eggs of coastal birds from the Eastern Cape, South Africa. Environmental Pollution Series B, *Chemical and Physical, 35,* 193e201.

De Oliveira, M., & Levkowitz, H. (2003). From visual data exploration to visual data mining: A survey. *IEEE Transactions on Visualization and Computer Graphics, 9*(3), 378–394.

De Veaux, R. D., Velleman, P. F., & Bock, D. E. (2018). *Intro stats* (5th ed.). Pearson.

Dee, T., & Goldhaber, D. (2017). *Understanding and addressing teacher shortages in the United States.* The Hamilton Project.

delMas, R., Garfield, J., Ooms, A., & Chance, B. L. (2007). Assessing students' conceptual understanding after a first course in statistics. *Statistics Education Research Journal, 6*(2), 28–58.

Descritan, J., Klieme, E., Kunter, M., Hochweber, J., Büttner, G., Fauth, B., Hondrich, A. L., Rieser, S., Hertel, S., & Hardy, I. (2015). Embedded formative assessment and classroom process quality: How do they interact in promoting science understanding? *American Educational Research Journal, 52*(6), 1133–1159. https://doi.org/10.3102/0002831215596412

Dewey, J. (1933). *How we think: A restatement of the relations of reflective thinking to the educative process.* Heath.

Dewey. J. (1938). Experience & education. Kappa Delta Pi.

Dewey, J. (1990). *The school and society: The child and the curriculum.* University of Chicago Press.

Dey, U., Mondal, N., Das, K., & Dutta, S. (2012). An approach to polymer degradation through microbes. *IOSRPHR, 2*(3), 385–388. https://doi.org/10.9790/3013-0230385388

Diamond, B. S., Maerten-Rivera, J., Rohrer, R. E., & Lee, O. (2014). Effectiveness of a curricular and professional development intervention at improving elementary teachers' science content knowledge and student achievement outcomes: Year 1 results. *Journal of Research in Science Teaching, 51*(5), 635–658.

Dick, W., & Carey, L. (1985). *The systematic design of instruction* (2nd ed.). Scott Foresman.

Dickinson, J. L., Shirk, J., Bonter, D., Bonney, R., Crain, R. L., Martin, J., Phillips, T., & Purcell, K. (2012). The current state of citizen science as a tool for ecological research and public engagement. *Frontiers in Ecology and the Environment, 10*(6), 291–297.

Dietz, S., & Henrich, C. (2014). Texting as a distraction to learning in college students. *Computers in Human Behavior, 36*, 163–167. https://doi.org/10.1016/j.chb.2014.03.045

Dissanayake, L., & Jayakody, L. N. (2021). Engineering microbes to bio-upcycle polyethylene terephthalate. *Frontiers in Bioengineering and Biotechnology, 9*, 656465. https://doi.org/10.3389/fbioe.2021.656465

Dixon, S. P., Birchenough, A. C., Evans, S. M., & Quigley, M. P. (2005). Children's knowledge of birds: How can it be improved and can it be used to conserve wildlife. *Transactions of the Natural History Society, Northumbria, 64*, 121–134.

Doble, C., Matayoshi, J., Cosyn, E., Uzun, H., & Karami, A. (2019). A data-based simulation study of reliability for an adaptive assessment based on knowledge space theory. *International Journal of Artificial Intelligence in Education, 29*, 258–282. https://doi.org/10.1007/s40593-019-00176-0

Doerr, H. M., Delmas, R., & Makar, K. (2017). A modeling approach to the development of students' informal inferential reasoning. *Statistics Education Research Journal, 16*(2), 86–115. http://iase-web.org/Publications.php?p=SERJ

Domínguez Figaredo, D. (2020). Data-driven educational algorithms pedagogical framing. *Revista Iberoamericana de Educación a Distancia, 23*(2). http://dx.doi.org/10.5944/ried.23.2.26470

Doomsday Clock. (2021). Bulletin of the Atomic Scientists. https://thebulletin.org/doomsday-clock/

Doren, B. M. V., Liedvogel, M., & Helm, B. (2017). Programmed and flexible: Long-term Zugunruhe data highlight the many axes of variation in avian migratory behaviour. *Journal of Avian Biology, 48*(1), 155–172. https://doi.org/10.1111/jav.01348

Douthwaite, R. J. (1989). Effects of DDT on the fish eagle *Haliaeetus vocifer* population of Lake Kariba in Zimbabwe. *Ibis, 134*(3), 250–258.

Driscoll, M. P. (2005). *Psychology of learning for instruction* (3rd ed). Pearson.

Druga, S., Vu, S. T., Likhith, E., & Qiu, T. (2019). Inclusive AI literacy for kids around the world. In *FL2019: Proceedings of FabLearn 2019* (pp. 104–111). Association for Computing Machinery.

Duran, L., & Duran, E. (2004). The 5E instructional model: A learning cycle approach for inquiry-based science teaching. *The Science Education Review, 3*(2), 49–58.

Dweck, C. (2015, September). *Carol Dweck revisits the 'growth mindset.'* https://www.edweek.org/leadership/opinion-carol-dweck-revisits-the-growth-mindset/2015/09

Eagles, P. F., & Muffitt, S. (1990). An analysis of children's attitudes toward animals. *The Journal of Environmental Education, 21*(3), 41–44.

Eagles, P. F. J., & Demare, R. (1999). Factors influencing children's environmental attitudes. *The Journal of Environmental Education, 30*(4), 33–37.

Echevarria, J., Vogt, M. E., & Short, D. J. (2000). *Making content comprehensible for English-language learners: The SIOP model.* Allyn & Bacon.

Edelman, L. (1893). Objects to the term jackass. *Journal of the American Medical Association, 21*(19), 711–711.

Ediger, M. (2006). Writing in the mathematics curriculum. *Journal of Instructional Psychology, 33*(2), 120–123.

Edwards, A., Edwards, C., Spence, P. R., Harris, C., & Gambino, A. (2016). Robots in the classroom: Differences in students' perceptions of credibility and learning between "teacher as robot" and "robot as teacher." *Computers in Human Behavior, 65*, 627–634. https://doi.org/10.1016/j.chb.2016.06.005

Egan, K. (2002). *Getting it wrong from the beginning: Our progressivist inheritance from Herbert Spencer, John Dewey, and Jean Piaget.* Yale University Press.

Ehlers, E., Moss, C., & Krafft, T. (2006). *Earth system science in the Anthropocene: Emerging issues and problems.* Springer Science+Business Media.

Eilat-Adar, S., Sinai, T., Yosefy, C., & Henkin Y. (2013) Nutritional recommendations for cardiovascular disease prevention. *Nutrients, 5*(9), 3646–3683.

Ellison, A. M., LeRoy, C. J., Landsbergen, K. J., & Bosanquet, E. (2018). Art/science collaborations: New explorations of ecological systems, values, and their feedbacks. *The Bulletin of the Ecological Society of America, 99*(2), 180–191.

Elsey, R., Miller, M., Lejeune, D., & Selman,W. (2016). Commensal nesting *Scincella lateralis* (little brown skinks) in *Alligator mississippiensis* (American alligator) nests and *Ondatra zibethicus* (muskrat) houses in southwestern Louisiana. *Southeastern Naturalist, 15*(4), 653–668.

Elsey, R., Selman, W., King, R., Miller, M., & Platt, S. (2013). *Alligator mississippiensis* (American alligator) nests used by other reptiles in coastal Louisiana. *Herpetological Review, 44*, 659–660.

Enriquez, A. G., Lipe, C. B., & Price, B. (2014). Enhancing the success of minority STEM students by providing financial, academic, social, and cultural capital. In *Proceedings of the ASEE Annual Conference & Exposition* (pp. 1–15). http://search.ebscohost.com/login.aspx?direct=true&db=asn&AN=115955349&login.asp&site=ehost-live&scope=site

Environmental Education and Training Partnership. (2002). *Voluntary citizen action: A new tool for environmental protection.* EETAP Resource Library No. 109. http://citeseerx.ist.psu.edu/viewdoc/download?doi=10.1.1.197.9917&rep=rep1&type=pdf

Espinosa, L. (2011). Pipelines and pathways: Women of color in undergraduate STEM majors and the college experiences that contribute to persistence. *Harvard Educational Review, 81*(2), 209–241. https://doi.org/10.17763/haer.81.2.92315ww157656k3u

Etheredge, S., & Rudnitsky, A. (2003). *Introducing students to scientific inquiry: How do we know what we know?* Pearson Education.

Evans, J., & Nicholson, K. (2003). Building a community of learners: Manhattan college elementary education program. *Teacher Education Quarterly, 30*(1), 137–150.

Fairbanks, L. (2011). Misconceptions in middle school life science and strategies teachers can use to change them. *Graduate Research Papers.* https://scholarworks.uni.edu/grp/179/

Fayer, S., Lacey, A., & Watson, A. (2017). *STEM occupations: Past present and future.* Bureau of Labor Statistics. https://www.bls.gov/spotlight/2017/

science-technology-engineering-and-mathematics-stem-occupations-past-present-and-future/home.htm

Feinstein, N. W., & Waddington, D. I. (2020). Individual truth judgments or purposeful, collective sensemaking? Rethinking science education's response to the post-truth era. *Educational Psychologist, 55*(3), 155–166.

Feynman, R. (1985). Quantum mechanical computers. *Optics News, 11*(2), 11–20.

Feynman, R. (1996). *Feynman lectures on computation.* Addison-Wesley.

Feynman, R. P. (1998). *Meaning of it all: Thoughts of a citizen scientist.* Perseus Books Group.

Fidler, F. (2005). *From statistical significance to effect estimation: Statistical reform in psychology, medicine and ecology* [Unpublished dissertation]. The University of Melbourne.

Field, J. V. (1999, April). *Johannes Kepler.* MacTutor. https://mathshistory.st-andrews.ac.uk/Biographies/Kepler/

Firestein, S. (2013). *The pursuit of ignorance by Stuart Firestein* [Video]. TED Conferences. https://www.ted.com/talks/stuart_firestein_the_pursuit_of_ignorance/transcript?language=en

Fisher, D., & Frey, N. (2014). Close reading as an intervention for struggling middle school readers. *Journal of Adolescent & Adult Literacy, 57*(5), 367–376.

Fisher, J. B., & Schumaker, J. B. (1995). Searching for validated inclusive practices: A review of the literature. *Focus on Exceptional Children, 28,* 1–20.

Fisher, R. A., & Mackenzie, W. A. (1923). Studies in crop variation. II. The manurial response of different potato varieties. *Journal of Agricultural Science, 13,* 311–320.

Fishman, B. J., & Krajcik, J. (2003). What does it mean to create sustainable science curriculum innovations? A commentary. *Science Education, 87*(4), 564–573. https://doi.org/10.1002/sce.10088

Folk, W., Miller, Z., Van Garderen, D., Lannin, A., & Palmer, T. (2020). "Flight of the Bumblebee": A middle school STEM text set to support development of disciplinary literacy skills. *Sci Scope, 43*(9), 40–48.

Foster, C. (2014). Confidence trick: The interpretation of confidence intervals. *Canadian Journal of Science, Mathematics and Technology Education, 14*(1), 23–34. https://doi.org/10.1080/14926156.2014.874615

Fraenkel, J. R., Wallen, N. E., & Hyun, H. H. (2019). *How to design and evaluate research in education.* McGraw Hill Education.

Frank, K. A., Zhao, Y., & Borman, K. (2004). Social capital and the diffusion of innovations within organizations: The case of computer technology in schools. *Sociology of Education, 77*(2), 148–171.

Franklin, C., Bargagliotti, A., Case, C., Kader, G., Scheaffer, R., & Spangler, D. (2015). *The statistics education of teachers.* American Statistical Association. https://www.amstat.org/education/SET/SET.pdf

Franklin, C., Kader, G., Mewborn, D., Moreno, J., Peck, R., Perry, M., & Scheaffer, R., & Spangler, D. (2007). *The guidelines for assessment and instruction in statistics education (GAISE) report: A curriculum framework.* American Statistical Association. https://www.amstat.org/asa/files/pdfs/GAISE/GAISEPreK-12_Full.pdf

Freinkel, S. (2011). *Plastics: A toxic love story.* Henry Holt.

Freudenthal, H. (1973). *Mathematics as an educational task.* D. Reidel Publishing.

Fricker, R. D., Jr., Burke, K., Han, X., & Woodall, W. H. (2019). Assessing the statistical analyses used in basic and applied social psychology after their p-value ban. *The American Statistician, 73*(sup1), 374–384. https://doi.org/10.1080/00031305.2018.1537892

Friendly, M. (2008). A brief history of data visualization. In *Handbook of data visualization* (pp. 15–56). Springer.

Friesen, S., & Scott, D. (2013). *Inquiry-based learning: A review of the research literature.* Alberta Ministry of Education.

Fuchs, J., Jäckle, D., Weiler, N., & Schreck, T. (2015). Leaf glyph: Visualizing multi-dimensional data with environmental cues. In *IVAPP 2015-6th International Conference on Information Visualization Theory and Applications* (pp. 195–206). SciTePress.

Fullan, M. (2010). *All systems go: The change imperative for whole system reform.* Corwin Press.

Funk, C., & Parker, K. (2018). *Women and men in STEM often at odds over workplace equity.* Pew Research Center.

Gallagher, S., Sher, B. T., Stepien, W. J., & Workman, D. (1995). Implementing problem-based learning in science classrooms. *School Science and Mathematics, 95*(3), 136–146. https://doi.org/10.1111/j.1949-8594.1995.tb15748.x

Gardner, H. (2008). *Five minds for the future.* Harvard Business Press.

Gardner, H. (2019). *Frequently asked questions—Multiple intelligences and related educational topics.* https://howardgardner01.files.wordpress.com/2012/06/faq_march2013.pdf

Garfield, J., & Ben-Zvi, D. (2007). How students learn statistics revisited: A current review research on teaching and learning statistics. International Statistical Review, 75(3), 372–396.

Garfield, J. B., & Ben-Zvi, D. (2008a). *Developing students' statistical reasoning: Connecting research to practice.* Springer.

Garfield, J. B., & Ben-Zvi, D. (2008b). Learning to reason about sampling and sampling distributions. In J. Garfield & D. Ben-Zvi (Eds.), *Developing students' statistical reasoning: Connecting research to practice* (pp. 235–260). Springer.

Garfield, J. B., Ben-Zvi, D., Chance, B., Medina, E., Roseth, C., & Zieffler, A. (2008). Learning to reason about statistical inference. In J. Garfield & D. Ben-Zvi (Eds.), *Developing students' statistical reasoning: Connecting research to practice* (pp. 261–288). Springer.

Gauchat, G. (2012). Politicization of science in the public sphere: A study of public trust in the United States, 1974 to 2010. *American Sociological Review, 77*(2), 167–187.

Gelman, A., & Greenland, S. (2019). Are confidence intervals better termed "uncertainty intervals"? No: Call them compatibility intervals. *British Medical Journal, 366.* https://doi.org/10.1136/bmj.l5381

Ghose, T. (2013, April 2). *Just a theory: 7 misused science words.* Scientific American -LiveScience. https://www.scientificamerican.com/article/just-a-theory-7-misused-science-words/

Gil, Y., Greaves, M., Hendler, J., & Hirsh, H. (2014). Amplify scientific discovery with artificial intelligence. *Science, 346*(6206), 171–172.

Gil-Pérez, D., Vilches, A., Fernández, I., Cachapuz, A., Praia, J., Valdés, P., & Salinas, J. (2005). Technology as "applied science." *Science & Education, 14*(3), 309–320.

Gilkerson, J., Richards, J. A., Warren, S. F., Montgomery, J. K., Greenwood, C. R., Kimbrough Oller, D., . . . , Paul, T. D. (2017). Mapping the early language environment using all-day recordings and automated analysis. *American Journal of Speech-Language Pathology, 26*(2), 248–265.

Gilliard, C., & Culik, H. (2016). *Digital redlining, access, and privacy.* Common Sense Education. https://www.commonsense.org/education/articles/digital-redlining-access-and-privacy

Giroux, H. A. (1992). *Border crossings: Cultural workers and the politics of education.* Routledge.

Goldenberg, E. P. (1996). "Habits of mind" as an organizer for the curriculum. *Journal of Education, 178*(1), 13–34.

Golinkoff, R. M., Hoff, E., Rowe, M. L., Tamis-LeMonda, C., & Hirsh-Pasek, K. (2018). Language matters: Denying the existence of the 30-million-word gap has serious consequences. *Child Development, 90,* 985–992.

Gonzalez, N., Moll, L. C., & Amanti, C. (2005). *Funds of knowledge: Theorizing practices in households, communities, and classrooms.* Lawrence Erlbaum.

Goodman, S. N. (2019). Why is getting rid of p-values so hard? Musings on science and statistics. *The American Statistician, 73*(sup1), 26–30, https://doi.org/10.1080/00031305.2018.1558111

Gopnik, A., Meltzoff, A. N., & Kulh, P. K. (1999). *The scientist in the crib: Minds, brains, and how children learn.* Harper Perennial.

Gorss, J. (2003). *The sin of synecdoche: David Quammen's epistemology and literary science journalism* [Master's thesis, University of Tennessee]. TRACE. https://trace.tennessee.edu/utk_gradthes/5229

Gotwals, A. W., & Songer, N. B. (2010). Reasoning up and down a food chain: Using an assessment framework to investigate students' middle knowledge. *Science Education, 94*(2), 259–281.

Gouvea, J., & Passmore, C. (2017). 'Models of' versus 'models for.' *Science & Education, 26*(1–2), 49–63.

Graham, S., & Perin, D. (2007). *Writing next: Effective strategies to improve writing of adolescents in middle and high schools–A report to Carnegie Corporation of New York.* Alliance for Excellent Education.

Grandjean, P., Bellinger, D., Bergman, Å., Cordier, S., Davey-Smith, G., Eskenazi, B., Gee, D., Gray, K., Hanson, M., van den Hazel, P., Heindel, J. J., Heinzow, B., Hertz-Picciotto, I., Hu, H., Huang, T. T., Jensen, T. K., Landrigan, P. J., McMillen, I. C., Murata, K., Ritz, B., Schoeters, G., Skakkebæk, N. E., Skerfving, S., & Weihe, P. (2008). The Faroes statement: Human health effects of developmental exposure to chemicals in our environment. *Basic & Clinical Pharmacology & Toxicology, 102*(2), 73–75.

Grant, T. S., & Nathan, M. J. (2008). *Students' conceptual metaphors influence their statistical reasoning about confidence intervals* (WCER Working Paper No. 2008–5). University of Wisconsin-Madison.

Grassé, P.-P. (1959). Reconstruction of the nest and inter-individual coordination in *Bellicositermes natalensis* and *Cubitermes sp.* The stigmergy theory: Interpretation of the behavior of constructor termites. *Social Insects, 6*, 41–81.

Gravemeijer, K., & van Galen, F. (2003). Facts and algorithms as products of students' own mathematical activity. In J. Kilpatrick, W. G. Martin, & D. Schifter (Eds.), *A research companion to principles and standards for school mathematics* (pp. 114–122). National Council of Teachers of Mathematics.

Gray, R., & Pak, K. (2015). *Flowers are calling.* HMH Books for Young Readers.

Greeno, J. G. (1998). The situativity of knowing, learning, and research. *American Psychologist, 53*(1), 5–26.

Gresalfi, M. S. (2009). Taking up opportunities to learn: Constructing dispositions in mathematics classrooms. *Journal of the Learning Sciences, 18*(3), 327–369.

Groth, R. E. (2007). Toward a conceptualization of statistical knowledge for teaching. *Journal for Research in Mathematics Education, 38*(5), 427–437.

Gu, J. (2017). Biodegradability of plastics: The pitfalls. *Applied Environmental Biotechnology, 2*(1), 59–61.

Guillette, L. J., Crain, D. A., Gunderson, M., Kools, S., Milnes, M., Orlando, E., Rooney, A., & Woodward, A. (2000). Alligators and endocrine disrupting contaminants: A current perspective. *American Zoologist, 40*(3), 438–452.

Guillette, L. J., Gross, T. S., Gross, D. A., Rooney, A. A., & Percival, H. F. (1995). Gonadal steroidogenesis in vitro from juvenile alligators obtained from contaminated or control lakes. *Environmental Health Perspectives, 103*(suppl 4), 31–36.

Guillette, L. J., Gross, T. S., Masson, G. R., Matter, J. M., Percival, H. F., & Woodward, A. R. (1994). Developmental abnormalities of the gonad and abnormal sex hormone concentrations in juvenile alligators from contaminated and control lakes in Florida. *Environmental Health Perspectives, 102*(8), 680–688.

Guillette, L. J., Pickford, D. B., Crain, D. A., Rooney, A. A., & Percival, H. F. (1996). Reduction in penis size and plasma testosterone concentrations in juvenile alligators living in a contaminated environment. *General and Comparative Endocrinology, 101*(1), 32–42.

Guillory, R. M., & Wolverton, M. (2016). It's about family: Native American student persistence in higher education. *The Journal of Higher Education, 79*(1), 58–87. https://doi.org/10.1353/jhe.2008.0001

Gutiérrez, C. D., & Rogoff, B. (2003). Cultural ways of learning: Individual traits and repertoire of practice. *Educational Researcher, 32*(5), 19–25.

Gwinner, E. (1989). Photoperiod as a modifying and limiting factor in the expression of avian circannual rhythms. *Journal of Biological Rhythms, 4*(2), 125–138.

Gwinner, E. (1990). *Bird migration: Physiology and ecophysiology.* Springer.

Hackling, M. W., Goodrum, D., & Rennie, L. J. (2001). The state of science in Australian secondary schools. *Australian Science Teachers Journal, 47*(4), 6–17.

Haji, M., Bui, T. D., & Suen, C. Y. (2012). Removal of noise patterns in handwritten images using expectation maximization and fuzzy inference systems. *Pattern Recognition, 45*(12), 4237–4239.

Halverson, R. R. (2003). Systems of practice: How leaders use artifacts to create professional community in schools. *Education Policy Analysis Archives, 11*(37), 1–35.

Halverson, R., & Halverson, E. (2011). Education as design for learning: A model for integrating education inquiry across research traditions. In C. F. Conrad & R. C. Serlin (Eds.), *SAGE handbook for research in education: Engaging ideas and enriching inquiry* (pp. 25–38). SAGE Publications.

Halverson, R., Prichett, R. B., & Watson, J. G. (2007). *Formative feedback systems and the new instructional leadership.* University of Wisconsin-Madison, Wisconsin Center for Education Research.

Hamilton, C. (2016). The Anthropocene as rupture. *The Anthropocene Review, 3*(2), 93–106. https://doi.org/10.1177/2053019616634741

Hammer, D., & van Zee, E. (2006). *Seeing the science in children's thinking: Case studies of student inquiry in physical science.* Heinemann.

Hancock, B., & Zografi, G. (1997). Characteristics and significance of the amorphous state in pharmaceutical systems. *Journal of Pharmaceutical Sciences, 86*(1), 1–12.

Handler, B. (2010). Teacher as curriculum leader: A consideration of the appropriateness of that role assignment to classroom-based practitioners. *International Journal of Teacher Leadership, 3*(3), 32–42.

Hanuscin, D. L., Rebello, C. M., & Sinha, S. (2012). Supporting the development of science teacher leaders: Where do we begin? *Science Education, 21*(1), 12–18.

Hanuscin, D. L., & Zangori, L. (2016). Developing practical knowledge of the Next Generation Science Standards in elementary science teacher education. *Journal of Science Teacher Education, 27*(8), 799–818.

Hapgood, S., & Pallincsar, A. S. (2007). Where literacy and science intersect. *Education Leadership, 64*(4), 56–60.

Hardin, G. (1968). The tragedy of the commons. *Science, 162*(3859), 1243–1248. http://www.jstor.org/stable/1724745

Harms, N. C., & Yager, R. E. (Eds.). (1980). *What research says to the science teacher* (Vol. 3). Science Education Information Report.

Harradine, A., Batanero, C., & Rossman, A. (2011). Students' and teachers' knowledge of sampling and inference. In C. Batanero, G. Burrill, & C. Reading (Eds.), *Teaching statistics in school mathematics: Challenges for teachers and teacher education* (pp. 235–246). Springer.

Hart, B., & Risley, T. R. (2003). The early catastrophe: The 30 million word gap by age 3. *American Educator, 27*(1), 4–9.

Hartley, R. R., Newton, I., & Robertson, M. (1995). Organochlorine residues and eggshell thinning in the Peregrine Falcon *Falco peregrinus minor* in Zimbabwe. *Ostrich, 66*(2–3), 69–73.

Hassan, S., & Haq, I. (2019). Pervasive pollution problems caused by plastics and its degradation. *International Journal of Online and Biomedical Engineering, 15*(10), 29–36. https://doi.org/10.3991/ijoe.v15i10.10873

Hattie, J. (2012). *Visible learning for teachers: Maximizing impact on learning.* Routledge.

Haverly, C., Calabrese Barton, A., Schwarz, C. V., & Braaten, M. (2020). "Making space:" How novice teachers create opportunities for equitable sense-making in elementary science. *Journal of Teacher Education, 71*(1), 63–79. https://doi.org/10.1177/0022487118800706

Havinga, H., & Smits A. J. M. (2000). River management along the Rhine: A retrospective view. In A. J. M. Smits, P. H. Nienhuis, & R. S. E. W. Leuven (Eds.), *New approaches to river management* (pp. 15–32). Backhuys Publishers.

Hayes, A., & Cheng, J. (2020). Datafication of epistemic equality: Advancing understandings of teaching excellence beyond benchmarked performativity. *Teaching in Higher Education, 25*(4), 493–509. https://doi.org/10.1080/13562517.2019.1689387

Hedges, L. V. (1981). Distribution theory for Glass's estimator of effect size and related estimators. *Journal of Educational and Behavioral Statistics, 6*(2), 107–128.

Heller, J. I., Daehler, K. R., Wong, N., Shinohara, M., & Miratrix, L. W. (2012). Differential effects of three professional development models on teacher knowledge and student achievement in elementary science. *Journal of Research in Science Teaching, 49*(3), 333–362.

Henke, N., Bughin, J., Chui, M., Manyika, J., Saleh, T., Wiseman, B., & Sethupathy, G. (2016). *The age of analytics: Competing in a data-driven world 2016.* McKinsey Global Institute.

Henriques, A. (2016). Students' difficulties in understanding of confidence intervals. In D. Ben-Zvi & K. Makar (Eds.), *The teaching and learning of statistics* (pp. 129–138). Springer.

Henson, H., Adams, C., Gutowski, V., Dove, D. E., Mundell, J. A., & Byer, G. B. (2003, May 7–9). *Magnetic exploration and data processing at the Mitchell Springs Ruins in Cortez, Colorado. GSA Abstracts with Programs,* 35(5).Geological Society of America Rocky Mountain Section Meeting, Ft. Lewis College, Durango, CO.

Henson, H., & Sexton, J. L. (1991). Premine study of shallow coal seams using high resolution seismic reflection methods. *Geophysics, 56*(9), 1494–1503.

Hernan, C. J., Morrison, J. Q., Collins, T. A., & Kroeger, S. D. (2018). Decreasing inappropriate mobile device use in middle and high school classrooms. *Intervention in School & Clinic, 54*(1), 47–51. https://doi.org/10.1177/1053451218762498

Herold, B. (2017). Facing an uncertain future: Automation and artificial intelligence are disrupting the labor market. What do K–12 educators and policymakers need to know? *Education Week, 37*(7), 3–6.

Hicks, S. C., & Irizarry, R. A. (2018). A guide to teaching data science. *The American Statistician,* 72(4), 382–391. https://doi.org/10.1080/00031305.2017.1356747

Hiller, S. E., & Kitsantas, A. (2014). The effect of a horseshoe crab citizen science program on middle school student science performance and STEM career motivation. *School Science and Mathematics, 114*(6), 302–311.

Hirsch, E. D. (1996). *The schools we need and why we don't have them.* Doubleday.

Hirsch, E. D., Kett, J. F., & Trefil, J. (1988). *Cultural literacy: What every American needs to know.* Vintage Books.

Hoekstra, R., Johnson, A., & Kiers, H. A. L. (2012). Confidence intervals make a difference: Effects of showing confidence intervals on inferential reasoning. *Educational and Psychological Measurement,* 72(6), 1039–1052. https://doi.org/10.1177/0013164412450297

Hoekstra, R., Morey, R. D., Rouder, J. N., & Wagenmakers, E.-J. (2014). Robust misinterpretation of confidence intervals. *Psychonomic Bulletin & Review, 21*(5), 1157–1164. https://doi.org/10.3758/s13423-013-0572-3

Holfeld, B., & Grabe, M. (2012). Middle school students' perceptions of and responses to cyberbullying. *Journal of Educational Computing Research, 46*(4), 395–413. http://eric.ed.gov/?id=EJ978842

Hollins, E. R., McIntyre, L. R., DeBose, C., Hollins, K. S., & Towner, A. (2004). Promoting a self-sustaining learning community: Investigating an internal model for teacher development. *International Journal of Qualitative Studies in Education, 17*(2), 247–264.

Hollweg, K., & Hill, D. (Eds.). (2003). *What is the influence of the National Science Education Standards? Reviewing the evidence, a workshop summary.* National Academies Press.

Holt, J., Huston, S., Heidari, K., Schwatz, R., Gollmar, C., Tran, A., Bryan, L., Liu, Y., & Croft, J. (2015). Indicators for chronic disease surveillance—United States, 2013. *Centers for Disease Control and Prevention MMWR Recommendations and Reports, 64,* 1–246.

Honey, M., Pearson, G., & Schweingruber, H. (Eds.). (2014). *STEM integration in K–12 education: Status, prospects, and an agenda for research* (Vol. 500). National Academies Press.

Hora, M. T., Bouwma-Gearhart, J., & Park, H. J. (2017). Data driven decision-making in the era of accountability: Fostering faculty data cultures for learning. *The Review of Higher Education, 40*(3), 391–426.

Hout, M., & Elliott, S. W. (Eds.). (2011). *Incentives and test-based accountability in education.* National Academies Press.

Hubalovsky, S., Hubalovsky, M., & Musilek, M. (2019). Assessment of the influence of adaptive e-learning on learning effectiveness of primary school students. *Computers in Human Behavior, 92,* 691–705. https://doi.org/10.1016/j.chb.2018.05.033

Hubbard, R. (2016). *Corrupt research: The case for reconceptualizing empirical management and social science.* SAGE Publications, Inc.

Hubbard, R. (2019). Will the ASA's efforts to improve statistical practice be successful? Some evidence to the contrary. *The American Statistician, 73*(supl), 31–35. https://doi.org/10.1080/00031305.2018.1497540

Hubbard, R., Haig, B. D., & Parsa, R.A. (2019). The limited role of formal statistical inference in scientific inference. *The American Statistician, 73,* 91–98. https://doi.org/10.1080/00031305.2018.1464947

Huff, D. (1954). *How to lie with statistics.* Norton.

Huff, K. L. (2016). Addressing three common myths about the Next Generation Science Standards. *The Science Teacher, 83,* 55–58.

Hunter, L. M., & Bhrem, J. M. (2004.) A qualitative examination of value orientations toward wildlife and biodiversity by rural residents of the intermountain region. *Human Ecology Review, 11*(1), 13–26.

Hurd, P. D. (1998). Scientific literacy: New minds for a changing world. *Science Education, 82*(3), 407–416.

Hutchison, L. F. (2020). Assisting preservice teacher candidates in accepting the need for using instructional strategies in content–area instruction. *Critical Issues in Teacher Education, 27,* 4–14.

Huutoniemi, K., & Klein, J. T., Bruun, H., & Hukkinen, J. (2010). Analyzing interdisciplinarity: Typology and indicators. *Research Policy, 39*(1), 79–88.

Huxham, M., Welsh, A., Berry, A., & Templeton, S. (2006). Factors influencing primary school children's knowledge of wildlife. *Journal of Biological Education, 41*(1), 9–12.

Ingersoll, R., Sirinides, P., & Doughtery, R. (2017). *School leadership: Teachers' roles in school decision-making, and student achievement.* Consortium for Policy Research in Education.

Institute of Medicine. (2005). *Dietary reference intakes for energy, carbohydrate, fiber, fat, fatty acids, cholesterol, protein, and amino acids.* The National Academies Press. https://doi.org/10.17226/10490

Isabelle, A. D., (2017). STEM is elementary: Challenges faced by elementary teachers in the era of the Next Generation Science Standards. *The Educational Forum, 81*(1), 83–91.

Israel, M. (2015). Shea butter: An opposite replacement for trans fat in margarine. *Journal of Nutrition & Food Sciences, S11,* 1–5. https://www.longdom.org/open-access/shea-butter-an-opposite-replacement-for-trans-fat-in-margarine-2155-9600-S11-001.pdf

Jarrahi, M. H. (2018). Artificial intelligence and the future of work: Human-AI symbiosis in organizational decision making. *Business Horizons, 61*(4), 577–586.

Jasanoff, S. (2017). Virtual, visible, and actionable: Data assemblages and the sightlines of justice. *Big Data & Society, 4*(2). https://doi.org/10.1177%2F2053951717724477

Javaheri, A., Moghadamnejad, N., Keshavarz, H., Javaheri, E., Dobbins, C., Momeni, E., & Rawassizadeh, R. (2019). *Public vs media opinion on robots* [arXiv:1905.01615].

Jenkins, D., & Kerrigan, M. R. (2008). *Evidence-based decision making in community colleges: Findings from a survey of faculty and administrator data use at Achieving the Dream colleges.* Community College Research Center, Teachers College, Columbia University.

Joel, F. (1995). *Polymer science & technology: Introduction to polymer science.* Prentice Hall.

Johal, W., Castellano, G., Tanaka, F., & Okita, S. (2018). Robots for learning. *International Journal of Social Robotics, 10*(3), 293–294. https://doi.org/10.1007/s12369-018-0481-8

Johnson, A. P. (2002). *A short guide to action research.* Allyn & Bacon.

Johnson, C. C. (2013). Educational turbulence: The influence of macro and micropolicy on science education reform. *Journal of Science Teacher Education, 24*(4), 693–715.

Johnson, D. H. (2006). Signal-to-noise ratio. *Scholarpedia, 1*(12). http://dx.doi.org/10.4249/scholarpedia.2088

Johnson, J., & Gove, M. K. (2017). Green heroes: Read write act! Thematic teaching units. Green Literacy Foundation.

Johnson, J. C. (2010). *Seeds of change.* Lee & Low Books.

Jones, T. (2014). *A historical look at probability & statistics.* https://www.tes.com/lessons/LgdX4UaznUk3rw/a-historical-look-at-probability-statistics

Jones, T., & Texas, L. (2017) *Strategic journeys for building logical reasoning: Activities across the content areas: 9–12.* Taylor & Francis.

Juarez-Orozco, L. E., Martinez-Manzanera, O., van der Zant, F. M., Knol, R. J. J., & Knuuti, J. (2020). Deep learning in quantitative PET myocardial perfusion imaging: A study on cardiovascular event prediction. *JACC: Cardiovascular Imaging, 13*(1), 180–182.

Judson, E. (2013). The relationship between time allocated for science in elementary schools and state accountability policies. *Science Education, 97*(4), 621–636.

Julian, S. D., & Ofori-Dankwa, J. C. (2006). Is accreditation good for the strategic decision making of traditional business schools? *Academy of Management Learning & Education, 5*(2), 225–233.

Kader, G., & Jacobbe, T. (2013). *Developing essential understanding of statistics for teaching mathematics in grades 6–8.* National Council of Teachers of Mathematics.

Kahn, K., Megasari, R., Piantari, E., & Junaeti, E. (2018). AI programming by children using snap! Block programming in a developing country. In *ECTEL practitioner proceedings.* 13th European Conference on Technology Enhanced Learning.

Kalinowski, P., Lai, J., & Cumming, G. (2018). A cross-sectional analysis of students' intuitions when interpreting CIs. *Frontiers in Psychology, 9,* 1–19. https://doi.org/10.3389/fpsyg.2018.00112

Kalman, C. (2010). Enabling students to develop a scientific mindset. *Science and Education, 19,* 147–163. https://doi.org/10.1007/s11191-009-9186-6

Kamenetz, A. (2019, October 31). *It's a smartphone life: More than half of U.S. children have one.* NPR. https://www.npr.org/2019/10/31/774838891/its-a-smartphone-life-more-than-half-of-u-s-children-now-have-one

Kaplan, J. J., Fisher, D. G., & Rogness, N. T. (2010). Lexical ambiguity in statistics: How students use and define the words: Association, average, confidence, random and spread. *Journal of Statistics Education, 18*(2), 1–6. https://doi.org/10.1080/10691898.2010.11889491

Karamikabir, N. (2012). Gardner's multiple intelligence and mathematics education. *Procedia—Social and Behavioral Sciences, 31,* 778–781. https://doi.org/10.1016/j.sbspro.2011.12.140

Karlan-Mason, G., & Shi, R. (2021, January 15). *Food Pyramid 2020 Basics & Money's Influence on USDA Guidelines.* GreenChoice. https://www.greenchoicenow.com/v/food-pyramid-usda-dietary-guidelines

Kastrup, H., & Mallow, J. V. (2016). *Students' attitudes, students' anxieties and how to address them. A handbook for science teachers.* Morgan & Claypool Publishers.

Kaur, M., & Kang, S. (2016). Market basket analysis: Identify the changing trends of market data using association rule mining. *Procedia Computer Science, 85,* 78–85.

Kazempour, M., & Sadler, T. D. (2015). Pre-service teachers' science beliefs, attitudes, and self-efficacy: A multi-case study. *Teaching Education, 26*(3), 247–271.

Kelce, W., Lambright, C., Gray, L., & Roberts, K. (1997). Vinclozolin and p,p'-DDE alter androgen dependent gene expression: In vivo confirmation of an androgen receptor-mediated mechanism. *Toxicology and Applied Pharmacology, 142*(1), 192–200.

Kellert, S. (1996). *The value of life: Biological diversity and human society.* Island Press.

Kelly, S. B., Lawrence, L., & Mercier, E. (2017). Engaging everyday science knowledge to help make sense of data. In *Computer-supported collaborative learning conference, CSCL* (Vol. 2). International Society of the Learning Sciences.

Khosravi, H., Sadiq, S., & Gasevic, D. (2020). Development and adoption of an adaptive learning system. In *Proceedings of the 51st ACM Technical Symposium on Computer Science Education* (pp. 58–64). Association for Computing Machinery. https://doi.org/10.1145/3328778.3366900

Kilb, D., Peng, Z., Simpson, D., Michael, A., Fisher, M., & Rohrlick, D. (2012). Listen, watch, learn: SeisSound video products. *Seismological Research Letters, 83*(2), 281–286. http://geophysics.eas.gatech.edu/people/zpeng/EQ_Music/

Kim, J., Merrill, K., Xu, K., & Sellnow, D. (2020). My teacher is a machine: Understanding students' perceptions of AI teaching assistants in online education. *International Journal of Human-Computer Interaction, 36*(20), 1902–1911. https://doi.org/10.1080/10447318.2020.1801227

Kim, M. K., Kim, S. M., Khera, O., & Getman, J. (2014). The experience of three flipped classrooms in an urban university: An exploration of design principles. *Internet and Higher Education, 22,* 37–50.

Kind, P., & Osborne, J. (2017). Styles of scientific reasoning: A cultural rationale for science education. *Science Education, 101*(1), 8–31.

Kitano, H. (2016). Artificial intelligence to win the Nobel Prize and beyond: Creating the engine for scientific discovery. *AI Magazine, 37*(1), 39–49.

Kitsantas, A., & Zimmerman, B. J. (2002). Comparing self-regulatory processes among novice, non-expert, and expert volleyball players: A microanalytic study. *Journal of Applied Sport Psychology, 14*(2), 91–105.

Klaassen, C. (1996). *Casarett and Doull's toxicology: The basic science of poisons.* McGraw-Hill.

Klein, A. (2019, July 05). *What every educator needs to know about artificial intelligence.* Education Week.

Kleist, V. (2015). Women in STEM careers: What is working well. *Sex Roles, 73*(5–6), 276–278. https://doi.org/10.1007/s11199-015-0522-9

Klingner, J. K., Arguelles, M. E., Hughes, M. T., & Vaughn, S. (2001). Examining the schoolwide "spread" of research-based practices. *Learning Disability Quarterly, 24*(4), 221–234.

Kloos, H., Baker, H., & Waltzer, T. (2019). A mind with a mind of its own: How complexity theory can inform early science pedagogy. *Educational Psychology Review, 31,* 735–752. https://doi.org/10.1007%2Fs10648-019-09472-6

Knapp, T. R. (2016). Why is the one-group pretest–posttest design still used? *Clinical Nursing Research, 25*(5), 467–472.

Knauer, L. (Director). (2011). *Jane's journey* [Film]. First Run Features.

Knox, J., Williamson, B., & Bayne, S. (2020). Machine behaviourism: Future visions of 'learnification' and 'datafication' across humans and digital technologies. *Learning, Media and Technology, 45*(1), 31–45. https://doi.org/10.1080/17439884.2019.1623251

Koba, S., Wojnowski, B., & Yager, R. E. (Eds.). (2013). *Exemplary science: Best practices in professional development.* NSTA Press.

Komar, V., & Melamid, A. (1997). *Most wanted and least wanted paintings.* http://awp.diaart.org/km/painting.html

Kotin, A. McGregor, S. A., Pellecchia, D., Schatz, I., & Liu, S. P. (2013). Speak up. Act out. Move forward. Disobedience-based arts education. *Harvard Educational Review, 83*(1), 190–200.

Kötter, M., & Hammann, M. (2017). Controversy as a blind spot in teaching nature of science: Why the range of different positions concerning nature of science should be an issue in the science classroom. *Science & Education, 26,* 451–482. https://doi.org/10.1007/s11191-017-9913-3

Krajcik, J. S., & Czerniak, C. M. (2018). *Teaching science in elementary and middle school: A project-based learning approach.* Routledge.

Kramer, G. (1951). Eine neue Methode zur Erforschung del' Zugoricnticrung unci die bisher damit erzielten Ergebnisse [A new method to study migratory orientation and the results thereby obtained thus far]. In S. Horstadius (Ed.), *Proceedings of the Xth International Ornithological Congress, Uppsala June 1950* (pp. 269–280). Almqvist & Wiksell, Uppsala.

Krashen, S. D. (1985). *The input hypothesis: Issues and implications.* Longman.

Krause, N. M., Brossard, D., Scheufele, D. A., Xenos, M. A., & Franke, K. (2019). Trends—Americans' trust in science and scientists. *Public Opinion Quarterly, 83*(4), 817–836.

Krebs, C. (1978). *Ecology: The experimental analysis of distribution and abundance* (2nd ed.). Harper & Row.

Kress, G. (2003). *Literacy in the new media age.* Routledge.

Kross, S., Peng, R. D., Caffo, B. S., Goodling, I., & Leek, J. T. (2020). The democratization of data science education. *The American Statistician, 74*(1), 1–7. https://doi.org/10.1080/00031305.2019.1668849

Krouse Rosenthal, A., & Linchtenfield, T. (2009). *Duck! Rabbit!* Chronicle Books.

Kuhn, T. S. (1996). *The structure of scientific revolutions* (3rd ed.). The University of Chicago Press. Originally published in 1962

Kuhn, T. S. (1970). *The structure of scientific revolutions.* University of Chicago Press.

Kukulska-Hulme, A. (2007). Mobile usability in educational contexts: What have we learnt? *The International Review of Research in Open and Distance Learning, 8*(2), 1–16. http://www.irrodl.org/index.php/irrodl/article/view/356/879

Kumar, R., Kanna, G., & Elumalai, S. (2017). Biodegradation of polyethylene by green photosynthetic microalgae. *Journal of Bioremediation & Biodegradation, 8*(1), 381–388.

Kupfer, J. A., Gao, P., & Guo, D. (2012). Regionalization of forest pattern metrics for the continental United States using contiguity constrained clustering and partitioning. *Ecological Informatics, 9,* 11–18.

Kushlan, J. (1974). Observations on the role of the American alligator (*Alligator mississippiensis*) in the southern Florida wetlands. *Copeia, 1974*(4), 993–996.

Kushlan, J. A., & Kushlan, M. S. (1980). Everglades alligator nests: Nesting sites for marsh reptiles. *Copeia, 1980*(4), 930–932.

Kuznekoff, J., & Titsworth, S. (2013). The impact of mobile phone usage on student learning. *Communication Education, 62*(3), 233–252. https://doi.org/10.1080/03634523.2013.767917

Ladson-Billings, G. (1997). It doesn't add up: African American students' mathematics achievement. *Journal for Research in Mathematics Education, 28*(6), 697–708.

Lamb, E. (2018, April 30). *The metonymy of matrices.* Scientific American. https://blogs.scientificamerican.com/roots-of-unity/the-metonymy-of-matrices/

La Merrill, M., Emond, C., Kim, M. J., Antignac, J.-P., Bizec, B. L., Clément, K., Birnbaum, L. S., & Barouki, R. (2013). Toxicological function of adipose tissue: Focus on persistent organic pollutants. *Environmental Health Perspectives, 121*(2), 162–169.

Landauer, T. K., & Dumais, S. T. (1997). A solution to Plato's problem: The latent semantic analysis theory of acquisition, induction, and representation of knowledge. *Psychological Review, 104*(2), 211.

Landivar, L. C. (2013). Disparities in STEM employment by sex, race, and Hispanic origin. *Education Review, 29*(6), 911–922.

Lane, S. N., Bakker, M., Costa, A., Loizeau, J.-L., Molnar, P., Silva, T., Stutenbecker, L., & Schlunegger, F. (2019). Making stratigraphy in the Anthropocene: Climate change impacts and economic conditions controlling the supply of sediment to Lake Geneva. *Scientific Reports, 9*(1), 1–11. https://doi.org/10.1038/s41598-019-44914-9

Langsdorf, M., & Smith, C. S. (2020). 1959: Science and art. *Bulletin of the Atomic Scientists, 76*(6), 363–365. https://doi.org/10.1080/00963402.2020.1847483

Larson, R., & Farber, E. (2019). *Elementary statistics: Picturing the world* (7th ed.). Pearson Education, Inc.

Lastrucci, C. L. (1963). *The scientific approach: Basic principles of the scientific method.* Schenkman.

Lattimer, H. (2014). *Real-world literacies: Disciplinary teaching in the high school classroom.* NCTE.

Le Pichon, X. (1968). Sea-floor spreading and continental drift. *Journal of Geophysical Research, 73*(12), 3661–3697.

Lederman, M. (2003). Gender/InEquity in science education: A response. *Journal of Research in Science Teaching, 40*(6), 604–606.

Lederman, N. (2014). Nature of science and its fundamental importance to the vision of the next generation science standards. *Science and Children, 52*(1), 8–10.

Lederman, N., & Abd-El-Khalick, F. (1998). Avoiding de-natured science: Activities that promote understandings of the nature of science. In W. F. McComas (Ed.), The nature of science in science education: Rationales and strategies (pp. 83–126). Springer.

Lederman, N., Lederman, J., & Antink, A. (2013). Nature of science and scientific inquiry as contexts for the learning of science and achievement of scientific literacy. International Journal of Education in Mathematics, Science and Technology, 1(3), 138–147.

Lederman, N. G. (1992). Students' and teachers' conceptions of the nature of science: A review of the research. *Journal of Research in Science Teaching, 29*(4), 331–359.

Lederman, N. G. (2007). Nature of science: Past, present, and future. In S. K. Abell & N. G. Lederman (Eds.), *Handbook of research on science education* (pp. 831–880). Lawrence Erlbaum Associates.

Lederman, N. G., & Lederman, J. S. (2014). Research on teaching and learning of nature of science. In N. G. Lederman & S. K. Abell (Eds.), *Hand-book of research on science education* (Vol. 2; pp. 600–620). Routledge.

Lee, C. D. (2008). The centrality of culture to the scientific study of learning and development: How an ecological framework in education research facilitates a civic responsibility. *Educational Researcher, 37*(5), 267–279.

Lee, E., & Hannafin, M. J. (2016). A design framework for enhancing engagement in student-centered learning: Own it, learn it, and share it. *Educational Technology Research and Development, 64*(4), 707–734.

Lee, L. (2019, July 26). *Computational thinking is critical thinking—and belongs in every subject.* Edutopia. https://www.edutopia.org/article/computational-thinking-critical-thinking-and-belongs-every-subject

Lee, O. (2020). Making everyday phenomena phenomenal: Using phenomena to promote equity in science instruction. *Science & Children, 58*(1), 56–61.

Lee, O., & Campbell, T. (2020). What science and STEM teachers can learn from COVID-19: Harnessing data science and computer science through the convergence of multiple STEM subjects. *Journal of Science Teacher Education, 31*(8), 932–944. https://doi.org/10.1080/1046560X.2020.1814980

Lehrer, R., & English, L. (2018). Introducing children to modeling variability. In *International handbook of research in statistics education* (pp. 229–260). Springer.

Lehrer, R., & Schauble, L. (2004). Modeling natural variation through distribution. *American Educational Research Journal, 41*(3), 635–679.

Lehrer, R., & Schauble, L. (2007). Contrasting emerging conceptions of distribution in contexts of error and natural variation. In M. C. Lovett & P. Shah (Eds.), *Thinking with data* (pp. 163–190). Psychology Press.

Leithwood, K., & Jantzi, D. (1998). *Distributed leadership and student engagement in school* [Paper presentation]. Annual Meeting of the American Educational Research Association.

Lemonidis, C., & Kaiafa, I. (2019). The effect of using storytelling strategy on students' performance in fractions. *Journal of Education and Learning, 8*(2), 165–175. https://doi.org/10.5539/jel.v8n2p165

Lenhart, A. (2012). *Teens, smartphones & texting.* Pew Research Center's Internet & American Life Project.

Lenhart, A., Ling, R., Campbell, S., & Purcell, K. (2010). *Teens and mobile phones.* Pew Research Center's Internet & American Life Project.

Lenton, T. M. (2016). *Earth system science. A very short introduction.* Oxford University Press.

Leung, A. (2019). Exploring STEM pedagogy in the mathematics classroom: A tool-based experiment lesson on estimation. *International Journal of Science and Mathematics Education, 17,* 1339–1358. https://doi.org/10.1007%2Fs10763-018-9924-9

Levy, J. (2016). *A curious history of mathematics: The big ideas from primitive numbers to chaos theory.* Carlton Publishing Group.

Lewis, S., & Maslin, M. (2015). Defining the Anthropocene. *Nature, 519,* 171–180. https://doi.org/10.1038/nature14258

Lewis, T. G., & Marsh, L. (2016). Human stigmergy: Theoretical developments and new applications. *Cognitive Systems Research, 38,* 1–3. https://doi.org/10.1016/j.cogsys.2015.12.001

Lewthwaite, B. (2006). Constraints and contributors to becoming a science teacher-leader. *Science Education, 90*(2), 331–347.

Li, J. (2015). The benefit of being physically present: A survey of experimental works comparing copresent robots, telepresence robots, and virtual agents. *International Journal of Human-computer Studies, 77*, 23–37. https://doi.org/10.1016/j.ijhcs.2015.01.001

Li, J., Kizilcec, R., Bailenson, J., & Ju, W. (2015). Social robots and virtual agents as lecturers for video instruction. *Computers in Human Behavior, 55*, 1222–1230.

Li, L., Shrestha, S., & Hu, G. (2017). Analysis of road traffic fatal accidents using data mining techniques. In *Proceedings 2017 15th IEEE/ACIS International Conference on Software Engineering Research, Management and Applications, SERA 2017* (pp. 363–370). IEEE.

Li, Y., Schoenfeld, A. H., diSessa, A. A., Graesser, A. C., Benson, L. C., English, L. D., & Duschl, R. A. (2019). Design and design thinking in STEM Education. *Journal for STEM Education Research, 2*(2), 93–104.

Liang, W., Yao, J., Chen, A., Lu, Q., Zanin, M., Liu, J., Wong, S., Li, Y., Lu, J., Liang, H., Chen, G., Guo, H., Guo, J., Zhou, R., Ou, L., Zhou, N., Chen, H., Yang, F., Han, X., . . . He, J. (2020). Early triage of critically ill COVID-19 patients using deep learning. *Nature Communications, 11*(1), 1–7.

Lidar, M., Lundqvist, E., Ryder, J., & Östman, L. (2017). The transformation of teaching habits in relation to the introduction of grading and national testing in science education in Sweden. *Research in Science Education, 50*(1), 151–173. https://doi.org/10.1007/s11165-017-9684-5

Lindholm, M. (2018). Promoting curiosity? Possibilities and pitfalls in science education. *Science Education, 27*(9–10), 987–1002.

Linnebo, Ø. (2017). *Philosophy of mathematics.* Princeton University Press.

Liou, Y.-H., Canrinus, E. T., & Daly, A. J. (2019). Activating the implementers: The role of organizational expectations, teacher beliefs, and motivation in bringing about reform. *Teaching and Teacher Education, 79*, 60–72. https://doi.org/10.1016/j.tate.2018.12.004

Liu, E. (2015, July 3). What every American should know: Defining common cultural literacy for an increasingly diverse nation. *The Atlantic.* https://www.theatlantic.com/politics/archive/2015/07/what-every-american-should-know/397334/

Lloyd, K., Tienda, M., & Zaiacova, A. (2001). Trends in educational achievement of minority students since Brown v. Board of Education. In T. Ready, C. Edley, & C. Snow (Eds.), *Achieving high educational standards for all* (pp. 1–25). National Academies Press.

Lock, R., Lock, P., Morgan, K., Lock, E., & Lock, D. (2013). *Statistics: Unlocking the power of data.* Wiley.

Locke, E. A., & Latham, G. P. (1990). *A theory of goal setting and task performance.* Prentice Hall.

Long, T. W., & Gove, M. K. (2003). How engagement strategies and literature circles promote critical response in a fourth-grade, urban classroom. *The Reading Teacher, 57*(4), 350–361.

Lopez-Jimenez, F., Simha, V., Thomas, R. J., Allison, T. G., Basu, A., Fernandes, R., Hurst, R. T., Kopecky, S. L., Kullo, I. J., Mulvagh, S. L., Thompson, W. G., Trejo-Gutierrez, J. F., & Wright, R. S. (2014). A summary and critical assessment of the 2013 ACC/AHA guideline on the treatment of blood cholesterol to reduce atherosclerotic cardiovascular disease risk in adults: Filling the gaps.

Mayo Clinic Proceedings, 89(9), 1257–1278. https://doi.org/10.1016/j.mayocp.2014.06.016

Loucks-Horsley, S., Love, N., Stiles, K. E., Mundry, S., & Hewson, P. W. (2009). *Designing professional development for teachers of science and mathematics* (3rd ed.). Corwin.

Louhab, F. E., Bahnasse, A., & Talea, M. (2018). Towards an adaptive formative assessment in context-aware mobile learning. *Procedia Computer Science, 135*, 441–448. https://doi.org/10.1016/j.procs.2018.08.195

Louv, R. (2005). *Last child in the woods: Saving our children from nature-deficit disorder.* Algonquin Books.

Luckin, R., & Cukurova, M. (2019). Designing educational technologies in the age of AI: A learning sciences-driven approach. *British Journal of Educational Technology, 50*(6), 2824–2838. https://doi.org/10.1111/bjet.12861

Luckin, R., Holmes, W., Griffiths, M., & Forcier, L. (2016). *Intelligence unleashed: An argument for AI in education.* Pearson Education.

Luehmann, A. L. (2007). Identity development as a lens to science teacher preparation. *Science Education, 91*(5), 822–839.

Lundholm, C. E. (1997). DDE-induced eggshell thinning in birds: Effects of *p, p'*-DDE on the calcium and prostaglandin metabolism of the eggshell gland. *Comparative Biochemistry and Physiology Part C: Pharmacology, Toxicology and Endocrinology, 118*(2), 113–128.

Lyman, F. (1981). The responsive classroom discussion. In A. S. Anderson (Ed.), *Mainstreaming digest* (pp. 109–113). University of Maryland College of Education.

Ma, K. L., Liao, I., Frazier, J., Hauser, H., & Kostis, H. N. (2012). Scientific storytelling using visualization. *IEEE Computer Graphics and Applications, 32*(1), 12–19.

Magrini, J. (2009). *How the conception of knowledge influences our educational practices: Toward a philosophical understanding of epistemology in education* (Paper 13). Philosophy Scholarship. http://dc.cod.edu/philosophypub/13

Makar, K., Bakker, A., & Ben-Zvi, D. (2011). The reasoning behind informal statistical inference. *Mathematical Thinking and Learning, 13*(1–2), 152–173.

Makar, K., & Rubin, A. (2009). A framework for thinking about informal statistical inference. *Statistics Education Research Journal, 8*(1), 82–105. http://iase-web.org/documents/SERJ/SERJ8(1)_Makar_Rubin.pdf

Maloy, R., Trust, T., Kommers, S., Malinowski, A., & LaRoche, I. (2017). 3D modeling and printing in history/social studies classrooms: Initial lessons and insights. *Contemporary Issues in Technology and Teacher Education, 17*(2), 229–249.

Maltese, A. V., & Tai, R. H. (2011). Pipeline persistence: Examining the association of educational experiences with earned degrees in STEM among US students. *Science Education, 95*(5), 877–907.

Mandinach, E. B. (2012). A perfect time for data use: Using data-driven decision making to inform practice. *Educational Psychologist, 47*(2), 71–85.

Mangochi, P. (2010). Endocrine disrupting chemicals and human health: The plausibility of research results on DDT and reproductive health. *Malawi Medical Journal, 22*(2), 42–45.

Mansour, N. (2020). The dissonance between scientific evidence, diversity and dialogic pedagogy in the science classroom. *International Journal of Science Education, 42*(2), 190–217. https://doi.org/10.1080/09500693.2019.1706114

Marginson, S., Tytler, R., Freeman, B., & Roberts, K. (2013). *STEM: Country comparisons*. Australian Council of Learned Academies. https://www.acola.org.au

Marsh, J. A. (2012). Interventions promoting educators' use of data: Research insights and gaps. *Teachers College Record, 114*(11), 1–48.

Martin, M., & Jones, T. (2019). Differentiating the teaching of statistics. In R. Brandl, G. Cobbs, & M. Shores (Eds.), *Proceedings of the 118th annual convention of the School Science and Mathematics Association* (Vol. 6). SSMA.

Martinez, S. L., & Stager, G. S. (2013). *Invent to learn: Making, tinkering, and engineering in the classroom* [E-book version 1]. Constructing Modern Knowledge Press.

Martín-Páez, T., Aguilera, D., Perales-Palacios, F. J., & Vílchez-González, J. M. (2019). What are we talking about when we talk about STEM education? A review of literature. *Science Education, 103*(4), 799–822.

Mason, L. H., & Hedin, L. R. (2011). Reading science text: Challenges for students with learning disabilities and considerations for teachers. *Learning Disabilities Research & Practice, 26*(4), 214–222.

Matthews, K., Janicki, T., He, L., & Patterson, L. (2012). Implementation of an automated grading system with an adaptive learning component to affect student feedback and response time. *Journal of Information Systems Education, 23*(1), 71–83.

Matthews, R. A. J. (2019). Moving towards the post $p < 0.05$ era via the analysis of credibility. *The American Statistician, 73*(1), 202–212. https://doi.org/10.1080/00031305.2018.1543136

Mattietti, G. K., & Peters-Burton, E. E. (2015). Student-centered visualization in general education introductory geoscience classes. In K. D. Finson & J. E. Pederson (Eds.), *Application of visual data in K-16 science classrooms* (pp. 333–355). Information Age Publishing.

Mayer, V. J., Fortner, R. W., & Hoyt, H. (1995). Using cooperative learning as a structure for earth systems education workshops. *Journal of Geological Education, 43*(4), 395–400. https://doi.org/10.5408/0022-1368-43.4.395

McClave, J. T., & Sincich, T. (2017). *A first course in statistics* (12th ed.). Pearson.

McClenney, K. M., McClenney, B. N., & Peterson, G. F. (2007). A culture of evidence: What is it? Do we have one? *Planning for Higher Education, 35*(3), 26–33.

McComas, W. F. (2016). The next generation science standards: How many dimensions of learning are there? *The American Biology Teacher, 78*(9), 707. https://doi.org/10.1525/abt.2016.78.9.707

McConnell, J. R., Bruster, B. G., & Smith, V. B. (2019). Predicting teacher effectiveness based on various preservice factors: Implications for higher education and the evaluation of teacher preparation. *International Journal of Educational Reform, 28*(1), 63–78. https://doi.org/10.1177/1056787918824204

McConnell, T. J. (2017a). *Conservation tales: Bats*. Airway Publishing.

McConnell, T. J. (2017b). *Conservation tales: Bees*. Airway Publishing.

McConnell, T. J. (2017c). *Conservation tales: Salamanders*. Airway Publishing.

McConnell, T. J. (2017d). *Conservation tales: The cerulean warbler*. Airway Publishing.

McConnell, T. J. (2018). *Conservation tales: Sea turtles*. Airway Publishing.

McConnell, T. J., & Brown, M. J. (2018). *Conservation tales: Seahorses*. Airway Publishing.

McConnell, T. J., & Stallard, S. (2018). *Conservation tales: Manatees*. Airway Publishing.

McCosker, A., & Wilken, R. (2014). Rethinking "big data" as visual knowledge: The sublime and the diagrammatic in data visualisation. *Visual Studies, 29*(2), 155–164.

McCoy, B. (2013). Digital distractions in the classroom: Student classroom use of digital devices for non-class related purposes. *Journal of Media Education, 4*(4), 5–14. http://digitalcommons.unl.edu/journalismfacpub/71

McDaniel, R. (2018, August 13). *Bloom's taxonomy.* Vanderbilt University Center for Teaching. https://cft.vanderbilt.edu/guides-sub-pages/blooms-taxonomy/

McDaniel, S. N., & Green, L. B. (2012). Using applets and video instruction to foster students' understanding of sampling variability. *Technology Innovations in Statistics Education, 6*(1), 1–17. https://escholarship.org/uc/item/1nh4n607

McGatha, M., Cobb, P., & McClain, K. (2002). An analysis of students' initial statistical understanding: Developing a conjectured learning trajectory. *Journal of Mathematical Behavior, 21*(3), 339–355.

McGreevy, P. (2019, March 20). More California students may be banned from using cellphones at school under a new bill. *Los Angeles Times.* https://www.latimes.com/politics/la-pol-ca-school-smartphone-ban-20190320-story.html

McKinney, S., & Hinton, K. (2010). *Mathematics in the K–8 classroom and library.* Linworth.

Mclaughlin, M., & Overturf, B. J. (2012). The common core: Insights into the K–5 standards. *Reading Teacher, 66*(2), 153–164. https://doi.org/10.1002/Trtr.01115

McMillan, J. H. (2012). *Educational research: Fundamentals for the consumer.* Pearson.

McNeill, K. L., Katsh-Singer, R., & Pelletier, P. (2015). Assessing science practices: Moving your class along a continuum. *Science Scope, 39*(4), 21.

McNeill, K., & Krajcik, J. (2012). *Supporting grade 5–8 students in constructing explanations in science: The claim, evidence and reasoning framework for talking and writing.* Pearson.

McPhee, J. (1982). *Basin and range.* Farrar, Straus and Giroux.

McPhee, J. (1998). *Annals of the former world.* Farrar, Straus and Giroux.

McPhee, J. (2000). *Annals of the former world.* Farrar, Straus and Giroux.

McPherson, G. R. (2001). Teaching & learning the scientific method. *The American Biology Teacher, 63*(4), 242–245.

Mei, X., Lee, H., Diao, K., Huang, M., Lin, B., Liu, C., Xie, Z., Ma, Y., Robson, P., Chung, M., Bernheim, A., Mani, V., Calcagno, C., Li, K., Li, S., Shan, H., Lv, J., Zhao, T., Xia, J., . . . Yang, Y. (2020). Artificial intelligence–enabled rapid diagnosis of patients with COVID-19. *Nature Medicine, 26*(8), 1224–1228.

Mentzer, G. A., Czerniak, C. M., & Duckett, T. R. (2019). Comparison of two alternative approaches to quality STEM teacher preparation: Fast-track licensure and embedded residency programs. *School Science & Mathematics, 119*(1), 35–48. https://doi.org/10.1111/ssm.12314

Menzies, C. R., & Butler, C. (2006). Understanding ecological knowledge. In C. R. Menzies (Ed.), *Traditional ecological knowledge and natural resource management* (pp. 1–17). University of Nebraska Press.

Merriam, S. (1998). *Qualitative research and case study applications in education.* Jossey-Bass.

Mesci, G., & Schwartz, R. (2017). Changing preservice science teachers' views of nature of science: Why some conceptions may be more easily al-tered than others. *Research in Science Education, 47*(2), 329–351.

Meyer, J. W., & Rowan, B. (1977). Institutionalized organizations: Formal structure as myth and ceremony. *American Journal of Sociology, 83*(2), 340–363.

Michener, W. K. (2015). Ecological data sharing. *Ecological Informatics, 29*(1), 33–44.

Migliorato, P., & Rahman, A. Z. M. S. (2017). Active-matrix LCD with amorphous thin-film transistors. *Materials Science and Materials Engineering.* https://doi.org/10.1016/B978-0-12-803581-8.10369-8

Miller-Struttmann, N. E., Heise, D., Schul, J., Geib, J. C., & Galen, C. (2017). Flight of the bumble bee: Buzzes predict pollination services. *PloS One, 12*(6), e0179273.

Milner, A. R., Sondergeld, T. A., Demir, A., Johnson, C. A., & Czerniak, C. M. (2011). Elementary teachers' beliefs about teaching science and classroom practice: An example of pre/post NCLB testing in science. *Journal of Science Teacher Education, 23*(2), 111–132.

Minchin, T. (2013). Foreword. In J. McCredie & N. Mitchell (Eds.), *The best Australian science writing 2013* (pp. 1–3). NewSouth Publishing.

Miranda, J. M., Anton, X., Redondo-Valbuena, C., Roca-Saavedra, P., Rodriguez, J. A., Lamas, A., Franco, C. M., & Cepeda, A. (2015). Egg and egg-derived foods: Effects on human health and use as functional foods. *Nutrients, 7*(1), 706–729. https://doi.org/10.3390/nu7010706

Mizrahi, M. (2013). What is scientific progress? Lessons from scientific practice. *Journal for General Philosophy of Science, 44*(2), 375–390. https://doi.org/10.1007/s10838-013-9229-1

Moll, L. C., Amanti, C., Neff, D., & Gonzalez, N. (1992). Funds of knowledge for teaching: Using a qualitative approach to connect homes and classrooms. *Theory Into Practice, 31*(2), 132–141. https://doi.org/10.1080/00405849209543534

Monhardt, R., & Monhardt, L. (2000). Children's literature and environmental issues: Heart over mind? *Reading Horizons, 40*(3), 175–184.

Moore, D. (1998). Statistics among the liberal arts. *Journal of the American Statistical Association, 93*(444), 1253–1259.

Moore, J. A., & Miller, J. D. (2008, October 7). Geological literacy during the Anthropocene Epoch: Public understanding of global climate change and public policy. *Global Warming Science: Implications for Geoscientists, Educators, and Policy Makers I,* Houston, Texas.

More, T. A. (1979). Wildlife preferences and children's books. *Wildlife Society Bulletin, 7*(4), 274–278.

Morigaki, K., & Ogihara, C. (2017). Amorphous semiconductors: Structure, optical, and electrical properties. In S. Kasap & P. Capper (Eds.), *Springer handbook of electronic and photonic materials.* Springer Handbooks. https://doi.org/10.1007/978-3-319-48933-9_24

Moses, R. P., & Cobb, C. (2001). Organizing algebra: The need to voice a demand. *Social Policy, 31*(4), 4–12.

MTSTatPAL Project Team. (2016). *MTSU math 1530 student workbook.* Middle Tennessee State University.

Mulder, I., dePoot, H., Verwijs, C., Janssen, R., & Bijlsma, M. (2006). An information overload study: Using design methods for understanding. In *Proceedings of OZCHI* (pp. 245–252). Association for Computing Machinery.

Nagle, C. E., & Pecore, J. L. (2019). A veteran science teacher's transitions to NGSS. *Electronic Journal of Science Education, 23*(4), 1–15.

Nagpal, R., Nagpal, P., & Kaur, S. (2010). Hybrid technique for human face emotion detection. *International Journal of Advanced Computer Science and Applications, 1*(6), 91–101.

Nasir, N. S. (2012). *Racialized identities: Race and achievement among African American youth.* Stanford University Press.

Nasir, N. S., & Hand, V. M. (2006). Exploring sociocultural perspectives on race, culture, and learning. *Review of Educational Research, 76*(4), 449–475.

National Academies of Science, Engineering and Medicine. (2017). *Building America's skilled technical workforce.* The National Academies Press.

National Academies of Science, Engineering, and Medicine. (2018). *Data science for undergraduates: Opportunities and options.* The National Academies Press. https://doi.org/10.17226/25104

National Academies of Science, Engineering, and Medicine. (2019). *Reproducibility and replicability in science.* The National Academies Press. https://doi.org/10.17226/25303

National Assessment Governing Board. (2014). *Technology and engineering literacy framework for the 2014 National Assessment of Educational Progress (NAEP).* https://www.nagb.gov/naep-frameworks/technology-and-engineering-literacy/2014-technology-framework/toc/ch_2/society/society3.html

National Center for Education Statistics. (2019a). *National Assessment of Educational Progress—The nation's report card.*

National Center for Education Statistics. (2019b). *State non-fiscal survey of public elementary and secondary enrollment by race/ethnicity projection model, 1972 through 2029.* U. S. Department of Education.

National Council of Teachers of Mathematics. (2000). *Principles and standards for school mathematics.*

National Council of Teachers of Mathematics. (2018). *Catalyzing change in high school mathematics: initiating critical conversations.*

National Governors Association Center for Best Practices. (2010). *Common core state standards for mathematics.* National Governors Association Center for Best Practices, Council of Chief State School Officers.

National Research Council. (1986). Earth system science. Overview: A program for global change. The National Academies Press. https://doi.org/10.17226/19210

National Research Council. (1996). *National science education standards.* National Academies Press. http://www.nap.edu/catalog/4962.html

National Research Council. (2000). *Inquiry and the national science education standards: A guide for teaching and learning.* National Academies Press.

National Research Council. (2001). *Knowing what students know: The science and design of educational assessment.* National Academies Press.

National Research Council. (2012). *A framework for K–12 science education: Practices, crosscutting concepts, and core ideas.* The National Academies Press. https://doi.org/10.17226/13165

National Research Council. (2013a). *Next generation science standards: For states, by states.* The National Academies Press. https://doi.org/10.17226/18290

National Research Council. (2013b). *The mathematical sciences in 2025.* National Academies Press.

National Research Council. (2015). *Guide to implementing the Next Generation Science Standards.* National Academies Press.

National Science Teachers Association. (2020, April 30). *About the Next Generation Science Standards.* NSTA. https://ngss.nsta.org/about.aspx

NCIRD. (2020, June 25). *COVID-19 mathematical modeling.* Centers for Disease Control and Prevention. https://www.cdc.gov/coronavirus/2019-ncov/covid-data/mathematical-modeling.html

Nersessian, N. (2008). *Creating scientific concepts.* MIT Press.

Newell, A., & Simon, H. A. (1976). Computer science as empirical inquiry: Symbols and search. *Communications of the ACM, 19*(3), 113–126. https://doi.org/10.1145/360018.360022

Next Generation Science Standards Lead States. (2013). *Next generation science standards: For states, by states.* National Academies Press. https://doi.org/10.17226/18290

Nguyen, A., Yosinski, J., & Clune, J. (2015). Deep neural networks are easily fooled: High confidence predictions for unrecognizable images. In *Proceedings of the computer vision and pattern recognition* (pp. 1–20). https://arxiv.org/abs/1412.1897

Niaz, M. (2018). Introduction: Understanding objectivity within a historical perspective. In *Evolving nature of objectivity in the history of science and its implications for science education* (pp. 1–22). Springer.

Nichols, M. (1967). *The graduate* [film]. Embassy Pictures.

Nicholson, N., & Leighton, G. (1942, August). Plastics come of age. *Harper's Magazine.* https://harpers.org/archive/1942/08/plastics-come-of-age/

Nifong, J., & Silliman, B. (2013). Impacts of a large-bodied, apex predator (*Alligator mississippiensis* Daudin 1801) on salt marsh food webs. *Journal of Experimental Marine Biology and Ecology, 440,* 185–191.

Niiniluoto, I. (2014). Scientific progress as increasing verisimilitude. *Studies in History and Philosophy of Science, 46,* 73–77.

Nilsson, P. (2020). Students' informal hypothesis testing in a probability context with concrete random generators. *Statistics Education Research Journal, 19*(3), 53–73. http://iase-web.org/Publications.php?p=SERJ

Nollmeyer, G., & Bangert, A. (2017). Measuring elementary teachers' understanding of the NGSS framework: An instrument for planning and assessing professional development. *Electronic Journal of Science Education, 21*(8), 20–45.

Norman, D. A. (1999). Affordance, conventions, and design. *Interactions, 6*(3), 38–43.

Norris, S. P., & Phillips, L. M. (2003). How literacy in its fundamental sense is central to scientific literacy. *Science Education, 87*(2), 224–240.

Novak, E., & Wisdom, S. (2018). Effects of 3D printing project-based learning on preservice elementary teachers' science attitudes, science content knowledge, and anxiety about teaching science. *Journal of Science Education and Technology, 27*(5), 412–432.

Novak, E., & Wisdom, S. (2020). Using 3D printing in science for elementary teachers. In J. J. Mintzes & E. M. Walter (Eds.), *Active learning in college science: The case for evidence-based practice.* Springer.

Nygård Larsson, P., & Jakobsson, A. (2020). Meaning-making in science from the perspective of students' hybrid language use. *International Journal of Science & Mathematics Education, 18*(5), 811–830. https://doi.org/10.1007/s10763-019-09994-z

O'Bannon, B., Waters, S., Lubke, J., Cady, J., & Rearden, K. (2017). Teachers and students poised to use mobile phones in the classroom. *Computers in the Schools, 34*(3), 125–141.

Odum, H., & Odum, E. (2000). The energetic basis for valuation of ecosystem services. *Ecosystems, 3*(1), 21–23.

Ogle, D. M. (1986). K-W-L: A teaching model that develops active reading of expository text. *Reading Teacher, 39*(6), 564–570.

Okasha, S. (2016). *Philosophy of science: A very short introduction.* Oxford University Press.

Oreskes, N. (2019). *Why trust science?* Princeton University Press.

Osborne, J. (2014). Teaching scientific practices: Meeting the challenge of change. *Journal of Science Teacher Education, 25*(2), 177–196.

Owen, J. C., Garvin, M. C., & Moore, F. R. (2014). Elevated testosterone advances onset of migratory restlessness in a nearctic-neotropical landbird. *Behavioral Ecology and Sociobiology, 68*(4), 561–569. https://doi.org/10.1007/s00265-013-1671-x

Paige, M. A., Amrein-Beardsley, A., & Close, K. (2019). Tennessee's national impact on teacher evaluation law and policy. *Tennessee Journal of Law and Policy, 13*(2), 523–574. https://trace.tennessee.edu/tjlp/vol13/iss2/4/

Palmer, M., & Mazzotti, F. (2004). Structure of everglades alligator holes. *Wetlands, 24*, 115–122.

Park, E., Kim, K. J., & Del Pobil, A. P. (2011, November). The effects of a robot instructor's positive vs. negative feedbacks on attraction and acceptance towards the robot in classroom. In *International conference on social robotics* (pp. 135–141). Springer.

Passmore, C., & Beauchamp, A. (2017, March). *Phenomena-Questions-Models* [PowerPoint slides]. NSTA National Conference 2017, Los Angeles, CA. https://education.ucdavis.edu/sites/main/files/file-attachments/phenomena-questions-models_nsta_2017_0.pdf?1493666608

Passmore, C., Schwarz, C., & Mankowski, J. (2017). Developing and using models. In C. Schwarz, C. Passmore, & B. Reiser (Eds.), *Helping students make sense of the world using next generation science and engineering practices* (pp. 109–135). NSTA Press Book.

Patterson, A., & Gray, S. (2019). Teaching to transform: (W)holistic science pedagogy. *Theory into Practice, 58*(4), 328–337. https://doi.org/10.1080/00405841.2019.1626616

Paul, A., & Herbig, H. K. (1994). The effect of information overload on the innovation choice process: Innovation overload. *Journal of Consumer Marketing, 11*(2), 45–54.

Paulu, N., & Winters, K. (1998). *Teachers leading the way: Voices from the National Teacher Forum.* U.S. Department of Education.

PBLWorks. (2021). *What is project-based learning?* https://www.pblworks.org/what-is-pbl

Peakall, D. B., Lincer, J. L., Risebrough, R. W., Pritchard, J. B., & Kinter, W. B. (1973). DDE-induced egg-shell thinning: Structural and physiological effects in three species. *Comparative and General Pharmacology, 4*(15), 305–313.

Pearson, P. D., Hansen, J., & Gordon, C. (1979). The effect of background knowledge on young children's comprehension of explicit and implicit information. *Journal of Reading Behavior, 11*(3), 201–209.

Pearson, P. D., Moje, E., & Greenleaf, C. (2010). Literacy and science: Each in the service of the other. *Science, 328*(5977), 459–463.

Peck, R., Gould, R., & Miller, S. J. (2013). *Developing essential understanding of statistics for teaching mathematics in grades 9–12.* National Council of Teachers of Mathematics.

Peck, R., Gould, R., & Utts, J. (2019, August). *Mathematics foundations for success in introductory statistics.* https://dcmathpathways.org/sites/default/files/resources/2019-08/Mathematics_Foundations_for_Success_in_Introductory_Statistics_20190809.pdf

Pelletier, T. A., Carstens, B. C., Tank, D. C., Sullivan, J., & Espíndola, A. (2018). Predicting plant conservation priorities on a global scale. *Proceedings of the National Academy of Sciences of the United States of America, 115*(51), 13027–13032.

Peng, Z., Aiken, C., Kilb, D., Shelly, D. R., & Bogdan, E. (2012). Listening to the 2011 magnitude 9.0 Tohoku-Oki, Japan, earthquake. *Seismological Research Letters, 83*(2), 287–293.

Pennock, R. T. (2019). *An instinct for truth: Curiosity and the moral character of science.* MIT Press.

Penuel, W. R., Harris, C. J., & DeBarger, A. H. (2015). Implementing the Next Generation Science Standards. *Phi Delta Kappan, 96*(6), 45–49. https://doi-org.ezproxy.lib.apsu.edu/10.1177/0031721715575299

Pérez, A., & Wise, J. P., Sr. (2018). One environmental health: An emerging perspective in toxicology. *F1000Research, 7,* 918. https://doi.org/10.12688/f1000research.14233.1

Perkins, D. N. (1986). *Knowledge as design.* Lawrence Erlbaum Associates.

Perkins, D. N. (2009). *Making learning whole: How seven principles of teaching can transform education.* Jossey-Bass.

Perrotta, C., & Selwyn, N. (2019). Deep learning goes to school: Toward a relational understanding of AI in education. *Learning, Media & Technology, 45*(3), 251–269. https://doi.org/10.1080/17439884.2020.1686017

Peters, E. E. (2012). Developing content knowledge in students through explicit teaching of the nature of science: Influences of goal setting and self-monitoring. *Science & Education, 21*(6), 881–898. https://doi.org/10.1007/s11191-009-9219-1

Peters, E. E., & Kitsantas, A. (2010). The effect of nature of science metacognitive prompts on science students' content and nature of science knowledge, metacognition, and self-regulatory efficacy. *School Science and Mathematics, 110,* 382–396.

Peters-Burton, E. E. (2015). Outcomes of a self-regulatory curriculum model: Network analysis of middle school students' views of nature of science. *Science & Education, 24,* 855–885. https://doi.org/10.1007/s11191-015-9769-3

Peters-Burton, E. E., & Botov, I. S. (2017). Self-regulated learning microanalysis as a tool to inform professional development delivery in real-time. *Metacognition and Learning, 12*(1), 45–78. https://doi.org/10.1007/s11409-016-9160-z

Peters-Burton, E. E., & Mattietti, G. K. (2011). Cognition and self-efficacy of stratigraphy and geologic time: Implications for improving undergraduate student performance in geological reasoning. *Journal of Geoscience Education, 59*(3), 163–173. https://doi.org/10.5408/1.3605042

Peters-Burton, E. E., Rich, P., Cleary, T., Burton, S., Kitsantas, A., Egan, G., & Ellsworth, J. (2020). Using computational thinking for data practices in high school science. *The Science Teacher, 87*(6), 30–36.

Phelan, P., Davidson, A., & Cao, H. (1991). Students' multiple worlds: Negotiating the boundaries of family, peer, and school cultures. *Anthropology and Education Quarterly, 22*(3), 224–250.

Pinter, N. (2005). Policy forum: One step forward, two steps back on U.S. floodplains. *Science, 308*(5719), 207–208.

Pinter, N., Jemberie, A. A., Remo, J. W. F., Heine, R. A., & Ickes, B. S (2008). Flood trends and river engineering on the Mississippi River system. *Geophysical Research Letters, 35*(23), 1–5.

Pinter, N., van de Ploeg, R., Schweigert, P., & Hoefer, G. (2006). Flood magnification on the River Rhine. *Hydrological Processes, 20*(1), 147–164.

Plank, S. B., & Condliffe, B. F. (2013). Pressures of the season: An examination of classroom quality and high-stakes accountability. *American Educational Research Journal, 50*(5), 1152–1182.

Plastics Europe. (2008). *The compelling facts about plastics for 2007.* https://www.plasticseurope.org/download_file/force/1114/181

Plouffe, L., Bosson-Rieutort, D., Madaniyazi, L., Iwai-Shimada, M., Nakai, K., Tatsuta, N., Nakayama, S., & Verner, M. (2020). Estimated postnatal *p,p′*-DDT and *p,p′*-DDE levels and body mass index at 42 months of age in a longitudinal study of Japanese children. *Environmental Health, 19*(49), 1–9. https://doi.org/10.1186/s12940-020-00603-z

Popper, K. (1983). *Realism and the aim of science.* Routledge.

President's Council of Advisors on Science and Technology. (2012). *Engage to excel: Producing one million additional college graduates with degrees in science, technology, engineering, and mathematics.* President's Council of Advisors on Science and Technology.

Preston, J., Wiebe, S., Gabriel, M., McAuley, A., Campbell, B., & McDonald, R. (2015). Benefits and challenges of technology in high schools: A voice from educational leaders with a Freire echo. *Interchange, 46,* 169–185. https://doi.org/10.1007/s10780-015-9240-z

Purcell, K., Heaps, A., Buchanan, J., & Friedrich, L. (2013). *How teachers are using technology at home and in their classrooms.* Pew Research Center's Internet & American Life Project.

Purtill, R. (1970). The purpose of science. *Philosophy of Science, 37*(2), 301–306.

Quince, C., Lanzen, A., Davenport, R. J., & Turnbaugh, P. J. (2011). Removing noise from pyrosequenced amplicons. *BMC Bioinformatics, 12*(1), 38–56. https://doi.org/10.1186/1471-2105-12-38

Quinlan, C. L. (2018). Use of crime scene investigations in anatomy and physiology: Potential for going beyond knowing in NGSS dimensions. *American Biology Teacher, 80*(3), 221–226. https://doi.org/10.1525/abt.2018.80.3.221

Rainie, L., & Funk, C. (2015). *Public and scientists' views on science and society.* Pew Research Center's Internet & American Life Project.

Raizen, S. A. (1998). Standards for science education. *Teachers College Record, 100*(1), 66–121.

Rafa, A., Erwin, B., Brixey, E., McCann, M., & Perez, Z., Jr. (2020). *50-state comparison: English learner policies.* Education Commission of the States. https://www.ecs.org/50-state-comparison-english-learner-policies

Ramenofsky, M., & Wingfield, J. (2007). Regulation of migration. *Bioscience, 57*(2), 135–143.

Ravizza, S. M., Hambrick, D. Z., & Fenn, K. M. (2014). Non-academic internet use in the classroom is negatively related to classroom learning regardless of intellectual ability. *Computers and Education, 78,* 109–114. https://doi.org/10.1016/j.compedu.2014.05.007

Rayor, L. S. & Jennings, C. (2016). Pollination: Trading food for fertilization in 3 minutes. *YouTube.* https://www.youtube.com/watch?v=Lu7AjOvznh8

Recht, D. R., & Leslie, L. (1988). Effect of prior knowledge on good and poor readers' memory of text. *Journal of Educational Psychology, 80*(1), 16–20. https://doi.org/10.1037/0022-0663.80.1.16

Reiser, B. J. (2013). *What professional development strategies are needed for successful implementation of the Next Generation Science Standards?* http://www.k12center.org/rsc/pdf/b1_reiser.pdf

Reiter, D. K., Brunson, M. W., & Schmidt, R. H. (1999). Public attitudes toward wildlife damage management and policy. *Wildlife Society Bulletin, 27*(3), 746–758.

Remo, J. W. F., Carlson, M., & Pinter, N. (2012). Hydraulic and flood-loss modeling of levee, floodplain, and river management strategies, Middle Mississippi River, USA. *Natural Hazards, 61*(2), 551–575.

Rhodes, H., & Feder, M. (2014). *Literacy for science: Exploring the intersection of the Next Generation Science Standards and Common Core for ELA Standards: A workshop summary.* National Academies Press.

Rhouma, B. K., Tebourbi, O., Krichah, R., & Sakly, M. (2001). Reproductive toxicity of DDT in adult male rats. *Human Exposure and Toxicology, 20*(8), 393–397.

Richards, P. G., & Kim, W. (2009). Monitoring for nuclear explosions. *Scientific American, 300*(3), 70–77.

Rieffel, E., & Polak, W. (2000). An introduction to quantum computing for non-physicists. *ACM Computing Surveys, 32*(3), 300–335. https://doi.org/10.1145/367701.367709

Ritchhart, R. (1999). Generative topics: Building a curriculum around big ideas. *Teaching Children Mathematics, 5*(8), 462.

Rittle-Johnson, B., Farran, D. C., & Durkin, K. L. (2021). Marginalized students' perspectives on instructional strategies in middle-school mathematics classrooms. *Journal of Experimental Education, 89*(4), 569–586.

Rivers, C., Martin, E., Meyer, D., Inglesby, T. V., Cicero, A. J., & Cizek, J. (2020). *Modernizing and expanding outbreak science to support better decision making during public health crises: Lessons for COVID-19 and beyond.* Johns Hopkins University.

Roberts, D., Laughlin, L., Hsheih, P., & Legters, L. (1997). DDT, global strategies, and a malaria control crisis in South America. *Emergencies of Infectious Diseases, 3*(3), 295–302.

Rogerson, K. (2003). Addressing the negative consequences of the information age lessons from Karl Polanyi and the industrial revolution: A note on the politics of theorizing technology. *Information, Communication & Society, 6*(1), 105–124. https://doi.org/10.1080/1369118032000068732

Rosen, L. D., Lim, A. F., Carrier, L. M., & Cheever, N. A. (2011). An empirical examination of the educational impact of text message-induced task switching in the classroom: Educational implications and strategies to enhance learning. *Psicologia Educativa, 17*(2), 163–177.

Rossman, A., Chance, B., Medina, E., & Obispo, C. P. S. L. (2006). Some key comparisons between statistics and mathematics, and why teachers should care. *Thinking and reasoning with data and chance: Sixty-eighth annual yearbook of the National Council of Teachers of Mathematics* (68th ed.; pp. 323–333). National Council of Teachers of Mathematics.

Roth, S., & Trumbore, C. (2018). *The mangrove tree: Planting trees to feed families.* Lee & Low.

Rowbottom, D. (2010). What scientific progress is not: Against bird's epistemic view. *International Studies in the Philosophy of Science, 24*(3), 241–255. https://doi.org/10.1080/02698595.2010.522407

Rowbottom, D. (2015). Scientific progress without increasing verisimilitude: In response to Niiniluoto. *Studies in History & Philosophy of Science Part A, 51*, 100–104. https://doi.org/10.1016/j.shpsa.2015.01.003

Royakkers, L., Timmer, J., Kool, L., & van Est, R. (2018). Societal and ethical issues of digitization. *Ethics and Information Technology, 20*(2), 127–142.

Rudolph, J. L. (2007). Epistemology for the masses: The origins of "The scientific method" in American schools. *History of Education Quarterly, 45*(3), 341–376.

Rudolph, J. L. (2020). The lost moral purpose of science education. *Science Education, 104*(5), 895–906. https://doi.org/10.1002/sce.21590

Rudolph, J. L., & Horibe, S. (2016). What do we mean by science education for civic engagement? *Journal of Research in Science Teaching, 53*(6), 805–820.

Rudwick, M. J. S. (1998). Lyell and the principles of geology. *Geological Society, London, Special Publications, 143*(1), 1–15. https://doi.org/10.1144/GSL.SP.1998.143.01.02

Rugai, J., & Hamiliton-Ekeke, J. (2016). A review of digital addiction: A call for safety education. *Journal of Education and e-Learning Research, 3*(1), 17–22. https://doi.org/10.20448/journal.509/2016.3.1/509.1.17.22

Russ, R. S., Scherr, R. E., Hammer, D., & Mikeska, J. (2008). Recognizing mechanistic reasoning in student scientific inquiry: A framework for discourse analysis developed from philosophy of science. *Science Education, 92*(3), 499–525.

Russell, S. J., & Norvig, P. (2016). *Artificial intelligence: A modern approach.* Pearson Education Limited.

Rutherford, F. J., & Ahlgren, A. (1991). *Science for all Americans.* Oxford University Press.

Sadker, D. M., & Zittleman, K. R. (2018). *Teachers, schools, and society: A brief introduction to education* (5th ed.). McGraw-Hill.

Sadler, T. D., Barab, S. A., & Scott, B. (2007). What do students gain by engaging in socioscientific inquiry? *Research in Science Education, 37*(4), 371–391.

Saldanha, L., & Thompson, P. (2002). Conceptions of sample and their relationship to statistical inference. *Educational Studies in Mathematics, 51*(3), 257–270.

Salsburg, D. (2002). *The lady tasting tea: How statistics revolutionized science in the twentieth century.* Henry Holt Co.

Samuel, A. L. (1959). Some studies in machine learning using the game of checkers. *IBM Journal of Research and Development, 3*(3), 210–229.

Sarmah, P., & Rout, J. (2019). Cyanobacterial degradation of low-density polyethylene (LDPE) by *Nostoc carneum* isolated from submerged polyethylene surface in domestic sewage water. *Energy, Ecology, and Environment, 4*, 240–252. https://doi.org/10.1007/s40974-019-00133-6

Sato, T., Yasuda, Y., Kido, A., Arakawa, A., Mizoguchi, H., & Valsiner, J. (2007). Sampling reconsidered. In J. Valsiner & A. Rosa (Eds.), *The Cambridge handbook of sociocultural psychology* (pp. 82–106). Cambridge University Press.

Saxe, K., & Braddy, L. (2015). *A common vision for undergraduate mathematical sciences programs in 2025.* The Mathematical Association of America.

Schmidt, W. H., McKnight, C. C., & Raizen, S. (1997). *Splintered vision: An investigation of US mathematics and science education.* Kluwer Academic Publishers.

Schreiber, J., & Asner-Self, K. (2011). *Educational research.* John Wiley & Sons.

Schroeder, M., McKeough, A., Graham, S. A., & Norris, S. P. (2019). Students' views of uncertainty in formal and personal science. *Research in Science & Technological Education, 37*(2), 239–257. https://doi.org/10.1080/02635143.2018.1541878

Schuchardt, A. M., & Schunn, C. D. (2016). Modeling scientific processes with mathematics equations enhances student qualitative conceptual understanding and quantitative problem solving. *Science Education, 100*(2), 290–320.

Schwartz, R., Lederman, N., & Crawford, B. (2004). Developing views of nature of science in an authentic context: An explicit approach to bridging the gap between nature of science and scientific inquiry. *Science Education, 88*(4), 610–645. https://doi.org/10.1002/sce.10128

Schwarz, C. V., Passmore, C., & Reiser, B. J. (2017). *Helping students make sense of the world using next generation science and engineering practices.* NSTA Press.

Science History Institute. (n.d.). *History and future of plastics.* https://www.sciencehistory.org/the-history-and-future-of-plastics

Scribner-MacLean, M. (2009). Making a leap toward concrete inferences. *Science Scope, 32*(6), 56–59.

Segel, E., & Heer, J. (2010). Narrative visualization: Telling stories with data. *IEEE Transactions on Visualization and Computer Graphics, 16*(6), 1139–1148.

Sellami, M., Ghamgui, H., Frikha, F., Gargouri, Y., & Miled, N. (2012). Enzymatic transesterification of palm stearin and olein blends to produce zero-trans margarine fat. *BMC Biotechnology, 12*(1), 48–55. https://doi.org/10.1186/1472-6750-12-48

Sellar, S., & Gulson, K. N. (2019). Becoming information centric: The emergence of new cognitive infrastructures in education policy. *Journal of Education Policy, 36*(3), 1–18. https://doi.org/10.1080/02680939.2019.1678766

Semisonic. (1998). "Closing Time." On *Feeling Strangely Fine* [album]. MCA.

Sen, S., Kim, S.-H., & Cohen, A. S. (2017). Comparative analysis of common statistical models used for value-added assessment of school performance. *Journal of Measurement and Evaluation in Education and Psychology, 8*(3), 303–320. https://doi.org/10.21031/epod.321840

Sewell, A. (2002). Constructivism and student misconceptions: Why every teacher needs to know about them. *Australian Science Teachers' Journal, 48*(4), 24–28.

Shanahan, T., & Shanahan, C. (2012). What is disciplinary literacy and why does it matter? *Topics in Language Disorders, 32*(1), 7–18.

Shor, I. (1992). *Empowering education: Critical teaching for social change.* University of Chicago Press.

Short, P. (2007). *Use of the Oslo-Potsdam solution to test the effect of an environmental education model on tangible measures of environmental protection* (UMI No. 304825292) [Doctoral dissertation, Southern Illinois University). ProQuest Dissertations & Theses Global.

Short, P. (2018–2019, Winter). Time for the science paradigm: A stalwart shift, not a tepid tweak. *Tennessee Educational Leadership Journal, 46*(1), 26–33.

Sikora, J., & Pokropek, A. (2011). *Gendered career expectations of students: Perspectives from PISA 2006.* OECD Publishing. https://doi.org/10.1787/5kghw6891gms-en

Sintov, N., Kar, D., Nguyen, T., Fang, F., Hoffman, K., Lyet, A., & Tambe, M. (2016). From the lab to the classroom and beyond: Extending a game-based research platform for teaching AI to diverse audiences. In *30th AAAI conference on artificial intelligence* (pp. 4107–4112). AAAI.

Skylar, J. (2013). *Why you don't actually 'F*cking love science.'* Mashable. https://mashable.com/2013/09/20/why-you-dont-love-science/

Slater, M. H., Huxster, J. K., & Bresticker, J. E. (2019). Understanding and trusting science. *Journal for General Philosophy of Science, 50*, 247–261.

Slattery, P. (2013). *Curriculum development in the postmodern era: Teaching and learning in an age of accountability* (3rd ed.). Routledge.

Slavin, R. E. (2002). Evidence-based education policies: Transforming educational practice and research. *Educational Researcher, 31*(7), 15–21.

Slavin, R. E. (2007). *Educational research in an age of accountability.* Allyn & Bacon.

Slavin, R. E., Lake, C., Hanley, P., & Thurston, A. (2014). Experimental evaluations of elementary science programs: A best-evidence synthesis. *Journal of Research in Science Teaching, 51*(7), 870–901.

Smith, A. P. (1978). An investigation of the mechanisms underlying nest construction in the mud wasp Paralastor sp. (Hymenoptera: Eumenidae). *Animal Behaviour, 26*, 232–240.

Smith, J., & Nadelson, L. (2017). Finding alignment: The perceptions and integration of the next generation science standards practices by elementary teachers. *School Science & Mathematics, 117*(5), 194–203. https://doi.org/10.1111/ssm.12222

Smith, K., Loughran, J., Berry, A., & Dimitrakopoulos, C. (2012). Developing scientific literacy in a primary school. *International Journal of Science Education, 34*(1), 127–152.

Snelling, J., Kemp, A., & Lincer, J. (1984). Organochlorine residues in southern African raptor eggs. In J. M. Mendelsohn & C. W. Sapsford (Eds.), *Proceedings of the second symposium on African predatory birds natal bird club* (pp. 161–168), *Durban, South Africa.*

Society for Mathematical Biology. (2020). History of the society. *Society for Mathematical Biology.* https://www.smb.org/history-of-the-society/

Somaweera, R., Nifong, J., Rosenblatt, A., Brien, M. L., Combrink, X., Elsey, R. M., Grigg, G., Magnusson, W. E., Mazzotti, F. J., Pearcy, A., Platt, S. G., Shirley, M. H., Tellez, M., Ploeg, J., Webb, G., Whitaker, R., & Webber, B. L. (2020). The ecological importance of crocodylians: Towards evidence-based justification for their conservation. *Biological Reviews, 95*(4), 936–959.

Sonnenschein, C., & Soto, A. (1998). An updated review of environmental estrogen and androgen mimics and antagonists. *Journal of Steroids Biochemicals and Molecular Biology, 65*(1–6), 143–150.

Sousa, E., Quintino, V., Teixeira, J., & Rodrigues, A. M. (2017). A portrait of biodiversity in children's trade books. *Society & Animals, 25*(3), 257–279.

Sowder, M., & Harward, S. (2011). Time for science? A study on the use of instructional time for teaching science at the elementary level. *Journal of the Utah Academy of Sciences, Arts & Letters, 88*, 186–203.

Spaulding, E., & Wilson, E. (2002). Demystifying reflection: A study of pedagogical strategies that encourage reflective journal writing. *Teachers College Record, 104*(7), 1393–1421.

Speier, C., Valacich, J., & Vessey, I. (1999). The influence of task interruption on individual decision making: An information overload perspective. *Decision Sciences, 30*(2), 337–360.

Sperry, D. E., Sperry, L. L., & Miller, P. J. (2019). Language does matter: But there is more to language than vocabulary and directed speech. *Child Development, 90*(3), 993–997.

Spillane, J. P. (2012). Data in practice: Conceptualizing the data-based decision-making phenomena. *American Journal of Education, 118*(2), 113–141.

Spillane, J. P., Halverson, R., & Diamond, J. B. (2001). Investigating school leadership practice: A distributed perspective. *Educational Researcher, 30*(3), 23–28.

Spillane, J. P., Reiser, B. J., & Reimer, T. (2002). Policy implementation and cognition: Reframing and refocusing implementation research. *Review of Educational Research, 72*(3), 387–431.

Spiro, R. J., Collins, B. P., Thota, J. J., & Feltovich, P. J. (2003). Cognitive flexibility theory: Hypermedia for complex learning, adaptive knowledge application, and experience acceleration. *Education Technology, 43*(5), 5–10.

Srivastava, N. (2018). *The relativity of theory.* https://arxiv.org/pdf/0902.3479.pdf

Stake, E. R. (1995). *The art of case study research.* SAGE Publications.

Stanford, P. (2003). Multiple intelligence for every classroom. *Intervention in School and Clinic, 39*(2), 80–85. https://doi.org/10.1177/10534512030390020301

Starčič, A. I. (2019). Human learning and learning analytics in the age of artificial intelligence. *British Journal of Educational Technology, 50*(6), 2974–2976. https://doi.org/10.1111/bjet.12879

Steel, E. A., Liermann, M., & Guttorp, P. (2019). Beyond calculations: A course in statistical thinking. *The American Statistician, 73*(1), 392–401. https://doi.org/10.1080/00031305.2018.1505657

Steffen, W., Crutzen, P. J., & McNeill, J. R. (2007). The Anthropocene: Are humans now overwhelming the great forces of Nature? *AMBIO, 36*(8), 614–621.

Steffen, W., Richardson, K., Rockström, J., Schellnhuber, H. J., Dube, O. P., Dutreuil, S., Lenton, T. M., & Lubchenco, J. (2020). The emergence and evolution of Earth System Science. *Nature Reviews Earth and Environment, 1*(1), 54–63. https://doi.org/10.1038/s43017-019-0005-6

Stember, M. (1991). Advancing the social sciences through the interdisciplinary enterprise. *The Social Science Journal, 28*(1), 1–14.

Stetka, B. (2017, March 6). *Unscrambling the nutrition science on eggs.* NPR. https://www.npr.org/sections/thesalt/2017/03/06/518152471/unscrambling-the-nutrition-science-on-eggs

Stewart, I. (2018). *Significant figures: Lives and works of trailblazing mathematicians.* Profile Books.

Strauss, J., & Corbin, A. (1994). Grounded theory methodology. *Handbook of Qualitative Research, 17,* 273–285.

Strauss, V. (2017, August 28). Teacher shortages affecting every state as 2017–18 school year begins. *Washington Post.* https://www.washingtonpost.com/news/answer-sheet/wp/2017/08/28/teacher-shortages-affecting-every-state-as-2017-18-school-year-begins/

Sullivan, P., & McCartney, H. (2017). Integrating 3D printing into an early childhood teacher preparation course: Reflections on practice. *Journal of Early Childhood Teacher Education, 38*(1), 39–51.

Susilowati, S. M. E., & Anam, K. (2017). Improving students' scientific reasoning and problem-solving skills by the 5E learning Model. *Journal of Biology & Biology Education, 9*(3), 506–512.

Sutcher, L., Darling-Hammond, L., & Carver-Thomas, D. (2016). *A coming crisis in teaching? Teacher supply, demand, and shortages in the U.S.* Learning Policy Institute.

Suter, R. (1939). Aristotle and the scientific method. *The Scientific Monthly, 49*(5), 468–472.

Swarat, S., Ortony, A., & Revelle, W. (2012). Activity matters: Understanding student interest in school science. *Journal of Research in Science Teaching, 49*(4), 515–537.

Swenson, R. (2004). *Margin: Restoring emotional, physical, financial and time resources to overloaded lives.* NavPress.

Symington, D., & Spurling, H. (1990). The 'draw a scientist test': Interpreting the data. *Research in Science & Technological Education, 8*(1), 75–77.

Szczesiul, S. A., & Huizenga, J. L. (2015). Bridging structure and agency: Exploring the riddle of teacher leadership in teacher collaboration. *Journal of School Leadership, 25*(2), 368–410.

Szegedy, C., Vanhoucke, V., Ioffe, S., Shlens, J., & Wojna, Z. (2014). *Intriguing properties of neural networks.* https://arxiv.org/pdf/1312.6199

Talanquer, V., & Pollard, J. (2010). Let's teach how we think instead of what we know. *Chemistry Education Research and Practice, 11,* 74–83. https://doi.org/10.1039/C005349J

Tall, D. (2013). *How humans learn to think mathematically: Exploring the three worlds of mathematics.* Cambridge University Press.

Tan, P.-N., Steinbach, M., & Kumar, V. (2013). *Data mining cluster analysis: Basic concepts and algorithms* [Lecture notes]. In H. Xiong (Ed.), Introduction to Data Mining. Lecture Notes for Chapter 8, Rutgers University, New Jersey.

Tao, Z., Yang, X., Lai, I. K., & Chau, K. A. (2018). Research on the effect of smartphone use, student engagement and self-directed learning on individual impact: China empirical study. *2018 International Symposium on Educational Technology (ISET),* 221–225. https ://doi.org/10.1109/ISET.2018.00056

Taylor, G. (2013). *Turn your smartphone into a 175x digital microscope for incredible macro photos.* Gadget Hacks. https://smartphones.gadgethacks.com/how-to/turn-your-smartphone-into-175x-digital-microscope-for-incredible-macro-photos-0149047/

Taylor, R. (2003) *Products for multiple intelligences.* https://cdn.shopify.com/s/files/1/0017/1920/5932/files/AHA_Product-Grid.pdf?17068620100210672204

Texas Education Agency. (2019). *Announcement of the single, statewide assessment for identification of English learners, effective 2019–2020 school year.* https://tea.texas.gov/about-tea/news-and-multimedia/correspondence/taa-letters/announcement-of-the-single-statewide-assessment-for-identification-of-english-learners-effective-2019-2020-school-year

Theraulaz, G., & Bonabeau, E. (1999). A brief history of stigmergy. *Artificial Life, 5*(2), 97–116. https://doi.org/10.1162/106454699568700

Tho, S. W., Lee, T. T., & Baharom, S. (2018). Scientific investigation through innovative use of mobile devices in the playground. *Teaching Science: The Journal of the Australian Science Teachers Association, 64*(2), 25–29.

Thomas, K., O'Bannon, B. W., & Britt, V. G. (2014). Standing in the schoolhouse door: Teacher perceptions of mobile phones in the classroom. *Journal of Research on Technology in Education, 46*(4), 373–395.

Tindell, D. R., & Bohlander, R. W. (2012). The use and abuse of cell phones and text messaging in the classroom: A survey of college students. *College Teaching, 60*(1), 1–9. https://doi.org/10.1080/87567555.2011.604802

Tintle, N., Chance, B., Cobb, G., Rossman, A., Roy, S., Swanson, T., & Vanderstoep, J. (2014). *Introduction to statistical investigations.* Wiley.

Tobias-Lara, M. G., & Gomez-Blancarte, A. L. (2019). Assessment of informal and formal inferential reasoning: A critical research review. *Statistics Education Research Journal, 18*(1), 8–25. https://iase-web.org/documents/SERJ/SERJ18(1)_TobiasLara.pdf?1559012429

Tomlinson, C. (2014). *The differentiated classroom: Responding to the needs of all learners* (2nd ed.). ASCD.

Touretzky, D., Gardner-McCune, C., Martin, F., & Seehorn, D. (2019). Envisioning AI for K–12: What should every child know about AI? *Proceedings of the AAAI Conference on Artificial Intelligence, 33*(1), 9795–9799.

Treffers, A. (1987). *Three dimensions: A model of goal and theory description in mathematics instruction–The wiskobas project.* D. Reidel Publishing Company.

Triola, M. F., & Iossi, L. (2018). *Elementary statistics* (13th ed.). Pearson.

Trygstad, P. J., Smith, P. S., Banilower, E. R., & Nelson, M. M. (2013). *The status of elementary science education: Are we ready for the next generation science standards?* Horizon Research.

Tufte, E. (1983). *The visual display of quantitative information.* Graphics Press.

Turner, S., Unkefer, L. C., Cichy, B. E., Peper, C., & Juang, J. P. (2011). Career interests and self-estimated abilities of young adults with disabilities. *Journal of Career Assessment, 19*(20), 183–196.

Turusov, V., Rakitssky, V., & Tomatis, L. (2002). Dichlorodiphenylchloroethane (DDT): Ubiquity, persistence, and risk. *Environmental Health Perspectives, 110,* 125–128.

U.S. Bureau of Labor Statistics (2017). *Spotlight on statistics.*

U.S. Department of Agriculture. (2011). *A brief history of USDA food guides.* https://myplate-prod.azureedge.net/sites/default/files/2020-12/ABriefHistoryOfUSDAFoodGuides.pdf

U.S. Department of Health and Human Services and U.S. Department of Agriculture. (2015, December). *2015–2020 dietary guidelines for Americans* (8th ed.). https://health.gov/our-work/food-and-nutrition/2015-2020-dietary-guidelines/

U.S. Department of the Interior. (1998). *Guidelines for interpretation of biological effects of selected constituents in biota, water, and sediment.* https://clu-in.org/download/contaminantfocus/arsenic/Dept_Interior_Guidelines.pdf

U.S. Fish and Wildlife Service. (n.d.). *Yellow perch.* U.S. Fish and Wildlife Service. https://www.fws.gov/fisheries/freshwater-fish-of-america/yellow_perch.html

ul Qamar, M. T., Alqahtani, S. M., Alamri, M. A., & Chen, L. L. (2020). Structural basis of SARS-CoV-2 3CLpro and anti-COVID-19 drug discovery from medicinal plants. *Journal of Pharmaceutical Analysis, 10*(4), 313–319. https://doi.org/10.1016/j.jpha.2020.03.009

United Nations Education, Scientific, and Cultural Organization. (1993). *Project 2000+; International forum for scientific and technological literacy for all.* UNESCO.

University of Maryland. (2018, August 28). *Responding to cholera before it strikes.* https://research.umd.edu/news/news_story.php?id=11656

Van den Heuvel-Panhuizen, M. (2003). The didactical use of models in realistic mathematics education: An example from a longitudinal trajectory on percentage. *Educational Studies in Mathematics, 54*(1), 9–35.

Van Rooij, A. J., & Prause, N. (2014). A critical review of "internet addiction" criteria with suggestions for the future. *Journal of Behavioral Addictions, 3*(4), 203–213. https://doi.org/10.1556/JBA.3.2014.4.1

VanMeveren, K., Hulac, D., & Wollersheim-Shervey, S. (2018). Universal screening methods and models: Diagnostic accuracy of reading assessments. *Assessment for Effective Intervention, 45*(4), 255–265. https://doi.org/10.1177/1534508418819797

Vélez-Ibáñez, C. G., & Greenberg, J. B. (1992). Formation and transformation of funds of knowledge among U.S.-Mexican households. *Anthropology & Education Quarterly, 23*(4), 313–335.

Verma, G., Campbell, T., Melville, W., & Park, B. (2020). Science teacher education in the times of the COVID-19 pandemic. *Journal of Science Teacher Education, 31*(5), 483–490. https://doi.org/10.1080/1046560X.2020.1771514

Vescio, V., Ross, D., & Adams, A. (2008). A review of research on the impact of professional learning communities on teaching practice and student learning. *Teaching and Teacher Education, 24*(1), 80–91. https://doi.org/10.1016/j.tate.2007.01.004

Vieira, R. M., & Tenreiro-Vieira, C. (2016). Fostering scientific literacy and critical thinking in elementary science education. *International Journal of Science and Mathematics Education, 14*(4), 659–680. https://doi.org/10.1007/s10763-014-9605-2

Vine, F., & Matthews, D. (1963). Magnetic anomalies over oceanic ridges. *Nature, 199*(4897), 947–949. https://doi.org/10.1038/199947a0

Vygotsky, L. S. (1978). *Mind in society: The development of higher psychological processes.* Harvard University Press.

Vygotsky, L. S. (1986). *Thought and language.* MIT Press.

Wade, A. (2015). Dots, fruit, speed and pills: The happy consciousness of Pac-Man. *Journal for Cultural Research, 19*(3), 248–261. https://doi.org/10.1080/14797585.2015.1021991

Walsh, J. A., & Sattes, B. D. (2005). *Quality questioning: Research-based practice to engage every learner.* Corwin Press.

Wan, X., Zhou, X., Ye, Z., Mortensen, C. K., & Bai, Z. (2020, June). SmileyCluster: Supporting accessible machine learning in K–12 scientific discovery. In *IDC '20: Proceedings of the Interaction Design and Children Conference* (pp. 23–35). Association for Computing Machinery. https://doi.org/10.1145/3392063.3394440

Ward, M. O., Grinstein, G., & Keim, D. (2010). Interactive data visualization: Foundations, techniques, and applications. *Choice Reviews Online, 40.*

Wasserstein, R. L., & Lazar, N. (2016). The ASA's statement on *p*-values: Context, process, and purpose. *The American Statistician, 70*(2), 129–133. https://doi-org.ezproxy.lib.apsu.edu/10.1080/00031305.2016.1154108

Wasserstein, R. L., Schirm A. L., & Lazar, N. A. (2019). Moving to a world beyond "*p* > 0.05." *The American Statistician, 73*(1), 1–19. https://www.tandfonline.com/doi/full/10.1080/00031305.2019.1583913

Watkins, J., Hammer, D., Radoff, J., Jaber, L. Z., & Phillips, A. M. (2017). Positioning as not-understanding: The value of showing uncertainty for engaging in science. *Journal of Research in Science Teaching, 55*(4), 573–599.

Watson, A. (2014). Consolidation. *Association of Teachers of Mathematics, 243,* 19–22.

Weintrop, D., Beheshti, E., Horn, M., Orton, K., Jona, K., Trouille, L., & Wilensky, U. (2016). Defining computational thinking for mathematics and science classrooms. *Journal of Science Education and Technology, 25*(1), 127–147.

Weng, S. F., Vaz, L., Qureshi, N., & Kai, J. (2019). Prediction of premature all-cause mortality: A prospective general population cohort study comparing machine-learning and standard epidemiological approaches. *PLOS ONE, 14*(3). https://doi.org/10.1371/journal.pone.0214365

Wertsch, J. V. (1993). *Voices of the mind.* Harvard University Press.

Westervelt, M. O., & Llewellyn, L. G. (1986). *Youth and wildlife: The beliefs and behaviors of fifth and sixth grade students regarding non-domestic animals.* Division of Program Plans, Office of Planning and Budget, U.S. Fish and Wildlife Service, Department of the Interior.

White, R. (2004). *Young children's relationship with nature: Its importance to children's development & the earth's future.* White Hutchinson Leisure & Learning Group. https://www.whitehutchinson.com/children/articles/childrennature.shtml

Whitehead, T., Smith, S., Park, J., Petreas, M., Rappaport, S., & Metayer, C. (2015). Concentrations of persistent organic pollutants in California children's whole blood and residential dust. *Environmental Science & Technology, 49*(15), 9331–9340.

Wieman, C. (2007). Why not try a scientific approach to science education? *Change: The Magazine of Higher Learning, 39*(5), 9–15.

Wiggins, G., & McTighe, J. (1998). What is backward design. *Understanding by Design, 1,* 7–19.

Wiggins, G. P., & McTighe, J. (2008). *Understanding by design.* Association for Supervision and Curriculum Development.

Wild, C. (2006). The concept of distribution. *Statistics Education Research Journal, 5*(2), 10–26.

Wild, C. (2009, June 26). *Early statistical inferences: 'The eyes have it'* [Conference session]. U.S. Conference on Teaching Statistics, Columbus, Ohio. https://www.stat.auckland.ac.nz/~wild/talks/09.USCOTS.wild.pdf

Wild, C. J., Utts, J. M., & Horton, N. J. (2018). What is statistics? In D. Ben-Zvi, K. Makar, & J. Garfield (Eds.), *International handbook of research in statistics education* (pp. 5–36). Springer.

Wilkinson, L. (1999). Statistical methods in psychology journals: Guidelines and explanations. *American Psychologist, 54*(8), 594–604. https://doi.org/10.1037/0003-066X.54.8.594

Willard, T. (2020). *The NTSA atlas of the three dimensions.* National Science Teaching Association.

Willems, P. P., & Gonzalez-DeHass, A. (2012). School–community partnerships: Using authentic contexts to academically motivate students. *School Community Journal, 22*(2), 9–30.

Willett, W., & Stampfer, M. (2006). Rebuilding the food pyramid. *Scientific American Special Edition, 16*(4), 12–21.

Williams, M. (2017). John Dewey in the 21st century. *Journal of Inquiry and Action in Education, 9*(1).

Williamson, B. (2020a). New digital laboratories of experimental knowledge production: Artificial intelligence and education research. *London Review of Education, 18*(2), 209–220. https://doi.org/10.14324/LRE.18.2.05

Williamson, B. (2020b). Bringing up the bio-datafied child: Scientific and ethical controversies over computational biology in education. *Ethics and Education, 15*(4), 444–463.

Williamson, B., & Eynon, R. (2020). Historical threads, missing links, and future directions in AI in education. *Learning, Media & Technology, 45*(3), 223–235. https://doi.org/10.1080/17439884.2020.1798995

Williamson, B., Bayne, S., & Shay, S. (2020). The datafication of teaching in higher education: Critical issues and perspectives. *Teaching in Higher Education, 25*(40), 351–365. https://doi.org/10.1080/13562517.2020.1748811

Willingham, D. T. (2017). Ask the cognitive scientist: Do manipulatives help students learn? *American Educator, 6*, 25–30.

Wilson, E. O. (1998). *Consilience: The unity of knowledge.* Alfred A. Knopf.

Wilson, J. T. (1968). Static or mobile earth: The current scientific revolution. *Proceedings of the American Philosophical Society, 112*(5), 309–320.

Wilson, N. (2013, January 21). *Perry's scheme of intellectual and ethical development* [PowerPoint slides]. SlideShare. https://www.slideshare.net/NoahWilson/perrys-scheme-of-intellectual-and-ethical-development

Wilson, P. S., Cooney, T. J., & Stinson, D. W. (2005). What constitutes good mathematics teaching and how it develops: Nine high school teachers' perspectives. *Journal of Mathematics Teacher Education, 8*(2), 83–111.

Windschitl, M. (2002). Framing constructivism in practice as the negotiation of dilemmas: An analysis of the conceptual, pedagogical, cultural, and political challenges facing teachers. *Review of Educational Research, 72*(2), 131–175.

Windschitl, M., Thompson, J., & Braaten, M. (2018). *Ambitious science teaching.* Harvard Education Press.

Winger E. P. (1960). The unreasonable effectiveness of mathematics in the natural sciences. *Communications in Pure and Applied Mathematics, 13*(1), 1–14.

Witten, I. H., Frank, E., Hall, M. A., & Pal, C. J. (2016). *Data mining: Practical machine learning tools and techniques* (4th ed.). Morgan Kaufmann.

Wolff, A., Gooch, D., Cavero Montaner, J. J, Rashid, U., & Kortuem, G., (2016). Creating an understanding of data literacy for a data-driven society. *The Journal of Community Informatics, 12*(3), 9–26.

Womack, A. J., Sadler, T. D., & Wulff, E. P. (2018, March). *Automated scoring of scientific practices through open-ended, scenario-based assessments* [Conference session]. NARST, Atlanta, GA.

Womack, A. J., Wulff, E., Sadler, T. D., & Romine, W. (2017, April). *Assessment of next generation science learning* [Conference session]. NARST, San Antonio, TX.

World Health Organization. (1979). *DDT and its derivatives* (Environmental Health Criteria 9). https://apps.who.int/iris/bitstream/handle/10665/39562/9241540699-eng.pdf

Worm, B., Lotze, H., Jubinville, I., Wilcox, C., & Jambeck. J. (2017). Plastic as a persistent marine pollutant. *Annual Review of Environment and Resources, 42*(1), 1–26.

Wysession, M. E., (2014). The Next Generation Science Standards: A potential revolution for geoscience education. *Earth's Future, 2*(5), 299–301.

Yacoubian, H. A. (2018). Scientific literacy for democratic decision-making. *International Journal of Science Education, 40*(3), 308–327.

Yan, L., Zhang, H., Goncalves, J., Xiao, Y., Wang, M., Guo, Y., Sun, C., Tang, X., Jing, L., Zhang, M., Huang, X., Xiao, Y., Cao, H., Chen, Y., Ren, T., Wang, F., Xiao, Y., Huang, S., Tan, X., . . . Yuan, Y. (2020). An interpretable mortality prediction model for COVID-19 patients. *Nature Machine Intelligence, 2*, 283–288.

Yang, J., Yang, Y., Wu, W., Zhao, J., & Jiang, L. (2014). Evidence of polyethylene biodegradation by bacterial strains from the guts of plastic-eating waxworms.

Environmental Science and Technology, 48(23), 13776–13784. https://doi.org/10.1021/es504038a

Yellow Perch. (2019, December 16). In *Wikipedia.* https://en.wikipedia.org/w/index.php?title=Yellow_perch&oldid=931021137

Yin, R. K. (2003). *Case study research: Design and methods.* SAGE Publications.

York-Barr, J., & Duke, K. (2004). What do we know about teacher leadership? Findings from two decades of scholarship. *Review of Educational Research, 74*(3), 255–316.

You, L., Casanova, M., Archibeque-Engle, S., Sar, M., Fan, L., & Heck, H. (2002). Impaired male sexual development in perinatal Sprague Dawley and Long-Evans hooded rats exposed in utero and lactationally to p,p DDE. *Toxicology and Science, 45*(2), 162–173.

You, L., Gazi, E., Archibeque-Engle, S., Casanova, M., Conolly, R., & Heck, H. (1999). Transplacental and lactational transfer of p,p'-DDE in Sprague-Dawley rats. *Toxicology and Applied Pharmacology, 157*(2), 134–144.

Ysoft. (2016). *3D printing in education: A 2016 report card* [Infographic]. Ysoft. https://www.ysoft.com/YSoftWeb/media/content/YSOFT-3DP-EduSurvey-infographic-final_1.pdf

Zalasiewicz, J., Waters, C. N., & Williams, M. (2015). When did the Anthropocene begin? A mid-twentieth century boundary level is stratigraphically optimal. *Quaternary International, 383,* 196–203.

Zammito, J. H. (2004). *A nice derangement of epistemes: Postpositivism in the study of science from Quine to Latour.* University of Chicago Press.

Zazkis, R., & Campbell, S. (1996). Divisibility and multiplicative structure of natural numbers: Preservice teachers' understanding. *Journal for Research in Mathematics Education, 27*(5), 540–563.

Zeide, E. (2019, August 26). *Robot teaching, pedagogy, and policy.* SSRN. https://papers.ssrn.com/sol3/papers.cfm?abstract_id=3441300

Zhai, X., Zhang, M., Li, M., & Zhang, X. (2019). Understanding the relationship between levels of mobile technology use in high school physics classrooms and the learning outcome. *British Journal of Educational Technology, 50*(2), 750–766. https://doi.org/10.1111/bjet.12700

Zhang, M., Lundeberg, M., McConnell, T. J., Koehler, M. J., & Eberhardt, J. (2010). Using questioning to facilitate discussion of science teaching problems in teacher professional development. *Interdisciplinary Journal of Problem-Based Learning, 4*(1). https://doi.org/10.7771/1541-5015.1097

Zhang, Q., Xu, E. G., Li, L., Chen, Q., Ma, L., Zeng, E. Y., & Shi, H. (2020). A review of microplastics in table salt, drinking water, and air: Direct human exposure. *Environmental Science & Technology, 54*(7), 3740–3751. https://doi.org/10.1021/acs.est.9b04535

Zhang, Z. H., & Linn, M. C. (2011). Can generating representations enhance learning with dynamic visualizations? *Journal of Research in Science Teaching, 48*(10), 1177–1198. https://doi.org/10.1002/tea.20443

Zimmerman, B. J. (2000). Attaining self-regulation: A social cognitive perspective. In M. Boekaerts, P. R., Pintrich, & M. Zeidner (Eds.), *Handbook of self-regulation* (pp. 13–39). Academic Press.

Zimmerman, B. J. (2002). Becoming a self-regulated learner: An overview. *Theory Into Practice, 41*(2), 64–70. https://doi.org/10.1207/s15430421tip4102_2

Zucker, A., & Noyce, P. (2020). Lessons from the pandemic about science education. *Phi Delta Kappan, 102*(2), 44–49.

ABOUT THE EDITORS

Philip C. Short has been an educator for more than 3 decades over a range of grade levels from Grades 5–12 through undergraduate and graduate students. He has also worked as an ecologist on projects ranging from environmental toxicology to community dynamics. Dr. Short has also served as a university instructor and department chair for biology and environmental sciences, a wilderness education guide, and an international science and environmental education workshop coordinator. He currently serves as science teacher educator and co-director (with his wife, Dr. Donna Short) of the Jack Hunt STEM Center at Austin Peay State University. Philip's favorite moments continue to be those when people, young or old, make a discovery from new experiences and allow their view of the world to change.

Harvey Henson is the interim director of the STEM Education Research Center and associate professor of science education and geology at Southern Illinois University–Carbondale (SIU). Henson has served in multiple positions as researcher, educator, and administrator at SIU since 1985. His research focuses on four main areas: (a) teacher partnerships and professional development; (b) preservice teacher education and literacy in STEM; (c) geohazards education; and (d) applied geophysical investigations. Henson leads teams of STEM educators and researchers at SIU and other universities, partners with K–12 educators, and mentors graduate and undergraduate students to conduct this research and advance STEM literacy. Henson has managed over $26 million in external grants from the NSF, Illinois Emergency Management Agency/FEMA, Illinois State Board

Age of Inference, pages 461–462

of Education, Regional Offices of Education, National Park Service, NSTA, and other agencies to support these research and scholarship activities.

John R. McConnell is associate professor of education research for the Eriksson College of Education at Austin Peay State University. He is a university educator, applied researcher, and former college administrator with over 10 years of experience in continuous program improvement, research design and analysis, and the use of predictive modeling and other advanced analytics. Prior to higher education, he helped develop and refine artificial neural networks in water monitoring and air traffic control systems and proudly served for 6 years as a secondary science teacher in an inner-city public school district.

ABOUT THE CONTRIBUTORS

Zhen Bai is an assistant professor of computer science and affiliated faculty of data science at the University of Rochester. Bai is an expert in human-computer interactions, augmented reality, tangible user interfaces, embodied conversational agents, and design for diversity. Her interests are in developing computational modeling of learning, creating intelligent and collaborative learning technologies in supporting socio-emotional learning, scientific inquiry in STEM education, learning for people with disabilities, K–12 AI education, and human-AI collaboration.

Arthur Beauchamp has expertise in the use of literacy techniques in science instruction, pedagogical design, and curriculum development. He has 21 years of high school teaching experience and served as the director of the Sacramento Area Science Project at University of California, Davis.

R. Alexander Bentley, an anthropologist, from the University of Tennessee, Knoxville, and co-author of *The Acceleration of Cultural Change: From Ancestors to Algorithms* (MIT Press, 2017), has enjoyed teaching big-data social sciences at multiple universities.

Joy G. Bertling is an assistant professor of art education at the University of Tennessee. Her primary research interest relates to how art education can be responsive to environmental concerns, particularly through critical place-based art curricula. She has published articles in various peer-reviewed journals including *Studies in Art Education, International Journal of Education Through Art, Art Education,* and *Environmental Education Research.*

Age of Inference, pages 463–470

Raffaella Borasi is the Frederica Warner Professor of Education, the founding director of the Center for Learning in the Digital Age, and is the former dean of the Warner School of Education at the University of Rochester. She has written extensively on the processes of learning and teaching mathematics through inquiry, and her current research interests are on leveraging online learning and digital technology for education more generally.

Dr. Bouwma-Gearhart's research program concerns STEM faculty work at research universities, specifically response to and implementation of education innovations and related individual and organizational learning and change towards teaching and programmatic improvements. She joined the science and mathematics education faculty at Oregon State University's College of Education in 2012 and is now also the College of Education's associate dean of research and faculty advancement.

Lingguo Bu is associate professor of mathematics education at Southern Illinois University–Carbondale. He is interested in model-centered learning and instruction and the integration of dynamic, design, and simulation technologies in STEM teacher education and professional development.

Jeneva Clark, from the University of Tennessee in Knoxville, teaches undergraduate mathematics, advises future teachers, mentors future mathematics faculty, and implements professional development for K–12 teachers.

Michael Daley is a clinical assistant professor of education and the director of higher education STEM outreach within the Center for Professional Development and Education Reform, in the Warner School of Education at the University of Rochester, and former environmental science faculty at Lasell College, where he conducted research on terrestrial ecosystems. Daley has published and presented extensively on both ecosystem science and science education. His current interests are on integrating technology into STEM teaching to support student inquiry.

Sarah Dugger recently completed her doctoral degree in the educational leadership program in the Eriksson College of Education at Austin Peay State University. She has taught science in a variety of public and private school settings since 1986. Her research interests include STEM education, teacher retention, and educational technology.

Kallina M. Dunkle is an associate professor of geology and associate dean of the College of STEM at Austin Peay State University. Dr. Dunkle teaches a variety of lecture/lab courses including physical geology, hydrogeology, environmental geology, and geomorphology. She regularly advises undergraduate research projects, which are typically local and involve stream and groundwater contamination, flooding, or other hydrogeologic issues related to the karst terrain. Her research interests also include pedagogy, groundwater flow modeling, and glacial geology.

William Folk leads research programs in plant sciences, human health, and science education. He has extensive experience with cross-cultural science research and education/learning.

Barbara Giorgio-Booher is a teaching professor of art at Ball State University. She teaches courses that include 2D foundations, drawing, figure drawing, and printmaking. Collaboration between the arts and sciences has helped to create new ideas, processes, and knowledge for her artwork. Barbara currently is the art director and co-faculty advisor for the Conservation Tales book series. Other interdisciplinary projects include the book *Amaya and the Court House Mouse* (CASA Activity Book), Neo Natural glass and drawing exhibition at Garfield Park Conservatory, and Fanatical Botanical a seminar in glass and drawing. Barbara's creative work includes drawings on glass, digital prints, printmaking, and traditional drawings on paper. Barbara is secretary and elected member of the board of Mid-America College Art Association (MACAA) that represents and supports college art concerns with a focus upon the practical and philosophical interests of studio faculty.

Mary K Gove, PhD, emeritus professor, in literacy education, Cleveland State University, is co-author of *Reading and Learning to Read* (Pearson), a textbook for 25 years, and has written extensively about environmental critical literacy and action research for teachers. She now lives in Gainesville Co-Housing.

Anna Strimaitis Grinath is an assistant professor of biology education research for the Department of Biological Sciences, Idaho State University. Dr. Grinath's research examines how students learn to participate in the specialized practices and discourses of science and how to design opportunities for such participation into biology learning contexts. She teaches undergraduate introductory biology courses and graduate courses in biology education teaching and research.

Rebekah Hammack served as a middle school science and engineering teacher for 12 years. She obtained National Board Teaching Certification in Early Adolescent Science and spent a year working at the National Science Foundation as an Albert Einstein Distinguished Educator fellow. She is also a recipient of the Presidential Award for Excellence in Mathematics and Science Education. Dr. Hammack researches science and engineering teacher efficacy and student engineering identity development at the K–8 level.

Lynn Liao Hodge is a professor of math education and director of the Center for Enhancing Education in Math and Science at the University of Tennessee. Her research interests focus on developing research-practice partnerships in order to address issues of access and equity in STEM education.

Leslie Huling, EdD, is a professor in the Department of Curriculum and Instruction at Texas State University. She serves as senior advisor of the LBJ Institute for STEM Education and Research and as program director of the NASA STEM Engagement & Educator Professional Development Collaborative. She also chairs the Association of Teacher Educators' Commission on STEM Education in the Future.

Laveria F. Hutchison is an associate professor of literacy education in the College of Education at the University of Houston. She has been awarded approximately $3.5 million in grant funding from the United States Department of Education and from the National Science Foundation for recruiting, academically preparing, and placing STEM professionals into high need Harris County (Houston, Texas area) public middle schools and high schools.

Jen Cullerton Johnson (MFA, MEd) is co-founder of Green Literacy with Dr. Mary Gove. She is the author of several books. For the past 12 years she gardens with incarcerated youth in Chicago.

Ryan "Seth" Jones is an assistant professor at Middle Tennessee State University. His research focuses on designing and studying learning environments that support students to use data, statistics, and models as epistemic tools to make inferences about the world around them.

Tammy Jones serves as an adjunct instructor in the Department of Mathematical Sciences at MTSU and is a consultant in mathematics, education, and technology providing professional development across 7 states over the past decade. Her interests are in effective techniques for being successful in the classroom, supporting instruction, and STEM integrations. As a K–12 math/science teacher for over 30 years, Jones currently is a T3 instructor for Texas Instruments and the author of 6 teaching methodology books.

Rachel Juergensen is an experienced educational leader and current doctoral student in special education with an emphasis in science. Her research interests include discovering ways to support teachers and diverse learners in elementary science.

Jennifer Kaplan is the director of the PhD program in mathematics and science education at Middle Tennessee State University. Previously she was an associate professor in the Department of Statistics at the University of Georgia. Her research field is undergraduate statistics education, and she has studied the effect of language on student learning as well as professional development of graduate students and faculty for teaching statistics.

She has been the PI on three NSF funded grants and serves as the editor for the *Statistics Education Research Journal.*

Dovie Kimmins is a professor in the Department of Mathematical Sciences at Middle Tennessee State University. Teaching mathematics content courses (sometimes including the history of mathematics) for pre-service and in-service teachers, mathematics majors, and the general education population, Kimmins has developed both undergraduate and graduate courses for mathematics education. She enjoys investigating student mathematical thinking at all levels and has directed or co-directed 21 grant-funded professional development projects for mathematics teachers in grades K–12.

Shande King's research interests center on small group discourse and mathematical argument development in K–12 mathematics classrooms as well as student interactions with verbal and visual representations of mathematics. Experiences with students and teachers across varied subjects and contexts have also expanded his research to include math and STEM classroom community development and pre-service STEM teacher pedagogical and identity development via constructive teaching philosophies in in- and out-of-school contexts.

Amy Lannin directs the University of Missouri's Campus Writing Program, a writing-across-the-curriculum program that supports writing instruction in the disciplines.

Vasileios Maroulas is a foundational data scientist, at the University of Tennessee in Knoxville, who develops data-driven models based on an interplay of statistics, machine learning, topology, and geometry.

Mary Barone Martin is a professor of mathematical sciences at Middle Tennessee State University. With research interests and background in commutative algebra and rindg theory, Martin has taught introductory through graduate level mathematics courses at MTSU for 22 years. Martin has also taught at Colgate University and Winthrop University and has directed or co-directed 6–12 STEM teacher professional development grants totaling more than $10M.

Giuseppina Mattietti is an associate professor of geology at George Mason University. Her research focuses on igneous petrology of the Greater Antilles. She has also worked at the Smithsonian Museum of Natural History, Department of Mineral Sciences with the Global Volcanism Program. At George Mason she has been involved in several initiatives concerning assessment and cognition in the geosciences.

Tom J. McConnell is a professor of science education in the Department of Biology at Ball State University. His research and teaching are focused on teaching science as inquiry, especially in connection with environmental education and teacher professional development. He is the lead author and publisher of the Conservation Tales book series, and the director of the Conservation Educator Academy at the Indianapolis Zoo. He is the lead author of the Problem-Based Learning in the Science Classroom series (NSTA Press), and is the managing editor of the *Global Journal of Transformative Education.* He is a past president of the Hoosier Association of Science Teachers, Inc.

Dave Miller is a clinical associate professor of education and the associate director for K–12 education of the Center for Learning in the Digital Age in the Warner School of Education at the University of Rochester, and also a member of the steering committee of the K–12 Digital Consortium. Miller is the former founder and owner of Knowledge Athlete, a company that developed an early LMS for K–12 schools. He has presented and published in the areas of data communication and networks, online learning, AI/ML in K–12 education, and produced a number of online instructional materials, as well as multimedia products.

Nicholas N. Nagle is a geographer at the University of Tennessee in Knoxville, who works on small area estimation and fusion of spatial data and who enjoys teaching students from both the physical science and social science sides of geography.

Euginia M. Nyirenda earned a BEd in biology secondary education at the University of Zambia, and received an MS and a PhD in curriculum and instruction at Southern Illinois University–Carbondale. She recently completed a post doctorate appointment in STEM assessment design and implementation at the STEM Education Research Center at SIUC. Her areas of research interest include assessment in STEM education, preservice teacher efficacy, preparation and development, equity in teacher professional development, hands-on strategies, and 3D design and printing.

Blanche O'Bannon is a professor of educational technology at the University of Tennessee in Knoxville. Her research interests include technology integration in K–16 classrooms, mobile technology, and interactive multimedia text development.

Torrey Palmer has worked as a classroom teacher, coach, and curriculum coordinator. She currently works for TNTP, a nonprofit focused on ending educational inequality. She supports teachers and leaders in leveraging college and career ready standards to yield improvements in teaching and learning.

Kristina Johnson Parrish (cover designer) is an art director who creates beautiful print books for Thought Catalog Books. She grew up in southern Illinois where she was once a creative and insightful science student of editor, Dr. Philip Short. Creativity was the greater motivating force, and she studied art in St. Louis before moving to Boston where she spent much of her twenties balancing artmaking and design with playing guitar in various bands in the underground music scene. Graphic design began as a hobby for making records and evolved into both a passion and career. Kristina is a graduate of the graphic design program at Massachusetts College of Art and Design where she learned to join her two loves for design and structure.

Cynthia Passmore is a professor in the School of Education at University of California–Davis. She has worked collaboratively with teachers to develop and implement innovative curriculum and study student learning with particular interest in modeling and model-based reasoning at the high school level.

Erin Peters-Burton is the Donna R. and David E. Sterling Endowed Professor of Science Education at George Mason University. She was a National Board certified young adolescent science and mathematics secondary teacher for 15 years before she served as an Einstein Distinguished Education fellow in NASA's Exploration Systems Mission Directorate. Erin's experiences have helped inform her work as an educational researcher, and she is currently pursuing research projects in the nexus of the nature of science, student learning, science teacher pedagogical content knowledge, and educational psychology.

Kristin Rearden is a clinical professor of science and middle grades education at the University of Tennessee in Knoxville. Her research interests include preservice teacher education, the integration of literacy and science, and effective practices for utilizing technology in content-area lessons.

Virginia Resta, PhD, currently serves as an evaluation specialist in the NASA STEM Educator Professional Development Collaborative project, LBJ Institute for STEM Education, and Research at Texas State University.

Kristen Roland is an assistant professor in the Department of Mathematical Sciences at Appalachian State University. She received her PhD in mathematics education at the University of Georgia with a research focus on student understanding of confidence intervals. Kristen was previously a lecturer in statistics at the University of Rhode Island where she earned an MS in statistics.

William Romine directs the Data Science for Education Laboratory at Wright State University. He explores public understandings and perspectives about biology and health and how these support learning and decision-making.

Teresa Schmidt is a lecturer teaching mathematics and statistics courses at Middle Tennessee State University in the Department of University Studies. With her academic and research interests and background in spatial visualization, lesson study, and student achievement, she also has 20 years teaching experience from middle school to collegiate level mathematics.

Fonya Scott is a PhD student in the math and science education program at Middle Tennessee State University with an interdisciplinary concentration. Her general research interest focuses on mathematics integration in K–12 science courses and how mathematics concepts can support student problematizing and argumentation in science classrooms.

Donna Short is an assistant professor of education at Austin Peay State University. She also has nearly 20 years of experience teaching middle school science in both public and private schools. Her research interests include evaluating effective strategies in K–12 science education and assessing the use of data-driven instruction by novice teachers.

Cassandra M. Smith is an experienced special education teacher and current doctoral student in special education with an emphasis in mathematics. Her research interests include discovering math interventions, strategies, and methods for secondary special education students.

Miranda Feliciano Tyson (Foreword) is a special education science teacher at a Title I high school in New York City specializing in educating disadvantaged youth on identity, leadership, and scientific literacy. Mx. Tyson co-founded and directed Ready& (Previously LADY), an organization dedicated to the socio-emotional development of Japanese youth leaders. As an undergraduate, to the end of popularizing science with Japanese teenagers, Mx. Tyson created the official Japan Aerospace Exploration Agency (JAXA) Instagram account.

Delinda van Garderen has expertise in teacher professional development and instructional practices in science and mathematics practices for diverse learners.

www.ingramcontent.com/pod-product-compliance
Lightning Source LLC
Jackson TN
JSHW010013311224
76273JS00004B/379
9781648027970